Dawn Atkins
Editor

Looking Queer
Body Image and Identity in Lesbian, Bisexual, Gay, and Transgender Communities

Pre-publication
REVIEWS,
COMMENTARIES,
EVALUATIONS . . .

"**I**n *Looking Queer,* Dawn Atkins has assembled an enormous collection of essays exploring the relationships between body form, self-reference, and sexual identity. Gender is very much a product of social action in these essays and the diverse racial, ethnic, and class backgrounds of the contributors show that gender is equally dependent on the details of social location. Both points are central points in the queer theory canon, but seldom has the truth of that canon been confirmed through such powerful and personalized means. *Looking Queer* may be the first collection to attack the demons of body fascism head-on. And if nothing else, these essays assure those of us unable to meet the expectations of these physical ideal(s)—we are not alone."

William Leap
Department of Anthropology,
American University,
Washington, DC

"*Looking Queer* offers searing, gutsy, and political accounts of looksism in and out of queer communities. True to its roots in gay, lesbian, bisexual, and transgendered activism, it includes articles from a remarkable array of writers.

This is a book you can read out loud to your lover—in bed or at the breakfast table; to a physician threatening to make a boy-girl one sex or the other; and to people who already know or want to understand the power of coming out and the healing power of touch. This book deserves room on the bookshelf with other writings on lesbian and gay life in the age of breast cancer and AIDS; with feminist writings that aim to account for race, class and sexuality; and with scholarship that keeps the body at the center of focus. As Dawn Atkins writes in her introduction, this book is about building a community that will look at our bodies differently and at different bodies with equal joy."

Becky Thompson, PhD
Associate Professor of Sociology,
Simmons College, Boston, MA;
Author, *So Wide and So Deep:
A Multiracial View of Women's
Eating Problems*

"Although one would never know it from examining the burgeoning queer studies literature, body image concerns are every bit as prevalent in lesbian, gay, bisexual, and transgendered people as among heterosexual women. This powerful book presents body image issues in a refreshing mix of academic theory and personal account, and fills a glaring hole in 'queer' or lesbian, gay, bisexual, and transgender studies. The book is appropriate for a wide variety of audiences, from academic classes on eating disorders or body image, to courses on gender and sexuality. It is also a powerful read for people in LGBT support groups or reading groups, or for individuals who struggle with body image issues themselves."

Mickey Eliason
Director, Sexuality Studies Program,
The University of Iowa,
Iowa City, Iowa

Looking Queer

Body Image and Identity in Lesbian, Bisexual, Gay, and Transgender Communities

HAWORTH Gay & Lesbian Studies

John P. De Cecco, PhD
Editor in Chief

New, Recent, and Forthcoming Titles:

The Golden Boy by James Melson

Barrack Buddies and Soldier Lovers: Dialogues with Gay Young Men in the U.S. Military by Steven Zeeland

Outing: Shattering the Conspiracy of Silence by Warren Johansson and William A. Percy

The Bisexual Option, Second Edition by Fritz Klein

And the Flag Was Still There: Straight People, Gay People, and Sexuality in the U.S. Military by Lois Shawver

Sailors and Sexual Identity: Crossing the Line Between "Straight" and "Gay" in the U.S. Navy by Steven Zeeland

The Gay Male's Odyssey in the Corporate World: From Disempowerment to Empowerment by Gerald V. Miller

Bisexual Politics: Theories, Queries, and Visions edited by Naomi Tucker

Gay and Gray: The Older Homosexual Man, Second Edition by Raymond M. Berger

Reviving the Tribe: Regenerating Gay Men's Sexuality and Culture in the Ongoing Epidemic by Eric Rofes

Gay and Lesbian Mental Health: A Sourcebook for Practitioners edited by Christopher J. Alexander

Against My Better Judgment: An Intimate Memoir of an Eminent Gay Psychologist by Roger Brown

The Masculine Marine: Homoeroticism in the U.S. Marine Corps by Steven Zeeland

Bisexual Characters in Film: From Anaïs to Zee by Wayne M. Bryant

The Bear Book: Readings in the History and Evolution of a Gay Male Subculture edited by Les Wright

Youths Living with HIV: Self-Evident Truths by G. Cajetan Luna

Growth and Intimacy for Gay Men: A Workbook by Christopher J. Alexander

Our Families, Our Values: Snapshots of Queer Kinship edited by Robert E. Goss and Amy Adams Squire Strongheart

Gay/Lesbian/Bisexual/Transgender Public Policy Issues: A Citizen's and Administrator's Guide to the New Cultural Struggle edited by Wallace Swan

Rough News, Daring Views: 1950s' Pioneer Gay Press Journalism by Jim Kepner

Family Secrets: Gay Sons—A Mother's Story by Jean M. Baker

Twenty Million New Customers: Understanding Gay Men's Consumer Behavior by Steven M. Kates

The Empress Is a Man: Stories from the Life of José Sarria by Michael R. Gorman

Acts of Disclosure: The Coming-Out Process of Contemporary Gay Men by Marc E. Vargo

Queer Kids: The Challenges and Promise for Lesbian, Gay, and Bisexual Youth by Robert E. Owens

Dry Bones Breathe: Gay Men Creating Post-AIDS Identities and Cultures by Eric Rofes

Looking Queer: Body Image and Identity in Lesbian, Bisexual, Gay, and Transgender Communities edited by Dawn Atkins

Love and Anger: Essays on AIDS, Activism, and Politics by Peter F. Cohen

Looking Queer
Body Image and Identity in Lesbian, Bisexual, Gay, and Transgender Communities

Dawn Atkins
Editor

Harrington Park Press
An Imprint of The Haworth Press, Inc.
New York • London

Published by

Harrington Park Press, an imprint of The Haworth Press, Inc., 10 Alice Street, Binghamton, NY 13904-1580

"Mirror" originally appeared in *Birthing*, copyright 1996, Woman in the Moon Publications. "Lesbians and the (Re/De)Construction of the Female Body" originally appeared in *Reading the Social Body*, copyright 1993, University of Iowa Press. "Faggot Rant" originally appeared in *Ritual Sex*, copyright 1996, Masquerade Books, Inc. "Love Poem" and "Body Language" originally appeared in *Anesthesia*, copyright 1996, The Advocado Press. "The Imperfections of Beauty: On Being Gay and Disabled" originally appeared in *Men's Style*, September/October, copyright 1995, Kenny Fries. Reprinted with permission from the author. "I like my Chi-i-sa-i Body Now" originally appeared in *Sinister Wisdom*, copyright 1993, Donna Tanigawa. "More Than a Sum of Parts: Rescuing the Body from Fundamentalism" originally appeared in *Sex and Spirit*, copyright 1995, White Crane Press. "A Matter of Size" originally appeared in *Outweek*, October 24, copyright 1990, Patrick Giles.

Cover design by Marylouise E. Doyle.

The Library of Congress has cataloged the hardcover edition of this book as:

Looking queer : body image and identity in lesbian, gay, bisexual, and transgender communities / Dawn Atkins, editor.
    p.   cm.
Includes bibliographical references and index.
ISBN 0-7890-0463-1 (alk. paper).
    1. Lesbians—United States—Identity. 2. Body image in women—United States. 3. Self-esteem in women—United States. 4. Gays—United States—Identity. 5. Body image in men—United States. 6. Self-esteem in men—United States. I. Atkins, Dawn.
HQ75.6.U5L66 1998
306.76'6—dc21
                                                   98-14678
                                                     CIP

ISBN 1–56023–931–X (pbk.)

To Michael Easton

Dearest little brother,
I wish I could have told you how much you meant to me,
how valuable your smile and your friendship was,
and how I wished you loved yourself even half as much as I loved you.
Maybe, if you could have seen yourself through my eyes,
seen how truly beautiful you were,
you would be with us now to read this book.
I miss you. Always.

CONTENTS

ABOUT THE EDITOR

Dawn Atkins is a thirty-six-year-old, bisexual, Wiccan, polyamorous, second-generation feminist. She has a BA in Anthropology and Professional Writing from the University of California at Santa Cruz, an MA in Feminist Anthropology, and is in a PhD program in anthropology at the University of Iowa. She is editor of upcoming special issues of the *Journal of Lesbian Studies* and the *Journal of Homosexuality* on sexual practices and identity. She worked for over ten years as a journalist, founded the Body Image Task Force, has given hundreds of presentations on body image, and is active in researching and writing about a range of body image and sexuality issues. She lives with her three partners and their young son.

CONTRIBUTORS

Andrea Askowitz has been, for most of her adult life, a student and an activist. She earned a bachelor's degree from the University of Pennsylvania and a master's degree in public policy at the George Washington University. Her activism took her across the country when, in 1991, she organized and participated in the Reproductive Freedom Ride. Eleven bicyclists rode from New York City to Seattle educating and organizing for reproductive rights and women's health. Andrea now works as a freelance writer and an environmental advocate at the Natural Resources Defense Council. She lives in New York City.

Sara Auerbach studied psychology and women's studies at Wesleyan University in Middletown, Connecticut. She currently works as a research assistant for the Departments of Psychiatry and Behavioral Science and Community Health at the University of Connecticut Health Center.

Michelle Bancroft is a graduate student/writer/artist living in Northern California. She holds a BA in Religious Studies and Women's Studies. She is an iconoclastic thirty-two-year-old stonefemme bottom. While not pleasing her Daddy butch, she is continuing her studies in religion, art history, iconography, mysticism, transforming arts, and the body. She has realized, thankfully, that the process of becoming is one that never truly ends.

Nancy Barron is a psychologist who evaluates changes in public mental health and substance abuse systems, teaches a course on self-image and body size, and practices as a psychotherapist. Her daughter cheers her on, and her son is making her a mother-in-law. She finds bell dancing, T'ai Chi, and outdoor activities, such as walking, canoeing, cross-country skiing, snorkeling, and scuba diving, delightful except for some rude aches in the joints. She was founder and board member of Ample Opportunity, a size-acceptance organization for women. Her new area of interest is an active, rural community for older lesbians.

Jay Blotcher has been a journalist, activist, and publicist in New York City since 1982, and has effectively intertwined these three lives by serving as media coordinator for the founding chapters of ACT UP and Queer Nation and by writing for *OutWeek, Out, POZ,* and several regional lesbian and gay newspapers. Blotcher was personal publicist for author Michelangelo Signorile for several years. He currently serves as Director of Media

Relations for the American Foundation for AIDS Research (AmFAR). A die-hard romantic Gemini, Blotcher still entertains notions of living happily ever after.

Boye is an Irish, working-class lesbian, raised in London. She now lives in Baltimore where she works as a healer and has a home with her master, to whom she is a lifetime slave. She is a published poet, an artist, and is currently completing a book of fine lesbian porn called *Letters to My Master.*

Rebekah Bradley is a teacher, therapist, and researcher. She is currently a graduate student in clinical psychology and in women's studies. She is also a student of guitar and biblical Hebrew.

Susie Bullington is a graduate student in anthropology and feminist studies at the University of Minnesota. She recently returned from southern Africa, where a recurring theme during her travels, and the source of many amusing stories, was the controversy that confusion about her gender inspired. For her thirtieth birthday, Susie bungee jumped 111 meters over the Zambezi River.

Wendy Chapkis is an author, activist, and educator. Her books include *Beauty Secrets: Women and the Politics of Appearance* and *Live Sex Acts: Women Performing Erotic Labor.* She is currently an Assistant Professor of Sociology and Women's Studies at the University of Southern Maine, Portland.

Cheryl Chase is the founder of the Intersex Society of North America (ISNA) and editor of ISNA's newsletter, *Hermaphrodites with Attitudes.* Born in the late fifties with intersexual genitals and ovo-testes, she was raised as a boy for a year and a half, then clitorectomized and raised thereafter as a girl. She feels transgendered but leans toward the female end of the spectrum and identifies as lesbian. She formed ISNA after her 1992 "constructive breakdown," and it has been an important part of her healing process.

Greta Christina is a white, female, queer, bisexual, feminist pervert. Her work, including essays, columns, features, book and film reviews, and assorted ad copy, has appeared in *On Our Backs, Penthouse,* and *Ms.* magazines, the *San Francisco Bay Times,* the anthologies *The Erotic Impulse: Honoring the Sensual Self* (1992), *Bisexual Politics: Theories, Queries, and Visions* (1995), and *Pornosexuals: Challenging Assumptions About Gender and Sexuality.* Her fetishes include books, films, weird music, reference materials, baseball, food, sex, and writing irate letters to the editor. She lives in San Francisco.

Laura Cole was born in 1967 to a large, midwestern Catholic family and has identified as bisexual since her early twenties. She currently works as an administrative assistant for a public health organization in Seattle, Washington.

Loree Cook-Daniels is a forty-year-old, white, queer-identified feminist. She owns Word Bridges, a writing and conflict resolution consulting firm, and is currently working on a book of essays, *American as Apple Pie: Confessions of a Queer Suburban Wife and Mother.*

Marcelle Cook-Daniels is a thirty-seven-year-old, queer-identified, transgendered feminist. Marcelle is a computer geek who resides in Vallejo, California, with partner of fourteen years, Loree, and son Kai.

Christine Cress was previously a counselor in the Career Services Center at Western Washington University. Currently, she is a doctoral candidate at UCLA where she is studying the effects of self-concept development on educational outcomes. In particular, she is examining the impact of campus climates on the academic success of LBGT students. When she's not working on her dissertation, she escapes into the mountains and canyons for hiking and quiet reflection.

Diane Griffin Crowder is Professor of French and Women's Studies at Cornell College. She has published research on the lesbian body, lesbian utopian fiction, lesbian pedagogy, semiotics, feminist criticism, and the works of Monique Wittig and Colette. Current research interests include lesbian theory, postmodernism and identity politics, and ongoing work on Wittig. She lives with her partner Margaret and their two cats.

Ozzie Diaz-Duque was born in La Habana, Cuba, on September 17, 1951 and raised in the rural town of Guanajay, near the port of Mariel. The son of immigrants from Austrias, Spain (Catholic father), and the Canary Islands (sephardic Jewish mother), he arrived in the United States on January 3, 1966, and lived in a home for boys in Miami, Florida, for a time. He moved to New York City to live with relatives and attended high school and Queens College, CUNY. He arrived in Iowa in August 1973 to complete graduate studies in romance languages and translation. Currently, he is teaching at the University of Iowa and working as a cross-cultural health care specialist and interpreter/translator.

Ganapati S. Durgadas was born July 5, 1947, in New York City as Leonard Tirado of Jewish and Puertorriqueno parentage and is a bisexual. He has been an anti-Vietnam war protester, welfare rights activist, ACT UPer and Queer National, Buddhist, and psychotherapist. Published in the *Bi Any Other Name: Bisexual People Speak Out* anthology, *James White Review,* and *Gay Community News*, he left Buddhism for Hinduism, changed his name legally, and was adopted into a South Indian Brahmin family. Nowadays, he looks critically at queer life from the perspective of this life experience.

Amy Edgington is a disabled lesbian artist and writer living in the South. Her work has previously been published in *Sinister Wisdom* (#39 on Disability), *Cats and Their Dykes, Wanting Women: An Anthology of Erotic Lesbian Poetry,* and other journals and anthologies.

Andrew J. Feraios has been a gay activist, AIDS activist, health educator, labor union organizer, student activist, and graduate student working on gay and lesbian issues. "If Only I Were Cute: Looksism and Internalized Homophobia in the Gay Male Community" is an adaptation from a larger work in progress called *The Adonis Complex: Homophobia, Patriarchy, and HIV Within the Cult of Gay Male Beauty.*

Kenny Fries is the author of *Body Remember: A Memoir, Anesthesia Poems,* and the play, *A Human Equation*, which premiered at LaMama E.T.C. in New York City. He is also the editor of *Staring Back: The Disability Experience from the Inside Out.* He received the Gregory Kolovakos Award for AIDS Writing and was Lambda Literary Award finalist for his sequence of poems, *The Healing Notebooks.* He has received a Ludwig Vogelstein Foundation grant and residencies at The MacDowell Colony and Yaddo. He teaches in the MFA in the Writing Program at Goddard College and lives in Northampton, Massachusetts.

Patrick Giles was born and raised in New York, where he still lives and where he came out while still a teenager. After years of participation in gay and lesbian and AIDS advocacy groups, he is now writing fiction and essays full-time and beginning to love working out at the gym and losing weight.

Amy Gilley has a PhD in Dramatic Art from the University of California, Santa Barbara. She has taught lighting design, set design, and theater history at the University of Georgia and Piedmont College. She left the South to teach creative arts and American literature at Concordia International University, Estonia. She has published fiction and poetry and presented papers on popular culture at a variety of conferences including the North American Studies Conference at the University of Tartu. A recovering victim of the fashion industry, she no longer thinks Kate Moss is the ideal.

Sandra Lee Golvin was born to Jewish parents in a Catholic hospital on Gabrielino land in the desert city named in Spanish by its founding African, Chinese, and European citizens for Our Lady the Queen of the Angels.

Her favorite childhood foods were tacos and brisket. S/he resists categories but will sign on for: writer/seeker/queer/femme/Sagittarius/lawyer. S/he has been published in the anthologies *Best Lesbian Erotica 1996 and 1997* and *Hers, Ritual Sex* and the journals *Fireweed* and *Spoon River Review.*

Paul EeNam Park Hagland is a gay Korean adoptee and an activist in LGBT Asian-American communities. He was the first chair and a founding member of Gay Asians and Pacific Islanders of Chicago (GAPIC) and was a board member of the Asian American AIDS Foundation (now Asian American AIDS Services) of Chicago. Currently he is a member of Gay Asians and Pacific Islander Men of New York (GAPIMNY), the Korean LGBT Group of New York, and a.k.a. (also-known-as), a New York-based organization of and for Korean and other intercountry adoptees.

Michael Hernandez is transitioning from lawyer to writer and is currently editing an anthology about transgendered men titled *Transgendered MAN-ifesto.* Mike's sexual orientation is queer. In other words, as both woman and man are embodied in one, Mike is a lesbian as well as gay. Needless to say, this self-perception causes a great deal of dismay in a world and society that requires a choice between one or the other. Mike's hope is that one day labels will be no longer necessary and that just being will suffice.

Gene-Michael Higney is a transplanted New Yorker who spends far too much time defending the Big Apple from the spiritually tanned denizens of the Big Orange and far too little time worrying about his appearance. The time he does not spend in the gym affords him ample time for fun, frolic, and, when his back is against the wall, writing.

Morgan Holmes is a founder of the Intersex Society of Canada (ISCA) and considers herself a force to be reckoned with. Thus, she finds herself slugging it out to finish her doctoral studies with two goals in mind: to teach many hundreds of students that we come in more than two varieties and to stop the unethical pathologization and medicalization of those deemed "intersexed." Morgan is definitely bent, and she likes it that way. Morgan is not sure where she lives right now, but her partner and son are with her, and the ambiguity suits them all quite well.

Claire Hueholt is a dyke woman without a nation. She has lived in Iowa for most of her life and has been struggling to overcome the barriers placed before her in the Bible Belt, as well as the barriers she feels daily because she is not an "appropriate" lesbian in her community. Much of what larger society demands of her as a woman is reflected in her inner struggle to rise up and reject the chains that come from her inner voices and the careful lessons she has been taught in her thirty-four years on this planet. She writes to give voice to her struggle and because she believes in the possibility of something better.

Sherrie A. Inness is Assistant Professor of English at Miami University. Her research interests include women's popular fiction, girls' serial novels, women's basketball, and lesbian fiction. She has published articles in *American Literary Realism, The Edith Wharton Review, Journal of Popular Culture, NWSA Journal, Studies in Scottish Literature, Studies in Short Fiction,* and *Women's Studies: An Interdisciplinary Journal,* as well as in several anthologies.

Raven Kaldera is a pansexual, intersex, F2M shaman/activist, writer, farmer, SM top, joyously married to an M2F shaman, polyamorous, and the parent of one child. Raven is the editor of *Hermaphrodeity: The Journal of Transgender Spirituality* and has published stories in the anthologies *Blood Kiss* and *S/M Futures.* Raven does not have a college degree and does not need one, thank you very much. Get over it. Raven is a Sagittarian with a Gemini moon and a Leo ascendant, if you're interested.

Dean Kiley is a (young)(queer)(Melbourne) writer, PhD candidate, and theorist currently lecturing in creative writing and hypertextuality at Melbourne University. His work includes (and often combines) theory, social commentary, and several modes of fiction. He is the author of *and thats final.* Some of his interests are, in no particular order: the interfaces between theory, criticism, and fiction; rollerblading; graphic design; what happens to textuality when it becomes hyper; the depoliticizing of popular gay media; queer theory, theorizing, and straightening-up; and his beautiful lover Jonathan. As to body concerns, he has the muscular build of a sexy pretzel crossed with a fifteen-year-old girl and is entirely happy with it, thank you very much.

Alexa Leigh is a righteous cultural critic. In the years since this piece was written, she has earned an MFA in Creative Writing from Mills College. She would like to thank the supermegaevilconglomerateubercorporations whose products appear in this piece without their permission.

Frank Martinez Lester went straight from the grit and turmoil of an inner-city high school in Pasadena, California, to the tree-lined, rarefied, ivory tower elitism of Stanford and Oxford (he studied at the latter for a year). He graduated from Stanford in 1988 and now works as a legal assistant and freelance writer in San Francisco. He has written articles for several local gay newspapers on city politics, health, and AIDS issues. His writing is informed by two factors: his upbringing, which was as a mostly (but not completely) white boy in a series of mostly racially diverse, culturally conservative, and economically impoverished neighborhoods, and the identity he has forged out of that mix. Lester seroconverted in January 1996. He plans to pursue a career in library and information science and, of course, to continue writing.

Catherine Lundoff is a white, bi-identified lesbian woman living in Minnesota with her long-suffering partner and cats. She likes tattooing, is a Wiccan, a women's festival organizer, a martial artist, and is just tickled pink to be writing this. She also doesn't have the social skills to sell out, so she's not too worried about the effects of law school.

William J. Mann is the author of the novel *The Men from the Boys* and the biography *Wisecracker: The Life and Times of William Haines*. His work has appeared in *The Advocate, The Washington Blade, Lambda Book Report,* and other publications around the country. His essays and fiction have been included in such anthologies as *Sister & Brother, Shadows of Love, Wanderlust,* and *Looking for Mr. Preston*. The winner of the 1994 Porn Press Award, he is currently completing a book of interrelated short stories involving ghosts, sex, our bodies, our souls, and small-town queer life.

Clancy McKenna is a lesbian who is surviving life with a fluid body image, as well as some gender nonconformity. She accepted the assigned label of "overweight" for about twenty of her forty-one years. These days she is described as big, not so bad, and she is an athlete, commuting daily by bicycle to and from work. In September 1995, she rode in the Boston-New York AIDS ride. Clancy lives in the West Village with her twenty-two-year-old son and their two cats. By night she is a student at Queens College, and by day she works for City University.

Jessica F. Morris is a PhD candidate in clinical psychology at the University of Vermont and a graduate of Vassar College. Her research, writing, and clinical work are focused on the psychology of women and particularly focused on lesbians. Her dissertation is titled "Lesbian Mental Health and the Coming-Out Process."

Anna Myers is a writer and a graduate student in the clinical psychology PhD program at the University of Vermont. She writes short fiction, non-fiction, and poetry. Her professional research has focused on issues related to the psychology of women, obesity stigma, and community mental health. Anna has been an out queer activist for over eight years. She graduated with a BA in Psychology and Feminist Studies from Hampshire College in 1991 and has spent her time since then expanding her various identities.

Jill Nagle is a skinny, white, Jewish, bisexual, Virgo chick who lives in the Haight-Ashbury district of San Francisco, where she experiments with, and cruises for: sex, gender, theory, Judaism, community, dance, social justice, and occasionally performance. Some of her documentation to date has been published in the volumes *PoMoSexuals, First Person Sexual, Bisexual Politics,* and *Closer to Home: Bisexuality and Feminism,* as well as in the periodicals *Girlfriends, Black Sheets, Spectator,* and *Anything That Moves.* Her latest book is an edited volume from Routledge titled *Whores and Other Feminists.* Her second, *Girl Fag,* looks at how women inhabit gay male identities, practices, spaces, and orifices. She is currently writing about white supremacy, sex industry consumers, and interparadigmatics, and is working on a screenplay. Her interest in social justice is grounded in *tikkun olam,* the Jewish injunction to mend the world. All she really needs is a good question.

Mark O'Brien was born in Boston in 1949. In 1955, he contracted polio, which paralyzed his limbs and forced him to use an iron lung. He graduated from the University of California, Berkeley, in 1982, with a BA in English. His journalism has been published by *Whole Earth Review, The San Francisco Chronicle, The Fessenden Review,* and *Pacific News Service.* His poetry has appeared in *The Sun, Margin, Berkeley Poetry Review, Rio Grande Review, Saint Andrew's Review, Spitball,* and *Saturday Museum.* He has two chapbooks, *Breathing* and *The Man in the Iron Lung.* He lives in Berkeley, California.

Conrad R. Pegues is a thirty-three-year-old, same-gender-loving black man. He completed his bachelor's degree (1991) and master's degree (1993) in English at The University of Memphis. At present, he teaches writing composition courses in the Memphis area. He is a Southerner born and bred in the buckle of the Bible Belt in Memphis, Tennessee. Living in the cultural milieu of the mid-South has fired an authentic vision of his racial and sexual identity while confronting the sometimes tyrannical powers of family, neighborhood, and church in Southern society.

Layli Phillips wrestles with and researches matters of identity. She is fascinated with words that begin with "i": inbetween, indeterminate, interstice, intersection, infiltrate, interrobang, and, yes, identity. She is Assistant Professor of Psychology and African-American Studies at the University of Georgia in Athens, Georgia.

Jim Provenzano's fiction has appeared in the anthologies *Waves, Best American Gay Fiction 1996, Swords of the Rainbow,* and *Queer View Mirror.* An editor of *Hunt, Wanderlust,* and staff member of *OutWeek,* the former dancer and performer was born in New York and raised in Ohio. With a BFA in Dance from Ohio State and an MA in English from San Francisco State, he writes the weekly column "Sports Complex" for the *Bay Area Reporter.*

Drama Rose is a thirty-year-old, radical, feminist, dyke mom living in central California. She has been out as a lesbian since age eighteen and has loved every minute of it. She is a speaker on body image and the dangers of dieting. She is also a massage therapist who works mostly on large womyn. She is happily married to a beautiful womyn, and they are the proud parents of four cats and one baby girl.

Esther D. Rothblum, PhD, is Professor of psychology at the University of Vermont and editor of the *Journal of Lesbian Studies.* She has edited the books *Lesbian Friendships, Lesbians in Academia, Preventing Heterosexism and Homophobia, Loving Boldly: Issues Facing Lesbians*, and *Boston Marriages: Romantic but Asexual Relationships Among Contemporary Lesbians*. Much of her research has focused on women and the stigma of weight.

Sandip Roy grew up in India and now lives in the United States. He edits *Trikone Magazine*, the world's oldest surviving magazine for gay men and lesbians of South-Asian origin. His work has appeared in *Christopher Street, India Currents Magazine, Queer View Mirror, My First Time, Men On Men 6, Contours of the Heart, A Magazine*, and *Bay Area Reporter* and other anthologies and magazines. When the rent is due, he also writes software.

Jo Schneiderman is a middle-aged dyke who is a recovering bulemic, director of a statewide child abuse prevention program, yoga and aerobics teacher, and community access television producer and news writer. In her spare time, she sometimes writes. She has been writing fiction, journalism, and essays since the late 1960s. Her work has appeared in *Outrageous Women, Gay Community News,* and *For Crying Out Loud*, among others. She is a contributor to and co-editor of *All the Ways Home*, a collection of short fiction about parenting and children in the lesbian and gay communities. Jo lives with her lover of eighteen years, Chaia Mide, who gives her enormous support and sustenance, and their cat, Ruach, who cleverly knocks things off her desk.

Darrell g.h. Schramm is a feminist gay man, trim at fifty, but utterly blind in the left eye, whose work has appeared in the anthology *A Member of the Family,* as well as in such magazines and journals as *Alaska Quarterly Review, Americas Review, Carolina Quarterly, Frontiers*, *Iris, Rain City Review, White Crane*, and numerous others. He teaches poetry and writing at the University of San Francisco. Recently, he conducted a year of weekly poetry workshops for HIV-positive gay men.

Nina Silver, a bisexual feminist, holds a doctorate in Transformational Psychology from the Union Institute and maintains a bodymind psychotherapy and healing practice. She is also a musician, artist, and social change author whose writing on feminism, sexuality, political theory, and metaphysics has appeared in *The New Internationalist, Off Our Backs, Flatland, Jewish Currents, Green Egg, Gnosis,* and the anthologies *Women's Glib, Childless By Choice, Closer to Home: Bisexuality and Feminism, Lesbian Bedtime Stories, Transforming a Rape Culture,* and *Society: Readings in Women's Studies.* Her volume of poetry, *Birthing,* was published recently by Woman in the Moon Publications. She is currently finishing a book that integrates feminism, depth psychology, and the bodymind principles of Wilhelm Reich.

Anna Snoute is a bisexual woman in her twenties currently living in Seattle. She feels as if she has something to say to other women. She would like to thank her sister, who was her best friend throughout childhood and who continues to provide her with challenges and opportunities to grow.

Margo Solod is a thirty-eight-year-old, white, lesbian poet, songwriter, second-generation American of Russian Jewish heritage. Depending on the time of day, the order of these labels can be switched. All the facets are important, and none defines her. Her poetry and fiction have been published in over fifteen publications, both gay and straight. No one who knows her can understand how a stranger could call her sir, or how she could be worried about her weight/body image. No one who thinks they know her does.

Michele Spring-Moore is a switch-hitting, code-switching, semi-butch, bisexual feminist activist poet, a founder of the Rochester, New York, Bisexual Women's Network, and a former editor of *The Empty Closet,* New York state's oldest lesbian and gay newspaper. She received an MA in Creative Writing at the University of Colorado in Boulder, and her poetry has been published in *Bay Windows, Fireweed: A Feminist Quarterly,* and *Hanging Loose.*

John Stoltenberg is the author of *Refusing to Be a Man: Essays on Sex and Justice, The End of Manhood: A Book for Men of Conscience,* and *What Makes Pornography "Sexy"?.* He lives in New York City with the writer Andrea Dworkin.

Donna Tsuyuko Tanigawa is a *yonsei* (fourth-generation), lesbian poet and artist of Japanese ancestry from the sugar plantation town of Waipahu on the island of O'ahu. She received her MA in American Studies from the University of Hawaii at Manoa. Her work explores the language and culture of her mother tongue, "pidgin" English. Her poems and essays have appeared in *Sinister Wisdom, Common Lives/Lesbian Lives, Hawaii*

Review, and *Asian Pacific Journal*, as well as several anthologies. She lives in Honolulu with her partner Lee Donna-Ann.

Jennifer Taub is currently a student in the clinical psychology PhD program at the University of Vermont. Her interests include community psychology, primary prevention, and children's services. Her other interests include bisexuality, constructions of desire, and politics within women's and queer communities. She also likes to play with her cat, brew beer, cook, travel, and waste way too much time on the Internet.

Silva Tenenbein, a fat, kinky, queer Jew who thinks a lot about power, privilege, and access, has been active in lesbian politics for twenty-five years. She lectures on a variety of topics, facilitates workshops, and teaches at a university in Vancouver, British Columbia.

Julia Dolphin Trahan is a crippled, queer, Hawaiian haole living in San Francisco. She earned her BA in Media Theory at Antioch College in Yellow Springs, Ohio. She comanages BUILD, a queer performance space, and is an active member of Corporation for Disabilities and Telecommunications, as well as Wry Crips Disabled Women's Theatre. Her writings can be found in *The Disability Studies Reader, Virgin Territory 2, Frighten the Horses, Sinister Wisdom*, and *Mouth: The Voice of Disability Rights*. On the outside she's a pretty young girl-thang, on the inside (depending on the circumstance), she's a debonair gentleman, glam-girl, or ABC's Cripple-of-the-Week.

Susanna Trnka is a graduate student in anthropology at Princeton University and the mother of a one-year-old daughter. Having recently finished her first novel, she is catching up on her sleep before she attempts to write another.

Naomi Tucker works as a teacher and battered woman's advocate in the San Francisco Bay Area. Virgo supreme, and a proud, pushy, Jewish feminist, she is the editor of *Bisexual Politics: Theories, Queries, and Visions*. Her writing has appeared in journals and anthologies including *Bi Any Other Name, Anything That Moves*, and the *International Journal of Eating Disorders*. Naomi's healing work and community education/organizing efforts have focused on liberating women from the tyrannies of homophobia and biphobia, body image, and domestic violence.

Darcy Wakefield is a Maine native currently living in Jamaica Plain, Massachusetts, and is working with her grandmother on her grandmother's oral history.

Julie Waters has been active in various queer communities for most of her adult life. She was one of the founding members of the first Internet resource expressly about bisexuality and has spent the last seven years maintaining one of the Internet's only free resources for transgendered people. She also has, on occasion, been known to compose music for classical and jazz guitar. She also devotes a great chunk of free time to maintaining Web sites on a wide variety of issues at http://drycas. club.cc.cmu.edu/~julie.

Kate Woolfe was born in Texas in 1969 and considers Austin her one true home. She has a BA in Anthropology and an MS in Community and Regional Planning from the University of Texas at Austin. She lives near the beach in California, with her lover, housemate, and too many cats. She has always wanted to be a writer.

Acknowledgments

In any work such as this, there are always so many people who have contributed to the ideas, the labor, and the inspiration. While I cannot possibly name them all, I will try to acknowledge people who were key in helping bring this book together. First, I owe a debt of gratitude for the "Fat Feminist" activists whose courage and creativity helped create the movement that brought me healing in my own struggle with my body. I would like to acknowledge the work of Judith Stein, Vivian Mayer, Karen Stimson, and Judy Freespirit, as well as all the members of the Fat Lip Reader's Theatre and NAAFA's Fat Feminist Caucus. Ruah Bull was my early mentor in leading body image workshops, whose encouragement created possibilities. And to all the women and men of the Body Image Task Force whose hard work, laughter, and intelligence have sustained me and taught me. In particular, I would thank Marius Griffin, Julie O'Reilly, and Drama Rose. Mary E. Atkins, current BITF co-chair, and copy reader for this volume, also shares with me her love and guidance as my mother.

Thanks goes to other members of my family as well. Lon Sarver spent hours entering material into the computer and filing correspondence, as well as reading and critiquing submissions. Troy McKee, my computer doctor and back fixer, continues to keep me and the equipment going even when overworked. Thanks go to my friends Timothy T. Murphy and Jay Linnell, who sometimes volunteered to do some of the clerical chores for me so I could concentrate on the editing. Klee Burke and Jay also painstakingly proofed the introduction for me. Thanks to Thomas Roche, my longtime friend, whose ideas and encouragement were crucial in both the development and the completion of this volume. Florence Babb, my mentor/advisor at the University of Iowa, has provided a supportive environment for my advancement as both scholar and activist.

Although I am grateful to all the contributors in this volume, several were instrumental in helping me work out the problems of editing, finding a publisher, and completing the manuscript. Jill Nagle, Naomi Tucker, John Stoltenberg, Esther Rothblum, Andrew Feraios, Wendy Chapkis, Julie Waters, and Michael Hernandez all provided crucial knowledge and support. An amazingly perceptive card from Naomi arrived at a moment when I thought I would give up, saying just the right thing to get me going again. Jill and Naomi both provided their expertise and encouragement from their own work editing collections.

Thanks are also due the hundreds of people from many different backgrounds who have over the years listened, questioned, and explored body image ideas with me in workshops. From you I draw my experience and my dedication.

Introduction: Looking Queer

Dawn Atkins

Darlin', I've been told all m' life that I'm goin' to hell 'cause I'm gay—but at least I'll be beautiful when I go!

—Michael Easton

His Texas drawl was beautiful, and his smile contagious, but the pain was unmistakable. My brother and I had never talked about his views of his own body before, even though I had been doing body image education for several years.

It was 1990, I was chair (and founder) of the Body Image Task Force (BITF), a volunteer education and activism organization devoted to promoting positive body image and educating people about the dangers of eating disorders, dieting, and appearance discrimination. BITF speakers had talked to colleges, high schools, and community groups. Now, we had been asked to do a workshop for the Lesbian and Gay Community Center in Santa Cruz, California. Suddenly we realized that we had never considered the specific issues that would be involved with lesbian, bisexual, and gay people's body image. Every book on the topic presumed eating disorders and body image dissatisfaction were the problems of straight, white, middle-class, young women.

This struck me as strange when I realized that two-thirds of the active members of BITF identified as lesbian or bisexual. Many of the other writers and activists involved in body image work were not heterosexual either. Why were so many of the leaders in this work lesbian and bisexual women with our own painful histories. In addition, many of us and our audience members were not all middle-class, young, or white. Clearly something important was missing.

And what about the men? At the time, it was then estimated that 5 to 10 percent of people with eating disorders were men (Barry and Lippmann, 1990:161). We knew from reports and anecdotal sources that a significant number of those men were gay or bisexual. One only had to be somewhat familiar with gay men's culture to see the emphasis placed on appearance.

Since we found academic and anecdotal sources scarce, we turned to our friends and families to prepare for the first couple of workshops. I sat down with my brother, Michael, to ask him about gay men and looks. After the initial camp humor, Michael explained:

> Women are bombarded with the idea that they must be slim, beautiful (blonde, blue-eyed—whatever the fashion is at the time). Men are given the idea that they should be attracted to someone who fits that stereotype. Gay men get this message from both sides "I should be attracted to someone who looks like this stereotype" AND "I must look like this stereotype if I want to attract other men because that is what they perceive as desirable."

What struck me most was that since he was my adopted brother, Michael and I did not share the same body type. He was tall and thin. Yet, he wore a girdle because his stomach "wasn't as tight as it should be." Michael said some people complained that he needed to "put on a few pounds," but he still worried about his figure.

I, on the other hand, was of average weight. But I was told by the weight charts that I was fat—even when I was anorexic. I ate little to nothing for months at a time. My rib and hip bones showed, and still I couldn't get within ten pounds of the supposed "ideal weight." Since I did not come out as bisexual until my mid-twenties, the pressures I faced to be thin came from "straight culture" and my family. It was feminism and the work of early size activists that helped me to break free of these pressures and to accept both my body and my sexuality. How had coming out helped me and not him?

Michael felt that internalized homophobia led to a gay men's culture that trapped him and others. He felt that many gay men have low self-esteem. "We are told that we are unnatural," said Michael, "so proving our sexuality and attractiveness becomes an obsession—a way of proving our worth." Michael also felt that much of gay life was centered in bars, a competitive environment where looks and money were the only things you could judge about people. Among gay men, how else was he supposed to meet someone to love and to love him except with his looks? I asked Michael how he felt it could change. He didn't think it would. For him, at least, it didn't. Michael died in 1991.

But things can change for the many of us—lesbian, bisexual, gay and transgendered—struggling with what it means to be queer and to live in these bodies that can bring so much pain and so much pleasure. I believe they are changing. I hope that this book will add some resources and energy to the work ahead.

In the Beginning . . .

Well, maybe not that far back. Karen Stimson, a longtime activist, observes that in 1969, the same year the first human set foot on the moon, a number of events occurred that would come to shape a generation (Stimson, 1993:1). That year saw: (1) the founding of the National Organization for Women and the second wave of the U.S. feminist movement; (2) the founding of NAAFA (originally the National Association to Aid Fat Americans, later changed to National Association to Advance Fat Acceptance), which would be a leader in the size acceptance movement; and (3) the Stonewall Rebellion, which would ignite the lesbian and gay (later joined by bisexual and transgendered) rights movement. What has come to be called the "body image" or "size acceptance" movement in the United States began with a fusion of these three elements. The first fusion was called "Radical Fat Feminism" in which feminist women, many of whom were lesbians, began to make connections between sexism and weight discrimination.

Throughout the 1970s, these activists published articles on both feminism, in size acceptance publications, and on size discrimination and dieting, in feminist publications. Some of the writings on these issues became part of a literature package developed by the Fat Underground, formed in Los Angeles late in 1973 and active until some time after 1977. According to Vivian Mayer, the movement was a blend of radical feminism and radical therapy (Mayer, 1983:x). Some of these early works were later published in *Shadow on a Tightrope: Writings by Women on Fat Oppression* (Schoenfielder and Wieser, 1983). This book contained several personal narratives (some previously published in feminist publications), which addressed the issue of weight discrimination in general, as well as within the lesbian feminist communities.

It was a struggle, but by the late 1980s, feminism and size acceptance were firmly (if not always comfortably) joined. Dozens of books were published in the 1980s and early 1990s that addressed the social pressures on women to conform to a beauty standard and helped change both the personal relationship women have with their bodies and the culture's treatment of women's bodies. At the time, I found only one book that took a more multidimensional approach, which included issues of sexuality and race, *Beauty Secrets* by Wendy Chapkis (1986). Although fat lesbian and bisexual activists continue to be an important part of the movement through founding organizations and publishing newsletters and articles, unfortunately, their unique experiences did not make it into the increasingly mainstream books and films on body image.

Homosexuality and Body Image

Meanwhile, in academia, most of the "early research on physical attractiveness consisted of studies of males perceiving females, reflecting researchers' implicit assumption that the phenomenon was limited to or most powerful when one of feminine beauty in the eyes of men" (Cash and Brown, 1989:362). In addition, reports of body image focused on women. Because of the focus on the male gaze as a prime motivator in developing eating disorders, men were not generally considered at risk for these illnesses. The heterosexual bias in these studies assumed that the only people interested in attracting men were women. The influence of body image disturbances on lesbians and bisexual women was not even considered by most researchers. This erasure can have a profound negative impact on the health of lesbian, bisexual, and gay people. They may face mistreatment by health care providers or avoid needed treatment because of neglect and prejudice in health care research and education (Stevens and Hall, 1991).

The first reference I was able to find to homosexuality and body image was a study on adolescent males' adjustment and self-image. Prytula, Wellford, and DeMonbreun found that homosexual males differed from heterosexual males in their "physical appearance, the perception of their physical appearance by others, and their perception of how their physical appearance was perceived by others" (1979:567). The gay and straight men were self-labeled. The same authors concluded that "homosexual males reported that they were significantly less adjusted during adolescence than heterosexual males" (p. 567). There is no discussion of the way in which societal factors, such as homophobia, may have influenced this result.

It wasn't until the early 1980s that psychological literature began to focus on males with eating disorders in an attempt to understand how and why these supposed female conditions were affecting them. In 1984, Herzog and colleagues published a report claiming significant "sexual isolation, sexual inactivity, and conflicted homosexuality" among their male anorexic and bulimic patients, unlike with their female patients. They reported that 26 percent of their male patients were homosexual but only 4 percent of their female patients. They cited "cultural pressure on the homosexual male to be thin and attractive" as possibly placing him at greater risk for eating disorders but did not elaborate on the cultural factors (Herzog et al., 1984: 990). Pope, Hudson, and Jonas followed in 1986 with a report that said they "found little evidence of increased homosexuality or 'sexual conflict'" among their male patients (p. 117). Both studies defined homosexuality as reported sexual behavior with another male, not by sexual identity.

In 1984, Kay Deaux and Randel Hanna published a report on the influence of gender and sexual orientation in personal advertisements (Deaux and Hanna, 1984). The personals have long been a popular way to meet, particularly for gay men. They looked at 800 ads, representing an equal number of male and female advertisers, heterosexual and homosexual, on both the East and West Coast of the United States. The identity of the advertisers was based on the gender given for the advertisers and the gender of the person they were looking for, not their stated sexual identity. Therefore, sexual identity was not explored as a factor, nor were they able to look at bisexuality. They did find significant differences by both gender and sexual orientation, as well as on the intersection of these. Men were more concerned with "objective and physical characteristics," while women were more interested in the "psychological aspects of a potential relationship" (p. 374).

Within gender, there were also significant differences by sexual orientation. Women looking for men were more likely to offer physical attractiveness, to search for financial security, specific occupational information, and sincerity. Women looking for women placed less emphasis on physical traits and more on personal information such as hobbies and interests. Men looking for men were more likely to place emphasis on physical characteristics of both themselves and their partners (Deaux and Hanna, 1984:374).

Another study also found emphasis by gay men on physical characteristics (Sergios and Cody, 1986). This study was done on a college campus among self-identified gay men. No description is given of how identity was determined or participants recruited. The participants were matched for "computer dates" through an "afternoon tea dance" arranged by the researchers. They found "the largest determinant" of how much a man liked the other man and would want to date him again was the partner's physical attractiveness. However, attractiveness did not seem to influence how often they actually did go out afterward (p. 71).

Fichter and Daser (1987) published a study on male anorexic and bulimic patients indicating "atypical gender role behavior" (p. 409). They reported that half of their patients felt they were less masculine than other men and that a quarter of them had had sexual contact with other men. The study confuses gender role with sexual orientation, reinforcing a stereotype of gay men as "feminine." The discussion section seems to imply that homosexuality and/or feminine mannerisms are "psychosexual development" disturbances, thereby pathologizing homosexuality and reinforcing male gender behavior as "normal." It implies that it is the lack of proper gender conformity that leads to eating disorders in men. They include no discussion of how homophobia or sexism may have contributed to the problem.

The first nonclinical sample study that showed a link between the development of eating disorders and gay men was by Yager and colleagues (1988). This study compared self-identified gay men from a Gay Men's Rap Group at UCLA with groups of other students on campus. They found:

> The homosexual men had higher prevalence of binge-eating problems, of feeling fat in spite of others' perceptions, of feeling terrified of being fat, and of having used diuretics than other male students. They also scored higher on the Eating Disorders Inventory scales for drive for thinness, interoceptive awareness, bulimia, body dissatisfaction, maturity fears and ineffectiveness. (p. 495)

This study implies that there may be many more gay men with or at risk of developing eating disorders and other body image disturbances than are indicated by the studies of eating-disordered patients. This may be because male patients less often seek treatment than female patients (Barry and Lippmann, 1990:163-164). It is possible that with the added stigma of homophobia, gay men may be even less likely to seek professional help with their body image issues.

Another study comparing self-identified gay and straight men found similar results (Silberstein et al., 1989). They found that "homosexual men showed more body dissatisfaction and considered appearance more central to their sense of self" than did the heterosexual men (p. 219). They also reported that heterosexual men were more likely to exercise for strength, while gay men were more concerned with exercise to improve their physical attractiveness. This study is the first to specifically mention gay culture.

> It has been observed that the homosexual male subculture places an elevated importance on all aspects of a man's physical self—body build, grooming, dress, handsomeness. (p. 338)

One of the more striking things about these early studies is the lack of theoretical discussion. Except for the one just mentioned, the only causal explanation given for the correlations between homosexuality and appearance concerns among men was to pathologize homosexuality. Most studies offered no explanation. In addition, all these reports are clinical in nature, and I have yet to find a piece written by a gay man on the topic in these early years. In contrast, this is particularly interesting given that almost all the work on lesbians and body image has come from lesbians themselves.

Women at Risk, Lesbians Immune?

The first academic material on lesbians and body image wasn't published until years after much of the personal and political work. Laura S. Brown had a theoretical article in *Lesbian Psychologies* (1987). Drawing on her and her colleagues' clinical experience, Brown proposes not only an evaluation of lesbian body image but an analysis of cultural factors and possible solutions to change conditions. First, she states that "lesbians appear to make up a smaller percentage of women with eating disorders than of women in general. Most of the women with eating disorders who are described in the literature are either clearly defined as heterosexual or their sexual orientation has not been the focus of inquiry" (Brown, 1987:295). She also notes that lesbians have been very active among "fat activists, that is, people who define fatness as a normative variation and the stigmatization of fat people as political oppression" (p. 295). She continues by outlining parallels between societal attitudes toward fat women and those toward lesbians, including the rule "for women in patriarchy that states that women are forbidden to love other women, because that would lead them to love and value themselves, and perhaps break the other rules" (p. 298):

> My clinical observation is that homophobia and "fat oppression" . . . can and do intersect in very particular ways in the lives of lesbians. . . . Lesbians and fat women are both valued negatively and stigmatized in patriarchal culture. Fear of being fat/being perceived as fat and fear of being lesbian/being perceived as lesbian are used by the institutions of patriarchal culture as a means of controlling women socially. All women will internalize homophobia and hatred of fat during their socialization in patriarchal culture. Lesbians are at risk from fat oppression in different ways than are heterosexual women. A lesbian's own internalized homophobia is likely to determine the degree to which she fat-oppresses herself. Specifically, I hypothesize that the more a lesbian has examined and worked through her internalized homophobia, the less at risk she is to be affected by the rules that govern fat oppression. The more a lesbian shames and stigmatizes herself for her lesbianism, the more likely it is that she will also actively fat-oppress herself. (p. 299)

Brown explains that lesbian "fat activists, a nonclient population, seem to be women who are comfortable with their lesbianism" (p. 300). She gives examples of clinical work where the more homophobia the client exhibited, the more problems she experienced with her body image. She warns that lesbianism is not a "magic cure for the problems with weight and eating" but does give us some possible explanations (p. 302).

Another theoretical piece by Sari H. Dworkin was published in *Women and Therapy* (1989). This work primarily draws upon *Shadow on a Tightrope* (Schoenfielder and Wieser, 1989) and other published lesbian fat activist work. She explains:

> Lesbians do not think of themselves as objects to be defined by male subjects. Therefore it seems lesbians ought to be able to escape from the negative body image and lack of self-acceptance that other women in our society suffer from. And yet as the lesbian literature suggests lesbians, even feminist lesbians, have bought the myth. Lesbians suffer from body image disturbance and discrimination against fat lesbians who do not fit the patriarchal standard of beauty. (Dworkin, 1989:28)

Dworkin reviews the lesbian body image literature (except Brown's work) and briefly explains fat politics. She concludes that lesbians suffer from body image problems because they "live and work within the heterosexual, patriarchal society" (Dworkin, 1989:33). She posits that the influence of the job market may play a major role in limiting lesbian self-acceptance.

The first clinical study on lesbians was not published until 1990. Ruth H. Striegel-Moore, Naomi Tucker, and Jeanette Hsu (1990) studied body image among lesbian and heterosexual students and found few differences in body esteem, self-esteem, and disordered eating. They did find lower self-esteem and other social difficulties among lesbians. They also found less dieting among lesbians but found more binge eating.

> Although lesbian ideology rejects our culture's narrowly defined ideal of female beauty and opposes the overemphasis placed on women's physical attractiveness, such ideology may not be strong enough to enable lesbians to overcome already internalized cultural beliefs and values about female beauty. Unlike other minorities, lesbians do not grow up with parental or peer models representing lesbian standards as an alternative to the majority culture's norms. (p. 498)

As they point out, age may also be a factor as the study included only women in their late teens and early twenties. The results might be different with a group of women who had been established in their lesbian identity longer and more comfortable with their lives. This study, similar to those with men, excluded bisexuals. According to Naomi Tucker (this volume), the study originally included bisexual women, but they were later dropped from the sample before publication.

Two years later, a study by Herzog and colleagues found "homosexual women were significantly heavier than heterosexual women, desired a significantly heavier ideal weight, were less often concerned with weight and appearance, and had less drive for thinness" (Herzog et al., 1992:391). Women in both groups were heavier than the weight they perceived potential partners would find most attractive and heavier than the weight they considered ideal. Yet, heterosexual women were more likely to be concerned about their weight and to diet, even though they were more likely to be underweight. More homosexual women were satisfied with their bodies. This study included a greater age range, eighteen to forty-five. Bisexuals were simultaneously included and excluded. Those with an affirmed bisexual identity were eliminated from the sample. Only women who categorized themselves as "exclusively" or "primarily" homosexual or heterosexual were included. This allowed that some of these women may also have been involved with men but still identified as lesbians.

That same year, Brand, Rothblum, and Solomon compared lesbians, gay men, and heterosexuals with results that illustrate the complexity of the issues:

> Heterosexual women and gay men reported lower ideal weights and tended to be more preoccupied with their weights than were lesbians or heterosexual men. However, gender was a more salient factor than sexual orientation on most variables, with both lesbians and heterosexual women reporting greater concern with weight, more body dissatisfaction, and greater frequency of dieting than did gay or heterosexual men. (1992:253)

The sexual orientation of participants was self-identified. Bisexuals were again dropped from the sample. The age range was larger for the lesbian and gay sample than for the primarily college-aged heterosexual sample.

A 1993 study found gay men and heterosexual women "showed greater actual concerns with appearance, weight, and dieting, and were perceived to possess greater body image disturbances and dieting concerns" when compared to heterosexual men and lesbians (Gettelman and Thompson, 1993:545). The mean age of participants was in the mid-twenties and, once again, bisexuals were dropped from the study. The discussion section emphasized the importance of cultural conditioning including the differences within lesbian and gay male subcultures.

Michaël D. Siever (1994) found similar results—heterosexual men were the most satisfied with their bodies; gay men were the least satisfied.

Heterosexual women were less satisfied with their bodies than were lesbians but more satisfied than gay men. Siever puts forward the theory that "gay men and heterosexual women are dissatisfied with their bodies and vulnerable to eating disorders because of a shared emphasis on physical attractiveness and thinness that is based on a desire to attract and please men. Although men place a priority on physical attractiveness in evaluating potential partners, women place greater emphasis on other factors, such as personality, status, power, and income" (p. 252).

One way to test Siever's hypothesis would be to look at the bisexual women and men and see what results their dual attraction had, if any. Unfortunately, as with all the previous studies, bisexuals were dropped from the study or lumped in with homosexual or heterosexual identities through the use of the Kinsey scale.

In 1994, Esther D. Rothblum, a leading body image researcher, published an analysis of lesbians and physical appearances. She listed six ways in which appearance affects lesbians:

> First, lesbians, as all women, grow up surrounded by institutions that value physical appearance. Second, lesbians are not in sexual relations with men, and this may lessen the importance of standard appearance norms. Third, research on stereotypes indicates that the dominant culture has extremely negative attitudes about lesbians, including lesbians' appearance. Fourth, the process of identifying with the lesbian culture may depend on the ability to recognize and be recognized by other lesbians, and thus on physical appearance. Fifth, lesbians who are also members of other minority groups may be invisible or may need to choose which group to identify with. Finally, the lesbian community itself has norms for physical appearance and these have changed over the course of the century. (pp. 84-85)

An important component of Rothblum's analysis is the effect of visibility and appearance norms. While some other works have pointed out the different appearance norms in the lesbian and gay cultures, none have explained how these norms may help as well as hurt. According to Rothblum:

> Appearance norms in the lesbian community have had two functions: (a) to provide a means for members of an often invisible and oppressed group to identify one another without being identifiable by the dominant culture and (b) to provide a group identity and thus separate norms from the dominant culture. (Rothblum, 1994:92)

In addition to helping members identify each other, privileging visibility is a tactic of identity politics whereby "participants often symbolize their demands for social justice by celebrating visible signifiers of difference that have historically targeted them for discrimination" (Walker, 1993:868). But the tactic has inherent problems. Those who do not fit the norm or are not visible such as a "femme lesbian" or an "invisibly disabled" person will sometimes be doubly marginalized by both the mainstream culture and the subculture. For those who have another visible marker such as race or disability, their less visible identity may be neglected.

A New Direction

So in 1990, when members of the Body Image Task Force began to design workshops for lesbian, gay, and bisexual people, the only books we had to draw from told us about straight women, their body image, and little else. We began by talking to people, surveying our workshop participants, and making connections with other issues.

We noticed several patterns. First, the cultural norm was (and still is) that women were valued for their beauty (appearance norms) and men for their power/money. Lesbian and bisexual women were brought up with these appearance norms, many even developing eating disorders as young women; it is noteworthy that some of us began recovery at or about the same time as when we "came out." We experienced a double freedom from having to be judged based on our appearance by female partners and the freedom from having to find a partner who "made a lot of money." For many of us, feminism and coming out combined to bring us into the body image movement or vice versa. Yet, people in my workshops showed me that many of us continue to struggle with body image even if we have been lucky enough to have this initial healing stage.

For men, this did not seem to be the pattern. In fact, many gay men's body image seemed in worse shape after coming out than before. It seemed that gay men were pressured to look for and be looked at for both their appearance and their money. They seemed to be taking on the worst of both mainstream ideals.

In my own workshops, I began to develop a "multiple axis" approach. I looked at how the six deadly "isms"—sexism, racism, ageism, ableism, classism, and heterosexism—all intersect in body image issues. I was increasingly frustrated in that there were no books which looked at these connections. So after a particularly powerful workshop as part of Pride Celebrations in June 1992, I began the process of soliciting and editing this book.

Since then, quite a number of works have come out that have begun to address these issues—though to date I have found no other book that tries to examine the way lesbian, bisexual, gay, and transgendered people think and feel about their bodies.

In contrast to the pattern with lesbians, gay men have only begun in recent years to publish more personal accounts of their experiences with body image and discrimination. Patrick Giles published a commentary titled "A Matter of Size" in *Outweek*, October 24, 1990. That was followed with a feature length article on the subject by Jay Blotcher, titled "A Matter of Gravity: How the Queer Community Trims the Fat" in *Outweek*, January 23, 1991. The second article included some interviews with lesbians as well as gay men. Both these groundbreaking articles are reprinted here. These works, and articles similar to them, have offered a bleak picture of the conditions for gay men and their weight and appearance. These materials still lack the political analysis that the feminist materials have included and are often short on solutions, but at least the silence had been broken.

To date, I have only seen two works by gay men on body image that articulate any solutions for change. Darrell g.h. Schramm's "More Than a Sum of Parts: Rescuing the Body from Fundamentalism," published in *White Crane Newsletter* in 1993 (reprinted here), offered a vision of change that included a reconnecting of the body and spirit for gay men. In 1997, well-known gay writer Michelangelo Signorile indicted the gay men's culture for it's "body fascism" in his book *Life Outside* with an appendix that called for changes among gay men.

Meanwhile, the lesbian story has gone from the personal narrative to the quantitative study to a fusion of the two. In 1995, Becky W. Thompson's *A Hunger So Wide and So Deep* became one of the most important books on body image to appear in a long time. Thompson is a feminist sociologist who, in 1984, began to conduct workshops on eating problems. She too noticed that the diversity among the women she worked with did not match the presumption that only middle- and upper-class, white, young women have eating disorders such as anorexia, bulimia, and compulsive eating. She interviewed eighteen women, including five African Americans, five Latinas, and eight white women. All of the white women, and some of the women of color, were lesbians. By focusing on women who were not white and/or heterosexual, Thompson illustrated that women of color and lesbians can be affected by eating problems and body image distortions.

As Thompson's and other works suggest, women of color whose families or life situations promote assimilation into the "mainstream," or "white," culture may be even more prone to eating disorders, as they try to cope with the stress of racism and the impossible ideals of beauty that make women of color invisible. As children, the women of color in Thompson's book experienced conflicts that negated even the body acceptance messages from their communities, when they did exist. Many attended all or mostly white schools so that they felt different. Some had families who internalized racism and passed it on in ways such as telling them that white women were more attractive. Some families were accepting at first but became caught up in the "culture of thinness" when they sought to move up socioeconomically. Over and over, it seemed that racism inside and outside the families was a key factor in these women of color developing eating problems.

Thompson also showed that "lessons about heterosexuality often went hand in hand with lessons about weight and dieting" (Thompson, 1995:39). In order to submerge or deal with their own and other people's homophobia, many young lesbians turned to food and fasting. Most found that "coming out" was a beginning, but not an end, to the healing process. Patterns started early in childhood did not simply disappear when they developed a positive lesbian identity. Feeling that this was expected, many had trouble talking about their eating problems with other lesbians. Coming out and healing was more of a "complicated maze" than stepping out of a closet, but it was a beginning. Thompson analyzes the cultural and personal situations that have perpetuated these women's eating disorders and makes suggestions for ways to change the problems.

Still, Thompson's book focuses primarily on women who have eating disorders—which doesn't tell us how some lesbian (and bisexual) women either recover from or never develop eating disorders. Nor does she address men at all, let alone gay men.

With the publication of *Looking Queer*, we enter what I hope is a new moment in body image. As with the early "Fat Feminist" movement, this book brings together feminism, body image, and sexual orientation—but with many more threads pulled into the weave. By looking at body image issues among lesbian, bisexual, gay, and transgendered people and including other axes of difference such as race and disability, this book attempts to bridge gaps left by earlier works and to provide a step toward new works.

Weaving the Threads

This book explores the questions of what "looking queer" means. The double meaning of "queer" as both "different" and representing "lesbian, bisexual, gay, or transgendered" is intentional. While I understand the objections some have to the word "queer," I feel its power to be both inclusive and evocative of the differences I felt were important to this book. Do we look different? What does it mean to "look gay" or "look like a dyke?" There is also double meaning in the "looking"—in both the seen and the see-er. How do we look at each other? What is it we are looking for? We are often both judged and judge—and by what standards?

When I set out to create this book, I realized that I could not write it alone; no one person could have the diversity of experience needed to explore what "looking queer" means. To do this, I would have to draw together as many different voices as possible. This collection is a large, often uneven, tapestry, drawing cloth from over sixty-five contributors from many different backgrounds, and the weave is not even nor smooth. It is pulled together from different types of cloth, tattered in places and rough to the touch.

The primary audience for this book are the subjects hereof—lesbian, bisexual, gay, and transgendered people. I also hope that those interested in our communities professionally, especially academics and health care providers, will learn from our words. Because this is a mixed audience, I have used a mixed medium with a balance of personal narrative, poetry, journalism, and research articles with what I hope is an accessible language style. Some of the authors in this collection are well-established writers and academics; others are published here for the first time.

This book was collected at a particular time and place, namely in the mid-1990s in the United States (though contributors include people in Canada and Australia). It reflects not only a time period in queer cultures but in the lives of the contributors as well. Even by the time this book went to press, some contributors' lives and ideas had changed. Similar to a snapshot which captures a moment, yet is forever archaic as life continues, so are these ideals. Indeed, we hope very much that our lives will continue to move beyond these points.

This book is also contradictory—like our lives. You will find both overlap and disagreement in the pages here, and I have made no attempt to settle these contradictions (even when I disagree with them). Instead, I feel it is important to show some of the breadth of experiences and ideas present in our communities. I make no attempt here to come up with the final or definitive word in queer body image. Instead, this is meant as a call to dialogue. I hope that this process will continue with more focused books to follow.

Diversity has remained a high priority in this work; of course, even a work that sets out to be as diverse as possible has limits. A work such as this can only include people who write. While this sounds obvious, too often forgotten in these discussions are people who either are not comfortable with, skilled, or interested in writing. Also missing are those for whom body image is "not an issue," so they have no interest in writing about it.

This work is also limited by racist and classist conditions that have left some, particularly people of color, in marginalized positions. First, as a white woman, my access to and acceptance from people of color is understandably suspect. Second, poverty and insecure environments may leave many people unable to write for anthologies. For example, I find it particularly agonizing that of the five works that were lost because the contributor moved and left no forwarding address, four were by people of color. Intensive phone, Internet, and publication searches did not locate their authors. These pieces could not be included without signed contracts and are sorely missed in this collection.

This collection was also constrained by time and size. After several years of collecting materials, I had to set a final deadline. It seemed there were so many issues to be covered that we could never address them all. At some point, the book had to be finished so that you could read it. Even so, the original draft was almost a third larger—too large for most presses and probably too expensive for most book buyers. Some pieces were cut while many others were condensed and tightened.

I knew going into this project that there were major differences in experiences between queer women and men. There was some logic, and even encouragement from others, to create two separate collections—one on lesbians (and bi women) and one on gay (and bi) men. I resisted this pull from the beginning, not knowing how important this resistance would become later. I knew and have confirmed that we had something to learn from each other, that lesbian and bi women, while still struggling, have something to teach about resistance and healing that many gay and bi men could learn from. I also felt strongly that queer women need to listen to and judge less queer men's struggles with appearance and sexuality. We can be allies to each other only if we can learn from each other. What I was not prepared for was the way transgendered people would shake up our worlds and our divisions.

When I began this project, I knew little about transgendered issues. Very little had yet been published by or about transgendered people, and the move to inclusion was only just beginning. Early calls for papers did not list transgender. It was only after I received the first submission, and encouragement/reminder, from a transgendered person that I amended my call. In the time since I began this work, Kate Bornstein (1994) and Leslie Feinberg (1993), among others, have unsettled the clearly divided gender lines among queers. The contributors to this volume have also made me reexamine old

ideas. I always knew that ideals of body and beauty are shot through with
gender ideals—so it should not have shocked me to find important explorations of these power dynamics in the contributions of transgendered people
(transsexual, intersexual, and third-gendered). They did surprise me, and I
am blessed for it.

Yet, among the gendered narratives, there emerged two other themes—
race and ability. Some authors were focusing on the importance of other
axes of difference in body image. Because these issues are so important, I
struggled with a way to highlight them. The inclusion of another section
would disrupt the pattern of gendered sections and threaten the potential
marginalization of these works. Yet, I felt that these authors were addressing
another focus other than reading gender and I wanted to ensure that they
would not become invisible in other sections. I settled (uneasily) on the
inclusion of another category that disrupted the neat pattern—which seems
quite appropriate given the disruptive nature of much of this book.

Having looked at the threads that have been included (and those that
have not), I now turn to the tapestry itself. What pictures appear in the
work?

Tapestry

Section A is titled "Women, Wommin, Womyn" to reflect the struggle
for renaming and recognizing gender differences by feminist women who
identify as lesbian and/or bisexual. Part 1, "Constructing Ourselves," looks at
the way queer women have deconstructed and reconstructed their sense of
the female body. Poet Amy Edgington begins with the beast—beauty.
Nancy Barron draws upon years as a fat lesbian activist to give us a brief
description of body image basics before going into her own struggles with
her body and her work to unite her feminism, size acceptance, and lesbianism. The next two works of original research take a more subtle and
grounded approach than previous studies. Anna Myers, Jennifer Taub,
Jessica F. Morris, and Esther D. Rothblum's study finds that many lesbians
and bisexual women continue to struggle with body image issues even
after coming out. Although many report that their views about their
appearance changed dramatically after coming out, some struggle with
lesbian appearance norms they might consider as restrictive as those of
mainstream culture. Sara Auerbach and Rebekah Bradley found too that
lesbians and bisexual women still struggle with body image issues and
experience pressure from media, families, and friends; though, many have
also received support from lovers, friends, and the lesbian community in
working through these body image issues. Naomi Tucker follows them
with a revealing look at her own previous research with lesbian (and bi)

women, and she faced both as researcher and research subject. And Diane Griffin Crowder brings the spotlight of theory to these issues and looks at cultural construction and deconstruction of lesbians and the female body.

Part 2, "Looking Dyke," explores questions of visibility and inclusion. Wendy Chapkis looks at the contradictory meanings of "dyke" and "beauty" as seen in lesbian and straight views. Weight, food, and sex are the humorous focus of Greta Christina's personal reflections and theories. Cristina Cress confronts the power and the problems of a workplace where "looking queer" can limit your opportunities. Anna Myers launches herself into the debate over femme conformity/resistance and lesbian standards with a personal story of femme self-expression as healing from weight obsession. Kate Woolfe explores questions of whether lesbian is "a look," an identity, or a sexual behavior and what the answers mean for her life and community. Hair, in all its political and personal meanings, is the focus of Andrea Askowitz's piece, including personal comfort, political meanings, and lesbian fashion. Michele Spring-Moore's narrative poem grounds us in the body as experienced in the midst of sexual politics and identity. Amy Edgington gives another look at beauty that we make and move.

Part 3, "Searching a Way Out," is about struggle and survival in the midst of pain, honoring the difficulty of healing. Margo Solod's poem evokes the trap so many of us are trying to break from. Amy Gilley explores struggles with food and sex, and the power, allure, and fear they generate in her. Alexa Leigh's story of fear and isolation experienced even after "coming out" is a poignant reminder of the danger in believing lesbians are free of body image conflicts. Clancy McKenna's story of her body's silent resistance to conformity, imposed on her most of her life, sees her finally freed through coming out. And tattooing as reinscribing and reclaiming of the body is the subject of Catherine Lundoff's piece.

Part 4, "A Woman's Love Heals," brings together stories from women for whom love shared with another woman was their path to healing. Nina Silver starts us off with a poem envisioning the mirror as a possibility for love. Drama Rose's story tells of how coming out did not heal her, only providing a place of self-hate and drug addiction with other lesbians—until a woman's love helped bring self-love. Susanna Trnka's ode to self-love through self-pleasuring shows that "the woman" can be oneself. Claire Hueholt shares the wounds of loving women in a world were women don't love themselves. The lesbian ideal, women's music festivals, and self-love are the focus of Susie Bullington's piece.

Part 5, "Coming Out, Leaving Behind," looks at the power of coming out into an affirming "women's culture" that, ideally, promotes the accep-

tance of sexuality and the body and rejects mainstream ideals of femininity. Darcy Wakefield's poem illustrates what, for many, is a route to affirmation. Silva Tenenbein asserts that, by refusing to serve men, lesbians are
not women but a powerful force against patriarchal views of women. Anna
Snoute explains how managing her weight was a way of controlling her
attractions to women, so that coming out freed her from both. For Jo
Schneiderman, coming out and recovering from bulimia went hand and
hand, much to the fear of her mother. Michelle Bancroft's piece gives us
precious moments in a process of discovery and healing that makes real
the knowledge that coming out and healing are not a moment, but a
process. Amy Edgington gives a poetic glimpse to the change of consciousness.

Section B, "One, Both, Neither," looks at the places both parallel to and
outside the vision of "woman" and "man," where we see the inscription of
the categories and the possibility for release. Part 6, "Crossing the Divide,"
contains stories from people who have crossed from one gendered body to
the other. Julie Waters' struggle with weight and a belief in the thin ideal
for women nearly brought *him* to suicide rather than face *her* life as a
woman. Yet, her courage in facing her own fears has brought a new level
of consciousness. Partners Marcelle and Loree Cook-Daniels explore, in
this honest and compelling conversation, Marcelle's transition from living
an unhappy life as a woman to the life and body of a man, complicated by
ideals of both men and women and of black men in particular. Michael
Hernandez takes on the journey of a young "girl" who knew she was a
boy, to coming out as a butch lesbian, to a final realization that she could
not be trapped by the expectations of *her* body. Living life as a man was
truer to his self.

Part 7, "Square Pegs," brings to us the stories of three courageous people
whose bodies have been altered against their will to fit the molds of female
instead of intersexual (both). Cheryl Chase, founder of Intersex Society of
North America (ISNA), takes a powerful personal and political look at the
system that mutilated her body to maintain gender purity. The sexism,
homophobia, and hidden shame that she documents is something everyone
should know about and work to change. Morgan Holmes, also with ISNA,
presents us with a personal story of how this mutilation of hir infant body
tried to render her "not queer" but the same and robbed her and others of
the pleasure of that difference. Raven Kaldera's story is one of rejection of
the medicalization of hir "hormonal imbalance" and the celebration of the
expression of "hermaphrodite" as sacred mystery.

Part 8, "Boyz, Grrls, Queers," looks at queers who take their difference
into gender as well as sexual desire—and for whom the two may not be

separate. Sherrie A. Inness and Laura Cole give us personal reminders that, while butch/femme roles may seem to mirror, they also reject man/woman roles. Inness begins with the bathroom (the site of many gender wars) and goes on to show how butch is a "gender outlaw" breaking free of the ideals for women in both gender and desire. Cole reclaims femininity as a lesbian and rejects what she sees as restrictive lesbian ideals. Sandra Lee Golvin and Boye creatively use, subvert, and re-create gender in their own body expression. Golvin takes shame as a place of power as she rejects it, through coming to know herself as a femme dyke and a faggot. Boye's prison of early distortion of self and body as those around her tried to make her into a girl/woman is finally broken as she comes to know herself as the feminine boy—neither one nor the other, but something more.

Section C, "Beyond the Pale," takes as its metaphor the visible difference that challenges the construction of "diversity" in "queer" communities. Here the struggle with acceptance of multiple difference is brought into focus. Part 9, "Color Vision," looks at the impact of race, sexuality, and the body. Layli Phillips finds herself at the intersection of race and sexuality as she struggles for acceptance in this place. Conrad R. Pegues takes a strong stance against internalized homophobia and racism in the black man as embodied in the penis. Searching for himself in two worlds, Sandip Roy does not find the gay Indian man in the images of India or America, gay or straight. With a critical look at gay press, Paul EeNam Park Hagland looks at the simultaneous erasure and colonization of the bodies of Asian men. Donna Tsuyuko Tanigawa's personal experience directly debunks the myth that eating disorders affect only straight, white women. Her innovative language style reflects both her Asian identity and her struggle with Western assimilation.

Part 10, "Access to the Look," is a critical look at how people with disabilities are systematically erased from what it means to "look queer." Mark O'Brien's fiction shows more than it tells and allows us to see everyday prejudice. Julia Dolphin Trahan's struggles with disabilities, gender identity, and sexuality give hir strength but not the secret to overcoming prejudice among other queers. Through poetry and narrative, the personal and the political, Kenny Fries explores issues of visibility, relationships, community, and the body as a disabled gay man.

Section D, "Men, Boys, and Trolls," draws from the language of gay men to look at deep divisions in gay male body and community. Part 11, "The Uniform Doesn't Fit," looks at the gay ideal and its restrictive power for both those who don't fit and those who do. Dean Kiley brings to us "Mr. Dummy"—in his provocative exploration of the personification of the gay ideal and embodied theory in Australia. Unfortunately, the situation is just as difficult in the United States. William J. Mann documents the hierarchy of beauty and self-hatred among gay men, including issues of AIDS and racism—with the thoughtful and provocative comments from leaders in the gay community. Reprinted here are the groundbreaking articles of Patrick Giles and Jay Blotcher. First published in 1990, Giles's essay is in the style of ACT UP: up-front and confrontational. He challenges that he had taken more abuse from other gays based on his weight than from the straight world in any form. Blotcher's article (1991) explores fatphobia and looksism among gay men and lesbians in gay New York and finds only moments of hope. Ganapati S. Durgadas notes the adoption of a mainstream "maleness" and the association of fat and femininity in gay male culture that brings together homophobia, misogyny, and fatphobia. Finding no acceptance in "community," he strives for self-acceptance.

Part 12, "Feeling the Burn," captures the pain embedded in the experience of the gay ideal. Gene-Michael Higney's tale of a fortieth birthday party, ageism, and looksism is funny, witty, disturbing, and empowering. Jim Provenzano captures the feel of "striving for the ideal" in his moment-by-moment account of what has become a common gay experience—working out in the gym. Frank Martinez Lester's poetic narrative is moving, sad, and courageous in its exploration of gay culture. John Stoltenberg, once part of the gay community, has become something of a pariah to many. In a deeply personal and painful account, Stoltenberg shows us the passage he took from fat kid, to unhappy gay man, to empowered feminist and gay outcast.

Part 13, "Reenvisioning Men," is a powerful look at a vision of what gay standards have brought us and where those with courage might lead. Ozzie Diaz-Duque starts us with a funny but troubled poem. Andrew J. Feraios takes us on a journey into the heart of the gay ideal. With experience as both an outcast and an insider, he now finds himself in the queer position of having escaped the trap and offers a kind of bridge for others. Reprinting Darrell g.h. Schramm's vision of reclaiming wholeness with mind, spirit, and the body presents a vision of the possible healing power of gay sexuality and community. Jill Nagle's vision of radical sex's power to enforce or challenge narrow ideals and dissociation from the body is powerful. She looks at her own position as "skinny, white chick," recognizing both personal struggle and cultural privilege but without giving over responsibility to guilt. What Feraios, Schramm, and Nagle effectively do is counter the stereotype that if you object to the gay or lesbian ideal, you are "sex negative." They show us a vision of wholeness, wherein sexuality is celebrated in all its forms with the power to heal all of us.

Queer Vision

During the same conversation as our discussion of body image, I tried to convince Michael to move from Texas to California. I told him about all the community resources and that I felt it would be a more accepting place. He shook his head. He explained that he couldn't imagine what acceptance would feel like and was afraid to try. He had grown accustomed to the role of outcast. Ultimately, and tragically, his isolation killed him.

I believe that we must have the vision to imagine communities where all of us are not merely accepted but welcomed and appreciated. We must begin to reshape our way of "looking," not necessarily the way we look. If we are able to see the beauty in diversity and experience the erotic of connection, I believe that we can build truly healthy communities where our bodies will become a source of joy and power. This collection has much to teach us. By looking at the pain, the struggles, and the healing that people have experienced, I know we can find ways to improve not only our own self-esteem and comfort in our bodies but create mutually supportive communities. "Looking queer," then, will mean looking at our bodies differently and at different bodies with equal joy.

REFERENCES

Barry, Archana, and Steven B. Lippmann. (1990). Anorexia nervosa in males. *Postgraduate Medicine* 87:161-165.

Blotcher, Jay (1991). A matter of gravity: How the queer community trims the fat. *Outweek,* January 23:38-43.

Bornstein, Kate. (1994). *Gender Outlaw: On Men, Women, and the Rest of Us.* Vintage Books, New York.

Brand, Pamela A., Esther D. Rothblum, and Laura J. Solomon. (1992). A comparison of lesbians, gay men, and heterosexuals on weight and restrained eating. *International Journal of Eating Disorders* 11(3):253-259.

Brown, Laura S. (1987). Lesbians, weight, and eating: New analyses and perspectives. In Boston Lesbian Psychologies Collective (Ed.), *Lesbian Psychologies,* pp. 294-310. University of Illinois Press, Chicago.

Cash, Thomas F. and Timothy A. Brown. (1989). Gender and body images: Stereotypes and realities. *Sex Roles* 21(5/6):361-373.

Chapkis, Wendy. (1986). *Beauty Secrets: Women and the Politics of Appearance.* South End Press, Boston.

Deaux, Kay, and Randel Hanna. (1984). Courtship in the personals column: The influence of gender and sexual orientation. *Sex Roles* 11(5/6):363-375.

Dworkin, Sari H. (1989). Not in man's image: Lesbians and the cultural oppression of body image. *Women and Therapy* 8:27-39.

Feinberg, Leslie. (1993). *Stone Butch Blues.* Firebrand Books, Ithaca.

Fichter, M. M., and C. Daser. (1987). Symptomatology, psychosexual development and gender identity in forty-two anorexic males. *Psychological Medicine* 17(2):409-418.

Gettelman, Thomas E., and J. Kevin Thompson. (1993). Actual differences and stereotypical perceptions in body image and eating disturbance: a comparison of male and female heterosexual and homosexual samples. *Sex Roles* 29(7/8):545-562.

Giles, Patrick. (1990). A matter of size. *Outweek,* October 24:32-33.

Herzog, David B., Kerry L. Newman, Christine J. Yeh, and Meredith Warshaw. (1992). Body image satisfaction in homosexual and heterosexual women. *International Journal of Eating Disorders* 11(4):391-396.

Herzog, David B., Dennis K. Norman, Christopher Gordon, and Maura Pepose. (1984). Sexual conflict and eating disorders in twenty-seven males. *American Journal of Psychiatry* 141:989-990.

Mayer, Vivian. (1983). Foreword. In Lisa Schoenfielder and Barb Wieser (Eds.), *Shadow on a Tightrope: Writings by Women On Fat Oppression,* pp. ix-xvii. Aunt Lute Books, Iowa City.

Pope, Harrison G., Jr., James I. Hudson, and Jeffrey M. Jonas. (1986). Bulimia in men: A series of fifteen cases. *Journal of Nervous and Mental Disease* 174(2):117-119.

Prytula, Robert E., Christopher D. Wellford, and Bobby G. DeMonbreun. (1979). Body self-image and homosexuality. *Journal of Clinical Psychology* 35(3):567-572.

Rothblum, Esther D. (1994). Lesbians and physical appearance: Which model applies? *Psychological Perspectives on Lesbian and Gay Issues* 1:84-97.

Schoenfielder, Lisa, and Barb Wieser (Eds.). (1983). *Shadow on a Tightrope: Writings by Women on Fat Oppression.* Aunt Lute Books, Iowa City.

Schramm, Darrell g.h. (1993). More than a sum of parts: Rescuing the body from fundamentalism. *White Crane Newsletter* 17:6-9.

Sergios, Paul, and James Cody. (1986). Importance of physical attractiveness and social assertiveness skills in male homosexual skills in male homosexual dating behavior and partner selection. *International Journal of Homosexuality* 12(2):71-84.

Siever, Michael D. (1994). Sexual orientation and gender as factors in socioculturally acquired vulnerability to body dissatisfaction and eating disorders. *Journal of Consulting and Clinical Psychology* 62(2):252-260.

Signorile, Michelangelo. (1997). *Life Outside.* Harper Collins, New York.

Silberstein, Lisa R., Marc E. Mishkind, Ruth H. Striegel-Moore, Christine Timko, and Judith Rodin. (1989). Men and their bodies: A comparison of homosexual and heterosexual men. *Psychosomatic Medicine* 51:337-346.

Stevens, Patricia, and Joanne M. Hall. (1991). Critical historical analysis of the medical construction of lesbianism. *International Journal of Health Services* 21(2):291-307.

Stimson, Karen. (1993). *Fat Feminist Herstory.* Largesse, New Haven, Connecticut.

Striegel-Moore, Ruth H., Naomi Tucker, and Jeanette Hsu. (1990). Body image dissatisfaction and disordered eating in lesbian college students. *International Journal of Eating Disorders* 9(5):493-500.

Thompson, Becky W. (1995). *A Hunger So Wide and So Deep*. University of Minnesota Press, Minneapolis.

Walker, L. M. (1993). How to recognize a lesbian: The cultural politics of looking like what you are. *Signs* 18(4):866-890.

Yager, Joel, Felice Kurtzman, John Landsverk, and Edward Wiesmeier. (1988). Behaviors and attitudes related to eating disorders in homosexual male college students. *American Journal of Psychiatry* 145(4):495-497.

SECTION A:
WOMEN, WIMMIN, WOMYN

PART 1:
CONSTRUCTING OURSELVES

Beauty Is a Beast

Amy Edgington

We are told it lies
no deeper than a woman's skin.
We are told it lives
in someone else's eye.
We starve ourselves and pad our breasts,
bleach or burn our skins,
curl or straighten our hair,
because beauty must be domesticated—
wolves don't worry about their appearance;
there is no Miss Bear contest.

But underneath the clothes
and the attitudes that cage us,
something paces, wanting out.
A wild woman longs to strut,
baring every scar and crease and bulge:
she knows her pack would not judge
but read what life has written on her.
They would delight to see how the spirit
spills through her frayed skin,
shining, like electric fur.

Living into My Body

Nancy Barron

After nearly a lifetime of silence, I am eager to write about lesbian bodies. As I weaken the stranglehold that sexism and homophobia have had on my ability to experience and communicate my lesbian body meanings, perhaps I also will find readers hungry for such reflections. Together, we may be able to experience the joyful, sometimes tearful, relief of seeing experienced realities *named* at last. We may feel the surge of vitality of simply *being* ourselves. Our expanded consciousness may also expand our power, giving us an opportunity to reduce oppression of lesbians. This is a personal essay with an unabashedly political aim.

In my earliest years, I challenged the heterosexist, patriarchal privileges within my family, yet I didn't hear the word "lesbian" until I was in my thirties (although I had once read it in my abnormal psychology course). It was not a word I said out loud until my forties. Now, in my fifties, I experience a vital integrity because lesbian is at the core of my identity.

I have studied body image for fifteen years (Barron, Eakins, and Wollert, 1984). Nonetheless, only in the last few years have I ventured professionally to speak of lesbian body image, for instance, in my university class on self-image and body size. In speaking of lesbian bodies, we are breaking a taboo, the taboo of silenced homosexuals, and no doubt every word we say will be fraught with our conditioned response to duck the anticipated societal blows. From this silence, my language suffers from a lack of names for experience and concepts that have relevance particular to my lesbian experience. Still, I am eager to speak and eager to listen.

Nancy Scheper-Hughes and M. Lock (1987) offer a definition of body image and three ways of viewing the body, which I find useful in my thinking about lesbian bodies as well:

> Body image refers to the collective and idiosyncratic representations an individual entertains about the body in its relationship to the environment, including internal and external perceptions, memories, affects, cognitions, and actions. (p. 16)

I paraphrase this as "Our body image is what we believe our body experiences, form, and actions mean in our life." Scheper-Hughes and Locke propose:

> . . . three perspectives from which the body may be viewed: (1) as a phenomenally experienced individual body-self; (2) as a social body, a natural symbol for thinking about relationships among nature, society, and culture; and (3) as a body politic, an artifact of social and political control. (p. 6)

Arthur Frank (1991) offers a typology of body use. The *disciplined* body becomes predictable through regimentation. It is perhaps *among* others, but not *with* them, dissociated even from itself. It is insufficient, and discipline sustains it. The *mirroring* body predictably reflects that which is around it. It reflects itself. It, too, is dissociated, assimilating only the objects made available for it to consume. The *dominating* body is a male body characterized by a sense of lack in the form of anxiety and fear, living through conquest. All is contingent on the insecure ability to dominate. The *communicative* body is a body in the process of creating itself. Relatedness is dyadic, and this body's desire is for reciprocal expression and the recognition of others rather than consumption, domination, or mirroring.

"Body image," as we use it here, implies a particular cultural/historical context. The eating disorder epidemic; the fitness craze; the preoccupation with personal, social, professional, and business image; the inescapable barrage of electronic images; a consumer economy of abundance faltering in the face of massive maldistribution creating richer and poorer; the need to save and preserve our global environment; and the second wave of feminism followed by backlash and possibly a third wave—these are among the powerful influences in which this writer-reader conversation takes place.

While certainly not *only* a body issue, being a lesbian certainly *is* a body issue. Intimate, sensual/sexual sharing with another of the same gender is a different experience from which to build body image than a heterosexual would have. The physical, emotional, cognitive, and spiritual differences that are coupled with loving women give alternative meanings to living in one's body. And, living identified as a lesbian in the social world offers others the opportunity to make judgments about lesbian bodies. The response of society—parents, teachers, friends, neighbors, employers—to our lesbian identity lets us know that the lesbian is very important and controversial, if not sinful, in their eyes. For them, the social body of the lesbian is fraught with danger. Lesbian reality becomes a political issue of control.

The reality of lesbian experience is hard to conceptualize, for the general culture has few words for our experience and relegates those words about our bodies to profanity and perversion or punishes us for speaking them. Our most tender exchanges are used as targets for disgust, fear, and derision.

Homophobia is an undeniable part of our experience. Here, in Oregon, the lesbian body politic recently narrowly escaped severe castigation through the defeated Measure Nine, which would have defined homosexuality as "wrong, unnatural, and perverse," forced teachers to teach that attitude in schools, and prohibited equal rights for homosexuals. Many lesbians and gay men became more visible and more vulnerable, and many people are now more aware of homosexuality through that political struggle.

As a culture, we have a great deal of body shame. As women, we bear a disproportionate share of that shame about bodily functions. As lesbians in a society racked by such quakes as the Oregon measure, informal social disapproval threatens to be bolstered by constitutional condemnation—and we would have the opportunity to carry a triple burden of body shame.

Yet many lesbians are happy and proud about their bodies. This may come through the crucible of differentiating how I feel about myself (the body image as experienced) from how others feel about me (the social body image). And the surge of gay pride/gay activism speaks of lesbian commitment to bringing choice and self-control to lesbian bodies (the body politic).

Several points of contrast promise to help clarify the dynamics of lesbian body issues. I will use myself as my best-known example to contrast the body image experience of living as a heterosexual woman and living as a lesbian, including information from others as possible. While my heterosexual and homosexual experiences are from different ages and eras, my basic personality and my cohort remain constant.

I will reflect on differences in body image and fatness for lesbians and heterosexual women. My experience in founding and leading the size acceptance organization, Ample Opportunity, has put me in contact with thousands of women interested in grappling with the societal meanings of fatness and the control of women through fat phobia. Some of these women are lesbian. Have the fat lesbians and the heterosexual women dealt with the same issues? Are there struggles particular to fat lesbian women? What are the dynamics when fat lesbian and heterosexual women attempt to work together on body image?

I will briefly describe the issues and resolutions from a lesbian body image support group.

MY BODY AS EXPERIENCED GAY AND STRAIGHT

I have a different relationship with my body living as a lesbian than I had before I came out. "My *lesbian* body" reflects a different experience within me and says more and different things about me than "my woman's body" or, simply, "my body." Homophobia has fostered a silence, a taboo, on issues of lesbian body image, which has made it very difficult to express these differences.

(My coming-out story in a nutshell: I have known sexism was not right and that I preferred women since I was three, had crushes on my sixth-grade teacher and girl friends since junior high, dated boys in college, married for twenty years after a Fulbright and a year and a half of graduate school, divorced and came out when my children were ten and thirteen, fifteen years ago.)

As a lesbian, I seldom feel "too." In contrast, during adolescence and while living as a straight woman, I felt "too" big, "too" tall, "too" intelligent, "too" capable, "too" independent, "too" masculine, and certainly, "too" fat. The anxiety and shame about my body has diminished markedly. The size and shape of my body has not.

Fatness is the characteristic I believe others accept least. Even so, I feel better about my fatness as a lesbian. Freedom, joy, fear, and at-homeness characterize my lesbian body experience. I moved from a heterosexual relationship in which my husband loved my body in spite of its fatness, to a lesbian relationship in which my partner loved my body irrespective of its fatness, to a partner who considers my ample proportions part of what drew her to me. I feel at home in this body, without shame or anxiety no matter where she touches me. My belly or the scallops of flesh on my sides are no longer flinch zones. I live in, make love with, and am loved in my body as an organic whole. My skin is an intimate communicator.

I feel less owned as a lesbian. My body belongs more to me. Although I'm excruciatingly aware of the political control over my body as a deviant from the heterosexual "right" way, being illegal in some states and countries, I still feel more in control of who touches me and how. I may consult others in decisions I make about my body, but I feel less pressure in how I make them.

I feel more at home in this body. I have been socialized into some of the gestures and postures of the heterosexual woman. I find some of them fitting to my basic self. However, many of the movements I am expected to make as a woman do not fit: keeping my knees together, holding my shoulders still as I walk, keeping my elbows in by my side, tilting my head to look up. Neither do I find a swagger comfortable. In fact, when I stride out, because of the structure of my body, I have quite a sway in my hips. I am content to move as best suits my body structure, without resentment of having to try to appear "feminine" when it doesn't fit and without fear of appearing "masculine".

Yet, assuming a lesbian lifestyle is not about becoming masculine, I was amazed that I felt so much more womanly after beginning to make love with women. For me, assuming a lesbian lifestyle was not about butch-femme, although I do feel these concepts carry significant experiences and feelings (which have little to do with masculine-feminine). Rather, as I have become lesbian, I have become more comfortable with moving, behaving, and dressing *as I feel I am* at any point in time, instead of how others think I should be.

Becoming lesbian is partly about reclaiming the neutral from being defined as masculine. For instance, hairy armpits are not masculine; they are human and as sensual as a woman's bush. Shoes that allow one to walk naturally are not masculine; they are human. Of course, one need not be lesbian, or even feminist, to reclaim the gender-neutral aspects of bodies. It may be easier if lesbian because of caring less about male approval or disapproval of one's body. Those intimately drawing pleasure from my body are not male.

Not only intimate relations shape and control my body image. Worrying about what people on the street think can be equally controlling. Clothing is far from trivial. It can still ruin my day to have "nothing to wear," and not just from personal insecurity. It is a constant battle to find clothes large enough. That battle is even more grueling when I want to exclude clothing that is extremely feminine or masculine because I often must shop at men's big and tall stores in order to find clothes that fit. Dyke finery also is often not available in my size. Both social acceptability and personal expressiveness are hampered by my size.

Socially and politically, being fat is still difficult. "Fat dyke" is the ultimate flinch word to keep women in line. That epithet condenses the union of two characteristics so negatively valued that people cringe.

Fat lesbians face double jeopardy in terms of dual discrimination for their threatening characteristics. Naomi Wolf, in *Beauty Myth* (1991), wrote incisively of young and thin as the mandates of patriarchal control—she neglected to add heterosexual. Examine the inverse of these, and you get "an old, fat dyke." Sound ferocious? Daring to exist differently from the patriarchal norm, such a woman threatens the cultural control. Such a woman risks social punishment for her being different, not only for being old, or fat, or lesbian, but also for being all three. I am a fifty-seven-year-old, fat dyke, and I am very fond of who I am, despite how those words ring in common parlance. Many of my friends also come in this category, and I delight in their women's beauty. However, they and I are at a social and occupational disadvantage within the mainstream.

Despite the double risk of "fat dyke," it was only after coming out that I felt secure enough to launch Ample Opportunity. AO is a size acceptance organization focusing on the health and happiness of fat women through joyful physical, social, and educational activities (Barron and Lear, 1989). Within a short time, I realized that, although mine was a body type many people didn't prefer, I probably experienced more feelings, and more positive feelings, in my body than nine out of ten people, including the so-called beautiful people.

Despite my shyness and body insecurity, I became a belly-dance teacher in order to be able to offer a situation in which fat women could take up space, make large movements, and dance with their whole body and spirit. I find an embodied wholeness in the dance. People often snicker at the idea; their discomfort usually gives way to enjoyment.

Why do I now feel more my own size, shape, intelligence, capability, etc.? I feel more integrity, more oneness with myself. My life is more congruent with my nature. I am working to become the best me I can rather than trying to be someone I am not. (I wonder if women who were extremely heterosexual but grew up in a compulsory lesbian society would feel that same sense of coming home after coming out as a heterosexual?)

Why did I found AO after becoming an active lesbian? Why did I defy my body shame and shyness to teach belly dance after I had become gay? Are lesbians more size acceptant? In the face of social opprobrium and sanctions, do lesbians seem to take the lead in social change? Perhaps we can see more clearly, being socially marginal because of our embodied affections. In order to simply become our*selves*, we must be and do some-what differently. Having the demand of differentiating ourselves from others because of our lesbian nature, yet also having a profound kinship with others because of our myriad commonalities and the need to live in the dominant culture, we can bridge multiple perspectives and perceive possibilities that might not be visible were we exceedingly well suited to prevailing roles.

Fat Women—Lesbian and Heterosexual

As I developed Ample Opportunity, I was struck by how difficult it was to come out as a fat person. Coming out as fat and coming out as lesbian are similar. (The major difference is that fatness is an undeniable visible quality while the obviousness of lesbian orientation can be somewhat increased or decreased by the individual.)

- Being ahead of the wave of what later came to be known as size acceptance, I had to speak of experiences that contradicted the unselfconscious rightness—and righteousness—of sizism. Similar dynamics occur around heterosexism/homophobia as a woman comes out as a lesbian.
- I was challenging stereotypes of the greed, self-indulgence, and psychological difficulties of fat people with empirical evidence to the contrary. In coming out as a lesbian, I faced analogous stereotypes.
- I had to come out as a fat woman to each person anew, similar to the constant decision of how much and how to reveal my lesbian identity.
- People often consider it embarrassing for me to speak of fatness, much as though I had loudly announced a fart when I could have had the decency to be silent. I was violating taboos of silence by saying the word "fat," by speaking of the fat experience. This resembles the "I don't care what you do in the bedroom, but I don't want to hear about it" position about lesbians. This position misses the point that being a lesbian defines affiliation, family, community, legal rights, etc., in addition to being an orientation toward sexuality. Both "don't talk about it" positions deny profound oppressions and maintain the silence which allow them to occur.

During the time Ample Opportunity has been in existence, there has been a shift in public knowledge and attitudes about lesbians, and certainly, a shift in my own. In 1984, when I began AO, I was positive about my own orientation but relatively new at the lesbian lifestyle and wary of being known as lesbian, especially in relationship to AO.

The initial advisory council was about half lesbian. This split was not deliberate but was a result of women I knew from my earlier fat groups and of who was available and interested. (There is, at least, the common opinion that lesbians are disproportionately frequent in many groups which focus on social services and social change.) I practiced a strong policy of "AO is for all women," trying in a relatively homogeneous and conservative community to promote acceptance of cultural diversity and acceptance of diverse sizes.

At one point, there was a donnybrook because some members of the council believed that only super-sized women should be allowed in AO, and some believed that it should be only radical lesbian feminists. The more clearly I understood that the whole culture was fat phobic and how sexist that fat phobia was, the less I wanted AO to be separatist and exclusive. On the other hand, I was often called upon by others to explain why fat women needed a group to themselves; we had to live in the world, didn't we? A safe space to heal and prepare was necessary. I had nothing against a lesbian or super-size-only group, but that was not this group. The advisory council disbanded before any consensus was reached, but the separatist lesbians did not to my knowledge act on their interest by forming a separatist group.

Making AO safe space for lesbian fat women was a continuing goal. Throughout the thirteen years of AO, fat women who were lesbians comprised an estimated 20 percent of AO, perhaps twice the number one would expect by chance. In a group focused on support and empowerment through personal growth and interpersonal activities, it would have been inconsistent and stifling for only heterosexual women to reveal about personal body image issues.

In AO participative workshops such as Fatness and Sexuality, it was impossible to share frankly about sexuality without revealing one's orientation. This was a special burden of homophobia that lesbians faced. While the heterosexual women involved often had personal barriers to surmount for meaningful disclosure, none of them had to contend with the likelihood that other members might respond with disgust, censure, or ostracism simply because their sexual responsiveness was toward men. In early years, other women and I had chosen not to self-reveal. Rather, we tried to use nongendered, ambiguous language, but then disclosure became more authentic, and it seemed to be accepted.

AO has been labeled "that bunch of militant lesbians" and other similar epithets—a misnomer, since AO has always been over three-fourths heterosexual women and has been both quiet and timid about specifically lesbian issues. One earlier board member assured me that, although I was OK, she did not want to be part of an organization identified with lesbians. When I wanted to hold a body image group specifically for lesbians, I chose to use the auspices of the local gay and lesbian social services organization rather than my own organization. It was only around the issue of Measure Nine (described earlier) that the two-year-old board and I (the only lesbian on the board) developed the resolve to make the headline article of our September, 1993, *Ample Information* newsletter a comparison of fat phobia and homophobia and a statement that AO supported neither.

As president of the small, busy organization, I come to know members in a variety of contexts—board meetings, newsletter folding, workshops, skiing, or swimming, etc. I do not hide my lesbian orientation, nor do I push it in their face. I simply let it be known as part of all the aspects of my life.

The lesbian community seems to accept some fatness more readily than straight society. Still, there is a certain flavor of fat phobia in their community too. It takes the forms of: (1) passing for professional acceptance, (2) wanting to appear "in control," and (3) believing that fatness is weakness, hampering physical activity.

Professional passing: Lesbian professionals in a homophobic society generally must modify their dress, hairstyle, etc., toward the dominant heterosexual norms to maintain professional credibility with their employers and their clients. Whether or not we are out, we must often deal with enforced professional dress codes. This is one of the areas in which heterosexist values often still rule lesbian appearance. These values include dress designed to emphasize women's body parts in a heterosexist, male-identified manner, which includes, above all, looking as slender as possible. Needing to look heterosexual, young, and slender regardless of how one *is* leeches confidence. And, as acceptability is judged on appearance, this inauthentic passing can block expression of actual capability and through biasing others' perceptions, hamper one in progressing professionally.

Susan Brownmiller wrote in *Femininity* of women "passing" by modified dress, manner, attitude, voice, etc., in enough ways to be perceived as feminine (weak) enough to be accepted. It is not surprising that Robin Williams in the film *Good Morning, Vietnam* joshed about lesbians as "women with sensible shoes." Ladies' shoes are carefully designed to hobble us, destroy our sense of balance, and inhibit our stride. I certainly teeter in how comfortable a shoe I dare wear in different work situations to still be acceptable. Idiosyncrasy credits are stretched to allow my lesbian body to show through as much as possible and still be OK. Add to that an enduring problem with a heel spur—will I wear my Avia walking shoes the podiatrist prescribed to work or to the after-work professional tea, or will I be appropriate? (I wore Avias to work, pain instead, to the tea.)

In control: Although research shows that the greatest influence on a body's degree of fatness is heredity (e.g., Stunkard et al., 1986), many people still believe that fatness represents the greed of eating too much. Lesbians are often breaking free of forms of control wreaked upon heterosexual women. Wanting to revel in and project an image of "in control of myself," lesbians may shun fatness because it implies lack of control to the uninformed. There is some understanding that plumpness rather than anorectic thinness is female. There is often not understanding that individuals are born with body types, and that some of those are markedly fat.

Fatness hampers strength: Lesbians often want to shed the weakness of the heterosexual feminine role and revel in their strength as women. Athletics or nontraditional occupations are examples of areas where this dynamic plays out. Fatness is believed to hinder performance; therefore, it is something to avoid in oneself or others. Indeed, performance is *not* as high in some sports, for example running or skiing. Performance can be as good or better in sports such as swimming, weight lifting, or discus throwing. There are roles for many body types in many activities, for example, dancing, softball, and the martial arts.

In our break with heterosexual conventions, as lesbians, we have the opportunity to break with oppression of fat and oppression of women. To a degree, we have and are. In some ways, we are still stuck in the boxes of the majority. Indeed, it is unrealistic to ask of an oppressed minority group that it overthrow conditioning and the majority's demands all at once. Sometimes we get stuck in boxes of our own subculture (for instance, a real dyke *must* be strong). It is freeing, exciting, and hope inspiring that we have done as much as we have to free lesbians to be real in our bodies and to have healthy, happy body images. Do other lesbians have the same balancing acts as I?

Notes from a Lesbian Body Image Support Group

The group was an eight-week support group facilitated under the auspices of the lesbian/gay social service agency of the metro area. We focused on current issues in members' personal lives and the development of positive body images. We did not have to deal with coming out and making others feel comfortable about our orientation, and we could concentrate on body image issues specifically as lesbians, as well as the way in which we, as lesbians, dealt with body image issues universal to women. We talked of what is beautiful, butch-femme, strong, graceful, and attractive.

Debbie (names are fictitious) shared having been handled and objectified by male doctors as an adolescent with an extended illness. She learned that she could catch glimpses in the mirror of herself as a self-determining, just-right woman and that she could visit those glimpses in memory when she felt depersonalized or objectified. Diane changed her belly from a hated barrier to loving her partner to a part of herself with which to love her partner. Samantha used the support of the group to come to believe that it was OK to be both femme and a tall, broad-shouldered woman despite an earlier nonsupportive experience within the lesbian community. Easterly was relieved to be able to integrate soft-jock, fat, womanly, and graceful within her lesbian self-concept with the group as witness.

The members who had come out as lesbians when they were adults agreed that there was some relief from the barrage of feminine body images but that the lesbian community expected strength and varied greatly in accepting fatness. Discussing body qualities with a supportive lesbian group gave an alternative point of reference. As Diane said, "I just don't feel so desperate about any of these issues now."

In Closing

This old, fat dyke yearns for the day when we can understand the beauty of those words. Age means a richness of experience, opportunities for wisdom, and a sense of nearly knowing the song of living. Fat is a natural way of being for some persons, complete with its own health and beauty. Living as a lesbian for those of us who *are* means living in harmony and integrity with our natures. Lesbians, and perhaps especially fat lesbians, have made inroads for ourselves and others in allowing body image to be a reflection of our intrinsic nature in communication with others. May we as lesbians continue to contribute to ourselves, our community, and the larger society the joy in our embodied being rather than the pain of never quite measuring up to the artificial standard imposed from outside.

REFERENCES

Barron, N., Eakins, L. I., and Wollert, R. (1984). Fat Group: A SNAP-launched self-help group for overweight women. *Human Organization, 43*, 44-49.

Barron, N., and Lear, B. H. (1989). Ample Opportunity for fat women. *Women and Therapy, 8*, 79-92.

Brownmiller, S. (1984). *Femininity*. New York: Linden Press, Simon and Schuster.

Frank, A. (1991). For a sociology of the body: An analytical review. In M. Featherstone, M. Hepworth, and S. Turner (Eds.), *The Body: Social Process and Cultural Theory*. London: Sage.

Scheper-Hughes, N., and Lock, M. M. (1987). The mindful body: A prolegomenon to future work in medical anthropology. *Medical Anthropology Quarterly, 1*, 1-14.

Stunkard, A. J., Sorenson, T. I. A., Hanis, C., Teasdale, T. W., Chakraborty, R., Schull, W. J., and Schilsinger, F. (1986). An adoption study of human obesity. *The New England Journal of Medicine, 314*, 193-198.

Wolf, N. (1991) *The Beauty Myth*. New York: William Morrow.

Beauty Mandates
and the Appearance Obsession:
Are Lesbians Any Better Off?

Anna Myers
Jennifer Taub
Jessica F. Morris
Esther D. Rothblum

"Being female means being told how to look."[1] For heterosexual women, the beauty standard is unavoidable: the images stare at us from magazines, billboards, TV screens, department store makeup counters— the list goes on. But what, if anything, does this heterosexual women's beauty ideal mean for lesbians? To date, there has been little examination of the impact of the dominant culture's beauty standards on lesbian communities. It is likely that, prior to coming out, lesbians are pressured to conform to the same appearance norms as heterosexual women. However, does coming out then free lesbians from these norms, allowing them to find their own, unique styles? Or, alternatively, is female beauty socialization carried over into lesbian communities? Do lesbians impose appearance standards of their own—standards perhaps as restrictive and narrow as heterosexual norms? Drawing on prior research, as well as on interviews with twenty lesbian and bisexual women from across the United States, this chapter examines ways in which female beauty mandates have impacted lesbians and raises questions about the relative freedom from such mandates currently experienced by lesbians in their own communities.

As girls and women, both lesbian and heterosexual women are socialized by the dominant culture to value physical attractiveness. Research suggests that this socialization remains with lesbians even after they come out. For example, in a study of body dissatisfaction among heterosexuals, lesbians, and gay men, Pamela Brand, Esther Rothblum, and Laura Solomon found that lesbian and heterosexual women were more dissatisfied with their bodies than were gay and heterosexual men.[2] The authors suggest that gender may, therefore, be a stronger predictor of body dissatisfaction than sexual orientation. A similar study found that lesbians, heterosexual women, *and* gay men experienced a similar degree of body dissatisfaction, significantly more than heterosexual men.[3] This study suggests that perhaps *both* sexual orientation and gender are implicated in negative body image.

Our interviews—with mostly white women from a variety of class backgrounds, geographic locations, and ages—supported the research findings indicating that lesbians continue to be affected by female appearance norms after coming out. Said one lesbian:

> Let's face it. The traditional standards of beauty for women are basically the same whether you're gay, straight, bisexual, or whatever. Looksism is as strong in the lesbian community as anywhere, if not more so. Women are more critical of other women than men are.

Said another:

> Even though my feminist and lesbian political awareness tell me that I am accepted, I am definitely affected by the beauty and size standards of this culture. . . . As a young woman, I used my beauty as a source of power. I used it for dominance over—and sometimes comfort from—lusting boys. I used it to manipulate, to gain friends, to get the attention I needed. . . . Now, I try not to pay attention to . . . the glory of women who have managed (even for a short time) to take off a few pounds.

A third woman added that she continually feels internal appearance pressure—to lose weight, in particular—even though she has recently come out into a lesbian community where dieting is looked down upon:

> I am not at all happy with my weight right now. . . . I think that fat acceptance is a stronger issue in the queer community than elsewhere, and I don't have a problem with that. What makes me feel funny is the [implication that being fat] is something you are supposed to be happy about and proud of, when I'm neither happy nor proud.

Thus, while beauty norms are still felt by lesbians even after coming out, some argue that coming out frees women, at least partially, from heterosexual appearance mandates. For example, Brand, Rothblum and Solomon's research found that heterosexual women and gay men—both groups of people concerned with attracting men—reported lower body weights and more weight preoccupation than heterosexual men and lesbians—groups not concerned with attracting men.[4] The authors suggest that because coming out removes women from competition for male attention, male standards of beauty become less important. Lesbians, then, may feel less pressure to conform to a certain appearance norm.

A number of women interviewed for this chapter remarked that in the lesbian community there *is* greater acceptance of physical appearances not consistent with the dominant culture's norms. Many lesbians stated that their views about themselves and their appearance changed dramatically after coming out. They reported feeling both freer to abandon traditional female appearance styles and to experiment more with those styles.

For example, one woman remarked:

> After I came out, I started to question the clothing I wore, the style of my hair, jewelry, makeup, the playing dumb thing. I cut off all my hair, I stopped shaving my legs and armpits, I stopped wearing makeup, and I literally burned my bra. I felt stronger, even more powerful than I had before. I wasn't playing dumb; I was playing tough.

Another stated:

> [After] I moved into a lesbian household, [a housemate] introduced me to lace and lingerie. I found out that as a lesbian—a femme lesbian—I could celebrate my body. I could *be* in my body for the first time. I could look in the mirror and have what I saw be okay. Be more than okay—be fantastic! For me, femme is the strongest, most powerful place I can be.

A sixty-year-old lesbian echoed this feeling of freedom:

> When I look at [heterosexual] women my age, they look frumpy. I'm glad I don't have to look like them.

Thus, while the idea that lesbians are less affected by the dominant culture's beauty mandate was not universally accepted among the lesbians interviewed for this chapter, the theme of "freedom" from appearance norms after coming out was a unifying factor.

This seeming contradiction—that lesbians are affected by the dominant culture's beauty norms and yet feel "freed" from these norms after coming out—raised other questions. How does the heterosexual beauty mandate creep into lesbian communities? Are lesbians truly "freed" from all appearance norms, or do they merely set up their own norms in opposition to those of the dominant culture? Although appearance norms in lesbian communities differ from heterosexual norms, are the lesbian norms any less rigid?

An examination of lesbian history shows that lesbian communities have always had norms for physical appearance. Rothblum notes that, as the dominant culture's norms for female appearance have changed over time, so have the norms of the lesbian community.[5] An important difference between the two norms, she says, is that while the dominant culture's norms have to do primarily with how women can attract men, lesbian norms have served a dual purpose: to allow lesbians to identify each other, and to provide a group identity that is distinct from that of women in the dominant culture.

In a review of U.S. lesbian history and culture in the twentieth century, Lillian Faderman found appearance to be an important part of lesbian life.[6] She notes that in the 1920s, being lesbian became chic among bohemian women. Black and white lesbians in Harlem and Greenwich Village began to form distinct subcultures, for which appearance lent a sense of group identity. Later, during World War II, women began to take factory jobs where they had to wear pants. This provided the opportunity for lesbians who hated dresses to continue to wear pants after the war, with less need to fear negative reactions.

By the 1950s, Faderman continues, the butch/femme style emerged in lesbian communities. Although butch/femme culture encompassed far more than just a dress code, appearance was nevertheless a significant feature. Butch/femme styles allowed lesbians to identify one another, as well as affording lesbians a way of expressing themselves as separate from the dominant culture. Among poor and working-class lesbians, butch/femme identity became a rigidly enforced code. Lesbians who were not clearly butch or femme were termed *kiki* and were unwelcome in places lesbians gathered. At least part of this rigidity had to do with fear. If a woman in a bar was not clearly butch or femme, other lesbians would be afraid to approach her, lest she turn out to be a policewoman who did not "know how to dress."

For refusing to be invisible to the dominant culture, working-class and poor butch/femme lesbians paid the price for their "free" expression during all-too-common police raids and beatings. In contrast, middle-class and wealthy lesbians of the 1950s usually avoided butch/femme styles and were more likely to pass as heterosexual. Faderman quotes the Daughters of Bilitis' newsletter, which urged its middle-class readership to adopt "a mode of behavior and dress acceptable to society" (p. 180). This idea that lesbians should conform to dominant appearance norms is still present in lesbian communities today, and it is a common source of conflict.

While the appearance norms of the dominant culture changed radically during the 1960s, Faderman reports that lesbian norms remained fairly constant until the dawning of the feminist movement in the 1970s. At this time, androgyny replaced butch/femme as the accepted appearance style. Flannel shirts, blue jeans, work boots, no jewelry or makeup, and short hair became *de rigeur*. Among lesbians, this norm was as rigidly enforced as the butch/femme code had been enforced in the years prior. In *The Lesbian Erotic Dance*, Joann Loulan describes how butch/femme lesbians of this time period were ostracized for aping heterosexual styles and how this attitude persists in lesbian communities today.[7]

According to Rothblum, the 1980s and 1990s have reflected "greater diversity" in the lesbian community.[8] She points out that in the last twenty years, lesbians of a variety of ethnicities and cultures have become more visible to the dominant culture, often forming communities of their own. Additionally, butch/femme styles have undergone a renaissance. The S/M subculture has become more visible. Lesbian mothers have had more success keeping custody of children, and more lesbians are getting "married" to one another and having babies. In the last twenty years, then, it is possible that lesbians have begun to be less rigid in the extent to which they hold one another to standards of "appropriate" appearance and behavior.

Among the women interviewed for this piece, though, there was no agreement about the relative rigidity or flexibility of appearance norms in lesbian communities. It may be that a woman's degree of involvement with the lesbian community, the number of years she has been out, her age, her area of geographic residence, and other factors affect the degree to which she is exposed—and feels she must conform—to lesbian appearance norms.

Among the women we interviewed, age and length of time since coming out greatly affected the degree to which lesbians felt they needed to conform to these norms. Younger and newly out lesbians felt more appearance pressure than did older lesbians and lesbians who had been out for a number of years. Two lesbians over forty, for example, expressed great satisfaction with their bodies and appearance styles:

> I've been out for fifteen years. As a sick, fat, middle-aged woman, being a lesbian is a wonderful gift. I love my aging body!

> I'm an outspoken dyke activist. I have no "clothes dilemmas." At work I wear comfortable cotton pants, blazer, white shirts. . . . I can always tell the straight women: they're the ones wearing sweaters.

A twenty-five-year-old bisexual woman who has been out for a decade said:

> As I've gotten older . . . it has become less necessary for me to blend
> in with the queer community. I know I'm queer now, and I don't
> need everyone else to be able to see it when they look at me.

Likewise, the lesbian quoted earlier, who said she "played tough" right
after coming out, stated:

> I don't feel restricted at this point to one standard of beauty. I no
> longer own a flannel shirt. My construction boots are buried under
> layers of pumps and granny boots. I wear lipstick when I want, and
> my hair is long.

In contrast, comments by teenage, newly out lesbians reflect frustration
with lesbian appearance norms and anxiety about "fitting in":

> It's very grouped out here. They want to make sure that people in
> their group meet all their requirements. It's very excluding. You have
> to meet specific requirements, or when they first see you, you're out.
> I think it's stupid. I could fit in almost any category.

> I dress differently [since coming out] . . . more pants, less skirts, no
> dresses . . . no heels. My hair is much shorter. I have also noticed that
> if I'm going to a festival, or a women-only event, I choose what I
> wear carefully. I think about it, which I normally wouldn't do.

Thus, it seems that women's experiences of appearance norms in the
lesbian community change over time. It may be that women feel more
pressure to "fit in" and to be "recognizably lesbian" when they first come
out, especially if one is actively dating. Later, and perhaps after having
found a partner, women feel freer to express their personal styles.

Another theme that emerged in our interviews was a feeling that there
are a variety of appearance norms within the lesbian community, with
corresponding pressures to conform to each norm. For example, contrast
the responses of women to the question, "Is there a lesbian aesthetic?"
Two women summarized the "androgynous" aesthetic well:

> I think there's a general aesthetic. It hasn't changed much since the
> 70s. It's the androgynous look: short hair, round glasses, scarf around
> the neck. . . . Some wear earrings; some wear leather jackets; some
> wear denim. . . . There are different versions, but they are all based
> on the same template.

> I think there's more tolerance for some types of "appearance" (e.g., facial hair, overweight, man-tailored clothing), but there is also so much suspiciousness about traditionally "feminine" norms of dress.

Others felt that there were different aesthetics for different subcultures within lesbian communities. For example, the butch/femme subculture was said to have its own appearance norms, different from those of other parts of the community:

> There's a butch standard. The classic butch is a diesel dyke: crew cut, broad shoulders, no tits, slim hips, able to pass as a man. . . . If you say "femme," people will say she has long hair, wears skirts, makeup, heels . . .

> We get pressure from both cultures: heterosexual and lesbian. They are different aesthetics. For heterosexual women, the image that is put out is . . . a fourteen-year-old boy with tits. Butch lesbian imagery comes from macho gay men. Nowhere is womanness allowed to be expressed. . . . I'm not sure if there is a femme aesthetic. We're trying to create it now.

Thus, while lesbians interviewed for this project seemed to feel that there are appearance norms in their communities, there was little agreement about what those norms are.

An additional theme that emerged in these interviews was that virtually all of the butch/femme lesbians complained that they are excluded and/or viewed as being overly "sexual" by others in their communities. Some of these women hypothesized that, because they represent a challenge to the "androgynous" lesbian aesthetic, they face harassment and exclusion:

> I get a lot of crap, hostility, anger—bullshit like that from other lesbians because I'm an extremely butch woman, very masculine-looking. I've been run off sports teams, out of towns, out of houses, and been falsely accused of sexually assaulting someone. Lesbians are very good at turning on each other. I find that butch lesbians tend to be aloof from groups of lesbians for just that reason.

> Femmes are not accepted because they're treated as if they are trying to pass as straight. Femme lesbians . . . may become invisible in the lesbian culture. [They] lose the support, the contact that may occur. I think the 1970s did [butch and femme lesbians] a huge injustice. The feminists . . . said, "Thanks for starting this movement; now vacate!"

Butch and femme lesbians also expressed feelings of being "left out" and "singled out":

> It's harder as a butch, definitely. I *am* the lesbian ideal as far as how butches are supposed to look: big, strong, masculine-looking, short hair. I have a great wardrobe. I have manners—you can take me anywhere. I make a good trophy. But that's not really what they want. What do women want? If I knew that, I wouldn't be single!

> It's scary . . . to be a femme walking down the street and getting all this energy and attention I don't want from people I don't want.

These statements suggest that there is no single conclusion we can draw about appearance norms in lesbian communities. Lesbian appearance norms are clearly different from heterosexual ones; however, the beauty mandate of the dominant culture has apparently been reproduced to some extent within lesbian communities. The heterosexual beauty mandate continues to affect lesbians to the extent that they still worry about weight and other factors that make up the dominant culture's ideal. In addition, lesbians create norms within their own communities, which to some may feel just as restrictive as heterosexual norms. The degree to which women feel pressured to conform to such norms may be a factor of age and the number of years of being "out," just as the degree to which heterosexual women conform to the dominant culture's norms changes over time. Other factors influencing the pressure to conform—or not—may be membership in a lesbian subculture, such as the butch/femme subculture. Lesbians in such groups may experience less acceptance by the larger lesbian community, and they might create different standards of appearance within their own groups.

Thus, while for many women coming out represents freedom from the dominant culture's ideal of beauty, mere coming out does not solve the problem. Although, in theory, lesbian communities afford women the opportunity to define themselves and to find the appearance they find most pleasing to themselves, our research suggests that appearance norms continue to exist among lesbians. Some lesbians experience these norms as being just as restrictive as those of the dominant culture. As one lesbian interviewed noted, it is ironic that a group which has so emphasized eschewing the heterosexual beauty aesthetic should create beauty standards of its own. Said she, "On a personal level, I find it all pretty tiresome." Thus, it seems that for lesbians, as for heterosexuals, the onus is on each individual to find her own ways of breaking free of the appearance obsession.

REFERENCES

1. Rothblum, E.D. (1994). Lesbians and physical appearance: Which model applies? In. B. Greene and G.M. Herek (Eds.), *Psychological Perspectives on Lesbian and Gay Issues, 1,* 84-97.

2. Brand, P.A., Rothblum, E.D., and Solomon, L.A. (1992). A comparison of lesbians, gay men, and heterosexuals on weight and restrained eating. *International Journal of Eating Disorders, 11,* 253-259.

3. Beren, S.E., Hayden, H.A., Wifley, D.E., and Grilo, C.M. (1994). The influence of sexual orientation on body dissatisfaction in adult men and women. *International Journal of Eating Disorders, 20,* 135-141.

4. Brand, Rothblum, and Solomon, 1992.

5. Rothblum, 1994.

6. Faderman, L. (1991). *Odd girls and twilight lovers: A history of lesbian life in twentieth-century America.* New York: Columbia University Press.

7. Loulan, J.A. (1990). *The lesbian erotic dance: Butch, femme, androgyny, and other rhythms.* San Francisco: Spinster.

8. Rothblum, 1994.

Resistance and Reinscription:
Sexual Identity and Body Image
Among Lesbian and Bisexual Women

Sara Auerbach
Rebekah Bradley

We'd like to begin with the context. It was our last undergraduate school year, and we (Sara and Rebekah) shared a small, cement square of an office in the basement of the psychology building. The context is important because that year we were doing more than studying lesbian identities and body image; we were doing lesbian identities, living the concepts with which we grappled in our studies. We were both, at that time, going through the long process of coming out as queer to family, friends, and the strange world around us. Along with heterosexuality, we found ourselves questioning contemporary rules that dictate the shape and size, as well as the color and presentation of women's bodies. The impact of these social pressures struck like an epidemic around us: dear friends struggled with anorexia and bulimia; our female classmates fueled their long hours in the library with tiny salads and diet cokes; and we began to question our own fears about whether we looked good enough to show ourselves as we were to the communities in which we traveled. Within this period of confrontation and change, the first author was completing her studies in psychology and women's studies with a thesis that blended the two disciplines under the supervision and encouragement of Dr. Ruth Striegel-Moore, whose research and teaching also focused on these areas of inquiry. The following chapter represents a summary of our year-long project.

The study began as an exploration of the ways in which lesbian identities interact with women's experiences of their bodies. A preliminary survey of the literature from empirical psychology revealed few efforts to examine sexual orientation as a factor in eating disorders and related body image concerns. Those studies we did discover presented mixed conclusions. In 1983, Ronald A. LaTorre and Kristina Wendenburg found that women who reported both opposite sex and same-sex sexual experiences were more satisfied with their bodies than were women with exclusively heterosexual experiences. Similarly, in a study of personal advertisements sent by heterosexual and homosexual women and men, Kay Deaux and Randel Hanna (1984) found that lesbians were the least likely of the groups to present information about appearance concerning themselves or their preferred partners. Pamela A. Brand, Esther D. Rothblum, and Laura J. Solomon (1982) also found from a survey of women and men of heterosexual and homosexual orientations that lesbians reported higher ideal weights than heterosexual women and described themselves as less preoccupied with weight.

In contrast, Ruth Striegel-Moore, Naomi Tucker, and Jeannette Hsu (1990) found lesbians and heterosexual women to express similar weight concerns. They also found that lesbians reported lower levels of self-esteem, which would suggest greater dissatisfaction with their bodies according to research which has linked self-esteem with body esteem (Fabian and Thompson, 1989; Silberstein et al., 1988).

Two conceptual papers present a similar mix of findings. In 1987, Laura Brown suggested that lesbians "appear to make up a smaller percentage of women with eating disorders than of women in general" (p. 295). As a clinical psychologist, she cited the relative absence of lesbians presenting for treatment of eating disorders in her own and others' practices. Furthermore, she pointed to the overrepresentation of lesbians among fat activists as another indicator that lesbian communities may foster greater body satisfaction. However, Sari Dworkin (1988) suggested a different picture. Using personal and clinical observations, Dworkin argued that lesbians suffer from negative body image to the same extent as do heterosexual women. As evidence of this similarity, she described the presence of discrimination against fat lesbians within lesbian communities as well as the abundance of diet advertisements in lesbian newspapers.

One of the most extensive and recent attempts to investigate the links between sexual identity and body image was a book-length presentation by Becky Thompson (1994) of a series of in-depth, loosely structured conversations she conducted with women of varying sexual identities and ethnic backgrounds. Through her exploration of women's life histories, Thompson laid a framework for understanding the importance of power and "otherness" as factors in women's experiences of embodiment.

Similar to Thompson's study, we used open-ended interviews rather than structured questionnaires to learn about ways women who identify themselves as lesbian or bisexual have confronted body image issues. The interviews themselves began with a short description of the project as a senior thesis on body image and sexual identity and an invitation to comment on any connections they saw between these two topics personally, socially, and/or politically. Interviewees were recruited through several different, informal, campus networks. The first notices about the project were written on the walls inside bathroom stalls in two women's bathrooms in the main campus center, which is used for informal, anonymous conversation spaces as well as a variety of campus issues and events. The project was also presented during several meetings of the Lesbian/Bisexual/Questioning support group on campus. Finally, we used word of mouth to locate potential interviewees and to ensure the relative diversity of the sample. The ten lesbian, bisexual, and bicurious women in the final sample included two black women, one Asian-American woman, six white women and one who described her background as black/white/and Native American. Eight ranged in age from nineteen to twenty-four and were undergraduates, one was an undergraduate in her late twenties, and one was a thirty-year-old graduate student.

Of the ten women interviewed, nine spoke at length about ways in which the development of their sexual identity was connected to their body image experiences. Only one participant felt that body image was not an issue in her life and, therefore, not familiar with this process. Throughout the remaining interviews, a common theme emerged: while in the process of reconfiguring their sexual identities, or "coming out," each woman in her own way shifted her expectations and practices surrounding weight, food, and body image. Although each interview presented different relationships between sexual identity and body image, the following stories highlight these links in vivid detail.

For example, Beth (all names have been changed), a white undergraduate who identified herself as bisexual discussed ways in which coming out marked significant changes in her attitudes about her body. In high school she had begun a serious regimen of diet and exercise after transferring to a coed school and experiencing increased pressure from her family to slim down. She started dieting "all the time, thinking about it all the time." These efforts continued until she entered college and soon after began questioning her sexual identity. During this time, her social circle shifted from high school peers focused on weight loss to a group of gay and bisexual college students who shared different attitudes about body image. "They helped me change my attitude," she explained, "and really helped me see my body as something to take good care of . . . really coming to terms with . . . just that my body is gonna look like what it is." She illustrated this shift with a story about her favorite jeans, ones she had worn since junior high school.

I wore these until they were tight, until the end of high school and they sat in my closet for a while as jeans that I wanted to get into.

> Finally I was like, god, I feel so shitty when I wear these jeans, I never wear them. I'll just do something about it. I'll open them. I opened up the sides, finally.

Through coming out as bisexual and later as a lesbian both personally and socially, Beth adopted a new, less restrictive, and more accepting view of her body.

Meg cited a similar shift in her experience from holding self-disparaging body ideals to self-nurturing ones with the support she gained within a lesbian community. Recalling a relationship with a boy in high school she stated:

> I remember myself, like, with the light on looking at myself as he would look at me, thinking like, if I turned this way then my thighs are gonna look bigger, and how that was running through my head when we were having sex.

She also felt that she had developed a sense of shame about her body from her ethnic background, Filipino and white. Because she was not as small as her family members in the Philippines, she consistently dieted before visiting during vacations. In college, she found what she described as a "difference between image in a straight context and in a lesbian context." She found that "in the lesbian or queer community, there's like a feminist focus or emphasis on not conforming to these societal standards of what you body should look like." She described a women's Take Back the Night march she attended early in the semester.

> They did this thing where everyone gets in a circle and someone shouts out something like women are powerful, and everyone repeats it and claps and says yes, right. And one of the things that someone shouted out was I can eat anything I want which was so great. And then I hear that and yeah, I can eat these french fries; give me some more. That's a really good feeling.

While she continued to struggle with the split between her cultural and family values and those within her social circles at school, Meg found that her growing alliance with the gay community socially and as an activist gave her more support to resist pressures to diet.

Jo's interview introduced the importance of gender in many women's body and self-image. A white undergraduate, Jo explained that she grew up feeling "inappropriately gendered" and "because of my body or how I felt in my body, I wasn't traditionally female." This feeling led to mixed self-perceptions. On the one hand, she felt different and special, "not buying into traditional feminine traits, able to indulge in sports, and to be "tough." On the other hand, she described feeling uncomfortable and disconnected from her body, which was growing more and more "feminine" as she matured. She explained:

> My mom used to take me bra shopping . . . and she wasn't comfortable with her body . . . wasn't comfortable with my body . . . she would try to get these minimizers . . . my breasts are so big . . . to try and make them smaller . . . I would be wearing these bras that were sort of ugly and made me feel like I had to hide my breasts.

As a girl, Jo learned that her body was something to be ashamed of and to hide. Continuing with the same subject of bra shopping, she suggested that her relationship with her girlfriend helped her confront her old ways of viewing her body.

> . . . And so when [my girlfriend] and I were in Europe last fall, she took me bra shopping and we got fancy lace bras and it was this totally different way for me to think about my body . . . I guess she helped me get more comfortable with the idea that if I wore these fancy bras and wore a shirt over it and you could see the outline of my breast, that's okay, that's good, that was nice . . . so that's part of the change.

Claire, also a white undergraduate, described ways in which, for her, gender, body image, and sexuality were intertwined. During the interview she asked:

> C: You remember Tab?

> I: The soda?

> C: The soda, second grade, the commercial . . .

> I: Yeah.

> C: . . . We were like six, seven years old . . . and here I was, this (laughs) total, flat-chested, flat everything . . . I was a big-time tomboy . . . little league ball and soccer . . . meanwhile all the girls were doing gymnastics and like that so I always had this kind of mentality, there's something about me that sets me apart and yet

wanting to drink Tab so I can be like that . . . like wishing I would do gymnastics, wishing I could be doing ballet but like hating it because it wasn't . . . I wasn't . . . it wasn't right for me.

When asked how she saw this conflict working in her current life she replied:

See, I think that's where the lesbianism thing comes in 'cause I feel like in a way that's bringing them both together . . . like yes, I can be a sexual person . . . but within what makes me comfortable which is the tomboy thing.

Claire believed that coming out as a lesbian was empowering on many levels for both herself and many of her friends. She explained:

Defining the lesbian community is a hard one, but in terms of my friends there is definitely, like the whole cutting off your hair thing, discovering your sexuality, dealing with your sexuality and discovering yourself and feeling very empowered by those things all coming together. There is this sense of being empowered by breaking away from what your society has told you you're supposed to be doing. And then, along with that, feeling comfortable with your body, like this is my body, this is great.

As the above comments begin to show, lesbian and bisexual identities brought possibilities of greater self-acceptance and appreciation to women from a variety of backgrounds and sexual histories. Still, through our own experiences and the narratives given by the participants in this project, being queer is not a simple answer to the problem of oppressive body ideals for women. For instance, after she described ways in which coming out as a lesbian is empowering, Claire suggested that this transformation is sometimes constrained by internal and external pressures.

I think that out of the idea that I'm this strong liberated woman, here I am; I'm lesbian; I'm bisexual; I'm whatever; I've cut my hair and like fuck you all, I'm not gonna deal with you anymore on your terms . . . but at the same time having this internal struggle, that I still feel like shit whenever I look at myself in the mirror. It's sort of this double dose of I feel like shit because here I am spouting off how empowered I am, but I'm really not, and not necessarily ever being able to talk about that amongst each other because there is this sense of we're such strong women; that's not an issue for us.

She described a division between messages circulated within the lesbian community and mixed feelings she and her friends actually had toward their bodies. She also raised the issue of silence within her community regarding ways in which lesbians were still affected by pressures which continue to play a role in their lives.

More doubts, about the freedom of all lesbians from body image concerns, were raised by two of the women of color surveyed. Xan, who is black, drew a contrast between the social circle of her aunt, who is an older lesbian, and the gay community she found at school. Her aunt's friends, she explained, are "large, small, medium, tall, short, skinny . . . more like the real gay community, the older gay community." In contrast, Xan found women on campus to be "thinking in heterosexual terms" by holding onto an "exoticized version of the lesbian," a lesbian aesthetic which has entered more mainstream media looking much the same in size and shape to heterosexual women in the media. She elaborated:

> What size people are becomes a part of the [aesthetic thing] because if you're in a room filled with really small white women and you're wearing like a tank top and a skirt and your belly's like . . . you're gonna totally stick out, especially if you're black.

Xan saw within the more visible lesbian social circles at school a look that conformed to mainstream images—thin, and no less important, white. As a black woman who found her body becoming larger the less she focused on sports, Xan felt out of place and unattractive among this crowd.

Similar to Xan, Taz, a black undergraduate in her late twenties, described dressing to hide her body because she found, "it's an issue here . . . most of the queer women that I've seen are very thin and have their bodies intact." Although she felt positive about her body when alone with her girlfriend and with other black friends, Taz felt insecure in the larger gay social environment on campus.

Jamie, a white graduate student, elaborated on the pressure to be thin that she saw coming from within the lesbian community.

> I thought for a long time that lesbians shouldn't, you know, feminists shouldn't have all these issues, but I don't think we can erase them, our subculture; they're so ingrained in us as children. . . . I mean, there's certainly a lot of movement going on within the lesbian community, of nonbody image oppression . . . and you certainly see a lot of large women that carry themselves beautifully, but I think . . . in the past few years, people are starting to worry more about body image.

As these women's comments show, lesbians experience the same cultural pressures and messages as do all women—those which filter down through media, families, and opposite sex sexual experiences, among others. A strong theme emerged from this research—that through coming out as queer, many women receive support from lovers, friends, and lesbian communities to work through body issues developed in their youth and young adulthood. In addition, coming out allowed many to return to their bodies and accept sexual desires that were rendered abnormal and invisible in a heterosexual context or were distorted by abuse in a culture that poorly protects its daughters. Others marked coming out as a process of exploring and embracing a gender identity other than traditional "femininity."

Still, as this study and other research has demonstrated, being a lesbian does not provide instant liberation from oppression of women's bodies. As Laura Brown suggested in her 1988 address to the American Psychological Association, lesbians are always, in varying ways, connected with mainstream culture and are, consequently, affected by those practices that are embedded in their cultures. Because sexuality is only one aspect of a woman's identity, her experiences are shaped at the same time by other marks of identity such as gender, race, and class, to name a few.

Although this study suggests that body images are formed through many cultural alliances and experiences, a closer reading of the stories told in the interviews reveals ways in which body image is interrelated with our relative positions of power within our social contexts. In her essay "Some Reflections on Separatism and Power," Marilyn Frye (1980) defines power as the right of access. She explains that those who are traditionally denied access to education, white-collar employment, marriage, etc., may gain power through the refusal to support those institutions designed to limit their access. Using these terms, compulsory heterosexuality empowers men by giving them an exclusive right of access to women's bodies through their sexuality, childbearing, and housekeeping services. In this context, women receive messages that their bodies must conform to certain standards in order to enter the domain of heterosexuality. In return, they are granted their "rights" as women, which include the economic contract of marriage, token positions in upper management, and tips at Hooter's restaurants.

Our interviews reveal that, insofar as lesbianism is understood and enacted as a right of refusal, it works to challenge body image oppression. This awareness of refusal was fostered during the events of the women's movement in the 1970s. The lesbian cultural identity that developed during this surge in the women's movement grew out of fervent dialogues about women's oppressions in all levels of society. Within this culture of resistance, lesbians saw women's hatred of their physical sizes and shapes in the context of structural oppressions based on heterosexuality and patriarchal power. A common phrase, attributed to Ti-Grace Atkinson (Allison, 1994, p. 136), circulated at the time was "feminism is the theory, lesbianism is the practice." These dialogues about power and injustice empowered lesbians to resist gender-based norms for body size and appearance as they defied compulsory heterosexuality.

However, when this refusal to accept a cultural and public identity of "straight" ceases to be understood as a refusal to perpetuate a culture of disempowerment, it appears that other structural inequalities go unchallenged. As demonstrated by the steady rise of media centered around gays and lesbians, more and more, gay identities in popular culture are moving from their roots in resistance from the civil rights and women's movements to a commercial market. While the increased visibility has resulted in decreasing stigmatization of gays and lesbians, the presentation of gay identities as "alternative lifestyles" disguises the imbalances of power embedded in sexual identity. Moreover, as Claire's interview suggests, the belief that, by claiming a lesbian identity, women will be instantly empowered, furthers silence within the community about the still present and powerful pressures on women to conform.

One apparent consequence of this growing silence concerning issues of power is a surfacing of structural oppressions within lesbian communities, such as discrimination based on race, class, and physical appearance. While on the one hand, most of the women interviewed described the positive impact of feminist ideologies and gay community support on their sense of self-acceptance, they also described a growing intercommunity ideal for the small and thin, the white and young. This growing conformity was most acutely felt by women of color in the sample who found themselves handicapped by their skin color when interacting socially with other lesbians.

Consider the following example. Within a politically rebellious context, a fat lesbian embodies resistance through her largeness and her refusal to shrink and disappear. Historically, lesbians have been at the forefront of fat activism. However, this same woman appears differently within a lesbian community in which her identity is configured as a lifestyle choice, and she is assumed to have the same rights and opportunities afforded the heterosexual population. If a lesbian is just another "woman" who happens to form intimate bonds with other women, then she is more likely to experience pressure to look like and act like a "woman," namely to conform to mainstream body ideals. She is no longer supported by her community as a heroine of resistance; she is once again considered a woman with a weight problem. Furthermore, the clear need for lesbian communities becomes less apparent in a context of assimilation and a false sense of inclusion in the straight world. If women who dare to come out as other than straight lose their vision of themselves as enacting a powerful refusal of heterosexuality, their refusal to nurture other cultural oppressions will fade as well.

Our research suggests that the interaction of body image and lesbian identity can only be described by a complex network of personal and cultural experiences. Because lesbian identities are unstable and partial, lesbians confront current body ideals in different and changing ways. In order to maintain efforts to conceptualize and reconstruct women's power, however, lesbian communities must continue to support and stimulate ongoing dialogues about structural oppressions generated both from within and from society at large.

REFERENCES

Allison, Dorothy. (1994). *Skin: Talking about sex, class, and literature*. Ithaca, NY: Firebrand Books.

Brand, Pamela A., Rothblum, Esther D., and Solomon, Laura J. (1992). A comparison of lesbians, gay men, and heterosexuals on weight and restrained eating. *International Journal of Eating Disorders, 11*, 253-259.

Brown, Laura. (1987). Lesbians, weight, and eating: New analyses and perspectives. In Boston Lesbian Psychologies Collective (Eds.), *Lesbian Psychologies*, pp. 294-310. Chicago: University of Illinois Press.

Brown, Laura. (1988). New voices, new vision: Toward a lesbian/gay paradigm for psychology. Presented at the ninety-sixth annual meeting of the American Psychological Association, Atlanta, GA.

Deaux, Kay, and Hanna, Randel. (1984). Courtship in the personals column: The influence of gender and sexual orientation. *Sex Roles, 11*, 363-375.

Dworkin, Sari H. (1988). Not in man's image: Lesbians and the cultural oppression of body image. *Women and Therapy, 8*, 27-39.

Fabian, Lisa, J. and Thompson, J. Kevin. (1989). Body image and eating disturbance in young females. *International Journal of Eating Disorders, 8*, 63-74.

Frye, Marilyn. (1980). Some reflections on separatism and power. In *The politics of reality: Essays in feminist theory*. Freedom, CA: The Crossing Press.

LaTorre, Ronald A., and Wendenburg, Kristina. (1983). Psychological characteristics of bisexual, heterosexual, and homosexual women. *Journal of Homosexuality, 9*, 87-97.

Silberstein, Lisa R., Striegel-Moore, Ruth H., Timko, Christine, and Rodin, Judith. (1988). Behavioral and psychological implications of body dissatisfaction: Do men and women differ? *Sex Roles, 19*, 219-232.

Striegel-Moore, Ruth H., Tucker, Naomi, and Hsu, Jeanette. (1990). Body image dissatisfaction and disordered eating in lesbian college students. *International Journal of Eating Disorders, 9*, 493-500.

Thompson, Becky W. (1994*). A hunger so wide and so deep: American women speak out on eating problems*. Minneapolis: University of Minnesota Press.

Contradictions of the Spirit: Theories and Realities of Lesbian Body Image

Naomi Tucker

The more financially independent, in control of events, educated and sexually autonomous women become in the world, the more impoverished, out of control, foolish, and sexually insecure we are asked to feel in our bodies.

—Naomi Wolf, *The Beauty Myth:*
How Images of Beauty Are Used Against Women

Apples, figs, pomegranates, peaches, milk shakes, Mother's Cookies—they are emblems of the Great Mother who fed us at her ripe breasts during our first sojourn in Paradise. That is why eating seems forbidden and food dangerous. When we eat we know. That is what the old stories tell us. What we know from eating will always lead back through a wandering train of primordial association to the mother-ground of first experience, before the father stole the garden, usurped the mother's power, established himself in her place.

—Kim Chernin, *Reinventing Eve:*
Modern Woman in Search of Herself

Feminist art and literature have reclaimed ancient portrayals of female bodies: wide hips, full bellies, strong arms, uneven breasts, differing body shapes and sizes. Lovingly and purposefully, nature designed women's bodies with these features. Feminism has helped many people understand women's negative body image as a product of sexism, a tool used to keep women psychically and physically hungry, and therefore, powerless. In particular, the lesbian-feminist movement of the 1970s took to task the myth of the "ideal" female body in Western culture. Rejecting the notions of body size norms for women, celebrating women's intrinsic beauty, protesting the societal mandates for "feminine" appearance codes, and naming the insidious damage caused by male-constructed beauty ideals, lesbian-feminists brought back healthy, realistic images of women. Lesbian-feminist ideology professed self-acceptance to and among women.

If feminism helped us to understand why so many women dislike our bodies, if lesbianism offered some models of self-nurturance and freedom from defining ourselves according to male standards, if the women's consciousness-raising movement taught women to value ourselves and control our own bodies—why then are women still literally killing ourselves to look "good?" And would it not be logical to assume that feminist women and women-loving women are less easily caught in the trap of food and body image terror?

Solutions to the puzzling relationships between sexual orientation, feminism, and body image are not likely to be found in traditional places. To begin with, "lesbian body image" is not a phrase found in psychology literature. Until recently there were no empirical studies on body image where the question of sexual identity was considered relevant. Second, most clinical treatments for anorexia, bulimia, and other self-destructive eating and body image problems are based upon psychopathological paradigms born of the very male-identified system that created the problems in the first place. The treatment models are often lacking in social context, and most would not go so far as to name the oppression of women as a root cause. Last, the lesbian and bisexual women's community itself offers few alternative support systems because of the general assumption that lesbian and bisexual women have "gotten over" body image problems.

Since mainstream organizations and literature have not offered any dazzling answers to questions about body image among feminist and queer-identified women, in 1987, I decided to conduct my own information gathering. With the support of the psychology department at Wesleyan University, I created a pilot project to study body image and eating disorders specifically within the lesbian community.[1] Through detailed written questionnaires and in-depth interviews, we hoped to understand sexual identity related to body esteem and eating disorders.

At the time, I was working with a group of women on a campus-wide food/body image educational campaign. Outwardly, many of those women spoke with a passion that suggested *they* would never succumb to sexist, self-destructive, culturally prescribed beauty norms. All of them knew the literature, understood how and why women are taught to hate and destroy our bodies, and possessed the tools with which to create a healthy relationship to their bodies and to food. But secretly, each shared with me her pained perception of her own body, expressed a desire to look different, confessed struggles with eating "disorders," and despaired over the gap between how she felt and how she wanted to feel.

This led me to believe that I might find a large disparity between perceived and actual attitudes about body image and food in the women's community. Because the majority of the campus "women's community" consisted of lesbian or bisexual women who identified as feminist, I also realized that it would be important to sort out what factors of body esteem were a product of sexual identity versus feminist politics and beliefs.

Overall, we found no significant difference in *body image* between lesbian and heterosexual students. Yet, group comparisons did show differences in *self-esteem* that were related to sexual orientation rather than to feminist beliefs. And our results revealed an interesting paradox. In the open-ended essay questions, an overwhelming number of women stated that coming out had greatly improved their body image and self-esteem. Some of the reasons they gave were freedom from compulsory heterosexuality; not worrying about being attractive to men; the positive self-images gained from relating sexually to other women with varying body types; the understanding of how heterosexist media shape women's body image; reinforcement from other women in the community who valued women and women's bodies; and lesbian images of strong, independent women not bound to heteropatriarchal norms or beauty standards. However, on actual scales such as the Eating Disorders Inventory,[2] many of these *same* women showed high ratings of eating disorder and weight concerns and low body esteem. In the lesbian group, significant correlations indicated that both weight concern and physical condition were strongly related to self-esteem. Although sexual attractiveness did not emerge as a significant predictor of self-esteem among lesbians, it is interesting to note that other attributes such as weight and physical condition did.

> For lesbian students, feeling good about oneself appears to encompass feeling good about one's body, whereas the link between self-esteem and body esteem may be more tenuous among heterosexual women. Satisfaction with how well one's body functions seems to be more closely related to self-esteem in lesbian than in heterosexual students, perhaps reflecting the great emphasis placed on physical strength in the lesbian subculture.[3]

In oral interviews, some of the same women later discussed how, although they no longer felt confined to heterosexist, male-defined beauty standards for women, they did feel restricted by a new, lesbian standard of beauty and attractiveness, including physical strength requisites and a particular dress code. Women described a shift from dieting to look thin, to

lifting weights or running compulsively to build musculature—from looking "feminine" enough to looking "dykey" enough. The liberation they
had initially felt upon coming out was soon clouded by attempts to fit in to
a community whose standards, though different ones, were standards nonetheless.

The specific age and context of the women surveyed—that is, students
at a small, private, liberal arts university—may explain some of the unex-
pected outcomes. First, this group is bound by factors of class, culture,
social status, and community background that could affect the outcome of
the research. Second, college is a major time of transformation and personal growth in people's lives, so these same women might test quite
differently five or ten years later. Finally, the standards of self-acceptance
that we expected to find amongst lesbian women might be less true for
young women who are just coming out, who are not yet confident and
established in their adult identities, or who are part of a newer lesbian
generation with different notions of appearance from the antiestablishment
leanings of 1970s lesbian-feminism.

Other limitations factored into our interpretations as well. Frameworks
of mainstream psychology research are intrinsically antithetical to feminist
practice. For instance, our results and conclusions were based more on
answers that could be computer analyzed (psychological scales, multiple
choice, and true/false questions) than on participants' detailed written and
verbal answers. The bias toward categorical, measured responses certainly
gives more "scientific" credibility, which was an important consideration
because lesbian psychology, body image, and the psychology of women in
general are marginalized (at best), if not trivialized, within mainstream
psychology. In essence, we made sacrifices so that we could at least get the
information widely distributed to psychologists and others who might not
otherwise even bother to read about lesbian body image. However, having
to leave out pieces of the puzzle was troublesome. Later, this contradiction
motivated me to continue writing about this subject in places (such as this
anthology) that provide more room for intuitive process and feminist
analysis.

One such omission was the outrageous elimination of bisexual women
from the study. Women were asked to self-identify on the Kinsey Scale.[4]
But later, when entering the data I was told to *eliminate all bisexually
identified participants* from the subject pool because "there was no data to
support research about bisexual women" at the time, nor to support the
conclusions we might reach. And such was the irony of doing feminist
research within a traditional, patriarchal framework. Given that many of
the women from both the "lesbian-" and the "heterosexual-"feminist

sample groups actually identified somewhere in the middle of the Kinsey scale, an entire component of valuable information was left out.

Not only was there no research on lesbian body image at that time, but there was even less research on anything to do with bisexual women. Prior to 1991, any clinical research that existed on bisexuality was either limited to middle-class, white, bisexual men or sensationalized bisexuals as promiscuous transmitters of HIV from the gay to the straight world. Here, in our hands, lay the opportunity to access new information and to interpret it from a feminist standpoint. It is a tragedy to me that this potential was not fulfilled.

Despite these limiting factors, I still believe that the study did break new ground. It came as a surprise, even to many of the study's participants, that body esteem was not significantly different between lesbian and heterosexual women. Some participants told me afterward that they had expected heterosexual women to "have more hang-ups." Yet the problems were equally prevalent among lesbians, with fewer avenues for support in that community.

Ironically, the lesbian-feminist standard of self-acceptance for women has created a *taboo* around worrying about weight and body image, going so far as to identify negative body image and obsessions as a "straight women's thing." Women with body image difficulties and food obsessions are therefore doubly isolated within the lesbian community. And isolation perpetuates the problem.

One woman who lived in a feminist co-op described the expectation in her household that lesbians should not have issues with food or body image. Because of that expectation, there was no room for her to express her own pain and confusion, no understanding for her discomfort with household meals, and no room for her to be anything less than a perfectly well-adjusted, self-loving, lesbian feminist. She carried not only the shame and self-hatred that all anorexic and bulimic women face, but also the shame that she should somehow be above all that. Her own community had turned against her.

Other women expressed similar difficulties. Slowly and painfully, they told me how the act of loving women had taught them the dreamy possibilities of loving themselves—but they could not seem to reach this idealistic goal. Lesbianism had given them the message that they *should* feel good about their bodies, but it had not taught them how. It had not given them quite enough ammunition to counter the media messages that continued to hound them daily. It had not given them a way to handle going home to their families, interviewing for jobs, or walking through department stores without buying into the American beauty myth.

> Although lesbian ideology rejects our culture's narrowly defined ideal of female beauty and opposes the overemphasis placed on women's physical attractiveness, such ideology may not be strong enough to enable lesbians to overcome already internalized cultural beliefs and values about female beauty. Unlike other cultural minorities, lesbians do not grow up with parental or peer models representing lesbian standards as an alternative to the majority culture's norms. Furthermore, even as the lesbian woman increasingly identifies with a lesbian community that ideologically professes self-acceptance, she is still a part of a greater cultural context that values beauty and thinness in women.[5]

In short, it is extremely difficult, if not impossible, to escape socialization around body image. Such difficulties may be even more intensified for younger women. For many lesbians, the gap lies between *intellectual* and *emotional* acceptance of lesbian-feminist ideology. The most frustrated women in the study were those who had all of the intellectual tools, had read all the books, and could even give lectures about sexism and body image—but who could not convince themselves of their own beauty and self-worth.

Many feminists experience a conflict between what they *know* ("my negative body image is a product of male cultural misogyny"; "we should be attacking the clothing and diet industries rather than our own bodies") versus what they *feel* ("I hate myself"; "I'm too fat") and how they behave in conjunction with those feelings. The same women in this study who reported that coming out as lesbian had taught them to love their body also tested high on scales of eating disorders and negative body image.

A woman who understands the possibility of positive body image but can't quite attain it often feels hopeless. Her beliefs may enable her to see the light at the end of the tunnel. But when, still a victim of deeply ingrained social messages, she fantasizes about excising parts of her own body—she is convinced she will never reach that light.

I believe that this sense of hopelessness comes from the unfortunate phenomenon of "shoulds." The lesbian community, in creating a counter-culture within U.S. American society, has developed its own standards of politics, music, fashion, sex, relationships, perhaps even cuisine—and many other attitudes about daily life. Though created to provide liberating alternatives to oppressive social institutions, sometimes these standards backfire. They do so simply by definition: standards imply a norm separating what is acceptable and popular from what is not. Lesbian standards of "political correctness," for instance, have attempted to narrowly define "lesbian" to the exclusion of leather dykes, bisexuals, sex workers, and transsexuals for not towing the lesbian purist party line. Such standards frequently apply to appearance, branding women who don't dress in enough queer-gear, work out at the gym, or keep their hair short as "straight-looking, straight-acting." Sometimes these standards apply to food, too: witness a community of earth-loving vegetarians that frowns upon the woman who adores Oreo cookies. What will become of her when she is relegated to indulging in her passion alone, in fearful secrecy?

We have simply exchanged one obsession for another. An obsession to replace body fat with muscle is just as destructive as an obsession to starve oneself into angular, bony bodies. Similarly, the pressure on lesbian and bisexual women to look butch enough, to be the femme fatale of the lipstick lesbians, or to be the most athletic, or tough, or sexy can be just as destructive as the pressure on heterosexual women to look "good" to men.

The gay male community is a glaring example of the queer body image dilemma. For ages we women have screamed about the thinness standard as a product of sexism; we have screamed about lack of gender equality. In an unfortunate twist on the equality concept, we now have men who are just as unhappy, neurotic, and self-destructive about their bodies as women. The gay male community seems to have combined all the looksism and objectification attributed to men, with the appearance-focused fashion standards attributed to women. There is such enormous emphasis among gay and bisexual men on looks—whether it is a well-defined chest, tight ass, big biceps, hair, no hair, the right clothes—that more and more men are judging their own self-worth on how they match up physically to these norms. Naturally, some gay and bisexual men are learning to diet, spend half their life at the gym, squeeze their bodies into uncomfortable clothes, take laxatives, vomit on command, give themselves enemas not for sexual pleasure but to lose weight, and become as miserable as so many women have been for so long. Is this what we meant by equality? Subjecting men to separate but equally destructive standards does nothing to liberate women from the tyranny of slenderness[6] or the beauty myth,[7] and it does not lessen the power of heterosexual male institutions over women's lives.

It seems to me that lesbian/gay/bisexual/transgender communities, by definition founded against the grain of mainstream society, have great potential to model healthy body image to ourselves and to those around us. We can untangle the web that ties food to body image, body image to self-esteem. We can deconstruct the need for standards instead of creating our own special brand. Predicated on the notion that relationships and attractions are neither gender-defined—nor bound to male dominance and female subservience—bisexual, transgendered, lesbian, and gay cultures undercut the very essence of heteropatriarchy by offering other options.

Thus, we have the potential to take the power away from the beauty standards that work so diligently to perpetuate women's subjugation.

But all of this idealism can only become reality if we are willing to scrutinize our own community's motives, politics, and culture. The key to shifting from the present reality to our ideal body image lies in breaking the cycle. If, for instance, the gay community can learn from what women have suffered, it might be able to stop itself from repeating the same mistakes that led white, heterosexual women of Western society into an abyss of literally self-effacing trauma.

Analogously, if we are to truly confront heterosexism, we must confront not only the symptoms, but also the roots. That means, for instance, that the answer does *not* lie in convincing all women to stop shaving their legs and then alienating the women who still shave. A more productive path toward healing would be to take away the powers that make shaving one's legs compulsory for women—to create a situation in which to shave or not to shave was truly a personal choice, both validated equally. Likewise, bisexual or lesbian identity can liberate women from hating our bodies only if we offer valid alternatives *and* understand the realities of living in a world where we are still continually bombarded with male-defined media images of women. It is insufficient to theorize about protesting traditional beauty standards if we forsake the women who don't manage to escape them.

Feminist bisexual and lesbian women of the 1970s contributed greatly to women's empowerment by rejecting traditionally feminine notions of dress and appearance. But they fell short of reaching their goal by virtue of their insistence upon such rejection as the only way to be a true feminist.

A friend once said to me, with respect to the question of monogamy and traditional roles for women in society, that "the *necessity* for monogamy is what's wrong; the *desire* for it is not."[8] That distinction parallels my perspective on women and appearance: the societal necessity to look feminine is the problem; there is nothing inherently wrong or oppressive about a woman who wants to flaunt her femininity or her sexuality.

Having moved somewhat beyond the 1970s categorical rejection of any focus on appearance, lesbian and bisexual women of the 1990s are now reclaiming and revamping fashion, even setting new trends. We are criticizing the dichotomous beliefs that all "feminine" clothing is intrinsically oppressive to its wearer. But in so doing, we have come back to placing *too* much emphasis on appearance. Why is it so difficult for us to see that the truth is somewhere in between?

Queers and sex radicals of all kinds can challenge the status quo of body image, fashion, and gendered appearance. Reclaiming lipstick, lingerie, or fishnet stockings (by people of any gender!) as symbolic rejections of social mandates can be an incredibly empowering statement, transforming these objects once used against us into tools of positive self-worth. But it is imperative to remember that we live in a world where those items bear significant cultural and sexual connotations. This reality will continue to weigh heavily on women's ability to make free choices about our bodies unless and until we untangle the beauty myth.

While I do not believe that miniskirts or high heels are inherently oppressive to women, I do think that we need to consciously discern what is personal taste or individual choice from what is social pressure to conform, submit, and suffer. This is no easy task since so many of our deepest desires are formed early on by socialization and enculturation. Lesbians and bisexual women have been leaders in the effort to overturn cultural mandates around women's appearance, but as of yet, we are a small force against the powerful institutions of society such as mass media, the fashion industry, the diet industry, the business world, and the entertainment industry.

Clearly, we have to fight this battle on several fronts. Externally, we must confront heterosexism in all its forms, especially the forces that perpetually subjugate us under male dominance. Internally, we must enter into a mode of critical thinking with respect to our own community and create models of queer women's community, social structure, and politics that do not re-create heterosexist paradigms of oppression. Only if we actively engage in these pursuits might we be able to bridge the gap between intellectual self-acceptance and actual internal transformation. And only then might we begin to transcend, rather than perpetuate, the societal beauty standards that haunt us.

NOTES

1. Striegel-Moore, Ruth H., Tucker, Naomi, and Hsu, Jeanette. (1990). Body image dissatisfaction and disordered eating in lesbian college students. *International Journal of Eating Disorders,* 9, (5), pp. 493-500.

2. The Eating Disorders Inventory is a detailed questionnaire that contains several scales measuring different attitudes toward food and body image, as well as specific behaviors such as compulsive eating and purging and anorexia. It is a widely accepted measure among psychologists (Garner, D.M., and Olmstead, M.P. *Eating Disorders Inventory Manual.* Psychological Assessment Resources, Inc., 1984).

3. Striegel-Moore, Tucker, and Hsu, p. 498.

4. The Kinsey scale is a seven-point scale that rates sexual behavior on a line from completely heterosexual (0) to completely homosexual (6). The scale was

not intended to describe sexual, social, or political *identity* but is rather a simple measure of incidences of behavior and fantasy, which is why it poses problems today as a measure of sexual identity. Many of the study's participants found the Kinsey scale too confining as the only measure of their sexual orientation (Kinsey, A.C., Pomeroy, W.B., Martin, C.E., and Gebhard, P.H. *Sexual Behavior in the Human Female*. Philadelphia: W.B. Saunders, 1953). See also *Sexual Behavior in the Human Male* by the same authors.

    5. Striegel-Moore, Tucker, and Hsu, p. 498.

    6. This phrase was coined by writer, activist, and consultant Kim Chernin in her groundbreaking work bearing the same name (*The Obsession: Reflections on the Tyranny of Slenderness*. New York: Harper and Row, 1981).

    7. For more on the notion of "beauty myth," read Naomi Wolf's book (*The Beauty Myth: How Images of Beauty Are Used Against Women*. New York: William Morrow and Co., 1991).

    8. Izakson, Orna. (1992). Personal communication. Berkeley, CA.

BIBLIOGRAPHY

Brown, Laura. (1987). "Lesbians, weight, and eating: New analyses and perspectives." In Boston Lesbian Psychologies Collective (Eds.), *Lesbian Psychologies*. Chicago: University of Illinois Press, pp. 294-310.

Chernin, Kim. (1981). *The Obsession: Reflections on the Tyranny of Slenderness*. New York: Harper and Row.

Chernin, Kim. (1987). *Reinventing Eve: Modern Woman in Search of Herself*. New York: Times Books, p. 187.

Garner, D.M., and Olmstead, M.P. (1984). *Eating Disorders Inventory Manual*. Psychological Assessment Resources, Inc.

Kinsey, A.C., Pomeroy, W.B., Martin, C.E., and Gebhard, P.H. (1953). *Sexual Behavior in the Human Female*. Philadelphia: W.B. Saunders.

Orbach, Susie. (1986). *Hunger Strike: The Anorectic's Struggle as a Metaphor for our Age*. New York: W.W. Norton.

Stein, A. (1989). "All dressed up, but no place to go? Style wars and the new lesbianism." *OUT/LOOK: National Lesbian and Gay Quarterly*, Winter 1989, pp. 34-42.

Striegel-Moore, Ruth, Tucker, Naomi, and Hsu, Jeanette. (1990). "Body image dissatisfaction and disordered eating in lesbian college students." *International Journal of Eating Disorders*, 9 (5), pp. 493-500.

Yager, J., Kurtzman, F., Landsverk, J., and Weismeier, E. (1988). "Behaviors and attitudes related to eating disorders in homosexual male college students." *American Journal of Psychiatry*, 145, pp. 495-497.

Wolf, Naomi (1991). *The Beauty Myth: How Images of Beauty Are Used Against Women*. New York: William Morrow and Co., p. 197.

Lesbians and the (Re/De)Construction of the Female Body

Diane Griffin Crowder

I cannot pretend to explore the mysteries of desire, of how one comes to define one's emotional and sexual attractions. Whether an individual desires members of her own or the other sex, she is subject to social pressures that define acceptable uses of her body. Many cultures impose upon the female body practices intended to orient behavior (if not desire) toward heterosexuality. When a woman becomes aware of her lesbianism, she must choose whether to conform to, or revolt against, such practices. The forms of imposed heterosexuality and of lesbian revolt against it are the subject of this study.

Formal studies of what lesbians do with our bodies, whether and when we use our bodies to make deliberate statements, how we conceive of our bodies as subjects and objects, are extremely rare. Broaching the topic risks overgeneralization and an analysis limited by culture, race, class, and historical moment (see Spelman, 1988). There is the danger of blurring the distinction between the body as a material condition and the social meaning attached to the body. If I take these risks, it is to begin a discussion of how sexualities intersect with the body in social discourse.

Discussion and passionate debate about the presentation and representation of the lesbian body are common among lesbians, but they do not find their way into the general press. More typically, such debate is found

I would like to thank Colette Guillaumin, Nicole-Claude Mathieu, Louise Turcotte, Stephen Lacey, and Jan Boney for their extended conversations with me, which helped shape my thinking on these subjects in invaluable ways. Catherine Burroughs and Jeffrey Ehrenreich were patient and helpful editors. My partner, Margaret Lieb, endured the lengthy process of my clarifying my thoughts and writing this article with unfailing good humor, insight, and common sense. The students in my 1990 Feminist Theory seminar listened to early versions and gave useful criticisms. Finally, I acknowledge an immense debt to all those lesbians, past and present, who have had the courage to live in proud defiance of their culture.

in informal community newsletters and journals such as *Lesbian Connection*, in more formal lesbian journals such as *Common Lives/Lesbian Lives* and *Sinister Wisdom*, or in the mixed gay male and lesbian press such as *Out/Look* or *Gay Community News*. Formal academic studies are almost nonexistent.

I have chosen to use the first person when talking about lesbians as a group. If this sometimes leads to awkward pronoun shifts, I feel the political importance of identifying myself as a lesbian among the lesbians I discuss more than outweighs any stylistic considerations. I make this choice in full knowledge of the problems inherent in the presumptuous "we," clearly articulated by Lanser when she finds herself facing "a dilemma that poses feminist discourse between the Scylla of 'we' and the Charybdis of 'they'" (1986:19). For me to say "lesbians/they" is, as Lanser says, a lie, but it is also a lie to use "we," since no one can speak for all lesbians. I shall attempt to make the referent clear, to avoid presumption, and to offend the reader as little as possible.

HETERSEXUALISM CONSTRUCTS THE FEMALE

The assumption of heterosexuality as a *natural* relation between male and female bodies has often been translated paradoxically into the literal (re/de)construction of the female body. On the one hand, the great weight of (Western) traditional thought views reproductive functions as defining sexuality, and the male and female anatomies as determined by reproductive function. The old crude jokes about a hole and a plug are only an extreme reduction of theories about sexuality in which the female's reproductive role determines her meaning within cultural praxis. That is, reproductive anatomy is sexual destiny.[1]

Yet somehow the female body is not sufficiently "female" or "feminine" as it occurs without social modification. It must be rebuilt by artificial means. Female flesh seems often, at best, inadequate, at worst, ugly or disgusting or threatening, unless tamed or improved upon. Such phenomena as foot-binding, stretching the neck with rings, genital mutilation, forced feeding, forced starvation, and cutting of Achilles tendons all function to construct a female body custom-made for male control (Daly, 1978; Dworkin, 1974; Guillaumin, 1993; Hosken, 1983). By limiting mobility, by rendering women more fragile and weak, or by excising the organs of female sexuality (but not reproduction),[2] such practices implicitly recognize that female anatomy does not, in fact, limit women to a reproductive role or dictate heterosexuality. Yet they are generally justified by that very reproductive role, that is, by "nature."

Westerners have sometimes seen radical modifications of the body in non-EuroAmerican cultures as extreme forms of physical construction designed to create a presumption of heterosexual inevitability. Such ethnocentrism has obscured the fact that, within Western culture, in ways usually not recognized before the advent of the current feminist movement, the female body has also been modified to enhance its attractiveness to men. That modification is, more often than we recognize, somatic, as in the case of cosmetic surgery, dieting, anorexia, or the molding of the body (through constraints such as corsets or through exercise to reproportion the body). In other cases it is more superficial—cosmetics, hairstyling, hair removal—but no less imperative and no less predicated upon viewing the female body negatively unless it is changed in ways designed to please men.[3] A recent American case illustrates the point most clearly. Under the guise of "love surgery," a physician repositioned women's clitorises so that heterosexual vaginal penetration would more easily stimulate the clitoris, thus alleviating the man of any responsibility for providing sexual pleasure to the woman so reconstructed (Brower, 1989; Harness and Kelman, 1989). Ironically, such surgery implicitly recognizes that "sex"—defined always as vaginal penetration by the penis—is not necessarily *naturally* satisfying, since it does not lead most women to orgasm. Less than half (estimates range from 25 percent to 45 percent) of women can achieve orgasm this way (Myerson, 1986). Rather than acknowledge the inadequacy of male-defined concepts of "sex," men mutilate women's bodies.

Finally, psychological pressures have determined the ways in which even an unmodified female body can experience itself. The terrorism exercised by the insistence of Freudian psychology upon the superiority of the "vaginal" orgasm as opposed to the "clitoral" orgasm and upon the necessity for female orgasm resulting only from penile penetration has caused millions of American women to deny the evidence of their own bodies and struggle to meet male-approved standards for having the "right kind" of orgasms.[4]

Such (re/de)construction of the body is seemingly designed to render the female body (1) accessible and (2) more attractive to men. Practices that render women fragile and relatively immobile guarantee male access to women's bodies, as do clothing styles that give no protection from intrusion. Anyone who has struggled to maintain a modicum of modesty in a miniskirt or to elude a pursuer while wearing high heels knows that power over others includes having unquestioned right of access to others.[5] Male definitions of attractiveness further overdetermine how female flesh will be sculpted. Chinese footbinding certainly limited mobility, but the attractiveness of the bound foot seems to have been stressed by those men writing to defend it. While acknowledging that bound women could not run away (and were therefore unable to prevent access to their bodies), Chinese male writers waxed lyrical about the erotic beauty of the deformed foot (Levy, 1966). In a recent example of how male concepts of attractiveness determine behavior, Brownmiller (1984: 97) notes that contemporary American gay men and straight women seem the most obsessed with clothing and appearance (while both lesbians and straight men dress relatively casually) because they are trying to attract male notice.

In some cases, a further goal is to prevent other men (and women) from access to a woman. Genital mutilation, especially infibulation, has been called a "living chastity belt" (Steinem and Morgan, 1983). It not only keeps a woman's sexual desire from leading her to extramarital heterosexual outlets but compromises the woman's ability to have sexual pleasure with other women as well.[6]

It seems clear that the female body is not, in fact, "naturally" destined to be heterosexual but must be made into a heterosexual creation, even through artificial means. Therefore, the implication might be drawn that the usual distinction between "sex"—the body—and "gender"—the social structures associated with masculinity and femininity—obscures rather than clarifies sexual meanings. Indeed, as Guillaumin (1984) has pointed out, it is suspicious that social sciences make this distinction, and yet, (un)coincidentally, there are exactly as many "genders" as there are "sexes."

I am suggesting not only that the physical body does not determine those behaviors and attitudes we call "gender" but that "gender" should be conceived of as a set of power relations that can and does determine not only the meanings we attach to the body, but the body itself. Further, the social institutions of heterosexuality, so far from being "natural," in many cultures call for mutilating or modifying the female body to impress the heterosexual imperative into the living flesh of women.[7] Hence, social constructionist theory, which posits a noncausal relationship between sex and gender, may not go far enough. My argument implies that there may be a reversed causal relationship: cultural gender definitions determine how the biological female is (re/de)constructed into a "feminine" woman.

DECONSTRUCTING THE FEMININE

Can we possibly, without apprehension, imagine two Ladies of Llangollen in this year of 1930? They would own a car, wear dungarees, smoke cigarettes, have short hair, and there would be a liquor bar in their apartment. Would Sarah Ponsonby still know how to remain silent? Perhaps, with the aid of crossword puzzles. Eleanor Butler would curse as she jacked up the car, and would have her breasts amputated.

—Colette, *The Pure and the Impure*

Colette's (1931/1966: 130-131) semifacetious suggestion that modern lesbians chop off their breasts illustrates a profound ambivalence toward the lesbian body as a female body. On one level, she implies that lesbian rejection of "femininity" is such a radical rejection of being female that it necessitates bodily mutilation. This mutilation is aimed at the breast since it is the only specifically female organ visible when clothed. On another level, Colette ties this act to behaviors (smoking cigars, working on cars) that we associate with masculinity, rather than with gender neutrality. Colette sees lesbians as rejecting femaleness, symbolized by the breast, and embracing masculinity, represented by cigars and cars.

I contend that lesbianism in twentieth-century America has simultaneously revolted against the heterosexual imperative of "femininity" and attempted to reconstruct the female body as a lesbian body. My observations here are limited primarily to Western, white, middle-class lesbians, since that is the milieu familiar to me, and should not be taken to extend to any other groups. I would welcome analyses rejecting or amplifying this paper from lesbians of all ethnic and class backgrounds.

Lesbians are reared within the same heterosexual imperative as all women and are subjected, therefore, to the same social definitions of femininity. That lesbians at some point in our lives revolt against compulsory heterosexuality and violate the taboo against loving other women does not mean lesbians do not experience the same pressures to conform as other women do. Indeed, both the pressures and the revolt are open to any woman, as suggested by Adrienne Rich's "lesbian continuum" (1980).

Thus, lesbians are invisible within the category of women unless we choose to differentiate ourselves. Lesbian "passing" has historically been a survival mechanism, allowing lesbians to avoid the harsh penalties meted out to "deviants." At the same time, it has meant that lesbians cannot escape the penalties of being female in an androcentric culture.

The ability of lesbians to blend into the general female population accounts for the fear mingled with titilation exhibited by many men confronted with lesbianism. The question, "Is she or isn't she?", provides the voyeuristic eroticism of Proust's characters Swann and Marcel when faced with the mystery of lesbianism (1954). That is, the lesbian may be any woman, and, as lesbian singer Alix Dobkin (1975) says, any woman can be a lesbian.

Thus, there is no lesbian body distinct from the female body until and unless a lesbian chooses to deconstruct the femininity imposed upon her. Coming out as a lesbian means making a decision whether to continue to "pass" or to revolt against the feminization (read heterosexualization) of the female body. Since a choice must be made, the lesbian is held responsible by both straight and lesbian society for what she chooses. Hence, the debate in recent years over whether or not lesbians should wear long hair or makeup has been partly a debate about whether lesbians should "pass" within a heterosexual society or should reject "heterosexual privilege."[8] This question is further complicated by the perspective of "femme" lesbians,[9] those who adopt elements of "feminine" style not to "pass" as heterosexual but to forge an autonomous lesbian look.[10]

This rejection of heterosexual feminization may, in fact, take the form of adopting "masculine" modes of appearance and behavior. In a society such as modern America, where almost every possible activity, attitude, and character trait has already been encoded as "masculine" or "feminine," it is perhaps inevitable that some lesbians seeking an alternative to heterosexual femaleness would gravitate toward "masculinity," as suggested by Colette's image of Lady Eleanor and Sarah. Indeed, some lesbians believe themselves to be "like men," for lack of any other way to express their refusal to conform to the social construction of the feminine (read heterosexual) body.

But lesbians have not so much adopted the masculine as deconstructed the feminine. This insight is not new. Sidney Abbott and Barbara Love summarized a central idea of the emerging lesbian feminist movement thus:

> She [the lesbian] sees "feminine" as confining in physical as well as mental terms, and to the extent that she is aware of the controls governing her in her assigned sex role, she tries to free herself from them. Her unauthorized freedom is sometimes mislabeled masculinity. (1972:61)

What so profoundly offends the "heteropatriarchy" about lesbians is not our supposed imitation of men (imitation being the most sincere form of flattery, as the saying goes) but the refusal to be women. Lesbians opt out of a heterosexual economy in which men and women mutually define each other. In the most radical sense, lesbians are not women (Wittig, 1980:110).

But by choosing to deconstruct femininity in physical appearance—refusing to "pass"—lesbians do more than seek a freedom that can be mistaken for an embrace of the masculine (pun intended). We go further and, through our presentation of the body, openly challenge the heterosexual imperative. By revealing the artificiality of "woman" as signified in the feminine body—that "natural" entity which heterosexual American culture so conscientiously constructs—the lesbian body undermines the very categories of sex and gender themselves. Three examples illustrate this dynamic: male disguise, camp, and butch/femme role-playing.

One can cite many famous examples of women who adopted male clothing in order to escape the confinements of the feminine role and enjoy the prerogatives of men (Dekker and van de Pol, 1989; Faderman, 1981; Grier and Reid, 1976). Although some were heterosexual, in many cases these women wooed and even married other women while passing as male. Nor are such cases confined to the past. In 1989, a jazz musician, Billy Tipton, was revealed to be female only at death, to the surprise of her ex-wife and three adopted sons (Associated Press, 1989:A18). Cross-dressing, with its attendant gender confusion, has been a staple of comedy from Shakespeare to the 1980s film *Tootsie*. But the audience enjoys the disguise only when they know beforehand that it *is* a disguise—that is, when the person's "true" gender identity is not in question for the audience, but only for the other characters.[12]

When women successfully pass as men in real life, eventual revelation of their sex causes a very different reaction. Many heterosexuals feel discomfort mingled with wonder, especially when the woman has "fooled" another woman into accepting her as a husband.[13] This discomfort reveals the extent to which people unconsciously recognize the passing woman's challenge to the definition of the body as male or female. For we know that simply wearing the clothing of the opposite sex is not enough, especially now that most women wear clothing that would have been considered very "butch" only a generation ago. To maintain the disguise successfully means using her body as a man would, demonstrating that the difference between the sexes is superficial indeed. When she marries or has affairs with other women and convinces them she is a man, even in the intimacy of sex, the challenge to gender dimorphism is profound. We want to know how she did it. Tellingly, we seldom wonder why she did it. We know why she did it. She did it to gain the advantages of men. Often those advantages include the right to love and even to marry women. In a culture such as that of contemporary America, which until recently denied that women are sexually active, the only way to escape enforced passivity has been to assert the "masculine" right to control over one's own body, one's own sexuality.

But what of women who cross-dress without trying to pass as men? The famous photo of Colette in male attire, cigarette held before her at a rakish angle, or the "page-boy" attire in which Natalie Clifford Barney and Renée Viven delighted to amuse their guests can stand as emblems here.[14] Dressing in male drag has long been a part of the repertoire of lesbian entertainers, such as the great black singers of the twenties (Garber, 1989). Whether or not accompanied with extremely short hair, cigars, a swaggering walk, and other signs of "masculinity," such cross-dressing does not gain a woman the advantages of being male since her female body is not disguised. Rather, outside the carefully circumscribed arena of the theater or music hall, a woman in drag is far more likely to be punished than praised for her efforts. Colette cites the laws against cross-dressing in *The Pure and the Impure* (1931), and, of course, refusing to relinquish male garb was one of the major charges leading to the burning of Joan of Arc.

Similar to other sumptuary laws, the prohibition against cross-dressing recognizes physical appearance as a sign of power, and those who assume the dress of the other sex are rightly seen as challenging a power structure based upon exaggeration of sexual dimorphism. When, as Joan of Arc, a woman dresses like a man in order to fulfill a male function, it is not the dress that is the offense but the performance of male activities, symbolized by the clothing (see Grahn, 1984; Shapiro, 1987, for historical context).

But in most cases of public cross-dressing, the woman is not appropriating a man's function in the world. Her challenge belongs often to the world of "camp"—that attitude so peculiar to the gay and lesbian subculture. "To camp" is to call attention to the artificiality of gender roles, to mock the very concepts of masculinity and femininity. In camp, as Susan Sontag (1966) has pointed out, one creates an aesthetic of artifice. In lesbian camp, the meaning of the role is precisely that it *is* a role, and the dissonance between the "masculine" appearance and the female body is precisely the gap from which meaning is derived.[15] For the lesbian does not here want to "be" a man, or even to "play" a man, but rather to be a woman playing a woman playing a man for other women who, of course, as lesbians, do not want a man at all! Judy Grahn sees such cross-dressing as having a "magical function" and the butch lesbian as the "equivalent of the traditional cross-dresser who may also become a magical/shaman of the tribe. . . . She keeps the idea of biological destiny untenable" (1984: 158). Indeed, the very function of camp—to elevate artifice to art—depends upon deconstructing the "natural" and invoking the magic of the gap between signifier and signified, "replacing the Lacanian slash with a lesbian bar" (Case, 1989:283).

It is in this gap between the female body and the meanings imposed upon it that the whole question of butch/femme role-playing enters into the construction of the lesbian body. Roles within the lesbian community cannot be isolated from the semiotic functioning of "masculinity" and "femininity" within the culture as a whole.[16]

The butch lesbian most flagrantly rebels against the restrictions placed on the female body. Beyond her clothing and hairstyle, she often makes a deliberate effort to eliminate any suggestion of "femininity" from her movements, gestures, and use of space. There is a conscious apprenticeship of the body necessary to achieve the desired corporal mastery, whether the individual is perfecting a physical style she feels is natural to her, or whether she must consciously overcome the effects of feminization. Ranging from the humorous to the overearnest, fictional and autobiographical accounts reveal an acute awareness of every aspect of "body language"—from how to hold a cigarette to how to squint the eyes.

It is, for my purposes here, irrelevant whether the butch defines her behavior as masculine or not. In any case, she is stating her rejection of femininity, her inclusion in the category of lesbians, and her nonavailability to men. In a culture in which women are defined by their availability to men, refusing male access often necessarily entails developing bodily skills (strength, martial arts, etc.) that are perceived as masculine, and that play a large role in the definition of the "bull dyke" able to defend herself and her lover from male attack. Pride in toughness, often (self-)defined as "out-machoing" men, must therefore be understood not as a desire to *be* a man but as a component of the rejection of male dominance.

The butch must develop such survival skills because, by her refusal to appear feminine, she constitutes a visible challenge to heterosexuality. She (and her femme lover) cannot hide in the closet.[17] Butch visibility explains the myth that lesbians want to be men, since Western culture reserves for the masculine all that is not marked as feminine. Regardless of her self-definition, by refusing to be feminine the butch is seen as masculine.[18] Under these circumstances, it is not surprising that, given the overwhelming pressure to identify as either masculine or feminine, some lesbians have equated their rejection of femininity with wanting to be like men. Indeed, sheer survival may have dictated such a choice.[19]

While both straight and lesbian feminists have demonstrated the crippling effects of heterosexually defined femininity and made an analysis of this central to feminist theory, until recently, the role of butch and femme lesbians in challenging both femininity and heterosexuality has been glossed over, if not overtly condemned. If it was not "politically correct" for feminists to wear dresses, high heels, elaborate hairdos, or to shave their legs,[20] it was equally "politically incorrect" in most feminist circles to dress as a classic butch. Butch lesbians have pointed out the double message here. A letter to *Lesbian Ethics* summarizes:

> . . . the nearly universal butch experience of being told you're like a
> man when you know you're the one person on earth that men hate
> and fear most: the woman who acts like a full human being. . . .
> [including being the] woman who does not obey. The woman who is
> in revolt against enforced femininity, who claims for herself the right
> not to dress and act and talk "like a woman" (meaning like a toy).
> (Anonymous, 1986:97)

The perception of butches as "male-identified" and the butch/femme roles as imitations of heterosexuality led to a criticism of roles during the elaboration of lesbian feminism in the early 1970s (Nestle, 1981; Smith, 1989). Yet the physical presentation of most lesbian feminists in that period—short hair, no makeup, androgynous clothing—could be seen as a modification of previous butch style. It is therefore doubly ironic that the movement excoriated butches while adopting a very butch look. Simultaneously, the femme look—feminine clothing and hair, jewelry, etc.—became identified as a politically incorrect imitation of heterosexual women. Yet many lesbians combined the more androgynous appearance with a cultural feminist ideology that reclaimed feminine traits, such as nurturance and nonviolence, and a concept of sexuality that sought to eliminate any hint of masculinity.

The high degree of opprobrium aimed at butches indicates the extent to which a revolt against culturally imposed femininity profoundly threatens the status quo. Further, this revolt and the criticism it provokes are most obvious as a question of physical appearance and comportment.

Finally, class and race play a role in attitudes toward butches. Many have noted that butches have been stereotyped as working class by a largely middle-class feminist movement (see Case, 1989; Ruston and Strega, 1986; Nestle, 1981). Smith notes that in the 1950s and 1960s, cover art and verbal descriptions from the lesbian journal *The Ladder* consistently depicted butches as dark and femmes as blonde (1989:404). Bev Jo Ruston and Linda Strega link such phenomena to overall hierarchical power arrangements in a patriarchal culture. They contend that more socially privileged lesbians tend to categorize as butch those lesbians who are "darker, larger, poorer, and/or older" (1986:32). *Difference from* therefore becomes, in a complex interaction between all sorts of social categories such as race, class, and gender, the key to *identification with* the social Otherness that constitutes lesbian culture in a heterosexist context.

This paradox underlies all the phenomena of lesbian revolt outlined above and goes beyond the question of "reading" and "writing" the lesbian body as social text. In a superb article, de Lauretis (1988) explores the ontological ramifications of creating a lesbian semiotics that does not (re)produce definitions of gender and sexuality centered on male models and ideals. For even if, as Case (1989) says, camp and the creation of a postmodern lesbian subject do present a possible escape from gender conceived as constructed difference (always defined as the difference of women from men), in reality at present, the refusal to be feminine is still read by much of society as the desire to be masculine. This paradox, which erases the possibility of an authentic lesbian subject, is what de Lauretis calls "sexual (in)difference" and "hommo-sexuality":

> The figure of the mannish female invert continues to stand as the representation of lesbian desire against both the discourse of hommo-sexuality and the feminist account of lesbianism as woman identification. (1988:162)

CONSTRUCTING THE LESBIAN

If the conventionally feminine or even female body is unlivable and the masculine body unthinkable, then lesbians must recreate the body. The problem is how to do so. One response is to transcend the categories of "masculine" and "feminine."

In both form and content, the works of Monique Wittig suppress the very concept of sexual difference, creating a discourse so radically at odds with Western cultural concepts as to force a fundamental shift in the production of meaning itself. Wittig states unequivocally that "Lesbians are not women" (1980:110):

> Lesbian is the only concept I know of which is beyond the categories of sex (woman and man), because the designated subject (lesbian) is *not* a woman, either economically, or politically, or ideologically. (1980:53)

It is no accident that one of her most important works is titled *The Lesbian Body*, nor that the physicality of the body is central to all her fictions (Crowder, 1983; Marks, 1979). Teresa de Lauretis cites *The Lesbian Body* for stepping outside the endless loop of sexual "(in)difference":

> Thus, the struggle with language to rewrite the body beyond its pre-coded, conventional representations is not and cannot be a reappropriation of the female body as it is, domesticated, maternal, oedipally or preoedipally engendered, but is a struggle to transcend both gender

and "sex" and recreate the body otherwise: to see it perhaps as monstrous, or grotesque, or mortal, or violent, and certainly also sexual, but with a material and sensual specificity that will resist phallic idealization and render it accessible to women in another sociosexual economy. In short, if it were not lesbian, this body would make no sense. (1988:167)

I have observed four major interrelated concepts underlying the various movements to "re-create" and make new "sense" of the lesbian body. First, lesbians want to develop bodily strength and express that strength physically. Second, a "natural body" ideology attempts to strip away culturally imposed physical values. Third, the lesbian body should be distinctive, not confused with that of heterosexual women. Finally, expressions of lesbian sexuality necessitate creating a new understanding of the relationship between the body and its discourses.

Physical strength is so strongly associated with maleness that almost every discussion of gender issues with nonfeminists eventually comes down to someone saying, "But men are stronger than women." The stereotype of the hulking (masculine) lesbian was used in my youth to discourage girls from developing muscles, which in any case were considered unattractive (to men), and I recall everyone looked with suspicion at girls who were good at sports. In a French article on "the lesbian look," the term "sportive" is used to indicate a butch appearance (Goldrajch and Jouve, 1984).

Yet lesbian singer Meg Christian's song "Ode to a Gym Teacher" invariably brings cheers and the laughter of recognition at lesbian gatherings, with its refrain celebrating the gym teacher who showed ". . . that being female/ Meant you still could be strong" (1974). Sports, especially softball, are an integral part of many lesbian communities in the United States, and other activities such as martial arts, weightlifting, and body building are ubiquitous. Long before "yuppie" trends and the 1980s fanaticism about health, lesbians placed a special emphasis on strength and physical development.

I believe there are two important aspects of lesbians' interest in strength. The most obvious, shared by many heterosexual feminists who practice martial arts and weightlifting, is the need for self-defense in a world where women are physically threatened with rape and other forms of violence. "Out" lesbians are a special target for "gay-bashing," and the incidence of violence against gays and lesbians is rising.[21] Hence, increasing physical strength is a survival mechanism.

Less evident outside the lesbian community is the valuation of strength as a form of self-validation. Many lesbians equate physical weakness with loss of identity and personal powerlessness. There is an obvious pride in having a strong body with powerful muscles able to perform difficult tasks. While this is partly a rejection of "feminine" passivity, its more important function is to create a new definition of physical beauty that makes strength and grace complements rather than opposites. Unlike some heterosexual female athletes, many lesbians find an obvious musculature aesthetically pleasing. The image of the Amazon, a symbol of power and strength as well as separation from men, was widely adopted by lesbians in the 1970s.

Along with strength comes a tendency to use space differently. Lesbians often cultivate movements (gestures, strides, motions of arms and legs) that, unlike the circumscribed movements of most women, occupy the full volume of space around the body. Although often read as "masculine" or even "aggressive" by straights, such motor movements instead should be understood as a refusal to constrain the body in conformity with social norms (see Guillaumin, 1993). One of the most frequent reasons lesbians give for choosing "unfeminine" clothing is the need for clothes in which one can move freely, extending the limbs fully and forcefully.

I would include in this reclaiming of space and volume another phenomenon seldom noticed or remarked upon even within the lesbian community. Lesbians frequently use the voice in a distinctive way, lowering the pitch or modulating the use of the higher registers of the voice. This is not a lowering of pitch to make oneself more masculine but rather a relaxing of the vocal apparatus to allow the voice to drop to its normal register. This phenomenon reveals just how artificial are the high pitch and weak tone of the "feminine" voice adopted unconsciously by many heterosexual women. Lowered pitch usually accompanies stronger volume and tone as well.[22]

It is a short step from seeing femininity as artificial to positing a "natural" female state which would obtain once patriarchal pressures are eliminated. A "naturalist" ideology explicitly or implicitly underlies many aspects of lesbian thinking about the body. It is necessary to separate out two types of naturalist thought. The first hypothesizes that the physical body should be allowed to develop and express itself with a minimum of societal intervention. Because humans come in many different shapes and sizes, this ideology seeks to strip away value judgments based upon physical attributes. The second type wants to eliminate those social interventions deemed harmful but places strong values on traits it considers "natural" to women.

"Fat liberation" is one example of a body discourse that illustrates how these ideologies work. Part of an overall feminist and lesbian tendency to fight negative attitudes toward the body, this movement begins with an analysis of the prejudices against fat ingrained in a heterosexual society that imposes an ideal of increasing thinness on women. The dangers of this ideal—anorexia, bulimia, constant dieting, damaged self-images—need no amplification here. The connection between the economies of race and class as they intersect gender and sexuality when it comes to fatness have also become clear (Sedgwick, 1986). Such procedures as wiring the jaws shut for enforced dieting, stomach stapling, liposuction, and other interventions that alter or mutilate the body, similar to the kinds of mutilations discussed in the first part of this chapter, shape the body in conformity with heterosexual ideals.[23]

On an ideological level, if prejudices against fat are part of a heterosexual mechanism that sets an unobtainable ideal of beauty that women must meet in order to attract men, they focus women's energies on meeting that ideal rather than resisting it. Two ideological strategies then become evident. One is to eliminate such prejudice, along with other prejudices based on bodily appearance, such that fatness or thinness becomes meaningless. Enough lesbians have become sensitized to make negative attitudes toward fat an issue in the lesbian community (Dworkin, 1988). This strategy corresponds to the first type of natural body ideology I mentioned above. The second strategy would valorize larger bodies, arguing either that "big is beautiful" (while thinness is a symbol of feminine deprivation) or that bigness accompanies strength.[24]

The difference between these two approaches to the problem is, I suggest, the difference between radical lesbianism and cultural feminism. The latter commits the fallacy of simply reversing cultural values—here it retains fat versus thin as a marker of individual worth and conformity to a norm, rather than eliminating the category altogether. Cultural feminism takes those traits negatively associated with femininity in the culture and tries to make them positive traits. Radical lesbianism calls into question the very valorization process itself.

Although certainly it is desirable to eliminate prejudices against the "natural" body in its various forms, I know of no human group that does not alter appearances to conform to ideas of what one should look like, and lesbians are not exempt. A major function of style is to create a group identity, to distinguish the group from others, and to make identification of members easier. Before the gay liberation movement of the 1970s, coded language, styles, and mannerisms allowed gay men and lesbians to find each other in a repressive culture. Today, distinctive presentations of the body serve to solidify group identification. Two current trends render the creation of a distinctive lesbian "look" difficult. First, the influence of feminist and lesbian revolt against constrictive clothing, makeup, and time-consuming hairstyles combined in the late 1970s and early 1980s with a sort of "radical chic" to extend what had been characteristic lesbian styles to the general American culture. Wearing pants to work, for instance, became fashionable, and the Annie Hall look was in. "Looks" cultivated by the gay and lesbian communities were at least superficially adopted by fashion-conscious straights.[25] This meant that the distinguishing function of style was blurred. I can recall semi-joking conversations about how one could no longer tell who was a lesbian.

This blurring combined with the virulent homophobia and antifeminism of the 1980s to create a second tendency. In reaction to what they perceived as the "clone" or "uniform" styles adopted by lesbian feminists in the 1970s, some lesbians saw the effort to creat a lesbian look as passé and repressive. Makeup, "feminine" attire, and long hair were reclaimed as valid expressions of a lesbian lifestyle. Other lesbians argue that this is just a way of "passing," accepting the privileges society awards to feminine heterosexual women, and negates the very concept of creating a lesbian (as opposed to homosexual) identity. Simply put, wearing high heels and a skirt is not a politically neutral action (see Klausner, 1990; Blackman and Perry, 1990).

Recently, a reclamation of butch and femme roles has led to experimentation with creating a variety of styles that challenge conventional meanings of clothing and body presentation. The goal, as with camp, is to invent a distinctively *lesbian* style that is easily recognized yet not androgynous.

The conflict between "lifestyle" lesbians and "political" lesbians over the lesbian "look" seems a minor skirmish in comparison to what one might term the lesbian "sex wars" of the 1980s (see Rich, 1986, Raymond, 1989, Valverde, 1989). At the heart of this conflict is the question of how to construct an authentic lesbian sexuality in a culture that defines the "sex act" in terms that do not apply to the lesbian body. Frye (1988) argues that we lack a vocabulary and ultimately a set of concepts that could even describe lesbian "sex." Clearly the creation of a lesbian body must include the creation of lesbian sexuality. As Barale says, "Genitals are the given: *what* we do with them is a matter of creative invention; *how* we interpret what we do with them is what we call sexuality" (1986:80).

In recognition that the female body has multiple erogenous areas, many lesbians have extended the concept of "sex" to include most parts of the body. A culture that defines as "sexual" only genital activities aimed at male ejaculation clearly has too restrictive a concept of sexuality, and lesbians have tried to eliminate the rigid dividing line between genital "sex" and activities involving other parts of the body. In the process, some risked defining as "masculine," and hence inappropriate, any goal-oriented genital behavior in favor of a generalized eroticism (Echols, 1983). Barale summarizes this utopian vision: "Lesbian sex was simple, blissful, tender, and endlessly satisfying" (1986:84).

One of the first stages in the reconstruction of the body was to transfer the focus of genital sexuality from the vagina to the clitoris and vulva. Rich notes that, " . . . in the 1970s, the sexual frontier moved from the vagina to the clitoris as decisively as the art world moved from Paris to New York after World War II" (1986:548). She sees an ambivalence toward penetration (of the vagina) as an underlying theme in debates of the 1980s over sexuality.

In opposition to this movement toward a "feminine" lesbian sexuality, other thinkers created a sexuality that "undomesticated" the lesbian body (Marks, 1979; de Lauretis, 1987). A totally new conception of sexuality and of the lesbian body became necessary to break out of the cycle of "feminine" aversion to the sexual versus "masculine" power-oriented sexuality. A notable example is the work of Monique Wittig, especially in *The Lesbian Body* (1973). Here, the lover and beloved dismember and reconstruct the body in all its parts.

What is most significant about efforts to construct a truly lesbian sexuality is that, for perhaps the first time in history, lesbians were *consciously* setting out to define what that sexuality might be. We were explicitly acknowledging the cultural basis of meanings attached to physical experience, and asserting that such meanings could be altered or created anew.

Thus, within contemporary American lesbianism, we find a movement to reconstruct a lesbian body that is neither "masculine" nor "feminine" but "Other" and radically different. The cultural interpretation of the body, and the power to determine what that interpretation shall be, is central to this effort. What is most remarkable about all the various modes of revolt against the heterosexual imperative that I have presented here is the degree to which lesbians have assumed that our bodies and even our sexuality can be (re)constructed through a conscious process of making choices. Articulated sometimes within a discourse of the "natural," these diverse efforts to deconstruct externally imposed definitions of what the female body ought to be show an underlying belief that lesbians can step outside the endless cycle of the opposition between the "masculine" and the "feminine," even at the most basic levels of sexual desire. Whether opposing existing definitions or substituting new ones, lesbians have insisted on the right to write the body as a social text.

NOTES

1. One would have to cite the entirety of Western thought on women and men to document this point. Suffice it to say that, whether the theory is biologically argued as in current sociobiology, or translated into psychological terms à la Freud or Lacan and their followers, the assumption of the body's configuration as naturally determined by reproductive function often leads to the belief that social destiny is overdetermined by anatomical difference.

Mathieu (1989) is a brilliant analysis of the possible conceptualizations of the relation between the body and gender identity. She traces the consequences for sexuality and identity of three major modes of thought: "sexual identity," in which gender translates sex and is homologous to it; "sexed identity," in which sex and gender are seen as analogic and gender symbolizes sex; and "identity of sex," in which there is a sociological correspondance between sex and gender, with gender constructing sex. She illustrates her argument with examples from numerous cultures, with special attention to how homosexuality fits into the various modes of thought. Readers should consult this article for a theoretical background to my work.

2. Of course, reproduction is not exempt from physical intervention. From forced sterilization and forced pregnancy through genocide and murder of women, women's (and sometimes men's) reproductive functions are often the target of social manipulation. Such practices are outside the scope of this chapter but cannot be forgotten. I thank Colette Guillaumin for her helpful comments on this point.

3. See Brownmiller (1984) for a discussion of the relationship between American ideals of femininity and body representations. The critiques of "fashion" and of bodily representations of femininity have been a staple in the modern feminist critique of sex roles. Further, the nineteenth-century women's movement also criticized corsets, dieting, makeup, and fashions, assuming maternal functions are good and criticizing fashions that might weaken the body to carry out those functions.

4. See Koedt (1968) for one of the first and most influential works on this topic within the early radical-feminist movement. See Echols (1989) for further discussion of Koedt's article and radical-feminist analysis of heterosexuality.

5. Frye (1983) argues convincingly that what men fear most is that women will deny them the total access to women that is at the heart of male power and hence male fear of separatism.

6. Note that genital mutilation often coexists with some forms of polygyny and purdah, situations in which access to sex with other women would otherwise be facilitated, not to say encouraged, by living conditions. Genital mutiliation therefore ensures not only that the women will not bear children to men other than their husbands—the usual explanation for the practice—but that they will not be tempted to experience sexual pleasure with no reproductive consequences—that is, lesbian sexuality. This fact may invite a modification of those theories of purdah based only on male economic power to hand on property to their own sons.

7. It is true that the male body is often subjected to some physical modifications to enhance its conformity to cultural norms of maleness (body building, ritual scarification, etc.). However, I know of no culture in which the male body is actually crippled or rendered incapable of normal functioning in the same ways

mutilations of female bodies almost always do. Further, many such rituals are not aimed primarily at preparing the man for his reproductive or sexual roles.

8. See the letters in *Lesbian Connection*, for instance, and the debate over "lipstick lesbians" at Yale ("Lipsticks and Lords: Yale's New Look," *The Wall Street Journal*, August 4, 1987:32). This debate recognizes that culturally defined "femininity" is limiting for women, while at the same time seeing that women who conform to the norms are safe from the taboos against lesbianism. See also Stein (1989). Blackman and Perry (1990) have done an excellent analysis of the underlying political ideologies of lesbian "style wars" in England. They note that, while "lipstick lesbians" reject the essentialist idea of a "natural woman" in favor of a social constructionist theory of style as arbitrary, they also are able to participate in the "good life" of Thatcherite England. This article also discusses how black lesbians in England have created a distinctive style using African elements.

9. In the vocabulary of the lesbian community, "femme" indicates someone who adopts certain aspects of the style and behavior conventionally associated with femininity, while "butch" indicates a lesbian who adopts aspects associated with masculinity.

10. A full discussion of the complex relationship between femmes and heterosexual "femininity" is beyond the scope of this chapter. See Nestle (1981) for a more thorough explanation. I thank Jan Boney for her criticisms and comments on this subject.

11. I borrowed this term from Penelope (1984a).

12. The spate of films in the early 1980s in which the "joke" was based on cross-dressing (*Victor/Victoria*, *Tootsie*, and *Yentl*, for instance) illustrates this point. The mass audience enjoys the comedy only because in each case the protagonist is securely heterosexual, and spectators know that from the beginning. Indeed, such cross-dressing reinforces, rather than questions, heterosexuality as "natural." Further, in some cases it suggests that men are better women than women, a tendency that invades real life, according to Showalter (1983). For an interesting analysis of gender roles and cross-dressing in Shakespeare, where male (boy) actors are playing women playing men, see Rackin (1987).

13. This same discomfort and wonder, of course, greet the unmasking of men who successfully pass as female, as David Henry Hwang's 1988 Tony Award–winning play *M. Butterfly* explores.

14. Jay (1988:91-92) points out that while Barney liked to dress in male costume, she disdained those who, like Colette's lover the Marquise de Belboeuf, wore men's clothes seriously. Colette associates men's clothing with the "androgyny" she attributes to the character modeled on the Marquise in *The Pure and the Impure* (1931/1966).

15. See Case (1989) for a sophisticated analysis of how "camp" and role-playing lead to the butch/femme couple as the ideal postmodernist feminist subject.

16. See Raymond (1989) on the question of depoliticization of sexuality and role-playing within the lesbian community. Unlike Raymond, I do not necessarily lump butch/femme role-playing with s/m and other "minority" practices, for reasons apparent in my arguments. However, I do find her analysis of the effects of liberal/libertarian approaches on the political movement convincing.

17. See Davis and Kennedy (1986) for a major exploration of the political meaning of butch/femme roles prior to the resurgence of feminism. See also Penelope (1984a and 1984b) for other points of view on these questions.

18. In her review of Holly Devor's *Gender Blending: Confronting the Limits of Duality*, Carol LeMasters (1990) reiterates that people assume maleness and that one "masculine" trait will override several "feminine" traits, causing people to make mistakes about gender in the case of "masculine" women.

19. Louise Turcotte (personal communication) notes the psychological impulse toward carving out an identity recognized as "real," even if seen as "deviant," in an environment where gender was equated with sex.

20. Unshaven legs and underarms have become something of a fetishistic symbol in the minds of the American public. Equated with radical feminists and having invariably a connotation of lesbianism, not shaving appears repeatedly in jokes, and in the press, as a negative indicator. For instance, in a recent *Time* cover article on the future of feminism, a college student is quoted as saying, "I picture a feminist as someone who is masculine and who doesn't shave her legs and is doing everything she can to deny she is feminine" (Wallis, 1989), and the article goes on to say, "Hairy legs haunt the feminist movement, as do images of being strident and lesbian" (1989:81). Further, the article quotes Erica Jong recalling a mood among feminists that was "anticosmetics, anti-lacy underwear" (1989:85). These quotations assume that the feminist critique of femininity was a regrettable "phase" and, thus, denies the validity of that critique. Why hairy legs are such a potent negative symbol for Americans remains to be analyzed.

21. In 1989, 7,031 incidents of violence and harassment against gay men and lesbians were reported to the National Gay and Lesbian Task Force Anti-Violence Project, according to a news release published in June 1990 (*Des Moines Register* June 8, 1990, and mailing from NGLTF).

22. I am indebted to Nicole-Claude Mathieu and Colette Guillaumin for their discussions with me on this topic.

23. Americans, male as well as female, are encouraged to diet and/or undergo surgery to lose weight for health reasons as well as aesthetic considerations. However, there is a crucial difference between maintaining a healthy weight and promoting the kind of excessive thinness that has become the ideal for American women.

24. Louise Turcotte gave me invaluable assistance in my thinking about the semiotics of fat in lesbian discourse and culture.

25. Sedgwick (1986) has noted the irony that gay men served as the standards of masculinity to many straight men, and recently, it has also been revealed that some fashion models purported to be women are in fact gay men (Jean Kilbourne, personal communication).

REFERENCES

Abbott, Sidney, and Barbara Love. (1972). *Sappho Was a Right-On Woman.* New York: Stein and Day.

Anonymous. (1986). Fmme and Butch: A Reader's Forum. *Lesbian Ethics,* 2(2):86-104.

Associated Press. (1989). Musician's Death at 74 Reveals He Was a Woman. *The New York Times,* February 2: A18.

Barale, Mechèle Aina. (1986). Body Politic/Body Pleasured: Feminism's Theories of Sexuality, A Review Essay. *Frontiers,* 9(1):80-89.

Blackman, Inge and Kathryn Perry. (1990). Skirting the Issue: Lesbian Fashion for the 1990s. *Feminist Review,* 34:67-78.

Brower, Montgomery. (1989). James Burt's "Love Surgery" Was Supposed to Boost Pleasure, But Some Patients Say It Brought Pain. *People Weekly,* March 27:13ff.

Brownmiller, Susan. (1984). *Femininity.* New York: Fawcett Columbine.

Case, Sue-Ellen. (1989). Towards a Butch-Femme Aesthetic. In Lynne Hart (Ed.), *Feminist Perspectives on Contemporary Women's Drama.* Ann Arbor: University of Michigan Press.

Christian, Meg. (1974). "Ode to a Gym Teacher." On *I Know You Know.* Olivia Records.

Colette. (1931). *Le pur et l'impur* (original title *Ces Plaisirs*). Paris: Gringoire. Definitive edition titled *Le pur et l'impur* (1941). (English translation [1966]. *The Pure and the Impure.* New York: Farrar, Straus, and Giroux.)

Crowder, Diane Griffin. (1983). Amazons or Mothers? Monique Wittig, Hélène Cixous and Theories of Women's Writing. *Contemporary Literature,* 24 (2):117-144.

Daly, Mary. (1978). *Gyn/Ecology.* Boston: Beacon Press.

Davis, Madeline, and Elizabeth Lapovsky Kennedy. (1986). Oral History and the Study of Sexuality in the Lesbian Community: Buffalo, New York, 1940-1960. *Feminist Studies,* 12(1):7-26.

Dekker, Rudolph M., and Lotte C. van de Pol. (1989). *The Tradition of Female Transvestism in Early Modern Europe.* New York: St. Martin's.

de Lauretis, Teresa. (1987). The Female Body and Heterosexual Presumption. *Semiotica,* 67(3-4):259-279.

de Lauretis, Teresa. (1988). Sexual Indifference and Lesbian Representation. *Theater Journal,* 40(2):155-177.

Dobkin, Alix. (1975). "View from Gay Head." On *Lavender Jane Loves Women.* Produced by Alix Dobkin, Kay Gardner, and Marilyn Ries.

Dworkin, Andrea. (1974). *Woman Hating.* New York: Dutton.

Dworkin, Sari H. (1988). Not in Man's Image: Lesbians and the Cultural Oppression of Body Image. *Women and Therapy,* 8(1-2):27-39.

Echols, Alice. (1983). The New Feminism of Yin and Yang. In Ann Barr Snitow, Christine Stanswell, and Sharon Thompson (Eds.), *Powers of Desire: The Politics of Sexuality.* New York: New Feminist Library, pp. 435-459.

Echols, Alice. (1989). *Daring to Be Bad: Radical Feminism in America 1967-1975.* Minneapolis, MN: Minnesota University Press.

Faderman, Lillian. (1981). *Surpassing the Love of Men.* New York: William Morrow and Company.

Frye, Marilyn. (1983). *The Politics of Reality.* Trumansburg, NY: The Crossing Press, pp. 95-109.

Frye, Marilyn. (1988). Lesbian "Sex." *Sinister Wisdom,* 35:46-54.

Garber, Eric. (1989). A Spectacle in Color: The Lesbian and Gay Subculture of Jazz Age Harlem. In Martin Baum Duberman, Martha Vicinus, and George Chauncey (Eds.), *Hidden from History: Reclaiming the Gay and Lesbian Past.* New York: New American Library, pp. 318-331.

Goldrajch, Muriel, and Christiane Jouve. (1984). Dossier: Le Look Lesbien. *Lesbia,* 20:6-10.

Grahn, Judy. (1984). *Another Mother Tongue: Gay Words, Gay Worlds.* Boston: Beacon Press.

Grier, Barbara, and Coletta Reid. (1976). *Lesbian Lives.* Oakland, CA: Diana Press.

Guillaumin, Colette. (1984). Unpublished lecture to Seminar, "L'anthropologie des sexes." N-C Mathieu, Dir. Paris: Ecole des Hautes Etudes en Sciences Sociales.

Guillaumin, Colette. (1993). The Constructed Body. In Catherine Burroughs and Jeffrey Ehrenreich (Eds.), *Reading the Social Body.* Iowa City, IA: University of Iowa Press, pp. 40-60.

Harness, Gerry, and Judith Kelman. (1989). My Gynecologist Butchered Me. *Redbook,* July: pp. 20,26.

Hosken, Fran. (1983). *The Hosken Report: Genital-Sexual Mutilation of Females.* Lexington, MA: Women's International News Network.

Hwang, David Henry. (1989). *M. Butterfly.* New York: NAL/Dutton.

Jay, Karla. (1988). *The Amazon and the Page.* Bloomington, IN: Indiana University Press.

Klausner, Kim. (1990). On Wearing Skirts. *Out/Look,* 8:18-20.

Koedt, Anne. (1968). The Myth of the Vaginal Orgasm. *Notes from the First Year: Women's Liberation.* New York: New York Radical Women. Reprinted in Leslie B. Tanner (Ed.), *Voices from Women's Liberation.* New York: Signet, 1970, pp. 157-166.

Lanser, Susan S. (1986). Who Are the "We"? The Shifting Terms of Feminist Discourse. *Women's Studies Quarterly,* 14(3-4):18-20.

Lemasters, Carol. (1990). Traitors to Their Sex? *Women's Review of Books,* 7(9):12. Review of Holly Devor, *Gender Blending: Confronting the Limits of Duality.* Bloomington, IN: Indiana University Press, 1989.

Levy, Howard S. (1966). *Chinese Footbinding: The History of a Curious Erotic Custom.* New York: Walton Rawls.

Marks, Elaine. (1979). Lesbian Intertextuality. In George Stambolian and Elaine Marks (Eds.), *Homosexualities and French Literature.* Ithaca, NY: Cornell University Press, pp. 353-377.

Mathieu, Nicole-Claude. (1989). Identité sexuelle/sexuée/de sexe?: Trois modes de conceptualisation du rapport entre sexe et genre. In Anne-Marie Daune-Richard, Marie-Claude Hurtig, and Marie-France Pichevin (Eds.), *Categorisation de sexe et constructions scientifiques.* Aix-en-Provence, France: Université de Provence, pp. 109-147.

Myerson, Marilyn. (1986). The Politics of Sexual Knowledge: Feminism and Sexology Textbooks. *Frontiers,* 9(1):66-71.

Nestle, Joan. (1981). Butch-Femme Relationships: Sexual Courage in the 1950s. *Heresies,* 12:21-24.

Penelope, Julia. (1984a). The Mystery of Lesbians Parts I-III. *Lesbian Ethics,* 1(1):7-33.

Penelope, Julia. (1984b). WHOSE Past Are We Reclaiming? *Common Lives/Lesbian Lives,* 13:16-36.

Proust, Marcel. (1954). *A la recherche du temps perdu.* Paris: Bibliotheque de la Pleiade.

Rackin, Phyllis. (1987). Androgyny, Mimesis, and the Marriage of the Boy Heroine on the English Renaissance Stage. *PMLA,* 102(1):29-41.

Raymond, Janice. (1989). Putting the Politics Back into Lesbianism. *Women's Studies International Forum,* 12(2):149-157.

Rich, Adrienne. (1980). Compulsory Heterosexuality and Lesbian Existence. *Signs,* 5(4):631-660.

Rich, B. Ruby. (1986). Feminism and Sexuality in the 1980s: A Review Essay. *Feminist Studies,* 12(3):525-561.

Ruston, Bev Jo, and Linda Strega. (1986). Heterosexism Causes Lesbophobia Causes Butch-Phobia Part II of the Big Sell-Out: Lesbian Femininity. *Lesbian Ethics,* 2(2):22-41.

Sedgwick, Eve Kosofsky. (1986). Labors of Embodiment. Paper for session S(e)izing Power: Gender, Representation, Body Scale. New York: Modern Language Association.

Shapiro, Susan C. (1987). Amazons, Hermaphrodites, and Plain Monsters: The "Masculine" Woman in English Satire and Social Criticism from 1580-1640. *Atlantis,* 13(1):66-77.

Showalter, Elaine. (1983). Critical Cross-Dressing: Male Feminists and the Woman of the Year. *Raritan Review,* 3(2):130-149.

Smith, Elizabeth A. (1989). Butches, Femmes, and Feminists: The Politics of Lesbian Sexuality. *NWSA Journal,* 1(3):398-421.

Sontag, Susan. (1966). *Against Interpretation.* New York: Farrar, Straus, and Girouz.

Spelman, Elizabeth V. (1988). *The Inessential Woman.* Boston: Beacon Press.

Stein, Arlene. (1989). Style Wars and the New Lesbianism. *Out/Look,* 1(4):34-42.

Steinem, Gloria, and Robin Morgan. (1983). The International Crime of Genital Mutilation. In Gloria Steinem (Ed.), *Outrageous Acts and Everyday Rebellions.* New York: New American Library, 1986, pp. 330-340.

Valverde, Mariana. (1989). Beyond Gender Dangers and Private Pleasures: Theory and Ethics in the Sex Debates. *Feminist Studies,* 15(2):237-254.

Wallis, Claudia. (1989). Onward, Women! *Time,* 134(23), December 4:80-89.

Wittig, Monique. (1973). *Le Corps Lesbien.* Paris: Minuit. English translation *The Lesbian Body.* London: Peter Owen, 1975. New York: Avon, 1976.

Wittig, Monique. (1980). The Straight Mind. *Feminist Issues,* 1(1):103-111.

PART 2:
LOOKING DYKE

The Ugly Dyke

Wendy Chapkis

Parents are always a good reality check, especially for those of us who live too long in gay ghettos. I recently took a new flame home to meet the family. During the seven-hour drive from San Francisco to the Los Angeles suburbs, I tried to imagine what my folks would see.

The woman is a beauty—green eyes, dark skin, and black hair. She also knows how to dress; she is one of the few women I know who is equally comfortable in the most delicate white lace and the most weathered black leather.

After my parents caught their breath, I thought that what would strike them most would be that she looks a little more femme than I do. This, I assumed, would be important to the family. My reasoning was that when daughter first comes out, they think "she's always been a feminist; it's a political phase." When daughter brings home her first girlfriend (who is absolutely riveting from her starched shirts and leather ties to her bad-ass boots), they think, "that one's the real dyke, not our daughter." But when daughter introduces them to a feminine beauty, the unavoidable question is posed: "Who is the boy now?"

At least that is what I had anticipated. On reflection, though, I think I got it only partly right. My parents' growing acceptance of the fact that I am a "real lesbian" may be due more to quantity (another girlfriend) than to qualities of fashion and gender self-presentation.

A clue I had missed the mark came in the midst of a wonderful talk with my mother. She was allowing me to fill her in on the romantic details of how we met: "And so there we were, in a crowded room. And suddenly from somewhere in the back I heard this voice you would die for . . . and the voice belonged to the most beautiful woman in the room!" The slight widening of my mother's eyes told me that we see women differently. Her next comment confirmed this: "Oh. I see. But does she always wear that leather jacket?"

She had only seen another lesbian in leather. Phrases such as "more feminine" or "most beautiful" probably didn't even occur to her. It made me think once more about the question of the Ugly Dyke.

"Ugly" is a strange word. So is beauty for that matter. Common sense and an endless number of aphorisms suggest that these are individual judgments, a question of taste, qualities present only in the eyes of the beholder, and so on. But we, as women, know that this is no description of social reality. While none of us could say exactly what beauty is, we each could probably list in depressing detail every single flaw that keeps us from fully belonging to that privileged category. And it's clear that beauty is culturally defined in ways that conveniently keep most of us out.

But, then again, lesbians are already outsiders. And from where we stand, the inside doesn't always look all that exciting. In fact, the straight world's idea of beauty can actually translate into bland and boring in a lesbian context.

On a good Saturday night in a gay bar in San Francisco, I, for instance, am hot. Give me a good haircut (a dyke imperative) and a pair of tight jeans riding between my motorcycle jacket and cowboy boots, and insecurity won't be my biggest problem. Surround me with women who, like me, are proudly strutting their unconventional stuff, and I will be able to match anyone glance for glance and hold a gaze with the best of them.

Transplant me to my parents' suburban community, though, and my self-consciousness will not be synonymous with self-confidence. Suddenly I look wrong: a woman in her late thirties with badly bleached hair, red lipstick, and a fuzzy blonde mustache. I can almost hear them thinking, "With a look like that, no wonder she's a lesbian."

Ugly Dyke. That's me too.

Ugly is more than a physical description. For a woman, it's meant to be shorthand for worthless, undesirable, and undeserving. And lesbians are by popular definition ugly women. This categorization of dykes as ugly serves a purpose. It's not only meant to make claiming the identity less appealing, it also provides a perfect explanation for why some women choose women over men. In fact, it's meant to rob us of that choice; presumably, we are involved with women because we are too ugly to attract a man's attention.

But the problem is, we don't seem to be aware of how ugly we really are. After all, if lesbians are such ugly women, where do we get off acting as if we deserve respect, civil rights, and perhaps most offensively, sexual pleasure? The media constantly remind us that only the "beautiful people" deserve love, lust, and life satisfaction. And only a very few—very heterosexual—women deserve temporary membership in this elite. Widespread female self-confidence could be dangerous. The self-confident, after all, tend to make demands, and women are not meant to be demanding.

Instead, commercial culture does its best to breed deep insecurity, endless attempts at physical transformation, and too often, a female sexual waiting game. She who does battle with her own imperfections may hold her desire in check while waiting for a more perfect moment or may settle for someone who will take her despite her shortcomings.

Lesbians generally aren't such nice girls. We are ugly women who pursue sexual pleasure. In fact, lesbian and bisexual women are the only categories of women defined by the pursuit of pleasure. Other female identities are only instrumentally sexual such as "mother" or "whore," or incidentally sexual as with "wife" or "girlfriend."

Lesbians and bi women, in contrast, are publicly defined by our sexual desire—a desire apparently so pronounced that we are willing to accept the burdens of the pervert and the outlaw in its pursuit. We are women out of control, and that is already a punishable offense. But the complicated labeling of lesbians as both ugly and sexual makes us particularly dangerous. For if we, in all our varied shapes, sizes, ages, and abilities, if we as "ugly dykes," deserve sexual pleasure, then maybe all women are deserving. The message we give is that beauty deserves nothing more than lip service from women. And who better equipped to perform that particular task than lesbians?

Woman Eats Brownies, Gets Laid

Greta Christina

At the beginning of 1993, I went through a mild and somewhat willful depression during which I watched a great deal of television. (Why I thought this would make me feel better, I'm not sure, but that's another story.) Toward the end of this spell, I told a friend that, although I was feeling generally better, I was going through a "bad body image period" (Jesus, do I really talk like that? I've been living in California too long), which I thought was at least partly brought on by spending hours slumped on the couch watching TV, snacking, and not moving very much. My friend thought about this for a moment and suggested that, perhaps, my unhappiness with my body was not so much a result of sitting on the couch snacking for hours but was more a result of watching lots and lots of very thin people on TV. (I don't know why he thought he had to tell me something so obvious. I'm sure I'd have figured it out myself in a couple of years.)

When I tell people how much I weigh, they are almost inevitably surprised. In fact, I rarely weigh myself at all and am not sure what my exact weight is at the time of this writing. I myself am almost inevitably surprised—and not pleasantly so—to see the actual number staring me in the face, irrefutably, undeniably, like a rude acquaintance telling you bald facts about yourself without even trying to be tactful.

Here's why I think this surprise takes place. I look, dress, carry myself, think of myself, and live in my body in a certain way. I usually like myself and usually enjoy my body. I enjoy sex and think of myself as desirable. I dress to call attention to myself and to my body, not to hide it. On good days, I swagger a bit and flirt a lot. If you saw me on the street or at a party, you might find me attractive, or you might not. Depending on how I was feeling when I got dressed that morning, you'd probably think of me as either relaxed and easy-going or as gaudy and outrageous. Your physical impression would most likely be of a short, solidly built woman, fairly compact, lots of curves on a square frame, great tits, curvy legs, long blue hair and big dark eyes and a big dumb grin and a loud laugh. You would probably not guess that, at five feet two inches, I weigh close to two hundred pounds.

I believe that you wouldn't guess this because most people have a mental image of what a woman who is five feet two inches and weighs close to two hundred pounds looks like. I have one myself. It doesn't look very much like me, but it's nonetheless quite vivid. The image is gross and depressing, an unhappy woman with low self-esteem and no discipline, gone to seed and sad indulgence. The reason that I rarely weigh myself (and try not to watch too much television) is that it's far too common, when I'm feeling tired and weak and worried about what people think, to look in the mirror and see that picture imposed on my body.

Now, seeing an image in the mirror other than the one that's actually present would, on the surface, seem to be a disturbing or even terrifying experience, the kind of stuff you see in trashy psycho-horror films about demon spirits from beyond the grave invading the minds of teenage girls. In fact, this experience is one that I have had more or less consistently throughout my adult life.

I can remember looking in the mirror at nineteen years and a hundred pounds, seeing an image of what I thought five feet two inches and a hundred pounds looked like on a nineteen-year-old girl—ripe, nubile, slender, sexy, energetic, the apex of female desirability. As I gained years and pounds, that image stayed on to scold and tease me with what I could supposedly become again with just a little hard work and sacrifice. It wasn't until friends told me how they thought I had looked at that time—scrawny, emaciated, and tense—that I remembered what it had actually felt like to live in my body then. At age nineteen, I smoked heavily, drank way too much coffee, took lots and lots of harsh drugs, got very little sleep, worked too hard and played too hard, and drove myself to my absolute physical limit as a matter of daily routine. It's no wonder I weighed a hundred pounds; I'm surprised I didn't weigh less. I was exhausted, strained, nervous, jumpy, distracted, repressed, and unhappy. To say that I was out of touch with my body would be like saying that Caligula was out of touch with the Marxist ideal. But hey—I was thin.

Now, I can say these things. I can say them truthfully, I can say them convincingly, and I can even believe them myself; and they can still not make very much difference. Because right next to the perception of big women as ridiculous is the perception of big women asserting their attractiveness and desirability as even more ridiculous. In films or books or on TV, if a big woman says she's horny, talks about cute guys, or in any way acts as if she has a sex life, 90 percent of the time it's played for laughs or pathos or both. She's seen as either self-deluded or saving face, deceiving either herself or others into denying the obvious, indisputable, objectively true fact that she is big and therefore not attractive to anyone except weirdos.

It's a very frustrating double twist. Big women are told that our bodies are repulsive and our sexuality is crippled; when we insist that this isn't our experience, we're told that this insistence is pathetic and laughable. Our sexuality is denied, and our assertion of our sexuality is then seen as denial. Our defense against the accusation is seen as proof of its accuracy.

The funny thing is this. I'm queer. (No, that's not the funny thing, that's probably the most normal thing about me.) I am attracted to and like to have sex with other women. I am particularly attracted to other big women (although not exclusively so). Oddly enough—or maybe not so oddly—I am extra-particularly attracted to women who are built somewhat like me. I like fleshy women, grabbable women, women with some meat on their bones. I like big breasts and round bellies and strong thighs and nice wide, curvy, shapely asses that you can sink your fingers into. There's no question of denial or self-deception or wishful thinking here—we're talking 100 percent pure and natural, heart-pounding, clit-thumping, head-swiveling lust.

So here's the funny thing (this is definitely it, the funny thing is coming right up): I have learned to convince myself of my own sexuality by a peculiar sort of proxy. Since I have terrible trouble believing in my own desirability, but no trouble at all believing in the desirability of other big women, what I wind up doing is seeking sexual affirmation, not by looking in the mirror, but by looking at other women who look like me. When I catch myself drooling over some hot babe with a nice meaty body that I'd really like to get my hands on, I remind myself that other people—especially other women—probably feel the same way about me.

"Well, duh," I hear you cry. "It doesn't take an atomic genius to figure that out." And yet I have to consciously and deliberately remind myself of it. It's such a patently obvious thought process that you'd think it would happen automatically, but it doesn't happen that way at all. I'll tell you what happens automatically—looking in the mirror and thinking, "Hey, whatta babe," and having that thought immediately followed by a derisive, "Who do you think you're kidding?" The self-appreciation takes practice; the self-derision happens at the drop of a hat.

This whole mess is made even more complicated and fucked up by the fact that there's not just one false image in the mirror; there are at least two, probably more. The ugly picture of the depressing fat woman that I'm afraid I've become is frequently accompanied by the beautiful picture of the exciting thin woman that I fear I've lost forever. At times in my life when I've been dieting and trying to lose weight, the sensation has been most peculiar—resisting one mirror image, yearning for another. Getting dressed in the morning becomes a daily exercise in hallucinatory self-imagery. I pick up an item of clothing, imagining what it will look like on the slender, sylph-like creature that I long for; then, when I put it on, I'm mocked by the hideous blob-monster I'm sure I've become. Not a lot of room in there for a simple glance in the mirror to see what I actually look like before I head out the door. What I actually look like isn't even in the picture. What I actually look like is meaningless, crowded out by the apparitions that inhabit the mirror-world. It's one of the reasons I like to change my appearance a lot—cut my hair short, let it grow long, bleach it blonde, dye it blue, dye it black, dye it brown again. The shock of seeing the new image jolts me into seeing what's really there.

I wonder sometimes how straight women deal with this stuff. They don't have the benefit of the "I have the hots for her, she's a lot like me, therefore, other people probably have the hots for me" equation. Plus, they have to actually deal with straight men all the time: they date them and sleep with them and listen to them babble about Michelle Pfeiffer. I don't know how they stay sane. One of the reasons why I don't sleep with men much, even though I am bisexual and not a lesbian, is that I've found, as a gross unfair reverse-sexist feminazi generalization, that dykes are far more tolerant and appreciative of other women's bodies than straight men are. Sure, there are exceptions; I know dykes with plenty of snot-ball attitude about women who aren't "fit and trim," and I know, and have in fact slept with, men who like me the way I am and want to fuck me because of my body and not in spite of it. But exceptions are exceptions. They do show that my generalizations are just generalizations; they don't show that, as generalizations, they're in any way inaccurate.

Here's another gross, unfair generalization, a cockamamy theory based entirely on personal observation and anecdotal evidence and with absolutely no scientific validity, but which I nevertheless believe to be true. I've noticed that gay men and straight women seem to have very similar attitudes about their bodies and that—conversely?—lesbians and straight men also have similar attitudes about their bodies. Fags and het women seem to worry about their weight, height, age, build, breast size, dick size, etc., much more than dykes and het men do. They compare themselves to an abstract ideal of physical perfection in very similar ways; and in very similar ways, they feel like shit because they never measure up. Whether they're obsessively dieting or obsessively working out, whether it's Tom of Finland or *Glamour* magazine that they're trying to live up to, the compare-and-contrast patterns for both het women and gay men look very much alike.

It's not that dykes and het men don't ever get anxious and stressed-out about whether they're attractive, but they aren't as likely to equate sexual attractiveness with a particular physical ideal. Issues such as status, intelli-

gence, income, hipness, sexual skill and experience, and what kind of car
(or motorcycle) one drives seem to have more effect on sexual self-esteem
for queer women and het men than how they measure up to some abstract
template of physical perfection. I've certainly noticed this in my own life
and experience as a bisexual woman. Over the last several years, as I've
gradually become more involved with women and less involved with men,
my body image has improved; this is despite the fact that my weight has
slowly but steadily gone up over those years. My confidence in my own
sexuality seems to be connected less with the bathroom scale and more
with the Kinsey scale.

So here's my cockamamy theory. When considering body image and
physical self-esteem, the determining factor doesn't seem to be which
gender you are—it's which gender you're involved with. Lousy body
image is not so much a result of being female in our culture. It's a result of
being looked at, desired, and most of all, judged by men. (I recently read
that most straight men who get penile implants don't do it for their wives
or girlfriends; they do it because they're worried about how they compare
to the guys in the locker room. It doesn't surprise me a bit.)

In all the motley assortment of ideas and judgments and bigotries that
are out there about big women, one in particular gets me seriously peeved.
The idea is that all big women use food as a substitute pleasure for sex. We
either can't or won't have sex, the thinking goes; we're either afraid of sex
for whatever the trendy neurotic reason of the month is, so we eat instead
and get fat, or we can't get sex because we're fat and nobody wants us, so
we eat instead and get fatter. In addition to the obvious fucked-upedness of
the assumption that fat women don't have sex, there is a seriously twisted
fucked-upedness to the assumption that one pleasure should have to substitute for another. The implication of food-as-a-substitute-for-sex is that
the two pleasures are mutually exclusive (for women, anyway); that the
enjoyment of one pleasure necessitates the sacrifice of the other (for
women, anyway); and that deprivation is an inherent component of
sensual enjoyment (for women, anyway). I can't tell you how mad that
makes me. I want to know who made up these rules. I want to know who
decided that I can't have both food and sex. I want to know who decided
that I can't enjoy getting fucked *and* enjoy eating brownies. I want to find
out who made this stuff up. And then I want to shoot them.

Please understand that I am not simply accusing Society. ("J'accuse," I
cry, pointing the finger of judgment at Society, and Society shrugs and
continues with its poker game.) As much as I would like to believe otherwise, I must acknowledge that criticizing society does not set me apart
from it. I am, however much I may dislike this fact, a member of my

culture. I don't simply absorb its tenets passively and against my will; I also act to perpetuate them, even those I oppose. God knows I've spent long conversations railing against the arbitrary and oppressive standards of beauty in our culture, only to turn around and dish someone for being too fat or too skinny or poorly dressed or having a bad haircut. It's not just some internalized yet somehow detached Society that jeers at me when I look in the mirror; I do plenty of jeering on my own. ("J'accuse," I cry, pointing the finger of judgment at myself, and thus judged, I cringe and cower and agonize about it for hours with my downstairs neighbor.)

I saw a film recently titled *Leaving Normal*, a film in which most of the primary characters are women (a rare and startling phenomenon—I think I saw a two-headed calf that same night). In this film there appears a secondary character, a woman who shows up for a short time in the lives of the two main characters and then disappears. This woman is a very large woman, a fat woman, who keeps saying to herself and everyone around her that she knows she is a beautiful, special person who deserves to be loved. When we first meet this woman, she seems a bit silly, spouting platitudes and affirmations and new-age, power-of-positive-thinking blather in the face of some dreadful upsets and the obviously insurmountable obstacle of her fatness. The movie carries on this way for a bit, and then, at a small-town holiday celebration in a park, while seated at a picnic table with her two slim and attractive newfound friends, a man comes over to the table and gracefully, respectfully, and adoringly, tells her that she is simply the most beautiful woman he has ever seen in his life and asks if she will honor him with the next dance. In that moment, you see that he is right—and that she was right all along. She is beautiful, she is special, and she does deserve to be loved by this gentle and lovely man.

This moment struck me very oddly and very strongly. It wasn't so much that the filmmakers skillfully took the prejudices of the audience, twisted them, and tossed them gently back into our collective face. It wasn't so much that they managed to show a rather subtle something about how people see each other by letting you believe, for a while, that everything you know is right after all, and then plucking your complacency from you like a flower. What struck me was that it worked on me. I sat in that audience, a big woman who knows she is beautiful, and I watched that character, a big woman who knows she is beautiful. And, until a man came along and confirmed it, I didn't believe what she insisted was true about herself.

So I'm not perfect. Big deal. It's not going to stop me from scolding Society and telling it to stand in a corner.

Or from getting laid.

Or from eating brownies.

Professionally Q:
A Day in the Life of a Career Counselor

Christine Cress

Living in a small town in the Northwest, I avoid the mall as often as possible. Built to lure Canadian consumers from across the border, the mall interior features palm trees and plenty of neon glitz. It's not exactly congruent with the resident Douglas fir and perpetual gray rain, but I guess all facades are designed for their own purposes.

After days of carefully placing nail polish over snags and runs in my nylons, I decided I had to purchase some new pairs. In a town this size my options are rather limited. The best place for a six-foot-framed, long-legged career counselor was to go out to the mall.

To avoid the typical crowds I planned to go immediately after work. Most folks around here take a dinner break (the last bastion of traditional values). As a career counselor at the regional university, I had spent part of this day talking with the parents of new freshman students. Representing the Career Center to this constituent meant I had diligently pressed my finest dress suit, polished my pumps, and made sure that those holes in my nylons were well hidden. Image is everything to people about to spend thousands of dollars on their child's education, and it was important that I fit their stereotype. Needless to say, this woman from the original land of grunge was the quintessence of professionalism as she walked into the Bon Marche.

Meandering past the perfume and makeup counter, I set my sights on "Beauty Secrets" a few doors down. I also needed to get shampoo and hair spray and thought I would make this my first stop. Picking up my pace and noticing the sound of my heels on the tile floor, I spotted a young man dressed like a model from *GQ* leaning on an espresso cart. Since he was just outside the men's department, I assumed he was one of those new college graduates still looking for the management position he expected but who was working retail to pay off student loans.

He was speaking to the espresso worker, a woman in her early fifties with short, sandy hair and a polo shirt with upturned collar. She sported a diamond ring on her left hand, and her voice was raspy from what sounded like years of smoking. The dark circles and drawn look on her face told me she hadn't had an easy life. And certainly, pulling lattes on the evening shift was not the highlight of her career.

The *GQ*-style salesman was obviously confiding in her as he leaned forward and endeavored to restrain his volume. He tried to appear nonchalant but he was noticeably tense, clenching the cart and speaking angrily,

"I just don't know what her problem is . . ."

The paucity of customers at this hour must have allowed time to gossip, but the last thing I wanted to do was overhear two employees discussing this man's relationship problems. I maintained my stride, which would take me directly past them as quickly as possible. I tried to ignore them.

"She's making this a problem. Telling me it's degrading to women. Degrading to women! How can it be degrading to women? She's the one with a problem."

This struck a chord in me. The *GQ*-style salesman couldn't see how any aspect of his behavior could be possibly degrading to women. Internally, I sided with this unknown woman. I knew nothing of the circumstances, but this man wasn't at all interested in trying to understand the situation. I fought to control my expression since I was almost next to them.

The espresso woman, attempting to console the man, said in her gravelly tone, "Some women can't keep their mouths shut. Always having to make waves . . . And you know, she's probably . . . a lesbian."

Something in me snapped. Why are women who ask to be treated fairly always considered troublemakers, somehow synonymous with lesbians?

Without breaking stride I turned toward them, smiled happily, and announced confidently, "That's OK, I'm ONE too!"

The woman stared at me in horror, with eyes wide and jaw hanging open—she looked as though she wanted to speak but was dazed.

I gaily waved my hand at her as I kept walking, maintained my smile, and said, "No really, I AM one." My long, blonde hair swayed back and forth across my tailored suit, and I clicked on down the hallway. I giggled to myself and wondered what got into me. Generally, I'm pretty much of an introvert and rarely engage people unless professionally necessary. It's not the kind of advice I would give to students on "how to win friends and influence people."

"Oh, yeah, the next time you want to enhance your career network, just go out to the mall and yell coming-out statements to strangers as you pass by."

But this episode was like a scene from a movie. The timing was perfect, and it was obviously a safe environment in which to raise the question of our collective image of lesbians. Then I pondered, what would have happened if I had told all those parents of freshman today that I was a lesbian? The career counselor that so impressed them with employment statistics and job search information is really a dyke with hair of uncharacteristic length.

"Excuse me ladies and gentlemen, just to give you a completely authentic image of myself, I don't always dress this way. Most evenings and weekends find me in T-shirt, shorts, Birkenstocks, and braless."

Of course, since this is the image most people have of lesbians, I would have been readily believable. Assuming they could have imagined me wearing clothes. The difficulty for most of us in coming out is that people mentally disrobe us and picture us in bed in wonderfully erotic positions. (Staying awake past 10 p.m. is about as exotic as I get.)

That fear of naked judgment is precisely what gay, lesbian, and bisexual students at the university face in questioning who, what, when, and where to out themselves. Not only with parents, roommates, and professors, but with employers. They ask me: Should I take off my pinkie ring/should I put on my pinkie ring? What about this earring, nose ring, nipple ring? Should I include working for the lesbian resource center under volunteer work on my resume? Can I ask about domestic partner benefits in an interview? I don't want to look lesbian but I don't want to look het . . . so can I wear slacks?

The relationship between our personal identity and our professional/career image is closely tied. About eight months ago, I was working with a senior who had achieved a 3.5 grade point average and who was preparing for her second interview with a major accounting firm in Seattle. The follow-up interview included a lunch with the director of the division.

We discussed possible questions, etiquette (don't order spaghetti or dump over your water), etc., and she seemed quite confident. It appeared that this second interview was a formality and the student had the position locked-in. When she got up to leave, I affirmed, "You're very qualified and very well prepared. Don't be nervous, just be yourself."

She paused at the door, turned around and said, "Being myself is precisely what I can't be. I'm afraid they may ask me questions about boyfriends, and I don't want them to know I'm a lesbian. I'm afraid I'll lose my position if I don't have a straight image."

This particular student was very proud of being a lesbian, but she didn't want to jeopardize her professional opportunities. Schoolteachers, especially elementary schoolteachers, have grappled with this dilemma for years, probably even centuries. However, another student told me, "If they're not gay positive, I don't want to work there. They take me for all of who I am or it's their loss." If only everyone could afford to model all the clothes in their wardrobe.

I was reviewing a videotape of a practice interview with an African-American student. He incurred a severe injury in a car accident in high school and when he spoke his head ticked ever so slightly. He was intelligent and very articulate. We discussed the possibility of disclosing to the employer the reason for his mannerism, although he knew that under the Americans with Disabilities Act he is not required to do so.

He told me, "You know, they can see that I'm Black. I can't hide that. And I can tell them about the hidden learning disability and assure them of my capabilities to compensate for it. But I don't want them to think that because my head bobs I'm too cu."

I thought he said "cute." "You don't want them to think you're too cute?" He did look handsome in his three-piece suit, but I wouldn't have characterized him as cute. Then again, my friend Jon might have thought so.

"Not cute. Q, like in queer. I want to have the image of a hard-working professional. Not the Black Professional. Not the Disabled Professional. Not the Q Professional. Just the Professional."

"And what about the personal?" I asked him. "Where does that fit in with your image."

He replied, "For me, the personal and the professional are all the same extension of the oneness of myself. I'm not talking about compartmentalizing myself. I don't see it that way. Yes, I want to be viewed as a professional, but wearing a suit doesn't make me less gay, and wearing leather doesn't make me less of a professional. I am who I am. And although I'm a little nervous right now about the confluence of all those images representing me to an employer, I just want them to give me a chance."

As I continued on my way down the mall, I turned over all these thoughts in my mind. Why can't people be a full range of images and personalities? Why did my current appearance and self-disclosure create such a shock? Must we always plant palm trees where they don't grow naturally and blind ourselves with neon?

But these questions seemed far too deep for further contemplation at the mall. I figured I had better finish my errands before a gay man mistook me for a transvestite (which at six-foot two in heels frequently occurs to me) or a byke dyke assaulted me for being too lipstick.

I remembered the comforting words a bisexual friend once shared with me, "It's OK to be a lesbian, Chris, and still nourish the Barbie inside of you."

I went ahead and bought my shampoo, hair spray, nylons, and two more dress suits that were on sale. Then I went home, kissed my partner, fed the cats, did the dishes, some laundry, went for a walk, and went to sleep.

The Beauty Norm:
A Femme Strikes Back

Anna Myers

The cult of appearance—I became a dues-paying member at age seven. Every Tuesday, my mother and I attended Weight Watchers together. It was our weekly mother/daughter ritual—a shared humiliation forging intimacy between us. Mrs. McKinnon, my first-grade teacher, presided over those meetings, greeting and weighing me as if she had not just taught me to read that afternoon. To Mom, Weight Watchers was just another diet, another attempt to lose those "last ten pounds." To me, Weight Watchers meant salvation. Weight Watchers promised to free me from the nagging voices of my peers, teachers, friends, and family—all urging me to lose weight now, "Before it's too late."

Weight was not my only concern at age seven, though. I worried—wondered why I was not like other girls, why I did not dress as they dressed, play "house" and Barbies, or scream at mice. I feared that something was amiss. Without knowing what queer was, I feared my queerness.

Perhaps because I had to hide, had to pretend I was a "real" girl, I took beauty all too seriously. I grew, and my appearance obsession grew with me. My sister was the "pretty one": thin, blonde, blue-eyed, and perfect—the princess from a fairy tale. I was the commoner: brown-haired, brown-eyed, freckled, and fat.

Each day brought fresh humiliations. "Eighty-two! Eighty-two! Eighty-two!" my father sang one night over dessert. I was ten, and the doctor had weighed me that day. Then came the Weight Watchers mailing, enticing me back to the thinness cult. "Put on a little weight since we last saw you?" the letter taunted. I was ten and already "relapsed."

I complained, "Mom, do you think someday I'll lose so much weight, you'll want me to gain it back again?"

"No," she said. "That will never happen."

Her "never" haunted me. *Never* is such an unlucky word.

I wondered, would another diet save me—deliver me from my father's cruelty, my mother's scorn, my schoolmates' laughter, and my friends' pity? *Maybe,* I decided.

Thus, when I was fourteen, I started the diet to end all diets—a diet to silence sneering voices and self-doubt forever. In six months, I lost thirty pounds. My critics held their breath, afraid at last to comment on my weight. My slow starvation silenced them as effectively as their disgust had silenced me. I lost ten more pounds, and my parents took me to a doctor. They told me he wanted "a blood test," drove me to the hospital, and left me there. Another patient told me I was anorexic.

My parents and I did not speak about this time, afterward. Weight and dieting became a forbidden topic, and "eating disorders" were mentioned rarely, if at all. We suffered separately, and I took comfort from the fact that, at last, I had silenced them. If only silence could have filled the hole in my self-esteem that the nagging and jeers had chipped away! If only food could have filled that hole; I had tried for years to do it. I would keep trying for eight years more, as a bulimic. My self-doubt remained.

As I recovered, I was reminded of the other doubts that had plagued me in the days before food became my life:

A high school teacher asked me, "Why don't you dress like a girl?" I'm not a girl, I thought in reply. How dare I dress like one?

I still did not do "girl" things. I was ugly, awkward, (queer). *How dare I?* Though I weighed only eighty pounds and could finally flaunt a thin frame, I clung to baggy, androgynous clothes. Afraid to look in mirrors, I lived from the neck up.

Later, in college, a hallmate commented on the different types of clothing I wore—jeans and sweatshirts sometimes, sometimes what he called "sophisticated woman clothes." I wondered what he meant. I had no idea how I looked—just wore what my mother bought. My dorm room was blessedly bare of mirrors, and I thought that was freedom.

To some, lesbians appear unaffected by negative body image. Our communities profess to welcome women who defy the beauty standard. The comfortably clothed, androgynous, lesbian look challenges the patriarchal ideal. Nevertheless, that patriarchal ideal affected me deeply.

When I was nineteen and newly out, I believed lesbians did not think about weight. I feared I would not be accepted into the lesbian community because I suffered from an eating disorder. I thought, "Surely I can't be a *real* lesbian and bulimic at the same time!"

Since then, I have wished I had been right. I learned that body hatred does not discriminate and will not be left in our forsaken closets. Body hatred plagues women equally, dogging lesbians and heterosexuals alike. Coming out cannot free us of our obsessions.

At the end of my first year in college, I finally acknowledged my silent companion—queerness. I came bounding from my closet: "Freedom!" I thought. "At last, I can wear baggy, sexless clothes and fit right in!" At last, I *was* the beauty ideal—the lesbian anti-ideal, at least.

And then, I was waylaid by a femme. I tried to tell her I thought I was butch.

"Butch? *Butch?*" she said. "No, no, no—look at your shoes! Look at your hair! Look at your jewelry!" she said. "That's not butch!"

I looked. "It's not?" I asked meekly.

The lingerie store in town was celebrating its thirteenth anniversary. "What better reason to shop?" she said, and off we went.

I had never tried on lingerie. Remember, I lived above the neck alone. I had never put on makeup, for doing so meant mirrors. Emily was patient, though. Love allowed me to accept her compassion as hesitatingly I tried on flimsy fabric. I found I loved the kiss of silk and lace! Slowly, amid the heaps of discount underwear, I began to find myself. We cried when I bought my first piece of fluff—a black lace bodysuit at 30 percent off. I was on my way to femme-ininity.

I realized I had abandoned my body somewhere around the age of seven, and slowly I set about finding her again. Finding her meant dressing up, or putting close to nothing on and dancing until the sweat ran freely through my hair. Finding her meant taking lovers and reveling in our shared curves and fleshy parts—or seeing that I was leaner than they, or hairier, or smoother. Finding her meant discovering sexual hunger—figuring out where I liked to be touched, and how, and how often, and by whom. I went to college an "A" cup, a virgin, never having periods. I left wearing "C" cups, fucking when I could, and bleeding once a month.

My eating disorder did not survive the transition. In 1991, somewhere between Overeaters Anonymous meetings, I left bulimia behind. With the help of countless women in my life, I finally relearned when to feed my body, when not to, and when to let her rest. I nurtured my seven-year-old body image and brought her to womanhood at last.

More time has passed, and still I gather wonderful femme friends to me. We do "girl" things: giggle, shop, gossip, share stories of our lives . . . none of us scream at mice. Did I mention that we shop? The lace bodysuit has company: silk shirts, miniskirts, tank tops, dresses. . . . My body rejoices as I reclaim her.

Unfortunately, I learned, one *can* be a lesbian and bulimic. Lesbianism, the queer community—neither can free us from the appearance obsession. I had to *choose* freedom and had to choose to accept my femme friends' help along the way.

I conceived this piece in response to lesbians who complain that as a femme, I perpetuate society's beauty standard. The beauty mandate is oppressive, they argue. Lace, lingerie, fetish clothing—all objectify women and rob us of our power. We must reject fluff to be free. I write as a woman who finds power and freedom in dressing as she wishes.

As a child, I learned to hate my body—to hate it for its commonness, to hate it for being different from the so-called "norm." I lived life in loose-fitting, comfortable, "androgynous" outerwear—denying I even had a body, abandoning myself as a seven-year-old. These clothes that hid my body's shapes and curves, hid her muscle, sinew, and bone—they hid my sexuality. Forgive me for eschewing these clothes that were my prison.

Last summer, I traveled to the Michigan Women's Music Festival. Other women took the opportunity to bare their breasts and revel in sunshine. I reveled in lace and ribbons—sometimes nothing at all. I worked with my body, built her muscles, and found partners to share her with me. I scared some women, I think, with all this revelry. But for the first time since I was seven years old, my body—and I—are free.

It's Not What You Wear: Fashioning a Queer Identity

Kate Woolfe

Oddly enough, it was my boyfriend Travis who spotted the first signs of lesbianism in me. "Men's jeans," he would say gloomily, "You know what *that* means." I didn't. I grew up in a white-bread, suburban town where lesbians were invisible. No one ever talked about lesbians, and as far as I knew, I had never seen a lesbian in person or in the media. I don't even remember hearing lesbian jokes growing up, although the hatred toward gay men expressed around my house through fag jokes seemed generally directed at women as well as men.

Somehow I had an idea that lesbians, as women-loving women, were hyperfeminine, with long, wavy hair and flowing, gauzy skirts, à la Stevie Nicks. It wasn't until my first Two Nice Girls concert that I glimpsed The Lesbian Look—short hair, funky glasses, maybe a little leather. Lesbians seemed a homogeneous group at that time, and I wanted nothing more than to be a part of them. Recognizing that I loved women was like finally giving reign to something long buried inside of me.

A series of transformations over the next year brought me closer to the Look, each one punctuated by a defeated sigh from Travis. I had stopped wearing makeup and shaving my legs a few years earlier when I discovered feminism, and the haircut and clothes followed quickly. I found the Look surprisingly liberating, discovering to my amazement that mascara, high heels, long hair, and fingernails were cumbersome in their own way and that without them I was free to be myself: to be intellectual, athletic, messy, hysterical, anything, without worrying about smudged makeup or torn stockings. I loved the serious, capable side of myself that emerged when I was free of those restraints. It was around that time that I stopped measuring my waist size, trying to get a tan, or worrying about the size of my breasts. I had always liked my body as it was, and if anything, I feared and disliked the unwelcome attention from men that came from having a body that more or less fit their expectations. Men now left me alone, which suited me just fine.

Travis and I parted amicably, and I immersed myself fully in lesbian culture. kd lang and Phranc were my new idols, and striding through campus in my Doc Martens and spiky haircut made me feel as if I could conquer the world. I saw myself reflected, validated, and loved through the queer images all around me, from Dykes To Watch Out For to my own girlfriends. I both loved and hated being mistaken for a man, and I pitied straight women, teetering on their high heels and fussing with their makeup. My greatest joy was that glance of recognition while passing another lesbian on the street that said, "I'm one, too." I was in the club, and the secret password was my image. Nothing thrilled me more.

Still, the Look had a certain tyranny of its own. Because it brought recognition and status as a lesbian, those women who deviated from it were often ignored or considered less worthy. Just as women are punished by society at large for stepping out of the traditionally feminine image created for them, I often saw that dykes who didn't look like dykes were considered unenlightened at best and traitors at worst.

My own dyke appearance, while crucial to my sense of self-worth at the time, seemed a little silly even to me at times. I wrote a country song for a high-profile lesbian in town called "Too PC For Me," about my unrequited love for her. Some of the lyrics went, "So I'm wearing turtlenecks and Birkenstocks/ And I'm reading Rita Mae Brown/ The hair is growing in under my arms/ But you're still not around / I even quit eating meat for you/ And I threw away my eye shadow . . . " and on it goes. My desire to be accepted was so powerful that I probably would have done anything to my appearance. Thankfully, I loved the way my dyke friends and I looked, and playing around with my image led to some truly exhilarating experiences.

One night I went in a rented tuxedo to a fundraiser for the rape crisis center where I volunteered. My date, who bore a striking resemblance to me in the right light, wore a femme, formal dress. Periodically throughout the evening, we would rush to the bathroom to change clothes. We would reemerge in each other's outfits and watch the heads spin. One rape crisis center staffer who was also a photographer adored us and photographed us all night. We played with our roles as well, alternating between butch and femme and feeling free to be anyone and everyone that we could be. I love those photos and the memory of our role-plays—the cavalier, Southern gentleman, the nagging wife, the nervous date. We were beautiful and brave and perfect that night. Being a dyke was a rare and wonderful thing to me, and my sexual identity was inextricably tied up in how I looked.

Much to my surprise, I fell in love with a man around that time. I tried at first to ignore it, and when that proved unsuccessful, I resolutely determined that I would identify as a "lesbian in love with a man," whatever that means. I feared losing my community's approval as well as my own identity. I had dreams that my hair had grown long again, and no matter how often I cut it, it kept coming back. Scott, the object of my affections, told me later that every woman he had ever dated initially thought he was gay, I suppose because of his sensitive, soft-spoken nature. This time, I was too caught up in misgivings about my own sexuality to worry about his.

We began a relationship, and I struggled with my identity constantly. He could never belong in my beloved lesbian community, and I shuddered at the thought of being mistaken for heterosexual. It was that fear that led me to be more out than I had ever been as a lesbian, and I found myself strolling through the supermarket, holding hands with Scott, and wearing a Queer Nation T-shirt.

I knew that my separatist friends objected to the heterosexual privilege I could claim with him, but that privilege seemed more like a curse to me. I hated the way I was treated with him. People could make all kinds of assumptions about our relationship—assumptions about power, sex, who did the dishes. I found it repulsive, and so did Scott, but it haunted me all the same. Perhaps that's why I clung so tightly to my dyke look. While I managed to look like a lesbian to straight people, I was still heterosexual to the queers who saw me with Scott, and I hated that.

As much as I feared assimilating into the heterosexual, mainstream world and losing my hard-won identity, our relationship was so untraditional that I didn't really have anything to worry about. Scott and I once stayed in a motel outside Houston, where we had gone to see a Paul Simon concert. We walked out of our room that evening, hand in hand, past a bunch of beer-swilling rednecks. As we passed, I heard them whisper, "Those are *fags!*" I had been mistaken for a man many times before, and people always thought my lover was gay, but together we faced a new and unusual form of gay-bashing.

Rednecks weren't the only ones who thought I was a boy. One night Scott and I went to eat in an Italian restaurant that was covered in mirrors on one wall. I hadn't bothered to look around the room very carefully, and I assumed that the reflection next to me was actually another dining room. Out of the corner of my eye, I glimpsed a fellow diner and said to Scott, "You know, that little red-haired boy looks a lot like me!" When I turned for a closer look, I realized I had seen my own reflection and mistaken it for a boy. I never again got mad at anyone for calling me "sir."

After a year or so, Scott and I moved to California, and I finally managed to claim the label "bisexual," thanks largely to the queer politics happening in San Francisco. "Coming out" to me now meant telling my gay and lesbian friends about Scott. I still feared rejection from lesbians and did encounter hesitation from some queer women, but my gay male friends loved our relationship, flirting with Scott and puzzling over how he could really be straight. The bisexual movement had made it acceptable for queers to talk about their sexual encounters with those of the opposite sex, so I began to know lesbians and gay men who slept with men or women without feeling that it diminished their identity or politics. With their support, I've begun to get my queer identity from within, and not necessarily from my clothes or haircut, or from the approval of my peers. I've even toyed with the idea of growing my hair out, taking on a more femme image, just because I love the look and feel of long hair.

I still feel a little distanced from the lesbian community, tending to idolize lesbians and pine away for those dyke days. I was amazed one day when my lesbian housemate, who looks quite femme but is always the consummate lesbian in my mind, said to me, "I love being out in public with you because then I get recognition as a lesbian." Sure enough, other dykes gave us that *look* that she didn't get when out on her own. I had begun to take that thrilling second of eye contact for granted and was amazed to consider that she didn't experience that in public. It seemed crazy to me that she got that recognition when she was out with me, who has been in a relationship with a man for four years now, but not on her own.

On the night I started writing this chapter, I was browsing in a bookstore in Berkeley and ran across *Out in America*, a collection of photographs of queers. I opened the book to a photo of Greg Louganis, looking for all the world like kd lang, with an impish grin and boyish hair. I couldn't believe it was a man and not a dyke I was so attracted to. I rushed to show Scott this beautiful person and remarked, "You know, the more bisexual I become, the less I even bother to figure out the gender of people I'm attracted to." (Don't worry, kd, Greg's got nothing on you, it was probably just a momentary lapse on my part.)

Over the years, I've come to find my own essential truth about the Lesbian Look: it has less to do with one's sexual preference and more to do with a rejection of our culture's values about women. The Look frees us up to be more than decorative, while pointing to new beauty standards for ourselves and other women. As we continue to expand the word "queer" to include gay, lesbian, bisexual, transgendered, etc., I am thrilled to see women of all sexual orientations looking queer as a way of reclaiming their own beauty and value. Still, we can hurt each other by trying to judge each other's politics and sexuality on those terms. A woman as dykey as myself can sleep with men, and someone as femme as my housemate can be the most radical, lesbian feminist.

As for me, it's been years since I even pretended to fuss over my looks, and I love the sight of large, strong, unadorned women. My haircut, clothes, tattoo, and glasses all represent my freedom to define beauty on my own terms and to respect other women's ability to do the same. I know now, however, that if I ever do let go of my look, my politics and identity will stay with me and could never be carted off to Goodwill with my dyke outfits.

Hair Piece

Andrea Askowitz

I wore my armpit hair to school today. I always wear my armpit hair, but today I wore it out. I brought a long-sleeved shirt to go over my tank top in case I get cold, or cold feet. But no, today I feel hot.

I feel like pushing myself. I want to speak out in class. I want to call my grandparents to tell them I'm a lesbian. I want to dress sexy with a woman and go to my high school reunion. I want to talk back to the men on the street.

Wearing my armpit hair is an act of defiance—a political action. In East Coast, mostly white, urban America, armpit and leg hair means lesbian. I know that body hair doesn't always implicate a woman as a lesbian. Maybe she's a "natural" or a "hippie chic," as my heterosexual, artist mother refers to herself, on occasion, when she's not in the mood for shaving. But lesbian is my guess when I see a woman with hair, and I think that assumption is held by most queer and nonqueer urbanites. Wearing my legs and armpits hairy in the summertime is like wearing a bold pink triangle.

My friends and I started shaving our legs in sixth grade, without question. Growing the hair out under the arms, on the legs, and above the lip is a conscious rejection of the social rules for women in this country. Hair on a woman is a matter of social consequence.

Body hair is also dyke high fashion, especially for urban, feminist lesbians. Part of the lesbian/feminist beauty requirement is acceptance of hair and body in its natural form. It is no wonder that lesbians, a fringe group, have created their own hair standards.

Hairy is my body—unaltered. When I let my hair grow out, I like to say that I'm exercising self-love as I pet the curly black fur on my thighs. Much of being a lesbian is a similar exercise—an unlearning of hatred toward women and women's bodies. I grew up thinking that vaginas smelled like dead fish. That wasn't a hard one to unlearn, not after lesson one. But the hair exercise is exhausting, and sometimes I need a rest. Then I remove it. This usually happens when I visit my family in south Florida where it feels to me as if there's not a woman with a hair out of place.

When Polly accompanied me on my visit south, her armpits and legs were in full bloom. I admire Polly, who is Greek American, for the courage to be as she is—dark and hairy. Polly identifies as a queer feminist and works hard to live true to her politics. My father had a different take.

"She's posturing just like anyone else trying to fit into a fashion trend," he argued. I tried to convince him that Polly was merely doing her body right.

"Body hair is the opposite of posturing; hair is natural and necessary," I retorted. I wanted to believe that Polly just is. But yes, Polly is conforming to an alternative regime.

Growing hair may defy traditional standards of female beauty, but women who do it are abiding by a new set of rules that may seem as strict as the standards they are rebelling against.

I was dating Martha during one of my hair growth phases. We were leaning back into a lazy sofa when she put her hand into the loose leg of my jeans. "I want to lick this," she said, caressing my calf.

"I'll never remove the hair on my legs again," I promised myself as if I had just been kissed by my teen idol, vowing never to wash my cheek again. But I couldn't keep that promise. Two weeks later, when I told Martha I shaved my legs, you'd have thought, by her reaction, that I told her I was engaged to a man.

Even if hair is not taken that seriously by all lesbians, hair is definitely on the top of our heads. Last summer I sat down with a group of ten lesbians hanging out in Dupont Circle, the queer section of Washington, DC. We were all in shorts and some in tank tops. Somehow hair became the central conversation. Polly called out, "Those with hairy legs or armpits on one side; no hair on the other." The ten of us divided up, jumping back and forth across our circle while laughing at the silly game. We were six with hair, four without. Jenn, now positioned on the hair side, described wearing short-sleeve shirts on the metro.

"Oh, I hate it," she began. "When I put my arms up to hold on to the rail I can see people sneaking peeks down my sleeve and eyeing my pits. . . . I know what they're thinking . . . they're all . . . this woman's dirty. She probably doesn't even brush her teeth. She's gonna fart."

Stephanie and I decided to grow our armpit hair because we think it's sexy. For Stephanie, armpit hair makes a woman look like a woman, not a prepubescent kid. For me, armpit hair is rebellious. I'm turned on by a woman with armpit hair because the gender play excites me—the contrast between breast and, what I have come to associate with men, hair under the arms. But both of us break down and shave sometimes. Stephanie shaves because the hair holds in sweat. I shave when I'm not in the mood for activism.

My first encounter with a lesbian happened during college. Lois was the BDOC (big dyke on campus) and spoke about being a lesbian at every public speaking occasion. I both feared and admired her. During a Women's Alliance meeting, Lois pulled up her jeans to show off her rugby injuries. The scabs and bruises were impressive, but not nearly as awe-inspiring as the hair which started mid-calf and continued up toward her knee. "I shave my ankles so I can tape," Lois said proudly. Apparently, taping is cool.

Lois the Lesbian was everything I knew about lesbians before coming out. As a baby dyke, I ventured out in search of love into my East Village, Manhattan neighborhood to a showing of lesbian short films. I went by myself and snuck in after the first film had started. The depictions of lesbian lives were dark and desperate. I was relieved at intermission until I noticed a woman with a full face of hair. The woman had a beard; I mean a bearded-lady-in-the-circus beard. This woman defied all of my assumptions about women.

Then I went to the Michigan Womyn's Music festival. I've never seen so much hair pride. Almost every one of the 7,000 women had hair where we've all been taught not to want it. At Michigan I felt wrong without hair on my legs. Shaving was the anomaly. One woman had a four-inch-long patch of hair growing right from her chin. It was wrapped with colorful string and beaded on the end. I asked her about her chin hair because it looked to me like it was there for the showing. She wore it proudly like a little girl wears her first pair of earrings.

"Wow! How did you grow your chin hair so long?" I asked.

"Well," she began as plainly as if she was talking about preparing a meal. "When you pluck and shave and pluck and shave, the hair grows back thicker. This is what happens. I just got tired of pretending it wasn't here."

The woman with the chin hair and all of the hairy women seemed right to me at the festival. At first I was shocked and impressed. Then I got used to it; after all, hair is natural. But I couldn't help wondering what the woman with the chin hair does professionally. What does her family think? Is she ever embarrassed by the hair? Doth the lady protest too much?

*　　*　　*

I didn't approach Licia although I'd seen her out several times since reading about her discrimination case in the newspaper. She looked intimidating under her hard-rimmed hat and behind her thin, black mustache. When I saw Licia again, in a more intimate setting, I cornered her for an hour and with a bold curiosity that could have been construed as rude, I asked Licia everything I wanted to know about a woman with a mustache. I was amazed. I couldn't help staring at her lip.

Licia was the audio-visual technician at the Ritz Carlton Hotel in Tysons Corner, Virginia. She had been setting up conference equipment for seven months before a memo was issued from the Executive Committee to the Audio-Visual Department stating, "We deem it unacceptable for a woman to have facial hair."

Licia's first reaction was fear. She told her immediate supervisor she would bleach to save her job. Her supervisor thought the memo was ridiculous and refused to enforce the ruling. Licia and her supervisor were both fired.

Licia was very forthcoming. I sensed that she was relieved to talk about her case and her everyday experience. I guessed that, to her, not talking about it would seem like a bigger deal than talking about it. It is no secret that she has a mustache, and it is no surprise that someone (like me) would think that out of the ordinary. But to Licia, the mustache is not a big deal at all.

"A lot of women stare at me," she said, "I don't know if they saw me on the news or what."

I suggested that maybe women are intrigued or freaked out. But Licia seems incredibly sure of herself; she doesn't try to guess what others might be thinking.

Licia has had a mustache since she was a teenager. Some of her friends cautioned her then, "You have a mustache." Licia responded simply, "Yeah." She has never shaved, although on occasion, like for a wedding, she has bleached her upper lip blond. I asked Licia if she was consciously making a political statement by growing her mustache. "It's not political," she said, answering my questions with no anger in her voice. "It's just part of my body."

"That sounds political," I prodded.

"Well, I know it's a personal choice, not being afraid to be different," she said.

"Why do you shave your chin hair?" I asked, wondering if vanity played a role.

"I don't like the way my beard looks. I don't feel as well-groomed." Licia continued. "It's not full. It's not groovy."

Several years ago, when Licia was completely immersed in a lesbian world, she grew out all her facial hair without trimming or styling. She admitted that during that time she refused to be affected by mainstream society. Today, although she is not consciously "shouting it from the rooftops," daring to be different *is* political activism. Licia wears her mustache as anyone wears lipstick or a hairdo—as fashion. And any fashion is political for women in our culture because we have always been, and continue to be, defined by our looks. Learning about Licia has enlightened me. What bothered me, at first, was a voice in my head saying with surprise, "She's pretty," as if mustache and pretty are mutually exclusive. I was taken by her, but countered my own thoughts about Licia being attractive. "I can't be attracted to a woman with a mustache," I thought. "What if we become girlfriends? What will I tell my mother?" I was getting crazy; these thoughts were hateful and, well, premature.

As I got to know Licia, her mustache became as ordinary as her nose. All in all, I know what it comes down to. Stephanie said it best when she was asked point blank, "Would you want a lover with fuzz on her face?"

"It depends on her personality," Stephanie answered. Because everything else is neither hair nor there.

Out-of-Body Experiences

Michele Spring-Moore

I camped out at the House of Edgewood, named after the cramped
    apartments in *Paris Is Burning*, where African-American New York drag
    queens sew tulle, invent costumes, create realness
real executive, real movie star, real prom queen, real homeboy homoboy
    hustler slut cheerleader model anything but.
You guys give me permission to be raucous, PI, out of line, out of step,
    offensive to anyone who hates what's queer in us
I can put away goddess-worship, politeness, quiet, solitude, fear of
    cattiness, dirt, sex, pain, camp
            fear of fear
can say *tit* and nobody will glare. No one cares to keep the boys and girls
    straight here
we vogue and limpwrist and runway up and down the halls all night, turn
    on the VCR and turn bad Hollywood movies into high camp, become
    academic queens, debate the functions of drag or the symbolic meaning
    of a poem's cocksucking scene

then go dancing at the gaybar, watch gayboys and girldykes, bykes
    and bi-boys
shake their asses and bulging crotches and unbra'd breasts under one-size-
    too-small shirts and silk blouses
till the lights come up at 2 a.m. last call last pickup
last chance last dance for love for
queers unafraid to move hips, thighs, rears, hands, arms, fingers,
    shoulders, heads, torsos, chests, feet, legs, knees
display themselves in mirrors, stare, play, posture, strut, gyrate, grind
some of us jerk our stiff limbs, shuffle awkwardly
as if we haven't met our bodies yet
snap divas, the newly-out awakening from long hibernations, fags soused
    in cologne, pool dykes at the table, cue sticks like oversized dildoes
    in hand

disco queens/drag queens/leather queens/size queens/chicken queens/
rice queens/potato queens/marriage queens/
new age queens/snap queens/do-me queens/drama queens/
grass is always greener queens
men who collect brown-skinned boys, intellectual bisexuals, PC lesbian
    feminist sometimes separatists, working-class diesel dykes in sneakers
    and jeans, gay women in designer sweaters,
lesbian hippies dressed for a Dead show in limp cotton T-shirts torn
    strategically to show off their shoulder and breast tattoos of Ishtar
    and the Egyptian goddesses' asps
and I have lusted after all: Black dreadlocked dykes
compact brown-skinned working-class Sicilians who eye me across
    the room
waspy blondes with miniscule ponytails who look like 12-year-old boys
    from the back
graceful femmes in black silk pants, dancing with arms akimbo
dark-eyed Chicanas with wind in their hair
the Anglo pair in black leather, she in a dress, she in pants, one's hands
    cuffed to the other's belt
light switches on
all stop dancing and drinking and drift out the door to little sports cars
    and big pickup trucks,
head for La Diner or the Royal Queen Restaurant or home with lovers
    to snuggle in bed or with tricks for more acrobatics than they could
    manage in the dance floor's dark corners

On Halloween the show's even better for tourists out slumming:
boys dressed as Miss Furr and Miss Skeene, the Terminatrix, Sisters
    of Perpetual Indulgence: the Order of Vagina Dentata
butch or femme girls, bitches, witches, virgins, and whores
silk stockings, black leather jackets and chaps, handcuffs, tit clamps,
    high heels, flats, flaming lipstick, jockstraps, g-strings
But we outdid this ritual once, in '79, and the second and third times, when
    we took over the capitol—Halloween and San Francisco Freedom Day
    Parade rolled into one and add half a million or so:
March on Washington 1987, 1993
queers, queers, everywhere
and not a drop to drink
Jack said
I just went to a bar and it was either
the cruisiest political scene or the most political cruise scene

I've ever seen. Dupont Circle wall-to-wall men till the wee hours,
the women all went over the D.C.-Maryland line to see a lesbian
    comedian, packed into little red Toyotas named Rojita and Gertrude
    for the ride back to the city,
sat up all night talking in hotel rooms, bars, baths, bookstores
I called Brian from a greasy phone at the Greyhound station where
    I waited for my bus north,
tried to tell him about meeting Michael Hardwick in nonviolent CD
    training and thinking, *he looks like a straight California surfer boy with big
    hair,*
about the dykes arrested on the Supreme Court steps, arms linked, kissing
    as cops in bright yellow latex gloves pried them apart, as hundreds
    of us chanted
Loud and clear! Lesbians are here!
Your gloves don't match your shoes! Your gloves don't match your shoes!
The whole world is watching! The whole world is watching! Cameras were
    watching.
            I was watching.
He didn't understand my tears and any explanation I could have given
    would have flowed like the Potomac through our lives

I went home, came out in the audience at drag shows,
at a Gay Alliance meeting, Boulder Queer Collective meeting, Bisexual
    Women's Voice meeting,
by saying *so am I* when you sneer *she's bisexual*
                        embarrassed
                        you fumble with apologies
but I don't have to come out at all because I can easily pass, can talk about
    my exes in class and throw in a *he* so all my students say is *you've had
    some weird boyfriends*
                        you don't know the half of it
I don't have to come out. I can shave my hairy legs, cram them into
    pantyhose, paint my plain cute face till I look like someone else
slip a dress over my head, stuff my feet into high-heeled pumps and listen
    to my professors:
You look really good   Michele, you have legs   You have a nice ass,
    Ms. Moore
I can pass, but I only feel at home in my short hair, boys' jeans
purple hightop sneakers I dyed myself, neon pink cap with the bill in back,
Queer Girl button in front   style stolen from gay men
Read My Lips T-shirt with the photo of two women kissing

I can pass as a dyke more easily   at bars, parties, meetings
            consider it a compliment when someone calls me *lesbian*
I slip back into my butch stance into my boys'-cut Levi's   spread
    my legs, drape my arms over chair backs, take up as much room
    in theater seats as men do,
sometimes even play dueling knees with those next to me
slide my hands into my pockets without realizing till my students write
    about it
and I become self-conscious: do I look dykey?   do they know?

I went to workshops, came out to Kim at one, Building Alliances Between
    Lesbian and Bisexual Women
She leaned on one elbow, sprawled in a sweatsuit on the overstuffed sofa
    so close to me I could smell the fear and attraction like cologne on
    her skin
One night that spring she and I in our leather jackets and five friends with
    short haircuts went out to the beach
where a gang of teenagers exclaimed *God! Fuckin' dyke mayhem!*
    Another bunch of boys walked to the end of the pier and screamed
    LEZZIES! LEZZIES! top of their lungs. We made them the butt of our
    jokes, designed T-shirts with *FDM* logos, strutted around and said,
    Tha's right! But I remembered
a man named Charlie who lived in Maine, killed in '83 or '84 when
    a couple kids threw him off a bridge and he drowned

I came out to you at a Lesbian Resource Center meeting when I was 18, to
    all 35 of you, the first dykes I'd ever seen outside of photos in books
I thought you'd all been sex partners at one time or another,
had no idea this is what it looked and felt like to be a member of a group
    that expressed friendship openly by hugging, kissing, holding hands,
    touching casually
So these are lesbians, I thought; *they look like normal people, just like
    everyone else.*

Cynthia and I came out to each other in print, met at the first meeting
    of the newborn bi women's group
spent the next two years wrangling with the same man and talking about
    dyke sex and lesbian porn, sat around her kitchen eating sugary fudge
    and discussing latex squares

and how to use them, embarrassing PI gossip in her living room among her
    collages and assemblages and hand-me-down chairs, Rapunzel plants,
    scraps scrounged from construction sites and the curb
she read my coming-out story in the *Empty Closet*

where I was hired as editor a month later, called my lesbian friend Anne
    long-distance to catch up
You're editor of the gay and lesbian paper and you've been seeing Ron?
    she asked
it dawned on me her tone said *betrayal*
thought of defensive replies till I remembered   *static on the line*
she'd been in a relationship with a woman for three years but had fucked
    the two most sexist men in our work brigade in Nicaragua
nights humid with the sea
palm leaves rustled like paper
dogs barked at people walking the dirt path to the cinderblock outhouse
roosters crowed every hour
norteamericanos snored under mosquito netting
Anne and Eric kissed on a sleeping bag in the cabin's corner
while I wrote in my journal *I don't know who I'm more jealous of—her for
    having him, or him for having her*
the next day in the fields my face said *betrayal*

I've come out to you and your namechanging sisters over and over
    you give me stern lectures on physical and spiritual cleansing,
why I shouldn't eat grilled cheese sandwiches or Milky Ways
 you womyn-loving wimmin not into material possessions who spend
    75 bucks to have the Venus of Willendorf
tattooed on your left cheeks   after you change
from Mary Jean Miller to Firewalk Stargazer

I too got my knowledge of lesbian feminism from books, but I started
    with magazines:
came out to myself by reading porn snuck from Dad's room when
    everyone was at work, stories of women having sex with women, stories
    for straights and the stray bi like me
My first lesbian thoughts, like yours, were theoretical, but mine were
    based in lust as
I rocked myself to sleep, childhood teddy bear stuffed between my
    twitching legs

I didn't know penetration was patriarchal and women weren't supposed to
    want each other that
way
and when I turned 18 and discovered the bars, I responded like
    Pavlov's dogs to butch,
that hand in the jeans pocket, little boy's tight round ass, that casual air
    as if she could take you and take you then leave you however she wanted to,
that barely perceptible once-over, slight smile, leaning on one hip
    and squinting across the green felt, chalking the cue stick, strolling,
    legs spread
that makeupless face so much clearer than so many straight womens'
that body, compact or fat, taking up space like a man, looking everyone
    in the eye
never apologizing for existing
How this plus a pair of hightop sneakers made my cunt salivate,
    I can't say,
nor why I was a feminist at 12, had my first crush on a gay boy the year
    before
but the feelings came from my gut, not my books
and when you fix me with that dead earnest stare and begin to drone about
    the evils of pornography
I wonder if your feminism has ever sent your fingers into a woman's
    soft wet vagina making loud slurping sucking sounds again and again
    till she sighs then groans then rolls over squeezing
like C-clamps
like a vise
till you know you'll never type with that hand again
Talk all you want about loving womyn energy
theory's fine, but sometimes I'd rather suck nipples

Your face says betrayal.
On we fight, both of us convinced deep inside we're not legitimate queers
I'm just bi, not a real dyke   you came out only last year, haven't
    had a girlfriend yet, a lover, a life partner, whatever word is in vogue
    this week
both of us ask *where's home?*
in a forest of crisp pubic hair, in a warm armpit, in a snake-tongued mouth,
    in my own body sitting on a cock standing ship's mast above the belly
inside the sea coves of a woman, heading toward the womb
inside the latex bags we can't fuck without
inside the head   the gut   the cunt

wherever lust is manufactured, then the theory to support it,
    the will to resist the world's crushing refusal of it

Why are you killing my people? Jim asks
    I must admit
that phrase has pretty good rhythm, like a brisk little stroll down the pier
When I get angriest I say *OK, fuckers, drown us, kill us, shoot us, mash our
    organs to pulp with baseball bats in alleys*
and who'll teach your kids and wipe their butts in daycare centers?
Who'll nurse your sick and care for your dying mothers in nursing homes?
Who'll take your photos, play your symphonies, make your touchdowns,
    shoot your movies, cook your burgers, serve your meals, perform
    your plays, drive your trucks, write your books, make your change?

Every day I live Colorado for Family Values, Citizens for a Decent
    Community
like deer ticks with Lyme Disease in the folds behind my knees and elbows
    after I walk in the mountains
I try to ignore them but they burrow beneath my tenderest skin and suck
    my blood
but they don't kill most of us with bats, fists, guns
most of us strangle slowly on our own blood
find our way to the bar, tell ourselves we're happy during 500 months of
    nights stuck on the vinyl stool, that the dim colored light shining
    through shelves of liquor bottles is pretty
trying to smile, talking to strangers, smoking another pack down to butts,
    skin getting dry, eyeing the younger and younger frames that cross
    the threshold
we join the priesthood, enter the convent, remain celibate, adopt stray cats
    and call them our babies, get married and have kids and try to wish it
    away, contract HIV from sex with nameless strangers in adult
    bookstores after work so our wives don't know,
get kicked out of the house at 12, sell sex on the streets, get knifed,
    get our ribs broken, get into and out of the hospital, get into drugs

we know we're worthless and no one will ever love us
we take dozens of sleeping pills
tattoo our wrists with razor blades in cold white porcelain bathtubs
put handguns into our mouths because a clit or a prick was in there last
    week
jump off bridges onto cement beds

drive too fast around curves so our families can say we were an accident
I tried in a dorm room at 18
after six drinks, nothing around to swallow but a bottle of aspirin
which doesn't mix well with vodka so I slept four hours, woke up,
    got sick, slept, got sick.
Probably didn't make any more fuss than the hundreds of bulemics
    and alcoholics on campus, so no one paid any attention

but we know our deaths are brought to us courtesy Armstrong,
    Dannemeyer, Tebedo, Macaluso, Reagan, Helms, and Bush
and those who say a holocaust can't happen here were wrong a decade ago
we remember our dead
our individual dead, our seventeen-friends-who-died-of-AIDS-last-year
the 152 of them who died in the last five
our memories like videotapes
patches on quilts so no one forgets the names
the quilt grown so big it takes an army of lovers to transport the damned
    thing and it can't be displayed in one place at one time
photos on walls, in books so no one forgets the faces
of the old and the young.

Movement

Amy Edgington

I want to see a ballerina
with hairy legs
and underarms;
a fat ballerina
with huge breasts;
a ballerina who
wears dreadlocks;
one who's old and grey
in ordinary clothes.
I want to watch
a ballerina stumble
and laugh or pirhouette
in a wheelchair;
I want to see her
clasp another woman
and lift her high.
Then I will be
moved.

PART 3:
SEARCHING A WAY OUT

Vanishing Point

Margo Solod

I can still pinch
some flesh around my waist
but it's much harder now,
I'm working on it all the time.
Growing in instead of up,
younger as I creep down the scale.
I know exactly how many calories
in a lettuce leaf smeared with mustard,
the burn of it in my throat
equals the burn in my thighs
running morning and night,
increasing the distance
between this body
and me.

Autobiographical Slices:
Life in the Queer Kitchen

Amy Gilley

I started to write about my relationship to popcorn. Plain popcorn is my staple. But is it a food or a plastic bit of popular culture? In addition to the movie theater popcorn in waxed paper buckets, stale cheese popcorn in the local A&P, and strings of popcorn on the Christmas tree, there is that ideal diet food, air-popped popcorn, only twenty-five calories a cup. Real popcorn, a blue porcelain bowl filled with hot popcorn which is covered with salt and at least half a stick of melted butter and eaten before the Bette Davis movie even begins, is a constant craving. In my persistent desire to disappear, I eschew even diet margarine and eat air-popped popcorn plain, carefully measuring out four cups.

Of recipes and sexual desire. We're here. We're queer. We're going to eat. Cooking a favorite recipe and sharing it involves the certain expectation that the recipient of one's work knows the lore; meeting the amused eyes of a dyke across a crowded laundromat in a rural town involves the understanding of the code. Once, I made some homemade sauerkraut for my sister who then asked for a recipe. I thought I could merely jot the recipe out by hand, but I threw away three drafts before I had a formula, an equation that would guarantee success for my sister, who owns an air popcorn popper and six can openers but no baking tins, mixing bowls, wooden spoons, or cookbooks. I had to explain why you soak cabbage in hot water, I avoided abbreviations, and I endlessly revised the proper chronology of cooking steps. All this, of course, masks the sensual pleasure of cooking, of altering recipes, of allowing the food to cook, to work out its own chemistry. Why was I worried about the proper verbs? Correct grammar? The knowledge of cooking is, I thought, part of the collective unconsciousness, especially of women. I ponder about the language of the kitchen and the language of the lesbian. What is a pinch, a dash? Did the bread fall flat because of the too careful kneading and a carefully timed rising period in my draft-free kitchen? There is something here almost Lesbian in nature, in this kitchen dialogue, this savoring of food. Cultivating, preparing, cooking, and eating—are all such sensual luxuries. Secret ingredients, recipes passed down the matrilineal line, nibbling on tidbits in the kitchen alone, or sharing rich cakes and ideas with women at teas or at lunch or at the park. Forbidden foods. One minute on the lips, a lifetime on the hips. Stay thin for the man.

The lesbian sensibility about food and body were made clear to me when I had shared a meal with A. I arrived in Durango, Colorado, for a job interview. Early January and a few inches of snow cover icy sidewalks. My first ordeal is a dinner with the department chair. The Victorian house looks smaller when I step inside. A huge golden retriever, a fireplace, and a few old armchairs fill the small, square living room. We eat in the kitchen. I stare at the countertop covered with bowls of pasta salad and two giant round loaves of whole wheat bread, and a ceramic bowl of soft butter. Exhausted and starved, I fantasize about consuming an entire loaf of bread, hacking off chunk after chunk, lying in bed back at the hotel. The daughter, a woman who has returned from an activist vacation in Central America, is chewing on a kosher dill pickle and laughing. Dressed in casual Colorado chic, jeans and a Gap turtleneck with well-worn Birkenstocks, she sits next to me at the table. What intrigues me, though, is the story that her father tells about her fierce all-night poker games, of the consumption of bowls of chips and six-packs of beer. At this point, we are spooning food on our plates. I note the cautious, almost disinterested, manner in which the family eats the pasta and fruit salad and, I decide that I must, as usual, suppress my appetite. Abruptly the conversation is broken by a phone call from a school friend, and instead of a conversation about women and Central America, I am grilled about art, my literary theories, and my teaching experiences; I no longer have much of an appetite. Only as we finish the meal does A return. My interest is keen again; my appetite returns. And again the phone interrupts. I leave exchanging smiles with A—who is again intently talking to her school pal. What can be as interesting as food, my lesbian instinct shrieks.

Although all that I thought about for a long time was a desire to eat more of that rich, whole wheat bread, it was perhaps A who really entertains me, who now possesses my imagination. I obsess currently about staying thin while A remains lush and almost zaftig, her appetites clearly a pleasure for her. I wonder about meeting her in the real world, perhaps a café—coffee shared, and aphrodisiac that sets the pulse racing. What sort of meal we could concoct. An Indian curry, an almost absurd mixture of bananas, orange juice, and carrots. The expensive cardamom pod is the key. Spicy basmati rice and crunchy chapiti to counter the spicy, creamy dessert curry. Sensual eating that requires a deliberate spooning of curry onto the rice. The spicy curry, too, requires frequent breaks from eating, and the intense eye contact can be broken by the need to scoop up drifting rice from the plate.

All I want to do is disappear. I weigh myself everyday, angry when I lose a pound, angry when I gain a pound. Is it water retention? I shouldn't have eaten that extra apple this afternoon. For a week, I drink coffee an hour before I work out, wishing to believe that it will burn the extra fat. I am five foot six and weigh one hundred pounds. Sometimes, I feel like a hundred pounds of muscles, a sinewy, long-distance runner. Sometimes I know I need to gain weight but am miserable when I eat that extra apple or indulge my craving for chocolate. I just want to disappear. I avoid mirrors but look quickly in the storefront windows as I walk by. Is that me? So thin. Fear. Fear of being out in public. Fear of causing trouble. Fear being seen. The long-standing belief that if I am good, polite, and quiet, harmony will reign at home. I equate assertiveness with heft; when I started graduate school, I was at a "normal" weight and I exercised for pure pleasure. Halfway through graduate school, my life began to mirror my childhood; demanding father figures criticized my intellectual and creative works, lovers demanded that I dress and act according to their standards, and the old feeling of always being outside resurfaced. Queer from day one. In order to cope, I begin a strict exercise regime; no longer was the leisurely five-mile run enough. Now I must run ten miles, cycle for an hour, and lift weights. All to cope with the stress, I claim. I cut back on food, pleading graduate student poverty, and ignore my constant craving for sweets and other cheap carbohydrates. I drink quarts of water, to filter my kidneys, I say, and cups of coffee to keep going on my term papers. Along the way I shed my old wardrobe, buying clothes in size five, now size three. Along the way I shed any notion that I was bisexual. I am a lesbian but am too busy, too stressed to do anything about it. I am too busy in school, and too busy working out.

I wish to correct my increasing eating disorder but the old fears and ambivalence regarding my identity, and attractiveness plagues me. I visit my local food co-op. Because it is located next to the lesbian bookstore, the store is swamped on the weekends with dykes: dykes alone, dykes with diaper bags, but mostly with couples buying bagels and organic bananas. I covertly cruise, consider asking that woman over there what jasmine rice tastes like, or that cute baby dyke whether the cream cheese is fresh. One Sunday, however, only one worker is there, filling bins from heavy sacks of bulk grains that he hefts over his shoulder. Somehow his presence means not buying that package of cream cheese, that half gallon of carob chip/ honey ice cream. But when I return the next weekend, she's there—not thin, not hefty, but pleasant and with broad cheekbones and glowing skin. The store is just opened and she's spreading a bagel with fresh honey then licking the knife. She giggles and waves at the tape deck. I love the Indigo girls she says and rings up my half dozen rye bagels. And throws in a free raisin one, too. I cannot imagine leaning over the breakfast table and biting into her toasted and cream cheese layered bagel. And yet I honestly fear becoming a stereotype—the type of lesbian who cares so little for the body. I want to move, to enjoy my body and eating, to be at peace, and yet, everywhere are the signs that being good means being thin, means being straight. To make the daily decision, to realize that every day means coming out all over again is tied to the body, and to food. To be honest means a danger; not playing by the rules means a potential disaster. Even cooking is fraught with the hazards. Do *Cosmopolitan*'s menus for two work for two lesbians? What if the politically correct lesbian does not own a microwave? To cook is to nourish the body, but if daily you are assaulted, told to deny the body and its sexuality, what role can food play?

I have no answers to the contradiction of the body faced by lesbians. Body is body, but whose body? What do you feed it? And where? Food is so loaded with memories and events. But now I remember that baking bread is perhaps a cure. Its demand for heavy pounding and then resting, a combination of calm and energy, makes it a healing cure. After years of not baking, I hesitantly prepare a loaf. It rises too fast. The bread is soggy and incredibly bitter. I throw it out remembering the heavy, whole wheat bread that, yes, A did make that night.

A woman in motion before the oven, stirring and kneading bread dough. Her hands so swiftly turning the dough, stretching it, pounding it. She turns around, hips brushing the counter. In her mother's kitchen, she is making bread for her lover. I sit at the kitchen table, drinking coffee, scratching the dough encrusted in my knuckles. My loaf of white bread lies cut and crumbing on the counter. She moves over to me, places her hand upon my shoulder, and brushes her lips against mine. Crumbs of white flour fall, drift onto my shirt.

That Other Girl Who Is Not Me

Alexa Leigh

I just got back this picture of myself taken on a day when I felt confident and proud. It's disgusting. My face is misshapen, my teeth yellow, and my smile crooked. I can't believe I went around with my hair looking that way. That dress looks entirely different from how it did in the mirror: I am enormous, huge, a tent, a blob. You can see my white undershirt through one of the button gaps and it's one of those things you wish you hadn't seen. I keep thinking about how I went around, smiling and almost flirting, acting for all the world like a pretty girl, and shame flushes my cheeks. But then I remember that inside I knew, and I was acting, and I pulled it off—even to myself, until now. There's a certain victory in that.

There were other lesbians there that day. They were older, had bad hair and bad fashion, and were there as family, not friends. My girlfriend and I were out, making the wedding party a little hipper, more 90s, while they just plain didn't fit in. They were fat, both fatter than me, and they didn't glide around and flirt and drink champagne and wear big dresses and fake it like I did. Maybe they knew better than to try. Maybe they were strong enough people not to want to. I didn't look at them. I didn't smile or say hi or purposely walk near their table or kiss my girlfriend where they could see or anything. I turned my back and got busy trying to be included in the glow of beautiful people, as though every year since I was sixteen had never happened. There are many shades of shame.

I am miraculously thin; still big-boned, but now my skin is drawn tight over muscle, sinew, limbs stretched long. There is a calm serenity in my face, the smooth triumphant look of a woman who has conquered control. My breasts are still large but fold neatly away, acceptably round and soft in their hiding. There is a hollowness to me, the glow of empty transcendence. Skin that was once sallow and mottled gleams like polished stone. My neck is elegant, my chest solid, my stomach a drum I play nightly. I marvel at the endless run of my legs, quietly and to myself. My bones, barely visible, announce my fortitude. I go silently through my days, wearing anything at all, looking striking and unflappably satisfied.

When I came out, I thought I had rounded the bend to the final stretch. I would never again be too big, too masculine, too strong, too loud, too opinionated or angry or political or serious or caring. A place in the world had been waiting for me and I was finally going to take it. Pride oozed from my pores. I was found. I was wet all the time, seeing women everywhere and knowing how I felt was okay and realizing I never had to sleep with a man by default again. I glowed—young in the best possible way—for once not worried that I was missing out. Naturally, I fell in love.

There were two weeks when my lover and I never left the house. The whole memory is a blur of incredible sex, and talks I'd always wanted to have, and kleenex, and deeply inhaled cigarettes. One scene is imprinted on my mind with the clear detail of certain dreams. I was sitting at the kitchen table eating homemade raspberry-pear pie and whipped cream, which was literally all we ate for those two weeks. I was drinking beer while she made coffee. As she padded around, I was watching how her breasts moved under her shirt, looking at her butt under her blue sweats, still unused to my own lust. I was shaking from hunger, and exhaustion, and disbelief and could barely lift my fork to my lips. But at the same time, my core was calm and still, warm and full, solidly planted. The heater was hissing. I felt drunk and giddy from the smell of sex that coated my hands and arms and neck. There was a snowy world outside the window and the phone was ringing, but we were too loose and proud to do anything about it.

I sparkle in the sun. Light comes from everywhere—my face, my feet, the grass, the sky. Sounds pour from my mouth. Life is rampant. My hair is a thick and shiny river. My smile stops your breath. I am irresistible, a craving to make your mouth water. There is no place like me to be today. Love is like snapping your fingers.

By the time I moved to Los Angeles with my girlfriend after graduation, I knew that I still had no idea what I wanted to do, I still missed all the other people I loved, and I was still capable of being alone, even though I was in love. We tried to like it there. We wanted to make friends, but even the dykes were starved, shaved, made up, and decked out, and they looked us up and down with flagrant judgment and disapproval. The butches wore blazers, women's jeans and boots, short-styled hair, and light makeup. It cost fifteen dollars to get into a club where no one looked like a dyke. They looked like one big aerobics class. It didn't take us long to stop going out.

Most of my nights were the same. I'd come back from a trip to the 7-Eleven, where the guy stared through my sweatshirt at my braless chest as I bought supplies, and put on Channel 13. I'd get my blankets, pour my drink, and make sure I had everything before sinking into the couch. The table would be lined with all I needed: Chee•tos, Kit Kat, Diet Coke, a new pack of Camel Lights, matches, and an empty ashtray. From 6:00 p.m. on I was set. *Roseanne* was on first, then *The Wonder Years, Jeopardy, Entertainment Tonight,* and the prime time shows. News came on at 10:00, another *Roseanne* at 11:00, Dave at 11:30 until she came home. On her late nights, there was a *Quantum Leap* at 12:00. My skin got cold and clammy from never moving, even under a pile of blankets, and some nights I'd shower during a bad news story. The air would be thick with smoke and flickering blue light. When I heard her car pull into the driveway, I'd get up and open a window.

> *There is a heavy-link chain covered with moss and rust and barnacles and slime. On one end, at the bottom of the sea, it is attached to an iron anchor sunk into the middle of the earth. The other end encircles my stomach. Only my head is above water, watching the world roll up and down, dreaming me a life. The sea air fills my nostrils and the taste of salt coats my throat. I float naturally and do not fear drowning. My body is pale, thick, and bloated. A lifetime of soaking has furrowed my skin into deep wrinkles. My flesh is rotting, far beyond soft. If it ever hits the air, the stench will be unbearable. My limits are impossible to delineate, making me boundless, ever expanding. This is how I live.*

It's easy to picture myself as an old woman. I'll sit on my wooden porch in the country, shelling something fresh from the garden, my hair in long, white braids. She will be inside making dinner because our children and their children are coming over. People will call me a crazy old lady and love to be in our house. I'll be at peace.

The present is not so easy, a scrambled signal I can't read. I love to be home, writing with the heat and music on, feeling clean and warm. But I find myself scanning the paper for the things I should be doing, writing down the names of dyke clubs: Faster Pussycat, Junk, the G-Spot. I fully plan to go, but when the time comes, the thought of all those skinny, little, hip dykes, pierced and tattooed and fine and already a part of things, makes me physically weary. I am weakened by fat, staying home for the most superficial reason there is. I just can't stand the way I look in the mirror.

> *A creeping web of blue spreads behind my eyes from the first groove on. The cool slithers down the back of my neck, releases my shoulders, straightens my spine tall and willowy as it weaves around my vertebrae. I have to move. My arms float up, billow, snap down the rhythm. The web pulses, skidding through the air around my skin.*

When my hips are caught, I finally believe I am alone in the dark. My favorite motion is a slow undulating wave curving from the top of my head to my hips to the soles of my feet. Beams of sound carry me from side to side, top to bottom, phrase to phrase. I am firmly anchored in myself, unshakeable: too slick to hold, too fluid to have shape, too sensual to touch. I am beyond you. This is a small taste of me, a peek, a momentary glimpse into a secret room you are not invited to enter.

So many places are not mine to fit into. I walk around feeling unsafe, entrenched in my fear. It's easy to forget the blanket protecting me, made of my privilege: my white skin, my long hair, my warm clothes, my new car with windows that close and doors that lock, the house I go home to, the money in my bank account, the people I can call if I get into trouble. These things cushion the way the world hits my skin. I don't know what it's like to live in a bigger body or to live without my blanket. It's hard to acknowledge that other people have it harder than I do without pretending to understand who they are.

I see dykes walking down the street—huge, mountainous, thundering, and tough. They immediately turn every asshole on the street into a fool. They wear leather jackets with stickers that say MUFFDIVER or FAT GRRRLS RULE. There is an eternal style to their wide-cuffed Levi's and steel-toed swagger. I am awed when I look at them, even as I cringe and look around. Their broad smiles are beautiful. I covet their pride. I know their blankets are as real and as deceiving as mine: genuine and exposing, foils, traps, disguises. I can't know who they are, how deep their pride goes, how steady it is, or at what price it was bought. To applaud their bravery may be to misunderstand their achievement. Their existence may make my own plight seem easier to bear. The affinity I feel with them is as close as I can get to an estimation of my identity, and I am standing on dangerous ground.

I am a tower, splitting the sky. Creatures like me are rare and unique. I am blessed with an understanding of the truth of things, the real core, the heart. I am made of a million stones sanded smooth. My voice is thunder. To stand behind me is to know fear, to be faced with what you've done, to get what's coming to you. To stand before me is to be cherished, to be writ large. I am the dividing line of the world. I rule and cannot be dismantled. My laughter rings mightily through the sky, thawing the ice that binds us.

Moving Like a Dyke

Clancy McKenna

How I've moved through space my whole life seems to have been some signifier to the world that I was one of those people outside the norm for my gender. I have a memory of coming home from school, maybe from fifth grade. My mom and my godmother were standing in front of our house chatting and watching me come walking along the boulevard. When I got close enough, I could hear their laughter. My aunt said to me, "Even from far away, I can always tell when it's you coming, because you walk like a longshoreman" (i.e., a laborer, a truck driver, a dyke). She didn't mean to hurt me, I know, but I was upset, angry—hell, they taught me how to walk, didn't they? Why is it my fault if I'm not doing it right? What should I do, go to charm school? Yes, my mother did try to "work on" (criticize and nag about) my posture and complain when I'd sprawl in a chair or on the floor. "Completely unladylike," she said. I remember her efforts to tame my wide stride and rolling gait by coercing me to walk around with a book perched on my head; all I got out of that was a stiff neck and more verbal abuse. I read a wise, farmyard axiom around this time, which made sense to me: "One should never try to teach a pig to sing. It will only frustrate you and annoy the pig."

I guess I always looked queer. I was called "Dyke," "Diesel," and "Dagger" a long time before I knew what those words meant. I remember, one morning in 1971, going to work and walking past a construction site in my new business clothes (office drag). I was eighteen, just out of high school, with long hair and "appropriate" feminine attire, and I had to hear "look at that fucking dyke!" Oh, I know it was done to keep us in our place; men were particularly angry then, at the beginning of the women's movement; but there was something there, in the way I moved, that caused them to call me dyke rather than cunt, bitch, or any of the other names angry men hurl at women.

The pressure to conform made me pretty miserable. I felt as if all the powerful people in my world were trying to change something innate about me. Unfortunately, I was not astute enough at the time to articulate my identity or even to be grounded and secure in my reality. I just always felt wrong—inadequate somehow—in the face of my family's and society's expectations. As a teenager, I turned to cigarettes "to help keep my weight down," but they really helped keep me numb. If I breathed less, I felt less. I began seriously to overeat on teen food—pizza, burgers, fries and soda—and got into the alcohol and drugs of my generation as well. Being conscious was too painful in the face of feeling so different, so wrong, so unlike anyone else. These were the painful things going on inside me, when all I wished for was to conform successfully and be like my friends.

Even though there was always something queer about me, I managed to be funny, outrageous, and crazy enough to alternately amuse and fit in with my various groups of friends throughout junior high and high school. I was a long way away from being honest with myself or anyone else about my thoughts and feelings—a long way from recognizing and acting on my authentic internal cues. I said what others wanted to hear and acted the way they expected me to act. Fortunately, during my teenage years, the sixties happened.

In my freshman year of high school, they abolished the dress codes so I was able to put on blue jeans and stop wearing the dreaded female attire, which never felt or looked right on my body. Finally, I fit in. I had the uniform of the sixties, and it worked to take the pressure off and allowed me to think about my body and my self-expression in a whole new way. I was in control of my clothing and, by extension, my body. I could stomp along the earth or sprawl out in a chair without much criticism. Now I was one of "those damned hippie-types" and so foreign to my family and society that their critique became focused on my politics and those of my group/sub-class rather than my body language or appearance. This movement was a perfect place for a queer to hide out and get some peace.

As a child, I was well trained to be very outer and other directed, and sadly, it is in that condition which I spent the first twenty years of my life. I married the boy next door as was expected of me, and I stopped the drugs but continued to use food, booze, and smokes to keep numb, in order to live a life that was neither wholly real nor satisfying. Happily, when I was twenty-one, I had a sweet baby son and had my first experience of unconditional love, which had nothing to do with how much I weighed, how I dressed, or how I moved. I began, via my role and experience as a parent, to grow up, to become autonomous, and to trust my inner voices.

Throughout these years until the very end of the marriage, I still didn't know I was a lesbian. Sex with my husband was never good for me, and it got worse once I acknowledged that and stopped trying. Clearly, I was using food for my primary physical comfort, cooking and eating whatever

I wanted, as often as I wanted. I was drinking about a gallon of wine per week. I kept alternately getting bigger and intermittently "dieting." Near the end of the marriage, I stopped seeing my body; I just didn't look. Internally I was conflicted; outwardly, I was becoming an uppity and loud feminist, a pain-in-his-ass, and the fights we were having got more frequent and more violent until I got out of there just barely alive.

All during this struggle for autonomy, I realized I was having strong sexual feelings for one of my female friends. At this point, all my peers were straight. I didn't know any real gay people. I'd seen some stereotypical film portrayals and read books where the miserable homo character ultimately commits suicide or leaves town. None of that had anything to do with me. Most of what I saw was depictions of men anyway; intimations about lesbian or bisexual women were clouded in such mystery that I never was sure what they really meant. I did know I always preferred the company of women, and my needs for intimate communication in a cold and unfriendly marriage were met by my relationships with my girlfriends. I was always the best bestfriend a girl could have: loyal and compliant. I had always had sexual fantasies about women. Nancy Friday's book, *My Secret Garden*, a collection of women's sexual fantasies, assured me this was OK. Many women in the book sometimes fantasized about other women, and *they* were not lesbians. This book gave me permission to think in a conscious way about things that I'd always kept veiled, even from myself. But it wasn't too long before I was struggling with real feelings I wanted to act on.

When I exited the marriage, I had one four-year-old child, a high school diploma, and apparently no marketable skills. The need to get a job brought forth the reality of my appearance again in a big way. I had to take a close look at my body and figure out a way to make it acceptable in the job market. By now, I was firmly grounded in my look as an over 200-pound, working-class, blue jeans/black sweatshirt sort of woman. My husband and I had worked together to rebuild our 100-year-old house over the seven years we were together, and I was equally comfortable hauling bricks, pushing a loaded wheelbarrow, or scampering up a ladder carrying tools, tar paper, or lunch. I looked and felt much more the laborer I was than any kind of housewife of my generation. In the late 1970s, women were still primarily dieting to lose weight. Jogging and aerobics were beginning to become fashionable, but working out at the gym to have defined muscles was just not acceptable. I looked more queer than ever. Yet suddenly, I needed a job that paid a wage I could live on.

I began with a career in uniform, driving a route truck for a laundry service. After nine months of that, I was hired for a job at The New York

State Corrections Academy. I went away to boot camp in Albany to be trained. If I survived this month of my life with any pleasure at all, it was in the joy of becoming lethally proficient with firearms, gaining the knowledge of how to fight and win, and feeling pride in finally being expected to stand up straight and strong and go marching in formation with the rest of my platoon. I was finally at home, moving publicly with my body. The reality of this job was so grim; I quit at the end of my training and went back to the laundry truck. But I was changed: I was still big, but now I was bad, too.

I changed jobs and began to drive a school bus and spent the next five years terrorizing the streets of New York City. I was a lunatic rage-aholic. I looked like a refrigerator with a head, often leaping out of the bus to scream at and hopefully throttle anyone who cut me off or gave me a "hard time." Given this city and this traffic, that was a daily occurrence. Not one of those men on the street or in the subway ever took me up on it. That was a very lucky, but also empowering, experience. I enjoyed making them back up and back down from their position of male superiority and dominance. I felt huge, strong, and powerful. Oddly, I felt most in control when I was out of control.

On November 16, 1986, I attended a concert at Avery Fisher Hall in Lincoln Center. It was the first time I'd ever purchased a single ticket to anything. I didn't know much about Holly Near or Cris Williamson, but I'd seen an advertisement that said it was "women's music"; I wondered if that was some sort of code. What a beautiful night! I was deeply moved by the sight of hundreds of women, obviously together in couples, holding hands, openly caring for each other, and happily decked out in their best clothes. Some were even wearing tuxedos.

I came out to myself at that concert. Holly Near sang a verse about a thirty-year-old mother who needed time and peace and choices. Sitting there in the dark, I began to weep with relief at the knowledge that these women, these songs were my story, and I wouldn't have to be alone. I wasn't crazy. The woman sitting next to me took my hand and just held it for a few moments, offering comfort. I don't know what she looked like—I never saw her. I don't know what her date must have thought either, but I am eternally grateful. It was a lovely welcome into my new world. The next day I went out and spent the grocery money on record albums so I could hear over and over these songs that treated women loving women as normal, as a positive and wonderful way of life. I knew I wanted the happy life that I imagined for all those women at the concert.

I traveled from Queens to the lesbian and gay community in Manhattan to find other women who, like me, were attracted to women. I went to the women's groups at Identity House, the local counseling center, and was perceived to be "butch," although I didn't really know how to fulfill those expectations yet.

In my early days in the community, I saw that there were many women who were like me or larger, and it was an acceptable way to be; here they were not ostracized or overtly insulted as the straight world I'd just left would do. Here, body size, differences in race, age, class, health, ability, and finances seemed to be lines that were crossed fairly readily. I assumed being lesbian/bisexual was enough common ground on which to build our relationships. Appearance wasn't so important. Oh yes, the beautiful, the young, the handsome, and healthy people had their place and held it with apparent ease, but none of that was a requirement. We'd stepped aside from the limited standards that Madison Avenue imposes upon the straight world. If we are not playing it their way, accepting and consuming their advertisements and images—sleeping with them—basically, we can reject what we no longer need when we enter the subculture that is our community. This helped free me to explore my individual and very personal way of expressing my sexuality and develop a gender identity based upon what felt good, rather than what someone else thought looked good.

For the first time in my life, I began to really care how I looked. Unpressured from outside, this was my desire, rising from a deep, authentic place. I wanted to wear nice clothes that looked hot. I went into the men's department of the local clothing store and began trying on clothes that pleased me. My attitude about my body began to change with my increased awareness of the possibility of actually finding a lover. I thought I looked OK in men's clothing. The styles are just cut better for the body I live in. I felt free and alive: charged up and excited in a way I'd never experienced in adolescence. Suddenly, I wasn't quite so interested in food.

On the Fourth of July, I met a woman at a discussion group and fell in love. It was fireworks that day and fireworks most of the way through, but she was wonderful to me and a great teacher for a while. I got sober about two years into our relationship, and it changed me so drastically that the relationship did not survive; we ended amid explosions, just as we had begun. When I stopped drinking and using food as a drug, I lost sixty pounds, unloaded tons of bad attitude and anger, and began another chapter in the book of my body.

One of my closest friends is a dancer and movement therapist who introduced me to an Authentic Movement group where I further explored my freedom to move how and when I please. I recommend this work for anyone with body, gender, or body image confusion. To move in a space while being respectfully witnessed by the therapist or experienced group member was an enormously helpful part of my defining my body, my boundaries, and my movements. I also learned a lot about different types of movement: how I feel when I define and expand my own movement vocabulary, as well as consciously trying on the movements of others; "leading, following, being"; to see what works for me and what feels bad, scary, or impossible. I have learned that I love to dance and I love to move. I love being in my body, and I know the difference when I am not fully in here. I breathe; I feel; I move. It's about being present, authentic, and alive.

What I've learned on this journey is that it's important *who* is living inside the body. Beauty, or conforming to some hetero-compulsory norm, does not signify honesty, decency, or goodwill. If I can't love my body exactly as I perceive it to be today, in this moment, then I can't let anyone else love it or love me either. Am I my body? Is that all, or is what goes on inside here something important, too? I work on this every day. Understanding and acceptance are key for me in this, as well as many other areas of my life.

I no longer smoke, drink, or "diet" in any conventional sense of the word. After I got sober I joined and participated in a support group for "overeaters," which helped me figure out what "normal" eating looked and felt like. Initially, I truly had no concept of "a portion." I eat a reasonable diet and exercise regularly by bicycling to and from work every day. My size fluctuates up and down one clothing size. Mostly, I don't sweat it. I guess The Universe is making me the size I need to be to do what I need to do in my life.

"Body image," for me, is my sense of my body—where I fit in the world, how much space I take up, and how entitled I feel to that space. Occasionally, my self-esteem can still get hung up on my size, or what I think my size is. Lessons from early life can take a long time to unlearn.

My body image is rather fluid, which makes sense, since my size isn't static. But, I am aware that the body image changes are not always connected to the bodily reality. On a good day I feel that I look fine, great, normal; on a bad day I can still feel that I look fat, old, tired. On a good day I am an athlete registered to ride in the Boston/New York Aids Ride in September this year. On a bad day, say with some PMS or a fight at work or with my lover, I think I'll never make the 250 miles that tour requires. It's all so subjective. The difference now is that I know it's just an image problem. The self is not fluid; just the image is, and to know that is reassuring.

Tattoo Me

Catherine Lundoff

I got my first tattoo put on in Texas by a biker dude about eight years ago. I got my second this year; it was done by a lesbian martial and tattoo artist in Minneapolis. A Chinese-style dragon in lots of colors rising out of clouds on my right shoulder was my first tat, transforming the way I felt about my body. The second, a Celtic knotwork of snakes and a crescent moon running around my left arm is my outward sign that I am a warrior, an Amazon. The first is about coming to some terms with my past; the second is for strength when I need it.

My parents' house was filled with pain, anger, and alcoholism; weight was used as a weapon—"Stop eating; do you want to get fat like me?" They put a chain around the refrigerator when I was five years old so I wouldn't eat so much. Until I took off for college at eighteen, if my mother wasn't harping on my body, my weight, or the way I looked, I was. I am, for the record, muscular and a whopping twenty-five pounds larger than the "ideal" weight/height ratio that we all get to see in stores, in magazines, and on health charts at the doctor's. Most of that twenty-five pounds is, and always has been, tits and muscle. Of course, in my mind, I was chubby and unhappy about it.

The event that started me down the road to body art was a museum exhibit that I saw in St. Louis in the early 1980s, on Maori art and culture. The Maori are the indigenous people of New Zealand who, along with a rich and vibrant cultural history, have some of the coolest tats I've ever seen. These include very elaborate facial tattoos, as well as full-body ones. I was seriously impressed. Plus, I come from a blue-collar neighborhood in Brooklyn where there were almost no out queers (I thought of myself as straight), and where women with tattoos ride around on the back of Harleys behind guys named "Puke." Having a tattoo is a way to broadcast that you don't belong, that June Cleaver is not in your future, the thing that the tough, bad girls do. Given that the "good" girls all wore tons of makeup and four-inch heels, it wasn't too difficult a choice.

Eight years ago, I was doing archaeology on construction sites in Texas, living as an out bisexual with my male lover, now a valued friend. He thought I was beautiful the way I was and never understood why I wanted a tattoo. For a design, I always knew that I wanted a dragon; in different mythologies, dragons are Earth spirits—wise, strong, beautiful, and both good and bad. I wanted to feel powerful, magical, and grounded all at the same time. I dreamed about it for two whole years before I found the nerve and the opportunity to get it done. At the time, I also worried that I might "sell out"—get a job not working on construction sites, wear dresses, shave my legs, and all that. I figured a tattoo would remind me that I wasn't always "establishment."

So, I had a day off, and a friend of mine from the dig and I went to the local tattoo artist, who was a buddy of hers. He was a big guy with long, black hair and a beard, covered with tattoos and wearing a Harley shirt. I picked a dragon design that I liked which got voted down for reasons of practicality, then moved onto my second choice, which I will wear for the rest of my life. It hurt like hell for an hour and a half, and anyone who tells you differently has no nerve endings. I had to ask him to change the TV station because I couldn't bear to watch Vanna White. He admired how tough I was, not whimpering or moving for an hour and a half, even though I was shaking everything but that shoulder, and he gave me a discount on the price.

It's a big piece, about six or seven inches long, covering my entire right shoulder blade. Within the week, I was pulling my shirt off at parties and at work to show it off. It was beautiful and I was beautiful, and I'd been strong enough to get it done, strong enough to handle the pain. The fact that the guy who was inked before me passed out might have had something to do with this feeling of great strength, but I like to think most of it was internal. It was one big high, changing me from a dumpy bookworm to the hottest thing on two feet. A day after it was done, I carried myself with pride and confidence; it was one of the best things I'd ever done for myself and it was permanent!

My second tat is new. I got it prior to starting law school and learning tae kwon do. Now, I'm calling myself "queer" or bisexual-identified lesbian, and living with my woman lover and our cats in Iowa. This tat is an armband, two intertwined Celtic knotwork snakes wrapped around a crescent moon. It's also wrapped around my martial arts–derived muscle definition. I love it because it's a beautiful piece of work, tattoo artistry at its best, and I've seen a lot. It's like joining a club; get one, flash it, and sooner or later someone wants to show you theirs.

In a way, I was disappointed when I got this one because it wasn't the "high" that the first one was—"I am woman, hear me roar!" This one had a quieter, more subtle feeling to it. All over the world, different cultures tattoo their warriors, and this tat is more like that kind of signal. It's about me being powerful and a fighter and about sending that signal to others. I am no natural athlete, and tae kwon do (a Korean form of karate) does not come easily to me. I am heavier and older than most of the women in my class, but I am an Amazon nonetheless. The tats place me in my body, some place that I have often not wanted to be, and let me be strong and powerful in that body. They are outward manifestations of how I feel about myself, reclaiming my body for me the way I want to.

Surprisingly enough, not many queer women write about their experiences with tattooing and piercing; it seems to be something you talk about but don't commit to paper. Susie Bright, in her essay "Absolutely Pierced" (1990), talks about the rush of pride and empowerment she felt when she got her labia pierced, and I can definitely relate (when I'm not curled protectively around my crotch). I have to admit that the idea of piercing still scares me, though it probably hurts a whole lot less than tattooing because it takes less time. It's that "good pain, bad pain" thing. It'd be fun to check out how tattooing and piercing are markers in the queer communities. I'm dying to know: do butches get tattoos and femmes get pierced, while softball players do neither? What about rugby players and drag queens?

My guess is that queers get tattooed for the same reasons that bikers, would-be bikers, and warriors and shamans from different cultures do it. In a world where you're an outsider, where someone always seems to want to control your body and what you're doing with it, a tattoo or piercing is a way to take it back, to say "This is mine." It's also a permanent thing, in general, being both difficult and expensive to remove; you're broadcasting to anyone who can see it that you're different. There's also the whole ritual aspect of body art: it hurts, no two ways around that, and to go through it you have to be pretty psyched to get it done. Regardless of what you may have been told, no reputable tattoo artist or piercer is going to work on you while you're drunk. For one thing, you bleed more and for another, you're more likely to pass out or just plain move around too much. Going through the ritual is a choice that you have to be conscious about.

Choosing to go through the ritual of tattooing becomes a test of endurance, a proof of bravery and strength. Complexity, content, size, coloring, and where and what you have tattooed on your body are the signals that you send to the world around you. It's a rite of passage: you know that you're strong enough to go through with it and, by extension, strong enough to take on the rest of the world with its homophobic, sexist, racist crap. The ritual can also involve healing; I know lesbians and bi women who get tattoos on old injuries or as part of their recovery from rape, incest, and/or bashings to make themselves feel good about their bodies again. Sometimes it's a combination of all of the above.

I'm tempted to say that the route to queer lib is found on the needle of a tattoo gun, but I can't say that I really believe it that literally. The flip side of marking yourself as permanently "different" is that you get treated that way by people already inclined to be prejudiced against you. This is particularly obvious with visible tattoos and really demonstrates how white, Western culture judges by appearances. Tattoos and piercings still have the mystique of representing outlaw cultures, and they're less accessible than buying a leather jacket. It can be one more way of being OUT in a big way, especially when you're judged by the way you look. Of course, one of the great things about choosing to be tattooed is that you can also decide who's going to see it afterward, depending on where it is; it's the effect on you personally that's important. If you want to share that feeling by having highly visible tats, that's even better!

After this celebration of tattooing, I'd like to say that I never felt "fat" again, but I do. I hate the way that we, as women, learn to think about our bodies and our body fat and muscle. It's all economics and sexism, you know: in times of economic prosperity, bigger women are seen as beautiful. At least that's how I remember it working out. I will say that I've never felt as bad about my body as I once did. I don't have to go to bed with someone so I can feel beautiful and desirable, or even loved, but that's another story. The confidence that I feel about my body shows in the way that I walk and dress. I love the way that my tattoos make my body even more unique, linking me with the Earth and the Goddess.

REFERENCE

Bright, Susie. (1990). *Susie Sexpert's Lesbian Sex World.* San Francisco: Cleis Press.

PART 4:
A WOMAN'S LOVE HEALS

Mirror

Nina Silver

My hips
mirrored silver sideways
        thinly polished
gleam softly back,
        shadowshapes gently arcing.
I pass.
But my bloated belly
        determinedly
sings coloratura curves
        as though beginning a babe,
        expecting miracles.

It would be a miracle
if facing the mirror
        frontways
facing my self
        (a miracle)
I could embrace
full roundness
        hips
        legs belly
        breasts
                all secret seekers
                of willowy flat.

But today
        picking up your paintbrush
you sighed
how you wished all women
curved like me.
If we weren't so linear
        thinking,
you said
everyone would rejoice
        over angles and dips
        turns and rotations
        canyons and valleys

each elegant arch
that delights you

whether your offering is strokes
for the canvas
or
        laying down your palette
for my own eager outline
        of purposeful folds.

Big Grrl

Drama Rose

I spent eight years of my life engaged in a compulsive dieting cycle. From the ages of twelve to twenty, it dominated my existence. Everything I ate was a source of worry and guilt. How much I ate, what kind of food it was, where and when I ate it, who I ate with (or didn't eat with)—all of these were crucial decisions that I agonized over daily. I took laxatives and I tried to make myself vomit (unsuccessfully, thank goodness). I would binge and then starve myself as punishment. I hated my body. I felt miserable in my body. There was no support, especially in my early teenage years, for accepting my body the way it was. My family encouraged me to lose weight. They felt I would be "prettier" if I lost weight and that "boys would like me more." It wasn't until later that I came to realize that I didn't want the boys to like me more! Everyone around me was supportive of what I now see as a very unhealthy cycle of dieting.

All of my friends (at that time they were all straight) were on diets of one form or another and totally obsessed with weight loss. We envied the girls who were anorexic! I hated my body and felt guilty whenever I ate. I lived my life in a state of waiting—waiting until I got thin. I couldn't wear certain clothes until after I got thin; I couldn't exercise until after I got thin; I couldn't eat until after I got thin. Everything good would happen to me *after I lost weight*. I would be able to be happy *after I lost weight*.

I had a brief reprieve from this devastating cycle when, at age fifteen, I got pregnant. Fortunately, I knew enough about pregnancy and health to not starve my baby by dieting while I was pregnant. I found out I was pregnant when I was three months along so that gave me six months of normal eating. Amazingly enough, that was really the only time in my teenage years that I felt comfortable in my body. I was healthy and enjoyed being pregnant, even though I had decided to release the baby for adoption. Immediately after my daughter was born, I went directly back to the same dysfunctional dieting cycle. Now I had a renewed interest in dieting in order to lose the weight gained during pregnancy. I was able to lose the "pregnancy weight" and an additional fifteen pounds. Now I was sixteen, almost at my "goal weight," and definitely the thinnest I had been in years. I was supposed to be happy! Everything was supposed to be perfect now, except that it wasn't. Nothing in my life had really changed, except that I had lost weight. Everyone was so proud of the way I had "bounced back" after the baby was born. I got a lot of attention for being thin. All of my friends thought I looked great and every one was encouraging me to keep it off. However, I still fought with my boyfriend, I still felt uncomfortable in my body, I was still unhappy a lot of the time, and I was still obsessed with food and dieting. Soon, I gained back the weight I had lost and an additional fifteen pounds. Then, I really felt miserable about my body and my "lack of self-discipline."

It wasn't until after I moved to California and came out as a lesbian that I had my very first introduction to body acceptance. The womyn I came to know in the lesbian community were much more accepting of different body types than the straight womyn I had grown up with. Suddenly I was part of a group of womyn who didn't diet! They talked about changing the image of womyn in our culture instead of changing the size of our bodies. For the first time, I realized that I did not have to buy in to the typical thin stereotype. Never before had anyone ever presented it as an option to love my big body without trying to change it. I never knew I had that choice. The idea of size acceptance opened doors in my mind that I never even knew were slammed shut. Womyn in the lesbian community put the question to me for the first time, "Why are you on a diet?" I began to hear alternative voices for the first time in my life. Lesbians said to me, "Don't destroy your body; you are beautiful the way you are." This was absolutely foreign to me.

Being with womyn sexually was a big part of this process for me. It felt comfortable. They didn't expect me to hold my stomach in. They loved my curves and roundness. For the first time, I had womyn around me who seemed to be relaxed in their bodies! It opened my mind to the possibility of not dieting anymore. I hadn't known that I could be sexy, happy, attractive, and still be big. I thought those things would only happen after I lost weight and fit into the societal image of what is supposed to be pretty. I was overjoyed at this new awakening, but I also found it scary and overwhelming. It shook the foundation of what my life had been built on. That was the first crucial step for my size acceptance. There have been many, many more in the last ten years.

I remember the last official diet that I went on. It was a liquid diet, and I was in my first lesbian relationship. She was not at all happy that I was dieting. She said it was unhealthy, and she encouraged me to quit. I thought that she was just saying that to be nice but that she *really* wanted me to be thinner. I didn't believe her when she said that she loved my body just the way it was. Then, I got sick from the liquid diet and ended up with a kidney infection. This was another big step in my process of size acceptance. I began to believe what my girlfriend had been saying. I began to see dieting as unhealthy, physically and mentally. I began to see dieting as a thing of the past.

The next level for me was realizing that I could not only be comfortable in my big body, but I could also be sexy. All of my images of large womyn were grandmas or old spinster aunts. They were *not* sexy! So, discovering that I could wear lingerie and leather and short skirts and feel good about it was amazing. I had always told myself that I could only wear those things *after I lost weight.* When I started dressing up and experimenting with sexy clothes, I felt attractive! It was delightful to see myself as a sexual body. I was excited to explore this newfound sexiness with my lover, even though it was often scary. To be big and wear a mini skirt, to be big and lay on top of someone (especially someone smaller than me), to be big and be naked and feel happy about it—all of this was new and joyous for me. To do those things right away instead of waiting for the magical (and unreal) time when I would be *thin* was hard for me to believe, and it often felt very scary as well as thrilling.

The acknowledgment that I could not only accept my big body but that I could revel in its largeness was incredible information that I got only after coming out as a lesbian.

Then, at age twenty-one, I became addicted to crystal meth. When I began doing speed, I did a drastic backslide into those old patterns. The more weight I lost from taking drugs the more I wanted to lose. Also, I was still trying to pretend that I wasn't dieting because I wasn't on an actual diet. I hadn't completely abandoned all of my newfound body acceptance. I was just fooling myself into thinking the speed was all for fun and not for weight loss.

I was heavily involved in doing speed for about a year. During that time I had many other self-destructive behaviors; I drank a lot, smoked cigarettes, and stayed up all night on a regular basis. All of these things were terrible for my body and my whole body image process. I had once again surrounded myself with people (both straight and gay this time) who were very fat negative, and who saw drugs as a great way to stay thin and "attractive." I was single by then, too, and felt desperate to get sexual attention for my newly thin body. I needed womyn to find me attractive in that body. The whole scene was a downward spiral of unhealthy behavior. If only I could do more drugs, then I would eat less and weigh less. That became my goal, my focus. It sucked me right back down into that mindset.

Quitting speed was literally a lifesaving decision. My physical and
emotional health had deteriorated to a frightening place. I hadn't cared for
my body for over a year, and it couldn't function properly. I felt very crazy,
and my brain also couldn't function properly. Lack of food and sleep and
an overindulgence in drugs, cigarettes, and alcohol had taken a mighty toll
on me. I knew I couldn't keep it up, but quitting drugs seemed impossible.
I thought the only answer was to kill myself. Dying seemed easier than
trying to get healthy.

It was through the strength and help of my birth family and my lesbian
family that I survived. People came to my rescue when I needed them the
most. They saved my life. I had crashed hard, and when I asked for help,
people came that I never expected. Lesbians I barely knew reached out to
help me. Part of my healing process during this time was to move away for
a while, back to my hometown in Idaho. I had to get away from the drugs
and the whole lifestyle that I had created for myself. I needed to make drastic
changes, and I couldn't do that staying in the same place. So my father came
to get me, and I moved away for a year and a half. My best friend Kayla
(who has since become my wife) came to Idaho to live with me.

Hitting bottom and making the decision to move away was a very powerful statement. Somewhere deep inside I respected my body enough to
know that I had to make drastic changes. I had to relearn everything that I
had learned years before about accepting my body and caring for it, and
learn it at a deeper level. It was a difficult and painful process, gaining
weight back, gaining my health back, and gaining back the safety and security in my physical self that I had lost in my year of doing drugs. While I
was away, I didn't need to feel physically attractive; I didn't need to be
sexy; I had no desire to look cool as I did when I was partying. I could just
be me, be plain, and do a lot of healing. I felt safe with Kayla; she supported
my process and helped me get healthy.

As I got physically stronger and healthier, I felt better about my body,
safer in it, and more comfortable. Being fat had always felt dangerous to
me, unsafe somehow, especially because of men and the harassment I often
got for being fat. Finally, through a long and wonderful process, being fat
began to mean being strong. The more comfortable I got in my body, the
safer I felt. When I compared myself to my thin friends, it was difficult
because I still saw them as more beautiful, but I always knew that I was
stronger and that was very important to me. When I was thin and on drugs,
I was weak, emotionally as well as physically. Now being strong is very
healing. After I quit speed, I once again gained back the weight I had lost,
plus twenty pounds more. This was hard for me to accept at first because I
had become used to the size of my body before, and now, I had to get used

to being bigger. Once again, I went through the old questions: now that I am even bigger, am I still attractive? Can I still wear sexy clothes? It was difficult, and I am still going through the process, but I feel good about it. I am bigger now than I have ever been, and I am also more comfortable and healthy than ever before!

Kayla, more than anyone else in my life, has helped me not only to accept my body but to enjoy and love it. She has helped me take the steps toward seeing myself as beautiful. The last eight years have taken me to a whole new level of positive body image. During my relationship with Kayla, I have come to feel the most comfortable in my body that I have ever felt. It's a feeling of rightness, as if I belong. Being in a healthy supportive relationship and creating a network of wonderful womyn friends is all part of my ongoing healing process.

Getting involved with the Body Image Task Force in Santa Cruz (an organization that presents information and education about body image and looksism in the schools and in the community) and finding out the facts about how detrimental diets are gave me powerful information to use when talking to people about my antidieting stance. Doing exercise that is not geared toward weight loss has been wonderful for me too. I do water aerobics regularly, and it is a pleasure, not a chore, as exercise was when I was dieting. Feeling my body get even stronger, but not smaller, has been an incredibly positive experience. It makes me feel so happy! I love the feel of exercise and am amazed by what I can do with my body now that I could never do before.

I am now a massage therapist. I especially love working with large womyn and helping them and womyn of all sizes have positive experiences with loving healthy touch. All of these things have taken me along the path to loving and cherishing my own body.

I have gradually realized that the things Kayla has been saying are true—I am beautiful, my body is worthy and sexy and powerful. That dawning has gotten brighter; that knowledge has grown into a whole way of being for me—an acceptance and a joy.

Ode to My Vibrator

Susanna Trnka

Making love to a man didn't do it. Making love to a woman didn't do it, despite what everybody says. It took making love to myself before I could make that long gaze down and be ready to see what met my eyes.

After three years of living in San Francisco, I finally got the nerve to go through that bona fide, queer rite of passage and bought my first vibrator. I bought it because I was filled with longing, curiosity, and fear. I bought it because I'd been staring at it in the catalogue for weeks. I bought it because I was in the store with my girlfriend and I knew the saleswoman and was cornered between the two of them; I couldn't really chicken out.

There is a definite love affair between queer women and our vibrators. It's not about phalluses or penises or the Empire State building but about power, power over sexual pleasure. As queer women we have by definition done some thinking about what turns us on and have taken certain, scary, risky, exhilarating steps to get it. Instead of literally lying back and accepting society's ideas about our sexuality or society's notions of what should and should not turn us on, we've developed our own ideas of sex and pleasure and been proud enough of these accomplishments to call ourselves gay, lesbian, bisexual, or queer.

So what is it about women and vibrators that is so alien? so frightening? so appealing? It's alien, obviously, in that we hardly ever get to see them. When was the last time a woman in a Harlequin whipped out her handy vibrator instead of swooning over Mr. Personification-of-Utter-Arrogance? Appealing? Well . . . that's obvious. But frightening—what could possibly be frightening about a woman giving herself pleasure? What could possibly be *more* frightening than a woman giving herself pleasure?

Using a vibrator was a gigantic step forward in developing my sexual independence. After I bought my vibrator, I took it home and stashed it under my bed where it sat patiently waiting for a few months until I finally dusted it off and gave it a whirl. And then, for the first time in my life, I myself, all by myself, made myself come—just like that. After I recovered from this awesome feeling, I went into the bathroom and grabbed a small mirror and a light. I had decided it was time to see that part of my body which can make the rest of me feel so magnificent. I didn't automatically find it beautiful, but it wasn't ugly either. It was just me, in color. Plain old me, but with the potential to blow my mind.

And contrary to popular opinion, the experience didn't doom me to a life of candlelight dinners with an electric whirlwind. A vibrator isn't a replacement for a warm, sexual body or for someone you truly care about, but it can change the way you relate to them. A woman who can give herself sexual pleasure enters sexual/erotic relationships on a different, more powerful, footing, as frightening and exhilarating as this may be.

I know that I'm expected to say that I learned to love my body the first time I made love to a woman, but that just isn't true. The first time, and a number of times after that, I got more anxious about my body than I'd ever been with a man. Forget about comparing myself to women on the TV screen or in a fashion magazine, now I had another real, live body right there in the bed with me to compare myself to. Hasn't anyone else caught themselves wondering; she's so beautiful, she's so strong, what must she think of me . . . ?

This is not to deny that making love with a woman makes me feel wonderful about my body. Hearing from a woman that she thinks my breasts are beautiful or that she likes the curve of my thigh makes the compliment all the more sincere. After all she has her own breasts; she knows what she's talking about. I know my body intrigues her because she likes it, not just because it's different.

Having sex with women has forced me redefine what sex is, to go beyond images of the male-female missionary position and wondering if, in our moment of passion, we look anything like they do in the movies, to asking what do I find erotic? If fun in the bedroom goes beyond just vaginal penetration by a penis, then what exactly does sex consist of? Redefining and expanding my ideas of sex and what is erotic has encouraged me to look beyond my body as a place where someone else can get pleasure. This is an idea that subtly, and at times not-so subtly, runs through most traditional, heterosexist, and misogynist ideas of sex as men getting pleasure from women's bodies and women, from the pleasure they give their men. Shattering this constricted definition of sex—by rethinking what is pleasurable and by having sensitive and imaginative lovers, both male and female, to explore this with—has encouraged me to identify my body as a space of pleasure for me.

Loving women has also forced me to think about what attracts me to a woman. The answer isn't that she looks as if she should be a fashion model on the cover of *Seventeen* but that she appears powerful, big, and strong, as if she is plowing through the air, making her presence known, taking up space and being proud of it. The realization that what I find attractive is different from the "ideals" of beauty drummed into my head has made me rethink my own body and begin to accept its eccentricities, its plainness, and its beauty, for what it is.

But it took stripping away all the social aspects of sex, all the worry and all the joy in relating to another person, before I could come face-to-face with my body, or maybe I mean face to crotch. In any case, it was the discovery of a lifetime. As much fun as it can be to make love to a woman, or to man, I'm not planning on retiring my trusty vibrator just yet.

Dressing Room Blues

Claire Hueholt

Shopping is something I used to love. I can remember as a child going to the big city with my parents and shopping all day, purchasing the required school shoes, winter coat, a pair of jeans to replace the ones that had ripped on the fence last week, and the assortment of trinkets that could only be accumulated by a twelve-year-old on a day spent tripping in and out of department stores and strip malls. When I'd get home, even though I was sleepy, I'd happily lay out each of my purchases, look them over, and try them on, modeling for my parents and little sisters. For days afterward I would marvel at these new things in my world.

Today, I do not like shopping. It makes me weary, nervous, and full of unresolvable anger. It must be done, I suppose, but each outing to a mall grips my heart with the fear of what the world has become since my last outing and how it will focus its eyes on me and those I love. I wonder what cruelty my culture has in store for me on this trip.

I'm accutely aware of my difference when I walk through the entryway to what is, seemingly, every other consumer's dream. I wince at the noise of the video arcade and the ambivalence of the teenagers ambling around its entrance.

I push my way through the crowds to the only store I feel remotely comfortable in. In my head, I know it's not an oasis but is also worn and tired, a cliché of classic styles and androgyny meant to make me just comfortable enough. My money spent here is not wisely spent but, rather, blown on overpriced shreds of fabric sewn together by third-world women being paid pennies each day to satisfy my materialistic, capitalistic soul. These articles sometimes end up carelessly tossed aside when they don't do what I hoped they would.

Being a woman openly loving women for twelve years now, I also approach these stores and these malls with hatred, knowing too well the pain they have in store for those hoping to recreate that innocent wonder of a child who has brought home magic.

I have loved many women—women who have taken different shapes and sizes: fat, skinny, tall, short, muscular, and soft. We have shopped and suffered together.

Today, every time I walk into a dressing room, its sterile, mirrored walls drip with the tears and rage of all of them. "Why doesn't this look good? Why doesn't it fit? Why am I so fat? So Ugly? So much celullite? How can you love me?" The words echo in my ears as I pull on a pair of jeans—my first new pair in a year—because I avoid these walls.

I remember my first love who gained 20 pounds over the four years we were together. I remember holding her as she cried, here in this room, because the largest size would not encompass her body. I remember how she pulled away from me in our bed, asking me with her eyes how I could desire a woman like her.

I remember another love who, though fit and muscular, could never find clothes that conformed to her body. Her shape was different—not long-legged and flat-bellied. When we broke up she asked, "Is it because I'm too fat?"

I remember my friend who had three sets of clothes of different sizes in her closet. She was constantly reading the latest diet book, joining the fitness club on the corner, and spending thousands each year on frozen weight-watching meals.

I remember my last trip here with my current girlfriend. She used to be a size 5, 103 pounds. Now she is twenty-eight years old, her hips are broader, her belly is softer; she struggles to fit into a size 9 and tears stream down her brown cheeks. She takes the jeans off, throws them down, and yells at me when I ask her to let me get her another style, another pair of denims, something better. She says, "I have to get out of here."

We go quickly. She is still the owner of a handful of torn, ripped, poorly fitting jeans she has rummaged from her brothers at home—nothing new, shiny, or magic.

Intellectually, we both understand the nearly unbreakable cycle that women have been thrown into, and its injustice. The diet industry, the fitness industry, the fashion industry—they all have much to gain from this dilemma. Clothing stores stocked with tiny sizes that every woman secretly or not so secretly aspires to fit. They have few sizes that normal, average-bodied women can pull over their hips, and fewer still that fat women can wear comfortably.

We know that these tears in this dressing room are institutionalized for us. We are supposed to feel this pain. And we feel complicity because we shed them.

We don't know how to stop. It is difficult to look in the mirror and say, "My body is not the perfect, hard-body, size 7 that every woman, including me, wants to be. I will never have the happiness that I have been promised if that body were mine."

It is harder yet to say, "I am not a size 7, and I do not want to be a size 7. I look at my naked, size 11 body and I love its curves, its hardness, and its softness. I love the strength I feel in my legs when I firmly plant them on the ground. I love the fullness of my breasts and the gentleness of my smile."

When I take my lover home and pamper her to make her forget the unforgettable, I think these things about her body. I wonder how I can communicate to her this beauty I see in her physicalness and the lust I feel when I touch her and smell her. I wonder how I can show her the magic that happens when she sheds the rags that clothe her and stands there, a woman living well in her body. I wonder how my vision can replace the vision in her eyes. And I am sad because I know that she has been taught well.

The voices of her past will always bounce around her head when she looks into a mirror, and she will always, for a moment, see something grotesque, undesirable, and hideous. She will feel guilty because she and I and so many others have failed as the women that this twentieth century demands.

My Ideal Becoming Real

Susie Bullington

(for Cynthia)
And there was a womon
    who defined herself by her body's imperfections
When she looked in the mirror
she couldn't see her sweet smile,
        her soft radiance
Her deep eyes filled with sadness
could only look with bitterness and contempt.

She longed to dance freely
    under the brilliant full moon
    to float to the stars
but the chains of her socialization weighed her down.

Her success was never enough
    her compassion and gentle strength
    she could never esteem
For she lacked that one thing,
    and could never forgive,
    sovereignty over her appetites
    looming out of control, washing over her
    and the perfect fat-free physique.

In talking about lesbian body image, it is essential to mention the Womyn's Music Festivals because Festival is about lesbian bodies. Everywhere you turn you see lesbian bodies: faces of all shapes and colors, legs (some hairy, some not), sunburned backs, vaginas peering at you when you come up for air in the pool, butts (some round, some flat, some stark white, some brown, some bronze with no tan lines, some painfully red), and breasts—large, shapely, drooping breasts, breasts larger than you've ever seen before, small, delicate breasts that hardly wiggle when walking, two breasts, one breast, surrounded by a sea of breasts!

Being at Festival is about being in your body, which is a struggle for many of us—feeling the solid boots on your feet, feeling the dust under them. It is the sensuous enjoyment of your body as it moves and stretches while you walk, as you glide through the icy water in the pool. It is being caressed by the sun on your shoulders and breasts, while a breeze delicately blows across your back. It is the shock as your body first hits the freezing water and then the rush as you swim like mad, exhilarated as your skin comes alive and ice shoots through your vagina and grips your head like a vise. It is feeling the wind in your freshly cut hair, feeling free, feeling strong, feeling the contours of another womon's body as you make love to her.

Maybe Festival is also about not being in your body, but becoming the collective body of the community, surpassing the limits of your own physical body. It is how you can sit freezing at the night stage, wrapped in your blanket, and manage to feel warm as you sit in the midst of thousands of lesbians. It is country-western dancing, gliding and turning together as one organism. It is standing in a drumming circle, losing yourself in the rhythm, becoming part of the energy.

Attending four years of Womyn's Music Festivals brought more healing concerning body image for me than years of self-help books, diets, therapy, exercise, and support groups. For the first time, I was allowed to see real womyn's bodies and to realize that mine wasn't as hideous and funny-looking as I'd imagined. I got to see my own body, since previously I'd spent all my time covering it, hiding it, controlling it. It had never really occurred to me that I could enjoy my body because I'd been too worried about what it looked like: how to stand and walk so my thighs didn't touch, how to sit so my legs didn't look fat, keeping my head up so my double chin didn't show, what exercises to repeat to get rid of my round butt and to obtain a concave abdomen. But I could walk around the land during Festival totally naked and it was *no big deal!* The intense freedom of that act was overwhelming—and addicting! I went from being too self-conscious to even wear a tank top to driving around Santa Cruz topless, where it is legal, upon my return from Festival. I would go read at the duck pond topless, hang out with my housemates topless, even play smash ball on the field topless.

Even at Festival, where unconditional acceptance is the underlying norm, talk is still sex- and appearance-oriented. Womyn check each other out on the dance floor and want to two-step with certain universally attractive dykes. MCs on the night stage make remarks about how hot a particular singer or performer is. And when you meet someone new, the first thing your friends say to you is "Oh, she's cute!" Attractiveness is still our primary critique, and our standards, though divergent from those expected of straight womyn, can be applied just as vigorously.

For me, my struggle with my body has always been intricately tied to my coming out. I grew up as a tomboy, always playing sports with the guys to the point that I thought of myself as a boy. I had fun in my body and never had to worry about my appearance nor my eating habits since I was very active. However, when my body started changing, I was in a panic. I didn't want to face being a female and rejected my developing breasts. I wore baggy sweatshirts every day to school and as much boy-style clothes as my mom would allow and asked all my friends to call me Sam. The curtailment of freedom that my period brought seemed overwhelming. My body was no longer my friend and I despised it. I changed for P.E. class in the bathroom and was bitter that it was no longer socially acceptable for me to play sports with the boys. Girls were totally alien to me, and I came to resent everything they stood for. I held out until the eighth grade before ever wearing a bra. My mom dragged me kicking and screaming to the mall, and we sat in the May Company parking lot for two hours as I cried and cried before she finally convinced me to go in. I bitterly resigned myself to my fate and felt completely alienated from my body and from anyone else, male or female. I began a pattern of compulsive eating to counteract the despair and loneliness and helplessness I felt and soon began to see myself as fat.

I graduated from junior high in 1980, as we headed into the diet and fitness decade—and that's exactly where my life headed for the next five years. I would be up at 6:00 a.m. swimming and fill my day with jogging, bike riding, tennis against the wall, basketball drills, running up and down the stairs and conclude with several hundred sit-ups and leg lifts every night. And all this was with minimal nourishment—mainly grapes and Wheat Thins! I had lots of energy because, you see, I'd fallen deeply in love for the first time. I couldn't eat for thinking about Paula, and all I cared about was being with her and thinking about her. We never became lovers, but while we were best friends, nothing could bring me down. When things fell apart between us, I was devastated. In my depression and jealous rage, food became my only friend and I gained nearly forty pounds in three months. My clothes no longer fit so I had to borrow my mom's jeans for school because I couldn't get into mine. Humiliated and ashamed, I could no longer eat around people. I felt people would look at me and think I didn't deserve to eat so I developed the habit of eating alone, staying up late into the night compulsively and desperately grabbing cookies, chips, and ice cream to fill up my empty heart, to counter the loneliness of not knowing who I was or how to make myself happy. I would wake up each morning with a food hangover, feeling totally out of control—a never-ending cycle. I'd have to face my family feeling weak, defensive, and ashamed. I completed high school enjoying sporadic moments of victory in the diet and aerobics routine (with great thanks to Richard Simmons, my makeshift friend on the TV) but without ever resolving the struggle concerning my body and my sexuality.

Away at college, it was terrifying to have to eat in the cafeteria in front of my friends. I was already embarrassed, and they would make matters worse by monitoring my food intake and not offering me cookies they were enjoying, saying, "I thought you were dieting." Home on vacation breaks, my mom would corner me and lecture "it's not good for your asthma or your heart to be so heavy" (after, she would send me care packages of snacks every week). I was involved with a Christian fellowship at the time, which reinforced my suspicion that your body was something evil and weak that needed to be mastered, and I became devout about fasting. It felt so wonderful to be in control, empty and clean at last, and I became afraid to eat, afraid to put anything into my system to offset the purification, afraid to let myself eat because the first bite may never end. I fought hard to control my food intake and my feelings, which were leaning dangerously toward womyn.

During my first relationship with a womon (my second year of college), I came to bed each night in sweats, a long-sleeved flannel shirt, and bra (nobody ever told me you were supposed to take it off when you went to bed). I was still totally ashamed of my body and alienated from myself as a womon. Anita was taking a feminism class at the time and tried to convince me to go, but an entire class about womyn seemed excruciatingly boring and foreign. When, one day in bed, she demanded that I look at my own vagina and then look closely at hers, I was absolutely horrified and frightened. Our relationship quickly succumbed to the pressure and guilt of living a double life within the Christian fellowship.

Meeting Carrie, another womon in the Christian fellowship, started me on the road to freedom from contempt for my womon's body. Her unconditional love settled me down, and I found strength in our growing relationship. Carrie also had body issues so we hesitantly, and often defensively, began to first talk about our feelings. This was the only time I had ever admitted to anyone my pain and shame and weakness. Over time I found I could even eat freely in front of her! Somehow, not having to hide what I ate, not regulating my food nor my exercise, I began to lose weight! It was only by refusing to diet and to participate in that up-and-down lifestyle any longer that my body size and my body image began to find any stability. I could begin to work on accepting my body as it was, instead of constantly trying to change, finding strength in knowing this was a revolutionary political act, not just a personal excuse for my own weakness. When I was asked to leave the Christian fellowship, I began to try to accept all of me, no longer making lists of my great faults and sins to work on and no longer praying to have control over my love for womyn.

Ultimately, however, it proved easier to accept myself as a dyke (somewhere between a man and a womon, in my mind) than as a womon. When Carrie and I left the Christian fellowship, we were alone. I was directed to a campus support group. As I began to meet other lesbians, I found myself attracted to the most androgynous of them. Sharon, with her short, straight, brown hair, boyish features, and thin physique was the ideal dyke in my mind. She was everything that I wanted to be and wasn't. I lifted weights constantly and dissected every inch of my body, looking with utter contempt and revulsion at every ounce of fat, every curve of my womon's body, and worked with any means possible to erase anything soft, any trace of weakness or roundness.

As I began to notice other dykes as attractive, I began to wonder if I was attractive. With the exception of my weight, which really bothered me, I had always prided myself on taking little care of my appearance—my style being no style—and that I was above all that superficial garbage. But coming out was similar to returning to junior high because for the first time I really wanted to be attractive and I really cared about my appearance. I cut my hair very short so I'd look and feel like a dyke; I worried if my clothes matched (before a match was if my T-shirt was consistent with my political views); I asked how to style my hair with gel. I felt totally inept and self-conscious, but sexy, too, for the first time. I began to make some peace with my body through dancing, where I could experience again some of that fun of being in a body after being shut down for so long.

I was trying to embrace my womonly body, to be able to see that roundness as attractive for myself and others. I thought that finding freedom from any beauty standard took the kind of courage and honesty which many queers have had to acquire in coming out, in having to face so much in being honest with ourselves. If we've already been stigmatized by "mainstream" society, hopefully we would be quicker to perceive and resist society's other limiting rules, or to avoid imposing our own. The socialization was still strong, however. My ideal dyke remained that androgynous, angular womon with a sexy attitude, and from what I observed at Festival, many others were moved by the same features. There's a sexual energy that comes from that body type, I think—the feeling that she is without a doubt a dyke and could be nothing else.

During this time, I played on a softball team. I was the only lesbian on the team, which can be a strange and lonely experience. A friend came and watched one of our games and told me afterward "you totally looked like a dyke," and I was so relieved! Apparently on this team, because I had short hair, no makeup, and carried myself like a dyke, it was obvious, but you never quite know sometimes what kind of image you're projecting to people. Especially in Santa Cruz, it can be hard to tell the dykes. Anyone looking like a "traditional" womon in a dress and heels is usually a male drag queen! So a womon in a loose dress and Birkenstocks with no makeup could be a dyke or she could be a deadhead. A womon in Levi's and a T-shirt, carrying a backpack, could be a dyke or could just be a student. I had a male therapist tell me once that of course everyone thought I was a homosexual because I was wearing the "lesbian uniform": jeans and a flannel shirt. This always amused me because even as a kid, I had a strict code of dress that I always adhered to, and it turns out that these standards are what many people associate with lesbians.

As a twenty-six-year-old, white, middle-class, self-identified soft butch (no leather, body piercing, or severe hair and definite soft personality), my personal style at the time, and what I found attractive about other dykes, was the athletic, outdoorsy look. Short, straight (or slightly wavey) hair (and was it ever difficult to get a good haircut in any kind of mainstream place. They always wanted to make it look girlish, and I ended up with a layered Dorothy Hamill style!) and a simple look—Levi's, shorts, or sweats; Festival or Gay Pride T-shirts or muscle shirts; no bra; flannel shirts or sweatshirts (any athletic attire); white athletic socks over hairy legs. Baseball caps made a good accessory. I was never interested in any earrings (though butches were wearing them), fingernails, or fingernail polish and, of course, never any dresses, skirts, sweaters, blouses, nylons, sandals, or pumps. I never carried a purse—only a wallet in the back pocket and a backpack slung over one shoulder. I never wore a nightgown—either sweats, men's pajamas, or nothing to bed. I never devoted much time to appearance; I shopped at Miller's Outpost, the Gap, or Outdoor World, if at all. Finally, the shoes were the most crucial: sneakers or boots (hiking, black, or cowboy) from the men's department. Even if there was a totally hot dyke out on the dance floor in tight jeans and a Levi's jacket, if she was wearing dorky shoes, it just ruined it for me.

Obviously, these unspoken and insidious rules about attractiveness show that the queer community is not immune to insensitivity and discrimination based on physical appearance. It would be impossible to live in a culture so obsessed with the physical, where we are taught to hate our own bodies, without bringing some of these values into our own culture. At twenty-six, it was difficult to be able to look at someone else with tenderness and compassion when I could not even accept my own humanity.

Now, at twenty-nine, the circumstances of my life have completely changed. As I think back to that time, I am embarrassed to remember feeling that way. Now, I am coming into myself, growing stronger every day, finally waking up from a long sleep. I feel alive and confident and happy. Yet this morning, I awoke for the fifth morning in a row hating my body, despising the flesh accumulating between my legs and around my waist, feeling as if I'll never stop growing. Even my underwear felt tight today, and I find myself wearing the same jeans I wore yesterday, as they are the only pair I feel comfortable in these days. So there is no magic cure, no fairy tale ending. There are only very human struggles, the ups and downs of a real life.

I now consider myself a hearty mid-westerner. I moved to Minneapolis in September to begin graduate school, and it felt like coming home. Here you can smile at people on the bus, talk with total strangers, and be on the dorky side without being subjected to that California "attitude." And people seem much more realistic about, and comfortable with, their bodies. I've been here for eight months and no one has publicly proclaimed nor privately confided to me a hatred for their bodies. This relaxed atmosphere is most remarkable in the lesbian bar scene, where there is an amazing diversity of body sizes and types out on the dance floor at any one time. This down-to-earth attitude has helped to free me of a lot of my shame and self-contempt.

Going to graduate school has helped to build my confidence as well. Deciding to go ahead with my studies was a major announcement that I was finally taking myself seriously, finally doing something just for me. It has been a struggle, feeling as if I don't have much to give back to others because I have all I can handle. It is hard not to feel selfish, but I am learning to value myself. I am learning to have needs, to be able to voice them, to be able to let people care for me, and I am refusing the shame that seems to come so easily and naturally. I moved to Minnesota alone, without Carrie, my partner of now nine years, and finally embraced myself as nonmonogamous. She and I are still exploring how to love and support each other in nontraditional ways.

I still seem to persist in believing that my quality of life is dependent upon my body size. When I'm not eating and feeling thin, I feel cute, confident, and energetic. When food issues are staring me in the face, I feel weak, ashamed, and unlovable. My life feels out of control and I feel as if I'm the only one, that no one else could possibly be that obsessed. I walk around subdued, unable even to stand up and look people in the eye.

I feel apologetic, lucky that people would bother themselves to love me, and not believing them even when they tell me they do. It is so painful and isolating.

But I'm learning that food and my body is not the problem. About a year and a half ago, I was perusing the local feminist paper and saw an advertisement for a therapist. It listed some food and body issues and concluded with "find out what you're really hungry for." We explored my compulsive eating and body hatred as valuable information for me about myself and what was happening in my emotional life. I'm learning, when those struggles come up, to remind myself I need extra tenderness and compassion during those times, not blaming and self-contempt. We discovered the understandable reasons why I turned to food as an escape, as an emotional comfort, and instead of being harsh with myself, I learned new tools to take care of myself. I found a wonderful inner calm in my body through the practice of yoga. I felt powerful from the inside out and learned to be attuned to my body with great inner clarity and precision, perceiving even subtle nuances where once I had felt totally numb. I am determined, in seeking to find freedom from these struggles, not to attempt to change or control my behavior. I, instead, intend to accumulate so many other good ways of taking care of myself that I no longer will need "food" in my repertoire.

My standards of attractiveness have changed considerably. That androgynous, angular womon holds little appeal for me any longer. Both of my present lovers are round womyn, and I think they're gorgeous. I don't follow after womyn with sexy attitudes anymore, or any attitude. I just want people in my life who are real and who allow me to be real. I have given up having endless infatuations with people, falling in love with their potential, trying to figure out what makes them tick, and what they may want from me. I have given up trying to be attractive. I just want to be myself, as unpretentious as possible. I don't care what people look like in their jeans or what shoes they wear. I just want good womyn around me, womyn who value themselves, womyn who are comfortable with their bodies and their sexuality, womyn who value me for who I am—exactly who I am, not who they want me to be. Most of all, I want people in my life who are comfortable with their feelings, who allow me to have mine, and who are open to talking about anything. I am turning away from my own fear and shame, opening myself to this life, cultivating in myself and in my relationships that which is life-affirming.

PART 5:
COMING OUT, LEAVING BEHIND

Coming Out

Darcy Wakefield

In junior high you knew you were different
so you read *Seventeen, Young Miss*
wore Bonnie Bell makeup even though it itched your face
had a boyfriend even though he tried to rape you.

Nothing worked because in high school you were still different
so you ate lunch with your girlfriends
said *I'm so fat*
sipped Tab
nibbled on rice cakes
secretly popped Dexitrims
exercised a lot
dated boys
slept with a boy
dreamed of walking through the Auburn Mall
holding your best friend Carla's hand.

At seventeen you met a lesbian
at eighteen you went to college
met more of them there
none of them were skinny
none of them wore makeup
so the first time you slept with a girl you ran from her
took up running and dating boys
slept with one, too.

Junior year of college you transferred to a women's college
cut your hair so people would know you were a lesbian
fell in love with a girl
worried when she overate
worried when she gained weight
worried you'd get fat
exercised when she left you.

Two years after college you hate rice cakes
don't date boys
don't weigh 118
your family isn't planning your wedding
your hair is shoulder-length
and everyone knows
you're a dyke.

Power, Beauty, and Dykes

Silva Tenenbein

I could smell her perfume and that meant she was sitting too close to me. She was heterosexual. I was uncomfortable with the assumed intimacy. I fidgeted on her sofa while she adjusted her guitar. Then she sang me a love song—a love song about her and me, about us being together. I was astonished (and flattered). I had never thought of her in a sexual context. I don't sexualize my relationships with straight women. It just doesn't occur to me.

I told her all these things. I told her that I had never wanted to be her lover. "You're not interested in me?" she asked. "Really? Good. That means my feelings are authentic. I was concerned that I was only reflecting something back."

That brave woman wasn't reflecting anything back because there was nothing to reflect. I really had no sexual interest in her.

I've been a dyke for my whole adult life, and I've never been attracted to women. This is not a riddle or some kind of semantic manipulation of words. I'm attracted to other dykes. There's a difference. If "woman" is a social construct, then lesbians aren't women. While this is a popular sentiment, it is by no means an official—or the only—lesbian position on the matter. In the early 1970s, the Radicalesbians produced a manifesto called the Clitpapers which warned that straight women are dangerous because they look like women. What these statements have in common is that they both claim an important difference between (heterosexual) women and lesbians.

The difference between lesbian and woman is not biological. It is social. Women around the world are defined by their social function, which is the service of men. The details of women's service to men vary by class and race, but many features are constants. Women perform personal services—the work of maids, butlers, cooks, personal secretaries, or, in other words, of wives. They offer ego services: encouragement, support, praise, and attention. They provide sexual services: fucking and sucking, and bearing his children, but also very much including "being nice," looking good, "being attractive for him."[1]

We're all familiar with the notion of looking attractive for a man. It makes an instant picture in each of our minds. The particulars of that picture may vary, depending on what country we're in, or what ethnicity we are, or what colour our skin is, but there are common themes. With cultural variations, an attractive heterosexual woman is the proverbial long-stemmed rose: she has long thin legs, and what's above (and between) them is delicate, vulnerable, and accessible.

We know what that looks like, and we know that women are "supposed to" look like that. Women are supposed to be attractive to men. When a woman is attractive, she becomes an object. What happens to those objects when they attract men? They get fucked. So attractive, for a heterosexual woman, means fuckable.

When I was a teenager, I used to hang out with a teenage boy who would, in my presence, look at a woman and say, "Not *great* looking, but fuckable." One time he looked at a woman with a round belly and said, "That would be flat when she's on her back. She's still fuckable."

We've all heard some variation on this theme. Fuckable—the bottom line of the heterosexual aesthetic. What does it mean to look fuckable? It means available, compliant, willing, or small, thin, flexible, and without anything that gets in the way, such as an attitude, or an opinion, or pubic hair, or big thighs, or an overriding preoccupation with a thesis, or a job, or a child. Men like women to look available, and women are supposed to enjoy looking available. Do you need evidence of this? Turn on the television. Go to a movie. Open a magazine.

So, we know what heterosexual men who are tuned into popular culture apparently enjoy, and we know that many heterosexual womens' aesthetics have been colonized by men. We know that mainstream heterosexual women largely accept these values promoted by that matrix of capitalism and patriarchy which we call the marketplace. Women want to look like the marketplace image because they believe that men want that, and they have learned to like whatever men like. So heterosexual women strive to look fuckable.

The primary component of fuckability in the straight world is thinness. In the marketplace, it's more important to be thin than to prevent nuclear war. (Remember that magazine survey of 33,000 women, in which 75 percent of the respondents, given three wishes, gave losing weight a greater priority than preventing a nuclear holocaust?) What this means is that after the flash, if a woman were not vaporized, and if her corpse were found, and if all the flesh were not burned away, then whoever finds the body will know that during her lifetime that woman was not fat and, therefore, was likely fuckable. As a considered set of priorities, this seems somewhat ludicrous, even if I do understand the need which many of us have to feel that something is within our control.

It's an interesting notion that being unnaturally thin gives women a feeling of control. What are they controlling? Their choices? Their appetites? Their accessibility? If a woman's body is primarily expected to be a small, firm container for her cunt, then it becomes the woman's responsibility to keep the container small and firm. If she does that, she will likely be perceived as a good girl who has her priorities straight. If she lets the container get large and soft, that is, if she gets fat, she will likely be perceived as ugly, lazy, stupid, greedy, belligerent, selfish, and pathologically out of control—and possibly as a dyke. She will be less sexually accessible, both physically because her genitals are less easily available and psychologically because she has demonstrated that being fuckable by a man is not her first priority.

One time when I was out for a walk, a man passing me on the street said, "I like your hair, babe." I ignored him. He backed up, running, until he was directly in front of me. "I *said* I like your hair." Looking him in the eye, I said, "I really don't care what you like." He was shocked. The idea that not every woman on the street cared about his opinion of them had simply never occurred to him. It's common knowledge that women care about that stuff. Just look at the contortions they go through to appear a certain way.

We learn in contemporary gender studies that male and female humans are essentially different from each other. One of the differences that we focus on in popular culture is that men's aesthetic is more visual and women's is more tactile. We don't really know if this difference is innate with the sex of the person or if it is a result of gender socialization. We also don't know the cause. But we base a lot of our commercial culture on the belief that men are attracted by what they see. Fuckable women in swimsuits can boost the sales of chain saws. What attracts women?

What attracts lesbians? Lesbians don't exist in commercial culture. How can we know what lesbians are attracted to? With no public role models to measure against (excepting kd lang) how can we know when a lesbian is attractive? What does it mean when a lesbian is attractive? Does that also mean fuckable? By whom? Men set the standards for heterosexual women. Who sets the standards for lesbians? Who gets to decide? Imagine driving around as I used to do with my teenage friend. Imagine looking at dykes on the street. Would you be able to know who's fuckable, as he did? Would you be able to judge just by looking?

What does it mean to you to find a lesbian attractive? Does it mean you enjoy looking at her? Does it mean you'd want to be with her? Talk with her? Touch her? Does it mean you'd like to fuck her; or that you'd want her to fuck you? What's the relationship between aesthetic pleasure and sexual pleasure for dykes? Does beauty depend on that person's physical appearance? When you think someone is beautiful, are you stimulated sexually? Are you stimulated other ways? What do dykes like? Are we tuned to men's aesthetic too, or have we developed values that are independent of the marketplace? Do the marketplace images turn us on? Are you sexually stimulated by those panty hose commercial photos of long, thin (men's) legs? Would you like to look at pictures of round, ripply legs? Would you be inclined to buy the product they'd be promoting?

Having an aesthetic that is independent of the mainstream is not an easy thing to accomplish. Having desires that are not automatically triggered by the images of popular culture is even more difficult. It's not easy to allow yourself to be turned on by what's not "normal."

Our North American, mainstream society insists on uniformity. Differences are not politically neutral. Differences aren't seen as choices. They're seen as sins, crimes, diseases, and mistakes.[2] And the different might not be welcome. Finding ourselves ostracized—even by people whose values we don't share—is hard on our self-images. If we're ostracized because of our sexual desires, we may find it hard to admit those desires publicly. So, for instance, a big, soft, fat dyke might be fun to stay home with and luscious to fuck, but it's hard to take her to the bar because an average-looking person doing so has a hard time experiencing a small fraction of the kind of social opprobrium that's in the fat dyke's face every minute of her public life.

Is there an exclusively lesbian aesthetic? Sure. Lots of them. It's unlikely that we would have just one. Many dykes are in the women's community by default because we're too belligerent to be anywhere else. We're unlikely candidates to have only one aesthetic. We certainly don't have that kind of consensus among us about anything else.

Becoming a lesbian is a conversion of attention. Attention is a kind of passion. Passion is beautiful. Passion is not just sexual passion. Passion grows out of our belligerence. Passion grows out of how much we care. We care enough to be different, to stand out, and to risk the dozens of daily societal rejections that we experience because we care enough about ourselves to be who we really are.

In our increasingly ersatz world, real passion is rare. The beauty it creates isn't recognized sometimes because of that rarity. A lot of us did not discover passion until we discovered each other. We're at our most passionate when we're together, when we recognize ourselves in each other's power. It took some of us quite a while to recognize that beauty. Many of us are still working on publicly acknowledging it.

We're told by mainstream culture that women have power in their physical beauty, and that being beautiful makes a woman powerful. We're told, we're shown, and we're taught, that a beautiful woman can experience her power by walking into a room and knowing that men get erections just from looking at her.

Think about that as a scenario. Who really has the power in that room? That fuckable woman? She isn't even safe there. Does being afraid mar her beauty? Or, in that aesthetic, is fear attractive too? Fear isn't attractive in my aesthetic. I don't go in for public displays of vulnerability. I want to reverse the beauty-is-power equation. I propose that for dykes it's not beauty which makes us powerful but power makes us beautiful. Seeing one another's power also turns us on. The relationship between aesthetic and sexual pleasure might be hard to articulate, but we sure can feel it.

I like power. I like it in myself, and I like it in other lesbians. I think that belligerence is really attractive. So, think about a new scenario. Instead of that "beautiful" woman, a dyke walks into that room. She's not heterosexually "attractive." She radiates power. She's a walking threat to the phallocracy, and it shows. Every man in the room goes limp. Think about having the kind of presence that makes men go limp. Does it feel good? Or is it missing the point because here you are reading a lesbian article, and some dyke is talking about dicks. Again.

I don't want to talk about lesbians as having negative value. I don't want to talk about being what men don't like. By definition, dykes don't care what men like. This is not an antiaesthetic we're developing as some sort of protest; it's a different and nonparallel universe.

Dykes are constantly, daily, in words and actions told by the rest of the world that we are ugly. We're ugly to straight people because they keep mistaking us for women who have our wires crossed. They don't see *us*. In the mainstream perspective, dyke identity doesn't exist. It's a one-way mirror in which they perceive us as a severely distorted image of themselves. So they don't see dykes. They see ugly women—women who are not fuckable because we're not *attractive* to men. Wrong context.

So what's attractive in a dyke? Gender ambiguity? Isn't that a hatred of femininity? No, it's a rejection of the mandates of gender socialization. Gender ambiguity is attractive because it disrupts the established balance of power. Gender ambiguity *is* attractive but not to the exclusion of anything else. Roles can be attractive too because they advertise a willingness to play. We mustn't underestimate the value of being able to play and have fun. Gender can be a sex toy, changeable with different partners, with differ-

ent moods, and with different times of day. If you live in a society that
wishes you didn't exist, anything you do to make yourself happy disrupts
that society's attempt to eradicate you.

Some dykes take up a lot of psychological space. They look like power.
They look as if they can take charge of another dyke's pleasure and be
responsible for it. They look as if they can take charge sexually. Sometimes we call this being butch. Some dykes have such a strong grasp on
their power that they can afford to give it away, and they can advertise that.
Sometimes we call this being femme. The sexual possibilities and the
number of options that are available to us are, in themselves, attractive,
don't you think?

The things that make lesbians attractive, truly attractive, are not about
physical appearance. Whatever and whoever we are, as long as it's what
we *really* are, is beautiful. What makes us beautiful is our passion, our
strength, and our courage to choose to be "other."

We aren't beautiful *in spite* of making the kind of choices in our lives
that mean that our appearances don't meet marketplace standards; we're
beautiful *because* of it. Our adamant refusal to be deflected from what we
want is beautiful, and it makes us beautiful. Think about us in all our
diversity of knowledge and talents and skills and desires and ages and
sizes and colours and shapes. Think about what we learn from each other.
Think about our belligerence, our strength, our potential collective capacity for civil disobedience, and the beautiful possibilities that grow out of
our passions. That's beautiful.

NOTES

1. Marilyn Frye. (1983). *The Politics of Reality.* Trumansburg, NY: The Cross-
ing Press, pp. 9-10. Sarah Hoagland. (1988). *Lesbian Ethics.* Palo Alto, CA: The
Institute of Lesbian Studies, pp. 61-63. Monique Wittig. (1980). "The Straight
Mind." *Feminist Issues,* 1(1), Summer 1980:110.

2. Pat Califia. (1988). *Macho Sluts.* Los Angeles, CA: Alyson Publications, p. 9.

My Big Fat Body

Anna Snoute

When I was fifteen, I was starving myself. My sister did it to make herself more beautiful; I did it to control myself and my desires. I remember being fascinated with female characters on nighttime soaps, carefully studying the images in glossy women's magazines, and closely observing other women at work and at school. Were they fatter than me? By how much? And where? Where did their bodies curve that mine didn't? What did they look like? What would it be like to *be* them? Who were they? And why was I so interested in their bodies?

As an adult, I can interpret my adolescent obsession with other women's bodies as a way to manage my emerging feelings of attraction to women. At the time, though, it just seemed a mess. My body seemed wrong; my body was the problem. If I just stayed an adolescent, everything would be OK. Somehow, staying a (thin) adolescent seemed linked to being male: if I stayed narrow and small-busted, could I get male power? Could I get women? I think at the time my "smart kid" stigmatization (the primary social identity I had) seemed linked to a neuter or male identity. Becoming a woman seemed both a challenge to that fairly comfortable, if difficult, role *and* a whole set of problems on its own.

Eventually my body won. I left home, gained weight, grew breasts and hips. And started dating men. They liked me: I was in general scared of them but liked the attention and affection. I acted stupid to keep my first-ever boyfriend around; I was happy that he didn't hate me for being smart, and he seemed to really like my body, or at least parts of it. We eventually broke up, and during this process he told me that for the majority of our multiple-year relationship he had thought of me as "too fat" to be attractive. He felt it was important to tell me that he'd recently gotten past his (still-present?) feelings about my body and seemed surprised that I wasn't flattered by this. I surprised myself by for once thinking of a clever line fast enough to deliver it; he really *was* less intelligent than most of the people I found attractive, and I probably *wasn't* going to get past it.

Once I relaxed into my adult body, I stopped having a weight-obsessed reason to look at other women. I had to accept that maybe I just wanted to look at them because their curves, my curves, our curves were compelling in and of themselves. Realizing I found other women's bodies attractive did wonders for my own body acceptance: once I'd felt overpowering lust for a woman with a body much like my own, it was hard to think of myself as "unacceptably" or "unattractively" heavy again. Unacceptable to who? And who did I imagine to be judging my attractiveness?

Ten years after adolescence, I've probably doubled in weight. Surprisingly, I don't *feel* twice as heavy. When I was fifteen, I hated my 100-pound body, felt I was disgustingly fat, and had enough presence of mind (or had read enough about eating/body image disorders) to realize that something was terribly wrong with this state of affairs. Now, I can accept and enjoy my 200-pound body, and it's comforting to know that my mental image and my physical body have at least a passing similarity to one another.

Having a bisexual identity that maps well onto my attractions to people of many genders is also comforting. I still have days where I need to work on actually being in my body, and some of my attractions to other people can still startle or confuse me. Being a queer-identified, fat woman, though, is a much better location for me to be working from than my former position as a semicloseted, anorexic adolescent.

My Mother's Journals

Jo Schneiderman

I probably should not have read the scrapbooks. But there they were in my parents' summer house, sitting on the shelf of the closet my mother had told me to use when my lover and I stayed at the house off-season. "1980," "1981," "1982." When I first took them down, I expected them to contain photos and other memorabilia from my parents' summers on the lake. The first page of "1980" displayed a program from the Acadia Players Production of *Blithe Spirit.* So, I figured the scrapbooks would provide an evening's entertainment, offer me younger images of my parents, and show me snapshots of people I vaguely remembered.

But as I turned pages, I realized my mother had saved much more than summer mementos. She had saved letters from me and from my sisters, journal entries, doodles on napkins, correspondence from an elderly artist to whom my grandmother had once lent money, even copies of letters she herself had sent.

In 1980, when I came out, I also started recovering from six years of bulimia. The more I read the scrapbook from that year, the more I felt as if I were invading my mother's privacy, but I couldn't put it down. There, amid thank-you notes from my aunt and photos of my father and the Kelmenson kids pretending to push over a boulder, was my mother's documented response to the changes in my life.

I knew my mother had not been happy to learn that her eldest daughter was a dyke. But I was shocked to read how much more strongly she reacted to the fact that I had also gained thirty pounds.

For the six years before I came out, I was first anorectic, then bulimic. My body size varied from gaunt to, as a women's magazine once described it, fashionably thin. For those six years, while I destroyed my gums and gastrointestinal system, my waking hours were almost entirely taken up with binging and purging.

My mother hadn't known that I was bulimic, but she certainly knew I was anorectic. She had often expressed concern to me about how little I ate. Regardless, after I came out, began the slow process of recovery from food abuse, and began to gain weight, my mother freaked out.

More than her fear that all lesbians have abusive relationships, more than her distress that therefore I was going to be hurt once again by a "bad" relationship, more than her self-blame that I had turned my back on hetero-sexuality, my mother was beside herself about my increasing weight.

Over and over in her journal entries she wrote that I was becoming obese. Soon, she wrote, I would no longer be able to cross my legs. I was, she surmised, using my fat to hide from the world and to make myself unattractive to men so I could pursue my new lifestyle. In other entries she imagined my weight gain to be a weapon directed at her and that I was punishing her by making myself ugly. And she berated herself for her own fat.

As I read these journals, I began to understand on a primal level my own reactions to food and fat and why I had numbed my feelings by becoming addicted to binging and purging rather than to drugs or alcohol. (I had already figured out why I numbed my feelings in the first place.)

The journals also offered a vivid example of the ways in which fat-hating messages are passed on from mother to daughter in American culture. As I read my mothers words, I remembered ways she and I used to bond. I remembered dieting together, making sotto voce cracks about other women's bodies at the beach, drinking Tab at picnics while the boys and men drank Coke, sharing a secret "illegal" snack and admonishing ourselves with promises of future deprivation.

Despite our obsession with dieting and weight, neither my mother nor I have ever been fat. Knowing this, her reactions both to my weight gain and to her own body size upset me so much that I often had to hold my arm over the journal to protect the pages from being damaged by my tears. It tore me apart to read about her hatred of her body, her interpretation of my weight gain as a punishment directed at her for being fat, and her consistent coupling of the words "fat" and "ugly" when she described both of us. Her reactions illuminated a whole set of lies that my mother had learned and that she then taught to me.

Since reading the scrapbooks, I've thought a lot about those lies. I've thought about what it means to women who really are fat when women who are not fat descend into a self-hating frenzy about their bodies. I've thought about how women's clothing stores carry a very limited selection of clothing larger than size twelve. I've thought about what my mother really looked like—how as a child I used to look through the mottled glass doors of the shower stall and think she was so beautiful, that she looked like an oil painting.

I wish my mother could have rejoiced that I had finally conquered an all-encompassing, self-abusive, behavior pattern in which I had been ensnared for six years. I wish she could have seen my weight gain for what it was—a sign of increasing physical and mental health. But most of all, I wish she hadn't hated her lovely body so much, and I wish she hadn't passed that hatred on to me.

Be, Being, Becoming

Michelle Bancroft

> Without that interplay between spirit and body,
> the spirit is always trapped . . .[1]
>
> —Marion Woodman

> From a distance, it looks like peace . . .[2]
>
> —Margaret Atwood

ONCE UPON A TIME . . . I beg my parents for a pottery wheel. Decade-old hands tremble as I open the box, sighing with relief, my mind engulfed in burning anticipation. I play. The clay, cool and pliable, comes alive in my innocent hands. The wheel spins a mystery, eternity. I am in a state of awed content as I watch the gray mass whirl. My imagination explodes as I dream of the bowls, vases, shapes, and beings I long to create. I place my hands on the gray. The smooth coolness has now become resistance. I do not understand. I cannot seem to make this work. I cry, but I dare not ask for help. I try again. When I place my hands on the clay, the wheel stops, and I greet fiery frustration. I try again, and again, and again—I no longer dream of bowls, vases, shapes, and beings. I only know I have failed.

ONCE UPON A TIME . . . I am walking to class; I am now in college. I look at other women's bodies. The hatred of my own sadistically spills over onto theirs. I rage in this bloody flood. She has shorts on. I study her thighs—envious, enraged. How dare she be so perfect when I never will be. Her chiseled thighs are a blatant reminder of my own intolerable inadequacy. Oh, how I have longed to possess that perfection she so blatantly displays. I loathe her. Yet, I am lesbian. Aren't I? I am supposed to *love* women. Don't I?

ONCE UPON A TIME . . . I am eight years old. The cool smoothness of my mother's bedspread calms my wandering, curious hands. Naked feet swinging rhythmically to my internal beat as I watch. I am being privy to a secret ritual. I was fascinated, wondering if I was to ever grow to be like her. It seemed unlikely; all I could do was admire her. She was beautiful. She would brush her hair as she gazed into the mirror. I can still smell her perfume and the scent of her lipstick. I remember the confusion I had when she would be angry at herself. Sometimes she would be angry and would throw down her brush in disgust. She hated her body, and the confusion it generated in me at that early age was profound. She was so perfect in my eyes, my mother. What did it mean that her stomach was slightly rounded, her thighs soft, her breasts full? How was this supposed to be "bad"? I would tell her how beautiful she was, but she would delete me from her world as if I didn't know a thing—my perception grotesquely false. "You don't understand, Michelle. . . . " Sometimes she would cry; it was a cry of anguish and despair. Other times her rage would ricochet around the room and off the mirror she stared into incessantly, terrifying me with its intensity. Sometimes her eyes would meet mine; I would bow my head sensing the seething desperation smudged with fear so reminiscent of the caged leopard I saw at the zoo last summer. I stood there transfixed as I watched the leopard pace back and forth, back and forth. I cried then, too. I think, "It doesn't have to be this way, Mommy. . . . " All I am left with now is the pain and the rage *I* now carry at a culture that makes body hatred a prerequisite for being a woman.

ONCE UPON A TIME . . . I sit in a therapist's office. I did not choose this. My lover made the appointment out of desperation; she says out of love. I have done my reading. I know my condition—bulimic, obsessive dieter, depressed, repressed, food addict, compulsive exerciser, distorted body image, etc., etc. Ha. The labels loom heavy in the air, cynically I laugh at them. I laugh at the man in front of me. He will give me a magic potion if I am good, if I smile, if I say what he wants to hear. I am good; I smile; I say what he wants to hear; I am given the magic potion. The potion is a powder—just mix it with water three times a day. I greedily drink this liquid "nourishment." I am told my problems will diminish in direct proportion to my diminishing body. I believe. I turned twenty-two that year.

ONCE UPON A TIME . . . I make love; the gift of my virginity was placed in a woman's hands. She thought I was straight, told me to slow down, to wait. But, I told her, I always knew I was crooked. She laughed. I don't look like her or any of the other lesbians I know. I am femme—heels and all. I soon find out that being femme, being me, is accompanied by an insidious air of suspicion that blows only around the isolated and the closeted. Maybe I imagine it, maybe not. Sadly, I feel different, even among difference.

ONCE UPON A TIME . . . I am fourteen. Above all else, I want, need, desire to be "OK." I look into the mirror and see how not "OK" I am. I HATE YOU, I scream. Everything is wrong, so very, very wrong. My hair is the wrong color, my body the wrong size as it dares to curve, my grades are too high, my clothes too loose, my friends too uptight. I am going to control this. Within a year, my hair is right, I starve my body to rid it of its disgusting curves—the genesis of severe eating disorders. I make my grades acceptably low, and my new friends are carbon copies of the new "me." I am rising like a phoenix above the weak, carried by the swirling gusts of judgment. Just look at how much weight Karen has gained over the summer; we sadistically laugh as we watch her walk. She is now the joke, not I. I revel in my supposed power because I am now "OK."

ONCE UPON A TIME . . . I tell my lover not to touch me. She cannot understand. Can't she see she would be touching a monster, a hideous mass of writhing flesh, dense in its vulgar intent? She is psychotic to not recognize this, to not be afraid and disgusted as I am. Her touch reminds me I have a body. Her touch awakens the dead zone I have created, a reprieve to the numbness. I cannot tolerate this. I scream.

ONCE UPON A TIME . . . I am twelve; my mother sits on the edge of my bed as she zips my eighth-grade graduation dress. I have just successfully completed my first round with Weight Watchers and lost thirty-five pounds. My parents, being middle-class to a fault, paid me for every pound of my unacceptable flesh that I lost and bought me a new wardrobe when my transformation into acceptability was complete. After my dress is in place, I turn to my mother and ask her, very seriously, "How could you love me before?" I am so ashamed and humiliated for looking the way I had. I start to cry and tell her how sorry I was for being so fat and what an embarrassment that I must have been. She looks shocked and says she and my father love me just the same whatever size I am—but I know the truth. I don't believe her. My parents' behavior spoke MUCH louder than my mother's words.

ONCE UPON A TIME . . . I am nineteen and decide to change. I want to become a "true" lesbian. I quit wearing makeup, save for some discreetly placed mascara. I quit wearing the clothes I love in favor of clothes they love. In loose jeans and tennis shoes, I strive to become as desexualized as possible. Visions of acceptance dance through my head, yet I am portraying an image of something/someone I am not. At that time, I didn't understand that the outer appearance does not a lesbian make. At that time, I didn't understand that the image we portray is to be a reflection of our inner self, of our inner worth. At that time, my neediness of acceptance was far greater than any need for true self-expression. At that time, I didn't care.

ONCE UPON A TIME . . . I am immersed in a dream that is a terrifying reality. I am being pursued, chased, hunted—their prey of the day, every day. I open my mouth to scream, but no sound emits. I try again, pushing the air out of my lungs, opening my mouth wider—still no sound, just panic, anger, outrage. This is the voice that has been kept silenced. This is the voice that is finding its voice within myself.

ONCE UPON A TIME . . . I hit bottom. My being convulses as I am raped by the word *HELP*. Sterile-steel cold assaults my face as it lays on the bathroom floor. I can no longer tolerate this insanity. I know I have performed my little self-destructive ritual for the last time. *HELP* . . . No longer will I wretch my anger, pain, frustration, humiliation, shame, terror, and inadequacy out of my body and into the toilet to hopefully be all flushed away. *HELP* . . . Because after the flush, everything used to be, once again, neat and tidy, neat and clean, neat and perfect. *HELP* . . . I can no longer reach the handle to flush it. I lay open, drowning in the mess that is myself as the illusion of this desperate "solution" has finally unveiled itself. *HELP* . . . I am left with Me.

ONCE UPON A TIME . . . I am in yet another therapist's office. Now I am here by *my* choice. I am surrounded by woman's art, woman's touch—soft hues of lavender, peach, and cream soothe the torrent of thought that I have come here to understand. She and I sit and stare at each other. I am not sure where to begin, yet her manner relaxes me. All I want to do is hide between the folds of her softly draping skirt forever and cry.

ONCE UPON A TIME . . . I believed I was a bad lesbian or maybe even not a lesbian at all. Perhaps I was some anomaly that had yet to be explained. So deep was my alienation, my misinformation. I read that very few, if any, lesbians suffered from eating disorders and body image disturbances. I knew that I bought into the patriarchal standards of what beauty meant, so much so that I wreaked havoc upon my body and soul to conform to those images. How could any self-respecting lesbian do that? How could I tell my lesbian friends that the only thing I really cared about was fitting into a size five? That I would give anything—even the love of the woman in my life—for that state?

ONCE UPON A TIME . . . I am on my knees; I pray. I am crying the cry of desperation, of fear, of help. I pray for release. I am praying? To whom, to what, I do not know. My eyes are shrouded in purple intensity as vague images appear. My hand is being held, and I am now sitting under a tree, my body resting on stone steps. I look up and see Her—long, blond hair cascading around a diffuse yet earthly body. I cry even harder as she holds me. I have missed Her so. I do not question how this can be since I was not even aware of her presence before this very moment. I am slowly becoming aware of a thankfulness, a gratefulness, that is so dense in its content I can barely contain it. Thank you, my God, my beautiful Goddess, thank you.

ONCE UPON A TIME . . . I am peeling the onion of spiritual awakening, the primal embrace of self. Layer after layer, I remove. Each time I go a little deeper, shedding my defenses. I peel, despite the tears and the wrenching pain I feel as the fumes assault my senses. I am forging a path to my core, the center, to the promise of living a life free of encasement. Previously shed layers insidiously lay in waiting on the floor, biding their time until I sweep them away permanently. Occasionally, I trip over them, sometimes bending over to pick one of them up, just one more time. I am grabbing at more protection for my core, my soul as woman. Those layers act as a blanket that clouds my clarity and muffles my true voice when speaking the truth seems to involve too much risk. I am comforted for a short while, just enough to allow me to continue this never-ending shedding, this process of rebirth.

> *My body Snake,*
> *Inside I shed the veil of disguise.*
> *As I shed, I give birth*
> > *To new realms.*
> *Shadows of truth dancing in my psyche*
> *Shadows moving into form, demanding to be heard*
> > *Once lying dormant, now*
> *Coiled for, ready for, vying for*
> > *Release.*

ONCE UPON A TIME . . . I realize. My body is their commodity to be bought, sold, used, legislated, molded, tucked, toned, reshaped, and diminished for *their* gratification. I see I am less of a woman if I am more than their prescribed image. And what do I get out of all that? I am simply given their nodding acceptance. I think I forgot to say, thank you, sirs.

THE NEXT MOVE

Take it,
    Rape it,
        Legislate it.
My body, your pawn.
Take it, not me
For I am two different women
I am body,
    I am soul.
I have learned to split
By your command, for my protection
I will not tell you when I am fused
But you will know, for I will say no
I will say no, I SAY NO.

ONCE UPON A TIME . . . I began to question that state of being
"OK"—that state I began to strive so desperately for when I was fourteen.
How "OK" was it, really? This being "OK" meant conforming to a
cultural size and shape. It was to know and accept women's supposed
inferiority and to contribute to it. It was the devaluing of the female ethos.
It was hating my mother for her weakness. It was the lack of positive
female role models. In my high school world, the only role models were
models. The message is, and was, to be a "real" woman was to be as
unreal as the women I saw in the magazines and worshipped. Their entire
being consisted of a picture, an image of one-dimensionality. I never questioned what was inside those images of perfection. I just questioned when
my body would be similar to theirs and agonized that it may never be.

ONCE UPON A TIME . . . I am celebrating my year anniversary—one
year of no dieting, no starving, no binging, no purging. I sit across from
my therapist and cry. She and I have begun a journey together. She is my
guide, my anchor, my vessel of trust that allows me to navigate these
uncharted waters. Does she know the incredible comfort I feel in her
presence? I finally feel understood for her past mirrors mine. She is a
lesbian. She has faced the same issues I am dealing with now. Sometimes
we cry together, sometimes laugh together. We share common pain but
common healing as well. She put me in contact with other lesbians dealing
with body image and eating disorders. I have finally come to understand I
am not alone. She is my light, my beacon guiding me to the other side.

ONCE UPON A TIME . . . I came to understand how crucial it is for
women to be aware of how they view their own process of growth. View-

ing psychological illness is similar to staring into a many faceted, brightly colored prism. Move it slightly, and new colors are illuminated and shape shifting occurs. This prism is our psyche. We must be extremely cautious how we label our fluctuations. Labels carry with them the ability to color how we interpret. We can use labels to hide behind, to buy into, and to use as another layer of protection. They become our justification for retreating from our inherent female power. Do we label ourselves depressed, codependent, neurotic? Or do we view ourselves as experiencing our depths, journeying to find our true self? Do we view this process as depression or as rebirth? What is the truth? Which way will we choose to view our prism? There is only *one* acceptable answer: woman *must* choose for *herself.*

ONCE UPON A TIME . . . I would scream at my body in hatred, fear, shame, disgust, and loathing. These messages kept me chained and bound— the shackles of misogyny at its most intimate, most terrifying level. I was given lessons on conformity, on hatred, on how to destroy not only my body but my very spirit, and I was a devout student. Are these the woman's mysteries of today? I pray. Oh, how I pray. I pray they are not. And even if they are, I pray we have the strength to rise above, for love of ourselves, for love of other women.

ONCE UPON A TIME . . . I was standing on a scale transfixed by those numbers ruling my existence. Those three numbers told me if I was acceptable or not, if I was a desirable woman or not, if I had any value or not, if I should be ashamed or not. Those numbers on the scale became the jury and executioner that categorized and labeled me—the imposition of judgment. Those numbers on the scale kept me fighting my body instead of the institutions that oppress(ed) me. I see that by getting on that scale without consciousness, I participated in alienating myself from my body yet once again. I took the scale to the garage and found a hammer.

DIE-IT

The sacrificial victim is our Self
We are trained to
Kill it, maim it, ultimately glorify in destroying it
We place body on block to be
    Slaughtered
Under the guise of Health
We do what we are told
They reinforce it

We allow it, participate in it, are seduced by it
believe it
When will we question it, rage at it, reject it
Instead of dying from it?
We die a death of spirit in our attempts to
cast their coveted reflection.

ONCE UPON A TIME . . . I make the decision to leave my lover, my long-term partner, my best friend. I could not sleep after I talked with her, desperately trying to understand this incredible change that we both knew must take place. I look in the mirror and watch as my image blurs, changes, retreats. I find myself clawing to get a glimpse of the woman in the mirror. Her image illusive, escaping me, yet she IS me. So, who am I now? Who am I without my lover's identity? Could I actually have one of my very own? Is it truly possible that I have not known the woman who was living intimately within my own twenty-five-year-old body? Who had taken her place, when, how, why? So many questions—the answers of which I am simply not ready for. The reflection gazes back, and I am caught by that fleeting image of a woman reclaiming her own inner power.

ONCE UPON A TIME . . . I undress as the bath water steams. Slowly, I am immersed into its heat. I rub my hands over my body, beginning with my feet and sensuously working my way up. My eyes are closed, focused on the sensation. A cartoon I saw at a woman's bookstore comes to mind—a picture of a woman carrying a sign that read, "If it weren't for your legs, your genitals would be in the dirt!" I begin to giggle. I realize at that moment my appreciation for this being called my body. As my hands caress it, I beg forgiveness. Cleansing tears heal compounded wounds. Amazingly, I realize I reside here in this profound miracle. A woman's sensuous body is my home. I profess my love and let go of the need to control this thing I called It, which I now call Me.

LOVE IS MENDING THE SPLIT

Needle in hand
I stitch
The thread that weaves
My Soul.
Poised, I insert needle
flesh closing in upon flesh.
Pain, blood sacrifice yet becoming
complete, coming together.
Mending the split

the slow merging,
The E-merging
of Body
of Mind.
Another stitch,
trembling of hand,
Stitches that heal, my hand that guides
The thread, the needle
The slow process of
Completion.
Another stitch
drops of blood
Full moon,
full Body,
In communion with Her
Another stitch
Complete.

ONCE UPON A TIME . . . I am listening to the radio. I hear a woman—a therapist, healer, teacher—discuss her program regarding weight loss without dieting and the healing of eating disorders, etc. What could this possibly mean? I listen intently wondering if this could be the piece of my healing puzzle that I have been missing. I have been in therapy for three years now. I know diets don't work. I know binging and purging solves nothing. I know further healing rests on my ability to love and accept myself. Yet, I have felt so stuck. I call and make an appointment with the woman on the radio.

ONCE UPON A TIME . . . I, in deep meditation, am gazing upon the collective pool of woman's psyche. I am looking into that mirrored reflection—glass that is the water of our souls. We touch the surface by questioning it; we create ripples causing temporary distortion. We are engulfed in disequilibrium. We learn, therefore, to gaze but not to touch. We fear the *distortion* when we touch our surface; we no longer see ourselves clearly. Who are we? The reflection we see is the image we have been taught to cultivate. It is the role we play to please, the acceptable definition of woman. It is being 36-24-36. It is our worth based on numbers. How do we measure up? We feel it is "right"; it is "beautiful." Smooth as glass, is this false perfection. Yet, if we can tolerate the distortion our questioning causes, we will see that our depths are illuminated with the essence of our true selves.

ONCE UPON A TIME . . . I understand. I have been trained not to listen to my inner self. I "forgot" who I was in favor of the "ideal" image

I was supposed to portray. I was encouraged to maintain and develop a relationship with *one* person—that *one* person, called Others. I was simply a machine—cold, hardened steel geared to meet everyone else's needs. I was taught to not only forget who I was but to *devalue* my true identity in favor of those prescribed roles and behaviors that benefited only others. Becoming absorbed in their external world, I left my internal world to atrophy. Oh, how I believed . . .

ONCE UPON A TIME . . . I am saying good-bye to my class, to my group, to courageous friends. This program, founded by Nancy Bonus (the woman on the radio), has altered the course of my life. This is in no way an exaggeration. She constructed this program based upon her own healing process. It is a holistic approach—the integration of mind, body, and spirit. I have learned what the body/mind connection is all about and how to apply that profound knowledge to myself step by step. It has been a process of loving myself. Class topics ranged from cognitive distortions and therapy to how to put food in its proper perspective—as substinance rather than a numinous enemy that ruled my life. I came in contact with the underlying issues that fueled my food/weight obsession and learned tools to effectively deal with those. I may not be a size five, but I am free.

ONCE UPON A TIME . . . I ponder my pottery wheel of long ago. I was missing an essential, primal ingredient—water. I was trying to create beauty in an arid wasteland. Water—the essential feminine element, representative of the Goddess herself, metaphor for love and creativity, possesses the power to turn aridity into fertility. Water. Goddess. Creation. Myself. I have no longer failed.

ONCE UPON A TIME . . . I honor my courage. I see that embracing my identity as a lesbian has become an integral part of and a sort of stepping stone on the path of discovering who I REALLY am. So many times I have taken for granted my ability and resolve to do this. I might not have chosen to be a lesbian, but I did choose whether I was going to express my lesbianism or not. A life of hiding, a life of constricting, strangling denial, was not for me. I can take pride in my courage to express my emotional and sexual nature that flies in the face of traditional societal mores. If I can do that, I know I can do just about anything.

ONCE UPON A TIME . . . I know that we hide our true power as woman. I am now coming to an understanding of what true female power is all about. A woman who is acting from her true self is a woman empowered—*is* power. It is *not* about control—external or otherwise. It is about creating our lives so that they mirror what is inside. Power is that feeling of being centered, of "acting from our gut." We become empowered when we know ourselves well enough—void of all the roles—to act upon our *own* truth, whatever that may be. Our power comes only by knowing ourselves at the most intimate level. I know when I connect with my higher self, I find the woman I was always meant to be. The is the essence of female power and of female identity, regardless of sexual preference.

ONCE UPON A TIME . . . I am looking at pictures of myself—me alone, me with others, me as a child, me with friends, me with lovers, me, just me. I tremble. Images are fragments of frozen time suspending further thought. Who is this woman, that woman? Here she is celebrating her eighteenth birthday. She smiles. Yet I know the other side of her—the terrifying side behind that smile, that false persona—the addicted, the ravaged. Yet, she smiles. Look at her here; she is eight and it's the first day of school, and she is clutching her lunchbox, her face straining into a pseudocomplacency—distanced, alienated, alone. Wow, here she is at fourteen in a family portrait, and still she smiles the smile she has learned so well to cultivate. In this one, she is much older; she must be twenty-five. She and her lover are on vacation celebrating their fifth anniversary. She is smiling the same smile, yet there are flickers of realness, sparks captured in print, fleeting but present. Ah, here she is at twenty-seven and miraculously, she is smiling a new smile. It is the smile of healing, of joy, of thankfulness, of being. Do I dare imagine this awesome possibility? I cry, my body contracting as I baptize myself with tears. I am released from the ice in true peace of spirit. I take the picture to the mirror, place it next to my face, and smile. In amazement I say to myself, "Yep, that's Me . . . "

NOTES

1. Atwood, Margaret. *Tha Handmaid's Tale.* New York: Ballantine Books, 1985, p. 17.
2. Woodman, Marion. *Addiction to Perfection: The Still Unravished Bride.* Toronto, Canada: Inner City Books, p. 16.

Boogeywoman

Amy Edgington

You would think the hump
and hairy chin would be enough,
but the scorn of others
has marked my face

like acid.
Warts thrive among my moles;
rheumatism gnarls my limbs.
Each time I lift my downcast

eyes, somebody cries foul.
I am the one who eats bad girls,
the one who drinks their monthly blood.
You were warned, someday I'd come for *you,*

if you didn't mend your wicked ways.
Stay home at night. Obey the rules.
And whatever else you do,
don't go into the woods alone,

lest you mistake me for a twisted oak
and fall asleep between my knees,
after circling for hours.
At dawn you'd wake in my arms, enspelled,

and suddenly find me
lovely.

SECTION B:
ONE, BOTH, NEITHER

PART 6:
CROSSING THE DIVIDE

The Razor's Edge:
Walking the Fine Line of the Self

Julie Waters

I sit in my tub, meticulously shaving my legs. I think about why this action is so important to me. I carefully stroke the razor across my right leg, and with each stroke, I shed a little skin as well as hair. Each stroke wipes away a portion of an old identity and an old way of life. Every slice of the razor is, in a sense, a new sort of freedom for me.

When I was a child, I was brought up to be male and frequently criticized for any aspect I presented that wasn't decidedly such. I've always had very "feminine" eyelashes, and at puberty, I found that while I started growing "male" patterns of hair, I also developed some very "feminine" breasts which got me sent to multiple doctors appointments and stigmatized beyond belief. I remember sitting in an office with a pediatrician who was talking to my parents about what he called my "enlargements," and explaining to them how I didn't need to be worried about anything, and about how I was "not turning into a girl." He then turned to me and explained that this "problem" would be more likely to go away if I "were to take care of that weight problem." I was taught that these were things to be ashamed of and to hide whenever possible.

I've known I was transsexual for many years, although I found it very difficult to face on a direct level. I've spent most of my life being what many people might call "obese" or "overweight," and this was a major issue for me. I grew up in the 1970s. Images of women popular at the time included Twiggy, Brooke Shields, Carol Burnett, and Jane Fonda. While it was acceptable to have a Dom DeLuise or Jackie Gleason from time to time, we didn't have any Roseannes or Kathy Najimys. Women of real size were practically invisible in the popular media.

So, when I looked in the mirror, I could not see a girl, even though I knew she was inside there somewhere. This wasn't because I wasn't feminine. In fact, I was very much so. It was because I wasn't thin.

Being both Italian and Jewish, I had a natural level of hairiness that developed when I hit puberty. From the age of thirteen, I had a mustache. From the age of seventeen, I grew a thick beard. These were masks. They were faces to hide behind. I developed an affinity for baggy clothes— wearing those, I wouldn't have to look at my body. Even now, when I think about those times I find myself feeling depressed, as though a severe weight is sitting on my shoulders and I just can't pull myself out from under it.

I'm sure that much of this despair is a result of many issues from my childhood. I grew up in inner-city Detroit and was one of the whitest people in my neighborhood. I felt consistently singled-out for this. During high school, I moved to a small town in upper Michigan. I found myself to be one of the darkest people within a 180 mile radius and then found myself singled out for that feature as well.

I do not know what to make of all this. I've been mistaken for at least twenty different races. When I lived in Detroit, I was taken for Lebanese by the people who owned the local grocery store, and they thought I was "one of their own." When I was in upper Michigan, I was consistently thought to be an exchange student from a wide variety of places including Mexico, Spain, anywhere in Latin America, South America, or Southern Europe. A friend of mine, someone I'd known for close to a year, once turned to me and asked, "How did you learn to speak English so well?" Being an awkward teen, I didn't have the composure necessary to come up with the appropriate response of "as opposed to what?" So I just sat there flabbergasted at the question.

The first time I went to college, it was in a very small, private, liberal arts school in the middle of Wisconsin. The school felt like a glass bubble within a glass bubble. The town was the birthplace of the archconservative Senator Joseph McCarthy, and while I was in school there, it became the national headquarters for the even more paranoid and rabid John Birch Society. Given the vast, for lack of a better term, "whiteness" of this town, I was routinely taken for a Greek exchange student. I had short hair and a thick beard back then, and I wore almost exclusively clothes that were gray, white, and dark blue.

It was sometime during that time when I first started to consciously acknowledge my own transsexualism. However, I still had what I would consider a "weight problem," and my own image of women was still restricted to people who were thin and pretty. So I found it impossible to imagine myself in that role.

The summer after my first year in college was the last summer I ever spent living in upper Michigan. I found myself spending most days hanging out with a group of friends and doing whatever possible to detach myself from my own body. Many of my friends smoked pot regularly, and though I had spent most of my childhood avoiding any sort of drugs, this time I decided I wanted to try it. However, I never found myself getting high or even experiencing the slightest buzz. I tried several times a week for most of the summer and not once did I get myself anywhere except stuck in my own miserable body.

The times I wasn't hanging out with friends, I found myself sitting in my room either writing or meditating. The meditation, oddly enough, succeeded where the drugs had failed. I found myself achieving states of transcendence that I still carry with me. I don't know whether this is fantasy or real. I make no metaphysical claims about the nature of the universe. All I know is that in the course of that summer I learned to experience things which by our physical laws simply do not exist. I would sit for hours and watch the walls melt in my room or drift my way into other lives and gain new experiences. Not having been interested in direct sexual activity in years, I found myself suddenly fantasizing about friends of all genders.

While I loved my friends dearly, I knew many of them to be openly homophobic. There was no one with whom I could share these feelings. I experienced a certain joy at understanding them, but once again, I was taught very quickly that they were things which I was expected to be ashamed of. The world around me was once again yelling at me to slice off those parts of myself that they didn't accept.

Despite this, I was sad to say good-bye to these people when the summer ended. They had been closer family to me than the people who had raised me from birth, and they had actually cared about me and shown caring for me that few others had.

When I went back to school, I found that several friends of mine were in their own process of coming out of the closet, and others were reacting positively to this. I realized that at school I had the opportunity to do the same. At first slowly, and then later quite vocally, I found myself coming out of at least one of my shells. Although I wasn't sexually active at the time, being one of the only out-of-the-closet bisexuals on campus in a small Wisconsin town was probably not the most safe thing to do. However, I found myself more willing to enjoy myself because at least one part of my life was no longer closed to my own mind. It was that year when I started to wear clothes of a wider variety of colors and started to let my hair grow longer.

Life continued to make itself more complicated around me. I developed relationships with people, but my own fears about my body kept me from being willing to go much deeper than close physical contact and intense kissing. While I enjoyed this physical contact, for some reason, anything close to real "sex" felt as if it was off-limits and totally inappropriate for me. Fantasizing about it didn't bother me, but the idea of actually engaging in it was relatively horrifying.

I eventually dropped out of school for a variety of reasons. I was going through some rather bizarre and intense personal problems. My own depression about myself was pulling me deeper inside itself and I fell victim to panic attacks and serious despair. It was that summer when I moved to Rhode Island, my current home, and found myself actually starting to deal with my own internal issues.

I'm not sure exactly what happened at the end of that summer, but many of my emotional problems reached a sort of a climax. I was living in a cooperative house, and I found myself one night unable to sleep in my room. I left my room and lay down on the couch in the kitchen and tried to sleep for four hours to no avail. I got up about four in the morning and looked at the mess around me (such messes are rather typical for cooperative houses) and decided to focus all my pent-up rage and anxiety on that mess. I found myself throwing silverware into the sink from across the room. I dealt with every item in the kitchen with some of the most brutal raw force I'd ever experienced. I rinsed every dish and loaded them into the dishwasher and cleaned everything I could for the next hour. And then, there was only one item left—a knife, sitting in the middle of the table.

I grabbed that knife with my right hand, and without thinking, without knowing, I found myself simply pressing it against my left wrist. Time froze. I stood there for what must have been seconds but felt like hours and simply wondered if I was going to live or die. I did not feel as though it were my choice whether or not to push the blade deep enough to cause wounds. It was just a force that was there on top of me.

Strangely enough, I had woken no one with my clatter of dishes and clanking of silverware. The room was suddenly silent, and the silence filled my head. Then I remembered. I remembered how when I was a child there was so much pain that I would deliberately inflict wounds upon myself to focus the pain on something external instead of the internal screams.

I remembered the fear, the intimidation, and the threats I had faced as a child for not "fitting in." I remembered the weapons with which beatings were threatened. I remembered the taunting about my size and my shape. I remembered the fear that came every time I had to shower with other children because I knew they'd see that I had breasts. I remembered how terrified that made me. I remembered when a group of kids tried to toss me into a locker and leave me there.

The knife dropped.

I fell to my knees and tried to scream, but no sound came out of my voice. Within days of that, I found myself taking a bus out to the Lincoln Mall to see some bargain matinee or another. While I was at the mall, I bought shaving cream and disposable razors.

The next shower I took, I shaved my entire beard and mustache for the first time in my life. Nobody in the cooperative house recognized me when I came down to dinner. The very next shower I took, I shaved my arms and chest and then shortly thereafter my legs.

I didn't know what was making me do this, but I just wanted to see what it felt like. It was shortly after that when I realized that Halloween was coming up. I finally started to acknowledge my desire to "crossdress" and talked to some friends about it. One of them had known several transsexuals before, and we had a long talk about weight and image. She told me that a lot of male-to-female transsexuals who are heavy-set actually are better off because the hormones tend to distribute body fat quite well.

It was at that moment when I realized I might actually be able to do something real with the ideas that were inside of me. Somewhere in there, I also began to realize that I was not a thin person and did not need to be a thin person and that being a woman did not equate with thinness. Finally, I was beginning to feel as if there was something positive and enriching I could do for myself.

Then I encountered a setback. I went out with a friend to search local stores for "women's" clothes that would fit me. I found very few. Skirts were almost entirely too small to fit around my waist, and blouses were a complete nightmare. I finally found a few wrap-around skirts that, alone, were too small but when combined worked fine.

For years, as a male, I had tried to think of myself as a "feminist guy." I had worked on being politically correct and understanding sexism and not buying into it. But never in my life had I ever really experienced what women go through on a day-to-day basis. The simple process of trying to shop for clothes that did not fit me (and finding that every item in the discount rack was sizes "s" and "xs") was the first time I'd ever experienced direct misogyny firsthand. Until that point, I don't think I'd ever really had a clue.

With a little work, I solved some of my clothing problems (many of them by seeking out clothing of a specifically non-American style), and I bought makeup and gel for my hair. I found myself approaching the upcoming Halloween celebrations with a lot of zeal.

I made myself up in what I could call nothing but "ultra-femme" mode, and I had a great deal of fun with the whole experience. I think I shocked a lot of my friends at first, but most of them got used to it. I think what confused them the most was that I was no longer ashamed of the fact that I had natural breasts, something they expected from someone they perceived as "a man."

This was four and a half years ago. My own perspectives have changed considerably in the meantime. My hair is now longer than it's ever been, and I've experienced amusement in changing its colors whenever I feel like doing so. I delight in feeling the long, curly lanks slip down along my back. In the summertime, I wear little but shorts and tank tops and am interpreted as female relatively often. In the winter, I wear sweatpants and sweatshirts and very frequently hear the phrase, "sir . . . uhm . . . miss . . . uhm . . . ," followed by a look of confusion. What I've learned is that my own body is just an obstacle to overcome. For whatever reason, there is some drive inside me to make myself as female as is medically possible. While I am saddened that I will never be able to bear a child, I know that medically I can have my genitalia altered and my physiology altered to match what I know inside is right for me.

None of this is any longer a deterrent from my living the sort of life I want to live. I know that eventually, thanks to electrolysis, my body will no longer grow hair where I don't want it to and that through hormones, I can have control over my own contours and body shape and can choose to do what I want with myself. The only true barrier to any of this is frightfully mundane—finding sufficient income to deal with it.

In the meantime, I've found that my own gender identity is no longer a function of how my body appears or what it looks like as much as it is my own attitude. In this process, I've learned a lesson that I think many women need to learn (and, fortunately, quite a few have): being a woman does not mean being thin nor does it mean fitting into specific social standards. It does not mean wearing high heels or makeup, and it does not mean shaving one's legs, though these are things I may do at times.

What being a woman means to me now is being myself, the best that I can be, in my own way and my own style. And finally, after all these years, I feel I am hiding behind nothing and living my own life in my own way. I have felt cuts and burns and blades and knives in my life. I have been scarred and hurt on occasions too numerous to list. It is possible now that what I am experiencing is a changing of hands. These knives that have been used against me are no longer weapons. I now hold the blades and rather than using them to escape I am using them to embrace. Rather than tools of violence these knives are now tools of sculpture.

My Life As an Erroneous Sonogram

Marcelle Cook-Daniels
Loree Cook-Daniels

L: Start by describing how you think of yourself at this point.

M: The phrase I've decided upon is psychological hermaphrodite. It's the only thing that sounds like something that's both and neither at the same time.

L: If the hermaphrodite is psychological, then what is the physical?

M: The physical is definitely more male. Where the female aspect comes in is emotionally and in my approach to life and the world. My communication style is a little of each of what is traditionally thought of as male and female. As far as relationships go, love is more important to me than sex. But, those things are just sort of broad-stroke stereotypes of male and female.

L: When I asked you about the physical, you said that it was definitely more male. But if someone were to see you now with your clothes off, they would have no question that your body is female. How do you resolve that? Or are you already living in the future?

M: I think I've *always* lived in the future; that's part of the whole dysphoria. Let's use an analogy. Say you think of yourself as being 5'10". In your mind or in your house, which represents your mind, all your chairs and furniture are scaled, proportioned, so that in relation to it, you seem 5'10". So in your own little, safe corner, you are a 5'10" person. Then you go out in the world, and the world is scaled the way it usually is, and you realize that you're 4'10", to the world, anyway. But the way you've always thought of yourself is as 5'10". What I'm doing is something akin to having my legs surgically lengthened so that, when I go outside, people will see on the outside the person I always see inside.

L: So you have been seeing yourself as male all along?

M: Basically. It's kind of schizophrenic. My problem is with mirrors and photographs and other people. I see myself a certain way, and then I'm faced with a "real" image that is very different from how I am in my mind. I feel I look a certain way in the world, am a certain way, and then reality intrudes.

L: Can you give a specific example of when reality intrudes?

M: Say I'm going out somewhere, and I'm picking out clothes. I'm thinking of a particular way I want to look, a particular image I want to convey. I take all this time and dress, and then when I check in the mirror to see how everything looks, there are these breasts that are staring back at me, and the shirt doesn't hang the way I thought it was going to. In my mind's eye, when I'm seeing myself, I don't see those problems. For instance, I like suspenders. But I'll put those on, and they bow out to the side because there are these huge impediments in the way. So I end up not wearing suspenders.

L: That's an example of when your reality crashes into the mirror. What happens with people?

M: There's the pronoun problem. I'm going out, and I think I'm really doing a good job of passing as a man, and I'll get "ma'am"ed. Sometimes it's nothing that obvious—going into a building, the guy in front of me stops to open the door for me.

L: You're assuming he's doing that because you're female?

M: Oh, yeah! It's not even an assumption sometimes. Sometimes I will open the door and try to wave the man on in front of me and he'll stop and say, "But that's not the way I was brought up!"

L: Is it the breasts that make you female?

M: Given my other physical characteristics, it's the breasts that are the deciding factor when someone's waffling on the fence, trying to decide which way to take me. They are the most noticeable, prominent feature I have, next to the freckles. Men can have freckles, but men usually don't have breasts, and if they do, they're not 42 triple Ds. I try to minimize them by the kind of clothes I wear, but they're a focal point. I've talked to men before. They're not making eye contact; they're looking at my chest.

L: Aside from the breasts, you think you present to the world as fairly androgynous?

M: I think I present to the world as fairly masculine. My body language, voice, facial expressions—I think all of those are sort of masculinizing cues. As Kate Bornstein said in *Gender Outlaw*, people are going to err on the side of male unless there's some feminizing cue, and so far, the breasts have been the feminizing cue.[1] I've been in situations where I've worn pretty, feminine earrings but concealed the chest some, and I've still gotten "sir." Even dangly, pearl-type earrings are not enough to convince someone that I'm anything other than a man wearing dangly, pearl-type earrings.

L: Which came first for you, looking masculine or feeling masculine?

M: Feeling.

L: So the looking masculine you've cultivated.

M: Looking masculine, I think I've accentuated more—to counteract the physical presentation. It's also part of who I am. I was always a "tomboy." Even before I had breasts, I was always told I was acting more like a boy than a girl. I'm just much more aware of *working* at the appearance more, of having to think about it. I don't know what I would be like if I didn't have to overcompensate for the physical stuff. I don't know if it would be much different, or if it's just a part of who I am—the way I sit, the way I walk. The testosterone helps too with the voice, the 5 o'clock shadow, the hair on my arms. I even have a receding hairline now.

L: You started by describing yourself as a psychological hermaphrodite, but we've been talking "male" and "masculine." How do you reconcile those two? Or do you?

M: When I'm talking "male," I'm talking about physical presentation. I don't know about the rest of it; I haven't come to a decision about that. I just know that when I think of myself after surgery, I physically present as male, but what my identity will be and what I really will be—I don't know that it has any antecedent.

L: Even though other people have changed their gender identities, you feel like you are forging new ground? A pioneer?

M: I'm not changing my gender identity; my gender identity has been fairly constant. What I'm changing is my gender presentation. I also don't think of myself as a pioneer. I'm not a follower. I'm not a leader. I'm just doing what I have to do.

L: In *Stone Butch Blues*, Leslie Feinberg talked about the problems faced by people she defines as "he-shes"—people who confound other people's sense of the dichotomy between male gender and female gender.[2] First, would you say the "he-she" analogy fits you, and second, do you think you've had problems by not clearly fitting into "male" or "female"?

M: I've definitely had problems with fitting in. Take job interviews, for example. I refuse to wear a dress to a job interview because I'm not going to wear a dress on the job. I wear pantsuits. I have no doubt that I've gone in and people have thought, "Oooh!" and not been able to deal with me on that level. I'm too butch.

There have been problems with other professionals, doctors in particular. I've called my gynecologist's office and the staff has said, "I'm sorry, sir, this is a gynecologist's office." I've said, "I know; I'm a patient; trust me." In dealing with salespeople, often I'll walk up to the counter, and they'll say, "Yes sir, er, ma'am." Then they're all flustered and they can't deal with me. I just want to say, "Pick one; it doesn't matter," and move on to the transaction. Leslie's definition of "he-she" is the same as my psychological hermaphrodite. I'm not all one or the other. I can't say how I'm going to feel two years down the road, but right now I think I "bend" gender and probably always will. At the same time, whatever part of my identity governs my physical self, that part is predominately what would be considered "male."

L: How early were you perceived as a "he-she" or as not fully fitting into the category "female"?

M: Probably from very early. As I said, I was a pretty severe tomboy, very physical, very daring. I did lots of climbing, rough-and-tumble stuff. I liked being around girls better than I liked being around boys; I thought the boys were awfully boorish. I enjoyed being a "boy" among the girls; the girls were more willing to play "doctor" with one of their own than with a boy so I got a lot of mileage out of that, particularly since I had a romantic interest in girls. But I almost felt like an infiltrator with the girls. I felt as if I was . . . that I was a pretender, that I was there in disguise.

The problem came when I hit puberty. All of a sudden, inside of weeks, I started getting breasts, which were totally wrong, in my opinion. They got in the way, and they drew attention to me as a girl. People started saying, you're growing up, you've got to stop all these tomboyish activities. I was not about to stop. I didn't want to. Beyond that, I knew it just wasn't right. What was happening was just not me.

L: The physical changes?

M: Yeah. Up to that time, I was fine. Up until age eleven, I had a flat chest, and I was fine. I had to deal with the period and what that meant, but by itself, that wasn't bad. That was hidden so it wasn't a big deal. But the breasts were very noticeable, very out there, and very damaging to my self-image.

L: If you could have had smaller breasts, would you have had an easier time staying in the female gender? Or settling into it?

M: I think if I had had smaller breasts, I would've tried passing more often, earlier. I would've tried to pass altogether. I would have come to the same decision sooner or later. Smaller breasts would just have allowed me to pass more easily.

L: Let's talk about images of beauty. How does either the body that the world sees now or the body you see in your head relate to images of beauty or attractiveness both in the society at large and in the lesbian/ gay community? How does attractiveness figure into all this?

M: I don't think of myself as an attractive woman. I just don't think I do "woman" well. I'm definitely far outside the mainstream beauty image, but then that ideal is so narrow very few women fit in. I've tended to play up the lesbian butch image, but I don't know that I necessarily fit that, either. When I think of lesbian butch I think white. More specifically, I think somewhat tall or medium height, short hair, handsome features, Caucasian. I'm kind of pudgy, lumpy, and big-breasted.

The body I see in my head leans more toward the masculine attractiveness ideal—trim and fit and well-muscled. I already have a muscular body that can be developed even more on testosterone. But the gay male ideal or the straight ideal for men—I don't think I fit those, either. One, I'm too short. Two, I tend to think of those ideals as being white, also.

L: So the fact that you're perceived as black almost by definition means that you can't be seen as attractive as either a male or a female?

M: No. I wouldn't say not seen as attractive, but not the ideal, which, as I said, fits very few people in this society. I have no doubt that some people may find me attractive—I think more so as male than female— but those would be people who don't necessarily accept society's view of ideal beauty. Even as a black, I don't have classic features. My complexion is too uneven. It would be better if I was all chocolate-brown, or all tan, not the mix that I have with the freckles. Other than that, I don't think I'm totally unattractive. I tend to think of my appeal as being somewhat idiosyncratic.

L: Has being black had any effect on how you see gender?

M: Yes, I think it has. In the back of my mind I always knew that gender realignment would make me a black male in a society where black males are tolerated at best and hated and feared at worst. That bias is something I have to get away from myself. I haven't had a real high opinion of most black men. I think of exaggerated macho, fathering babies and abandoning them, that kind of thing. If anything, being black has stood in my way of accepting my maleness.

L: It would have been easier for you to have your gender feelings if you had been white—

M: Oh, definitely!

L: —because it would've been easier to imagine yourself as a white man than a black man?

M: Most definitely. Take the TV show Mod Squad. I didn't identify with Link so much as I did with Pete. If I had been white, it would have definitely been a lot easier to accept my masculinity. But I gave up on being "white" when I was a kid. I didn't want it anymore.

L: Given all that, when you're in that in-your-mind "house" we talked about, are you seeing yourself as a black male or a white male?

M: Actually, I see a male of indeterminate race. I see a mixture—brown-skinned, decidedly, but mixed.

L: But that's not necessarily how you define yourself out in the world, is it, brown-skinned and mixed?

M: I'm leaning more toward it. When I filled out a survey recently, they had a question about race. They had African American, European American, Asian American, Native American, and Other as choices. I put down "Other" and wrote in African American, European American, and Native American. Maybe that's what I have to do now to accept the male—somehow downplay the "black" part.

L: Because it's too scary to be a black man in this society?

M: Maybe. Or maybe because I'm challenging what is male and female and whether one has to be one or the other, and that's making me wonder about all the categories.

L: When we were talking about images of beauty, you talked about being pudgy. When we met, you were *not* pudgy. You'd lost a lot of weight and were working out. You were also taking testosterone and planning on surgery. Then you began putting on weight and got out of shape. In retrospect, those were the years in which I blocked you from going forward with the surgery. Do you think there is a connection between your weight gain and being "stuck" in being female?

M: There is *definitely* a connection. I stopped taking the hormones in 1986, and it was right after that time that I started porking out again. Looking back, I think I had an investment in my body before then. When I was around seventeen and decided that I definitely wanted surgery, I started to work out and lost weight. When I was eighteen or nineteen, I started taking the hormones. At that point I also started to develop other physical characteristics I wanted: body hair, deeper voice, more muscles. My body was starting to be shaped more and more the way I wanted it to be so I started to take more care of it and appreciate it more and like it more. After we got together and it became clear that I wasn't going to be able to go through with surgery, I stopped taking the hormones. I figured, "Why? Why bother anymore?" I started to lose that investment in my physical appearance again, and I just didn't care anymore. Now that surgery's planned, I've started to care more what I look like; I have a little more investment in my body. Unfortunately, it's a little harder now to get in shape than it was when I was seventeen!

L: One reason it may be a little harder now is because you've had a baby. Can you talk about what it was like, as someone who's dealing with gender issues, to try to get pregnant and then being pregnant?

M: Originally, I decided to carry the child because I thought that it would help me "be in my body," that it would help me "ground" myself in my female body. I thought the experience would make me accept the way I was more so that I wouldn't have to keep dealing with the gender stuff. It didn't turn out that way.

Getting pregnant was so goal-oriented; I don't know that I thought about it much. BEING pregnant felt almost as if there was some kind of parasitic creature in me. It didn't feel real, somehow. It just felt as if some strange thing was controlling my emotions and my body and making me eat when it wanted to. If I didn't eat enough, it took all my energy, and I didn't have any left. And the movement inside—it was very *un*grounding as opposed to grounding. I dissociated a lot from my body. I wasn't able to deal with the experience in a positive way. I was sick all the time, and tired, and in pain. I definitely think part of the problem was the idea of me being a pregnant woman. The more people paid attention to that, the more pissed off I was. I didn't want anybody at work to know until absolutely the last minute.

L: How did it feel when people reacted to you as a pregnant woman, either people on the street or people you knew?

M: I don't think many people on the street related to me as a pregnant woman because I didn't do "pregnant" stuff: I didn't dress pregnant; I didn't walk pregnant (as far as I can tell); I didn't act pregnant. At work, when it all came out, I had all these people walking around giving me unsolicited advice: [falsetto voice] "Oh, well, you've got to do this and you've got to do that and now you've got to breastfeed and this, that, and the other." All of a sudden everyone was in my business. People were telling me what I should and shouldn't do: I shouldn't be lifting that; I shouldn't be doing this. As a butch, I was functioning at a lower level and I couldn't do many things. I couldn't lift stuff, I couldn't reach for things, and I had no energy. So my whole butch self-image that I'd cultivated all this time got really out of whack. The care people were giving me, making sure they carried things for me, opened doors for me—it made me very angry.

L: You breastfed the baby for awhile. Given how much upset your breasts have caused you all your life, was breastfeeding a problem?

M: That was another dissociation. I didn't think of them as my breasts so much as the source of his food. They ceased to become, in lots of ways, a part of my body. It was just sort of his meal; that's the way I looked at it. I wouldn't bare my breasts in public in order to breast-feed, but I get uncomfortable when other women do that, too. I really did a good job of separating myself from what was happening.

L: The baby we were expecting based on sonograms was a girl, but you bore a boy. Given your gender issues, what did it mean to you immediately and then later to have a boy?

M: The first time I heard he was a boy, I was coming out of the anesthe-sia [from a C-section] and I refused to believe them. I think I asked them about four times: "What did you say it was again?" "A boy." I was like, "How did *that* happen?" So there was shock. But I was also just plain relieved that it was over and he was here, and in some ways, it didn't really matter that it was a boy.

There was a little bit of disappointment. I was struck, actually, by what I took as sort of a metaphor for my life. We thought our child was a girl, and prepared for a girl. We had a girl's name picked out and were all ready to receive this female, and it turned out to be a male! I thought about that as a metaphor for my life in that by all appearances—my life being the erroneous sonogram—I was a girl, but surprise!, I wasn't; I was a boy. Very early, within a few hours, I remember thinking, well, I wonder if this is a message—that this means I'm supposed to go through with it (gender realignment).

Later I started dealing with my disappointment that he wasn't a girl. I had to examine my feelings about males in general and my feelings about my being male, or my maleness. . . . I realized that I had to do some work to accept him being male, and that was the same work I needed to do to accept me. So in lots of ways, Kai's gender was another positive push.

L: What do you mean, you have "to do some work" to accept Kai's and your maleness?

M: I had to start identifying the problems I have with men in this society. How many of those problems stem from the way males are socialized, and how much is irrevocably "male"? I had to sort of broaden and loosen my thinking about what males were and females were, and what they are capable of. I had to start looking at more of the paths or, sometimes, the lack of paths, that we're given to pursue based on perceived physical limitations, gender, height, or color, or any other sort of arbitrary means of measuring people. In lots of ways, it's making me less rigid about why people are the way they are, and how much of that is intractable (biological), and how much of that is sociological (how much we buy into the system).

L: Given that, what do you think your transgender identity is going to mean for Kai? What are your hopes and fears about that?

M: I don't have a lot of fears. Hopes are that he won't be so rigid in his gender expectations, that he might be more capable of seeing people as people, and that he might be able to see degrees of maleness and femaleness and "otherness." Hopefully, he'll be able to see that being a male or being a man has very little to do with just the physical, that it's a whole package which has to be developed. Most people just go through life saying, "I am what I am." They don't have to think about what they are and what it means to be what they are. I would hope that, given my experience, he would be more self-aware, more self-examining about who he is and what he is and why he is what he is. I would hope that it would make him a much more conscious person in general and teach him not to take things at face value.

L: What are your hopes and fears about what will happen to *you* when your surgery is complete, your papers changed, and everyone accepts you as male?

M: I do fear I'll be perceived as "selling out." Regardless of what some people think, this is not about male privilege. That's something else that I had to fight in myself all along: am I doing this just because men supposedly have it better in this society? That's another realization I had to come to. No, I don't necessarily think men have it better. So my fear is that people will assign the wrong motives to what I have done and make certain assumptions about me based on those motives. They may, for instance, think that I think being a woman in this society is so awful that I couldn't do it, that I had to cop out. Although, they do that *now*—make assumptions about me based on my perceived gender, or my sexual orientation, or my color.

My hope is that I will be able to live openly as a transsexual or transgendered male, be up front about that and have people accept me for that and not try to make assumptions about who I am.

L: So what are your motives?

M: My motives are just to have my . . . to have things in sync. I don't know how else to put that. I don't believe that when I have the chest surgery there are going to be any really profound, immediate effects on my life. I'm not going to be suddenly richer, or handsome, or anything like that. I just feel I'll be more at peace with who I am and happier with the way I am. That's the whole point in going through all this. As for any long-term effects, changes—I'll just have to see as I go along. I can't really say what the future will hold. I just know it'll be better.

NOTES

1. Bornstein, Kate. (1994). *Gender Outlaw: On Men, Women, and the Rest of Us.* New York: Routledge.

2. Feinberg, Leslie. (1993). *Stone Butch Blues.* Ithaca, NY: Firebrand.

Holding My Breath Underwater

Michael Hernandez

As a child I knew that I was different but had no clue as to how or why. I just knew that I was. I assumed that I was a boy and acted as one. In the eyes of this child, there was no difference between the genders. It was unfathomable that there could be differences between boys and girls.

When the adults in my family told me that there were differences and that I was a girl because little boys had penises and testicles, I did not believe them. I did not know what a penis was nor did it matter to me. While my cousins could pee standing up and I could not, I just assumed that I had not mastered that technique. It was who I perceived myself to be not what others told me that I was. I knew that I was not exactly a boy, but then again, I was not exactly a girl either. I became genderless in my eyes, although my outward form of gender expression was always masculine. My mother and I had constant raging arguments from as young as age three about my having to wear a dress.

I played sports and rough-housed, hated the fact that I had long hair, and developed the habit of spitting from watching my cousins. My mother was mortified. Eventually, people told me that I was a "tomboy" and that I would grow out of this phase. After hearing that a couple of thousand times, I was conditioned into thinking that it must be true.

As I approached puberty, I was in for quite a shock. I eventually learned that I was female but also refused to give up being masculine as well. I continued to be genderless on the one hand and a hybrid of female and male on the other, although never feminine. Unbeknownst to me, not only were hybrids disallowed, but being latin, there was a more stringent gender code to be applied. I was expected to catch a husband, have kids, and spend the rest of my life sacrificing myself for my family (not likely). Women were and are still expected to look and act in a particular fashion. According to societal expectations and those of my culture, women are not supposed to be 6' tall, have broad shoulders, large hands, a booming voice, or facial hair. Society continues to demand petite, birdlike appearances and demure behavior, but I wanted everything that my culture and society said was not right for women. I wanted big muscles, facial hair, broad shoulders, to be taller than the 5′3″ that I grew to be, and more. I wanted freedom from domesticity, wearing dresses, marriage, childbirth, and the chains that I perceived the women of my family to be bearing. Housework and cooking be damned.

Puberty revealed that what I wanted could not be. My body had betrayed me, and my behavior would not be tolerated. I tried to conform and do the makeup, long hair, dress, panty hose thing. I even tried nail polish. I never quite mastered the art of walking in heels. Femme was something that I was not. The hopes and dreams of others that I was a princess were not to be. When the other girls in school were fantasizing about that knight in shining armor galloping toward them on the white horse, I secretly fantasized about being the knight. Despite these fantasies, I remained clueless about my sexual orientation. As I got older, I had a number of relationships with straight men. All of them were fine in the beginning, but then little by little they too wanted me to be more "feminine" or at the very least docile. As time passed they felt threatened, and the relationship inevitably ended as we both grew more and more frustrated just interacting on a basic level. I was forever doomed to relationship hell and just could not understand why.

The answer came much later when I learned that there were others like me. For some reason unknown to me, they had kept hidden. I had heard talk, all derogatory, about gay men, but the topic of lesbians had failed to even come up. I was clueless to the existence of lesbians until very late in my teens, but even then I denied it to myself. In my early twenties, something miraculous happened. Like a curtain being parted, it all came into view. I remembered having fallen in love at age five with a twenty-year-old woman named Diana who lived in the same apartment complex as my family. I had the crush to end all crushes and followed her around like a puppy dog. She was married, of course, and I spent time with her and her husband, Dave. Then there was Dawn, the girl in fourth grade with the brown curly tresses and the shoulders of a Pittsburgh Steelers lineman. Then—you get the picture. It turned out that all of the women that I had related to and identified with in high school were lesbians. I just didn't know about it at the time.

I tried to duck the responsibility of labeling myself by asking a friend who was a lesbian whether I too was one. She told me that only by sleeping with a woman would I truly know the answer to that question. I was not thrilled with what she told me, but it turned out to be the best advice that anyone has ever given me. I realized that I had to decide for myself who I was. No one else could define me but me. Subsequently, discovering that I was a dyke, I was off and running. At last, I had found my niche, my community. I embraced lesbianism as my salvation. It gave me the permission to break away from society's constructs and expectations regarding gender, body image, and behavior.

I altered my gender expression by looking and acting even butcher than before. This change in gender expression manifested in the way in which I dressed and acted: that I swaggered rather than swayed when I walked, how I talked, in what and who I projected myself to be. I could be as butch as I wanted and there was a place for me. For a time I had found peace. Getting to know the rules was just a matter of trial and error. However, while experiencing a great deal of freedom, I remained ill at ease without knowing the reasons for it. The feelings of being a misfit continued to surface at the most inopportune moments, but I became quite adept at batting them aside. What I was left with were a lot of questions, no answers, an incredibly negative body image, and a strong sense of foreboding.

The dreams of having a mustache and beard that were prevalent in my youth returned full force and grew during my dykehood. Waking in the morning to find myself smooth-faced proved disappointing. I kept these dreams and disappointments to myself. The taboo was too great for me to share with others. When I did see women with facial hair at the women's music festivals, I just about fell over. That was exactly what I wanted, but more—more hair, a lot more hair. I began to look forward to menopause, which was just too far out of reach to be a reality. I had resigned myself to the fact that facial hair would never be. It was then that I saw two friends appear at a party fully cross-dressed, sporting theatrical mustaches. I had definitely died and gone to heaven! I followed them quite speechless all night. That very weekend they both took me to buy my first mustache. Now the dilemma was where could I wear it. It was exciting and nerve-wracking all at the same time. I did eventually wear my mustache to a couple of events and parties and found that I was being cruised by gay men. It was definitely nice to be cruised, but being a dyke and all, I was not interested in gay men, or was I? A whole new can of worms plopped itself into my lap. Oh, goodie, new issues and dilemmas to pour over.

This predicament died down for quite awhile and then reared its ugly head at a workshop where gender play was discussed. The fact that I might be transgendered had eluded me just as during my youth my lesbianism had. Right in the middle of this workshop I felt as if someone had grabbed me by the ankles and proceeded to hold me facing head down from the twentieth floor of some office building. I did not want to tell my lover what I was going through. These feelings were just too deep, dark, and personal for me to discuss with her until I could figure them out for myself. I stewed and mulled for the next twenty-four hours and assumed that, because the women around me who identified as butch were just that, I could not possibly be transgendered. This theory broke like a piece of fine crystal when two out of three who had been present at that workshop revealed that they too were having gender issues. The third woman revealed that she had thought about it seriously on prior occasions, but that it wasn't for her.

I thought long and hard about who I was and why something as simple as a talk had triggered so many emotions. In the span of a few hours, my entire world had gone topsy-turvy. I was afraid that I would lose my lover, my friends, my job, the support and love of my family, my community, etc. Try as I might, I could not hide from myself, although I continued to attempt it. Altering my gender expression had worked until that moment of clarity when the transgendered sign flashed before my face. I was going to have to do something about it fast before my big guts ate my little guts. An ulcer definitely loomed on the horizon. Intensive therapy and soul-searching followed.

I realized, in addition to a variety of other things, that I was incredibly uncomfortable with my body. Body image problems surfaced and persisted during the doubt phase. When I did come to terms with the fact that I was transgendered, it was primarily my physical appearance that proved problematic for me. It was not misogyny that brought me to this place. It was the total and complete dichotomy between how I perceived and felt about myself and how the world at large perceived me. I was afraid that I would not be able to "pass." I was afraid that the lesbian community that was my home would ostracize me as a straight male despite the fact that I am neither straight nor male. I was afraid that I would grow bald.

It seemed that no matter what I did, bodies and body images remained constantly on my mind. It played a huge role in my metamorphosis. I continued to worry about "passing." Could I pull it off? Would I be called ma'am today? Was my voice deep enough? When would the facial hair come in? I worried that my hands were too small or that my hips were too wide. In part, these worries stem from a rigid code of what is deemed a man and what is deemed a woman in society. In the United States, even our fragrances have genders. Here, perfume is worn by women whereas cologne is worn by men. In Europe, these are just fragrances. I knew from personal experience that in this fashion and in other subtle ways society teaches that the identification of gender is first and foremost. Appearances and other cues provide distinguishing markers between men and women, the only two gender options presently available. I had often observed others become obsessed in determining a person's gender. I became terrified that I would give off the wrong cues, that I would be humiliated or worse, beaten to a pulp.

Needless to say, the testosterone helped assuage these worries considerably. During the first year, the most noticeable changes are as follows: There is a substantial change in body chemistry. Body odors increase and become more acrid. The clitoris enlarges and grows. The voice takes on an almost gravelly quality as it begins to change and crack. There is increased energy, water retention, and acne. Breasts appear to become slightly smaller or at least change shape. A friend has described the image as "soup in a baggie." Facial and body hair starts to thicken and darken. There is a constant ache or sensation that makes you feel as if you want to stretch all the time. Shoulders broaden so that shirts no longer fit. Muscularity increases. Body fat redistributes to the upper belly as opposed to the lower belly. Hands and feet get larger. In some instances, the individual grows an inch or more. I was not so lucky. Jaws and the facial structures square off. There is a change in hair line, and mine was and is more dramatic than some of those around me. However, I am also substantially hairier that most genetic men that I know.

Explaining to others the monumental discomfort that I felt became an insurmountable task. The phrase "trapped in the body of the opposite sex" was coined in a poignant attempt to explain what I and others like me feel. While easy to understand, the phrase has been used too often and oversimplifies the complexities of the issue. I did not feel "trapped" within my body so much as I felt trapped by the expectations that accompany the body which I occupied. What I felt was remarkably uncomfortable with only some aspects of my body. I know of some cases where the individual has felt discomfort with all aspects of body image. The term uncomfortable is the understatement of the century, but I can find no other word to explain it. It's like holding your breath underwater. At some point in time you know you're going to have to inhale. The price that I paid for body comfort was the continuing saga of relationship hell. Finding people who can deal with the visual and physical disparity has proven quite challenging, but they are out there.

From the moment that I come out to someone as transgendered, the inevitable questions arose: "Do you have a penis? Which bathroom do you use? Does your boyfriend/girlfriend know? Are you straight now?" People tend to forget that everyone is different. Not all transgendered men (formerly known as female-to-male transsexuals) want penises. Some of us do and some of us don't. Some of us identify as straight, some as gay, some as bi, and some as queer. We come from all walks of life and take quite different approaches to transition.

In retrospect, some of these questions seem silly. Sporting a full beard, I doubt that I could escape arrest were I to enter the women's restroom at this time in my life, even if I shaved. But gender and body image are so firmly entrenched in the psyches of those that knew us before hormones, that these questions are not silly at all. Frankly, questions and our willingness to answer them in an open and honest manner are what promotes a better understanding of transgendered folk.

* * *

Maybe that is what these disclosures will do—promote a better understanding. Not all of us have severed our ties with the lesbian community. Despite the changes in my body, I continue to consider myself a lesbian as well as a gay man, but that is another story and a can of worms unto itself. I, for one, am thankful that I have been socialized female and that I have had these experiences in my life. After all, life is an adventure of epic proportions.

PART 7:
SQUARE PEGS

Affronting Reason

Cheryl Chase

"It seems that your parents weren't sure for a time whether you were a girl or a boy," Dr. Christen explained, as she handed me three, fuzzy, photostatted pages. I was twenty-one years old and had asked her to help me obtain records of a hospitalization that had occurred when I was a year and a half old, too young for me to recall. I was desperate to obtain the complete records, to determine who had surgically removed my clitoris, and why. I wanted to know against whom my rage should be directed. "Diagnosis: true hermaphrodite. Operation: clitorectomy." The hospital record showed Charlie admitted, age eighteen months. His typewritten name had been crudely crossed out and "Cheryl" scribbled over it.

Though I recall clearly the scene of Dr. Christen handing me the records and dismissing me from her office, I can recall nothing of my emotional reaction. How is it possible that I could be a *hermaphrodite?* The hermaphrodite is a mythological creature. I am a woman, a lesbian woman, though I lack a clitoris and inner labia. What did my genitals look like before the surgery? Was I born with a penis?

Fifteen years of emotional numbness passed before I was able to seek the answers to these and many other questions. Then, four years ago, extreme emotional turmoil and suicidal despair arrived suddenly, threatening to crush me. "It's not possible," I thought. "This cannot be anyone's story, much less mine. I don't want it." Yet it *is* mine. I mark that time as the beginning of my coming out as a political intersexual, an "avowed intersexual," to borrow the epithet that until recently adhered to homosexuals who refused to stay invisible.

The story of my childhood is a lie. I know now that after the clitorectomy my parents followed the physicians' advice and discarded every scrap of evidence that Charlie had ever existed. They replaced all of the blue baby clothing with pink and discarded photos and birthday cards. When I look at grandparents, aunts, uncles, I am aware that they must know that one day Charlie ceased to exist in my family, and Cheryl was there in his place.

The medical establishment uses the terms *hermaphrodite* and *intersexual* to refer to us. The word hermaphrodite, with its strong mythological associations, reinforces the notion that hermaphroditism is a fantasy, not your neighbor, your friend, your teacher, or—especially—your baby. And, because it falsely implies that one individual possesses two sets of genitals, it allows my clitoris to be labeled as a penis and the clitorectomy performed on me to be justified as "reconstructive surgery." For these reasons, I prefer the term intersexual. Kira Triea, one of many who has joined me in speaking openly about her intersexuality, also feels strongly about this point. "It irks me so when I am trying to explain to someone who I am, what my experience has been, and they begin to quote Ovid to me." For Triea—an intersexual assigned male at birth, raised as a boy, who began to menstruate through her penis at puberty, and who now lives as a lesbian-identified woman—hermaphroditism is a real presence in her life every day; she need not look to poetry penned in Latin two millennia ago.

At the beginning of my process of coming out as intersexual, I chose to examine again the three pages of medical records that I had set aside for fifteen years. The word "hermaphrodite" was horribly wounding; it drove me to the brink of suicide. I thought back to my earlier process of coming out as lesbian. The way out of this pain was to reclaim the stigmatized label, to manufacture a positive acceptance of it. This second coming out was far more painful and difficult. As a teenager recognizing my attraction to women, I visited the library, stealthily examined Del Martin and Phyllis Lyon's *Lesbian/Woman* (1991) and Radclyffe Hall's *The Well of Loneliness* (1990). I learned that other lesbians existed, that they somehow managed to live and to love women. Somehow I would find them; there was a community where my lesbianism would be understood and welcome. No such help was available to reclaim my intersexuality. The only images I found were absolutely pathologized case histories in medical texts and journals, closeups of genitals being poked, prodded, measured, sliced, and sutured, full body shots with the eyes blacked out.

For many months, I struggled to reclaim the label "hermaphrodite." I knew that I had been horribly mutilated by the clitorectomy, deprived of the experience of sexuality that most people, male or female, take for granted. What would my life be had I been allowed to keep my genitals intact? "No,"

I thought. "I don't wish to have a penis between my legs, for my body to look like a man's body. I could never relate sexually to a woman as if I were a man." The physicians who removed my clitoris considered instead performing a long series of surgeries to make my genitals look more male, to support the male sex assignment rather than changing it to female. Though I can offer little evidence to support the idea, I am convinced that, had I been kept male, I would now be a gay man.

"Never mind, just don't think about it," was the advice of the few people to whom I spoke, including two female therapists: "You look like a woman." There is a powerful resistance to thinking about intersex. Because they look at me and make a female attribution, most people find it impossible to imagine that my experience and my history are not female. The resistance to thinking about what my sexual experience might be is even more profound. Most people, including the two therapists mentioned above, are paralyzed by the general prohibition on explicit sex talk. But sex radicals and activists are little better. They assume that I am having "vaginal orgasms" or even "full-body orgasms." If I persist in asserting my sexual dysfunction, many patronize me. "I am completely confident that you will learn how to orgasm," one man told me, then continued his explanation of how male circumcision was just as damaging as clitorectomy, my experience to the contrary.

What is most infuriating is to read, nearly every day in popular media, denunciations of African female genital mutilation as barbaric abuses of human rights, which fail to mention that intersexed children's clitorises are removed every day in the United States. Such writers occasionally note that clitorectomy has been practiced in the United States but always hurry to assure the reader that the practice ended by the 1930s. Letters to these authors receive no reply. Letters to editors pointing out the inaccuracy are not published. In 1996, Congress passed H.R. 3610, prohibiting "the removal or infibulation (or both) of the whole or part of the clitoris, the labia minor, or the labia major" (p. H11829). However, the next paragraph specifically excludes from prohibition these operations if they are performed by a licensed medical practitioner who deems them necessary. As early as 1993, Brown University Professor of Medical Science Anne Fausto-Sterling had joined intersexuals to ask Congresswoman Pat Schroeder, in drafting the prohibition, not to neglect genital surgery performed on intersexed infants. Ms. Schroeder's office made no reply. Newspaper accounts in 1996 lauded the bill's passage as an end to clitorectomy in the United States.

It took months for me to obtain the rest of my medical records. I learned that I had been born, not with a penis, but with intersexed genitals: a typical vagina and outer labia, female urethra, and a very large clitoris.

Mind you, "large" and "small," as applied to intersexed genitals, are judgments that exist only in the mind of the beholder. From my birth until the surgery, while I was Charlie, my parents and doctors considered my penis to be monstrously small, and with the urethra in the "wrong" position. My parents were so ashamed and traumatized by the appearance of my genitals that they allowed no one to see them—no baby-sitters, no possibility of tired parents being spelled for diaper-changing by a helpful grandmother or aunt. Then, in the moment that intersex specialist physicians pronounced that my "true sex" was female, my clitoris was suddenly monstrously large. All this occurred without any change in the objective size or appearance of the appendage between my legs.

Intersex is a humanly possible but (in our culture) socially unthinkable phenomenon. In modern industrial cultures, when a child is born, the experts present, whether midwives or physicians, assign a sex based on the appearance of the infant's genitals. They are required—both legally and by social custom—to assign the child as either male or female. Were parents to tell inquiring friends and relatives that their newborn's sex was "hermaphrodite," they would be greeted with sheer disbelief. Should the parents persist in labeling their child "hermaphrodite" rather than "male or female with a congenital deformity requiring surgical repair," their very sanity would be called into question.

Thus, intersexed children are always assigned to either male or female sex. In making these problematic sex assignments, specialist physicians are generally consulted; the assignment may not be made for several days, and it is sometimes changed, as was done with me. In fact, there are documented cases in which the sex assignment has been changed without soliciting the opinion of or even *informing* the child, as many as three times.[1]

Most people take for granted, even assume as "scientific fact," that there are two, and only two, sexes. In reality, however, about one in two thousand infants is born with an anatomy that refuses to conform to our preconceptions of "male" and "female." Few outside the medical profession are even aware of our existence. I now know that hundreds of thousands of people in the United States alone share my experience, and we are organizing ourselves through the Intersex Society of North America.[2] My ability to embrace the term hermaphrodite, at first halting and uncertain, has grown in depth, conviction, and pride, as I have met other intersexuals; we have shared our stories, our lives, and our anger.

Struggling to understand why society so utterly denies the phenomenon of intersexuality, I read widely in such diverse fields as philosophy, history, psychology, and ethnography. I was excited to discover that in recent years a number of scholars in these fields have begun to examine the ways in which sex and gender are socially constructed (Butler, 1990; Foucault, 1980b; Kessler and McKenna, 1978; Laqueur, 1990; Vance, 1991). These and related works constitute a recognition that the paradigms of previous investigators have caused them to overlook information about nonreproductive sexual conduct, practices, and categories. Data that were at odds with their culturally determined, heterosexist, dimorphic point of view were ignored because they could not be accounted for.

In many other cultures, however, the phenomenon of intersexuality is well known, and an intersexed child may be recognized and assigned as such at birth. Unfortunately, interpretations by ethnographers have been straightjacketed by the absolute sexual dualism that has dominated Western thinking since Darwin. Recently though, ethnographers have given us examples of cultures in which intersexual assignment confers high status, low status, or even condemns an infant to death by exposure, as an evil omen (Edgerton, 1964; Furth, 1993; Herdt, 1994; Nanda, 1994; Roscoe, 1991). The Jewish Talmud discusses hermaphrodites in many locations and lays out regulations governing matrimony, priesthood, inheritance, and other matters for intersexuals (Berlin and Zevin, 1974). The Talmudic sages held variously that the hermaphrodite was: of uncertain sex, but in some essential way actually either male or female; part male and part female; definitely male, but only in respect to certain laws. And, in an eerie echo of modern medical practice, one Talmudic writer even differentiates the hermaphrodite, whose sex can never be resolved, from the *Tumtum*, whose sex is ascertainable through surgery.

Americans, though, are apt to express disbelief when confronted with evidence of intersexuality. Modern Western culture is the first to rely upon technology to *enforce* gender dichotomy: since the 1950s or so, surgical and hormonal means have been used to erase the evidence from intersexed infants' bodies. Medical literature speaks with one voice on the necessity of this practice, even when it concedes that surgical intervention may damage sexual function (Conte and Grumbach, 1989; Emans and Goldstein, 1990; Hendricks, 1993). Silence has been considered evidence of patient satisfaction.

For over forty years, some form of clitorectomy or clitoroplasty has been used to treat little girls with adrenogenital syndrome (one of dozens of reasons why an infant may be born intersexed). The only indication for performing this surgery has been to improve the body image of these children so that they feel "more normal" . . . *Not one has complained of loss of sensation even when the entire clitoris was removed. . . . The clitoris is clearly not necessary for orgasm* (Edgerton, 1993, p. 956).[3]

What are genitals for? It is my position that *my* genitals are for *my* pleasure. In a sex-repressive culture with a heavy investment in the fiction of sexual dichotomy, infant genitals are for discriminating male from female infants. It is very difficult to get parents, or even physicians, to consider the infant as a future adult and sexual being. Medical intersex specialists, however, pride themselves on being able to do just that.

For intersex specialists, male genitals are for active penetration and pleasure, while female genitals are for passive penetration and reproduction: men have sex; women have babies. Asked by a journalist why standard practice assigns 90 percent of intersexed infants as females (and surgically enforces the assignment by trimming or removing the clitoris), one prominent surgical specialist reasoned, "you can make a hole, but you can't build a pole" (Hendricks, 1993, p. 15). Notice how John Gearhart, a noted specialist in genital surgery for intersex children, evades questioning about orgasmic function following the presentation of his paper on additional surgeries for repair of vaginas surgically constructed in intersexed infants. (Dr. Frank, in attendance at the presentation, shares a professional interest in such surgery; the discussion was published in the *Journal of Urology* along with the paper.)

> *Dr. Frank:* How do you define successful intercourse? How many of these girls actually have an orgasm, for example? How many of these had a clitorectomy, how many a clitoroplasty, and did it make any difference to orgasm?

> *Dr. Gearhart:* Interviews with the families were performed by a female pediatric surgeon who is kind and caring, and who I think got the maximum information from these patients. Adequate intercourse was defined as successful vaginal penetration. . . . (Bailez et al., 1992, p. 684)

Gearhart has since condemned outspoken intersexed adults as "zealots" (Angier, 1996, p. E14), and minimized reports by former patients of damaged sexual function after clitoral surgery because "some women who have never had surgery are anorgasmic" (Chase, 1996, p. 1140).

Intersex specialists often stress the importance of a heterosexual outcome for the intersexed children consigned to their care. For instance, Slijper and colleagues state, "parents will feel reassured when they know that their daughter can develop heterosexually just like other children" (Slijper et al., 1994, p. 15). Dr. Y, a prominent surgeon in the field of intersexuality, agreed to be interviewed by Ellen Lee only under condition of anonymity. He asserts that the ultimate measure of success for sex assignment of intersexed children is the "effectiveness of intercourse" they achieve as adults (Lee, 1994, p. 60). Intersexuals assigned female who choose women as sexual partners, and those assigned male who choose men as sexual partners, must then represent failures of treatment in the eyes of our parents and of intersex specialists. Indeed, my mother's reaction upon learning that I was sexual with women was to reveal to my siblings, but not to me, my hermaphroditism and history of sex change and to regret that she had allowed physicians to assign me female, rather than male.

My mother and father took me into their room one day to share a secret with me. I was ten years old, still utterly ignorant about sexual matters. "When you were a baby, you were sick," they explained. "Your clitoris was too big; it was *enlarged*." The way they spoke the word *enlarged*, it was clear that it was being given some special, out of the ordinary, meaning. "You had to go into the hospital, and it was removed." "What is a 'clitoris'?" I asked. "A clitoris is a part of a girl that would have been a penis if she had been a boy. Yours was *enlarged*, so it had to be removed. Now everything is fine. But don't ever tell this to anyone else."

Who am I? I look at my body. It *looks* female. Yet I have always harbored a secret doubt. I remember myself as a withdrawn, depressed adolescent, trying to steal a glance of a woman's genitals. Do hers look like mine? I had never seen a naked woman up close. I had no idea that my genitals were missing parts. In fact, one cannot discern the difference between my genitals and those of any other woman without parting the outer labia. I do recall learning, from a book, about the phenomenon of masturbation. Try as I might, I could not locate a focus of pleasurable sensation in my genitals, couldn't accomplish the trick that I had read about. I wasn't able to associate this failure with the secret about the *enlarged* clitoris that had been removed. I simply couldn't take in that such an irreversible harm had been done to me and by adults who were responsible for my well-being. I often woke from a nightmare in which my life was in danger, my gender in question, and my genitals were somehow horribly deformed, spilling out of me like visceral organs. It wasn't until I became a young adult that I was able to make the connection between the removal of my clitoris and my feeble sexual response and inability to experience orgasm.

Who am I? I now assert both my femininity and my intersexuality, my "not female"-ness. This is not a paradox; the fact that my gender has been problematized is the source of my intersexual identity. Most people have never struggled with their gender, are at a loss to answer the question, "How do you know you are a woman (a man)?"

I have been unable to experience myself as totally female. Although my body passes for female, women's clothing does not fit me. The shoulders are too narrow, the sleeves too short. Most women's gloves won't go on my hands, nor women's shoes on my feet. For most women, that wouldn't be more than an inconvenience. But when the clothing doesn't fit, I am reminded of my history. Of course, men's clothing doesn't fit either. The straight lines leave no room for my large breasts or broad hips. Still, I experience something about the way that I work and move in the world as relatively masculine. And when a man expresses an intimate attraction to me, I often suspect that he may be wrestling with a conflicted homosexual orientation—attracted to a masculine part of me, but my feminine appearance renders his attraction safely heterosexual.

As woman, I am less than whole—I have a secret past; I lack important parts of my genitals and sexual response. When a lover puts her hand to my genitals for the first time, the lack is immediately obvious to her. Finally, I simply do not feel myself a woman (even less a man). But the hermaphrodite identity was too monstrous, too other, too freakish, for me to easily embrace—a medical anomaly, patched up as best the surgeons could manage. I had an article from a medical journal that stated that only twelve "true hermaphrodites" (the label applied to me by my medical records) had *ever* been recorded (Morris, 1957, p. 540).

For whose benefit does this mechanism of medical erasure and social silencing operate? Certainly, it does not benefit intersexed children. I have been brutally mutilated, left to wonder and to search for the truth in utter silence and isolation. When at age thirty-six, I finally confronted my mother, I asked her how she could possibly have kept her silence for all those years, left me to learn my history as Charlie and the label of hermaphroditism from medical records. Her response? "Well, you could have *asked* me." (I wonder what other improbable questions I should be certain to ask while she is alive . . .)

At first, I was horribly vexed by this issue of identity. My earlier experience of coming out as a lesbian helped me to see the solution to my predicament. The terms homosexual and lesbian, as with the term intersex, were inventions of medical discourse used to pathologize disapproved sexualities. I must proudly assert my identity and insist that the medical construction of intersexuality as disease is oppression, not science. I must find others who share my experience—others who will speak out with me. A community can provide emotional and logistical support for its members and mount a much more powerful resistance than individuals acting alone.

It wasn't easy to overcome my feelings of intense shame. I remember furtively using the printer, copier, and fax machine at the office, heart pounding with the fear that someone would see the documents that I was working with—medical records, articles from medical journals, a journal of my emotional progress. I still believed that intersexuality was so rare that I might never find another whose experience was similar to mine. Instead, I first sought out and spoke with transsexuals. Alice Walker had just published *Possessing the Secret of Joy*, a novel which focused Western attention on the African cultural rite euphemistically referred to as female circumcision. I thrilled to read the elderly midwife, whose long life had been spent performing clitorectomies, castigate her former victim for suggesting clitorectomy might be justified for hermaphrodites, if not for females. "It's all normal, as far as that goes, says M'lissa. You didn't make it, so who are you to judge?" (Walker, 1992, p. 257) I located and spoke with African women mutilated in this way, who are now organizing in the United States against the practices of their homelands. The examples of all these brave people helped me to deal with my shame.

I began to speak, at first indiscriminately, with friends and acquaintances about what had been done to me. Within a year, I had turned up half a dozen other intersexuals; most of them were also genitally mutilated; two were living with their atypical genitals intact. A woman clitorectomized during her teens, though she knew from masturbation that her clitoris was the focus of sexual pleasure, she was unable to express this or otherwise resist the pressure of parents and doctors; a child who had been clitorectomized just two years previous (in 1990); a woman who was grateful that her mother had resisted years of medical pressure to remove her daughter's large clitoris; a man who had been raised as a girl, switched to living as a man (with intact intersexed genitals) after he developed a masculine body at puberty; a man whose penis had been severely damaged by repeated surgeries to "correct" the position of his urethral meatus;[4] a man who had discovered that the childhood surgery which no one would explain to him had actually removed his uterus and single ovary. None of these people had ever spoken with another intersexual.

Surgeons assert that the reason why they fail to provide us with counseling is that they cannot locate mental health professionals with experience in dealing with intersexuality (Lee, 1994). Yet, surgeons perpetuate this situation by mutilating, traumatizing, stigmatizing, and silencing us, their intersexed patients. We grow up with so much shame that as adults we are not able to discuss our experience openly, and the phenomenon of intersexuality remains invisible. Indeed, as recently as 1996, one entrant in a medical ethics contest won a cash prize for her essay encouraging physicians to lie to their intersexed patients in order to prevent them from knowing their diagnoses (Natarajan, 1996). In adulthood, many who were treated as children by medical intersex specialists feel so betrayed that they shun all medical care.

What do I see when I look in the mirror? I see a female body, though scarred and missing some important genital parts. When I interact in daily life with others, though, I experience a strange sort of bodily dissociation—my perception of myself is as a disembodied entity, without sex or gender. I view healing this split as an important element of personal growth that will allow me to reclaim my sexuality and to be more effective as an intersex advocate. My body is not female; it is intersexed. Nonconsensual surgery cannot erase intersexuality and produce whole males and females; it produces emotionally abused and sexually dysfunctional intersexuals. If I label my postsurgical anatomy female, I ascribe to surgeons the power to create a *woman* by *removing* body parts; I accede to their agenda of "woman as lack"; I collaborate in the prohibition of my intersexual identity. Kessler quotes an endocrinologist who specializes in treating intersexed infants: "In the absence of maleness, you have femaleness. . . It's really the basic design" (Kessler, 1990, p. 15).

Must things be this way? In all cultures, at all times? Anthropologist Clifford Geertz contrasted the conceptualization of intersexuals by the Navajo and the Kenyan Pokot—"a product, if a somewhat unusual product, of the normal course of things"—with the American attitude. "Americans . . . regard femaleness and maleness as exhausting the natural categories in which persons can conceivably come: what falls between is a darkness, an offense against reason" (Geertz, 1984 p. 85). The time has come for intersexuals to denounce our treatment as abuse, to embrace and openly assert our identities as intersexuals, and to intentionally affront that sort of reason which requires that we be mutilated and silenced.

Even before intersexuals began to speak out, there were a few stirrings of awareness that something fishy was going on at the boundaries of the sexes. In 1980, Ruth Hubbard and Patricia Farnes pointed out that the practice of clitorectomy was not limited to the Third World but also occurs "right here in the United States, where it is used as part of a procedure to 'repair' by 'plastic surgery' so-called genital ambiguities" (Farnes and Hubbard, 1980, p. 9). Reacting to intersex specialist John Money's explanation to a three-year-old girl that clitorectomy "will make her look like all other girls," Anne Fausto-Sterling wryly noted, "If the surgery results in genitalia that look like those shown in [Money's] book, then [he is] in need of an anatomy lesson!" (Fausto-Sterling, 1985, p. 138). Five years later Suzanne Kessler, whose work has been influential in motivating the current discourse on gender as a social construction, interviewed physicians who specialize in managing intersexed children. She concluded that genital ambiguity is treated with surgery "not because it is threatening to the infant, but because it is threatening to the infant's culture" (Kessler, 1990,

p. 25). Finally, Fausto-Sterling suggested that genital surgery should not be imposed on intersexed infants (Fausto-Sterling, 1993).

A letter to the editor in which I responded to Fausto-Sterling's article, announcing the formation of the Intersex Society of North America (ISNA), brought emotional responses from other intersexuals (Chase, 1993). One, Morgan Holmes, has completed an extended analysis of the reasons why medical technology has been used to erase intersexuality in general, and from her own body in particular (Holmes, 1994). Until she contacted me, Holmes shared her experience of intersexuality with no living being. The only other intersexual in her universe was Herculine Barbin, the nineteenth-century French hermaphrodite whose journals were edited and published by Foucault (Foucault, 1980a). Barbin's life ended in suicide. By 1996, ISNA had grown to include more than 150 intersexuals throughout the United States and Canada, and several in Europe, Australia, and New Zealand.

In Britain, as well, intersexuals have begun to speak out against the extreme secrecy, shame, and freakishness surrounding their condition. The British movement was given a boost when the respected *British Medical Journal* carried an exchange that led to publication of an address for a support group.

> Mine was a dark secret kept from all outside the medical profession (family included), but this is not an option because it both increases the feelings of freakishness and reinforces the isolation. (Anonymous, 1994b)

> It's not that my gynecologist told me the truth that angers me (I'd used medical libraries to reach a diagnosis anyway), but that neither I nor my parents were offered any psychological support but were left to flounder in our separate feelings of shame and taboo. (Anonymous, 1994a)

Both writers have androgen insensitivity syndrome (AIS). During gestation, their XY sex chromosomes caused them to have testes, and their testes produced testosterone. But because their cells were incapable of responding to testosterone, they were born with genitals of typical female appearance but having a short vagina, without cervix or uterus. Raised as girls, with bodies that develop many adult female characteristics at puberty, women with AIS are often traumatized to read in medical records or texts that they are "genetic males" and "male pseudohermaphrodites." The publication of these letters led to a swell of visibility and participation in Britain's AIS Support Group, which by 1996 had chapters in the United States, Canada, the Netherlands, Germany, and Australia.

In Germany, intersexuals have formed the Workgroup on Violence in Pediatrics and Gynecology for mutual support and in opposition of medical abuse. In Japan, intersexuals have formed Hijra Nippon, with a similar agenda. In the United States, HELP and the Ambiguous Genitalia Support Network were separately founded by mothers who opposed the drastic surgical interventions and secrecy that medical specialists recommended for their intersexed children.[5] One of these women has a suit pending against physicians who removed her son's testes against her stated wishes.

Some intersexuals whose bodies resemble mine have an XX, some an XY karyotype; others have a mosaic karyotype, which differs from cell to cell. There is no possible way to discern my karyotype without sending a tissue sample to a laboratory. If the result were "XX," should this information bolster my identity as a female? As a lesbian? If "XY," should I reconceptualize myself as a heterosexual man? It is ludicrous that knowledge of the result of a laboratory test in which cell nuclei are stained and photographed under a microscope should determine the perception of anyone's sex or gender.

The International Olympic Committee has learned this the hard way. Since the IOC began to karyotype women in 1968, one in 500 female athletes tested have been rejected because of their unusual chromosomes; in some cases, the decision was made only after the event, and the woman was stripped of title and barred from future competition. To this writer's knowledge, only one person treated in this way has thus far been willing to speak openly about her experience. When meet officials presented Maria Patino with the news that she was "genetically male," they advised her to fake an injury and leave quietly (Pool, 1994).

When I first began to seek out other intersexuals, I expected, I wanted, to find people whose experience exactly matched mine. What I have discovered is that in one sense we are very different—the range of personalities, politics, and anatomies in our nascent intersexual movement is broad. Some of us live as women, some as men, some as open intersexuals. Many of us are homosexual, if that term is narrowly understood in terms of the social gender roles of the partners. Some of us have never been sexual. But, in another sense, our experiences are surprisingly coherent: those of us who have been subjected to medical intervention and societal invisibility share our experience of it as abuse.

I claim lesbian identity because women who feel desire for me experience that desire as lesbian, because I feel most female when being sexual, and because I feel desire for women as I do not for men. Many intersexuals share my sense of queer identity, even those who do not share this homosexual identity. One, assigned female at birth and lucky enough to escape genital surgery through a fluke, has said that she has enjoyed sex with both women and men but never with another intersexual. "I'm a heterosexual in the truest sense of the word" (Angier, 1996, p. E14).

Healing is a process without end. The feeling of being utterly alone may be the most damaging part of what has been done to us. My work as an activist—listening to, counseling, and connecting other intersexuals, and working to save children born every day from having to repeat our suffering—has been an important part of my own healing and of feeling less overwhelmed by grief and rage.

NOTES

1. Money describes a child who was assigned male at birth, female a few days later, male at age three weeks, and female at age four and a half. She was clitorectomized in conjunction with the final sex change. Her history of sex reassignments was kept secret from her, tabooed from family discussion, although she recalled it in dreams (Money, 1991, p. 239).

2. Intersex Society of North America, P.O. Box 31791, San Francisco, CA 94131. E-mail info@isna.org.http://www.isna.org.

3. Although this statement was written in connection with an article about "clitoroplasty without loss of sensitivity," the authors provide no evidence that this standard procedure, which removes nearly the entire clitoris and relocates the remainder, leaves sexual sensation intact. On the other hand, Morgan Holmes, who was subjected to it as a child, characterizes it as a "partial clitorectomy" (Holmes, 1994). Another woman, who had the procedure performed as an adult and is able to contrast her sexual experience before and after the surgery, calls it "incredibly desensitizing" (Chase, 1994, p. 3).

4. Approximately one in three or four hundred infants is born with a condition called hypospadias, in which the portion of the urethra that traverses the penis is partially or completely open. This condition is rarely harmful; it looks unusual, and the boy or man may have to sit to urinate. Hypospadias "correction" surgery is probably the second most common form of cosmetic genital surgery performed in the United States, following "routine" male circumcision.

5. AIS Support Group US, 4203 Genessee #103-436, San Diego, CA 92117-4950. E-mail <aissg@aol.com>. AG Gewalt in der Padiatrie and Gynecologie, Brandtstrasse 30, Bremen 28 215, Germany. E-mail <aggpg@t-online.de>. Hijra Nippon, Suita Yubinkyoku Todome, Honami cho 4-1 Suita shi, Osaka T564, Japan. HELP, PO Box 26292, Jacksonville, FL 32226. E-mail <help@jaxnet.com>. Ambiguous Genitalia Support Network, P.O. Box 313, Clements, CA 95227.

REFERENCES

Angier, Natalie. 1996. Intersexual healing: An anomaly finds a group. *The New York Times* (February 4): 14.

Anonymous. 1994a. Be open and honest with sufferers. *British Medical Journal* 308 (April 16):1041-1042.

Anonymous. 1994b. Once a dark secret. *British Medical Journal* 308 (February 19):542.

Bailez, M. M., John P. Gearhart, Claude Migeon, and John Rock. 1992. Vaginal reconstruction after initial construction of the external genitalia in girls with salt-wasting adrenal hyperplasia. *Journal of Urology* 148:680-684.

Berlin, Meyer, and Shlomo Josef Zevin. 1974. *Encyclopedia Talmudica.* Jerusalem: Phillip Feldheim, pp. 386-399.

Butler, Judith. 1990. *Gender Trouble: Feminism and the Subversion of Identity.* New York: Routledge.

Chase, Cheryl. 1993. Letters from readers. *The Sciences* (July/August): 3.

Chase, Cheryl. 1994. Winged labia: Deformity or gift? *Hermaphrodites with Attitude* (Winter): 3.

Chase, Cheryl. 1996. Re: Measurement of evoked potentials during feminizing genitoplasty: Techniques and applications (letter). *Journal of Urology* 156 (3):1139-1140.

Conte, Felix A., and Melvin M. Grumbach. 1989. Pathogenesis, classification, diagnosis, and treatment of anomalies of sex. In *Endocrinology*, edited by L. J. De Groot. Philadelphia: Saunders, pp. 1810-1847.

Department of Defense Appropriations Act of 1996, 104th Congress, second session, H.R. 3610 Sec 645, Congressional Record: September 28, 1996 (House), p. H11829.

Edgerton, Milton T. 1993. Discussion: Clitoroplasty for clitoromegaly due to adrenogenital syndrome without loss of sensitivity (by Nobuyuki Sagehashi). *Plastic and Reconstructive Surgery* 91 (5):956.

Edgerton, Robert B. 1964. Pokot intersexuality: An east African example of the resolution of sexual incongruity. *American Anthropologist* 66 (6):1288-1299.

Emans, S. Jean Herriot, and Donald Peter Goldstein. 1990. *Pediatric and Adolescent Gynecology*, third edition. Boston: Little, Brown, and Co.

Farnes, Patricia, and Ruth Hubbard. 1980. Letter to editor. *Ms Magazine* (April): 9-10.

Fausto-Sterling, Anne. 1985. *Myths of Gender: Biological Theories about Women and Men*, second edition. New York: BasicBooks.

Fausto-Sterling, Anne. 1993. The five sexes: Why male and female are not enough. *The Sciences* (March/April): 20-25.

Foucault, Michel. 1980a. *Herculine Barbin, Being the Recently Discovered Memoirs of a Nineteenth-Century Hermaphrodite.* Translated by Richard McDougall. New York: Colophon.

Foucault, Michel. 1980b. *The History of Sexuality, Volume I: An Introduction.* Translated by Robert Hurley. New York: Viking.

Furth, Charlotte. 1993. Androgynous males and deficient females: Biology and gender boundaries in sixteenth- and seventeenth-century China. In *The Lesbian and Gay Studies Reader*, edited by Henry Abelove, Michellé Aina Barale, and David Helperin. New York: Routledge, pp. 479-497.

Geertz, Clifford. 1984. *Local Knowledge*. New York: Basic Books.

Hall, Radclyffe. 1990. *The Well of Loneliness*. New York: Anchor.

Hendricks, Melissa. 1993. Is it a boy or a girl? *Johns Hopkins Magazine* (November): 10-16.

Herdt, Gilbert. 1994. Mistaken sex: Culture, biology, and the third sex in New Guinea. In *Third Sex, Third Gender: Beyond Sexual Dimorphism in Culture and History*, edited by G. Herdt. New York: Zone Books, pp. 419-446.

Holmes, Morgan. 1994. Medical Politics and Cultural Imperatives: Intersexuality Beyond Pathology and Erasure. Master's Thesis, Interdisciplinary Studies, York University, Toronto.

Kessler, Suzanne. 1990. The medical construction of gender: Case management of intersexual infants. *Signs: Journal of Women in Culture and Society* 16 (1):3-26.

Kessler, Suzanne J., and Wendy McKenna. 1978. *Gender: An Ethnomethodological Approach*. Chicago: The University of Chicago Press.

Laqueur, Thomas. 1990. *Making Sex: Body and Gender from the Greeks to Freud*. Cambridge: Harvard University Press.

Lee, Ellen Hyun-Ju. 1994. Producing Sex: An Interdisciplinary Perspective on Sex Assignment Decisions for Intersexuals. Senior Thesis, Human Biology: Race and Gender, Brown University, Providence.

Martin, Del, and Phyllis Lyon. 1991. *Lesbian/Woman*. Volcano, CA: Volcano Press.

Money, John. 1991. Biographies of gender and hermaphroditism in paired comparisons. In *The Handbook of Sexology*, edited by J. Money and H. Musaph. New York: Elsevier.

Morris, John McL. 1957. Intersexuality. *Journal of the American Medical Association* 163 (7): 538-542.

Nanda, Sarena. 1994. Hijras: An Alternative Sex and Gender Role in India. In *Third Sex, Third Gender: Beyond Sexual Dimorphism in Culture and History*, edited by G. Herdt. New York: Zone Books, pp. 373-418.

Natarajan, Anita. 1996. Medical ethics and truth-telling in the case of androgen insensitivity syndrome. *Canadian Medical Association Journal* 154:568-570.

Pool, Robert E. 1994. *Eve's Rib: The Biological Roots of Sex Differences*. New York: Crown Publishers.

Roscoe, Will. 1991. *The Zuni Man-Woman*. Albuquerque: University of New Mexico Press.

Slijper, F.M.E., S.L.S. Drop, J.C. Molenaar, and R.J. Scholtmeijer. 1994. Neonates with abnormal genital development assigned the female sex: Parent counseling. *Journal of Sex Education and Therapy* 20 (1):9-17.

Vance, Carol S. 1991. Anthropology rediscovers sexuality: A theoretical comment. *Social Science and Medicine* 33: 875-884.

Walker, Alice. 1992. *Possessing the Secret of Joy*. New York: Simon and Schuster.

In(to)Visibility:
Intersexuality in the Field of Queer

Morgan Holmes

I would like to illuminate what it has meant for me to grow up as a mutilated, intersexed woman. I want to write about stolen physical potential, emotional harm, and the loss of years within a potentially legitimate identity/community of queer and intersex culture. It is a robbery and loss that I share with a mostly silent and invisible population, and I hope that telling my story will draw out the potential for others to recognize "kin" instead of remaining in the poverty of isolation.

I want to focus on what it means to grow up in a world in which there is no name, at least no *spoken* name, for what you are—a world in which you search through all the sex education materials in the fifth grade, looking for a description of the body you were born with. I want this chapter to be inflected with some of the pain I have felt living in this body.[1]

Entering the Closet

I was born in 1967, three months early. In an unsuccessful attempt to avoid premature delivery, my mother was given androgenic drugs (presumably progesterone).[2] I suffered from a number of complications related to being born so early. I was also born with "ambiguous" genitalia[3]—specifically a clitoris large enough that it threatened the possibility of growing into a certifiable phallus (if not exactly a penis).

When I was very little, from the ages of about three to seven, I think I was a psychologically healthy child. It's a little bit ridiculous of me to speculate about the past this way because, of course, the position from which I recognize myself now influences who I thought I was then. However, even with that knowledge, I think it is possible to begin to tell at least a somewhat illuminating story of who I was as a child and who I am now.

As a child, I was continually reminded *not* that I was weak but that I was strong. When I had pneumonia on repeated occasions, my family did not fret about how sickly I was but, instead, reminded me that I always beat the sickness before and would do so again. I couldn't play with other children because I couldn't be immunized for illnesses without contracting the actual diseases. But I was assured that the day would come when I'd be strong enough to resist all infections and roll in the muck with the toughest of them. I knew that I was small—about the size of a two-year-old at age four, of a four-year-old at age six—but I also knew that for my size, I was strong and fast, even if my peers did think I was a plaything and my elders mistook me for a walking doll. I considered myself "special," a "miracle," an "accomplishment"—a sort of Evel Knievel of toddlers. I did not consider myself peculiar in any negative sense—though perhaps a little distinguished from the masses of usual children who lacked my extraordinary medical history.

When I was seven I learned that, not only was I "special," I was inappropriately different from my peers. In March of 1975, I was admitted to Toronto's Hospital for Sick Children and spent eleven days there. I was not sick when I went in, and I was not healthy when I came out. Indeed, I was so unhealthy when discharged that I didn't actually *come out* for another fourteen years afterward—and even then, only in the "safest" of circumstances.

During those eleven days in the hospital, I was subjected to many of the same tests that I had been undergoing for several years—tests that I had assumed were just "routine" checkups that "made sense" in taking care of an infection daredevil such as myself. Urinalysis, more blood-tests, more buccal smears—most of the time that I spent in the hospital was time spent waiting for the results of tests. Of course I didn't know that so much time was taken up with testing until quite recently when I finally obtained my medical records from Sick Children's Hospital. What seemed like a horrendously boring time to me then has had its banality revealed for the more insidious testing ground that it was.

There were three other children in my ward; I remain uncertain about what was done to the others, but Anna, the little girl in the bed beside me, had what I now know was a bladder exstrophy and at least a partial cloaca of the colon—meaning that these organs were exterior to her body. I remember that I was fascinated by her because she was funny and somehow poignant in a way that I couldn't assimilate with my own reasons for being in her ward. Anna was *Other* to my *Self.* Now I know, from innumerable texts on pediatric gynecology, that Anna and I sit in the same medical space—the unworldly realm of sexual/genital "ambiguity." What I don't know about Anna is whether or not she had any surgeries similar to my own. I know what I do because I asked her directly why she had bags

attached to her body, and in some way, she responded—something I suspect she was able to do because even very young children possess a
language with which they can speak about their evacuating/excreting
functions. But if Anna ever asked me why I was in the hospital, I'm sure I
wouldn't have been able to respond in any clear way. I did not know why I
was in the hospital, and I did not know what would be done to me and,
indeed, did not have any clear idea of what had been done to me after the
fact.

This latter statement is, in some sense, absurd. Of course *I knew* what
had been done to me. I could see quite clearly that my body had been
painted orange from navel to knees (iodine sterilization), and it hurt like
hell to take a piss because it would run along the fresh wound that marked
the spot where that piece had previously been. But this is just my point—I
did not *know* what that piece was. I had no name for it. I could not have
articulated what had been done to me even if I had wanted to—which I am
not convinced I would have wanted to talk about. After all, having one's
"privates" altered never seemed appropriate conversation to me when I
returned to school just a few days later, or at any point after that until I was
twenty-one (at which time I slowly began learning that inappropriate
behavior can be the most appropriate response available).

Coming "Out"

In *Getting Specific,* Shane Phelan makes the following comments on
Nietszche's Zarathustra:

> In *Thus Spake Zarathustra*, Zarathustra replies to a hunchback's
> demand for a "cure" by suggesting that such a cure would take away
> his "spirit"—what makes him distinctively him. . . . Zarathustra
> teaches the contingency of all norms, and in doing so he teaches the
> value of each of our positions and knowledges. Our value does not
> rest in approaching "the" norm, nor does it rest in our potential for
> being other that what we are; it rests in being well what we are.
> (1994, 1)

This idea that the point of our lives should not be to be the same as
everyone else, to be indistinguishable from the rest, to even "approach the
norm" but, rather, to be specific is, in short, what "Queer" has offered and
continues to offer up: a potential for me to "be well what I am."

As an adolescent I considered myself "bisexual" and came out as bi
when I was sixteen at an alternative high school, and again at age seventeen at a mainstream high school, and yet again at age nineteen in a final

mainstream high school. In those four years I had three sexual relationships with women, none of them lasting very long. Yet, I continually
risked myself by coming out even when I had no intentions of being in a
relationship with anyone. I came out in contexts in which one might not
see any obvious reason to be "out"—when the closet does, after all, make
promises of security and safety (however illusory).

Why is this narrative relevant? First, I think that I wasn't bold enough
to just walk away from the hetero world; second, I was unable to sustain
physical intimacy with women because I felt quite certain that they'd *know*
I wasn't authentic—that I was a "skin-job";[4] finally, (pro)claiming my
bisexuality was as much as I was able/willing to risk. In retrospect, I am
quite certain that this list of reasons is the direct product of my medicalization and surgical mutilation.

Not long after the surgery, I figured out that it was not standard procedure for my classmates to have genital surgeries, and I surmised from that
fact that I had been made "normal"—that what I'd been before was
deformed. I spent years obsessed with "freaks," searching through books
on famous circus personalities, looking for someone similar to myself.
Unfortunately, I didn't know what I was looking for. Knowledge of myself
and where I fit in is what was stolen from me by being medicalized and by
having my body altered against my will.

If it had been up to me, I wouldn't have had my body changed; after all,
I didn't think there was any reason to change it. And now, twenty years
later, I feel with the conviction of queerness behind me, that I was right—
there was no reason to change my body.

Eventually I gave up looking for someone who was similar to me. The
vacuum that I lived in permitted no one to speak of what had been done to
me or of how my body had looked before the surgery. It became the great
unspoken in my family, I think, because, as Anne Fausto-Sterling states,
intersexuality " . . . raises the haunting spectre of homosexuality" (1993, 26).

When I fell in love with my girlfriend in seventh grade, I thought it was
because I was physically "different," and so I wasted close to a decade not
telling—only to find out that she too had been in love with me, at certain
points. But I was quite certain that what had happened to me as a child had
not happened to her, so I kept silent about that part of my story. I learned
then that my desire wasn't necessarily linked to my physical difference.
However, even that knowledge could not assuage the fear that my lovers
of whatever sex, but particularly female, would "know" I had a "fake"
cunt and would abandon me. Even as a queer I was hung up on the idea
that I was a monster—not "normal"—even though I should have seen that
there is much to be lost in believing in the binary opposition which privi-

leges sexual normality in contrast to sexual deviance. In this friendship, which has now spanned sixteen years, it has only been about seven months since I broke my silence about my intersexuality. And she didn't run way from me—a fact that astonishes me even now.

However, I think a point about the "not running" needs to be made. Of the people whom I have told about my past and with whom I have also had sexual relationships, their first response is always to assure me of how normal I am. As well intentioned as this might be, it echoes the notes in my medical file from 1984 that state "She has certainly had a very good surgical result. She has perfectly normal adult female genitalia. You wouldn't know she had any surgery if you did not know this in advance." I *know*. I have never forgotten. When people tell me how normal I look now, it raises the issue of how horrible I might have otherwise appeared in their eyes.

This reminds me of an old commercial in which an expensive clothing detergent was compared to a cheap one with identical twins modeling the same clothes while two others inspected the cleanliness of the garments saying: "I can't see the difference. Can you see the difference?" This has been the approach taken to my postsurgical body. But part of what I'm getting at here is that the reassurance I used to seek and the one that is still often given ("I can't tell the difference") fails to acknowledge two things: first, I can literally feel the difference on both physical and experiential levels and, second, just because an external viewer can't recognize the difference, that doesn't mean there isn't one.

My point here is that although I find myself in a committed relationship with a man, and have produced a child in that relationship, I am not just another happy het. This is not just because I'm pro-queer but because I am queer. I refuse to allow my mutilation to rob me any longer of my difference. I should have been left alone to mature in a body that quite feasibly could have penetrated another with its phalloclit. I should have been allowed to grow up to blur the physical markers of sexuality, but I wasn't given that freedom. So I want to take it back by force. I do so by insisting that people think about my marriage as that between a man and an intersexual. Having my genitals mutilated has made me no less intersexual; it has merely made me a mutilated intersexual—just as a woman whose genitals are mutilated is still a woman, as a person who loses a limb is still a human being.

It is my hope that in a future perfect world, queers will not question the validity of calling oneself "queer" even if no one can *see* their difference. It is my hope that hetero-normative culture will be made to account for its oppressive function and will stop insisting on robbing all of us who don't fit in of our rights to self-love, sexual freedom, and community. As it is, I am sitting in a netherworld, but I do feel the doors to the queer community are more open to me than are those of the heterosexual one that will only take me in if I promise to shut up about my difference. "Queer" makes a promise, which I believe can be fulfilled, and that is for all of us "different folk" to be able to achieve freedom from oppression—which is distinct from the freedom to oppress.[5]

NOTES

1. It is a body on/in which the medical model instills a sense of nonbelonging and monstrosity. These feelings are common to all the members of the Intersex Society that I am currently in contact with—approximately twelve persons.
2. This is indicated in my initial assessment in 1971 from my personal medical file.
3. This occurred possibly as a side effect of the drugs, possibly as an "idiopathic" condition—meaning that the condition has no traceable cause.
4. "Skin-job" is the derogatory name given to replicants in the film, *Blade Runner*. I am indebted to Cheryl Chase of ISNA for this imagery.
5. I am indebted, for this idea, to Simone De Beauvoir's *Ethics of Ambiguity* (1948) for the distinction between freedoms.

REFERENCES

De Beauvoir, Simone. 1976 (1948). *The Ethics of Ambiguity*, New York: Citadel Press.
Fausto-Sterling, Anne. 1993. "The five sexes: Why male and female are not enough," *The Sciences,* Spring 1993, pp. 23-26.
Phelan, Shane. 1994. *Getting Specific: Postmodern Lesbian Politics*, Minneapolis, MN: University of Minnesota Press.

Agdistis' Children:
Living Bi-Gendered
in a Single-Gendered World

Raven Kaldera

When I was ten I found the word "hermaphrodite" in a book on Greek myths and looked it up. A thrill of excitement ran through me upon finding the definition. There was a word for what I was, what I felt myself to be inside my head. I knew what my body looked like—a girl's body, though large and sturdy for my age. I knew what my mother wanted me to be—something pink and fluffy and delicate, something I was never quite able to manage, being something of a tomboy. And now I knew what I really was—the secret "me" no one else knew. Then I realized that this word referred to a mythical creature. How could I be one? It was quite impossible. I should just go by what my eyes could tell me, not what my heart already, somehow, knew.

I pulled down my underwear and looked thoughtfully. I think this is the point in life when most transsexual children realize that something is wrong. For me, it wasn't so much that my genitals were the wrong ones than that they were incomplete. Something was missing, and I wondered how I knew.

Then puberty hit me like a double-barreled shotgun—literally. I grew breasts and hips and began to menstruate, irregularly and painfully, but it was happening. My skin broke out and my voice started to crack, just like the boys in my junior high school class. Stubble began to show up on my chin, and my sex drive caromed upward like a speeding car. Boys, girls—it didn't matter. I wanted to jump on all of them, and I was too ashamed to touch any of them. My secret fantasy was real; I was really becoming what I thought was impossible.

I remember reading a story about a man in a repressive dystopia who wakes up and discovers he has a horn growing out of the middle of his forehead. Over the course of the next few weeks, he slowly becomes a unicorn, while his family and society refuse to admit that it's happening. I could relate. I was becoming, little by little, a creature of myth and legend.

Of course, I never made it there in my teen years. In the real world, my mother freaked out and dragged me to the doctor, who diagnosed a hormone imbalance and put me on female hormones. No more shape-shifting; I was stuck with just being a girl again. My condition, for the record, is an intersex condition known as secondary congenital adrenal hyperplasia, but those are just words. It doesn't reveal the wonder and mystery of all that I am.

The hormones stopped the development of masculine secondary sexual characteristics, but they also made me dangerously hypertensive and psychotically depressed. I was to take these hormones off and on for the next dozen years until the doctors finally became worried and made me stop. In the meantime, terrified of the near hysterical reaction of my mother to any hint of crossing gender boundaries (she was a self-proclaimed feminist who swore she could never love a son), I decided to forget what I was. I repressed my bisexuality (Yes, I'm a Kinsey 3, what did you expect?), got married, and proceeded to put my body through a hideous round of hormone treatment in order to have a child. I felt it was necessary to prove, once and for all, that I was a real female. The hormone treatment left me sterile, still depressed, with a premature infant—and nothing had changed. I still didn't feel female. I'm grateful that my daughter came into existence, but the price I paid for her was high.

Years later, sans husband and hormones, things began to change back. At first it was rough, as all change is. Coming to terms with my true sex, a sex barely recognized by humanity outside of freak shows and medical oddities, took years of work and soul-searching. I finally ran across the budding transgender community and breathed a sigh of relief. Here was a whole roomful of bi-gendered people all together! I had varying reactions when I explained my situation. Some were envious ("you've got a medical reason!"), some were supportive, and some, very invested in being seen as single-gendered individuals, were uncomfortable at being compared to me.

I also had to come to terms with my sexual preference. I call myself pansexual because bisexual implies that there are only two genders. There are at least three; even if you discount my transgendered friends, I'm living proof. I like girls; I like boys—but other androgynes are at the top of my list. It doesn't matter which direction they're going in; if it's gender ambiguous, my head will snap around as they go by. Does that mean I'm gay, in the strictest sense of the word? Is it a new sexual preference? There's a new word in the community for people who go for genderfolk: transfrienders. Most are bewildered by their preference, wondering what it implies about their visions of male and female.

Coming to terms with what my body wanted was another hard issue. I function best on testosterone—no depression, no lethargy, better physical health. My brain was somehow bathed in it while I was still a fetus, creating my endocrinal disorder (Is it a disorder? I prefer to think of it as a variation.) I need it to be healthy. Letting the male hormones take back my body pushed me into a category I hadn't expected—that of female-to-male transgender. I grew my beard out and was surprised to find that I loved it. I heard the male pronoun used on me for the first time and liked that, too. I joined a support group of F2M transsexuals that has been my lifeline in times of crisis, but although we have much in common, there are many ways in which I'm somewhat different.

I ended up marrying one of those tempting androgynes in the gender community; my wife is a male-to-female transsexual. In California parlance, we're a reverse couple. Are we gay? Are we straight? I'll tell you, it sure doesn't feel straight to me, although it obviously isn't lesbian or gay male. Queerest of the queer? Perhaps even beyond labels? I like to explain us in terms of a butch-femme dynamic. Butch-femme is a dynamic of same sex, different gender—all the common ground of the same sex along with all the tension of opposite genders. (By this definition, far from butch-femme being a poor copy of heterosexuality, heterosexuality becomes a truncated, incomplete version of butch-femme! Those poor heterosexuals! How do they manage! I'm so glad that it's physically and mentally impossible for me to be one, no matter who it's with.) There are butch-femme lesbians and also gay men who I'd say fall into that category. My wife and I are just the butch-femme version of the third sex.

Male culture provided the really rough part of the change. I was utterly not invested in either cultural or countercultural versions of womanhood. On the other hand, I was politically educated enough to realize that cultural maleness wasn't any better. I wanted to keep my hair long. I wanted to wear black leather, and lace, and brocade, and occasionally skirts. I wanted to make eye contact. I wanted to do all these things and do them in a masculine body. I also figured that if there were men like that, they probably got beat up a lot. I went in search of role models to teach me how to survive—men who challenge the dominant system and stay alive and sane and aware. I found them, too. (Okay, so they were almost all gay or bisexual.) They taught me the male mysteries—the real ones, not the fake ones offered up by society. No, I'm not telling. They're mysteries, OK? Get together and figure them out yourselves.

This brings us to the sticky question of gender dysphoria, which is the shrink word for what transgendered people suffer from that makes us so durn intractable when it comes to neat gender segregation by genitals. I divide it into two parts—body dysphoria and role dysphoria. Role dysphoria is simply being unhappy with one's assigned gender role and preferring that of the opposite gender. Obviously, this is highly dependent on the context of the society the individual is in—some are bad enough to create a small amount of role dysphoria in anyone with a functioning brain! An example of role dysphoria might be my friend Ailsa, a butch dyke who wears a suit to work and wants to be a good husband but still identifies as female.

Body dysphoria is a cat of a different color. Even those of us who have it don't really understand it, and it must seem completely incomprehensible to those who've never experienced it. Body dysphoria makes you desperately wish the gender of your physical form were different, regardless of social role. It's not about lipstick or privilege. It's about wanting to stand naked on the street corner and have people point and say, "Oh, that's a guy (girl)." It's not about aesthetics; you'd rather be an ugly opposite-sex critter than a beautiful member of your birth gender. It infuriates psychiatrists because it has no apparent cause and can't be budged. (I think it's biological, but then knowing where I'm coming from, you'll understand why I like this theory.)

Of course, intersex people aren't supposed to have gender dysphoria. They're supposed to fall placidly and obediently into whatever category the doctors and parents hammer them into; at least this is the myth that the doctors desperately push. Some do and seem to be fine. Some end up in the sex change office; we don't know how many statistically, but I know quite a few personally. The sins of the medical profession against intersex children are varied and hideous. (Are you ready for this? Got the Dramamine out?) If, for example, you bore a child with mixed genitalia and reproductive organs, the doctors immediately set out to "fix" it by surgical alteration. Ours are the ultimate outlaw bodies.

Most intersex children are assigned as girls. No child with a phallus/penis/enlarged clitoris that's smaller than normal gets to be a boy because of the "humiliation factor" later in life—no dick, no male gender. If the dick is big enough but there's a vagina, it gets sewn up. If the child is assigned as a girl, the doctors perform one of their complicated medical procedures on the baby's phallus/penis/enlarged clitoris. That is to say, they cut it off. Yes, just like the clitoridectomies of those million or so women in Africa. If there are female reproductive organs but no connecting vagina, one will be constructed. The parents will then be informed that their "daughter" can now have a normal sex life, meaning that there is now a (albeit insensate) hole for some future male to stick a pole into. They won't be told that sexual pleasure is now impossible for this child. They certainly won't be told that this child may end up with gender dysphoria or that the child will probably be queer. (Two studies, done twenty years apart, of individuals with my "disorder" showed they only had a one in four chance of being heterosexual. No, Ma, it ain't your fault.) At puberty, of course, the child has to be pumped full of whatever hormones the adults think they need.

All the parents are told is that if they do their best to carefully delineate the differences between boys and girls and carefully reinforce fairly stereotypical behavior and punish opposite sex behavior (I'm serious here!) the kid will turn out OK. Uh-huh. And pigs fly. This is one circus freak the treatment didn't take on. How do I manage? Well, I'm a shaman, a pagan priest(ess) of the Dark Goddess and the Lord of the Dead. Thousands of years ago, I might have been seen to be a shaman at puberty, been acknowledged and valued for the living, breathing, magical, mythical beast that I am. Those of us in the gender community who consider ourselves shamans, such as myself and my wife, are starting to move. We want our birthright back.

I remember the first time I asked for an answer. Sometimes you just throw up your hands and ask "Why?" and you get a sudden answer from your deeper power that knocks you over—one that is utterly inarguable. I still recall it: "I'm sending you where you're needed most!" It's become my mantra now that I'm an activist for the transgendered community.

There's a myth in the gender movement that two bi-gendered people together on the street attract too much attention; they inadvertently "out" each other and create a danger of bashing. My beloved and I reject this, and not just because we're always "out." Let me lay a different situation on the table. A whole gang of genderfolk walking down the street *together* and not seeming the least bit intimidated is enough to shatter the world view, blow the mind—and scare the hell out of—any would-be basher. I know. I've been there. We need community. And we need the gay community, too, for various reasons, and they need us. I march in Gay Pride, not because I'm intersex or transgendered, but because I'm pansexual. I'm not the only one, either.

There's a Greek/Middle Eastern ancient myth I found about a wild, laughing hermaphrodite named Agdistis who ran about the mountains screwing who s/he pleased.[1] The gods decided that s/he was too dangerous, because s/he knew both the male and the female mysteries and could command too much power. So they offered Agdistis a choice: cut off the male member or sew up the female one. Choose.

And Agdistis said unto them, "Fuck you," and ran away laughing.

And the gods became very paranoid, and they determined that it should be done anyway, but no one wanted Agdistis' blood on their hands because something "strange" might happen to them. (Gee, wonder what?) So they tricked a young god into doing it, and it ended up killing Agdistis, whose death sparked a whole chain of reactions, but that's a different story.

If there is a bi-gendered mystery, that's it in a nutshell: our very existence affects people, whether they like it or not. We don't even have to talk to them. We can just stand around and exist, and they'll have to struggle with their world views. We are walking catalysts. People have different reactions to this, of course. Maybe they find us fascinating. Maybe they want to categorize us. Maybe they want to obliterate us.

Remember the gods' reason—too much power! We are the walkers between worlds, the bridgers of opposites. We have always lived in mythology—as Dionysus, Shiva, Tiresias, Pales, Baphomet, the Bearded Aphrodite of Cyprus. And now, in this time of the war between the sexes, we are needed more than ever. After all, who are going to be the ambassadors in the cleanup of this mess? We are here to help, but the price is getting used to us.

Be warned. You stand in the presence of a mystery. And believe me, there's a hell of a lot of spiritual clout in being a mythical beast.

NOTE

1. Vermaseren, Martin. *Cybele and Attis.* London: Thames and Hudson, Ltd., 1997.

PART 8:
BOYZ, GRRLS, QUEERS

Flunking Basic Gender Training: Butches and Butch Style Today

Sherrie A. Inness

The women's room is a war zone for my girlfriend and me, as well as for countless other butches across the United States. Dressed in leather jackets, jeans, button-down men's shirts, and boots, with our haircuts barely brushing the tops of our ears, we strike fear into many women's hearts, as they glance pointedly from the sign on the door to us. The women at the sink glare at us as if we have committed some unspeakable crime. Not uncommonly, a braver woman will walk up and tap one of us on the shoulder and say, "This is the *ladies'* room." This happens with such frequency that I enter a public restroom only with trepidation. I smile and try to appear nonthreatening, attempting to diffuse any hostility or confusion. Yet, I still am stared at and have caused women to bolt out of the women's room, muttering, "I thought this was the ladies' room." The bathroom is supposedly the place where gender solidarity is taken for granted, yet for a butch lesbian the experience can be exactly the opposite. Yet, what is the alternative? Certainly not the men's room. Metaphorically the butch's lack of "belonging" in either the women's room or the men's room points out her place in the society at large, where neither heterosexual women nor men are tolerant of her style, presentation, and attitude.

First, what does it mean to be butch? Alisa Solomon (1993) calls butchness "a style of self-presentation, as a way of asserting or displaying oneself—one's lesbian self—in 1990s America" (p. 36). Using this broad definition, butch has much more to do with attitude, style, and dress than it has to do with particular sexual practices. As one butch commented, "If I were celibate for the rest of my life, I would still be butch." What we can say is that the butch blatantly refuses to assume what many think should be her "normal" role and appearance. She might reject lingerie in favor of men's underwear or insist on a butch swagger instead of a dainty, mincing step. She might shop in the men's department. Whatever way she seeks to create her personal style, the butch rejects culture norms about how women should act, behave, and dress.

In many ways, the butch who refuses to pass as straight is a social outcast, who might be denied jobs, professional advancement, or social acceptance because of her butch appearance and actions. No wonder that many butches strive to pass as not butch or seek a variety of nontraditional positions (computer programming, truck driving, construction work) that place less of an emphasis on looking feminine. We must recognize that a butch is subject to discrimination almost every day of her life in addition to open harassment and threats. Although butches certainly do not comprise the entire lesbian community, they are frequently the ones who have to bear the brunt of being lesbian and face the hostility of heterosexual society. They are the lesbians who stand out from the crowd; whether Radclyffe Hall or Gertrude Stein, the butch is an unmistakable presence.

Being butch means that friends, associates, and strangers remind you constantly that you should be more feminine. As far as landing a job in the first place is concerned, a butch learns fast that her chances go up with each feminine signifier she adds. With a crew cut, pants, and leather jacket, her chances of employment are dim. But if you appear more feminine one day, perhaps wearing a skirt to work, your heterosexist co-workers will enthusiastically proclaim how good you look in a skirt and that you should wear skirts more often. A butch who adopts feminine adornments such as long hair and skirts may discover that males in power, who were formerly cold and difficult to work with, will warm up, lean over the desk to talk, and take a clear interest that they never did before.

Why is it that presenting oneself as butch calls up the wrath of mainstream heterosexual society? Why do so many straight women seem to believe that they need to praise a butch when she wears a dress and pumps, but never say a word when she wears a pin-striped men's suit, no matter how dashing she looks? A butch makes heterosexuals uneasy because she rejects the role of a female as a commodity to be exchanged and bartered by men. She refuses to accept the feminine behavior (such as flirting with men) that identifies her sexual availability. Quite to the contrary, the butch openly advertises her sexual unavailability to men, which marks her as an open threat. At the same time, the butch also advertises her sexual availability to women and her ability to subsume the role that men assume is theirs. Critic Alisa Solomon writes astutely about the threat posed by butches and their images: "Adopting and often transforming traits traditionally associated with men, butches threaten masculinity more than they imitate it; they colonize it. Making aggression or toughness or chivalry or rebelliousness their histrionic own, butches reveal the arbitrariness with which such traits are said to belong to men" (1993, p. 37). Solomon continues, "Being butch isn't simply to flunk basic gender training; it's to scoff at the whole curriculum. And in doing so, it reveals the artificiality of the entire system" (p. 38).

Given the hostility of the general society, why do butches still insist on shopping in the men's department, despite the glares they might receive? Why do they insist on wearing ties, when scarves are so much more "feminine"? Why do they still get haircuts that frequently make them look as if they just got out of the military? Even though society in general might look askance at these manifestations of butchness, there is another side to the coin. Whereas heterosexuals might scorn butches, other lesbians adulate them, often regarding them as even semiheroic figures. You can even find entire books, such as Lily Burana and Roxxie Linnea's edited collection *Dagger: On Butch Women* (1994), that focus solely on the butch's alluring image. Scan any page of the personal ads in a large city gay newspaper and you will see scores of advertisements for "butches wanted," advertisements far outnumbering the similar requests for femmes. Butches are larger than life characters in the lesbian community, frequently acting out by their appearance and behavior an attitude toward society that others can never imitate. With her 500cc motorcycle, soot-black leather jacket, and Ray•Bans, the butch acts out the fantasies that so many lesbians have, but might be unable to fulfill. The butch flaunts her difference. She proves that a woman can have power on a man's terms. Her very existence denies the essentialist claims that women are "naturally" weaker, "naturally" incapable of performing as men perform. Of course, not all butches have motorcycles or even Ray•Bans, but this does not stop them from still embodying the fantasy of escape from gender norms.

One of the fantasies that the butch fulfills is that she no longer seems obsessed with being "a girl." Gender no longer seems to have the same constraint on her that it does on many other women. The butch glories in leather jackets, men's shirts, pants, ties, and shoes—all signifiers that mark her as a gender bender, someone who intentionally plays with what gender means in our culture. Nor is the butch confined to one particular masculine style and appearance:

> There are at least as many ways to be butch as there are ways for men
> to be masculine; actually, there are more ways to be butch, because
> when women appropriate masculine styles the element of travesty
> produces new significance and meaning. Butches adopt and trans-
> mute the many available codes of masculinity. (Rubin, 1992, p. 469)

The butch can be a boyish, soft butch, flat-chested and narrow-hipped,
or an impressive diesel dyke, heavyset and tough enough to brawl with
any man who makes a slur about her appearance; she can model her
appearance on Steven Gordon, Gertrude Stein, or Leslie Feinberg. The
possibilities are endless, and all of them result in an image that is a
political statement—whether the butch wants it to be or not—a statement
that makes it clear that the butch refuses to accept her place as a "properly
feminine" woman in society. Because masculine garb and attitude marks
the butch as someone who is rebelling against society's restraints, it also
makes the butch sexually attractive to many; as Gayle Rubin writes, "The
coexistence of masculine traits with a female anatomy is a fundamental
characteristic of "butch" and is a highly charged, eroticized, and conse-
quential lesbian signal" (1992, p. 468).

Nor does being butch mean that a woman is simply trying to mimic
men, as many heterosexuals wrongly assume. Butch is a word to describe
a woman with a certain attitude, a certain look, a certain energy and way of
self-presentation and self-identification. This self-presentation, however,
has far more to do with other butches than with men. The butch must
constantly read the behavior of other butches in order to understand her
own role as a butch. Even in the 1940s and 1950s, as Elizabeth Lapovsky
Kennedy and Madeline Davis point out in their study *Boots of Leather,
Slippers of Gold: The History of a Lesbian Community* (1993), younger
butches modeled their appearance on that of more experienced butches
(p. 158). Today, a butch looks to other butches in order to rate herself as a
butch: Am I as butch as her? Am I butch enough? Maybe I should try
wearing my hair like that. Where did she buy those Doc Martens? Hunting
for a sense of style, the butch looks at other butches in order to affirm her
own place in the world. Theorist Judith Butler, in her groundbreaking
study *Gender Trouble: Feminism and the Subversion of Identity* (1990),
does an excellent job explaining why it is that butches are not simply
trying to be men. "Within lesbian contexts, the 'identification' with masculinity that appears as butch identity is not a simple assimilation of
lesbianism back into the terms of heterosexuality," Butler writes. "As one
lesbian femme explained, she like her boys to be girls, meaning that 'being a
girl' contextualizes and resignifies 'masculinity' in a butch identity" (p. 123).
Butler is describing a crucial aspect of butch appearance and identity.

Because she is a biological "girl," the butch inevitably reshapes the masculine clothing and style that she adopts. On the butch's body, "men's" clothing suddenly goes radical. A butch always reshapes masculinity in a way that is truly subversive, suggesting as it does the intrinsic instability of gender.

The butch, as with the transvestite, is a gender outlaw, someone who pushes at the edges of gender, forcing us to recognize that gender has little to do with biological sex. Even a seemingly trivial incident, such as being called "sir" in the ladies' room, is enough to make someone examine her preconceived notions about how women are expected to dress and behave— and look. To be acceptable, I ask myself, must I be willing to conform to all the stereotypes that are supposed to represent femininity? If I let my hair grow longer, put on lipstick and mascara, wear high heels, no one again will ever question my right to be in the women's room. But—and this is why I will continue being butch and not attempt to pass as anything else—I am not willing to accept having to conform to whatever the prevalent ideas of femininity might be. I only hope I never have to use a restroom.

REFERENCES

Burana, Lily, and Roxxie Linnea (eds.). *Dagger: On Butch Women*. San Francisco: Cleis P., 1994.

Butler, Judith. *Gender Trouble: Feminism and the Subversion of Identity*. New York: Routledge, 1990.

Kennedy, Elizabeth Lapovsky, and Madeline Davis. *Boots of Leather, Slippers of Gold: The History of a Lesbian Community*. New York: Routledge, 1993.

Rubin, Gayle. "Of Catamites and Kings: Reflections on Butch, Gender, and Boundaries." In *The Persistent Desire: A Femme-Butch Reader*, Joan Nestle, (ed.). Boston: Alyson, 1992, 466-482.

Solomon, Alisa. "Not Just a Passing Fancy: Notes on Butch." *Theater* 24(2) (1993): 35-46.

Frankly Feminine: Rejecting and Embracing Standards for Beauty

Laura Cole

I lean toward the mirror, my lips parted and pursed. Steadily I trace my mouth with the richly colored lipstick I hold at my fingertips. I stand back, snap the cover on the tube, and evaluate the image before me. Some of my hair is combed out of my face and propped back with a barrette. The rest cascades past my shoulders in waves and soft curls. I am wearing a colorful, cotton-poly T-shirt, nondescript black pants, knee-high nylons, and low-heeled pumps. I wear a watch and earrings, but no rings; my manicured nails are painted. The nail polish and lip color are the only cosmetics on my body, if you don't count the perfume. I like the image before me. It can be either flashy or understated, depending on where you let your eyes rest. I perceive it as pretty, and that makes me feel good.

If my identity could be summed up under a label, it would be "lipstick," but that's not accurate either since I am bisexual. Regardless, it is an image I am comfortable with, and I have no plans to change. I know that I defy the straight world when I limit or forgo the use of cosmetics, refuse to shave my legs, and accept my 130-pound frame. I also know that I've raised the hackles of a few dykes with my occasionally painted lips or a lacy tank top that reveals clean-shaven underarms. But my integrity rests on creating an image that I am comfortable with. If I conform to the standards of any group for the sake of inclusiveness or approval, I am sacrificing personal honesty. Before I am bisexual, before I am a feminist, before I am a woman, I am an individual. Hopefully, that is what one sees first when they look at me. The lesbian and bisexual circles I have been a part of have made an honest, if not successful, attempt to reject the traditional, mainstream standards for how we should look. In these groups, hair tends to be cropped in a functional cut. Dresses and skirts are rare. Makeup is nearly obsolete. Fashion is dictated by personal style and practicality; comfortable shoes are the last word. It makes for an androgynous crowd, with the occasional butch or femme to tip the scale. But it is not me.

I like to wear my hair in a feminine style. Occasionally, I like bright lipstick. I'm not afraid to wear a skirt and heels to work—even when it's not required. No, they don't have the mobility of Birkenstocks, but I have a desk job and the minimal awkwardness is worth the boost in confidence. When I go out at night, I wear clothes that accentuate my sexuality. I shave (in places).

I find this style appealing in myself as well as other women. I'm attracted to traditional femininity—"traditional" in the sense of what other lesbian or bisexual women may refer to as "patriarchal." Figure-flattering clothes, long hair, a pretty face, and a body that is height/weight proportional are some of the things that turn my head. A woman's physical attributes would not be the first or last word on whether we became romantically involved. However, if she had an androgynous or tomboyish look, it would not be her appearance that attracted me to her.

These are honest reflections on what I find beautiful. I should add that I think physical beauty is important. I cannot imagine becoming sexually involved with someone whom I did not think was attractive. I have tried to forge romantic liaisons with both men and women without using their appearance as a criterion. It seemed to be the politically correct thing to do: focus on personal qualities and ignore the superficial ones. In all cases I got what I asked for—a friendship with substance but little or no sex life. It felt dishonest and forced.

So I reject pressure from both the queer and straight communities to date according to their criteria for attractiveness. And I reject pressure from both groups to look the way they think I should look. Personal appearance is a highly subjective issue and should therefore remain personal. Certainly society can impose standards, but it is up to the individual to discern whether those standards are reasonable or not. The only role our respective communities should play is to give us permission to express ourselves as we choose. They should not impose their own set of standards.

Faggot Rant

Sandra Lee Golvin

I'm on a mountain somewhere in New Mexico with a hundred dykes and faggots trying to vision a way to come together beyond the boundaries of boy and girl and figure out what is this thing called queer and I am wearing my shorts, my leather jacket, and my favorite baseball cap when this lovely black-haired man—Latin like my longtime woman lover—takes my hand, draws me into him, looks at me deep like he really sees me and says: "You really are a two-spirit. Because sometimes I look at you and I see a woman and sometimes I look at you and I see a man." And suddenly, after forty-three years, I am arrived home.

I said my body is a shame and what I meant is the force of life. The things I want flayed away I cannot even name but it has something to do with always wanting to please and always wanting to be liked and whether or not you think I'm a nice nice girl. Fuck that shit. There's a faggot inside of me wanting to come out. A speedy young guy who likes it from the pelvis. He's a pleaser, a hustler, a carpenter white boy from down south.

See everyone wants to know what do dykes and fags have in common so there's this mental masturbation about whether our politics overlap and what the boys owe the girls who've helped so much with the AIDS crisis and what the girls owe those boys who understand abortion is their issue too. No one's talking about the faggot dykes who just want to do it with those boys you know like a big sister with baby brother. No one's talking about the lesbo fags who want to put their lips to their sister's lips and turn their butts to some lovely strapped-on cock. And let's be clear now that we're not just talking the S&M queers who understand all of this and don't let gender get in the way of descent or ecstatic arrival. No we're talking about the hardcore feminist dykes who fantasize about being a boy with another boy and all those button-down daddies who dream of wearing a dress and going pussy to pussy with some scary Amazon from the bar down the street.

Faggot Rant was first presented at P.S. 122 in New York City on November 19, 1994 as part of The Franklin Furnace in Exile series funded by the Franklin Furnace Fund for Performance Art Award.

Someone called us gay and said that's about you have sex with the same sex and yes, sex with the same sex is part of it, we all like sex but there is something more that connects us for which no language seems to exist but it has something to do with how my boy-daddy inside is faggot and my girl-mommy inside is dyke and that the whole goddamn inner landscape is utterly and completely queer.

"You really are a two-spirit." It's not that I haven't heard this before. I have. But not in this way. It's always been a shaming, a shaming of the boy in me. My muscular body, the calves too big for a girl, the hair there thicker than most men's. Hair on the face, the beard, the mustache, between the dark-set brows. Hair on the arms, between the breasts, around the belly and down to the pubis. So many times like in Berkeley twenty years ago when I tried on the golfer's cap and the man behind the counter said to my girlfriend, "That hat looks great on the little guy." All the times the trainers at the gym cautioned me, "Don't lift too much weight or you'll get muscles too big for a woman." I want to tell you, though, I am not a man trapped in a woman's body. Though I honor those who are. Because my body is a woman's only by virtue of the pussy and the breasts. Why are these the determining factors? With a flat chest and a dick nothing else changes and I am a guy. Why do I have to make a choice? I'm not a man and I'm not a woman, but some strange combination of the two. And that has been my shame.

I said my body is a shame and what I meant is the force of life. Because if I can figure out how to occupy that territory that is neither man nor woman and yet is both man and woman, how to truly stand at the point of intersection into which my body says I was born, then I can perhaps begin to see who and what I really am.

And the place of the shame is the place of power. There's a reason people like me cannot be allowed and it has to do with possibility, that possibility that the line between boys and girls is not nearly so clearly drawn as some would have us believe. And if that boundary is fluid, and there is a large unmapped erogenous zone that lies between the territories of boy and girl, then the assignment of gender which is the very foundation of the culture is rocked to its core and every rigid dualistic structure built upon it must crumble.

I hate the words man and woman. I hate the words male and female. I can't choose one place or the other. Even dyke, which is a word I love, without major redefinition doesn't seem to include my serious erotic attraction to men in beards and dresses. Further confused by not being a butch but a femme dyke who is also a faggot—what is this category? What am I, some kind of freak? Yes, I am some kind of freak. I claim my place as a freak.

I said my body is a shame and what I meant is the force of life. It's the strange vibrant place of possibility that must be ground to dust in the first moments after we're born because it threatens the heart of what has been constructed around it. What I am saying is that the occupation of the not-man-not-woman-all-man-all-woman-fag-dyke territory is the war zone, where my battle has always been fought without a fucking map or mythology. I've been fighting my way into that shadow land of my obliterated history every day of my life, my body the scarred earth of what I never understood, of what I could not name, of my utter lack of language to serve as compass home. But I'm starting to see it now, forty-three years later.

"You really are a two-spirit." There is an ancient holy office of the double-gendered body, a queer tradition of life in service to the erogenous zone between the genders, a calling of the sacred body. What if someone had told me I was special? My body a precious gift, hair to be welcomed, muscles to be sculpted and oiled and adorned. They say that in some Native American cultures the parents of such a child consider themselves as blessed. My father said "one of nature's little oddities." Yes, nature has a way of recruiting us to her service. And having refused it for so many years only now do I begin to be able to offer myself in service to her mystery, to walk her land as a living reminder to all who see this man-woman, woman-man that the body does not lie. And this body says yes this is my shame. Yes, this is my heart. Yes, this is my desire. And, yes, this is the force of life.

Beautiful Boy:
A Girl's Own Story

Boye

She calls me her beautiful boy. Beautiful boy, words from her lips that touch the heart of me. I am the boy who makes her smile. This little body of mine is beautiful to her. This woman's body of mine, once a curse, has become a wonderful thing. This little body pleases her. I am learning to allow it to please me. My baggy jeans hang on my hips without the fat to expose my female condition. My boy self has made the woman beautiful. She calls me her beautiful boy, with a beautiful woman's body.

This woman's body of mine was a place of darkness, a home of demons and shadows. This body of mine was an alien thing. The essence of who I am cowered inside, baffled by its limitation. Old spirit, young soul, I watched as one-third of this lifetime slipped away. Born little girl, the body and its social implications ran counter to the spirit. Not male, not female, an undefined third sex, inherently unacceptable. A walker between worlds with no place to call my own.

As soon as I was able, I fought my mother's need to "dress up" her little girl doll. I felt naked in dresses. I resisted her desire for patterns or flowers, her need to play with my hair, make me pretty. My sad eyes dominate family photos. I loved the tie of my school uniform but hated the skirt, the shame of the breeze between my legs. I made sure my socks always fell to my ankles and my knees were always dirty. Rebellion without breaking the rules, my survival. Failing as a good girl, I devoured books about "naughty" girls. I wanted so to be one. I dreamt of private convent schools and special friendships, secret societies and hidden clubhouses. I had an altar in my room at home. I knew the Mass by heart. I was going to be a priest.

The chance to be with my father in his workshop was a much sought-after treat. I wanted to learn to build things, not bake them. I wanted my own set of tools. My best friend was Mark. We terrorized the neighborhood. We raced our bikes and fought wars. His mother let me wear his swimming trunks to play with the hose in the garden. It felt forbidden, exciting, powerful to run with no shirt, to wear "boy" clothes. We both knew I was the bravest because I went into the boys' bathroom in the park and he wouldn't go into the girls'. I broke my arm doing a cartwheel in his yard and didn't tell any grown-ups for nearly two weeks. By the age of six, I had learned not to show or feel the pain in my body.

For my eighth birthday my godmother gave me ten classes to learn how to swim. In the water I was strong. In the water I was free, no restrictions of expected ladylike behavior. In the water I didn't have to wear a dress. In the water I felt my body as a good thing. At ten, I was the best in the county. In the team photo I stand to the side, arms folded against my chest, looking like a little boy wearing the wrong bathing suit. I look lean, muscular, and strong, which surprised me as an adult because I experienced that time as a fat kid—distorted body image, a family inheritance.

I did not want to be a girl. I did not want to be a boy. I despised the weakness of women, the arrogance of men. More than a child's disdain for grown-ups was the recognition that neither sex bore a mantle that I could see myself being willing to bear. As my body grew, I was frequently shocked at my reflection; it had no resemblance to the boy I felt inside. As an adult, my therapist asked me to complete the sentence "A woman is . . . ". Of one hundred versions, less than 25 percent were empowered, positive statements. At thirty, my resistance to acknowledge myself as a woman was still a powerful force. This revelation added feminist shame to the family pile.

As a teenager, I fucked boys but dreamt of women. In love with my art teacher, I sat in a school assembly of 700 girls, looking for the others like me. I got married at sixteen. Freedom came in the form of a man who liked my hair too short, my clothes too masculine, a man who relished my differentness, who didn't want an appropriate girl. In private, we laughed about finding a woman for us both to fuck. In public, my husband was frequently asked, "How old is your son?" We laughed about that too. Laughter protected me from the festering fear inside, fear that they would make me be what I knew I could not, fear that fed the rage of my impotent rebellion.

I came out as a lesbian into the feminist climate of the eighties, when "too much male energy" was the most fashionable insult. The noncommitment of androgyny gave me the protection of asexual conformity but no sense of self. I saw the butch and femme women of our past as far more of a statement to society of who we are. I wanted the world to know. I would not be hidden. I became a professional queer. I wore the label "baby butch" with attitude and pride. However, my desire for a leather jacket and my blossoming interest in handcuffs remained suppressed. I was not willing to risk the isolation of being that politically incorrect. I thought I had to grow up to be a "real" butch but had no actual skill for manual trades or a desire for softball and backslapping. It seemed even in a culture that claimed to accept me I didn't belong.

With an inherent sense of feminist protocol, I had always argued against my mother's compulsion with dieting. I weighed 180 pounds and hid myself in sweats. I told myself I was proud of my size, my perceived power. The bigger I was, the more invisible I became to men. That was my power. I embraced the fashion of baggy men's clothes. I liked being a big woman. I was safe.

Then, my comfortable cocoon was shattered by a stomach flu during which I lost thirty pounds in a month. Men started noticing me on the street again. I did not want their attention, but the flu had shown me a new outlet for my pain. I found the powerful emotional purification that throwing up could bring. As my body shape changed, the boy began to recognize himself again. He wanted the body for himself. I knew the fat I saw in the mirror was not real, but I continued losing weight, proud of the twenty-nine-inch jeans I could wear and the ribs beneath my tight, white T-shirt.

This body of mine, taken from me as a baby by stimulation and invasion, had no value. I claimed the right to its destruction, the right to remove the burden. As I sat on the bathroom floor, I mocked their power to define me—my dinner in the toilet bowl, endorphins pumping the illusion of safety. This female body of mine, with too many soft edges, hips, and thighs, had betrayed my weakness. I drowned it in alcohol, captured it in cocaine, abandoned it with opiates. I sought strength in other people, power in sexual conquests. Searching always outside of myself for a sense of peace, for the semblance of sanity, for a way to feel comfortable in my own skin. Balance was the place I crossed between extremes.

I walked into queer bars with the arrogance of the boy to protect me. I knew I was being noticed. I rarely had to go home alone. If you were my friend, I would fuck you. If intimacy reared its head, I would fuck you. I would fuck you to prove I cared. I would fuck you to stop you getting too close. Redefining its value, I made this body my most potent legal tender, clinging to the belief that the chasm of need inside me could be filled.

This body could not be comforted. I learned not to ask for comfort. I gave up any expectation that this body could be pleasured by another. I did not know how to trust myself; how could I trust them? I gave up searching. There was no place for this body, this spirit, to call home. I retreated further into the darkness of my addictions—rage at the world turned inward. The ultimate aloneness of suicidal insanity and chronic depression created a glamour of safety as all else began to fail. My only hope was to find a way to leave the planet.

Friends took me to a psychic who spoke of the need to stay. The need to stay in this body that didn't belong to me. This body with no place. This body that could not bear patient touch. This body full of shame. My boy/girl child self screamed, "No! this body is too big. It hurts too bad. No!" The psychic spoke of the black box inside that needed to be opened to the light, of trust and solution. The child chanted alone.

The body began to remember, despite me. The box started to open. The boy, the girl, the woman walked toward the pain. There was not enough of anything to take it away. The woman became willing to hear both the boy and the girl. The need to grow up or die pushed me from my island of isolation. The spark of life within me that should have perished took a new breath and became a flame. Although I could not acknowledge it at the time, the will to live became stronger than the desire to die. With the brazen courage of one who had nothing to lose, I became willing to trust. No booze, no food, no sex to protect me—the pain in this body became my pain. I became able to do, feel, and believe that which I could not do unaided on my will alone. I became willing to accept this human condition and to believe I could have the power I wanted as a woman. I became willing to entertain the concept of choice.

Many years later, I heard a voice inside that I have come to recognize as mine. The voice is clear and strong. I am Boye. My name is my number. Boye, the feminine of boy. Boye my name, my attitude, my body. Being called "Sir" no longer embarrasses me or causes shame; it empowers me. "That's the Ladies' Room," they helpfully explain. "Yes, I know," I reply, as I walk through the door with pride and a smile. Society's narrow ability to define does not take power from who I am. This boy has biceps, baggy jeans, and a flirting eye. This boy wears a prick when she wants to. This woman's body is small and strong, with breasts to tease, cunt to fill, and hands to touch. This boy loves women; she will fill you, touch you as only a woman can. This body is mine. This body is mine to give honorably. This body I am learning to trust tells me what it needs, what it wants. I wear my leather jacket and handcuffs with pride. This body likes to expand the boundaries of pleasure and be tenderly tortured. This body has no need to hide behind mounds of fat or to find solace in secret bathroom fixes. The boy and the woman are finding balance between the picture of his/her body in the mind and the size of her Levi's.

She calls me her beautiful boy. This body of mine, my most valuable possession, I give to her willingly. The power of my submission feeds the strength of this woman that I have become. The searching has led me back to the beginning, back to this body of mine, this heart of mine, and this transgendered spirit. I walk in this world, but I am not of it. There is no limit to what this woman can do. There is no limit to who this boy can be. In this body, this Boye has found home.

SECTION C:
BEYOND THE PALE

PART 9:
COLOR VISION

"I" is for Intersection:
At the Crux of Black and White
and Gay and Straight

Layli Phillips

I have often felt like I am several people, not in the multiple personality kind of way, but in the personae kind of way. It's not that I haven't wanted to be one, it's just that it's been impossible. I've always had to choose between being whole and being intelligible, being whole and being loved—between the desire to "be" and the desire to "be with." My body is not simple; it forces people to think about uncertainty: Is she black or is she white? Is she gay or is she straight? Where are the lines?

AUTOBIOGRAPHY:
MY BODY IS MY IDENTITY

My body has always been a symbol—a symbol of race conflict and a symbol of the state of race relations at any given point in time. It has been a symbol of threat, a symbol of subversion, a symbol of boundary crossing and taboo. That defiant attitude which is my birthright later permeated my sexuality and gender beliefs as well. While I might not have chosen such a controversial existence as a child or adolescent—it seemed nearly unbearable during my youth—I now revel in it, and its tensions and conundrums structure who I am, what I value, and how I love and work. My body has become my identity, and the way I look has become the way I think.

My parents—black mother, white father—were married in 1962 at a time when interracial marriage was only legal in seven states. Both new Baha'is, they were full of religious idealism about bridging race relations. In 1965, two days after the assassination of Malcolm X and on the ninety-seventh anniversary of the birth of W.E.B. DuBois, I was born. Our family life revolved around the Baha'i faith: We moved from place to place as "pioneers" to teach the faith (traversing New York, Georgia, and Florida), and all our social activity revolved around the Baha'i community. This was a diverse community, comprised of people from virtually all races, nationalities, and social classes. Because it was visually utopian and I was a child, I took it at face value and was shielded from knowledge of racial, class, and gender conflict within the Baha'i community as well as outside it. Although my experiences as a racially anomalous person in the world outside the Baha'i community (e.g., public school) made me acutely aware of race as a problem area, it wasn't until my high school/college period that I became aware of the depth, extent, and virulence of racism. Furthermore, it was not until this same period that I fully realized that most people viewed me as black; until the day one of my white friends referred to me as her "black friend," I assumed that others viewed me as I viewed myself—as somebody who was "Mixed."

Much of my early identity was structured by the fact that, as a person with a "Mixed" self-identity, I had never really fit in with other kids. My body was always signifying: The white master's rape of the black slave woman one day, "jungle fever" the next. My race was always questioned: "What are you??," "Are you Black enough??," "Are you trying to be White??" I was more often called "zebra" than "nigger," as much by blacks as whites. To some people, this meant that I couldn't possibly know what it means to be a "nigger" in America; to others, this meant, "You're not like the rest of them." I had a hard time finding acceptance, a peer group, a niche: Either kids didn't like me because I was "weird"—racially indeterminate, socially flexible—or I felt awkward because I was "different"—I talked different, I looked different. I was called "high yellow" and "half-breed"; depending on my hair—it's been long and straight, long and nappy, short and straight, short and nappy, near-dreaded and near-bald-headed—I was approached, avoided, reproached, or rewarded. Anxious in almost all social situations involving my peers (and invited to very few), I struggled to learn the "rules" of race-based identity and activity so I could—hopefully—eventually fit in. I was in a constant state of frantic yet earnest self-revision and experimentation, but to no avail. I kept thinking, if only I can stumble upon the magic formula—of mannerisms, interests, friends, music, hair, clothes—everything will fall into place. But it never did. The best that could be said is that I became a good chameleon.

My obsession with race matters and finding social acceptance was so intense and consuming that it left no room for exploration of my other identity issues during my early formative years. Most notable was my realization at the age of twelve or thirteen that I was sexually attracted to females as well as males. While I was well aware of my feelings and never tried to suppress them, they held no social or behavioral significance for me until after I was twenty-five, and I was not aware of any community of others with similar desires until well past the age when most people have already entered into it.

In my early twenties, I "hit bottom." An ill-fated college marriage and my failed attempt to play the perfect bourgeois black mom and wife had brought to my attention the reality that, however strong my desire for acceptance, conventionality was not my strong suit and ought not be played. This realization necessitated a break not only with my marriage but also with my religiosity; acknowledgment of my queer desire was the straw that broke the camel's back with the latter, and acknowledgment of the nontraditionality of my beliefs about gender followed on its heels, forever altering the way I viewed all social categories.

The years that followed constituted something of an odyssey, to first repair my relations with men and then enter the queer community and initiate relations with women. During this phase of my life, explorations of race and racial identity took a backseat to sexual, gender, and political self-development. Central to this process was bodily self-expression through dress, dance, and sexual activity. The genteel pumps and the long khaki skirts of the Atlanta buppie housewife were traded in for the combat boots and black lycra minis of the Philadelphia alternachic. Long, straightened, feminine hair was exchanged for androgynous nappy twists and head shaving. Modestly spaced, boyfriend-only dancing was superceded by everything from full-contact, bisexual dancing to moshing, raving, go-go dancing, and dragging. Sex was relational, recreational, experimental, and bisexual. I had had to travel 180 degrees with my body to find expression for what had always been in my head.

While I experienced an extraordinary and exhilarating feeling of freedom and authenticity during this experimental period, I experienced the reemergence of race-based yearnings beneath the surface. My core social group—not to mention the greater portion of the "scene"—was comprised primarily of white people with White cultural roots. While there were some black people (primarily men), many of them self-admittedly preferred the company of whites. I, on the other hand, despite my punkish appearance, considered myself both mixed and black, and I identified strongly with the Black struggle against White hegemony and oppression. Although many of my radical white friends felt similarly, I began to miss certain aspects of the Black experience—the historically rooted politics of resistance, the historically forged sense of solidarity, the home-bred and mandatory etiquette, the improvisational and style-conscious speech, the bass-heavy, booty-shake music, the simple and satisfying food, the common-sense way kids are raised, the presence and participation of elders. I found myself taking a psychocultural detour around many of the people who had been the first close friends in my life and being unable to articulate what was happening.

This psychological movement coincided with a professional/vocational one as well. I was finishing up graduate school and on the job market. My goal was to move back South and to take a job with an African-American focus, and it was achieved in the form of a joint appointment at The University of Georgia. This new job offered me an opportunity to integrate my various professional and personal concerns—race, queerness, womanism/feminism, identity, and education—in a new, synergistic, and transformative way—as well as presented certain foreseeable yet stirring challenges based on the particular history of the place.

When I first arrived, my engagement in Black, queer, and womanist issues was about equally strong. Although I had not revealed my sexual orientation during my job interview, I fully intended to plunge headlong into queer social activity upon arrival. To my own surprise, however, I soon became involved in a very consuming long-distance relationship with a straight (albeit queer-cool) black man—an old friend. In the course of spilling bits of information about this relationship to my colleagues, however, I became outwardly agitated about the prospect of having to revise the straight image I was assuredly presenting and inwardly beleaguered about issues of bisexuality and passing. My desire was to be upfront and out, but my growing perception was that, while the town of Athens was a queer haven, the university itself and Athens' very church-based Black community were bastions of sex-and-gender conservatism; thus, being out might be injudicious and antithetical to some of the important good that I was already showing the potential to achieve. I did not want to trade my politically transformative currency—for example, the inroads I had made infusing the White-dominated curriculum with Black studies courses or infusing the androcentric Black studies content with womanism—for whatever self-serving commodities I might obtain by coming out, and I knew that this was a real risk. I also realized that despite, as the slogan says, "Racism—Sexism—Homophobia: Recognize the Connections," not everyone was ready to deal with all three at once, and sometimes a step-wise approach is best. Yet somehow, even though I had never lied about my queerness, even though I had shared the fact of my queerness with a number of colleagues and students, even though my research and vitae are infused with queer theory and subject matter and my office is replete with queer paraphernalia, I continued to feel like a fake and a fraud because I had not made "The Big Announcement" or was not the queer mouthpiece in every situation. The Anxiety had reared its ugly head again.

In true dialectical fashion, The Anxiety precipitated my coming out at work. Only I did not come out as bisexual—I came out as lesbian, a dyke. Leaving no room for my queerness to be watered down by ambiguity or further masked behind the smoke and mirrors of an elidable label, I proceeded further with my social and academic radicalism. I incorporated queerness into my black and white curricula and race into my queer academic products (e.g., research). I invited even more controversy by becoming attached to a white woman. Without flinching, and to my own surprise, I took on the implications that this interracial union symbolized for many—including the putative dilution of my blackness, the perceived complicity with an enemy, and the further reification of my social and bodily indeterminacy—because, for once in my life, I felt secure in the knowledge that not everyone who might render judgment on me could possibly know all the intimate details of my journey—details without which any judgment rendered would, in a most profound way, be meaningless and void of merit. While my choices were not without fear, as Audre Lorde (1984) said, "[W]e have been socialized to respect fear more than our own needs for language and definition, and while we wait in silence for that final luxury of fearlessness, the weight of that silence will choke us" (p. 44).

ANNOTATION:
THE BEAUTY OF DIFFICULT THINGS

As a mixed-race, mixed-culture body, I embodied the visibility/invisibility paradox of anomaly in the flesh: I-as-a-body was highly visible as a deviation from expectation, but I- as-a-psychological-self was invisible behind the shadow of that body. I learned that, without the costumery of race, gender, sexuality, class, and politics, one was invisible, and with it, one was expected to be equivalent to the sum of the parts—nothing more, nothing less. Without these boxing adornments, one was outside the running for love, popularity, and the ultimate commodity, cool—the stuff of life by kid standards. I further learned that, when one is invisible, one contorts or invents oneself to become visible because visibility is just that strong of a psychic need. One tries everything, for better or for worse. Likewise, when one is in need of love or connection, one does what one perceives it to take—whether this involves contortion or invention—to get it, even to the detriment of oneself or others. I learned that we use our bodies as canvases for what is inside and the rages and desires we can find no other place to articulate. I learned that visibility and love are linked, but how they are linked is subject to the social order we generate by choice and tradition as well as the representational milieu we surround that order with. I came to feel strongly that everyone deserves a place in the representational realm and that no one deserves to be swept under the rug like unwanted human detritus. I came to believe that representations of others manifestly like ourselves are singularly important to our development as children and adolescents; once we find ourselves—once we see our reflections in the social mirror—we find happiness and can concentrate on becoming generous and compassionate human beings. This is particularly true in our information society, as the intergenerational transmission of "reality" becomes more and more media-driven.

Growing up as a member of perhaps the first generation to actually be raised by TV and pop music, I was acutely aware that I was nowhere to be found in the representational realm. I could read magazines such as *Seventeen* or *Glamour* and see my skin color but not my hair type; I could read magazines such as *Essence* and see my hair type but not my skin color. From any of these, I could get advice about how to pursue boys, but not girls; later, from queer magazines such as *The Advocate* and *Out*, I could learn how to pursue my same-sex desire but could find no validation for my other-sex experiences. On TV, when I was a child, there were the Jacksons and the Osmonds, but it was either-or—as school-children, we had to choose our loyalties. On the radio, there was Black music and White music, but not both. Being into Black music wasn't just being into Black music, it was being into Black culture, Black people, Black life, Black struggles, Black dance, Black hair, Black food, Black talk, and avoiding white people; being into White music wasn't just being into White music, it was being into White cultural referents, White privilege, White hegemony, and White dreams. It was about drawing lines and staying within them. Needless to say, there was nobody queer on TV or the radio, much less the representation of any kind of queer community; race and gender seemed to be about all the consuming audience could handle.

MTV changed all that, beginning when I was a teenager. Despite its blatant commodification of multicultural difference, it began to validate difference as well as coalition—first across race, nationality, and class, later across gender, sexual orientation, and individual expression generally—in ways that were important and intelligible to youth. Although I was an adult before many of these changes took place, the emergence of MTV onscreen and alternative music subcultures offscreen, along with the attendant emergence of differently queered icons such as Madonna, Michael Stipe, and RuPaul, proved ultimately transformative for me.

Beyond these examples, reading has provided many of the key resources for rethinking and reframing what has essentially been my central dilemma: How to queer a life and live to tell (changing the world in the process). Early in my Philadelphia coming-out phase, I picked up a publication called *BiFocus: A newsletter for Philadelphia's bisexual community* in the Giovanni's Room bookstore. Right there on the front page in big letters, it said, "GEN*DER*FUCK—to fuck with or confuse the notions and prejudices of others around gender" (Burke et al., 1991-1992). I thought, why isn't there a concept like this for everything?? Like also "RACE*FUCK." It suited me. At that moment, all the social reformist desires that had been born of my Baha'i utopianism and all the radical political convictions I had cultivated in the course of thinking Black, thinking feminist, and thinking queer merged in one explosive epiphany. It was the beginning of the end of my desire to seek comfort or acceptance in boxes, and the beginning of the beginning of my desire to learn—contrary to everything I had been taught—to think improvisational, think indeterminate, think transgressive, and enjoy the beauty of difficult things. Incipiently, my body had taught me this; I embodied this knowledge long before I could articulate it, but other books, from *But Some of Us Are Brave* (Hull, Bell, and Barbara, 1982), *HomeGirls* (Smith, 1983), and *Black Feminist Thought* (Collins, 1991), to *Fear of a Queer Planet* (Warner, 1993), helped fortify both self and voice. There was pleasure in the discovery of the fit I found inside these new concepts and cognitions and in the discovery and exercise of their articulation—*the pleasure I had always been seeking.*

REFERENCES

Burke, Pat, Cartwright, Woody, Gales, AAn, Harrison, Cappy, Jackson, Sharon E., and Nagle, Jill. *BiFocus: A Newsletter for Philadelphia's Bisexual Community*, Vol. 2, No. 1, Winter 1991-1992, p. 1.

Collins, Patricia Hill. (1991). *Black Feminist Thought: Knowledge, Consciousness, and the Politics of Empowerment.* New York: Routledge.

Hull, Gloria T., Scott, Patricia Bell, and Smith, Barbara (Eds.). (1982). *All the Women Are White, All the Blacks Are Men, But Some of Us Are Brave: Black Women's Studies.* New York: The Feminist Press.

Lorde, Audre. (1984). "The transformation of silence into language and action." In *Sister Outsider*. Freedom, CA: Crossing Press, pp. 40-44.

Smith, Barbara (Ed.). (1983). *Home*Girls: *A Black Feminist Anthology*. New York: Kitchen Table, Women of Color Press.

Warner, Michael (Ed.). (1993). *Fear of a Queer Planet: Queer Politics and Social Theory*. Minneapolis: University of Minnesota Press.

Piece of Man: Redefining the Myths Around the Black Male Phallus

Conrad R. Pegues

While sitting in the mall, I watched people passing in all of their diversity. I saw the usual mix of people in all shapes and sizes and colors and sometimes sexual orientations. A young, black guy walked toward where I was sitting, dressed in a jacket, jeans, boots, a sweater, a single earring in his ear, with his hair pulled back in a processed ponytail. He was very attractive, but this was not what I noticed most of all about him. I followed his eyes as he checked himself out from head to toe after another guy passed him by. In his tight jeans, running down his right thigh was a big lump—his penis.

I began to wonder about the considerable number of black men, regardless of sexual orientation, who place such high value on this one part of their body. The brother at the mall evidently wasn't embarrassed about his penis being on view for everyone to see. It was a prized possession in which he'd found some profane confidence.

I was raised around black people who, spoken and unspoken, taught you not to go around with your penis running down your leg. I'll never forget a black woman commenting about a brother who came through the door at a party with tight pants on through which his penis could be so obviously seen. He was known for doing this, and she, along with some other women, simply frowned on him. She called it nasty. Another time, I overheard another brother talking to some male friends: "Did you see Mike? What is his problem coming down the street with his shit down his leg?" They all laughed at him.

So, when I saw the guy at the mall, I thought that he ought to have been embarrassed, but he wasn't. He was displaying his penis like a walking billboard with the rest of his body reduced to a caption to what was between his legs.

In American history, no other part of a black man's anatomy has ever had such a maelstrom of controversy surrounding it. There have been so many negative racial myths built up around it as the symbol of an uncontrollable libidinous energy coursing through our bodies that might break forth at any moment to violate some white woman's presumed virtue. As black men, we could have our genitalia cut off while still alive, at a public lynching, picnic baskets and all, to exorcise white projections of a super-sexed presence from American society (See Ginzberg, 1988).

But the black penis had become something else to the brother at the mall; it was a trophy straining against his jeans in a mall teeming with more white people than blacks. No panic, no upset—but I, another brother, was disturbed.

As a homosexual black man, I had to wonder about the juxtaposition of the racial myth with homosexual desire. Within the confines of homosexual desire, the black penis is still seen as representing a super-sexed stud who is ever ready to please any white male takers; every black man's penis is huge and simply waiting to burst forth from briefs or boxers at any moment for the sake of another's pleasure. And there are those black homosexual men who buy into the racist myths, as well as thinking them complimentary.

With black homosexual males, the genital stereotype adds more complexity to our dilemma in a racist and homophobic society. Black men, not readily accepted into mainstream society, are relegated to the place of negative other, whether we want to be or not. In a racist atmosphere, it becomes necessary to find some definition of self that inflates a wounded male ego. Black homosexual men have taken the stereotype given to us by white males of the "big black dick" that's eager to please and made it our own. Little thought is given to the fact that being thought of as super stud can limit the definitions of one's humanity. Black homosexual men become contextualized within the perceptions of their penis, rarely realizing a greater human capacity to have feelings and the need for emotional bonds to find deeper fulfillment. Black homosexual men become sexual performance artists on a mythic stage created by racism. We play out the sexual caricatures of a society steeped in hatred of both our skin color and our genitalia.

In American culture, there is a seed of distrust embedded early in the black psyche where our color and bodies are concerned because they are associated with darkness, fear, the irrational, decay, and last, but not least, the devil. Many of us have not learned to recognize those seeds of destruction that deny us viability as human beings, and we act out unhealthy behavior in public and private. We perpetuate our own violence and oppression when we don't stop to ask ourselves why we allow our penis to play such a central role in our self-concept, to the exclusion of our whole self. When we allow this limited interpretation of ourselves, we become what the sisters call "a piece of man."

I've often heard the sisters refer to men who make no real contributions to their lives as a "piece of man." Such men are thought of only as providing some semblance of masculine presence by just being around. A piece of man is better than no man at all. These brothers may provide some sexual satisfaction but are rarely making emotional or economic contributions to the sisters' livelihood. These brothers are present in body only. They are men in name only. I have come to apply the epithet "piece of man" to those black homosexual males who, as with their heterosexual counterparts, refuse to be fully present in relationships and have accepted the racial stereotypes created around their lives.

When we as black men see ourselves in pieces, we bring along the negative conceptions about who we are into our relationships. Instead of recreating ourselves in an image that promotes a more complete sense of self, including all parts of body and soul, we can only end up with the stereotype wreaking havoc with our ability to love.

Too often, I'm met by black homosexual men with two basic concepts of self that promote psychological sickness. Some men like to show off their penises publicly, barely veiled under clothing; others, who become his adoring audience, promote his piecemeal self-concept by haggling after this one particular aspect of him, reinforcing his ignorance as well as our own. We rarely stop to ask ourselves who he is and what he feels as a person. We will concentrate on that one aspect of him that cannot reveal to us the depth of his humanity because too many of us do not know what it is to care beyond the erection. We will silently agree to keep him centered on his penis (the bigger the better) by taking a romp in the bed and thinking that we have experienced a natural and basic expression of humanity; all we've done is experience the length and width of him. Inches does not a human being make. We've had sex; sex and nurture are not always synonymous. For those sensitive enough to feel a lack of fulfillment afterwards, we're often told to ignore it; we think too much.

The basic sexual desire is mere impulse for a deeper desire to connect with the brother, but that desire has no conscious, mutually agreed upon somatic language through which to convey itself favorably. As black men, we have yet to take the time out to create it; we are too busy living inside contrived roles about what it means to be a man.

I have used the term *somatic language* and define it as one in which individuals seek to affirm one another's humanity and the soul's needs within a nurturing context through their bodies. Sexual stimulation is not compulsory in the union. The other is given a sense of being valued as an individual, and their body is in actuality sacred space. Sacred space is created by two or more people coming together to integrate and balance mind, body, and spirit and can include a sexual dimension. A whole new world of possibilities of existence are created. Mircea Eliade states the ontological importance of sacred space in the life of human beings: " . . . the experience of sacred space makes possible the 'founding of the world': where the sacred manifests itself in space, the real unveils itself, the world comes into existence" (Eliade, 1959:63). Upon entering sacred sexual space, the individual is given a deeper sense of himself as being wanted and loved as a valuable entity and not just desired as a sexual object. The individual realizes that he or she has a right to be in the world, to find meaning within it that gives life a sense of wholeness, and to realize a connection to a higher spiritual principle. To willfully inflict pain to gain a sense of power or to see another as a piece of flesh is intolerable in sacred space because a sense of connection between self and other cannot be born. The aspiration for community is desecrated, the aspirant's humanity diminished.

A concordant somatic language has yet to be invented because the right questions about our impulses or those of the brother thinking his penis a prize are not asked. We become stuck in our own sexual and psychic oppression and never understand why we sometimes feel so unfulfilled in black male social circles. The obstacles to a healthy relationship and self-perception of the black male body as derived from racist myths are many. Not only does the black penis become problematic by its very existence but also in its function.

The fear or denial of the penis often leads to a repulsion of semen that is not only about the fear of AIDS. The Christian church has played a significant role in setting limitations on the penis and its usage in human relationships. Theologian Matthew Fox says that sex and the Western church's teachings on it have been about silence and moralizing: "Telling us all the sins we are capable of performing with our sexual organs . . . in the name of moralizing, the mystery of sexuality has been so often reduced to problems of morality" (Fox, 1988:163). Seminal fluid not expended for the reproductive act was reason for censure in the Judeo-Christian tradition and still is today. The biblical story of Onan spilling his seed on the ground, which was viewed as a waste because it was not ejaculated into the body of a woman to propagate the race, has often been used as argument against nonreproductive sexual activity. Spilling seed "on the ground" becomes identifiable with a waste of semen through masturbation or sex between men, who cannot bear children. Semen becomes a commodity in the performance of heterosexual duty in traditional male roles.

Traditional Christian ideology along with white supremacy via slavery have combined over the years to further distort perceptions of the black male's body and genitalia. Black men were given limited roles in slavery, which consisted of two jobs: work and being a "buck" who was to impregnate black women like an animal, dehumanizing him and her. Herbert G. Gutman, in *The Black Family in Slavery and Freedom: 1750-1925,* writes:

> Reproducing the slave labor force required only the simple biological dyad "mother and child." The social dyads "husband and wife" and "father and child" were not essential. Neither was the completed "nuclear family." . . . Slave women mostly counted in the calculations of their owners as mothers, and slave men counted mostly as laborers. (Gutman, 1976:79)

His body and seed were more important than what he felt as a person. Her womb was not her own. Their humanity and emotional life was null and void, and a system was maintained to teach him and her as much. The only modes of self-expression were labor and sex, which, under capitalism, turned into issues of economic production. Black male semen was a commodity in the production of more slave labor. Like chattel, it was cheaper to produce one's own slave labor force than to have to buy or import slaves from Africa, especially after the import of slaves was outlawed.

The dehumanization of slavery combined with the soul/body split of Western thought leaves black men with a historically derived psychological view of themselves as important only in the context of what they could produce by body (labor) and semen (more slaves).

Reduced to a production tool, the erect penis is placed in a state of ambivalence because it can also give and receive pleasure; it bears a negative connotation, but it's good. Pleasure is always of a doubling nature when the penis is aroused with the aid of another. It is a point of union whether entering the body of another, mutual stimulation, or self-stimulation. In *The Phallus*, Alain Danielou says that the phallus is more than a simple procreative symbol and "represents a place between two worlds, a point of contact between being and nonbeing, where life manifests itself and incarnates the divine spirit" (Danielou, 1995:24). In the case of masturbation, pleasure may be thought of as an isolate endeavor, but it is not. The act of fantasizing about another, self-stimulation, or an external stimulant such as a dildo initiates arousal so it is still a matter of doubling. Physically and psychologically, another is needed to bring pleasure to the self, but in the historical context of racism in America and heterosexism in the Church and society, the need for another human being, emotionally, is either denied or limited to reproduction. Historical precedent and human need inevitably clash in black male relationships. A black man's penis, whether homosexual or heterosexual, is no longer his own but is the object by which he validates his worth in the world. He is not worthwhile simply because he is here. His erection always points externally to another's world at the expense of his own inner world.

In relation to homosexual men, penetrating through the anus or mouth is still the performance of a duty with their "tool" (a term often found in so-called erotic literature), reduced in language to the act of a machine: "He forced his big black throbbing tool . . . " Black homosexual men are faced with a sexual act that violently splits us in two, body from soul.

Homosexuality has the potential to break sex away from its exploitative economic basis where semen and the sex act are concerned. It can put sex within the context of play instead of keeping it within a fixed heterosexual model of reproduction. Having no history to psychologically counter the products of a racist myth system, some homosexual black men very easily come to believe that there is something fundamentally wrong with their sexuality and their bodies.

It has been my experience that black homosexual men who will not fully acknowledge the act as being homosexual come to see the sexual act as "fuckin' around," distancing any sense of soul from the act itself. They're not fully present. That absence of presence createes a vacuum of a sense of time, place, and space, which are all the foundations for the creation of a healthy self-concept. Often, when one lacks a sense of place, the personality is forever in an incubated state and cannot develop into the foundation for an authentic expression of one's humanity. The penis, through which the body can merge with another human being, only exacerbates the problem of being present. To act and deny the act is to live the lie that what is done in the body has no spiritual or psychological significance. The penis is merely the object through which another human body is entered. Nothing of it can be known beyond the erection, for example, developing the "[v]isionary experiences, clairvoyance, and clairsentience—all aspects of psychic opening—often accompanying spiritual awakening in sexual experience" (Bragdon, 1990:148).

Black men have to decide whether or not to view our bodies as a center for nurture, as the basis for our actions within the community. A state of nurture is one that is inclusive of sexuality but is not limited to reproduction only. There are those who spitefully hate the black homosexual male presence because we are not using our bodies, primarily, as a tool for propagating the race. We can produce children just as any other healthy male, and some of us do want them. Black homosexuals break faith with the heterosexist script that says we *must* be sexually attracted to women, that we *must* marry a woman, and that we *must* produce children. Regardless of sexual preference, a new myth grounding black male sexuality within a propitious spiritual context has to be established.

Blacks in America descend from an African worldview that sees the words and experiences of the ancestors as the creative ground for the quality of life for the present generation; thus, the past is the present. If black male relationships are tainted by the myths of white supremacy and patriarchy concerning what it means to be a man, then no deeper sense of community can be passed on. Only the stereotype and limited perceptions of masculinity will remain as the tradition. Our ancestors in America were too busy surviving the ravages of white supremacy to sit down and contemplate all the psychological limits placed upon them. But certain aspects of the African paradigm still remained beneath the surface of every day existence and have been passed on just the same, which could offer a key to reversing the negative mythologies around black male masculinity. Consideration of past modes of ancestral behavior and its legacy could be considered as points of reference to countering the damage done to the black male psyche and offer a point of reference for healing.

Traditionally, in the African paradigm, people are not seen as isolate personalities floating free in the social space. Rather, everyone's actions (the living and the "dead"), past and present, and spoken words help to create the larger community's sense of interconnectedness and self. Janheinz Jahn writes in *Muntu* that, "[o]nly through the effect of a muntu, a man, living or dead—and that includes the ancestors, the orishas and even God—can 'things' become active and in their turn influence other 'things'" (1990:121). Individual psyches in the black community are woven together like the strands of a spider's web and are about as delicate, influencing other lives and being influenced.

Also taken from Africa is the idea of community that includes departed souls. Departed souls are constantly influencing their descendants' lives and returning to this world to make contributions to the larger community's needs. The younger generation is sometimes seen as reborn souls who have come to fulfill personal and collective destinies and to maintain the community's stability as the Dagara tribesman Malidoma Patrice Some writes about in his book *Ritual* (1993:54). Souls are thought to return out of a sense of commitment to helping the community define its purposes in line with its needs at a particular moment in history. Sometimes that destiny can be forgotten, which leads to a community in chaos. Returning souls can be recently deceased family members, friends, or ancestral spirits who may have walked the earth in times past. So a soul is never born tabula rasa.

In spite of Christian and European influences to the contrary, the idea of reborn souls and interaction between the living and dead is a persistent belief in the black community in America. It is not unusual for me to hear some black folks say, "That chile has been here before," or "That's an old soul," in reference to a child whose perception of the world stretches far beyond his or her age. I believe many souls born in this day and time may very well be the bearers of changing notions of black masculinity from one generation to the next. That sign of change would manifest through the black male's body and its treatment as the center of his existence.

Within an African paradigm, flesh and spoken word are both manifestations of spirit. What is born in the spirit must find its parallel in the flesh. Some states that, "our soul communicates things to us that the body translates as need, or want, or absence" (1993:43). The body becomes a "spoken" language of its own via dance, gesture, stance, walk, or activity. So, it would not be unusual that the black male body is the point where traditional notions of black masculinity are questioned. Due to the presence of AIDS, it is a very dangerous time where sexual activity is concerned. I believe many younger black males are experimenting sexually with one another although not making any claims publicly or privately to being "gay." The experimentation may have less to do with a breakdown in moral fiber or gender confusion, but may have more to do with the strain of restrictive ideals around black masculinity as have been passed on to them. The younger generation is searching to redefine themselves sexually and, in the process, are muddling the extremes of heterosexuality and homosexuality.

Just as important as what younger black males are doing behind closed doors is what they're doing in public where their sex is concerned. I'm thinking of the clutching of their crotches. In a racist myth system where the value of the black male body has been established through the penis, to see black males clutching their own opens the door to a deeper and provocative sense of reality of which they may not be conscious. Clutching the legendary penis of power and presence may be a question of potential. The message may be distorted by racism, sexism, and sex without commitment to human affirmation, but that doesn't disregard the essence of the message or the messenger. The black male's penis can be the point at which to redefine the black male's sense of self in America since, historically, it has been under constant attack. It is my supposition that black male youths are publicly signifying where their sense of their own masculinity is in need of deepest healing.

Crotch-clutching isn't only common to black youths; it's just more pronounced and has come to be viewed as a "subcultural" phenomenon with the popularity of the rap and hip-hop culture. Youths simply don't care where they do it, and the media has helped to broadcast the behavior to the larger community. The same behavior can be seen amongst black males in all social circles. It is different from the guy at the mall in that he sees his penis as a trophy because of its size and the perception of it and is conscious of the fact. The black men bonding in a group are using their bodies in a context that establishes a sense of community and it is unconscious. Common with the behavior amongst black men is that crotch-clutching expressions are usually done in the midst of a group gathering. Of course, there are exceptions, but it is much more common than some would like to admit. As I've seen, it's an atmosphere of sharing through the spoken word whether through discussion, jokes, storytelling, or gossiping. The spoken words weave together a larger, shared, masculine identity. At various times, they'll each grab their crotch. It's similar to an "Amen"—a physical mode of agreement and affirmation of things said. It is done without any of them giving it a second thought. It is a ritual of bonding within their particular group and the body's participation in reaffirming the spoken word.

Bonding through genitalia is nothing new. It is a very old phenomenon and has Afro-Asiatic roots. The testicles, in particular, are seen as the nexus through which the community may arise as far as it depends upon males. Through them, the ancestors and the unborn can enter the world. In addition, the testicles are seen as a point where the spirit of the ancestors' knowledge converges with the knowledge of earthly experience. Respect for the genitals as bearing such spiritual import becomes the point at which contracts and promises are established between men who were respected even after death.

For example, in the Old Testament, the patriarch Abraham makes covenants with other men by placing the hand under the thigh (Genesis 24:2 and 47:29). In actuality, the covenant was established by holding a man's testicles. The testicles were seen as a point where the divine manifested in the body of men to maintain the patriarch's line. The English translators chose to use "thigh" instead of testicles; the thought of one man holding another's genitalia was too similar to homosexual encounter so the truth was distorted.

In Africa, the testicles are viewed in a mystical sense unto the present day. Syl Cheney Coker, the Sierra Leone poet and novelist, writes of the mystical nature of the testicles in his novel *The Last Harmattan of Alusine Dunbar* (1990). Throughout the novel, the testicles of the mystic Alusine Dunbar glow and radiate to phenomenal size and length as he develops a deeper insight into the multiple dimensions of reality intersecting our own. Coker's use of "the eye of the testicles," as they are called in the novel, is not simply a literary motif; it is a mythological motif, within the novel, drawn from African tribal philosophy concerning the esoteric nature of the testicles.

Amongst the Yoruba of West Africa, the penis and testicles are seen as holding the fecundating force of nature to initiate change and evolution out of a state of complacency. The erect phallus of the trickster deity Eshu is a prime example. Eshu's erect member is viewed as the bearer of change, which would come via the potent seminal fluid. Through his phallus would come clarity to maintain the balance between the world of the spirits and the human community.

In the various philosophies mentioned above, the body is viewed as a center for culture and community. How it is treated illustrates the nature of a people's value of the body within a particular culture. It becomes the point at which a person establishes the sense of self and relation to the larger social order. Genitalia, in particular, seem to play a major role in the degree of male bonding allowed within a culture. "The man who scorns the very symbol of the life principle abandons his kind to the powers of death" (Danielou, 1995:1). Where there is disdain for genitalia outside the context of reproduction, male-to-male bonds cannot flourish. Homosexual interaction is always a fear. Heterosexual interaction amongst males is overshadowed by the fear that same-sex affection will turn into same-sex desire. The male body becomes a prison. Only a new spiritual paradigm sensitive to black historical experience can unlock the door to a better quality of black male relationship.

Since crotch-clutching is very common amongst black men from the "homeboys" to the "professionals" to the men drinking and hanging out on the corner, I believe an ancient mode of connection may be making a return to the fore of the conscious mind, though not necessarily recognized for what it actually is. Clutching the genitals may be a call to healing in black male relationships. Changing the nature of black male relationships could not come at a better time. The high rates of death by murder and suicide are nothing short of genocide born of psychological trauma in a racist society. The numbers of black men in jail, in trouble with the law, on drugs, or suffering from physical ailments such as hypertension, heart disease, AIDS, and prostate cancer are at phenomenal highs. The minds and bodies of black men are calling out for a change in how we treat ourselves and in how we treat each other.

Genitalia that was once used to establish contractual faith or viewed as a symbol for change and evolution have been cut off to the point that black men are unconsciously signifying where the sense of self and community has been literally and figuratively cut away. Realizing the racist view of our bodies created by white supremacy and patriarchy, we can create a sense of self not rooted in its labor and production only. Quality of presence in the community comes to be of primary importance.

Our various modes of black male bonding, formed under the auspices of the slave system, don't cause deeper bonds beyond the penis. The greater responsibility falls to us as black men to literally and symbolically re-create ourselves in the image of our own needs without compromising our own preferences sexually as unique individuals. If we don't, we'll continue to produce dehumanized black men whose most basic sense of self is drawn from what's swinging between their legs, how big or small it is, and how hard it can become.

Because I am a black homosexual male, I'm moved to consider my own plight in the face of a historical process that has trained me, before deeper awareness, to find my center and sense of self through my penis. I don't want to live like that, and I do not want to perpetuate such a tradition amongst my brothers: homosexual, heterosexual, bisexual, celibate, virgin, don't know, can't figure, experimenting, or just don't like to be labeled—whatever! Acting out of stereotypic behavior only maintains us all in centuries-old oppression.

The black penis of American racial myth has to be transformed into the black phallus of primordial myth that reconnects the part of him to the whole of him and more. In times past, the phallus represented "harmony, the beauty of the world, the respect of the divine work, and the infinite variety of forms and of beings in which the divine dream is embodied" (Danielou, 1995: 111). Historically, in Africa and places far and wide, the phallus represented the fecundity of the universe. Not simply in its capacity for procreation, but symbolically, in its priapic state along with the feminine principle of the universe, it represented energy necessary for matter to manifest in the world. It represented social order and meaning where the divine enters into culture. Whether the horns worn on crowns, phallic carvings from Nigeria, the obelisks of Egypt, the pillars holding up ancient temples, or ritual masks, arrows and spears, rock paintings, or huts, it was never about sex and reproduction alone. It was about the quality of spirit and human relationship to the world at large. Returning to a deeper mystical perception of the black phallus places it within a mythological context where it is reconnected with the cycles of the body (youth, adulthood, and old age), culture, the natural world, the realm of spirits, and the cosmos.

As a black male, I have to see the brother at the mall in some other light than that passed on to us by a history not of our own making, which has had influence in creating who we perceive ourselves to be. We must create a new myth system in which to thrive that affirms the value of the black phallus reconnected to a strong, black, nurturing body, widening the conception of masculinity beyond aggression and violence. No one is more qualified than black men to do the work of creating the new myths to counter the racist ones that have led to our being torn to pieces in America. The seed for that new myth is as close as our own black bodies.

REFERENCES

Bragdon, Emma. *The Call of Spiritual Emergency: From Personal Crisis to Personal Transformation.* San Francisco: Harper & Row, 1990.

Cheney-Coker, Syl. *The Last Harmattan of Alusine Dunbar.* Portsmouth, NH: Heinemann, 1990.

Danielou, Alain. *The Phallus: Sacred Symbol of Male Creative Power.* Trans. John Graham. Rochester, VT: Inner Traditions, 1995.

Eliade, Mircea. *The Sacred and the Profane: The Nature of Religion.* Trans. Willard R. Trask. New York: Harper & Row, 1959.

Fox, Matthew. *The Coming of the Cosmic Christ.* San Francisco: Harper & Row, 1988.

Ginzburg, Ralph (Ed.). *100 Years of Lynchings.* Baltimore, MD: Black Classic Press, 1988.

Gutman, Herbert G. *The Black Family in Slavery and Freedom: 1750-1925.* New York: Vintage, 1976.

Jahn, Janheinz. *Muntu: African Culture and the Western World.* 1961. Trans. Marjorie Grene. New York: Grove Weidenfeld, 1990.

Some, Malidoma Patrice. *Ritual: Power, Healing, and Community.* Portland, OR: Swan Raven & Company, 1993.

Mapping My Desire:
Hunting Down the Male Erotic
in India and America

Sandip Roy

They didn't even kiss on Indian cinema. The lovers would draw closer and closer. The camera would zoom in. The audience waited with bated breath. The hero swooped down for the kiss. The camera skittered away to show nodding flowers and cooing birds. The shrill voice of the female playback singer burst into tremulous song. The magic moment was over.

The old movies had The Woman and The Other Woman—the kind you sowed your wild oats with. The Woman was demurely dressed, often in light colors, to symbolize her chaste beauty. The Other Woman wore dark clinging dresses with plunging necklines. She smoked cigarettes and had names such as Miss Rosie and Miss Lovely. She danced in the dens of evil smugglers—her padded bosoms heaving, her sequined skirt flying up to show her hefty thighs. Men growing up in India were torn between these two poles. They knew they were supposed to marry the virtuous woman in her pale saris. But oh, when the music started and the vamp wiggled on to the screen, they couldn't help throwing money at her. I was even more confused. I was interested in neither women. I was ogling the hero. But all the heaving breasts and pouting lips kept getting in the way.

The problem was in Indian cinema, the hero did not have to be handsome or young. Or more accurately, he could go on being a hero long after he was neither handsome nor young. So while each year seemed to throw up a fresh crop of nubile heroines, I was growing up with some of the same heroes my parents had seen on screen. A popular matinee idol apparently buttoned his collar to hide the signs of age creeping up his neck. Another one wore a toupee. And, a third gave up a losing battle against his paunch. It didn't matter—they were men.

"Hmmm," said my great-aunt peering at the new baby, "he will be dark."

"Well, at least he is a boy," said my aunt. "It doesn't matter so much."

The market was full of herbal pastes guaranteed to make my sister fairer.

"Don't go out in the sun like that," admonished my mother.

"Try this new cucumber paste," suggested my aunt.

I, on the other hand, was a boy and my parents were putting me through the rigorous manly paces of tennis and swimming—all guaranteed to burn my skin a dark brown. But as long as I studied engineering or medicine it did not matter. Not that men were devoid of all standards of beauty. A man was considered good-looking if he was tall, fair, and handsome. Actually, if he managed to be tall and fair, handsome usually followed automatically—in a sort of a package deal. We all knew this harping on fairness was archaic and nonsensical—a ridiculous hangover from a colonial past. On the abstract, we could theorize about how foolish it was. In practice, every Sunday, the newspaper matrimonial ads would be offering "Fair, 5'3", educated (MA), slim" women to doctor/engineer husbands. The darker ones were described as having "lustrous" complexions. The ones that said nothing about complexions tried to compensate with litanies about singing abilities and domestic skills.

Everyone knew the British had imposed a whalebone corset of Victorian morality around our hot-blooded, tropical selves. Before the British came, women did not wear blouses with their saris. The more diaphanous and sheer a sari was, the more its worth. The British, shocked at such tropical licentiousness, brought in blouses and petticoats. Everyone knew that our old texts and sculptures were replete with illustrations of sex in every possible form and permutation. Yet even today, India as a nation is not ready to lift the antiquated 100-year-old, antisodomy law that the British imposed on us and have themselves revoked in Britain. We know what we once had or at least have some idea of it, but we have become too used to living in our corset.

In the West, for better or for worse, the media has in the last few decades produced images of desirability in males just as it has always done for women. Those Calvin Klein and Soloflex ads are probably in large part responsible for men feeling the need to go to health clubs and strap themselves into Nautilus machines and heave and pump and check the mirror every day for the first signs of a budding muscle or flattening abdomen. In India, we laughed at men who looked into the mirror too often. The only male models I could identify were the Wills Filter man (a ruggedly handsome type who drove Jeeps and smoked Wills Filter cigarettes) and the Zodiac man (who posed wearing only Zodiac ties). Apart from a few coat-hanger types who modeled what was always called "suiting and shirting," the only other men were mustachioed ones who marveled at their wife's cooking with XYZ brand of sunflower oil.

In India, the family was the most important institution; it dominated our lives and determined their course. For me, being gay was similar to betraying the family. It wasn't their rejection I feared; it was more whether my father would be able to hold his head high again. What would the neighbors say? Being gay was almost an act of selfishness—after all your selfless parents did for you, is this their reward in their old age? Coupled with the shame of being gay was an embarrassment about desiring men. Desiring men not for the jobs they had, not for their economic potential, but for their male beauty. It had been branded into our heads that beauty was a word that went with females, sunsets, and paintings. Beauty was an "unmanly" thing for men to concern themselves with. And here I was, a little freak, turning around to look at men on the street, missing my stop on the bus so I could follow some stranger a little while longer.

It was uncharted territory—this wilderness of male eroticism. But I was learning to look, to draw my own maps, and to chart my own desire. I was looking at college boys in faded jeans and the way the jeans clung to their asses. I was looking at those grainy ads of long-haired men in old tattered copies of Rolling Stone at the United States Information Services library. I was looking at the vegetable sellers and their sweaty bodies stained teak-brown by the sun. I remember the boy bathing at the tube well on the street—the coppery brown slopes of his back and shoulders, the hard wet planes, the sleeping muscles in his arms, and the surprising fullness of his chest—clad only in a pair of faded torn underpants, his sex straining the threadbare fabric. How acutely I memorized the grace of his interlocking muscles as he poured a bucket of water over himself and his hand with those thick, coarse fingers burrowing under his pants to soap himself. His skin wet and brown, his hair in his eyes, the ballet play of his muscles as he vigorously rubbed himself dry—he remains frozen in my memory in an electric shock of unabashed youth.

It seemed to me that just as I needed guidelines in every sphere of life, so I needed pointers in my desire. Were hairy chests sexy? Dark skin? Mustaches? Recently, I came across an old cardboard box stuffed with the scraps of images I had torn from magazines—an underwear ad, a group of laughing youths in swimsuits advertising some cola, a row of bare-chested hill tribals in shorts—these were all I had by way of building blocks for the construction of desire.

I thought that in America it would all be different. We would know; the papers, the magazines, the gay porn would tell us what was sexy, what was not. And I found they did—only too well. After countless interchangeable

274 *LOOKING QUEER*

films of smooth-skinned boys with brown-blond hair and tan lines on their butts fucking each other, I was ready to turn back to my cola ads for stimulation. And, what there was by way of erotic images for Asian men was corroded by the dubious politics behind their creation. Who made it and for whom? Was this exoticization or plain exploitation?

I remember a little glossy book of photos of a young Indian man on the beach. His name was Arjun, and he emerged from the ocean, wet and glistening and inviting. It was one of the first unabashedly male-erotic images I had seen of an Indian man in an Indian setting. Yet, because the pictures were taken by one Wolf Nikolas about whom the book said nothing, they raised many disturbing questions. Who was Wolf Nikolas? How did he get Arjun to shed his clothes for the camera? Did Arjun know his wet body was on sale in every gay bookstore in the West? Later, I found that Arjun was well aware of what he was doing and had also secured Nikolas' help to emigrate from India. But every time our desirability is framed in the lenses of someone from outside our culture, these prickly questions will arise and haunt our desire.

So I was quite pleased to see a calendar on Asian men by an Asian photographer. Here at last we were on safe ground; we could unabashedly wallow in our desire without fearing we were playing into the hands of colonialist, exploitative, keeping-Asian-boys-as-pets, white men. The pictures were superb—buff Asian men liberally coated with glistening oil dallied in various stages of undress on rocks, under palm trees, and in gardens ablaze with tropical flowers. The foreword explained that this calendar hoped to shatter the stereotype of Asian men as passive, geeky nerds with smudged glasses and hunched shoulders. Another Asian man leafing through the calendar with me exclaimed, "Wow, these pictures could be right out of some fancy Western catalog. I mean these models are just as good." He meant it as a compliment, but it sent shivers down my spine. I looked at those pictures again; this time I noticed the perfectly straight aquiline noses and the smooth, tanned, oiled skins. These men were as close to white as an Asian man could get. I had hoped that by controlling the camera we would be controlling the definition of erotic. But that definition had been set long ago by others; these pictures were just trying to live up to it.

While the high-society models on the catwalks of Bombay aimed for the high cheek-boned, long-necked look of their counterparts in the West, in films, especially in South Indian cinema, the women often tended to be well-padded. That is how a woman's appeal was defined there—big-breasted and wide-hipped. While it is true that these women had no say in the way their sexiness was being defined for them, at least that definition came from the land and was not pirated out of glossy, foreign, fashion magazines.

I saw a line drawing of two men sitting in a field. One was sitting behind the other, his hands resting on the other's shoulder and thigh. The men wore *dhotis,* which had ridden up to their thighs. They had turbans on their heads. In the distance was a little village temple with a three-pronged *trishul* spire. I looked at their turbans, the plain bangles called *karhas* round their wrists, and the amulet around the one's neck. They showed no distended organs as with the drawings of Tom of Finland. Yet the picture was unbelievably sexy. They were sexy because of the *dhoti,* the *trishul,* the *karha*—small everyday objects, so intrinsically Indian, it is difficult to find words for them in English. As with those objects, the eroticism in the image was untranslatable.

In the gay magazines of the West, which I lusted for in India, there are many sexy men. The pictures are artfully taken; the bodies have been sculpted in gyms. The pool or the beach the men are posed near could be anywhere. In the effort to make their appeal universal, their sexiness has been deodorized of the piquant smells of their particular cultures. They have been carefully deculturized and homogenized in the American melting pot.

But the men in my drawing are unmistakably Indian. Their sexiness stems not from their looks; they are not even naked. They are erotic because to look at them is to remember the hot, unrelenting, blue sky of an Indian summer. To look at them is to remember those lazy, sluggish, summer afternoons spent lolling half-dressed on the bed waiting for the first dark, pregnant clouds of a thunderstorm. I can once again feel the first fat, warm drops of rain. I can smell the rich, earthy odor of the parched ground as it soaks up the rain. I can taste the sticky juice of the mango running down my chin.

These men are exciting because I recognize them. They are exciting because they have not been stripped of their cultural context. They are exciting because their Indianness has not been carefully airbrushed out of them in order to make them "sexy." In fact, they are sexy *because* their roots are showing and the artist, instead of being embarrassed by them, has chosen to celebrate them. And in doing so, he has given me the image that I have been searching for—Indian *and* erotic—unabashed, unapologetic, uncensored.

"Undressing the Oriental Boy": The Gay Asian in the Social Imaginary of the Gay White Male

Paul EeNam Park Hagland

INTRODUCTION

The relationship between lesbian, gay, bisexual, and transgendered (LGBT) communities and Asians and Pacific Islanders (APIs) within their midst is fraught with misunderstanding and clouded by ethnocentrism. Unfortunately, LGBT individuals are often no more enlightened on issues of race and ethnicity than are their heterosexual counterparts.

Indeed, LGBT society to some extent may have replicated the larger straight society's attitudes to APIs. This is especially apparent among gay white men (GWMs) who are "admirers" of Asian men, often referred to, somewhat derisively, as "rice queens," in gay slang. Relations between GWMs and APIs are reflected in publications catering to such men.

Such "rice queen magazines" (RQ magazines) reproduce what can be termed an "orientalist discourse of power," in which the Asian male is "constructed" or portrayed as an exotic but ultimately pliant sexual creature whose sexuality is directed outward toward the GWM. Here, "discourse" may be understood simply as a way of thinking or talking about a topic, an approach to or understanding of the subject, which in this case is the Asian male.[1] "Orientalist" in this context refers to the objectification of Asian and the Asian as foreign, exotic, and fundamentally different from the West.[2]

Those publications and the discourse that informs them are part of a "social imaginary" of the gay white world in which Asians are imagined and then reified as the "exotic Other," limiting and marginalizing their presence in LGBT communities and excluding from view those APIs who do not conform to the reified image.

But the implications of the phenomenon in question go far beyond the gay community itself: the specifically gay-oriented discourse which such

277

gay male erotica reproduces is part of a larger discourse of orientalism that structures Western understanding of Asian and Pacific cultures and of individuals of Asian/Pacific heritage in their own societies.

THE "RQ MAGAZINE" GENRE

Probably the best known of these "RQ magazines" is *Oriental Guys* (OG), based in Sydney and distributed in Australia, Asia, the United States, and Western Europe.[3] A second publication in this genre is *The Male Club* (which I will abbreviate as "MC"), a self-described "art card mag," also published in Sydney and distributed in Australia, New Zealand, the United States, Southeast Asia, and Japan.[4] Third, and finally, is the magazine *Passport: Crossing Cultures and Borders*, which is published in San Francisco and distributed in the United States, Canada, the United Kingdom, the Netherlands, and Japan.[4]

Of the three publications, *OG* and *MC* can be described as lavish and expensively produced, while *Passport*, despite its glossy cover, has a cheaper, matte-finish look to its text. *Passport*, it must be noted, is not solely Asian in focus, including some Latinos and Latin Americans between its covers, but the overwhelming focus is on APIs.

Male Club is primarily pictorial, with only the occasional article or interview interspersed between elaborately choreographed, artsy photographs of Asian men. In contrast, *Passport* is primarily text, with a few photos and a substantial personal classifieds section; the articles focus on travel and gay life in Asia and Latin America; in addition, regular features include letters, news from around the world, an events calendar, a bulletin board, and a regular review of new, pornographic, video releases.

In format, *OG* is midway between the other two publications, including substantial written text such as feature stories on gay life in Asia, AIDS, and travel, as well as erotic fiction and a substantial "personals" section; it also includes professional-quality photographs of Asian men in various states of undress and even an elaborate centerfold.

THE ORIENTALIST REPRODUCTION
OF THE "MYSTERIOUS EAST"

While the genre's reproduction of orientalist discourse has important implications for relationships between gay Asians and GWMs, the implications are much broader and the stakes much higher: it is our understanding of Asia and the Pacific, as well as those of Asian/Pacific origin, that is in question. This becomes apparent when we examine some excerpts from the RQ magazines, including a profile of a certain "Jamie." The article's author, Victor Davis, gushes:

> It hardly seems possible for one man to possess such languid, tropical grace and also call forth such heat and passion before the camera
> . . .
>
> Jamie is playful and mischievous. There is a boy still playing inside
> . . . . Jamie is proud. He knows his heritage and his roots . . . He is a rare blend. Tenderness and strength. Playful innocence and unexpected wisdom . . . He exemplifies exactly what is most enticing and mysterious about all of Asia itself.[6]

Through his description of one young man, Davis constructs an entire continent, characterizing the individual as well as this vast region of multitudinous and diverse cultures. Jamie apparently possesses both the childlike innocence of a Japanese geisha and the "wisdom of the East" of an "oriental" sage from central casting.

The portrayal of Jamie as a kind of a "geisha boy" recalls the most famous of geishas, Cio-Cio San, the central character in Puccini's opera, *Madama Butterfly.* Cio-Cio San is a delicate Japanese flower who is crushed by the betrayal of her trust by the American navyman, Pinkerton, and commits suicide rather than live with the dishonor of an illegitimate child. The Italian opera was partly the inspiration for David Henry Hwang's hit Broadway play, *M. Butterfly.*[7] The same Italian opera also inspired a Broadway musical, *Miss Saigon,* but the decision by the Lambda Legal Defense and Education Fund to use the musical as a fundraiser provoked a series of demonstrations by Gay Asian and Pacific Islander Men of New York (GAPIMNY) and the Asian Lesbian Organization of the East Coast (ALOEC), who eventually organized a broad coalition of Asian American groups to protest the fund-raiser.[8]

Hence, OG's Jamie is a latter-day, gay male Cio-Cio San, exemplifying an "inscrutable East" that is both enticing and mysterious—a strange, foreign, perhaps ultimately unknowable land peopled by exotic creatures blending childlike simplicity with a smoldering sexuality open to entreaties from the West. Significantly, of the ten photographs in the OG spread, four of them portray the young man partially veiled in white drapery. The choice of such drapery is a curiously apt one for this brief exercise in orientalism, given that the description of Jamie draws a metaphorical veil across Asia, partially obscuring it in narrative fabric of the author's own construction.

Positioning the "Oriental" as Subject

Despite the inclusion of articles in each of these publications written by APIs, as well as editorial staff, it is apparent that the perspective is that of the white subject and the Asian object. Hence, *The Male Club* invites us to:

> Appreciate the whole physical structure of the Modern Asian Youth. He is bigger at the right places, taller and more self-confident in manner and speech. He exudes an unique oriental charm and flavour born and bred of a carefree and yet disciplined adolescence. There is a cool gentleness about him which exudes slow warm sexuality and a restless animal spirit beneath.[9]

Here, the attractive young Asian looks out to return the gaze of the observer, implicitly assumed to be non-Asian. In establishing the relationship of non-Asian subject to Asian object, the text and photograph implicitly construct a binary opposition or stark dichotomy of Asian/non-Asian and Asia/non-Asia.[10]

While the text begins by celebrating the "Modern Asian Youth," the anonymous author predictably reverts to the use of the term "oriental," linked significantly to the quality of "charm," creating an "Orient" that is a charming but necessarily foreign and exotic—the Western imagination's view of Asia as the "exotic Other," in contrast to the familiar but ultimately more human Occident. The "restless animal spirit" marks the "Oriental" as in some ways subhuman, or only partly human, in contrast to the presumably fully human being emblematic of advanced, Western civilization. The "Oriental's" sexuality is "slow and warm" and implicitly instinctive, presumably in contrast to the perhaps more analytic and self-conscious sexuality of the Westerner.[11]

Significantly, what distinguishes the "Modern Asian Youth" from his predecessor—presumably the "Antique Oriental Youth"—is a set of largely physical characteristics: he is "taller" but also "bigger in the right places" (though the author discreetly avoids specifying which places). The new Asian boy is also "more self-confident in manner and speech"; it is not clear whether one is to interpret this passage as suggesting that he is perhaps less inhibited sexually and more open to sexual encounters with Westerners or whether he has attained an enhanced masculinity; in either case, the "Modern Asian Youth" clearly is advertised as a new and improved product, assumed to be more appealing and more marketable to the unseen but omniscient Caucasian eye behind the "gaze."[12]

That Obscure but Youthful Object of Desire

The Asian celebrated in the pages and pictorials of *OG*, *MC*, and *Passport* is no generic Asian Everyman but instead, a specific type: as the description of the "Modern Asian Youth" suggests, he is almost invariably masculine, but he is also boyishly young. One ad in the "OG Connection," for example, makes this explicit:

> . . . I seek youngish Oriental partner willing to live almost anywhere.[13]

In one issue in which the "OG Connection" is devoted exclusively to "Malaysian pen pals" (though inexplicably, one of the seven is Japanese), the seven young men whose photos and names and addresses are included range from twenty-one to twenty-eight years in age. One of the few references to an older API, a forty-three-year-old, "international pen pal" from the Philippines, includes his name and address and a short self-description but no photograph.

And yet the "pen pal" directly to his left on the same page, a blue-eyed, "straight-acting" American from Kansas City, declares that he would

> like to correspond with or meet Asians/Hispanics under thirty-five—prefer short, slender build, hairless, boyish.[14]

The "look," then, is that of the adolescent boy ripening into manhood. One enthusiastic *OG* reader writes:

> I enjoyed OG 8 very much, and being attracted to boys who fall into the pretty category, I must say I found the Street Urchin to be incredibly sweet-faced and angelic. He has that irresistible combination of sweet innocence and powerful, almost overwhelming sexual attraction . . . [15]

One Asian featured in *MC,* under the title "The Boy Crooner," is described as "boyish and handsome," a "twenty-six-year-old man" who is "Singapore's Peter Pan of pop music."[16] The reference is significant when one considers that Peter Pan is the boy who cannot grow up. According to one of the artsy captions in *MC:*

> Categorically I assure you that being young . . . vulnerable offers
> plenty of sensual delights and thrills of all sorts and kinds. It is
> dangerous in today's context. But what is excitement without the
> element of danger?[17]

The ageism evident in the orientalist text becomes paradoxical when one considers that the lifetime partnership that some of the GWMs advertise for cannot continue to be consonant when the twenty-something Asian boy lurches into middle age. And yet, the invisibility of older APIs is one of the most striking features of the genre of RQ magazines.

This omission calls our attention to the curious asymmetry of the RQ magazines, as reflected in their personals, fiction, and photographs: while the caucasians ogling the Asians portrayed in these magazines implicitly and often explicitly express a strong preference for attractive, nubile, young Asians, the APIs themselves are not given the option of being so selective.

In none of the "traveler's tales" or fictional accounts in these publications does an API actually reject a Caucasian as sex partner, no matter how old, overweight, or unattractive he may be. The narrative constructed by the orientalist apparently does not grant the Asian such an option. In fact, the Caucasian partner or would-be partner is rarely described at all; we do not know whether he is a wrinkled, pot-bellied, aging "troll," but it does not matter in the universe of the rice queen: his physical profile is not at issue.

GENDER IN THE ORIENTALIST IMAGINARY

Equally evident as ageism is the general insistence on the masculinity of the subject, as traditionally defined; in fact, ageism and heterosexism often go hand in hand, as made clear by one *OG* reader who writes, in a letter to the editor:

> I find *OG* 5 a slight deviation from your previous issues. The models, except for the darling Poh of Hong Kong, are too old! Please stick to your original concept so apparent in *OG* 1-4—that of using fresh young faces with hard and masculine bodies to match. This is what your readers want to see . . . [18]

It is apparent that the reader does not feel in the least bit compelled to inform the editor whether he, too, meets this standard of being sufficiently young, hard, and masculine.

One of the glossy features in *OG* is titled "Boy in a Cave: Masculinity," and features the following text strung across seven pages of photos of one young man:

> A man . . . his body . . . sculptured . . . well-endowed . . . finely tuned and engraved . . . with deep sensuality . . . a man is divine.[19]

The irony of this very butch, young man featured in generally butch poses is captured by the fourth in the series of photos, showing only his torso, buttocks, and legs from behind, with the tip of his glans hanging down as the sole conclusive evidence of his maleness; such a pose is clearly meant to show his vulnerability, his attraction as an object of anal penetration—the nonmasculine subject position in homosexual sex, at least as traditionally conceived.[20] In the text created by orientalist discourse, this boy is both "man" and "woman," if by "woman" one means the passive partner of penile insertion. His masculinity, apparent from the rugged backdrop and masculine apparel of the photos, paradoxically makes the "femininity" of his pose for the camera all the more alluring to the unseen observer, who has reduced the boy to a "woman" by the penetration of his "gaze."

Elsewhere in this same publication are other photos of young men in masculine attire, such as tennis togs and other sportswear (p. 8), a feature on "Jamie" posing in an obi (a Japanese robe for both men and women) and in drapery veiled across his body in a way that suggests women's clothing (pp. 17-20), and an article in "The World of OG" on police harassment of transvestites and transsexuals in Bangkok (p. 9).[21]

There is also an article by one young Filipino who describes himself as the following:

> I was, and still am a sissy. I like to wear my mother's wigs and smear my face with her makeup . . . My fingers float in the air when I walk and whenever I sit, I cross my legs like ladies do . . . [22]

Significantly, though, the feminine-identified Solis is not constructed as an object of overt sexual attraction for the reader: the small photograph of him wearing only a bathing suit contrasts with the full-page, lavish photos of other Asians in the issue, and the article itself is written as an "open letter" to his father from a gay son.

The other image of a nonmasculine Asian in the same issue seems to have been included almost inadvertently. A photograph accompanying a short news story on a gay beauty contest in Bangkok shows the winner, and standing slightly behind him and to his right, what appears to be a transvestite in an elaborate dress and wearing a floral headdress.[23] Such references to feminine-identified or transgendered males constitute an anomaly in a publication that largely excludes any images of "effeminate," feminine, or clearly transgendered Asians.

Ironically, perhaps, in this genre, the API is often constructed as somewhat androgynous. For example, in another issue of *OG*, "B.B.," a tourist from Perth (Western Australia), in his contribution to "Travelers' Tales," describes a young Hong Kong Chinese he came across as having

> long almost silky hair down to his fair and slender neck and his facial features were almost beautiful, like those of a girl, but without any feminine airs.[24]

The author's description contributes to the orientalist discourse by admitting into the narrative a description of womanlike but not womanly traits; the young creature described here has characteristics associated with the feminine but without effeminate gestures to "spoil" the image.

In a photographic profile of Chinese Canadian Wang Zheng, the photographer captures the young man in nineteen different images, only two of which are distinctly nonmasculine.[25] In one photo, Zheng is shown dancing in a red, tank-top unitard, waving a long, red banner attached to a short stick; in another, Zheng is shown wearing a woman's dress with a tight-fitting, black bodice and a loose, gray skirt, with a gray bow in his hair and a black fan held up demurely to cover his face below the eyes.[26]

These two images, rather campy and coy, and a bit pretentious, contrast strongly with the imagery of masculinity and athleticism in the rest of the series; but while they diversify the imagery of the photographic profile, they paradoxically reinforce the narrative of masculinity articulated by the profile: Zheng might "play" at being a woman, but in fact, he is "all-boy" underneath it all—as revealed, graphically, in the two later photos that show a flaccid male member to the viewer.

Hence, in many images and fictional narratives, the Asian boy is gendered ambiguously but in such a way as to exclude the "excessively effeminate" and the self-consciously transgendered. While cast in the narrative in the role of "the woman" or woman-substitute, the API nevertheless clearly reflects a traditionally masculine and masculinist concept of gender.

Intra-Asian Coupling in the Orientalist Narrative

What is particularly curious, but especially revealing upon further examination, is the inclusion of intra-Asian coupling in the orientalist narrative. At first glance, it might seem an anomaly, on the one hand, to portray the Asian as not only available for Western "consumption" but even oriented sexually toward whites but, on the other hand, to portray the Asian in fiction, photos, and illustrations as coupling with other Asians.

But the apparent contradiction can be resolved with reference to the audience. The intra-Asian coupling portrayed is constructed largely by Caucasians for their own gratification: the Asians, whether constructed in fictional narrative or choreographed in pornographic video and film, perform for the "gaze" of the GWM much as the "lesbians" in heterosexual pornography perform in the genre of "fake lesbianism."

One pair of Japanese videos, *The Best Friend* and *Tropic in Dream* (Atelier Imago Videos, 1993) for example, includes:

> . . . smooth models who are fucking and grinding Olympian machines. They suck, they fuck, they rim, they kiss, in twos and threes. For all you pretty boy lovers, there are a couple of soft-lit, romantic scenes for you too. But what I got off on was the solo jack-off scenes where the boys would pose as boxers or body-builders and flex their young muscles for the camera.[27]

Clearly, the narrative structures a rice queen's fantasy in which the participants are performers in a drama constructed for his gaze. With the videos being distributed in advanced industrialized countries such as the United States, the audience invariably will be largely Caucasian. And the pornographic sex video itself is a Western genre, in this case produced with APIs for Western consumption.

An attempt to connect the porn video to the culture from which it ostensibly emerges is apparent in a recent series of videos produced in Thailand, aptly and significantly, from "Exotic Productions." The series, reviewed in *OG*, includes titles such as *Red Hot Beaux Thai, Boys of Pattaya, Tales from the Thai-Side,* and *Memories of Bamboo Island;* while the second of these includes Eurasians and the fourth features a European American, the others feature all-Thai casts. *Red Hot Beaux Thai,* for example, is described as follows:

> Shot on location in the enchanting and exotic world of Thailand, OGGI combined the elements of sensuous foreplay, erotic fantasy, and authentic Thai-style lovemaking, to guide you through the dimensions of Thai culture and male eroticism with the introduction of three handsome young men.[28]

The effort to ensure "authenticity" in the portrayal of "Thai-style lovemaking" is curious since one must presume that few if any Thais will be able to afford the video, even if they had the inclination to watch it. With the video undoubtedly distributed largely to a Western and Caucasian audience, "authenticity" instead constitutes an element in the orientalist discourse of the exotic.

The video description is reminiscent of advertisements for straight porn videos featuring "real lesbians" in "hot lesbo action"; as with the fake lesbian porn, this genre of "Asian" porn ironically promises an "authenticity" that contributes much to the reproduction of the orientalist discourse of power while contributing little or nothing to the cultivation of an autonomous, gay Asian sexuality.

THE DISEMPOWERING DISCOURSE
OF THE PLIANT AND APOLITICAL

One of the most striking features of the RQ genre is the way in which the API is constructed as being willing if not eager to engage in sex with Westerners. Erotic fiction and tourist stories in the RQ magazines invariably center on the seduction of an Asian, usually by a non-Asian. That this fantasy is the basis for virtually all of the fictional and "real-life" stories in this genre has been decried as somewhat repetitive and tiresome, even by the editors of *OG*. In giving potential contributors guidelines, *OG* declares, revealingly:

> While OG has, in the past, published stories detailing readers' sexual encounters with guys, often in explicit detail, we want to encourage writers to go beyond the man meets Asian man, man seduces Asian man story the end . . . Plot, pace, and characterization are extremely important in developing the story and holding the readers' attention. A story should have something to say or be entertaining or thought-provoking, not just titillation which is forgotten in five minutes.[29]

It is the introduction of monetary transactions into the orientalist narrative that draws the construction of Asian men closely parallel to that of Asian women. This point is conveyed implicitly in "Manila Manic," an article by Robin Sharpe in *Passport* that consists of a nine-page compendium of diary entries of a Canadian sex tourist's visits to the Ermita district of the Philippine capital from 1984-1991.[30] Visiting a Manila bar named the "Adams 12," Sharpe observes naked Filipino dancing boys as follows:

> However, the boys do not understand erotic dancing; they could learn a lot from, proud to be a Canadian, the naked dancing girls who

perform with so much dedication and style in our peeler bars and pubs.[31]

Thus, the author himself links male prostitution and erotic display in the Philippines to its female equivalent back in North America, though locating the former lower on a hierarchy of skill, authenticity, and commitment to customer service. Even in such matters as sexual performance for paying male customers, Asians are reduced to a position in which they are to learn from their "betters" in an act that is patterned after its heterosexual equivalent in the advanced Western civilization.

Significantly, Sharpe justifies patronizing the "mabini boys" as a contribution to the economic development of the Philippines, declaring in self-satisfied tones that

> Noel, my muscular friend from Puerto Galera . . . and his brothers have done well by foreigners who've paid their school fees, bought them clothes and expensive gifts, and helped their parents build a better house . . . The father is not unconcerned about these relationships and has always insisted that his sons never suck the foreigner's cock or let themselves be fucked.[32]

In the discourse of male prostitution as economic development that Sharpe's narrative constructs, questions of the unequal distribution of wealth and power in a relationship of Asian "boy" to white "man" are ignored, and paternal concern is limited to preventing the sexual feminization of the boy through passive anal penetration. Ironically, this concern, while perhaps not shared in its specifically sexual form by the diarist, appears to parallel the general preference for those boys who do not transgress gender rules through extreme "effeminacy" or transgendered expression.

Even more significantly, Sharpe's narrative constructs a discourse in which criticism of male prostitution, including patronage of young boys, is a form of cultural imperialism. According to Sharpe,

> Moral imperialism has forced Filipino authorities to crack down on presumed pedophiles and the more serious of them have moved to Thailand, which has traditionally resisted all forms of imperialism.[33]

In explaining to one mabini boy his country of origin, Sharpe tells him that Canada is

> not part of "America" but "independent," and with intended but unappreciated irony, I add, "like the Philippines."[34]

But in his smug superiority over the Filipino boy in assuming that the boy would not appreciate the irony of his comment, Sharpe himself fails to see the irony of his own commentary: issues that have been raised by Canadians (in particular, francophone Québecois) about the political independence and cultural autonomy of Canada from the United States parallel those raised by Filipino commentators about the continued neocolonial status of the Philippines in relation to the United States.

Even more important, the author equates resistance to the cultural and sexual subjection represented by transracial prostitution with "moral imperialism," all too neatly reversing the patterns of dominance and submission in the relationship of patron to prostitute. Thailand's heretofore more casual acceptance of boy prostitution is lauded as an act of "independence" and resistance to "moral imperialism."

An article in *OG* on homosexuality and the sex industry in Thailand, at first glance at least, appears to move further than most contributions in the RQ magazines to breaking out of the orientalist discourse of power. The anonymous author of "Thailand: Behind the Bars" acknowledges the complexity of Thai attitudes toward homosexuality and questions the predominant image of Thailand as a "gay paradise."[35]

The anonymous author attempts to address the issue of whether prostitution constitutes exploitation. His approach here is rather more subtle than that of Robin Sharpe; in attempting to answer his own question in the negative, the author uses native Thai voices to advance his own position. Toward this end, the author quotes one Thai as saying the following:

> The real problem is not prostitution or sex tourism but the fact that Thailand is an under-developed country with a huge gulf between the very rich and the very poor. The sex industry is merely a symptom of deeper inequalities . . . [The bar boy scene] is, to some extent, an expression of the resourcefulness and determination of poor people to survive in the face of immense poverty.[36]

Once again, we see the erasure of race, gender, and inequalities of power in the discourse of prostitution as economic development; the fact that most prostitutes are young women and men, including adolescent and even prepubescent girls and boys, and most of their clients are male heterosexual Westerners, although all the prostitutes are Southeast Asians, is conveniently ignored.[37]

The anonymous author uses another Thai to suggest that the relationship of bar boys to Western customers may be one of mutual exploitation; yet, although mutual exploitation and the exploitation of clients by prostitutes may be an element of the transaction, the uneven distribution of wealth and power in the relationship is not addressed.

Most significant, the author quotes a Thai journalist writing for the *Bangkok Post* to articulate the counter-critique of cultural relativism, echoing Sharpe in his indictment of "moral imperialism":

> What right do liberal Europeans have to condemn the sex industry? Them telling us what to do is just plain neo-colonialism. It's up to Thais to sort out our own problems.[38]

What is most insidious about this sometimes insightful commentary is the way in which the author calls upon Asian voices to articulate a discourse that privileges the pleasure of Western sex tourists through the sexual submission of Asians. The irony of it all is that the author, who remains anonymous, introduces the names of native Thais into his commentary, in effect attempting to implicate Asians in an assent to their own oppression.

In the discourse of orientalist power, any insertion of critique or even cultural or historical context, much less resistance, represents an unwanted disruption of the narrative of the seduction of the pliant and apolitical Asian boy. Examples of frustration with political consciousness abound, as evidenced by two brief descriptions of pornographic videos in one issue of *Passport*. In reviewing the video, *Inner Circle* (OG Video Network, 1994), "Kino, our intrepid movie reviewer," writes:

> You have to be a die-hard rice queen to like this one! The dicks in the video are nice but you have to wade through the quasi-ethnographic and documentary footage to reach it . . . It's cute that the video contextualizes homosexuality and homophobia in China by juxtaposing interviews of gay Chinese men living in subterfuge with the sex scenes, but when I want dick, I WANT dick . . . People would rather see Asians giving head than talking heads.[39]

In reviewing the video, *Young Love, Sweet Lust* (Blue Lotus Productions, 1994), Kino writes:

> They don't make guys like these in the States. They're not the ACT UP, in-your-face, I'm-a-fag type. Sometimes too much empowerment can be a real turnoff. No these guys are good friends who happen to enjoy each others' dick.[40]

The reviews are rated on a scale of one to five, with the highest rated videos marked by an illustration of five half-peeled bananas, one assumes chosen because of the phallic imagery of the fruit. Whether the reviewer or editors are aware that "banana" is a pejorative term for an Asian with no ethnic or political consciousness is an intriguing question. In the world of the rice queen, consciousness is sexually deflationary, and Asian empowerment is the ultimate transgression of sexual mores.

CONCLUSION: MARGINALIZING THE API

In short, the API in these publications is constructed as almost invariably young, boyishly cute, yet butch, and implicitly sexually pliant—an Asian or Asianized version of the sexual partner of choice reflected in so many pornographic gay magazines. Excluded are the mature, the obviously "effeminate" or transgendered, the overweight, and the unattractive. Hence, in producing and reproducing a certain image of the "cute, young, Asian boy," RQ magazines contribute to the marginalization of APIs who do not fit the extremely limiting specifications of the genre.

Instead, the rice queen's universe is peopled by a relatively narrow spectrum of APIs, predominantly the young, traditionally masculine yet boyish, and appealingly pliant Asian boy who is oriented toward sexual encounters and relationships with white men. The idealized Asian boy of the RQ magazines, as described in the orientalist narrative, is perhaps as unselective regarding age and physical condition as his white "admirer" is selective; he is, above all, apolitical, and not one who will insist too stridently on the autonomy of his own sexuality and life choices.

The orientalist narrative excludes an entire range of possibilities, such as the potential for satisfying intra-Asian relationships, for political consciousness and activism consistent with the construction of an autonomous sexuality, for significantly transgendered sexualities, and for sexualities informed by Asian and Pacific spiritual traditions.

Hence, the "orientalist discourse of power" found at the heart of the RQ magazine genre, while ostensibly "celebrating the beauty of Asian men in erotica," functions in practice to disempower Asians and Pacific Islanders. One might respond by pointing to the relatively small circulation of these publications, but what is noteworthy here is the lack of publications by and for gay APIs themselves; one of the few examples of which is a special issue of the *Asian Pacific American* (APA) *Journal* published in 1993.[41]

What is yet more marginalizing is the general exclusion of APIs from gay publications outside of the specialized confines of the RQ genre, whether pornographic or nonpornographic. The general invisibility of Asians from the social imaginary of gay culture consigns gay Asian men to the margins of the subculture. The focus on APIs in specialized publications such as the RQ magazines therefore has the effect of constructing the API as a specialized and perhaps acquired "taste," as a bit of exotic color to add to the predominantly white hue of the black/white binary of race or as the object of desire of only the "connoisseur" of Asian male beauty.

Above all, the disempowering discourse of "oriental guy-dom" constrains social understanding of Asian Pacific Americans (APAs) and APIs more generally and limits the possibilities for an autonomous sexuality and spirituality. Hence, the implications of the construction of gay Asian identity in the RQ genre go far beyond the confines of the genre itself to challenge our understanding of gay API sexuality and international society as a whole.

NOTES

1. See Michel Foucault, *The Archaeology of Knowledge,* A.M. Sheridan Smith, trans. New York: Pantheon, 1972. (In French, *L'Archéologie du Savoir,* 1969); *Discipline and Punish: The Birth of the Prison.* Alan Sheridan, trans. New York: Pantheon, 1977 (In French, *Surveillir et Punir: Naissance de la Prison,* 1975).
2. See Edward W. Said, *Orientalism.* New York: Vintage, 1978. For Said, Orientalism

> . . . is, rather than expresses, a certain will or intention to understand, in some cases to control, manipulate, even to incorporate, what is a manifestly different (or alternative and novel) world; it is, above all, a discourse . . . (p. 12)

Said develops the concept of "discourse" found originally in the work of Michel Foucault.

Since the publication of Said's *Orientalism* in 1978, Asian Americanists—scholars of Asian-American studies—have appropriated the term to describe the social and cultural construction of Asian Pacific Americans (APAs) and APIs in general in ways that perpetuate the image of APAs as the "exotic Other."

3. *Oriental Guys (OG)*, no. 6 (spring 1990); and no. 10 (spring 1992).
4. *The Male Club,* no. 2. (March/April 1992); and no. 3 (spring 1993).
5. *Passport: Crossing Cultures and Borders,* no. 78 (August/September 1994), p. 2.
6. Victor Davis, "Jamie," *OG,* no. 10 (spring 1992), pp. 17-22.
7. See Marjorie Garber, *Vested Interests: Cross-Dressing and Cultural Anxiety.* New York: Harper Perennial, 1992.
8. Yoko Yoshikawa, "The Heat is On 'Miss Saigon' Coalition: Organizing Across Race and Sexuality." In Karin Aguilar-San Juan, ed., *The State of Asian America: Activism and Resistance in the 1990s.* Boston: South End Press, 1994, pp. 275-294.

9. *MC*, no. 2 (March/April 1992), p. 7.

10. It is not insignificant, I think, that the leading publication in this genre is called "Oriental Guys;" the editors clearly could have renamed the publication "Asian Guys" long ago; and in fact, *OG*'s motto on its cover is "celebrating the beauty of Asian men in erotica." One could speculate as to whether the publication retains the term "oriental" in its title because many readers still have not come on board with the use of the term "Asian." But the continued use of the term "oriental" can be interpreted as being consistent with the general discursive practice of reproducing the notion of the "exotic Orient."

11. Here, one may be forgiven for seeing shades of the "Noble Savage" so beloved of some Enlightenment and Romantic thinkers.

12. That the primary audience for these publications is GWMs in the developed West becomes even more evident from the personals, in which the GWMs all specify an interest in APIs (and/or Latinos).

13. *OG*, no. 10 (spring 1992), p. 85.

14. *OG*, no. 10 (spring 1992), p. 85.

15. *OG*, no. 10 (spring 1992), p. 6.

16. *MC*, no. 2 (March/April 1992), p. 3.

17. *MC*, no. 3 (spring 1993), p. 5.

18. Steven Lee (Amsterdam), letter to the editor, "The OG Forum: Comments and Viewpoints," *OG*, no. 6 (spring 1990), p. 6.

19. *OG*, no. 10 (spring 1992), pp. 31-38.

20. *OG*, no. 10 (spring 1992), p. 33.

21. *OG*, no. 10 (spring 1992), pp. 8, 9, 17-20.

22. Wattus Solis, "Of Sissies and Men," *OG*, no. 6 (spring 1990), p. 25.

23. "Mr. Handsome Boy: A Bangkok Gay Tradition," *OG*, no. 6 (spring 1990), p. 10.

24. B.B., "The OG Forum: Travelers' Tales," *OG*, no. 6 (spring 1990), p. 7.

25. *OG*, "Free to Choose: A Chinese in Canada Takes a Stand," *OG*, no. 6 (spring 1990), pp. 11-21.

26. Ibid., pp. 13-14.

27. Kino, "Blue Movie Review," *Passport*, no. 78 (August/September 1993), p. 23.

28. Exotic Productions, "Red Hot Beaux Thai," *OG*, no. 10 (spring 1992), pp. 112-113.

29. *OG*, "Attention Writers, Poets, and Artists," *OG*, no. 6 (spring 1990), p. 106.

30. Robin Sharpe, "Manila Manic," *Passport*, no. 78 (August/September 1994), pp. 8-16.

31. Ibid., p. 28.

32. Ibid., p. 14.

33. Ibid., p. 12.

34. Ibid., p. 13.

35. Anonymous, "Thailand: Behind the Bars," *OG*, no. 6 (spring 1990), pp. 22-24.

36. Ibid., p. 24.

37. Here, the question of Japanese sex tourism is not addressed; the role of the Japanese in the gay sector of the Thai sex industry, as far as I know, has never been the subject of sustained analysis. The fact that Japanese are Asians does not undermine the critique of race but, in fact, arguably reinforces it, given the widely held view among Japanese that they are a distinct "race," superior to other Asian peoples as well as Westerners.

38. Ibid., p. 24.

39. Kino, "Blue Movie Review," *Passport,* no. 78 (August/September 1994), p. 23.

40. Ibid., p. 23.

41. *The APA Journal, Witness Aloud: Lesbian, Gay, and Bisexual Asian/Pacific American Writings,* vol. 2, no. 1 (spring/summer 1993) (Asian American Writers' Workshop, New York). This admirable publication is all the more noteworthy on account of the precedent it sets as the first LGBT journal issue, but what is regrettable is its singularity and the lack of an autonomous LGBT API publication enterprise.

I Like My Chi-i-sa-i Body Now

Donna Tsuyuko Tanigawa

Before time, I got plenty things for feel shame. Whoever said that one Asian woman is exotic never come talk to me. Eh, I wish that I was told my body was something desirous. From small-kid time, I when think that for be Japanee was kinda ugly. More worse, I was kinda fat. Whoever saw one not-so-skinny Japanee in magazines at Tani's Superette? Not me. I never even see one Japanee in papa-san's dirty magazines (the ones under the sink by the Ajax). Wow, I never believe that haole-folks when think Asian women stay exotic. Even okay looking. 'Ass why hard. Maybe my life would be different if I knew this kine stuff. Maybe I would never try for look like one haole, yeah? Da kine, put Scotch tape on my eyelids for make 'um double. And maybe I would never think I had for go on one crash diet. Dis kine thinking when make me hate myself.

I stay struggling now. My lover Lee-Ann thinks that I got one great body. She loves the way my two chi-chis grew from one "almost A" to one cup size "C" in the last two years. Japanee women get small breasts, yeah? I used for tell her that I wanted to kapu her chi-chis because they stay big.

Good to have Lee-Ann in my life. She safe for talk story with at night. I tell her more and more about my hanabata days as one kid in Waipahu. I tell her any kine about my family. About my small-kid friends. After about one year, I tell her about me, Donna.

Eh, I was one fat Japanee girl. I used for eat adult size meals at Funaba's Family Restaurant. I ate plenty ono foods at home, too. I used for grind the New Year's mochi. The rice all white and soft. Only thing I had stuck doo-doo that never like leave my okole-hole when I ate too much.

I think that my life when really change at Alphabet Land. I was the only fat kid in preschool. I began for feel shame about the size of my body. All the kids was skinny, I think. I used for cry when they called me "Donut" and not Donna. "What did you do?" Lee-Ann when ask me. I ate more. Mama-san when think that one fat child was healthy.

At Alphabet Land I fell in love with my classmate Laurie, one haole girl. She was skinny and had short, blond hair. She ate plenty carrot sticks for lunch. I put myself on one diet so I could look like her. Just think, one

295

seven-year old kid going on one fucking diet in the 1970s. Geez, this was even before health food was in the markets. I remember I made a list of all the fattening things I ate but had for stop eating. I wrote down andagi, shrimp tempura, and milk at the top of my list. Had about twenty foods I never like eat, bumbye I get fat. Laurie was pretty and had nice thighs that kinda looked like carrot sticks.

I lost plenty weight. I came skinny, too. I noticed that my school teacher when think I was so cute. She when say that I was "petite." Wow, I when love Miss White that year. After I when pull down, nobody called me "Donut" or tease me. More better I stay skinny, I thought.

So why, you ask, I no can believe that me, one Asian woman, stay ono-looking? I never see the Hollywood movies of us-folks as Chinatown playthings? I did. Or all the dirty magazines from Japan with plenty beautiful naked women? I did. (My uncle had some under his mattress.) I think that I when always hate my body. First I was fat, then ever when I was one "petite" girl I when still see myself as fat. Or at east not like the other girls. Maybe that's why my doctor when tell my mother I was suffering from anorexia nervosa when I went for my physical exam. I was one teenager and my rags when stop for three months. Nothing. Not even enough for soil one Stayfree panty liner. Anyways, I like to be skinny just like Laurie.

I never think that I had problems. Later in college I never see that I was suffering from bad self-image. Only nowdays I can see that I really when hate myself. I stay four feet, eleven inches. I always weigh less than 100 pounds, even before I get my rags. My waist stay twenty-four inches and now I get decent size chi-chis. So why I hate my body, you like ask? Ask, sistah.

I think that I never like feel good anymore. Not only did I think that nobody when like me because I was Japanee and fat, but then I when also think that for be da kine "sexual" was shame. As one small kid, I used for play on the monkey bars after school. I used for be real still and move my legs like one scissors. Back and forth in the air. Felt good. Used for feel good right under my stomach. Sometimes more better do this after drink-ing four glasses water. All the shi-shi made the feeling more strong. I had the same feeling when my pen pal from the mainland came Hawaii for the summer. We when Eskimo kiss and move our legs like one scissors until her aunty got all huhu at us. "Sick," I think she when yell at me.

So later when Martin made the same feeling come for me I thought, "Sick, Donna." He was my classmate in the sixth grade. He put anykine stuffs between my legs. Mostly his hands. I think that that's where I learned to leave my body in the canefields and go someplace else, even if

Martin was there on top of me. I only had for think that I was someplace else.

So as one adult, I when still hate my body. All the times those haole men when date me I was thinking that maybe they heard about me and Martin. Silly, yeah? Here I was on the mainland far, far away from Hawaii and I when think that some stupid childhood memory when inform these men. Maybe they made me feel the same way, 'ass why.

I think that the only really ugly thing about my body is the scar on my left forearm. Stay look like one mouth, all red on the inside and thick brown on the edges. I made this badge myself. Curling iron works good for create it. I burned my arm every night. Later, I used for peel off the scab and swirl around whatever flesh I could see. One time I even bit the hole. But I no eat red meat anymore. (Only get stuck because Asian people no can digest too much meat and dairy.) I used for lick the blood. All this when help me with my pain. Fuck my arm, I when think. The pain feels kinda good. I never feel "sick" like I did when I was with my pen pal (Secrete-kine, felt kinda good with her).

Eh, I was all prepared for the rape. I had my mind all psyched. I know it's not true, but I used for think that I was raped because it was easier for me, as opposed to some beautiful woman, to take the rape. My therapist first thought that I hated my body because my rapist when violate me. True, the guy was one fucking animal but my small-kid days when prepare me. Later she agreed. She was good for me. She when help me not only with the rape but also with myself. We dug deep. We made sense out of one of my hana hou dreams. I'm standing naked in a room full of naked women. Oddly, I feel comfortable, like I've "come home." This was my coming out. Laurie, the many girlfriend "crushes,", my pen pal—all clues.

Now I like my body. I see dykes check me out. Especially when I get all femme-out and go to the women's bar in Waikiki. Lipstick and heels. Strangers mistake me for straight. Fuck them. I no care anymore if I don't look like a dyke. I am one. I know the "sick" feeling I have with women is actually a good and healthy one.

So what, Donna? How you feel now? Think your body still no good? No. I like who I am now. No big thing for be Asian. Or that my eyes no more space for fit eyeshadow. And that shit when happen to my chi-i-sa-i body. Now I know that it's no good destroy myself. No starve or carve yourself, Donna. No even hurt anymore for look in the mirror. My lover makes the space between my legs feel good. And you know what, sistah? I stay make that place feel good, too. I make my whole body feel good. I even eat andagi now.

GLOSSARY OF "PIDGIN" WORDS

andagi: fried Okinawan doughnut
'ass why: That's why
before time: long time ago; earlier; formerly
bumbye: later on
chi-chi: female breast
chi-i-sa-i: small; tiny; petite
grind: eat
hana hou: recurring; one more time
hanabata days: childhood (literally, a time when you had "butter" running from your nose)
haole: Caucasian; white; Hawaiian for "foreigner"
huhu: upset
Japanee: a person of Japanese ancestry
kapu: to reserve; to claim
kine: kind (of); sort of (e.g., da kine, dis kine, anykine)
mama-san: grandmother
mochi: steamed and pounded Japanese sweet rice
okole-hole: anus
ono: delicious; tasty
papa-san: grandfather
pull down: lose weight
shi-shi: urine

PART 10:
ACCESS TO THE LOOK

When Pigs Have Wings

Mark O'Brien

"I don't know how to say this." Len's voice, usually breezy and confident, sounded tense and confused as it came out of the speakerphone. "Chuck, you know I love you, I do, but . . . "

"But what, Len?" Chuck barked as he peered through the darkness of his cramped studio apartment at the icy green numerals on his clock radio. "It's three in the fucking morning and you're telling me you love me? Don't you think I already know . . . "

"Please Chuck, I have to . . . " Chuck heard Len's voice rise until it broke into a sob.

"Len . . . Lenny-benny, Punch, I'm sorry, so sorry. Please tell me . . . what is it?"

"It's . . . it's my father. He had a stroke at his office and he's totally zonked—can't talk, can't understand, can't . . . he may live, I mean, a long time—ten, twenty years. Christ, I sound like I want him dead, don't I?"

"I'm sure you want him to live."

"I don't know, I haven't been a good son to him . . . I mean, if only I had . . . "

"Look, Punch, how many times have you told me that he spent so much time with his accounting firm that he never noticed you?" Chuck heard nothing but the sound of a car's motor until the digital clock clicked off another minute. 3:08. Its engine was so loud that Chuck thought it must be an old Volkswagen beetle. Finally, he asked Len, "You still there?"

"Yeah, kinda." Len sniffled, then blew his nose.

"And he never took you to ball games or out on his boat."

"Yeah, the boat was strictly to impress clients or potential clients. He said he didn't want to lose business 'cause some client slipped and fell and broke his neck on a deck slippery with kids' barf." Len snorted.

"Bastard. Probably didn't want us to see him get boozed out of his mind with his cigar-stinking cronies."

Len sighed and paused. Chuck imagined him sitting naked in his bed, his hair rumpled, his eyes squinting without his glasses, and his torso gleaming and beautiful.

"Maybe I wasn't . . . "

"Wasn't what?" Chuck asked.

"Oh, maybe I wasn't such a worthless son . . . but I do have to go back. Only way we can pay for long-term care is for somebody to take over the business."

"So you're leaving, really leaving?"

"Got to catch United Airlines flight two-two-nine at eight. It'll be the red-eye for me. Been up all night."

"Len, you can't go," Chuck shouted. "I don't know what I'd do without . . . shit, you're no accountant; you're an astronomer; why can't someone else take over the damned firm? You can't leave; I'll miss you horribly."

"You think I haven't argued with my mom about this? No, she can't do it; she says she's a teacher and too old to take on a new trade, and my Dad's brother Rich has this cushy job as travel writer for the *Advertiser.* They both say what invaluable experience I had working summers for a tax attorney. Besides, and it's true, I've studied so much math—"

"Yeah, but that was so you could be an astronomer," Chuck interrupted, now frightened and desperate.

"I know, but the stuff I've studied makes accounting math look like two and two equals four."

"You sound like you've already made up your mind," Chuck said after a silence. "Do you need a lift? You could use my van."

"No, I already got a cab to pick me and my shit up. But I'll drop by to say good-bye."

"No, Len, you don't have to . . . I mean . . . shit, the meter'll be running and . . . " Chuck surprised himself with the loudness of his sobbing.

*   *   *

"I see your friend was over here last night," Trudy said as she switched on the light and entered Chuck's apartment five hours later. "Why didn't he straighten out your bed?" she asked as she stepped over piles of books, magazines, newspapers, and medical supplies. "He always has before. It's just a mess, and who gets to fix it up but long-suffering me, Trudy Goldman?"

A short woman with a flat Jersey accent, her streaky reddish hair fell loosely over her denim jacket and rust Jansport backpack.

"Trudy," Chuck said, "Len's gone. He's left Berkeley. For good. He just came last night, this morning, to say good-bye on his way to the Oakland airport. Has a family crisis."

"Chuck," she said, rushing to embrace him, "you must feel awful."

"I do. I don't want to go to school today. I don't want to get up in the wheelchair. Too tired to cry." Silently, she held him until a thought came to her.

"You like Spence, don't you?" she asked.

"Like him? I think he's gorgeous. You sure do have good taste in men. You're lucky to have him."

"Hmmm, way you talk makes me wonder if you guys have been having secret rendezvous. Come on, Chuck, fess up. Or I'll put you in your manual chair and push you to Biz Ad 73."

"No, no!" he screamed in mock terror. "Anything but that."

She let go of him.

"Trude, old girl, you make me laugh, even when I'm feeling horrible."

"Then why don't you come over for dinner tonight?"

"O Jesus, not tonight. I just want to die or watch the channel seven news or something."

"That's why you've got to come over tonight. I'll make you laugh some more, accuse you of base behavior involving Spence and his brother, Theo. Theo's going to eat with us tonight, did I tell you?"

"No, you've never told me Spence even had a brother. Is he like Spence?"

"Yup. Same long hair, same wire frames, same mumble. Only he doesn't like girls."

"He doesn't?" Chuck asked. "Well then, maybe I'll go. Can't hang around here mourning the loss of Len . . . looks like Spence, huh?"

"Uh-huh," she said lasciviously. "Coming?"

"Like my grandfather used to say, nothing like a good double helping of lust to chase the blues away."

"Which grandfather said that? The stuntman or the preacher?"

"Why, the preacher, of course."

For a second, they looked at each other seriously, then burst into laughter.

The September heat simmered incongruously amid the dying leaves on the trees in front of the small house on Carlton. Children raced on skateboards in the car-deserted street and made the loudest sounds in the neighborhood with their venomous arguments. Chuck eyed the steps with trepidation.

"Okay, Theo, you grab the wheelchair under the seat on that side; I'll grab this side; Trudy, you supply the sarcasm," Spence directed.

"I hate being lugged up and down stairs," Chuck said. "When are you guys getting a ramp put on this old Victorian?"

"When you start paying me twenty bucks an hour."

"One two three UP!"

"When pigs have wings, Trudy, when pigs have wings, when pigs have . . . there, made it."

"Thanks to the great big hunks I supply you with," Trudy said.

Spence made a muscle while Theo growled, "Meat, meat, kill, red meat."

"Theo," Chuck said, "hasn't Trudy told you the specialty of the house is nonmeat?"

"We're having a chef's salad," Trudy said cheerfully.

"Arghh," said Theo, clutching his throat.

"Followed by fish-flavored tofu," she continued, undismayed.

"I'd rather eat shit-flavored fish," Theo said. "Spence, has this little twit turned you into one of those godawful lettuce freaks?"

Chuck inhaled deeply as he watched Trudy shoot an "is-this-guy-for-real?" look at Spence.

"Hey, I like Trudy's cooking," Spence said softly. "You will too if you give it half a chance."

"Well . . . I ate part of a dead cow on the flight up from Anaheim; I guess I can survive another day without protein."

"Theo," Trudy said, "the tofu has more protein and . . . "

" . . . iron than a pound of calves' liver," Theo said, rolling his eyes toward the sky in exasperation. "Yeah, I've heard that Ted Mack speech."

As they sauntered into the dim entrance hall, Chuck saw the tension in Trudy's face and asked her to help him in the bathroom, which was small and just barely accommodated the two of them. She opened the backpack strapped to the back of his wheelchair and pulled out a white plastic urinal.

"You want me to empty your legbag?"

"Yeah, that'd be nice. Mostly I just wanted to get you away from Theo before you strangled him."

"I don't believe in violence; I don't believe in violence; I don't believe in violence," she muttered, clenching her fists.

"Nice mantra. Almost as good as 'when pigs have wings.' "

She put the urinal on the floor beside his foot before placing the tip of his legbag into the urinal. Then she opened the tip and squeezed the accumulated urine out of the legbag.

"Is that why you were saying that over and over?"

"Yes."

"I could kill him. Put some ground glass in his tofu like the slaves used to when dear ol' marse got too oppressive," she said with a tight smile that immediately burst into rage. "That motherfucker! Who's he to tell me what to cook or how to cook it, or to imply that I've brainwashed Spence into . . . as if he could be led by the nose like a . . . oh shit! Shit, shit, shit!"

She began to cry.

"How can a sweetheart like Spence have such a cuh-reep for a brother?"

"I didn't know the old-timey slaves made tofu."

"What are you doing messing up my metaphors with something as petty as reality? You want me to give you a quick shampoo with this stuff?" she asked, holding the urinal aloft.

"I think it might cover up my cologne."

"Oh, all right," she said. "You get off this time."

She dumped the urine into the toilet and flushed it.

"I don't know why I bothered with cologne in the first place," he said as she put the urinal into his backpack. "He only looks like Spence. Has all the charm of Idi Amin."

"Let's get out of here and go please the menfolk."

"Trudy, you okay?"

"Yes, definitely yes," she said grimly. "I'll just get through this like a good little girlfriend and slash my wrists later. Let's go."

*   *   *

"Well, I'll admit I was kind of down when I split up with him," Theo said as he stroked his reddish beard and glared at his blocks of tofu. "Even the people at StarSoft, where I work, they noticed it. One of the other writers tried to set me up with a guy from sales, Vin something. I was looking forward to meeting him, but my God, he had a limp, can you believe it? Guy's twenty-five, my age, and he walks with a friggin' limp. Looks like Grampappy Amos. I can't be seen with a guy like that. People'll think I'm desperate. That's what I told that writer later. And he gives me all this shit about how kind and sensitive this Grampappy Amos guy is and I say look, if I want kind and sensitive, I'll watch Mister Rogers. What I want is to fuck, not perform missions of charity."

"Theo," Chuck said, "have you happened to notice that I tend to be somewhat disabled myself?"

"Sure, I noticed it. I carried you up the goddamned stairs, didn't I? Look, I feel for you. I know it must be rough. If I ever found myself in your position, I'd want to die. But I have the right to sleep with guys I like, guys I find attractive; wouldn't you agree, Spence?"

"I don't want to get involved." Spence said as he dabbed at some white wine on his chin.

"Well, I do have the right. Says so right in the Constitution," he said and gave a harsh laugh. "And if I don't want to be in the sack with guys with limps or wheelchairs or spit drooling down their faces, hey, that's my business."

Trudy put her elbows on the table and her face behind her hands as Chuck withdrew from the table.

"I think I'd better go."

"No, Chuck," Trudy said, surprised.

"You asshole," said Spence to his brother.

"What'd I say? I didn't insult him or anything."

"Theo, you've always had a talent for getting people pissed at you."

"Ah, for God's sake—"

"Gentlemen, if I may interrupt, I'll need your assistance to get down the stairs."

"Chuck," Spence protested, "don't pay any attention to this jerk."

"The jerk is willing to help," Theo said as he stood, "if it will restore domestic tranquillity."

"Thank you," said Chuck as he headed for the front door.

*   *   *

"Now, you remember how to lift the wheelchair, don't you, Theo?"

"Sure, just put my hands under here."

Chuck, whoozy with fear, gazed down at the little front lawn. I have to be crazy to trust Spence's shithead brother to get me down these steps. I'd have to be a doormat to stay, though. He tried to think of something to say before they lifted him, something carefree to impress them, as well as himself, with his fearlessness.

"Mares eat oats and does eat oats and little lambs eat ivy," he sang in a deliberately off-key screech. "There, touchdown."

"Touchdown on planet Earth, Chuck," said Spence, slapping him on the shoulder. "Where'd you hear that dopey song?"

"Old Bob Hope movie. I'll be going now. Thanks for the lift, guys," he said while looking at the brothers. Christ, they're both beautiful. One's hetero and the other's as sensitive as Reagan's dentures.

He had gone a block when he heard Trudy calling him.

"Wait, Chuck, wait!"

If I put this thing at top speed, it'll do seventeen miles an hour, faster than she or anyone else can run. Remembering how sad she had been in the bathroom, he decided not to.

"Wait, Chuck," she said, breathing hard. "I want to give you some tofu. Thought you might want to eat it at home."

"Theo's serving, I assume?"

"Look, I'm sorry, really sorry," she said as she put a Tupperware bowl into his backpack. "I know you're upset with Len leaving and now tonight . . . but I know you'll find someone, someday."

He heard her zip his backpack shut.

"When pigs have wings," he said as he left her at top speed.

Inside/Outside

Julia Dolphin Trahan

Sometimes, when a pretty girl touches me I hide my hard-on. I'm very shy and wouldn't want to be considered rude. I can't help it. I like being touched by pretty girls. I'm talkin' the grown-up kind. The kind so smart so sweet so tough my mouth waters, my nose twitches wondering what their skin smells like.

But I get tongue-tied when my brain sinks down to my ten-inch cock and all I want is to be thrusting inside her. Warm, juicy, and synchronized. Even more confusing is when I remember I don't have a cock and she can't see my hard-on (maybe she can). Then she says "But Julia, I don't think of you as *disabled.*" That's when my heart drops. I die inside. Now, it's my tears I try to hide.

I keep my fragile body image hidden at the bottom of my favorite coffee cup, protected inside the secret pocket of my leather jacket. It lingers behind a long-haired voluptuous Viking know-it-all who's body is modeled for theatergoers, photographers, painters and exposed every time I walk down the street with my florescent-colored crutch. I have several body images. I flaunt my flexible Shirley Temple butchness and partially paralyzed pride, cajoling mix-matched audiences of queers, feminists, and disability activists. On stage, I regally swing my strap-on overhead, thrust my erect crutch from between my legs like a giant cock while Madonna sings, "Your voice can take me there." I wait patiently while some lovely femme strips me of tuxedo tails and leather belt to reveal my lacy, low-cut bustee. Then, in sync with flamboyant queens throughout history, I don purple feather boa drag as Bowie sings, "You've got your mother in a whirl./ She don't know if you're a boy or a girl."

But the body image frozen behind my eyes is the determined little girl terrified of the sterile hospital lights, the obedient charmer who smiled her way through neglect and sexual abuse disguised as "normal medical procedure." That stubborn little girl holds my hand and whispers, "Don't leave me," whether I am lugging buckets on women's land or getting all worked up about some fearless, pretty girl in a red silk dress.

My sex life died when I moved to San Francisco, the queer Mecca, in 1991. Except for a two-night stand and two hassled relationships, it hasn't reincarnated. It has been a difficult death to grieve. Since childhood, exchanges of sexual energies have been my foundation for identity. Choosing semicelibacy has been a curse, a cleansing and a hazardous venture. I understand love and affection physically. Expanding my vocabulary has been important, but I long for a country where I understand the first language. For my spiritual and emotional balance, I masturbate and come everyday. When I come, my entire body, ghost-cock and cunt explodes. At times it surprises me how feminine my face, body, and voice are. I couldn't pass as a man. If I could live in the world as male, I would temporarily—long enough to check out sexism and privilege from the other side. Sometimes I plan out what I'd look like and whether I'd be straight, bi, or gay. I think I'd either be a flaming bisexual romantic-poet or a vigorous straight dude.

But surgically changing genders isn't for me. I've had too many operations already, my ghost hard-ons feel real, and Good Vibrations, the dildo store, is right down the street. The plushness of my female body is an exotic turn-on, and I can buckle on/off any size and stay hard infinitely. As a nondisabled kid, I hated the ways I was mis/treated because I was a girl, and I certainly didn't want to be one. My wrestling partners, favorite animal toys, and imaginary friends were boys, but I never wanted to be "like that" either. I wasn't sure where I fit in or if I did at all. Today, more aware of my options, I want to be a sweet dyke and find women who are as sexually appreciative and assertive toward me as men are.

It's been difficult to find others willing to match my inside/outside puzzle pieces together. As a kid, I played a sword-wielding Robin Hood rescuing Maid Marian. At age twenty-nine, I'm a crutch-wielding, long-haired, tomboy dyke playing Billy Idol teaching harmony through lust. My love for adventurous, anonymous sex, previously done with men, decreased as I kept running into baffled dykes who wanted to process about "what I could manage" before we undressed. Condescension doesn't pass as negotiation. Uninterested in adapting my pheromones or spontaneous eroticism with men, I decided to experiment with longer relationships.

When I tried to tell Jessie, my first self-defined "FTMish/prissy butch" girlfriend, about my lonely little cripple girl who wants to cry when people are rude, she compared me to a straight man with a car, a wife, and a wheelchair; "he doesn't have any problems being disabled." Jessie started feeling like an enemy so I took her to my Contact Improvisation dance class with disabled and nondisabled dancers to give her an opportunity to interact with a continuum of races, classes, genders, and abilities. We communicated better after that until she expressed her appreciation of my gentle, sexual prowess, since I was the first woman to flip her. We broke up soon after she announced, "you might be disabled, but you give great sex!".

When I asked my new silk-dressed girlfriend if she was ashamed that I was disabled, she looked at me as if I had announced that I could fly and answered, "No, I'm lucky to have you." She got everything she asked for after that. I was happy. She accepted that strangers would interrupt our conversations to give unwanted medical advice or to ask about my injuries. When it came time to do "normal" things, such as go to the beach, I started getting nervous. How would she feel about us/me being stared at while being exposed and just having fun? I have scars from toxic attitudes and surreptitious glances that I'm ashamed to show. My need to have everything look "good" no matter how uncomfortable I am, because of physical pain, stairs, or stares, twists my comfortable body image. When it gets combined with others' fear of fragility, resentment is the main result. It wasn't until my girlfriend saw me limping in pain that she understood that I really did need days off to physically rest and I didn't just have a "fear of intimacy."

It's not easy being inside my body. I want to feel loved and at home. I often feel cut up. I can't afford to decide between my subcultures or pretend one part of me is more important than another. I felt freakish enough as a nondisabled kid: arguing with Mom for blue corduroy pants instead of frilly, coordinated outfits, arguing with Dad that I could be Captain Kirk, and hiding my precocious breasts with smarter-than-the-teachers aggressiveness. After my childhood car accident, I didn't know that my swelling hips, pendulous breasts, and bruised-looking, reddish, purple vulva weren't part of being Disabled, Fat, Lazy, and Disfigured. My blossoming body and sexuality felt disgusting and embarrassing. I wanted to hide, but bedpans and bras were unavoidable. Complete strangers demanding to know, "What horrible thing happened to such a pretty young girl?" was fame and kindness I would've enjoyed doing without. It wasn't until I studied and made love to other female bodies that I caught on that all vaginas have little bumps and women's bodies are naturally soft and curvy. Unrequited crushes on nurses and therapists kept me constantly confused. What to do with these dreadful longings for certain women when their touch made my pain bearable or their pride in me gave me incentive to heal? As an adult, sex reminds me that I don't have to bite my tongue and feign disinterest when a paramour touches me intimately or whispers compliments. I'm still astonished when my lust and love of fucking are desired and encouraged. Without sex, I still need the strength of connection to feel good in my body. I hesitate to show or receive affection, still living under the internalized rule that patients and staff shouldn't get emotionally involved. In my predominantly straight, disabled, activist culture, I am welcomed and nurtured as a beautiful, gutsy, pioneering, nationally-known writer/performer/videographer. In my nondisabled, sex-radical, pleasure-activist, queer cultures, I barely escape the Patient role. I am an accepted, at times inspirational, but often faceless, Weird, Disabled Artist.

It seems strange that achievements in one world are sources of pity, overglorification, and alienation in the other. I simultaneously hate, adore, and am in awe of my body. Living through twenty-one days in a coma, thirteen major operations, an adolescence of isolation and hospitalization, and still putting out for hemiplegia and chronic pain from a brain stem injury, damaged vertebrae, a reconstructed pelvis/femur and intrusive flashbacks, is undoubtedly my best performance. Although I got a standing ovation at age twelve, when I returned to my elementary school after a year in the hospital, my reviewers disappeared when I lost my tragic, poster-child charm. Of course I grieve my lost, four-minute-mile body, but what cripples me is 98 percent of my lifelong, nondisabled, queer friends disappearing when I need an operation or express too much anger/grief about being shoved into an "icon of despair" social role.

My nondisabled, lesbian-feminist friend, Sarah, when I told her of my head and brain stem injuries, said, "Congratulations, no one would ever know." I am blessed with good fortune, stamina, and a certain amount of privilege. I worked strenuously to relearn basics things I'd taken for granted. At the same time, I want people to know and value who I am. I want people to understand that while they might have been getting their first kiss behind the jungle gym, I was in the hospital struggling for my life, and that effects what we talk about today or if we talk at all. I want potential lovers to understand that hundreds of strangers' hands have been between my legs—some gentle, some businesslike, some violent. I grew up in and out of hospitals, where men are men and women are underpaid, overworked nurses rubbed in the devalued role of women—an unwanted role but better than Patient. Coming out was hazardous in a world where the person with the needle in my arm wanted to know if I had a boyfriend because I'm so pretty. My scars mark my history and are more glorious than the Olympic gold medal I trained for as a child athlete.

When caught between differently abled and differently gendered, I cut my breasts until I bleed and feel whole. Stuck in hopelessness about ever finding joy or people who speak my language, I started this habit about a year after moving to San Francisco. Cutting has kept me in touch with my essence. However, I struggle to find a more compassionate way of piecing my worlds and myself together. Extreme disharmony doesn't go with my self-image of the heroic outlaw who always gets kissed in the end. But Robin Hood was never a little girl raped in the hospital by nurses and doctors under the guise of tests or bed baths; he never has flashbacks to his molestations or car accident, and his nondisabled peers never ask him, "Were you born THAT way?"

I learned from nondisabled lesbian-feminists and queer women that self-mutilation is a common tool used by sexual abuse survivors. Hoping to find help healing, I've spent much time in these communities. Instead of finding connection and trust, I lost myself even further, neglecting my goals to explain my physical disability and that I'm not a femme just because I'm often quiet and have long hair. Adding extra catch-22 complications, my sexual abuse flashback/panic attack triggers were women laughing or looking into my eyes. Because fear and self-abasement would only raise their ugly heads if there were power inequities, I debilitated myself trying to develop enough trust to talk about why I was terrified to trust. Cautiously careful to whisper about how I wanted to be treated, I worried others would be overwhelmed. Often friends, therapists, teachers, and lovers, all some sort of queer, are intimidated by the extent of my injuries.

In Luna Sea, the hip, queer women's performance space, I listened to 100 women clap for a poorly written piece about a mother drowning her two-year-old, blind/deaf child because she couldn't bear watching it struggle. I felt betrayed. Just two weeks prior, on the same stage in "The Butch Show," I had performed *Billy Idol Sings the Blues*, a piece on the healing power of self-respect and self-love. I glimpsed my way out of the black hole of abuse. I realized if I wanted to feel good in my body I needed to stop trying to change myself or fit in and find people I could relax around. I linked up with several of my androgynous counterparts, effeminate gay men, as mentors and friends. I've found relief from my flashbacks and body hatred, steadfast encouragement, and people with whom I enjoy taking risks. I partially attribute this to men not seeming to personalize my experiences and beliefs as much as women. Whatever the reason, finding people who appreciate my drag makes the right side of the bed much easier to find in the morning.

Sometimes I believe if you're good to people, they'll be good to you. Loving support is a personal, situational thing beyond gender, ability, etc., but it's paradoxically entrenched within Who-You-Are. When the first weekend showcase I produced, *Body Talk = Survival: Intersections of Disability, Sex, and Race,* sold out, it was mainly queer women doing behind-the-scenes work and filling the audience. I am always grateful to the pervy-girls who identify with and support my work whether I'm talking about masturbation, circus freaks, or receiving blow jobs. I adore my men, but it's a rare, admirable fag who overcomes his sexism, shares his privilege, and learns from dykes.

I have a strong body with powerful instincts that guide me to who or what I need. So . . . what about the pretty girl in the red silk dress who got me all worked up? What about my last girlfriend with her lipstick on my tux, champagne, and ultra-femme sighs of desire? Of course I packed and fucked her on floors, against walls—anywhere she wanted—just like Billy Idol. I rescued her from a life of princess servitude just like Robin Hood. I even bought her a dick of her own. But when it came to fragility, dealing with old wounds acting up or wanting a back rub and a soft belly to cry on, I had to start explaining, defending, and banging my head against the wall all over again.

My body aches with need sometimes. But, I don't care who or how many stunning, well-connected, wealthy admirers drop inspiration and promises of social acceptance at my feet; unless they can be vulnerable, hold my hand, and love profoundly, they make me hurt more.

I am an outlaw. I gather my merry knights around me and commemorate the mixed blessing of escape from the proper way to live. I gather stolen moments to mix my worlds together: a kiss from a sexy femme in a power chair who also gives me Advil, a fan letter and poetry from an iron-lunged transvestite, onstage praise from a prestigious pleasure-activist who doesn't hesitate to zip and buckle my tired, backstage, motorcycle boots, a (straight) girlfriend who sings me love songs as she massages my wounds, an old-time butch who stubbornly grooms and tattoos my concealed, young Marlon Brando. My happiness is an endless array of slides in which my inside/outside colors are enhanced.

During an interdisciplinary arts and disability conference in Ann Arbor, Michigan, Andrea, a beautiful academic femme I had known for several hours, bought me a gourmet dinner and volunteered to undress me onstage. She wore a long, blue dress and long, white gloves for the occasion of my defrocking. After carefully folding my tuxedo jacket and setting it aside so it wouldn't get dirty, she whipped my belt out of my pants, flung it over her shoulder into the audience, ripped open my jeans, and tore them off without a pause. As I posed in my queenly lingerie, I stared adoringly amazed into her eyes, my scars and hard-on in full display. I laughed, feeling Whole, with ample amounts of love to spare.

Body Language

Kenny Fries

What is a scar if not the memory of a once open wound?
You press your finger between my toes, slide

the soap up the side of my leg, until you reach
the scar with the two holes, where the pins were

inserted twenty years ago. Leaning back, I
remember how I pulled the pin from my leg, how

in a waist-high cast, I dragged myself
from my room to show my parents what I had done.

Your hand on my scar brings me back to the tub
and I want to ask you: What do you feel

when you touch me there? I want you to ask me:
What am I feeling now? But we do not speak.

You drop the soap in the water and I continue
washing, alone. Do you know my father would

bathe my feet, as you do, as if it was the most
natural thing. But up to now, I have allowed

only two pair of hands to touch me there,
to be the salve for what still feels like an open wound.

The skin has healed but the scars grow deeper—
When you touch them what do they tell you about my life?

The Imperfections of Beauty: On Being Gay and Disabled

Kenny Fries

Five years have passed since I wrote my first article based on my experiences being a gay man who lives with a physical disability. During that time the Americans with Disabilities Act, the civil rights legislation passed by Congress in July, 1990, has become law; Academy Awards have been given to Daniel Day Lewis for his portrayal of disabled writer Christy Brown and to deaf actress Marlee Matlin; and this year, books such as Lucy Grealy's recent *Autobiography of a Face* have received much attention. But even though AIDS still causes the disablement of too many gay men, the gay men have yet to develop an understanding of those among us who live with physical disabilities. Why?

Last year I was taken out to lunch by a nondisabled gay editor who pitched the idea for me to write a memoir based on my life as a gay disabled man. During lunch, this editor, whom I had never met before but whom I had talked to on the phone and corresponded with, seemed to take more than a casual interest in the more lurid aspects of my past, which made me uncomfortable but also intrigued me. I wanted to find out what lay at the bottom of his interest.

At lunch that sunny California afternoon, I learned that the editor had a cousin who was disabled. As he spoke, I sensed that growing up he had an obvious affection for this cousin which had something to do with his own sense of feeling different, of being ostracized by his family for being gay.

When I told the editor how, as I wrote, my book was becoming more and more sexual, he said: "Well, people are very interested in how disabled people have sex, aren't they?"

For a moment I was taken aback. My first internal thought was that not too many people would be interested in the way I have sex, being that my sexual practices are probably similar to the experiences of most nondisabled men I had talked with. My next unspoken response was: "No, but you obviously are interested."

Taking into consideration that I might have to work with this well-intentioned man sitting across from me, my verbal response was to correct his assumption. "Actually, most people do not think of persons with disabilities as being sexual at all," I informed the editor.

This brought to mind a lunch I had had with another gay man during the time I lived in San Francisco, when I was working for the theater services organization that served the Bay Area. In the capacity of my job, I was asked out to lunch by a man interested in getting to know his way around the San Francisco theater community. During what was supposed to be a business lunch, he looked at me and asked, point blank, "Do you like to be humiliated?"

Right away I knew what he was talking about, even though no one had ever asked me such a question before. "Why do you ask?" I responded, wanting to know where his question was leading. His response: "Because I know this one disabled guy in Los Angeles who told me that's the only way he can enjoy sex. Pain and humiliation bring up all the times he got attention when he was a kid, so he gets off on it."

For me, the operative words in his response were "this one disabled guy in Los Angeles." This nondisabled man with whom I was having lunch, reasonably intelligent and successful in the theater, took an experience from one disabled gay man he knew and assumed that all disabled people got sexually aroused by pain and humiliation. I could have answered him by pointing out how many nondisabled gay men might enjoy experiencing sex that way or offered other enlightened responses. But at the time, all I could muster in response was: "Really?"

*   *   *

Even though many of the gay male participants at OUTWRITE '91, the national gay and lesbian writers conference, were disabled due to HIV infection, and even though the conference was being held in disability-conscious San Francisco, accessibility was poorly organized. During the overcrowded plenary session, nondisabled attendees filled the seats reserved for those of us who were disabled. When I mentioned this to one of the organizers the next morning, he innocently, but angrily, asked me what could have been done. "Perhaps, you could have made an announcement informing those in the wrong seats that they would have to move?" I offered.

Because of my contact with the planning committee, accessibility was well planned at the next OUTWRITE, held in Boston. Not only were seats reserved for disabled participants at all conference events, but there was ample space for people to maneuver between sessions, a room reserved for those who might need to rest, and interpreters available for those in our community who are deaf.

However, at the conference the following year, also held in Boston, which was planned by many of the same people as the past year's gathering, accessibility problems once again were apparent. When the preconference reading was held in an inaccessible church and friends of one of the keynote speakers could not get in, members of the planning committee excused themselves saying: "We were told it was accessible." If there was a member of the planning committee who lived with a disability, accessibility would have been assured. But, too often, persons with disabilities are not included in the organizing or in other positions of power. Imagine the uproar if the event was held in a place in which African Americans or Jews were denied entrance?

A well-known, politically savvy writer I know will not appear on a panel where there is only token representation of people of color. However, my friend always appears on panels where there is no representation of those of us who live with disabilities. (After doing so for a few years, I no longer speak on panels that are solely about disability, wanting to make disability visible in wider contexts.) When I ask my friend, who is sure to represent the underrepresented in her novels, why there are no characters who live with disabilities depicted, she responds that, even though I am a close friend, she does not know enough about disability to write about it. This writer is contrite when I point out that in a well-publicized speech about censorship, her litany of the oppressed excluded the disabled. But when the speech appeared recently in a collection of her nonfiction, although she had rewritten much of the previously published material, the disabled still were not mentioned.

A few years ago at the Lambda Literary Awards, I watched in disbelief as Allen Barnett, who left the hospital to receive two awards that evening, had to get up out of his wheelchair and climb the steps up to the stage in order to make his acceptance remarks. Earlier in the evening, I realized that, standing just over five feet tall, I would not be able to reach to podium when it was time to accept my award.

The inaccessibility at these community events is reinforced in other social situations. I was denied admission to a gay bar in Florence, Italy, because I was disabled. And a blind friend in Minneapolis, who at the time did not have a Seeing Eye dog but used a cane for assistance, was approached by a man in a gay bar who asked him: "Are you lost?"

*   *   *

When I lived in Provincetown, I met an artist who was hired to draw the illustrations for the *New Joy of Gay Sex*. The artist wanted to include all types of men in his depictions of gay sex and asked me if I would be willing to pose for him so a disabled gay man would be represented in the book. For the cause, I agreed to take off my clothes and be intimate with a nondisabled man I had never met.

Before we began the session, the artist told us that the part of the book that we would model for would be "Biting". Although this gave my partner and I the opportunity to explore each other's bodies, the artist finished his photo shoot before the sex got past the stage of arousal.

Later that week, I viewed the photos as well as the drawing the artist had begun. I was relieved at my reaction. Both the photos and the drawing were quite beautiful. But when the artist submitted the finished drawing to the publishing house in New York City, the art director was not pleased. He said that in the drawing "the disability did not read."

The artist was disappointed. He did not want to simply put a wheelchair by the bed as two men made love. He wanted to depict an actual person with an actual disability in the act. In order to call more visual attention to the disability, the art director told the artist to take off one of my legs. During an uncomfortable conversation, I told the artist if he could not use my body as it is, he could not use my body at all. Thus, no drawing in which I appear is included in the published book. Instead, there is a drawing of a man with one leg, and there it is, the wheelchair in a prominent position. Once again, it is the disability which predominates, which defines the man, instead of being part of the man. A person defined *as* his disability instead of being portrayed as a person *with* a disability.

*   *   *

Mental health professionals also sometimes make similar mistakes. Yes, people with disabilities certainly have issues, both physical and emotional, to deal with that are related to their disabilities. But many of the people I talk to (some in the mental health field themselves) realize that sometimes a therapist will see the disability *as the problem*, not simply as one problem among many. It is difficult to see a disabled man as whole.

Some of what happens between disabled and nondisabled gay men, just as what sometimes happens between those who are gay and nongay, can be attributed to ignorance. But when friends who have known you for years continue to talk about what great legs a man has when someone passes in the street, or how tall last night's trick was, insensitivity is more likely the culprit.

When I was in my early twenties, I was basically able to do anything I wanted, so it made it easy for people to forget about my disability. The man with whom I was intimately and sexually involved would never mention, in or out of bed, the obvious physical difference of my legs. One man told me when I appeared in his dreams I was not disabled.

But as I grew older, my congenital physical disability began to cause more and more physical problems. At the same time, my identity as a disabled gay man has solidified. I no longer will accept such behavior, which causes internal conflict when I have to point out oppressive behavior to an old friend. My awareness also will occasionally cause rifts in my relationship with my lover, who is, at his best, willing to learn and be supportive.

A gay man I know who is, due to a spinal cord injury, quadriplegic and gets around using a wheelchair, told me that many men with whom he has sex feel they are going to crush him in bed. When this man asks why his partner is acting strangely, the partner looks at him dumbfounded. "Why doesn't he just ask me if I have physical limitations that he should be aware of during sex?" he asks.

Our fears often get the best of us, leaving the disabled person in the position of having to take care of their partners. It is such a relief when a partner just asks. As a good disabled friend of mine says, "We're not eggs."

I was sitting alone on a crowded beach in Provincetown a few summers ago when I saw a tall bearded man sitting nearby. After we exchanged glances, the man came over to where I sat on my towel. This stranger bent down and told me that if I needed any assistance in getting to the water his lover and he would gladly help. I remain friends with this man and his lover still.

* * *

A common misconception is that a disabled man is attracted to other men because he couldn't "make it with women." I remember a drive I took with my father over fifteen years ago. At the time, I had just finished my freshman year at college, was just coming out and dealing with, for the first time, my identity as a disabled person. My dad, a generous, loving, and supportive father if ever there was one, told me that he was afraid I was gay because I felt rejected by women because of my disability. I should have told him right then and there that if there was a reason for my being gay it was because I always felt so loved by and close to him. That might have turned his misperception around.

Other times, a disabled person's homosexuality is perceived as a disabled man's need for a more perfect reflection of his own body, which he views as incomplete, unwhole. Although I confess to wanting to explore my lover's knees and ankles, parts of his body that are structurally different from mine, I am also aware of what my body has that others might not have. It seems to be that sexual attraction between men, whether disabled or not, is located somewhere between the need for similarity and the need for difference, between what we know and what we long for.

                           *   *   *

When I asked a gay male psychologist who has worked with many gay male couples what was the major difference between how male homosexual relationships differed from heterosexual relationships, he mentioned the issue of power. How does the issue of power play itself out in a relationship between a disabled gay man and a nondisabled gay man?

Of course, every disabled/nondisabled relationship has its own set of unique issues, many having nothing to do with disability. However, a few things were commonly mentioned by the disabled gay men with whom I have talked. One was the idea of the disabled person borrowing the privilege of being able-bodied from their partner. This helps them feel safer, is easier, and helps the disabled person to sometimes feel some relief, some escape from their disability, especially in public.

However, the flip side is that relying on the nondisabled partner in this way reinscribes many of the negative feelings that the disabled person has internalized. Or it shields him from feeling these feelings at all, keeps them buried. It makes the disabled partner feel they need the nondisabled partner to pass, to have access to the nondisabled world. The nondisabled partner becomes a calling card, of sorts, a validation. Needless to say, this affects the power dynamics of the relationship.

On the other hand, the nondisabled partner, especially for those involved with a disabled person who experiences a lot of physical pain, often starts to feel that their needs are not being met in the relationship because their disabled partner's needs are always paramount. This leads to an imbalance and it is necessary for both partners to realize that each of their needs be seen as requiring equal attention and care.

The gay quadriplegic I mentioned earlier tells me that most of the men who get involved with him want to take care of him. When they find out that this man can clearly take of himself, they lose interest. Conversely, many disabled people play out the caretaker role themselves because that's the only way they think they will be loved, accepted, needed. These issues, commonly referred to as "codependency," are found in relationships where neither of the partners are disabled, but these issues, however, become more complex and more difficult to untangle because of the added emotional baggage disability may cause.

This gets even more sticky since many disabled people have a history of physical or sexual abuse. This points to how important it is that we think about and become conscious of the power dynamics underlying our relationships. Being aware of these issues does not make them go away, but knowing what you're up against surely makes it easier to go beyond it.

*   *   *

Making things more complicated for all of us, disabled and nondisabled alike, is HIV infection and AIDS. As treatments improve, keeping people alive and healthier longer, disability has become a central issue within the gay community. Over the past decade, I have been able to offer my knowledge of how best to maneuver within the medical and social services system to others who did not yet have that experience. Those of us who live with disabilities can offer insight into the effects physical limitations and pain have on one's life, and how to best negotiate such difficult changes.

Although AIDS continues to demand so much of our attention, we cannot forget that many gay men who are disabled are not HIV infected. My first lover and best friend continues to battle testicular cancer. The issues with which he grapples remind me why it is so difficult for us to come to terms with those among us who live with disabilities. Someone else's disability reminds us that we are all mortal and, as we live our days, vulnerable to becoming, in some way, disabled. It is this fear of disability that is a partial answer to the question with which I began this article.

*   *   *

Imagine living in a world in which you never see images of yourself or the way you live. This should not be too difficult for gay men, who from birth are bombarded with images of heterosexual love.

This is even more prevalent in the lives of gay men who are disabled, who not only have to confront the absence of affirming images (yes, we do exist) but must contend with the images of the gay male body to which we are exposed. The preponderance of these images—in advertising, literature, film, and pornography—are images of what is perceived as perfection. There is little room, even in our subculture, for images of what is perceived as different. Wouldn't it be more interesting and artistically challenging to explore the imperfections of beauty? To locate understanding and attraction within physical difference?

Now in the mid-1990s, as the more community-oriented press is replaced with larger, dollar-conscious, slick magazines, these images of perfection take an even more pernicious hold on the gay male psyche, fueling the perception that all gay men are white, have gym-toned bodies, and have plenty of money to spend. Surely, this reflects only a small fraction of those who identify as gay.

These images of the idealized gay male go back to classical times. But today, the segment of our community that has access to visibility, to money, and to power broadcasts the message that we must put our best foot forward, so to speak. We must behave, conform, in order to be accepted by what they perceive as the mainstream.

Lurking beneath the inability of gay men to embrace physical disability is not only the fear of the body's inevitable decline but the yearning for an acceptance by this so-called mainstream that has historically ignored, or been hostile to, gay men and homosexuality. You need to only scratch the surface of this desire to be accepted to find the lack of self-acceptance and self-esteem that feeds the cycle of disappointment.

The flip side to this is the reaction of nongay disabled men who, when I am among them, do not quite know what to make of my sexuality. This leads me to the conclusion that there is something in the way that men, gay and straight, are socialized which leads to the obstacles in their inability to deal with the disability of another man.

*   *   *

What all this points to is the central truth of identity—the way we perceive difference. But what is perceived as different by one society is not perceived as different by another. As writer Hugh Gregory Gallagher, who is disabled, has pointed out, before eyeglasses were widely available, poor eyesight would be a harsher physical condition with which to live than it is today. And, as too many gay men know, it is societal attitudes toward persons living with AIDS that make an already troublesome situation that much more difficult.

Though a part of the identity of a person who lives with disability has its origins in physical limitation or physical difference, a large part of what makes one disabled is the access society, in its attitudes and physical barriers, puts in our way. When society affords access, many of us are not disabled at all.

Five years ago, when I first began writing about my experiences being both gay and disabled, I received many letters from those who thanked me for bringing to light portions of their untold stories. Through my writing and my travels during the past five years, I have met gay men, like Tom Vickery who has started Rainbow Bridge, an organization for gay disabled men outside Chicago. I have also come up against many obstacles, whether it be the "looksism" so prevalent in, or portrayed in, gay male culture or by inaccessible bookstores where I have been asked to read. I impatiently await the maturation of gay men as they learn to further embrace physical difference, and as I do so, I will continue to write about my experiences of being a gay man who lives with a physical disability, making visible the imperfect bodies, and imperfect fates, that wait for us all.

Love Poem

Kenny Fries

On the narrow bed. Patterns of light
and shadow across your body. I hold

your face in my hands. Tell me, before
I kiss you, what is it like to be

so beautiful? I want to know how other
hands have touched you. What other

eyes, beneath your clothes, imagine.
And how do you imagine me? Do you

feel my calloused skin? See my twisted
bones? When you take off my clothes

will you kiss me all over? Touch me as
if my body were yours. Make me beautiful.

SECTION D:
MEN, BOYS, AND TROLLS

Queer Crash Test Dummies: Theory, Aging, and Embodied Problematics

Dean Kiley

DUMMIES? OR...

I want to examine—in queer communities, the media and the academy— the crash between analysis and image, rhetoric and logic, the written world and lived experience. Throughout, there are ironic interruptions by voices from bystanders (glossy gay magazines) which resuscitate the very myths and stereotypes that gay-and-lesbian studies and queer theory had allegedly mowed down. There are live eyewitness reports from victims and survivors of our body-as-commodity, body-as-text, body-as-identity subcultures.

Is there a "new" or "real" gay/queer "Man," is there a "body perfect" or a perfectible body or a queer body? Can we buy it or make it; can we play with it, or are we just manufacturing dummies? If we build or lease ourselves a good body, does it come with a warranty, and what happens when it gets older? Possible answers to such questions are neither short nor easy, but I promise to keep my theorizing practical and my ideas tethered to examples and illustrations.

... *POSTMODERN BODIES?*

The mudwrestling between "social constructivist" *versus* "essentialist" views on homosexuality is, despite a last-minute tag-team entry from genetics, long over. Foucault won. But we live in postmodern times, and we seem to be seeing the *literal* triumph of constructionism. Subjectivity becomes text becomes surface. We textualize bodies, we "construct" our bodies as if they were theatrical sets for identity, then we stage our selves: for the community as warrior-heroes, for sex as objects of desire, for lovers as consumer durables in relationships, etc.

> *Campaign* and *OutRage* are glossy Australian gay magazines based in Sydney and Melbourne, respectively. Middle-of-the-road reading, large sales, wide distribution in Australia and UK. In reading back through every copy to January 1990, a trend emerges. There's a big bundle of In-Depth-Look-At-The-Issues[TM] articles that focus on overlaps between body, body image, sex, sexuality, culture, subcultures, and aging. The majority are reductive, overgeneralized, under-researched, self-serving. and romanticized (i.e., representative). They reduce the body to an anatomy. They set up aging as, not a social issue, but a personal problem with an objectified body, an illness to be treated, a mechanical problem to be fixed. You too, they urge, can reset the biological clock by a combination of preventive maintenance, upmarket renovations, cosmetic/s consumption, and optimistic idealism.

Theory and journalism are on the same expressway here: both treat flesh as if it were plastic. But theorists say *You can play with this*, while gay media and the images they recycle say *THIS, this is the body for you (to rent or buy or lay-by)*. It's mass produced in fixed molds. It's fashionable. It's sexy. It sells things. It's a Crash Test Dummy. It is designed to test and to survive the collisions between different ways of looking at body image and body concept. It is designed to be almost, always almost, within your reach, if only you spend a little more, work a little harder. Now let's *really* stretch the metaphor: I want to explore the runaway sales success among the gay niche of one generic-brand mold or template for this dummy; some of the preconditions, means, and processes of its production; its marketing strategies; some structural flaws; some repackaging techniques; and above all, the stress fractures that develop as the product ages.

... *MADE INTO POSTERS*

The most "comprehensive" media article, *Campaign*'s "Face the Future,"[1] is interrupted after the first half-page of text by a full-page photo of a naked, young, attractive, short-haired, smooth-bodied, defined, muscular (emphasis on pecs, biceps, abs, thighs) white man (whom I will call The Dummy). He is badly posed as Michelangelo's David. In a desktop publishing update of nineteenth-century anatomical manuals, the model's body parts are mapped and labeled with future deterioration: (TESTES—shrink, loss of sex drive, etc.) Hanging above his head is the title, *How We Fall Apart.*

Aging, it seems, is mostly about the effects of, and resistance to, Mr. Dummy's degeneration. The problem is that in queer male communities we massively overinvest (all senses, from financial to psychoanalytic) in bodies. Physicality accumulates myths, and the body is used as a guarantee, indicator and proof of image, style, esteem, sexual competency, attractiveness, peer acceptance, fidelity, relationship survival, role, and identity. This is the body made, to the fullest, self-evident: evidence of my self. As we begin to age, however, what happens when disjunctions between societal expectation, the template body, and physical feasibility/reality emerge? Because the body has been constituted and reinforced as a primary site of self and of self-control, identity can be destabilized and—in cultural, let alone individualized, terms—sexual role, response, image, and marketability can all end up depreciating.

With such high stakes in the body, it acts as a map and diagram of control. It seems such a reliable depth-reading of my positioning, legitimation, and power, in sexual economies and within the life course. And if you're twenty-three and built like a pretzel or a potato, you're old or ill or abnormal or not working hard enough by definition or analogy.

WITH THE BASIC BODY KIT...

Even before Freud discovered the penis as the basic building block in all our psyches' playpens, the male body had a privileged position in formulations of masculinity, normality, and heteronormativity, from seventeenth-century ethnography through eugenicist sex education to the "prehistory" of sex-role studies.[2]

> Letter to the Editor: "I am gay and a man, and I like men. I do not like men acting like girls."[3]

The body, body image, body concept, the identities built on them, and our embodied experience—all these are as socially constructed as anything else. In Western cultures we also retain a leftover Cartesian mind/body split. We typically know our bodies as "other," separate from ourselves but material and metaphoric vehicles for our real essential *self.*

Then there's the semiosis (ways of signifying) of psychic development. These are crammed with architectural, mechanical, and archaeological imagery, with logic and stories: the psyche as being constructed, put together, integrated, restructured, and so on. In the semiosis of gay/queer bodies and of aging processes, these two kinds of imagery—body as external machine and body as framework assembly—are made more literal. Thus, gay men sculpt and build and tone and shape bodies, maintain them, condition them, pump them up—making and transforming themselves. Mold yourself (into) a Mr. Dummy. The metaphysics of the gym. The phrase "workout" is both noun and verb, and bodybuilding means much more than it says. It's not something you do, still less something you do to yourself. It's a process of becoming, like time-lapse photography of an identity metamorphosis, a natural evolution. Thus it sponsors Disney-like mythologies of transformation, Schwarzenegger success stories.

> Editorial: [W]orking out (both aerobic and anaerobic activity) can be highly satisfying and healthy. In the age of AIDS, one could argue that this is more important than ever. There is also a kind of vengeful satisfaction in seeing a slim, well-built gay man in his thirties or forties and comparing him with a heterosexual male in the same age bracket—usually a ruddy-faced, pot-bellied lounge lizard. *Vive la difference!* More power to poofters![4]

The problem is that, in middle-age, cracks appear in such symbolic constructs because they also work in reverse. What's *built* can *collapse*, and what's *put together* can *fall apart*. The body you live in becomes subject to the stress of imagery based on disintegration and degeneration. You remain the same, but your body doesn't work anymore. This is, as *Campaign* magazine discreetly put it, "How We Fall Apart," and it is complicated by a diverse range of factors.

> Is it true that middle-aged gay men now avoid the bars because they can't cope with the deluge of biceps and triceps, or is it because they are content with their dinner party circuit and detest the endless drag routines, loud music and cigarette smoke? I have heard a story about a young gay man who is HIV positive and who is almost certainly damaging his health by continuing to take steroids so that he can go out on the scene looking healthy and fit. Can the gay media really be held responsible for this? Frankly, I don't think that if some dumb queen decides to trade in months (or years) of health to maintain

some parody of "fitness" the responsibility can be laid at anyone else's door but his own. [5]

... *YOU TOO CAN MAKE THE "NEW" GAY BODY*

Now, if *gender is drag*,[6] if we fetishize it, objectify it, and theatricalize it (i.e., if there's no "essential maleness"), then why do we keep "straight-acting" or the so-called "New Masculinity" in business? And why do we buy Mr. Dummy wholesale and straight out of the (porn) catalogue?

Justifications for Mr. Dummy are suspiciously excessive. Health and fitness are consistently cited, even as basher protection,[7] though the work required to mold recalcitrant flesh into the template is far beyond necessary preventive maintenance of the body-product. Discipline, the work ethic, hedonism, and spectacular consumption are no longer contradictory, let alone exclusive, terms. Rhetoric then becomes circular because, having invested so much in body assemblage, the builders have the "right" to promote and display the finished product.[8] Gyms often become body-works where the New (gay) Man goes for major reconstruction of the ego or identity: how else to explain the psychosomatic addiction to body-building and the alarmingly widespread addiction to steroids and their equivalents?[9] Studies of gym users consistently confirm the level of steroid abuse and the underground but burgeoning steroid industry. Most point explicitly to peer pressure and the subcultural idealization of the body as major causes,[10] perhaps most clearly seen in "pumping up" and reconditioning for specific events.[11]

> Swaggering Muscle Marys with attitude dominate many an inner city gym. They get a lot of reinforcement from the longing looks of "ordinary" others whom they summarily dismiss. For men who accept this philosophy of entitlement—this iconography of desire— there seems to be an increasingly narrow, almost concentric pattern of existence. [12]

AIDS, as always, shifts every boundary and category here. HIV-positive men fear losing lovers as their looks leach out,[13] gym work equals fitness, and more alarmingly, bulk is seen an integer of health (=HIV negative).[14] *He can't be HIV positive, he looks so healthy.* Pectorals double as condoms. Such misreadings of the body and of disease (still a major problem for safe-sex education) intersect with both techno-faith and amateur immunology: aging is imaged and experienced as illness (thus, potentially, expensively, curable), and misdiagnosed as such in the real world of sex and sexual arenas.

> Get away from text and textuality! What about real live men? I conducted a series of semistructured interviews, via snowball sampling—three hours each, in focus groups of five or six, with forty-seven men self-identified as entering (or living in) middle age. This is not an empirical verification of hypotheses. No generalization can validly be made from such a small sample, which is biased socioeconomically (by the recruitment method) and epistemologically (a target group sufficiently hidden that the decision to be interviewed presupposes a relatively high level of self-esteem and political consciousness). Twenty-three interviewees experienced being misrecognized as ill because of age. In the traditionally supportive environment of the sauna (ho ho), four were explicitly rejected on grounds of suspected AIDS.

Another marketing technique for Mr. Dummy is that he will magically, and on his own, reclaim the image-making initiative and forestall recuperation by heterosexist society or cooption by newly sexuality-fluid capitalism. Muscle apparently makes the stereotypes go round: after decades of miscasting as effeminate, weak, oppressed masses, we can become avenged, empowered, strong, autonomous, cohesive, resilient, decisive, visible, potent as embodied Men.[15] If this sounds itself too much like a mass-produced, gender-role stereotype, *it is*. And the most convenient thing to do with such stereotypes is to ascribe them to someone else.

> "We grow up and live in a society with masculine stereotypes: the tradesman, the farmer, the man in the armed forces. All these types fulfill stereotypes of masculinity." Darryl Hood, a senior research assistant with BANGA [Bisexually Active Non-gay Attached Research Project], suggests that this sexual dynamic may be more the province of older gay men. "I suspect that it may be more of an issue with gay men in their forties, fifties, and sixties. Since they were born and grew up in the decades before gay liberation and gay rights, they are more subject to the historical times of these decades."[16]

Nevertheless, in warrior-hero guise, Mr. Dummy is the epitome, mascot, long-term marketing strategy, and visibility-meter, as well as symbolizing the spirit, of the community. An array of feminist analysis, cultural anthropology, sociology, and clinical psychology corroborates this mistranslation from surface to depth, image to identity, fetishized gender markers to essential gender traits,[17] and beauty to positive qualities (i.e., you look good, therefore you are good).[18] And beauty, despite its multiple forms of corsetry, has a proven track record as acceptable compensation for societal subordination.

> SMART is an anti-Dummy group: Slim Men are Real Treats. It was attacked in Sydney newspapers for negativity, accused of ordinary jealousy, of demeaning the beauty that all gay men revere in the arts, and of suffering self-esteem dysfunctions because "an attack on beauty is an attack on nature."[19]

Moreover, the body has a tactical and centuries-old history as stand-in, metaphor, morality play, and classifying system for social structures:[20] that's how we got the phrase "body politic" and AIDS allegories.[21] This is reinforced by political paradigms of visibility, visual statement, destereo-typing, and protest or conflict as social theatre. There's also the long painful history of homosexuals' bodies as sites of contest and intervention seeking definition and control, from etiology (in our heads, our pants, our Mothers, our souls, our genes) to cures to immigration policies to safe-sex regulation and so on.

> "Well," says David,[22] "What I look like stops me from going to dance parties or nightclubs or saunas. I don't go to Oxford Street [main, Sydney, gay commercial area], I feel locked out from the whole scene, sometimes as if I'm not part of the community at all, like there's no place for me; I'm not real. It's like a new kind of discrimination, a new sort of homophobia."

But the most elaborated analysis of Mr. Dummy is the gay (eventually queer) facility for manipulation of imagery,[23] juggling style, conjuring ironic élan from nineteenth-century proto-camp to the Sydney Mardi Gras' most recent controversial postmodern satire. As subordinate forms of masculinity, the gay lifestyle and its styles of bodies are necessarily foregrounded, as constructed and oppositional, never as "natural" or unproblematic.

> And let's not forget the element of play. For many gay men who have resolved issues of self acceptance and self esteem and who have had a number of sexual encounters with "straight men," the notion of "being straight" is a role play, a construct to be satirized and poked fun at.[24]

So We Get the "New" Queer Body

The basic idea of most queer body theory is that gay/queer men self-consciously fabricate, then distance themselves from, gendered body images. They use tactics of parody and mimicry, thus enabling them through incongruity[25] (butch goes poof) or excess (hypermasculinity and its emblems) to criticize or ironize "normal," standard masculinity. This is an allegedly innovative and transgressive playing with, and at, being Real Men.[26] Basically, though, the theory behind this is that of the High Literature canon's satirical poetics—Swift, Dryden, Pope, and others—cross-dressed with the Divine Miss S (Susan Sontag) and her "Scribbles on Camp,"[27] put in a wheelchair with go-faster stripes and trundled back onstage. And I have four major reservations about this "new," "queer" body and what it can do or be.

> Perhaps it's just me. Perhaps the exclusionary boy's club ethos of body sculpting,[28] the hierarchies and regimes of desire based on how closely you attain Mr. Dummy's template, the myths of entitlement that exchange an iconography of desire for a topography of identity politics cashing out as an economics of consumption . . .

The first problem is that "incongruity" tends to rely on situation and context and is thus unreliable, momentary, amorphous, and politically unformulated. So it is open to mis- or noninterpretation. As with all forms of irony, models of camp commentary (gay/queer/whatever) all depend on a decoding interpretive key. Here, it is supplied by a conspicuously unexamined notion of gay sensibility that will somehow provide the "real" or "true" rendering of the new masculinity as ironic or oppositional.

> . . . perhaps the sense of reflex rejection at dance clubs marketed as venues for HARD TIGHT BODIES, the student discounts at saunas and sex venues, the muscle photos filling the front page reportage of *OzQueer* newspapers . . .

The same criticism applies to the second issue, that of "excess." Can the hypermesomorphic (gym-built) body or super-masculine (butcher-than-butch) body image really become readable or decodable as critique, despite the fact that what is appropriated and exaggerated is taken holus-bolus from the iconography of unreconstructed hetero-masculinity? When and how does "straight-acting" become queer?

> . . . perhaps the Aussie Boys clothing ad which runs:

"The rubber moulds to the body, enhancing every ripple and toned muscle it screams SEX-SEX-SEX."[29]

My third reservation is that the style-as-resistance argument is decrepit and wrong. Styles—*for bodies* and *of bodies*—are easily and comprehensively commodifiable as chic and repackageable as coopted mainstream trends. This defuses, by diffusion, any subversion. It depoliticizes possible radical motivations by detaching the object from its discourse, the hypermasculine body from its alleged antihetero-masculine context, the image from any critical practice—and mass marketing it back into something approaching a norm, both normal and normative. The idea that gay men are identifiable and then *readable*, able to be decoded as "un-Real" or "non-Real" or "pseudo-Real" Men: this yet again assumes some kind of "clever gay reader." And it also assumes reading strategies that can separate Pseudo from Hetero. The unexamined reliance on text/book metaphors becomes clearer. Such Queer Theory often simplistically textualizes bodies.

. . . perhaps this anti-euphemistic hard-sell—[30]

> **BODY HIRE**
>
> (Private)
>
> **20 yo
> MASCULINE
> 6'2"**
> Well Hung
> Guy
>
> **Shane**

or perhaps the cross-translations of body image articles with porn-sourced graphics and of classifieds with ads for porn, sex venues, sex toys, protein supplements, independent sex workers, escorts, masseurs, electro muscle stimulators, phone contacts, beauty therapists, HIV social research, body sculptors, introduction agencies, and singles clubs . . .

. . . perhaps all these are actually unconnected, the obsessive focus on . . .

. . . And perhaps not.

The fourth problem is that there is little discernible sense of humor, let alone sophisticated flexible irony, in any of the formulations of the new masculinity and its body images. Lots of Highly Serious playfulness and low-grade camp, yes, but always framed by the intense work ethic necessary to construct full-scale Mr. Dummies. And making a profit, let alone making markets, has never been a terribly ironic activity. Instead of fluidity and play, what we get is the commercial and cultural version of a classified ad saying "seeks same."

> U.S. comparative studies of 800 heterosexual and homosexual Men's and Women's Personals found that gay men place disproportionate emphasis on age parity, sexual criteria, physical characteristics (including race), and specific positioning on a masculinity-femininity continuum.[31] Even the most cursory scan of Australian gay classifieds would confirm this analysis. Other studies have researched ideal-partner profiles of gay men, with similar results.[32]

Several influences are meeting, here, in the technological and socioeconomic changes that converge in the first few decades of American industrial history. The quantum jump in consumerist ideology and consumption strategies enables a market explosion and a marketing percolation. With the saturation of the image came body image as pastiche of objectified body parts; with the advertising industry came the cosmetics and dietary and fitness industries *as lifestyles*; and with the availability of body construction techno-sciences came the fascist body-fashion democracy. Everyone *can* have a good body if they work or buy hard enough—thus everyone *should*, then everyone *must*—all still comfortingly egalitarian, materialistic, and individualistic.

> When Mr. Dummy appears in Versace undies to sell Cameron's Fitness next to "Getting a great body is 90 percent perspiration and 10 percent inspiration. Here's the 10 percent,"[33] he is object, product, status, and goal: we want to *have* him, *make* him and *be* him.

... WHICH BECOMES THE POSTMODERN BODY PRODUCT

The body becomes the ultimate postmodern product, never perfect but always about to be perfected, open to inexhaustible marketing, itself marketing the self to others, reflexively producing new markets. It's aspirational: "You want to look like this don't you?" hides "Why don't you look like this?" underwritten by the regular "discovery"[34] of the gay dollar, the brand loyalty, trends, and high-consumerist lifestyle.[35] Then there's window-selling. Over the last decade, objectified male bodies have increasingly entered the advertising vocabulary, so a shorthand imagery able to be appropriated by (not necessarily overtly targeted at) gay men is accomplished with small modifications.[36] Such proliferation of images is not unconnected with the gay media's origins[37] and continued revenue sources, in the full spectrum of commercial sex.

> Editorial: Recently *OutRage* has started experimenting with its covers, using wider angle shots and avoiding such stereotypical notions of youth and beauty. The result has been a small, but quite noticeable, drop in sales.[38]

Another parallel unexpectedly relevant here is that of the high aesthetic Nude in sculpture and painting, complete with the phallic enterprise of artistic creation as possession, control, and proof of virility: the perfectionist craftsman produces the work of art that is his own body. The privileged mythology of the Nude (unity, universality, form, perfection) separates it from its complement, pornography.

> Peter Genet photographs a contemporary classic—April's *OutRage* Hunk, Falcon video star Brad Stone.[39]

But, says the media, photos stolen from porn magazines and other storehouses of Mr. Dummy are vital to "increase reader interest in the issues that *really* count"[!][40] Besides, body packaging, both two-dimensional and gym-made, also offers a bonus, being a prefab, safe, known identity. It comes with its own myths and is already positioned within the community.

AND THE OZ BODY PRODUCT,
BOTH EARLY MODELS AND LATE...

The Australian version of gay studies tells a specific story about masculine bodies that might as well also be that of bodies of theory. It goes like this: in the beginning there was camp, effeminacy, the underground, and close-knit networks in which middle-aged men acted as mentor/patron/guide. Then there was Stonewall, the Cultural Big Bang: gay men achieved self-consciousness, came out, liberated themselves, built communities, radicalized sex and sexuality, pluralized identities, and developed macho and other clones (put together from things like mustaches, body hair, denim, leather, etc.). Then they went through a "silly" antimasculinist phase during the mid-seventies called "Effeminism"[41] and gradually worked up their Mr. Dummy through slim tanned 1970s boys through late-1970s proliferating clones[42] to early-1980s athletic jock to gym bunny and thus, to the Credible Hulk of the 1990s.[43] On the way, gay men discovered that they just couldn't keep the differences between "butch," "real," and "straight-acting" straight.

The Australian gay early 1970s promised the most epochal radicalization and reconceptualization of sex, sexuality, gender, and gender roles. This is a tired and much-told old fairy tale. I mention it because the Marcusian idea of pan- or omnisexuality and the resulting fluid play of gendered body images resonates through current queer body theory. And today's celebrity theorists have about as much chance of being proved correct in post-1990s postmodernity as Altman did when he announced the end of the homosexual in 1971.[44]

> Who knows, maybe we can look forward to a future sexual stereotype of cuddly, furry, middle-aged "daddies."[45]

... ARE FAKES

Instead of any relativist fluidity, open multiplicity, and ironic manipulation, what we actually get is homogenization. Any body is acceptable so long as it's built on a Mr. Dummy franchise structure, like McDonalds. And while we're on the subject of disposability and mass marketing: the gay/queer chic fashion costuming of today is merely a stretch-fit, ready-to-wear template. This "radical" commodifying commodity is in great demand by up-to-date male/female Dummies from queer to straight, mainstreamlining the style and effectively limiting any chance of any queer critique.

> The manager of OZ ON fashion's Paddington store, Kevin Metcalfe, says straight guys are: "cautious at first but their expressions quickly change when they see how good their bodies look. This whole town is a narcissist's heaven; anybody that spends hours each day in the gym wants to show their bod to its best advantage."[46]

So, what happens to the idea that gay men aren't complicit in sexism or misogyny and aren't exclusionary or discriminatory of the anti-bodies of thin/fat/effem/old because they consciously construct their masculine bodies and can thus distance themselves with irony, incongruity, or excess?

> Does Kevin apply high camp; does he radically decentre stereotypes? No. He buys the whole het-up masculinity deal: "Turn-Offs: Gay guys dressing effeminately, except at special events like Mardi Gras. If they go that far, they may as well wear lipstick and eyelashes as well."[47]

... AS ARE THEY ALL

The queer theories of body image, Oz or imported, are sustainable only at a rarefied level of abstraction, framed on literary critical textual parallels and quarantined in poststructuralist space. Deconstruct them, or prick them with sociological perspectives, and they deflate into their own covert essentialisms. In the process, embodied experiences, particularly those of aging, implode into theory and textuality. Real people are not, and are not much like, texts.

"This isn't going to be one of those obscure theory things is it?" says David.

THE AGING BODY PRODUCT...

All my interviewees confirmed the pervasive sexualization of almost all sites on the subcultural map, experienced as the automatic assumption of a sexual subtext to everyday places and interactions. At cafes, restaurants, movies, bars, pubs, parties, and parks, the stares of others are felt as evaluations (I don't measure up) or, worse, as deliberate unseeing (I'm invisible). Even in these homo-social spaces, let alone at sex-specific premises like saunas, the specter of the Desperate Old Poof lurks. Behind it hides the old homophobic myth of the Dirty Old Man:[48] after all, sexuality stops (or should) at age forty.[49] A common explanation for the disproportionately high level of use by mature men of saunas and other sex venues is to circumvent the just-as-commercialized sexual sports going on everywhere else.[50] Such sports allocate amateur, retired, or incompetent status to mature men while ascribing ulterior motives. The controlling presumption is of predatory intergenerational sex, one of the lowest and most stigmatized in the homosexual hierarchy.[51] "*Narcissus wilting into middle-age, youth destined to repeat itself first in reverse, then in rejection.*"[52]

For a rough sketch of the ways in which body/body-image disjunctions are tangibly written on midlife bodies, you could look at that useful medical fiction Correct Body Weight, and how it exacts its pound of mental problems in increasing eating disorders[53] and related psychoses in men.[54]

This often bitter sense of cognitive dissonance and social estrangement deriving from an inadequate or inappropriate or unacceptable or unassimilable self-presentation—being out of shape hence out of place and out of the running—is consistently reported by both mature men and researchers.[55] The context, logic, language, and imagery of gay physicality, and its relentless eroticization, are experienced as alien and alienating. In return, mature men are popularly and conveniently categorized as inherently conservative such that social isolation becomes voluntary separatism, lifestyle accommodation and negotiated visibility becomes closet-clinging, and ideological critique becomes neopuritanism.[56]

> Or you could examine the component of steroid addicts comprised of mature, well-educated men, and related trends of exercise abuse.

Lacking a true community voice, it is easy (and empty) to politically label mature gays, particularly in the cartoonish characterizations of them as tired Returned Services League chatterers, back from the holy wars of Gay Liberation and unable to comprehend the Queer agenda as other than betrayal or collaboration.

> You could investigate what some psychologists call "Last Chance Syndrome"—a fuck, at any price up to and including high levels of risk, is worth it at my age with my looks—and its ramifications for physical and mental health, let alone AIDS.[57]

This is why, if you have been searching for "my" definition of middle-age, I suggest you give up. The men participating in interviews ranged from thirty-four to sixty-three and almost all categorically refused to set chronological parameters. Many self-identified as "middle-aged" only as a preliminary to reconceptualizing themselves as "mature" and/or entering "midlife" (somewhere in the thirties and forties to somewhere in the fifties and sixties), or comprehensively critiquing the hidden politics of life-cycle positioning. Similarly, their assessments of how they would be age-defined by others (invariably older) does not tally with covert (i.e., negatively constituted) definitions in Men's Personals, itself mostly consonant with sex marketing ("MATURE [mid-thirties] MALE VISITS YOU at your home").[58]

> Re-examine the methodological and practical problems experienced by researchers in health promotional communication with such hidden population subgroups.[59]

Stigmatized, excluded, marginalized, stereotyped, invisible—sound familiar? How's this for an equation: homo is to het as lesbian was to early women's lib and as mature gay men are to the subculture. Is it as easy (and complex) as a shifting along axes of discrimination from sexual identity to age? Perhaps. Probably.

I have neither expertise nor space to further develop these "hard" research aspects here, but it's vital to acknowledge that these issues are not just textual or theoretical or in any way limited by this exploratory analysis.

... *VERSUS THE GENUINE PRODUCT!*

There is nothing *genuine* about Mr. Dummy or his template in any of his incarnations, r/Real (gay) m/Man or otherwise. The crisis of authenticity in the masculine body is specious, having always been a gender fabrication. And while we focus on queer theories, representational identity politics, and discursive strategies, genuine people are authentically affected, bodies and other bits, by the Nietzschean will to manhood and by the Foucauldian technocracies of a perfectible body as postmodern product. These are implicated in, and made by, externalized (mechanical, architectural, plastic, etc.) figurings of corporeality; the commercial subculture, its markets and marketing; and a conveniently unfixed web of ageist assumptions, ideology, logic, iconography, and language. There is no queer body, only bodies queered by uncritical theory.

NOTES

1. Cuthbertson, "Face the Future," *Campaign* 196, July 1992, pp. 26-31.
2. Traced in, for example, T. Carrigan, B. Connell, and J. Lee, "Toward a New Sociology of Masculinity," in H. Brod (Ed.), *The Making of Masculinities: The New Men's Studies*. Boston: Allen and Unwin, 1987, pp. 65-80.
3. G. Callaghan, "Editor's Pen," *Campaign* 217, April 1994, p. 4.
4. G. Callaghan, "Pumping Ironies," *Campaign* 204, March 1993, p. 48.
5. C. Dobney, "Pretty as a Picture," *OutRage* 110, July 1992, p. 43.
6. J. Butler, "Imitation and Gender Subordination," in H. Abelove, M. A. Barale, and D. M. Halperin (Eds.), *The Lesbian and Gay Studies Reader.* New York: Routledge 1993, p. 317.
7. W. Harris, "Steroids and the Quest for Perfection," *Sydney Star Observer* 207, April 6, 1993, p. 8.
8. G. Callaghan, "Pumping Ironies," *Campaign* 204, March 1993, p. 51.
9. Ibid., pp. 47-48.
10. Dr Dick Quan's study reported in: *Campaign* 207, June 1993, p. 7; W. Harris, "Steroids and the Quest for Perfection," *Sydney Star Observer* 207, April 6, 1993, p. 8.

11. S. Shadwell, "Sweaty Bits," *Sydney Star Observer* 195, October 30, 1993, p. 31.

12. I. Cuthbertson, "The Beefcake Backlash," *Campaign* 208, July 1993, p. 20.

13. A. Creagh, "Living and Loving With HIV," *Campaign* 204, March 1993, p. 17.

14. Noted also by W. Harris, "Steroids and the Quest for Perfection," p. 8.

15. Callaghan, "Pumping Ironies," pp. 49, 51.

16. P. Mitchell, "Straightjacket," *Campaign* 217, April 1994, p. 40.

17. A. Goodman and P. Walley, *A Book About Men: Quartet Books.* London: Quartet Books, 1975, p. 32.

18. For example, K. Dion et al., "What is Beautiful is Good," *Journal of Personality and Social Psychology* 24, 1972, pp. 285-290.

19. D. Monteguesu, *Sydney Star Observer* 32, April 16, 1993, p. 4.

20. E. Cohen, "Who Are 'We': Gay 'Identity' as Political (E)motion," in D. Fuss (Ed.), *inside/outside: Lesbian Theories, Gay Theories.* New York: Routledge, 1991, pp. 76-81.

21. A footnote cannot cover an industry, but writers on this particular point include: Susan Sontag, Cindy Patton, Simon Watney, D. A. Miller, Sunil Gupta, Douglas Crimp, Donna Haraway.

22. Not his real name.

23. G. Callaghan, "Pumping Ironies," p. 50.

24. P. Mitchell, "Straightjacket," p. 24.

25. J. Butler, *Gender Trouble: Feminism and the Subversion of Identity.* New York: Routledge, 1990, p. 123.

26. S. Kleinberg, "The New Masculinity of Gay Men and Beyond," in M. Kaufman (Ed.), *Beyond Patriarchy.* Oxford: Oxford University Press, 1987, p. 130.

27. S. Sontag, "Notes on Camp," in *Against Interpretation.* New York: Octagon Books, 1978, pp. 275-277, 279-281.

28. I. Cuthbertson, "The Beefcake Backlash," *Campaign* 208, July (1993), p. 20.

29. *Sydney Star Observer*, February 19, 1993, p. 9, (emphasis in original).

30. *Campaign* 206, May 1993, p. 82.

31. K. Deaux and R. Hanna, "Courtship in the Personals Column: The Influence of Gender and Sexual Orientation," *Sex Roles* 11 (5-6), 1984, pp. 363-375; M. F. Lumby, "Men Who Advertise for Sex," *Journal of Homosexuality* 4, 1978, pp. 63-72.

32. T. Boyden, J. S. Carroll, R. A. Maier, "Similarity and Attraction in Homosexual Males: The Effects of Age and Masculinity-Femininity," *Sex Roles* 10 (11-12), 1984, pp. 939-948.

33. *Campaign* 204, March 1993, p. 29. Or: "I want your body!" for Olympus Fitness Gym, *Sydney Star Observer* 188, May 15, 1993, p. 28.

34. T. Carrigan and J. Lee, "The Male Homosexual and the Capitalist Market," *Gay Changes* 2 (4), 1979, p. 39. Locate it in 1979, and it has been discovered regularly since.

35. "The Hard Sell," *Campaign* 206, May 1993, pp. 27-30. Interestingly, this article has no author.

36. C. Dobney, "Pretty as a Picture," p. 42.

37. "The Hard Sell," p. 30.

38. C. Dobney, "Pretty as a Picture," p. 43.

39. P. Jordaan, "The Naked VCR," *OutRage* 131, April 1994, p. 45.

40. Callaghan, "Pumping Ironies," p. 49.

41. G. Bennett, "Categories: Activism, Community, and Change," *Gay Information* 7, Spring 1981, p. 9.

42. C. Johnston, "Fragments of Gay America," *Gay Information* 8, Summer 1981/1982, p. 8.

43. Callaghan, "Pumping Ironies," p. 48; M. Simpson, "No Effems, Please, I'm Straight-Acting," *Campaign* 201, December 1992, pp. 48-50.

44. D. Altman, *Homosexual: Oppression and Liberation*. New York: Outerbridge and Dienstfrey, 1971, p. 229.

45. C. Dobney, "Pretty as a Picture," p. 43.

46. S. Short and M. Kwasniewska, "Dressed to Thrill," *Campaign* 206, May 1993, p. 49.

47. Ibid., p. 50.

48. R. Booth, "When We're Old and Gay," *Campaign* 207, June 1993, p. 28.

49. C. Shively, "Old and Gay," in P. Mitchell (Ed.), *Pink Triangles: Radical Perspectives on Gay Liberation* Boston: Alyson Publications, 1980, p. 75.

50. Booth, "When We're Old and Gay," p. 30; J. Dawson, "Saunas and Sex: An Open and Shut Case," *Sydney Star Observer* 194, October 16, 1993, p. 16; confirmed by most of the men in interviews.

51. G. S. Rubin, "Thinking Sex: Notes For a Radical Theory of the Politics of Sexuality," in Henry Abelove, Michellé Aina Barale, and David M. Halperin *The Lesbian and Gay Studies Reader*. New York: Routledge, 1993, pp. 14-15.

52. N. Triffitt, "Old Within His Time," *OutRage* 105, February 1992, p. 37.

53. M. M. Fichter and C. Daser, "Symptomatology, Psychosexual Development, and Gender Identity in Forty-Two Anorexic Males," *Journal of Psychology and Medicine* 17 (2), 1987, pp. 409-418.

54. For more detailed perspectives, see P. Craig and I. Caterson, "Weight and Perceptions of Body Image in Women and Men in a Sydney Sample," *Community Health Studies* XIV (4) 1990, pp. 378-379.

55. Booth, "When We're Old and Gay," p. 30.

56. Variations on this theme are to be found throughout *Gay Information* 2, May-June 1980, pp. 4-18.

57. W. A. Myers, "Age, Rage, and the Fear of AIDS," *Journal of Geriatric Psychiatry* 20 (2), 1987, pp. 125-140.

58. "Men's Personals," *Campaign* 206, May 1993, p. 83.

59. "Social Aspects of the Prevention of AIDS Study A," *SAPA Report No. 1*. Sydney, Australia: AIDS Council of New South Wales and the School of Behavioural Sciences at Macquarie University, 1987, pp. 14-15.

Laws of Desire: Has Our Imagery Become Overidealized?

William J. Mann

The boy sitting across from me is, by anyone's definition, beautiful. He's barely eighteen, with dark hair, dark eyes, long lashes, and pouting lips. Anyone's definition, that is, but his own.

"I'm ugly," he says, and I'm dumbfounded. He's a member of a gay youth support group that I facilitate, and this is what he has come to talk with me about. Call it a case of typical teenage insecurity, but it's more than that.

"You're not," I protest. "You're very attractive." I struggle with boundaries: how far do I go in detailing his physical beauty before I cross the line between mentor and seducer? But that particular dilemma is swiftly replaced by another.

"Here," he says, standing up and walking over to my bulletin board, where I have tacked up a photo, torn from a gay newspaper, of Mr. Hotlanta 1994. "Here," he says, taking it from the wall and handing it to me. "*This* is attractive," he tells me. "I'll never have a body like that."

I take it and look at it, remembering the compulsion that prompted me to tear it out and tack it up on my wall. A thought strikes me hard: am I part of this young man's oppression? Have I contributed to his feelings of inadequacy? And what should I tell him now? That *of course* he could have a body like that? That all he needs to do is *work* at it? Or do I take the opposite tack, and tell him that such bodies are not—or at least, *should* not—be the only barometers of beauty? But I suggest neither. All I say is, "Who does?"

"Lots of guys," he tells me, and he's right. "I've got to start working out," he says, "or I'll never be attractive."

I flash on my own time in the gym, my own pursuit of the ideal. It's the definition of that word—*attractive*—that is so troublesome. How much is subjective, at least anymore? Has that definition become too limited, too restrictive? I wonder suddenly if I was wrong: if by anyone's definition the

---

Based on interviews conducted January-March 1995.

young man across from me might *not* be considered beautiful. But that's *absurd,* I tell myself.

Yet is it? In a recent issue of *Out* magazine, columnist Michelangelo Signorile asked what kind of message we send to our youth as images of gay male beauty become more and more precise: hard, chiseled, buff, smooth. "Looking out at the hordes of shirtless, pumped-up men, each virtually indistinguishable from the next, it dawned on me just how much pressure is put on young gay men as they enter gay community—more than ever before," Signorile wrote. "It's true that there have always been paradigms in the gay world, but it seemed in the past there were more choices, more leeway about what was considered a gay stud. Today only one very precise body type is acceptable—one that few gay men have or can achieve."

How many gay kids fit that ideal? Or feel they ever will? How many gay kids are just the opposite, struggling through identity issues that often result in physical manifestations of difference—being overweight, or socially awkward, or ill-groomed? What does the image of the pumped-up, pretty white boy—plastered all over our magazines, our advertising, our literature, and our erotica—say to the nonwhite or skinny queer kid, looking to find a place in a community that seems to have no place for people who look like him?

And it's not just the young. Several of my older (read, thirty-five and up) friends declined to accompany me to the big dances at the Stonewall 25th anniversary celebrations in New York in June 1994. "But there will be lots of hot boys there," I protested, urging one friend to join me on board the U.S.S. Intrepid. *"Precisely,"* he said, and I understood.

The reverberations go deeper, especially now, as more and more of us take on the unmistakable appearance of living with HIV. How is beauty defined then? What do the proliferating images of buff young boys say to someone whose muscle tone is shot? And how much of our obsession with appearance is, in fact, a direct response to the increased numbers of us who look emaciated and frail?

And yet, if it's oppressive, am I a part of that oppression by tearing out Mr. Hotlanta and hanging him on my wall? How about when I choose a hunky, blonde twenty-three-year-old to go home with from the bar instead of the more ordinary Joe closer to my own age? How much of that is perpetuating a societal oppression, and how much of it is merely the acknowledgement of an ideal, an archetype of beauty? And if there is such a thing, how do we reconcile that fact with the very real implications it has in the very real world? For this chapter, I spoke with several observers of the gay male scene: writers, activists, political scientists, and pornographers.

THE HIERARCHY OF BEAUTY

"There is a hierarchy of beauty," the late Michael Callen, activist, author, singer, and flirt, said shortly before he died in 1994. "It is naive or foolish to think that everyone has to be included in that aristocracy." Callen, who had an advanced case of AIDS when he made those remarks, argued that sexual desire should be "placed in a natural preserve" like "wetlands that are filled with bugs and harsh conditions but have a certain integrity all the same. This place ought to be off-limits to charges of political incorrectness."

Douglas Sadownick, author of the novel *Sacred Lips of the Bronx* and *Sex Between Men,* a study of the connections between gay male sexuality, identity, and politics, adds another level to Callen's argument. "Let's hypothesize, for argument's sake, that there are at least two different realms," he says, coming from a deep psychological approach. "There's the archetypal, with its idealizations and compulsion to worship, and the human, with its imperfections and foibles. On the one hand, the objects of desire are created by an exploitative Madison Avenue that senses an opening in the intersection between the two. On the other, if the images strike a chord within us, that feeling might actually be honored as archetypal. The challenge is how to resolve these two levels, how to come up with a language that lets us honor our feelings while seeing how we might be being exploited unawares."

Such a theory, Sadownick admits, is controversial. Are the images featured in Catalina videos and on *Genre* magazine's "Who's that Guy" photo page archetypes—and, as such, to be respected, not repudiated? How much impact has Madison Avenue—i.e., the consumer culture, the media, and other outside influences—had on establishing this ideal? "Most people say the image creates the desire," Sadownick says. "That's where I differ. The images awaken something that was already there."

Regardless of where it comes from, however, there *is* an ideal: although individual appreciation obviously fluctuates, that ideal has become more standardized in recent years, as witness the majority of images in gay porn and advertising. How that has happened is open to question. "There are *hierarchies* of beauty, not just one hierarchy," said the late Victor D'Lugin, who was a professor of political philosophy at the University of Hartford and a gay and AIDS activist. "What is considered beautiful changes profoundly and significantly over time. None of these ideals have remained."

"There are cultural ideals that people cannot conform to," says Michael Bronski, author of *Culture Clash: The Making of a Gay Sensibility.* "To be fair, however, we should blame it on the Italian Renaissance and not *Mandate* magazine." Nevertheless, our pornography often reflects as well as informs what we consider erotic. "We can say fantasy is just fantasy," Bronski adds. "But fantasies do have resonance in the world. Pornography *does* have an impact. It's not what Ed Meese or Andrea Dworkin say it is, but it is there."

That resonance can be, for some, oppressive—even for those who might not appear, at first glance, to be affected. "In spite of the fact that everyone will say I've obviously benefited from it, I agree the culture of beauty is an oppressive thing, and it oppresses the very people it benefits," says porn star and *Steam* magazine publisher Scott O'Hara.

"One of my favorite people in the porn industry is a boy who achieved success very early," O'Hara explains. "He has a lot of smarts, but he's never had to do anything but smile and everyone goes weak in the knees. And he's made no plans for anything else. One of these days he's going to wake up and he'll be forty." He laughs. "Occasionally I've wished that I was ugly so that I didn't have to wonder whether people were responding to me only because they think I'm cute," he says.

Beyond the implications of self-esteem, some would argue the current physical ideal also has the effect of suppressing our erotic imagination. "The image is muscular and very white and very young and very clean," said D'Lugin. "That very cleanliness seems to imply there are certain limits with what one would do with that body. The image is so clean and ultimately so safe and nonthreatening that it doesn't allow for us to explore our sexuality, to see what the limits of our fantasies might be."

That's especially ironic within the gay community, whose movement began with a mission of sexual liberation. "At the point where the gay movement decided it wanted to be more mainstream," Bronski argues, "that's when people started to be excluded."

Michelangelo Signorile, who uses the term "body fascism" to describe the current hierarchy of beauty, says we have created a new elite—the "beautiful, healthy, and young." And although that is clearly a part of a wider obsession on beauty and youth in the culture at large, Signorile says "it is much bigger in the gay community than in the straight world." He explains, "I think it's part of the whole cultural experience we have. I think it's because we were all insecure, we all feel inferior. One way we deal with that is to set up hierarchies of beauty. Gay men are made to feel effeminate, and that's seen as being bad. One way to feel superior is to overcompensate in being macho."

That dynamic has further implications. "When we look at the imagery, it's both 'I want to *look like* this person' and 'I want to *have* this person,'" Bronski points out. A straight man who defines beauty only by the ideal of

Cindy Crawford does not simultaneously want to *look like* Cindy Craw-ford. "It's a very complicated relationship," Bronski says.

But not necessarily an entirely undesirable one. "It's oppressive because we don't have the tools to understand it," Sadownick argues. "I would suggest that there is a place in the psyche that may be off-limits or even immune to our particular political considerations and hidden agen-das. I happen to be as oppressed and fucked over by the ideal beauty as anyone else. But I refuse to go about hating the ideal—or my own attrac-tion to it—and I don't always attribute my desire to outside influences. To do so is to give the psyche short-shrift."

THE PURSUIT OF THE IDEAL

But it's hard to ignore those "outside influences." On a recent night out in New York, for example, I stood in line outside a trendy, mixed club waiting for the "guards" to determine whether I—and my friends—were attractive enough, hip enough, to be let inside. The fact that we were (eventually) chosen over others in line produced an odd, artificial sense of triumph, as if we were somehow "better" because we had been deemed, by the powers that be, more "attractive" than the others.

Then there's the private sex parties that send scouts out to the clubs, instructing that invitations to the after-hours sex fest be distributed only to the cute boys—read: the boys who come closest to the ideal. Even some safe-sex party throwers like the OBoys! in Los Angeles, who by all accounts have made tremendous headway in helping a plague-weary population over-come sex negativity, have restrictions based on looks for attendance. At a Creating Change conference sponsored by the National Gay & Lesbian Task Force a few years ago, Marshall OBoy! attempted to defend his group's policy of exclusion. "I like good-looking men and can't get hard around people who aren't," he said. "If you don't like what we do, why not start your own group?" As reported in the gay press, the audience booed.

The OBoys! are blatant in their exclusion. But *de facto* discrimination occurs as well, in the advertising and media coverage that promotes the burgeoning gay party circuit, from the Black Party in New York to the Morning Party on Fire Island to Provincetown to Hotlanta to Russian River. The message is clear: if you don't look like these boys, you can't come. And if you try, you'll fail.

"Of course people should be able to do what they want to do," says Signorile. "I would never say people have to start opening doors. My concern is that this is what we have come to glamorize in our community. The message has become: If you don't go, you're worthless."

Although O'Hara agrees that an "open door" policy usually means more innovation and thus more fun, he—like most of those interviewed for this article—believes that private parties have an absolute right to allow admission based on looks. "There's no question it's discrimination," O'Hara admits. "But the real question is: Is discrimination always a bad thing? The word discrimination has gotten a bad rap. We've changed the meaning. It used to mean you had taste."

That doesn't mean that the effects such discrimination might have on those who are discriminated against shouldn't be at least pointed out. It's *that* discussion many chafe against. "I'm not going to feel guilty going to a party that keeps out the trolls," one friend told me.

Bronski says he shouldn't feel guilty; he should just recognize the implications such a policy might have on others. "The minute someone points out something where we should be more culturally sensitive, there's this cry of 'political correctness,'" he says. "People see it as an attack on them, a loss for them. But nobody's saying you can't find Marky Mark and his kind attractive."

But that's just it: "Marky Mark and his kind" have become the ideal, and the ideal has increasingly become less and less attainable for most men. O'Hara, who made his first porn film in 1983, says he has seen a change in the prevailing erotic imagery during that time. "Muscles were already pretty common by then, but not as much," he says. "It was still fine to have a natural body and be a porn star. Now a natural body doesn't make it in a porn flick." Signorile adds, "Before there were all sorts of body types. Now there is only one."

"We've created a standard where eventually we all have to fail," D'Lugin pointed out. "We set up this system that's planned for us to fail. We are going to get old. Two summers in Provincetown, then it's over. I'm not sure adulation of the elders was a better system, but at least it was something we could grow into, rather than out of."

But it's even more specific than that. Young is a given. The image is also buff and smooth. "Hair means experience," Signorile speculates, "and experience means AIDS. So everyone feels this pressure to shave their bodies."

Too simple a connection? Maybe just glaringly obvious. For as AIDS became more and more entrenched over the last decade, the ideal became more and more youthfully healthy—or at least healthy-appearing. "As our commitment to health and fitness got bigger and bigger, our images changed," Signorile says. "I do think that the coming of AIDS changed the ideal, with people wanting to look the opposite of being unhealthy. It's trying to recapture a youth, an innocence."

D'Lugin said, "People are trying to prove they're healthy, and this includes people already infected. If the external signs are healthy, then we are. For a long time, outside and inside the community, the face of AIDS was the emaciated body. The image of gay men, both inside and outside the community, has become just the opposite—hunky, healthy bodies."

He described standing in front of Spiritus Pizza, the traditional late-night cruising spot in Provincetown, and how he, as a man in his late forties living with AIDS, felt out of place. "And it wasn't just ageism," he says. "I didn't see any long, thin bodies. I certainly didn't see KS [Kaposi's sarcoma]. Even though a significant percentage of the men standing there were surely infected, the visual image they were projecting was that they were healthy. Anyone who didn't look like that was not welcome. It's a desperate attempt to appear healthy."

Some of that attempt comes through in another way—which specific body parts are now prioritized in the erotic pecking order. The (in)famous ad slogan for the David Barton Gym in New York proclaims "No Pecs, No Sex." It's not just a reflection of gay men's increasingly body-conscious outlook; it's also a clear refocusing of our sexual attention.

"I don't hear people talking about baskets and buns anymore," D'Lugin said. "We accentuate those areas that are sensuous but not sexual—pecs, biceps, triceps, nipples, washboard stomachs. You can manipulate these areas without ever really having sex. At least baskets and buns deliver. Nipples do not deliver. They're supposed to be foreplay."

"It's an unwillingness to be directly sexual, to refer directly to what it is you want, a shying away from saying 'I want to have sex with you,'" O'Hara adds. But O'Hara, who himself has AIDS, would caution against reading too much into it. "It may simply be that Madison Avenue is more willing to sell pecs than sell crotch," he says. "I think that contributes more than AIDSphobia."

D'Lugin strongly disagreed. "As we became more fearful of sex, we show off more of our bodies, but in a redirection of energy. Instead of sucking and fucking, we're pumping. It's a way of having your body exposed, but in a safe way. In the 1960s and 1970s, there wasn't this flaunting, this display, of the body. You took off your shirt in a bar, to be sure, but it wasn't on the dance floor. It was in the back room for sex."

Still, Sadownick would argue, maybe the answer is to become more comfortable with this notion of an ideal. "On the bad level," he acknowledges, "the ideal has gotten so much more perfected that it is hard for any human being to attain it. But on the good level, maybe this means that ideal has gotten stronger—the need to worship something, anything, is being fine-tuned."

COMING TO TERMS WITH THE IDEAL

Just as it seems the perfected ideal has become all pervasive, there are signs that some are rebelling against it. "I counted forty-three ostensible porn magazines at Glad Day Bookshop [in Boston]," says Bronski. "Eighteen had nontraditional body types. Almost half the magazines now feature hairy men or big men or men who like to put pieces of metal through their dicks." Signorile adds, "On America Online there's now a category [of electronic personal ads] that says 'Shaved Need Not Apply.'"

O'Hara, whose *Steam* magazine has tapped a pulse of rejuvenated sex radicalism, feels that the imagery will change again, moving away from the unattainable ideal and back to a more realistic—and multifaceted—depiction. "Body hair and other signs of maturity are becoming more fashionable," he says. Erotica based solely on idealized looks, he contends, results in a "homogeneity of product that is boring and insipid."

Whether the image may also become less white is not clear. The inherent racism in the prevailing ideal of gay male beauty is obvious: few porn films have mixed-race casts, and advertising in gay magazines and for the party circuit rarely feature hunky nonwhite men. "Once in a while [filmmakers] will fetishize something like Latin gangs," Signorile says, "but they completely miss the range." The implications of race on the discussion of a hierarchy of beauty demand an article of their own. But there's no question that just as nonmuscular, average Joes with body hair and body fat who happen to be white find no reflection in the prevailing imagery, so too do nonwhites of whatever body type feel excluded, except as erotic fetishes or occasional exotic diversions.

"We need to empower people who don't feel attractive," Signorile says. "I'm not saying that for vast numbers of people the club and party scene is not fun, is not great. But those who don't fit in need to see other images. Lots of people don't see themselves in what they see of gay culture. The range of what's attractive needs to be expanded, not because it's a good thing we *should* do, but because the range really *is* broader. The bottom line for [filmmakers and other image-makers] should be, if they want to make more money, they should be showing more of what's out there."

But what about those of us who admit to finding the guys in the RSVP cruise ad really attractive, or find Mr. Hotlanta so hot we tear his photo out of the paper and tack him up on our wall? Should we, metaphorically, take him down—or at least pin up a wider diversity of images?

"Ultimately this hierarchy of beauty, and our participation in it, is wrong," D'Lugin said conclusively. "Socially, politically, ethically wrong. But ultimately why it's wrong is that we've limited our own sexual freedom." Take the white guy who says he's simply "not attracted to" black guys. Or Asians. Or the older man who only sleeps with twentysome-things. Or the gym clone who buys David Barton's adage, "No Pecs, No Sex." What if they say it's too late for them to change what gets their dicks hard? "Then they're missing out on some potentially great sex, and the opportunity to discover their own sexual limits," D'Lugin said.

"There is both a political and an ethical response, which is to develop a way to talk about the feelings the images evoke," Sadownick says. "Yes, there may be oppression, but if the images make one feel bad, then maybe the answer isn't to take the pictures down—or to hurry out to the gym and try to keep up—but rather to contain some of the hysteria and see what's going on."

The oppression we might feel, Sadownick argues, could come as much from our own hurt and pain as any outside influence. That the "hordes of shirtless, pumped-up men" Signorile wrote about have become practically indistinguishable from each other may result from a desire to finally fit in, and fit in so completely that we end up rendering ourselves invisible. What could be safer?

"The images have become overidealized partly as a way to compensate for our own pariah status," Sadownick says. "The first thing that usually comes up [in his workshops on sexuality] is a quiet and even secret sense of hurt. The hurt over never being able to love completely or have sexual relations the way we want them—lots of profound disappointment over the way life has turned out." It's this pain and rejection, Sadownick says, that frequently causes many gay men to become so angry and resentful of the archetypes around us.

"According to Plato," he continues, "in the *Symposium,* Eros always loves what it is not. Eros is, by definition, a little ugly. It wants the Beloved to provide the wholeness it lacks. I would go so far as to suggest that the secret behind our idealizations is a sense of our own hideousness, pariah status, lack of worth. Even beauties feel this—especially beauties."

Perhaps, then, it is this: honoring the archetype, the ideal of Mr. Hot-lanta tacked up on the wall, should not necessarily create a demand that we reproduce him, not in ourselves nor in others. But neither should it compel us to take him off the wall. A difficult conundrum. How do we respond?

"Whatever you're attracted to, that's great," Signorile says simply. "No matter what people say, say fuck you. But if *you* feel there's a problem, then you need to do something about it."

And that's the hard part. "We can work on this as a community," Sadownick says, "but ultimately it seems that the hard work has to take place on an individual level, through honoring the subjective. That's the way we'll be able to resolve all this finally for ourselves."

A Matter of Size

Patrick Giles

At ACT UP, at Queer Nation, at healing circles, meetings, parties, and dances across queer New York (even in *OutWeek*), I hear "liberty, justice and equality" cried with a fervor once reserved for exchanging names and phone numbers. Queer New York has changed, everyone assures me, for the better—more sensitive and aware, truly concerned with fairness and justice both in and out of our own tribe. I've been tolerating this eruption of enlightenment with angry doubts.

In seventeen years of being out of the closet, none of the shit I've dodged from the straight world has matched the hostility, ostracism, and enforced anonymity flung in my face by my own queer kind. Ignored, avoided, not served at bars and stores, turned away at entrances to gay hangouts—that's my status in the old and new queer nation (the entity, not the organization). I've even been bashed—yes, bashed. One night during a protest of a local club's no-Blacks door policy, the bouncer panicked and let the Double A's in—then held me back. "No whales in here," he sneered, and when I objected, he punched me out.

At six-foot, three-inches, I weigh 315 pounds. In the gay world, this makes me a bona fide nonperson—an invisible fag. I must insist that I am not speaking here of lesbians, only gay men. I've never had the nerve to ask the big lesbians of my acquaintance if they have as unhappy a time being queer and fat as I do. I think that I am afraid that they'd say yes.

Now, I'm not talking about the lack or kind of sex available to big men: for us, dating, cruising, and fucking are another nightmare entirely. I'm talking about even being noticed by my fellow gays. I'm talking about the fear and annoyance so many radicals display when I try to speak at an ACT UP meeting. I'm talking about the way most of my own brothers can't look me in the eye when I'm addressing them. I'm talking about being accepted as a queer human being as fine and valuable as the gym daddies or the little boys or the kids of the club scene (the center of the universe, it seems, according to *OutWeek*), by my queer, alleged brothers.

Despite GMHC, ACT UP, 12-steps, Louise, Larry, and crystals, I don't find our community more sensitive since AIDS and activism. We are as deeply obsessed with appearance and "normality" as we've ever been. Clonism has been succeeded by gym bodies, little-boy bodies and ACT UP *couture*. Ostracism of big men thrives, usually in the most enlightened places, often among our most enlightened brothers. Some would call this obsession with a uniform appearance a betrayal of shallowness, others, a passion for "beauty." The implication is that someone like me is not beautiful or desirable, which, no matter how brainwashed some of you have been, is just not true. As long as we are bigots ourselves, all this fine talk of solidarity and community will never grow beyond talk. As with straights and homophobia, many gays I've addressed this issue with are unaware of any problem. Or they consider the problem to be the big people themselves (sound familiar?). Then there's the New Age edition of this lash: I must have an attitude problem or lack of self-esteem. But attitude was a nonissue ten years ago, when I weighed 190 pounds. Then I "passed" and was more than welcome as a brother. Now, when I step out into my own community, the reception from my peers is nearly unanimous: Lose weight, or get lost.

According to a recent article in *OutWeek*—which survives by marketing sex lines and other services which may give people lots of fun but also perpetuate this bigotry—Girth & Mirth is the answer to my dilemma. But discrimination of any kind is our dilemma, not mine alone. And as for G&M, I find the queer ghetto too small for my whole life as it is: Why should anyone have to cram himself or herself into an even smaller one? How can we rage with integrity at straight prejudice when we don't even admit to our own? When *OutWeek* was brand-new and seemingly open to covering every strata of queerness in captivity, I called and suggested an article on queers and weight issues. An editor huffed, "That's not an article for us."

So, amid this new wave of solidarity, who the fuck are we? Who will be welcome in our ideal queer nation? Only muscle boys? Only skinny boys? Only politically correct, muscular, skinny boys? Recently, some gay men have at last accepted that lesbians are us, too. So, now what about queers who don't look like Falcon Video wannabees or one of Chip Duckett's boys of the minute? Do I count for less because of how I look? Am I welcome only in my little corral—Girth & Mirth dances?

The solution then becomes "Let's find some safe, distant harbor for our queer whales—not welcome them wholeheartedly into our freedom dance." "You dance?" a boy asked me skeptically on Gay Pride Day. Yeah, I can dance. Better than a lot of you, I'm willing to bet.

I don't exempt myself from this intolerance. Earlier this year, I suddenly found myself losing weight again, and sure enough, as the pounds peeled off, I started buying into the prejudice, too! Does being thin also thin out your conscience? If I drop 100 pounds, will I get a job as a bouncer at Quick! to keep out the chubbies on Thursday nights?

Whatever happens, may I make a suggestion to my reluctant brothers: Don't start talking about freedom unless you've worked really hard on your own bigotry against people who don't look the way you think you do; unless you can look me in the eyes without flinching; unless, when you start orating justice, you know you really mean it.

Justify My Love Handles:
How the Queer Community Trims the Fat

Jay Blotcher

When queer talk of politics and disease is momentarily exhausted, conversation returns to weightier issues—specifically, body image. Who's fat and who's thin. The queasy subtext: Who's perfect and who's unacceptable, by dint of their pec size or waistline. This is no mere parlor game. Among the countless mortals living among queer gods and goddesses, few are content with their physical appearance. My friend John is an award-winning writer and adorable WASP. When the tire forming around his belly became oppressive, he ran off to a health club. Now, weight lifting competes for time with work on his new novel. Roy, a dear pal with boyish good looks and a frame of respectable dimensions, coaxes friends weekly to feel the progress of his Megafitness Gym biceps. My own beau, Dave, is a handsome blond. His thin flame is enviably proportioned, yet he still strips down with a groan and dismisses my hoots of approval. And there's a similar story for every other friend.

Obsessed as they are, these people know the score. In our queer community, appearance counts. If you're looking for compassion or justice, try another culture. It is a nice but naive notion that AIDS has moved us to greater love for one another. If anything, the epidemic has moved us to worship these values even more so, to run from the hellish sight of wasting bodies to embrace the youthful, the lean, the muscled, the attractive. Chubby, fat, and obese queers register for outcast status—likewise for extremely thin folk. We are a community that has given its approval to a culture of body fascism.

The impact of this issue can be measured vividly: never before in researching an article have I been told so often to use aliases, to accept statements off the record, or been simply denied an interview. Body fat is serious business.

It is a Tuesday night at the Tunnel Bar, an East Village hangout for neighborhood artists, activists, old clones and new. The Christmas decora-

Originally printed in *OUTWEEK*, January 23, 1991.

tions still twinkle and blink, vying for attention with the porn films on the television. Jim, a tall, dark-haired man of twenty-five, is talking body image with a couple of friends. Like Jim, these guys have little to worry about. They are better than average looking, and the body definition beneath their T-shirts is apparent.

Jim (an alias), the son of an international diplomat, has lived all over the world. He insists that appearance is an oppressive factor in the American gay community. Europe has no parallel. He chalks it up to a masculinity standard foisted upon us by straights—and readily accepted. In a queer community where self-esteem comes from another's adulation of you, he says, AIDS gives that standard a pathetic twist.

People get their self-worth from the attentions of others, he explains, and they thrive on it. Finding out that they're HIV-positive has not had the effect of reevaluating the way they get their self-worth. Instead, it has made them frenzied about getting as much attention and self-worth as they can in a short time. "And it freaks them out absolutely to think that they're going to lose that one thing that gives them self-worth."

Phil (not his real name) says that he was "a sexual nonentity" in high school. Then he began working out, obsessively. He sculpted his thin, short frame into a tight, highly defined machine. Now he considers himself a sex symbol—so do others. He makes extra money dancing in his scanties at an East Village club. He is ambivalent when it comes to talking about body image. Gyrating on top of the bar, Phil obviously basks in the adulation. "It's not entirely unpleasant," he admits. "I don't mind being objectified, to some degree. As a man, I feel it's liberating—striking a blow for gender equality—to be purely a piece of meat. Of course, I expect to be appreciated for more than that," he adds quickly. "I'm not interested in someone who's incapable of appreciating my other qualities."

Phil splits his time between East and West Coast life. His relationships are numerous, their duration brief. Phil finds himself the victim as well as the champion of his crusade for physical beauty. "Our predilection for muscled bodies comes obviously from society's emphasis on physical perfection," he says. "It should be gotten beyond rather quickly because it ends up just aping that superficiality. At a point, it isn't liberating, and it leads to rotten objectification and not-niceness."

What of lesbians? Do they fare better? Legend says yes. The traditional vignette has portrayed lesbians in love, their middles expanding effortlessly. Deb Brown (her real name) is a twenty-eight-year-old lesbian. She lives in Copiague, Long Island, where a different breed of lesbian dwells. Brown calls them "mall girls" and identifies them by big hair and slacks.

Brown works in the state health department's AIDS epidemiology program. At night, she's a waitress. Between the two jobs, there is little time for eating. Although she considers herself "fairly big," the two jobs keep her weight steady. Brown has battled weight gain for several years, but she scoffs at the fat dyke stereotype: "The myth of fat lesbians began because heterosexuals needed an excuse for why women wanted to be with women." She claims to see more compassion in the women's community for overweight people.

A long-term relationship was unraveling three years ago when Brown decided to join Weight Watchers. She had ballooned during the time spent dating another woman. "You know the old saying: get in a relationship, get fat and happy." It was the only program she found effective; within forty-five days, she shed twenty-five pounds. On her own, she lost twenty-five more. Her succinct appraisal of the body image obsession? "A lot of people are just way too superficial. It's existed before, and it will continue."

Siobhan (not her real name) is a thirty-five-year-old lesbian living in Manhattan. Her 165 pounds cover a 5'7" frame. She has been in a relationship for eight years with another woman, but she is vulnerable to the same standard as single lesbians and women in general.

"This culture treats fat as a moral issue, which is completely out of place. Lesbians don't take the same moralizing and punitive position as those in the general culture. Gay men do—I think it may have to do with being men." She feels that the lesbian world claims a different party line on body fat policy. "I've not found a lot of discrimination against fat with lesbians. Women are a lot more willing to overlook physical specifics in the search for an ideal personality."

In the past year, Siobhan has bought the same pair of pants in three sizes. Her lover doesn't care nor does she. This is quite a switch from her last relationship, which lasted six years. The woman was anorexic. She was also sadistic. If Siobhan's weight rose above a certain level, her lover would refuse to sleep with her. Eventually, Siobhan buckled under. After a traumatizing move to New York City from Washington, DC, compounded by family crisis, Siobhan became neurotic about eating. Her appetite faded out. She took to picking through the refrigerator, throwing out uneaten food because she was convinced it had spoiled. She stopped short of seeking professional counseling and forced herself to overcome anxiety and eat.

It is Friday night at Crazy Nanny's, a lesbian bar in the West Village. On the video screen, David Lee Roth is ogling a fleet of bodybuilder women. Few patrons are watching; they're more concerned with making small talk. The manager, a strong-featured, dark-haired woman in a pull-over, is guarding the door for under-twenty-ones and hetero men who are merely shopping for kicks. Both levels of the bar are filled comfortably with a variety of women. Some are the "mall girls" of Deb Brown's neck of the woods. Others are lipstick lesbians in fashionable evening attire. Some of the women are overweight. Others are not.

Ovidia, twenty-nine, is a thin, nicely dressed woman with a sharp but pleasant English accent. She comes from Singapore. Speaking loudly over David Bowie's "Rebel, Rebel," Ovidia describes the sedate, somewhat-closeted queer bar scene of her native city. She doesn't feel that lesbians dress up for one another. She is vague about the existence of body fascism in the clubs. Her preference, when pressed, is "well-toned people, but not muscular." I ask her what her feeling is when she sees an overweight lesbian? "She's probably a nice person." Ovidia giggles. Would she be attracted to her? She stops, her eyes narrowing. "How overweight?" She expresses an interest in the bartender downstairs, who is not thin but not fat. "She's heavy. Heavy is nice. Then I don't feel bad. I think bigger than me is good." Has Ovidia ever turned down a woman because she is overweight? "Only because she was short. If she were the same weight and taller, she wouldn't be overweight, would she?"

Sharing a table with Ovidia are her friends, Bill and Leah, both from Iowa City. Bill is a timid, rosy-cheeked, man-boy with glasses and unruly brown hair. He is dressed in a sweater, shirt, and slacks. Bill admits that he feels oppressed by "gay culture" standards: "I feel a little bit inadequate about the appearance of my body, but I'm too lazy to do anything about it."

For some, the societal standards of queer body image are a constant reminder of inadequacy. Siobhan recognizes a lifelong struggle with the time-honored ideal. "When I can't find clothes that fit, that's oppression," she says. "When I listen to fat jokes, that's oppression. When people ask me why I can't diet, that's oppression."

For others predisposed to obesity, living in the queer community means a tortured existence. Consider Ron, twenty-seven, who asked that an alias be used. He is a gentle-eyed, brown-haired man with expressive hands. At an attractive weight of 160 pounds, Ron seems at ease with his tall body. But there are emotional scars. At one point, he carried an extra seventy pounds. His family background is an emotional minefield, all issues concerned with weight. Ron was raised in a Jewish middle-class family near Los Angeles. The only problem was, his parents wanted to be slim WASPs instead and were unable to cope with the reality of the situation: his father weighed 350 pounds; his mother was bulimic. The obsession with image maintenance took its toll. Ron became a battered child. He began overeating to cope with his problems. Naturally, they worsened. "I had a choice: I could either hurt other people, which is what my parents did," he recalls, "or I could hurt myself. And I did. I ate compulsively and got fat."

As a fat young adult, Ron even attempted suicide. Therapy was needed in tandem with a diet plan. Slowly, the suppressed feelings came to the surface. A major problem was Ron's inability to accept his homosexuality. Since he was not attracted to women, he gained weight to keep them away. Experts in the field of eating disorders recognize the plight of homosexuals. Dr. Ellen Shor-Haimoff is a clinical psychologist practicing in Gramercy Park, a fashionable area of Manhattan's East Side. Her associate is Regina Hausler, PhD, a licensed psychologist. Both women have counseled people with bulimia and anorexia for several years. In fact, back in 1978, a weekend workshop they held for bulimic females attracted many lesbians. The workshop was so successful that it ran for two years. "If you have mixed feelings about your homosexuality, and you have the extra burden of an eating disorder, your self-esteem is really going to suffer," Shor-Haimoff says. "If you hide who you are, you're really going to hurt yourself."

Among their clients, Shor-Haimoff and Hausler have seen many gay men. These men were wrestlers, bodybuilders, dancers, and models. They were in the business of body and definition; their bodies were their business. They were living under the constant pressure of maintaining perfection, lest they lose their job. Says Shor-Hamioff, "They suffered from the same tight restrictions that society usually puts on women insofar as looks [are concerned]."

Hausler says that there is no essential difference between eating disorders for heterosexuals and homosexuals: "They both have something they keep as a secret. They can't get to this secret that they consider so terrible, so they introduce an eating disorder as a way to avoid dealing with the problem."

Dr. Steven Levenkron, a psychotherapist practicing on the Upper East Side of Manhattan, is the author of several books on the subject of eating disorders, including *The Best Little Girl in the World*. Karen Carpenter came to him to be treated for her anorexia. Levenkron says that he has observed eating disorders in gays and lesbians. Anorexic males are often gay, he adds. Yet the patterns and character structure are the same for gays and lesbians as they are for heterosexuals. The pressures of sexual identity facilitate the eating disorder. "One pressure I infer is the lack of long-term unions, the fear to tell folks," he says. "There is a sense of being separate from one's family. There's a greater tendency to obsessionality because they have always felt different. They have to compensate for all those years of perceived separateness."

Losing weight takes its emotional toll. Personal revelations flood in as the weight—the only barrier between the individual and reality—is shed. Ron found powder diets to be most effective, and he bought every fad product from Dick Gregory's Bahamian Diet to SlimFast. Over-the-counter drugs such as Dexatrim did not work. A short stint with bulimia came in desperation. As the weight came off, Ron began to realize dire fears of intimacy. Now that he was physically attractive to many more men, he was scared to death of their advances. He was also angry with his newfound admirers: "I resent people who are attracted to me. I still want to be loved for the way I was. I feel I'm bluffing people." The sensitivity of a shunned person remains with him. Ron feels great compassion for other overweight people: "I still identify with the underdog. I still have a fat person's personality."

Patrick Giles, thirty-three, works at Gay Men's Health Crisis and is an activist with Queer Nation. These qualities are not immediately apparent. What is apparent to everyone who meets him is that Patrick is very large. In fact, he weighs more than 300 pounds. Giles will not mince words about his condition, nor will he apologize for it. He has already distinguished himself in the pages of *OutWeek* with an article about big men in gay society, or rather, their status as outcasts looking in. "Weight bigotry is present in society," he says, "but it is intensified in queer society."

Giles has seen both sides of the experience. An anorexic child, he became a fat teenager. Then the native Brooklynite slimmed down at the age of sixteen, "when I realized I wasn't going to have much chance as a queer unless I looked a lot better than I did." The 190 pounds fit nicely on his 6′ 3″ frame. He hit the bars in triumph. "I was totally lionized for about three years. I was a youth in heat on the piers and at the Ninth Circle."

As an adult, Giles began putting on the weight again, and his appeal dropped as the scales tipped. At the time, he suffered slipped vertebrae, and his doctor ordered him to join a gym. Giles was walking a half-mile each day on the track at the local YMCA. After he lost fifty pounds, he observed the same phenomenon: suddenly, he was getting compliments again. While big men have their admirers (called by the dubious term "chubby-chasers), Giles identifies bigotry in their preferences, as well. At a meeting of Girth & Mirth of New York, Giles was asked home by an admirer. The next morning, the man admitted that he was disappointed by the sex. He expected Giles to behave passively, not aggressively. "I really don't like the way we did it," he said to Giles. "You have sex like a thin man."

Ernie Harff is a member of Girth & Mirth of New York, a group founded in 1978 for heavy men and their admirers. Its male-only policy has never been challenged. Harff agrees with Giles that big men suffer most at the hands of their own queer brothers and sisters: "The discrimination is evident. Before we point the finger at anyone else who has prejudices against us, we have to put our own house in order."

Girth & Mirth does not preach about weight loss. Its purpose is to provide a positive environment for people who are shunned elsewhere. The approach has its merits, Harff says. Many times a person has come to Girth & Mirth obese and poorly groomed. After a few months of interacting with those who accept him, he begins to lose some weight and pays more attention to dress. But Harff is quick to mention that losing weight is not the only virtue: "Not everyone in this world is meant to be skinny."

While Girth & Mirth allows its members to be who they are, Overeaters Anonymous starts with the premise that overeating is a disease and that you must overcome it. The approach is based on the twelve-step model from Alcoholics Anonymous and can be very strict. Since confidentiality is the cornerstone of the program, the source of this information requested anonymity.

My source says that Overeaters Anonymous people bring their own feelings of self-loathing into the program, to the point that they discourage other members. It is necessary to work with a sponsor on a personal food plan. However, he says, some people refuse assistance unless you give up certain foods. Others commit you to exercise. My source lost thirty pounds in a month and was taken to a victory dinner by other members. Incredibly, they told him that he wasn't going to feel better, despite the weight loss. Moreover, they warned that he would probably have hanging flaps of skin. "They just demolished my hopes," he states. He became so depressed that he gained fifty-five pounds.

It is Sunday afternoon at the Athletic Complex, a huge fitness center on Park Avenue at 34th Street. Despite the raw, rainy day, men and women are jockeying for the exercise cycles and stair machines, hoping to absolve themselves for the excesses of Saturday night. According to one employee's estimations, the clientele here is 65 percent gay. "Overweight people come here, and they need more help with exercises. They want to lean up, lose weight. They're not so interested in muscle." Other patrons are kind to them.

Alan, twenty-seven, is a recent arrival from New Brunswick, Canada. His face is boyish and Spiegel-catalog handsome. He has a husky but solid frame and an eager face. Alan resembles a chubby man in transition. His goal is simple—to have a great body by summer. He started the mission a year ago. His incentive? Going to clubs such as Private Eyes and the Men's Room, where boy-beauty proliferates.

Ask him if he's pumping up to impress the Adonises, and Alan will tell you, "I'm doing it for me, basically." He does this for himself six days per week. He even quit smoking and drinking. Talk shifts to his lover, whom Alan describes as "totally out of shape." His lover feels insecure because Alan is suddenly into bodybuilding. Alan laughs and adds that he doesn't try to make him feel less insecure. At clubs, he dances while his lover sits and drinks. He thinks, then offers this bit of introspection: "Basically, we don't have a whole lot in common."

A year after he began his new regimen, Alan is getting come-hither looks from the same guys who snubbed his weightier frame. But he feels no resentment. "I just laugh because they don't recognize me." The first thing people ask when they meet him is, "Where do you work out?" When quizzed about body types, Alan balks, "I'm not really into looks so much. If I'm attracted to somebody, they don't necessarily have to have a great body." He goes back to the exercise cycle. And so does everyone else.

Don't look for an upheaval in body image trends. The new queer generation promises to uphold the same values as their predecessors. And we're not dismissing them as empty-headed, nonpolitical queers, either. Just drop into a meeting of ACT UP/NY. Body fascism goes hand in hand with AIDS activism, as well.

In a perfect world, how would the overweight fare? Patrick Giles had a taste of that fantasy last summer during Gay and Lesbian Pride Day. He was on the pier for the annual dance. It was nearing dusk. As the energy heated up, the deejay played the Pointer Sisters' "Jump." Giles peeled off his shirt and began to dance wildly. Soon, those closest were laughing at the mountain of flesh gyrating in their faces, until they noticed the grace and excitement of his dancing. The jeering gave way to whoops of applause, as Giles spun and writhed to the music in the setting sun on the Hudson. "I'd like that to happen more often," he says, his voice dreamy with recollection. "It was a nice moment."

Fatness and the Feminized Man

Ganapati S. Durgadas

Once, during the height of the Glitter Rock era, I decided to further androgynize my physical appearance. It was a few days before a David Bowie concert, and I wanted to go in style. I bought a large bottle of Nair hair remover and went to work eliminating my natural hirsuteness. After applying the container's entire contents, I let the shower's rush of luke-warm water burst upon me, following the time alotted by the bottle's instructions. As both my hands moved across my body, literally shoving off the falling hair from my skin, I watched the brown follicles flush down the shower stall drain with a mix of anxiety and fascination. Newly uncov-ered, pale and pink flesh, soft and round, revealed itself.

I was fascinated with the new self I saw emerging from beneath that water. This new self also awakened an old anxiety and returned to nag me with an almost stabbing quality, perhaps recurring because of the willful-ness of my flaunting of it, despite my earnestness in being a newborn, sexual outlaw. I knew I had really stepped over the lines enforced by the gender police. The womanlike breasts that being fat has given me were exposed, free of any masculine covering. I examined my fleshy thighs, noticing the only remaining hair around my genitalia, then back up my abdomen to the curve of my belly. I was voluntarily exposing what I had always been afraid of having others, especially men, notice. Inwardly, I relished the sensual pleasure of seeing myself this way. But I was acutely aware of the penalties that could be exacted upon me for having done so.

In Living Color, the television series, is nearing its end. I sit watching it in its last year, viewing its last gasps in a puerile sketch taking place in a prison. The fat, Caucasian male member of the comedy company is paraded out in character as the involuntary contestant in a convicts beauty pageant, wearing a bra, pushed out to the appreciative leers and catcalls of the assembled black, latino, and okie prisoners. It's a cheap joke. I chuckle but also acknowledge the seriousness of what this folk humor expresses in our continuing realm of sexual politics.

Around the time I was coming out as bisexual, exiting my former hippie phase of countercultural identification and participation, it was suggested I grow a beard. I would "look more masculine." But looking manly was furthest from my mind as I was transitioning into gender-fuck. Yet, despite my challenging of sex role stereotyping, I was very, very aware of where I was placing myself in the sexual economy, and the risks this entailed.

Being fat already put my male status on shaky ground. Fat men are automatically suspect: they are visibly, palpably soft and round, neither lean and lithe, nor robustly muscular, enjoying a physically questionable male status, upholdable only through boisterous clownishness or blustering bullyhood provided by sheer girth. Fat men are already suspiciously womanish. Conscientious androgyny only sets off the social alarms with undeniable certitude. One's womanishness is confirmed, meaning you can be fucked, in more ways than one, within the patriarchal hierarchy as your relative male status is revoked. Such revocation comes in various degrees, from not being taken "seriously" as a man to being rendered or avoided as a surrogate female.

It has been an object lesson in itself watching the local chapter of Girth & Mirth trying to get off the ground here. Try as I might, I've been unable to get any of my fellow fat gay and bisexual men involved. One declines because he prefers "boys with washboard stomachs." Another chooses to cruise our Washington Park, where he's bashed and robbed by an unfat hustler-trick, instead of attending a Girth & Mirth party held in the relative safety of an area gay bar. Other fat men sit furtively at the downstairs bar, glancing in the direction of those going upstairs where Girth & Mirth meet. Avoiding guilt by association, I guess.

These men would never be seen dead with another fat man in an erotic situation. They pursue slimmer men. Their partners often treat them brusquely, if not abusively. These men frequently engage in nonreciprocal relationships. They service their pursued partners orally or submit anally; often they caretake these partners emotionally or financially. In either case, there is rarely any reciprocation demanded from the partner. It's as if they feel they don't deserve better. As for their partners, there's a patent disdain in the partners' attitudes and behaviors toward these fat men. The interactions take on characteristics similar to those of abusive, heterosexual relationships. It's as if these partners possess a quality status the fat men can never achieve by themselves. And these partners know it.

I'm forty-seven now and have been "in the life" for more than two decades. There's not as much energy or naive idealism to my androgyny as there used to be. But it's enabled me to notice a thing or two about the changes that have occurred since my youth concerning the issues of fatness among queer men. The situations I've just described represent questions I want to address according to the thesis I presented at the start.

Fatness is equitable to feminization for a man, for heterosexual men, but even more so for gay and bisexual men.

I say this in light of the three male "types" most predominant in the community's media: the buffed, sleek and boyish preppie, the well-oiled and muscled bodybuilder or butch-type, and the smooth, Key West, Southern Cal, or upper West Side Manhattan sophisticate. No fat in sight. Obviously this represents a select few, but these few images so dominate as to monopolize the playing field for most men.

The reason lies in the "success" that the commercialization of the gay ghetto has achieved. It's a very dubious success because a ghetto, no matter how well-provisioned with cafes, bars, gyms, baths, clubs, etc., remains a ghetto and is a cramped and contained existence when compared with the diversity of human interchange, expansive time, and social space, and the degree of individual personal mobility available in the world outside.

Because available time and social space is so comparatively contained and compacted within the gay ghetto, appearance becomes all. Appraising others' "looks" and acting accordingly becomes the quickest and shortest means by which to find and form relationships within these limits. The trouble is by whose standards these means are established. Here's where the space between gay ghetto and the outside world overlap.

Despite the societal homophobia that has created and still enforces ghettoization, the majority of gay and bisexual men seem to have internalized the mainstream's "beauty" standards. True, in instances such as drag and leather, heterosexual cultural ideals of femininity and masculinity are often exaggerated and eroticized to a subversive extreme. But the drag queen's and leather man's appeal is calculatedly that of the gender or sexual outlaw. They constitute the foundation to a queer counterculture that is tacitly imaged in opposition to the gay assimilationist adoption of the mainstream's monopoly on prescribed appearance. They usurp heterosexuality's dictates by blatantly subverting its image ideals for their own mock-serious or rebelliously erotic purposes in a manner calculated to attack straight "norms." The way in which they are frequently and vehemently attacked for how they present to the media by the the image/status-conscious gay establishment indicates how threatening they are. They carry to an utmost extreme the heterosexual gender definitions of male and female, thereby rendering their blatant arbitrariness and nonabsoluteness patently obvious.

After all, the heterosexual political scheme of things is pretty much a shell game once scrutinized closely, instead of automatically buying its assertions as absolute truths. Behind notions of scientific, naturalistic, or religious rectitude, heterosexism confounds and confuses psychological and biological sex (not necessarily synonomous) with sex role and gender assignation with self-gender identity, usually to affirm or defend its own favored, ascribed status (and power exercised therein). Everyone either rushes to fit in as best to their advantage as possible, or rejects, or is rejected and placed outside of it.

The majority of gay and bisexual men seem to have chosen the first option. They genuinely embrace the image ideals of straight "maleness," not only in the area of erotic choice-type (not necessarily wrong or unhealthy in itself), but more important, it seems, for the vicarious and refracted social status and power the system built upon it awards. In the process, they affirm and uphold the explicit homophobia which heterosexism breeds upon the grounds that lesbians, gay men, and bisexuals are intrinsically unacceptable. They are unacceptable either because they exist on their own self-defined terms, or psychobiologically dysfunctional or maladaptively unable to. This is an unacceptability initially decided almost completely by expressed or perceived appearance.

I've lost count of the number of times gay men have complained about the appearance of many lesbians during street conversations. They can't understand how these women could "let themselves go" like that—meaning putting on weight. The irony of their complaints doesn't seem to strike them: their negative judgment of lesbians are according to standards of ideal, heterosexual, female body weight. Of course, I wonder what they think of yours truly when not face-to-face. But I wonder even more about what they think about themselves, so that they have volunteered themselves to be the straight world's policemen of queer appearance. The assumption is that a lesbian or bisexual woman would necessarily have to look satisfactorily heterosexual to deserve societal approval. She would have to customize herself heterosexistly to be a happy nonheterosexual. The absurdity, if not outright craziness of a notion such as this is obvious. A fat lesbian or bisexual female is less a woman and more a man by these standards adapted from straights.

For fat gay and bisexual men, there is a similar situation. They are less like men and more like women. Fleshy bulk or stoutness in females implies inappropriate strength or toughness. In males, it represents womanlike weakness or physical impressionability. We are reminders of the feminine stigma with which heterosexism still tars queer men. To fit into homophobia's rule system, many queer men feel it appropriate to oppress us so they can feel more accepted and comfortable with themselves. They reject us for the straight man's acceptance, hoping they'll slide by approved or unnoticed when compared to us.

Yet, what does this really say about them and about what the straight world they so fervently court thinks of them? I have my doubts whether these men really care about anything except fitting in and avoiding the twin terrors of looking queer (i.e., nonmanly) and fat (womanly and "weak"). I have to be honest and confess I used to feel bitter because of the rejection and segregation forced upon me as a consequence of being fat. Rejection by many prospective male partners, thin, chubby and rotund, all caught somewhere on the spectrum of desire between these two poles. This rejection is only reinforced by the societal stereotypes of all round people being lazy, or pathological overeaters, selfish, or repressed. The thought of fat folk as sensual beings, or sensually attractive to others, whether round or slim, is considered either criminal, sick, or incredulously ludicrous (Madonna being one of your more famous size-fascists, a commentary in itself, considering how she maintains goddess status in her one-way exploitive relationship with the gay world). "Chubby-chaser" is a name ascribed to our admirers with a pejorativeness that is half mockery, half disbelief, which begrudges the vague kinkiness it might suggest.

My anger was the result of the realization that I was an outcast in what had once been an outlaw community where there had been a possible chance of acceptance for me. Over the years, the possibility has dwindled as this same community has increasingly distanced itself from its counter-cultural origins and has become dominated by a strata only dimly connected to the original past—a strata arguing for integration into the scheme of things instead of liberation from them, and so accepting the standard of "looks" to fit in. These standards exclude people like me or allow me entry only as a second-class citizen.

I could continue in bitterness, and thus—if you will excuse the pun—eat my heart out to no avail except to consume myself in frustrated rage. Or I can acquiesce to the status others try to accord me. Instead, I prefer to adapt an adversary role, nor do I fail to perceive the irony involved. If my community increasingly refuses to maintain its former outlaw position, I can only rebel and embrace my fatness in defiance and the feminization implied as an outlawry counter to that community, as much as it is to the rest of society at large. I rewelcome my androgyny, now in its mellower middle-aged ripeness. I revel once more in my womanlike breasts, the jut of my belly, the thickness of my thighs, the quiver of my ample flesh when slapped, (for what is sensuality, if not such fleshiness itself). I have tattooed the images of the Gods—Shiva, Durga, and Ganesha—and their yantras (diagrammatic, mandala-like symbols) upon my flesh as reaffirmation of a belief in the Divine's embodiment in me, as I am. It's all the acceptance I need—self-acceptance.

PART 12:
FEELING THE BURN

But to Hear THEM Tell It . . .
Or: Looksism, Beauty's Evil Stepsister

Gene-Michael Higney

Ever wish you could be invisible and listen in on your friends while they talked about you? Well, I got that wish. I wasn't exactly in*vis*ible, but I cleverly concealed myself in a friend's closet. (To hear *them* tell it, I *locked* myself in there, upset because I'd turned forty years old, but that's not relevant to *this* story.) (I said it *is not*.) (Besides, *if* I should ever have reason to hit forty years old, *I* will let *you* know, ungrudgingly, with my usual cheery, good nature.) I got quite an earful from my secret vantage point.

It was before a dinner in my honor, given by a friend whom I shall refer to here as Benedict Arnold for reasons that will become unattractively obvious. The fiesta was to celebrate something, I forget what. (To hear *them* tell it, it was my fortieth birthday, but it would take more than turning forty to force me to hide in a closet.) (Though not *much* more.)

So there I was in the (you should pardon the expression) closet, only because I was thoughtfully waiting until everyone was distracted so I could slip out unobtrusively without frightening someone into cardiac arrest. (So much for that "Gene-was-locked-in-there-sulking" story *they're* telling!) It's amazing how many conversations are started at a person's doorway (in front of the person's hall closet door). Seems some people can hardly wait 'til they've crossed the threshold before they start hacking away, like Jason in a hockey mask, at (supposedly) absent friends.

"Glad you could make it!" exclaims Benedict Arnold to someone. (Not sure *who*; it's tough when you can only see boot and sneaker soles from an otherwise great location.)

"Is our guest of honor here yet?" That's Ronnie!—a great guy, Phys Ed from USC. He exercises for *hours* without shedding a *drop* of perspiration. I've examined him myself repeatedly—out of strictly scientific curiosity, of course.

"How *is* our bubbly, bouncing birthday boy?" That's Kay, Ronnie's sister, Psych Major, also USC. She singlehandledly dispels that myth about lesbians not having a sense of humor.

Benedict's voice is not muffled enough by the closet door to hide that note of treason of which I'd been previously and innocently unaware: "Don't mention the b-day! *You* know Gene! He's forty and getting *melodramatic* about it." (I am *never* melodramatic. I could just open a vein when people tell such scurrilous lies about me.)

"But he doesn't look forty at all!" (*Love* that Ronnie!)

Treacherously, Benedict adds: "No, but he's *acting* like I'm trying to put him in a home in Senile City." Okay, Benedict Arnold, I regret that you have but one life to give for your treason. I'm considering sending over a very butch, mob-involved friend of mine, Otto "Babymasher" Dogdroole, to rearrange your . . . priorities.

"Well, *I* think he's a doll!" (What a sweet, *sweet* gal, that Kay!) "I just wish," she continues, "that he'd take better *care* of himself, maybe lose a little weight." (Bitch.)

"I try to get him to go joggin' with me," says Ronnie, the sweatless one, "but he always says he can't go 'cause he's got menstrual cramps. *That* can't be . . . can it?" (Guess I can't use *that* excuse anymore.) Laughing, they move out of closet range, so I don't quite catch the rest of the assassination of my character. Have you begun to think that perhaps you detect the scent of burning martyr? Not so. I like to think of myself as, well, *comfortable*-looking, like an old mattress—plenty of stuffing and I usually look as if I've been slept in. But to hear *them* tell it, I'm guilty of heinous crimes against the community, such as wrinkled shirts, of which I am the patron saint. They're not "politically correct." And *I* had to get locked in a closet to find that out! (Well, all right, it *was* true. I *did* get locked in, but it could happen to *any*body.) (I said yes it *could*.) Also, I was informed that if my body isn't comparable to Mister Arnold Schwarzenegger's, then people consider it poor taste on my part to show myself in public. Now, Mr. S. and I *do* share some bodily similarities: we have the same number of eyes, one nose each, and I bet (though without the benefit of eyewitness assurance) that we put our pants on the same way. With further comparison, the similarities between him and me become more difficult to find. Maria's husband has enhanced *his* physical person with a sculpted physique, while *I* enhance mine with a dash of cologne and a sense of humor. (You only need to look at me to realize that the cologne might be optional, but the sense of humor is mandatory.) Ronnie even recommended (and I thought he was such a *nice* kid) that I should spend a portion of my day lifting heavy objects repeatedly so that I can irritate my muscles (they're in there *some*where) into shape and earn respect from the gay community at large.

I hereby apologize to the gay community at large. Sorry, gay community at large. I'd be at my less than attractive best, heaving hunks of metal around, lathered in perspiration, unable to gasp out my opinions of DePalma's latest film. Exertion should produce something worthwhile, such as a finished manuscript, a clean apartment, or a mutually satisfactory conclusion to an intimate experience. *They* say that "getting into shape" *is* a worthwhile result to such exertion. I reply, ruefully, that for *me*, working out would be like rearranging the deck furniture on the sinking *Titanic*. *Un*like some houses, some people are just *not* "fixer-uppers."

Unfortunately, my more militant siblings aren't content to leave bad enough alone. They inform me that my attitude and my disastrous personal appearance will get me *ignored* at best, and at *worst*, get me denied admission to certain exercise or dance establishments geared toward the more attractive and physically oriented of us. Furthermore, my physiquey, freaky acquaintances intone, my lack of muscular definition earns me disgusted glances and critical comments from those looks connoisseurs who undergo great expense and effort to elevate their bodies to the state of gorgeous, and so feel justified in frowning upon others who do not "go and do likewise."

My experience has been that some people feel free to be as rude as they please to chunkies such as myself. One self-appointed wit asked me, "When was the last time you saw your *feet*?" And though I detest violence, I was forced to reply, "The last time I kicked a wiseguy in the butt." My response to those who object to my blithe acceptance of my own appearance is simple: I believe it was Shakespeare who once said: "Tough Titties."

That same evening, (The Night of the Living Closet) we all went to the theatre, and then to dinner, which was where *it* happened. Now, dinner conversation with a group of lesbian sisters and gay brothers ideally ranges from passionate discussion of meaningful subjects to heart-gratifying gossip and significant bitchery. The restaurant was pleasant, tastefully decorated by gifted gay hands; the food was excellent, spirits high. Let me give you a cast of characters and then toss you into it so you can make up *your* mind about what happened. I need an *un*biased opinion. You've already met Benedict Arnold, whose *real* name is Perry, a paralegal who bears more than a passing resemblance to Marky Mark and could model for other than legal briefs if he wanted to. I was to meet some of his friends for the first time.

You remember Ronnie, (who runneth and sweateth not, neither doth he tire), and his sister Kay, whose fancy-schmancy Psych Major will not help her win friends and influence dumpy people if she keeps up that "he should lose a little weight" routine. Also present was Edward, whose styled, formed, and microclipped mustache looked oddly false, as though it had fallen off the face where it really belonged and landed on Edward's by accident.

Lon, a young man acquired earlier by Edward, for some temporary company, wore a muscle shirt (complete with muscles) and dazzling white cords that matched the candlepower of his equally dazzling white teeth.

Harvey was an accountant who'd failed an assertiveness training class. When his lover found out and laughed, Harvey smacked him in the face, asserting himself right out of a relationship. He wore an "I can't even THINK straight" T-shirt and designer jeans embroidered with sequins in select places. His hair was cut assertively short, and his mustache was long and exquisitely tailored, as though he sent it out frequently for alterations and dry cleaning.

Then there was Desmond. Had he been a knight of the round table he'd have been dubbed "Sir Desmond of the Perfect Shirt." A Marlboro Man, he sported a tastefully greying coif that gave new meaning to the words, "not a hair out of place." (There really wasn't. Not a one. I looked and looked.) Desmond's belt defied gravity by laying perfectly in the center of the belt loops of his slacks, sliding neither up nor down no matter how he moved. The creases in his slacks were supernaturally sharp; a person could shear off a limb on even casual contact with such creases. And the shirt—we're talking a shirt touched by the gods, not a wrinkle in it, not even where it slid with abandoned perfection into his slacks. It fit *more* perfectly than skin, since skin wrinkles eventually and Desmond's shirt would do nothing of the sort—ever.

Then there was me, resembling two of the lesser-known dwarves, Dumpy and Frumpy, wearing one of my comfy, self-designed shirts, black sweat pants (I intend to be buried in them), longish hair (showing no ear, and a complete stranger to the ministrations of West Hollywood stylists), and my beard, formless and wandering over the deservedly hidden terrain of my face. By the main course, the talk had gone from Siskel and Ebert-ing the play we'd just seen (none of the fingers that went up were thumbs) to the merits of pure silk sheets, and from gay marriage possibly being legalized in Hawaii, to making West Hollywood a truly gay town. By dessert, I'd caused a small tempest, and by the coffee and Sweet 'N' Low course, I was a prime candidate for lynching. To hear *them* tell it I was "cruising for a bruising," ready for an altercation, having not gotten over being suddenly called forty years old for no good reason. *You* tell *me . . .* Let's pick up on Desmond speaking, his perfect shirt molding to his every move: "So I told him West Hollywood *should* be independent *and* proud."

"Really!" Harvey chimed in. "Enough of this hetero bullshit dragging their feet on housing rights and—"

"Never mind all that," Edward chirped, "did you know that Carl and his lover—what *was* his name?! *You* know Harvey, the beach blanket body with the huuuge—"

"*Billy!*" Harvey replied just in time to keep this piece from offending the NEA.

"Oh, right. *Billy.* Well! Carl and this Billy were *evicted* for just *being* gay!"

"*And* for giving lively parties into the wee hours. Every night," Harvey added. Harvey believes honesty is the best politics.

"I think the landlord just used that as an excuse."

Desmond shook his perfectly coiffed head. "Well, that won't happen in the *new* West Hollywood."

Lon agreed. "Yeah! Everything'll be like one big awesome *par*ty!" There was a beat of silence, during which and afterward poor Lon was generally ignored.

"So," my pal Perry pursued paralegally, "no housing discrimination at all, eh?"

Edward answered, "Just against *straights!* Show *them* what it feels like. We should evict *them* for *breeding!*"

Turning to Perry, I muttered, "Original thinking, lavender neo-Nazi." I never meant anyone to actually hear me. (No, really.) Edward snorted, as though he was about to hurl a mucus missile in my direction. Wisely, however, he did not actually do so.

Perry said to me out loud and plainly, "Shut up, dear. Please. Personal favor."

But Desmond was on a roll. "The point *is*, we have to make a statement to the community. On *every* level. Professional, personal . . . *every* way."

I asked him innocently (I swear), "How do you do *that?*"

Desmond warmed to his subject. "Well, people watch us, you know? How we live, dress, act. So we need to *present* ourselves in the best possible light."

Recalling my entrapment earlier that evening, I ventured, "You mean like coming out of the closet?"

"Oh, that's just the bare minimum. We've *got* to be totally out and visible. Well, except for drag or leather queens. People need to see us at work, at play, looking as normal and straight as *they* do. Being politically active—"

Lon volunteered some information freely, "I *voted* once!"

Desmond darted an exasperated look at Edward, muttering, "Can't you keep that piece of fluff quiet?"

There were *two* beats of silence this time from everyone at the table while I patted Lon on the back in approval and said, "Don't tell us *who* you voted *for*, Lon. That'd be like telling your wish after you blow out your birthday candles."

"Wow," he answered, impressed, "thanks for stopping me in time."

Edward scooped up the conversational ball with, "Well, having our own city will make a *big* difference."

Ronnie grinned. "Haven't you heard? We already *had* our own city! San Francisco!"

While the rest of us laughed, Lon seemed confused. "When did they give us San Francisco?"

I tried to help out. "The Republicans turned it over to us when they heard there'd be another major earthquake there. *Ouch.*" (The "*ouch*" was due to a well-aimed kick under the table from Perry, who, I'll point out, is Republican.) (There, Per, now the *world* knows.)

"Gene, you sound a little flippant about this," Desmond said, eyebrow lifting ominously. Perry didn't give me a chance to reply, he just shot me. But only with his eyes, while telling Desmond, "Gene is flippant about *every*thing."

Lon asked innocently, "What's 'flippen'?"

I answered as innocently, "Perry is."

Lon just said, "Oh."

Like the fake nails on TV, Desmond pressed on: "Actually, Gene, I don't think it would do you any harm to do some, well, personal assessment."

"Anybody seen any good *movies* lately?" Perry asked everyone, a little too loudly.

"Desmond, are you referring to my political views?" I asked, all wounded dignity.

"Those I don't know about. I meant, your, uh, appearance. Your uh, clothes for example."

"You wouldn't criticize my clothes if you knew what they *spared* you from seeing."

At that point Perry used his famous patented warning tone: "*Geee*-ne. A *grip* is called for at this time."

"Well, no offense, of course—" Desmond began weakly.

"Of *course*—" I said, sounding maybe a tad unconvinced.

Desmond, perhaps foolishly, went on: "but, uh, it's actually not just your clothes. Um, for example, you *could* do a little more with your hair. And, there's your uh, *weight*. Don't *you* think you would impress people more if you made an effort to be more attractive, stylish . . . "

"Keep going," I urged, "you're liable to hit an adjective that fits me yet."

Perry interjected *so* helpfully, "How about 'obnoxious'?"

"Bingo!" I crowed. "But I wanted Desmond to guess it."

"No offense, Gene," Desmond reiterated with possible undertones of guilt, "but gay men are supposed to be very fashion and looks conscious, you know?"

I patted him on the arm. "Okay, I'll start telling everyone I'm a lesbian. That'll let *you* guys off the hook and the only one I have to worry about now is Kay, and I can beat *her* up."

"Not on your best day, buster." I don't have to tell you who said *that*. As soon as I mentioned the word "lesbian," Kay playfully tossed a sticky bun at me. (I *think* it was playfully. Anyway, I dodged it, and it hit Edward so that turned out okay.)

I added, "Tomorrow I'll start Richard Simmons' 'Swishing to the Old-ies'. Now can I look a mess in peace?" And I really wanted that to be the end of it. (No, really.) It was Desmond who forged onward into the valley of death. "But don't you have any desire to improve yourself? Look better? *feel* good? *Date* more often?"

"You sound like a Hair Club For Men commercial, Desmond."

Ronnie interposed on my behalf, "But, Desmond, Gene dates all the time! And with really good-looking guys! *I* always ask him what's his secret."

After a shocked pause, Desmond fumfered: "Well, I mean, the *point* is, he's making such a negative statement by looking so, so—"

Okay, there *are* limits. I said, "*Care*ful Des, if history teaches us any-thing, it's that many people have been slain over unfortunate choices of adjectives."

Luckily, Lon gave us the benefit of his youthful taste by playfully ruffling my lengthy locks and saying, "Geez, guys, *I* think Gene looks *Rad*! Like this major Teddy Bear." This did not help my case with Desmond, but I smiled my thanks at Lon anyway. I am infrequently referred to as looking "Rad," (though I *have* suffered the Teddy Bear thing before). Still, no point looking a gift compliment in the mouth.

Rather wistfully, Perry murmured, "Anybody read any good *books* lately?"

Never one to have it said about him that he could take a hint, Desmond continued boldly where few have dared to go before. "But Gene, don't you see that the statements we make individually speak for us as a *group!* One rotten apple can spoil—"

"Anyone for more *cake?*" Perry offered feverishly. There were no takers except Lon who cheerfully extended his plate for another slab of sugar buzz. I decided it was no longer worth it to give peace a chance.

"Desmond, let me tell you a little something." I raised my voice *just* a little to be heard over Perry's groaning. (He sounded like his water just broke.) "I believe in truth in advertising. As Popeye used to say, 'I yam what I yam.' What *you* might wish to chew on if you ever take a break from your role as schoolmarm, is that every area of our lives doesn't need to be submitted for the approval of some self-appointed Image Police, straight *or* gay. Get a clue here, you Gay Goebbels. I didn't fight like hell against being homogenized by the *straight* world only to let some gay, buff, big brother determine what I have to look like."

"Goebbels? *Goebbels?*" repeated Desmond tiresomely.

"Get a grip, Des, you sound like a turkey. And it isn't the *first* time this evening! Why do we protest physical gay bashing by straights but then bash each other psychologically over something as transitory as looks? Not every gay man has to make his entrance to 'Send In The *Clones*.'"

"Cool," said Lon, "I *love* that song!" There was a great gust of silence from everyone else though. Desmond sat there with his every hair in place and still not a wrinkle in his shirt, but somehow the very *air* around him ruffled. He finally said, "Are you implying that I'm a *clone?*"

"Why, good rollicking *heav*ens, Des! You? A *clone?* When *you* were made they threw away the *mold*." (I felt safe making this remark because it's only when written down and spelled out that it can be proven to be an insult.)

Desmond criticized me for my attitude of callous indifference to the, shall we say, negative visual impact I have on my environment. But I've got quite a few friends of the gorgeous persuasion who've overcome whatever aversion they might've had to being seen with me in public, and they don't seem any the worse for wear. And every time I nurse a gorgeous friend of mine through his or her latest broken heart due to a case of the decrepit blues, I count my chubby little blessings. *You* know how the decrepit blues go, don't you? Something like this:

The phone rings at six in the a.m. I have been in deep, luxuriant sleep for two hours and have to disentangle myself from my dreams, pillows, sheets, and companion in order to say something like, "Hmmoh?"

I hear: "Gene! Can I come over right away? You are *not* going to be*lieve* what just happened to me!" I visualize a 747 jumbo jet crashlanded and still smoking in gorgeous' living room. I'm wrong about this. I've failed to grasp the true extent of the tragedy. Gorgeous continues: "I found a *wrinkle!* On *my face!* Can you be*lieve* it? Nothing covers it *up!* What am I gonna *do?* Can I just come *over* for a while? I don't think I can be *alone* at a time like this! Maybe you could help me go through the phone book and find a good plastic surgeon? Gene, what's it gonna be next, *age spots? You believe in God; what kind of God would let a thing like this* happen?"

I answer: "Uh . . . who *is* this?"

Maybe it's because I will never be mistaken for Richard Gere that my suddenly deteriorating gorgeous friends assume I am the most likely to understand and have words of wisdom for them on how to cope with looking like Quasimodo's cousin. But I personally think that looks are *not* (he said with rip-roaring originality) everything. And those who think they *are* everything are often shocked at how fast "everything" fritters away to "nothing." Like it or not, muscles mush up, definition droops, "lats" go flat, barrel chests roll ever downward; all your spare tires are *not* in the trunk of your car, and "laugh lines" become less than hysterically funny. Although diamonds are forever, the dappled freshness of a Gorgeous Face is often superceded in value by the ability to make truly great popcorn with which to curl up together and watch *Plan 9 From Outer Space* for the fortieth time.

As long as nature (or expensive supplements *to* nature) has allowed a rift to occur in our ranks between the "hunks" and the "chunks," we have a choice: we can allow ourselves to *be* categorized and to categorize each other into one group or the other, *or* we can relax and be happy with *who* and *what* we are and look like—while at the same time freely acknowledging that others have the very same right. If you *want* to lose weight, gain weight, style your hair, wear designer jock straps, lift weights, lift faces, sculpt your points and plugs, or simply just leave it all the hell alone—*do it!* If *you're* not happy with what you have, change it if you can. If you *are* happy with what you have and somebody else *isn't,* as the case might be with our looksist siblings who insist on hob-*s*nobbing only with their "Body By Fischer" peers, then you may quote me quoting Shakespeare again: "Tough Titties." We aren't on this planet long enough to waste our time dancing on the end of *any*one's strings. The right and privilege to like ourselves as we are, and others as *they* are, is ours to exercise every day. And *that's* a kind of exercise even *I* can get into. (Maybe the *only* kind . . .)

And *that's* basically what I said to the retreating back of Desmond and his shirt that night, ending with the part about the titties. But to hear *them* tell it, I preached a sermon.

Gee. Maybe I did. Oh, well. *No*body's perfect. So *I* say, "people who live in tin houses shouldn't throw can openers."

Reps

Jim Provenzano

They're sticking their heads through a cardboard cartoon of a muscle guy with their own skinny heads on top. It's a picture I saw on TV or in a dream. No, that's not me, is it? Naturally curved and tight. I'm liking it. Come here every other day. It's good. Should come more. Be big soon enough, if I don't die first. If I'm already dying, I won't get big. Keep working to get big while I waste away, like climbing a greased pole. Pole. Rod. Dick. Guys looking at me. Supposed to cruise a guy and pretend you don't care at the same time.

Funny T-shirts get me chatting with guys. Sharing a bench helps. Gotta work with a guy who's doing your weight range. Beauties are all over at the free weights. Wimps. Ha. Me, who used to pass out in gym class now pumping iron and calling guys wimps. Ha. Me, with gloves and a weight lifting belt. Ha. Wait till Christmas. No, better I should go home in the summer. Show off my bod. The farts who pushed me around getting beer-gut fat and hating their wives. Me getting harder. Ha. Not for them. For me. For the Italian guy over there with amazing pecs. Another rep of lat pulls while I zoom in on one leg hair of his thigh. Waiting for my tongue. Eight. Just to lick his. Nine. Thigh. Ten. He walks over to the barbells, does forty pounds on the incline. Me at twenty-five. Gotta rate before you mate. No pecs, no sex. His shorts, like the lifeguards at Rehobeth Beach. Faded red cotton, baggy, soft, with a light crotch smell, I imagine. His legs are skinny. My legs are bigger than his. That's because I'm a running faggot. He probably hauls TVs for a living, works on his tits like a real man. Looks at me. Doesn't turn away. A good sign. Don't rush it. He goes to the drinking fountain. Don't go. He'll be back. He'll always be here afternoons. He's devoted. Commited. Endorphin junkie.

Shoulder press. Gotta get big. Seventy pounds? Pin in. Shiny bricks, layered. Stick the pin in. Smile like a geek at any joke that'll get me through this torture. And one. That blond is watching me. Two. This weight's too light. No matter. I look cool. Threeee. Was he in a movie? Looks away. Fooooour. I'm not standing right. Fiiiiive. Is he looking at me? No. Fine. Siiiix. I like it when my veins pop out. It's all going into my forearms. Seveeennn. I'll end up like Popeye. Breathe out and distribute the labor. Aaaand. Won't look like Popeye. Two more. Niiiiine. Get big. Urgh. Tee-clunk!

Nobody saw that. I'm cool. Stand back. "No, sure, go 'head. I'm through." He probably saw me drop it. But he's lowering the weight. Ha. I'm tough. Getting big. This will get me a big neat guy. We'll work out together. Be buddies. Fuck buddies. Only we won't fuck. Can't fuck anymore. Gotta stay healthy. Don't think about sex anymore today. Drink water. Eight glasses a day. Sweat. Guys with towels wiping off the seats. Afraid of sweat. Who's straight here? Anyone? Would whoever's straight please raise your hand so we can hunt in an orderly fashion? Next year a gayer gym. No. No fun. No adventure. The furtive glance. Could mean romance. Ah, Janet Jackson on the radio. Work harder with good music.

Dips. Climb up. I'm good at this. Up higher. People naturally watch. One. Now I'm in control. Twoo—oops, can't do it with the music. Too fast. Hate that. Three. My legs are swinging too much. Steady. Firm. Make my lips tight, like Robert Conrad. Yeah, *Wild, Wild West,* pulling myself out of some dastardly machine. Just a body like his. No freak pecs, just nice. Wait. Four? Nine? Lost count. Somebody's waiting. Go till fatigue. Up. Down. I'm cheating. Not going down all the way. Wish Max would come and help me. Big beefy German trainer. Amazing. How long? Up. Before I'm big as you, cupcake? Down. Hop down. Time? Can I leave yet? 5:35. Quit at six. Two hours. Bigger guys spend less time. I'll catch up. Making up for lost . . . no. Six. Yes. Breathe. Look around. Fat guy on a bicycle. Good for him. Grind. Grind. Look at the Italian guy, his beautiful brown pecs peeking out from the frayed edges of that sweatshirt. Sleeves cut off. Busting out all over. What is he doing? He's feeling his own pecs. Making sure it's working. He looks at me again. Turn away. He's probably pissed I'm staring. Hates coming here because of all the homos. Or loves it. Goes home with a different guy every night. Or maybe just one guy he keeps locked up who worships him like a moving shrine— STOP. The right time will come. He wants me, he'll say it. His chest and my legs. Together they'd make one perfect body. Of course then there'd be a real wimp left over from the trade. Ridiculous. Imagine telling him in bed. He'd laugh. Right after he's shot all over my new chest. Soon to arrive. How long? How many hours lifting metal? Two months? SEE RESULTS! A cartoon. Become addicted to megavitamins and protein powders? Just wanna be proud. Proud enough not to have to think about what my T-shirt should say at Gay Pride, since I won't even wear a shirt. Become my own logo. My face doesn't go with the muscles. My face fits a lanky body. No. That's negativity. An excuse. I'm not even tired. WEIGHT

LIFTING IS AN ANAEROBIC EXERCISE. COMPLIMENT YOUR WORKOUT WITH AEROBICS. The sign. Right over the drinking fountain. Bullshit. Ain't burning a calorie that I can turn into a muscle instead. No need to lose weight. Swim. Yes. Should have joined a club with a pool. Next year. All these clubs are too tiny, scummy. Don't know what's in them. Is this part of the workout? Work myself into a shell? Exoskeleton of muscle fiber?

Tricep curls. Ninety pounds. Ten reps. Do it. Enjoy it. Hup. Up to ninety. I'm such a show-off. Window view. People down in the street actually walking while I'm pulling a bunch of metal blocks up and down. S-e-e-even. Don't think like that. Cute guy waiting for me to finish. Don't get exhausted. Don't grunt. So stupid, guys who grunt. Breathe. Stare at the geek who did grunt. That one there. Smooth. Shaves his butt sometimes. The muscles are right. Play it cool, babe. I don't grunt. Don't mess my face up like some guys, grimace so hard they smile. Smile through the pain. Spaz all over. Don't work the muscle smooth. Not me. Max taught me right. Kip ze stummik down. Touch me, Max. In here. I wanna be your muscle dog.

Back to work. Do it for Max. Do it for the Italian guy. Do it for the blond who was in a movie. Do it for a photographer. Do it for your future boyfriend, whichever machine he's at. Do it for yourself, maybe, even.

Incline flies next. Start easy. Fifteen pounds. The big guys have bigger weights. Calm down. They've been at it a while. They don't care. "You using this bench? Thanks." Sit. Breathe. Set the weights on my knees. Cool shiny metal machines. Strap ourselves in. Peel the metal poles off and there'd be chocolate. Silly. Concentrate. Scoot back. Share the bench. Head, shoulders, upper back lying on the bench. Ass free. Look up at the ceiling. White dial. Gas light fixture a hundred years ago. Your sun for the day. Pump. Pray to it. Push your crotch up. Steady. Arms up, and . . . one . . . Somebody standing nearby. Twoo. Don't look over. Three. You're doing fine. Foooour. He's admiring me. Five. He's just waiting to use the bench. Glance over. Siiix. It's him. Red shorts. The Italian guy. Seven. Losing it. Standing over me, just like as if we were in bed. Eight. Don't lose it. Look back up at the ceiling. Nine. His leg inches away. Ten. He's lifting his shirt to wipe his face. The stomach. Clunk!

Shit. Sit up. Don't let it roll on his foot! Sit up. "Sorry. No, I'm done." He's waiting.

"Trade reps?"

"Sure." Flood of adrenaline. This I like. Buddy systems. As long as it doesn't get competitive. No tension. He didn't bother to wipe off my sweat. Good sign. His curls ringed, glistening with sweat. Italian fresco. Tanned.

Florida? No. Bermuda? Maybe. The Pines. I'm pale. Wish my hair was black like his. Or blond like the movie actor. He still here? Who cares. "Done? Thanks." Sit. Do it again. He watches. Admiring? Checking. Ghosts of gym classes past. Urgh. Pick it up.

"Keep your arms even," he says, touching me.

Thanks. Ooo, I like helpful corrections. Probably means he'll wanna be on top in bed. No. Equal. It's gotta be equal. No guru boyfriends, no power play. But would he be worth getting it and not giving it?

"Better," he says. Thanks. Three. A possibility. The whole deal. What if he's straight? Probably a real jerk. Water. "Be right back." Leave. The drinking fountain. Walking on the new carpet. Soft. The fountain by the desk. Cute guy ahead guzzles water. My turn. Press. Giggling tube of water shot in my mouth. Swallow. Go back. Don't stall. Walking back. Pretzeled grid of metal tubes and leather seats. The arena.

Back to the bench. Italian guy's still there. Some other guy waiting to get on. Get on him. Or in him. No, he just wants to use the bench, I guess. Not me. Warm Caravaggio eyes. Big arms. No ass. Most of the guys here not working on their asses or legs. Great uppers. Half-inflated circus balloons. Hot dogs. Clowns making balloons. Cartoon from a drive-in: IT'S REFRESHMENT TIME! Hot dogs diving into buns.

Time? Five to six. Two hours. Good enough. Won't come overnight. And neither will he. Another look at the Italian. He's doing curls. Back turned. Soon. Strut into a bar. Strut down the street. Watch the eyes. No cares except sore all over. Always sore. Enjoy. Feel the factories in the veins.

Locker room. Moist warm air. Damp carpet. Locker. Take off my shirt while . . . oops. The combination. 14-4 . . . ? Check the Asics. Written on the inside. 4-14-28. Right. Do it slow. Damn lock. Doesn't work. Must be mine. All the locks look the same. Cheap. Master. Black. Leather cap.

Chlunk.

Open. Love that sound. A locker opening. Like the first beer can on a Friday night. Like a car door slamming. Like a full fridge heavy with all kinds of food. The door slamming shut. Chlunk.

Peel off my shirt. Warm salty sweat. Toss it in. Wait. Put it on the bottom. Get out the towel. Sneakers off. Getting damn near naked now. Anybody watching me strip? Anybody interested? Cute guy over there. Fat Hasidim guy nearby. Both looking. Shuck off the shorts and the strap. Slow down. Enjoy this. Be cool and as unsexual as possible even though just smelling myself makes me think the warmest, sexiest thoughts.

STOP. Don't pull a boner. Think of dead people. Tragic events. Reagan, hate, dead people. Hang your towel up. Walk bare feet over the clammy tile. Turn the water on. Cold. Keep it that way. Don't look at the tall, lean guy over there, sudsing up his . . . Jesus, is he half hard or is that his real dick?

STOP. Think of money you owe. Trip back home next month. Airfare. Planes. Airport restrooms.

STOP. Cold water's doing the trick. Freezing, good, that'll keep it down. But then I think of that porn movie with the guy jacking off in the waterfall. Freezing cold and him hard as a rock.

STOP. Easier to hide in the sauna with a bone, but how long can I hide in all that steam? Might meet that guy from *Tales of the City,* when his butt shows, just at the door . . .

STOP IT. Whistle. Yes, that should do it. Singing requires concentration. Now I'm in control. Shrink, little wonder weapon. Tilt my head back, like Warren Beatty in *Splendor in the Grass*. Fine. Being admired won't give up a boner. Open my eyes, get relaxed, and look who's coming into the shower. The Italian guy! Stark naked, his legs so hairy, his dick cut so nice, friendly bouncing dick and balls tucked under and pecs like turkey dinner. Jesus, he's smiling at me. I'm getting a boner for sure. Quick gesture of return, offer him my shower. Here you go.

"Thanks, guy."

Yes, whoo, yes. Enough. Exit. You're exiting. Your dick's getting conspicuous. He sees it. Smiles. Uh oh. The towel. Wipe, wipe, scrub. Think of dead people. Think of gramma, rotting in her grave. Being admired in the doorway. Let him watch. Saved. Quick, to the locker. 44. Sit. No. 4, 14. Think. 28.

Chlunk.

Ah, my stuff, still there. Relax. Stand and dry off. Yeah, no problem now. Get the jeans. Nobody's really looking. That first contact of denim. Get that skin back on. Dry and safe. Well, almost dry. Dick's comfortable, back in his place. Stand around nonchalantly with the zipper down. Fingers through the hair. Yes. Enjoy the scene, the festivities. Where's the Italian guy? Still in the showers. Dinner with him, movies, corny dates, holding hands, sucking cock, going too far. He can't be sick. He looks so healthy.

Get my shirt. Slip it on my new body. One more inch on the chest and I'm perfect, according to that magazine chart. Was that perfect or average? Dressing, undressing, a ballet of personal strippers. Cadmus tableau.

Got everything? Everything. No one to walk up and ask for a phone number? No one to walk with? Not today. What makes one dick better? Safer. Shooting sperm. Might as well be acid. Turn, leave, catch the Italian guy just leaving the shower. No, I'm not going to wait for you. I'm too busy trying to catch up. Wait for hours when you're late for a dinner date, sit by the phone like a pathetic teenager reading *Glamour,* wait for you to come with me as you slide your wonderfully average-sized cock in and out of me, watching your abs and lats flex and release as you cry out like a baby falling down stairs as your acid shoots into the little rubber dam with me on the other end. I will wait for you to say the first words, to ask the questions, to come up with the right opener, but I'm not gonna wait for you to get dressed. Not today. I know I don't rate today. In a month. In a year. I will rate. And when that time comes, I will charm the pants off you.

Your Dreamworld
Is Just About to End

Frank Martinez Lester

No amount of make-believe can help this heart of mine. An unde-servedly popular dream dictionary has it that a dream of gaining weight means different things depending on your sex. If you are a man, it means you are getting freedom. If you are a woman, it means you are losing a lover. Setting aside the gender-specific absurdity of the distinction, I won-der what such a dream would mean for a gay man or a lesbian. This is the tug of war in the world of sexual identity: it would probably mean both things at the same time because the gay man is ambivalence personified.

* * *

He is the wanderer, even more now than he was in the 1970s. He wanders in and out of bars and coffeehouses and gymnasiums and parks, looking for his double to conquer. At the same time, he hopes he does not find him. He does not want to lose the ability and the urge to conquer. And with it, the urge to wander: the idea of settling down is as noxious as the smell of gasoline fumes. We are the fickle ones. Our heartbeats synchro-nize themselves to the footstep of the prettiest boy to come in our line of vision, even if what walked in two minutes ago was just as pretty, just as porcelain-skinned, just as sculpted, just as exotic, just as bulimarexic. Our love pours itself out for the smallest possible percentage. It is like a food chain in reverse, with the plankton wagging the tail of the whale. We are the fickle ones. We gain freedom, we lose love. Repeated over and over, this dance becomes the *pas seul* in an increasingly chimerical ballet.

* * *

I stand in for many things. I am the other. I am the victim, the plotter, the predator, the subverter. I am the satyr, the slut, the sinner. I am the destroyer of the nuclear family, the unbridled exhibitionist, the glory hole patron, the friend of chiffon and organdy. I am Bacchus, Herod, Wilde, Divine. I rape, whip, plunder, pillage, laugh, mince, ride the stationary bike, order a Bloody Mary, throw a limp wrist. I am fickle. I am faggy, ferocious, fun, fantastic in bed, fiddler on the roof. I stand in for everything that the world at large wants to use to define the homosexual male. But when I turn to look at myself in the mirror, I stare right into a field of pointing fingers and snickering lips. Even among my own kind I am the other. There are too many of us trying to be the same thing. Difference gets transformed into dichotomy. Otherness becomes a zoo attraction. I turn from the mirror and walk away.

*   *   *

Statistics are curious as fuck. One of five gay men belongs to a gym or health club. Also, one of five gay men is an alcoholic. How do these numbers overlap? How many gay men are in both categories? How many gay men go to the gym to inflate their muscles and then head for the nearest bar? What emotions are at play when I work out and then pound down? Who am I trying to impress? Dare I look at the dark side of gay life? Jeremiads, after all, are so uncool. They are so tired, so unfunny, so predictable. Lord knows that a gay man without a sense of humor is like a clipper without sails. *Get over yourself, girlfriend.*

*   *   *

If it is true, as Michelangelo says, that beauty is the purgation of all that is superfluous, the gay community is in serious need of a fashion make-over.

*   *   *

I change to fit circumstance. I become what is desired, or demanded; or else I escape the desire, escape the demand. In college, this meant giving female dorm mates stuffed unicorns and roses and then retreating glumly to my journal to scribble about the hot, bursting crotch of the guy in shorts I had just seen lounging on the common room sofa. Ten years later, this means walking down Castro Street with my gut sucked in wearing an oversized shirt. It means a gym membership to which I stand in relation in the same way that a Catholic stands in relation to the confession booth. I turn from the mirror and walk away.

*   *   *

His body was firm and muscular—not a hulking muscularity, but a solid frame packed with rockhard pecs, broad shoulders, and a wide, muscular back that gave way to the most gorgeous set of cut-up abs that I have ever seen. Over and over again we are bombarded with the representations that come from the beauty myth—the cock that goes for days, the chest as big as K2, the butt worth bronzing and hanging over the fireplace like a bear's head, the insatiable sex drive that sweeps you off your feet into an ocean of forgetful ecstasy. These are the myths that I and my brethren hold like cherished boxed jewels in the back of our heads when we walk up Christopher Street, through Dupont Circle, into West Hollywood. We throng the bars as though time never ends. We look around for doppelgängers and are confronted with aliens. "Life is short," wrote the late John Preston in a letter to Andrew Holleran in 1990, "and you should be taking advantage of its gifts when they occur."[1] But is life as short as a roller-coaster ride? What is out there that is not already within myself? Who is paying attention to what is going on? There is such a thing as the slippery slope, and we are closer to it than we think.

*   *   *

"Every man bears the whole stamp of the human condition," wrote Montaigne.[2] We ignore that proverb at our own peril. I was on Market Street the other day and was flagged down by an indigent. He said that he had codged only six cents in the past hour. It was the height of afternoon; the sun was out bright; and the sidewalk was crowded with people, including many laughing gay couples, hand in hand. While the bum could have been lying, and while the couples I saw could have been fresh from handing other bums on other corners substantial portions of their disposable change, I doubt it. We wonder why the stereotype arises that we are airheaded money-burners with more cash than we know what to do with. Although that stereotype is demonstrably false, acts beget images. We grow our bulked-out, pretty-boy bodies off the sweat of those beneath us on the ladder of privilege. And we stomp their heads as we scurry up it trying to acquire as many track lights and money market funds as all the straight DINKs in Sausalito.

*   *   *

Statistics are curious as fuck. We conform without thinking why we conform. We shape ourselves to fit circumstance. We do not command it; we fall under its thrall. Coming and going through each day and week, we lose a bit more of our link with the rest of humanity and become as much of a ghetto as the men with gavels in courtrooms and conference rooms across the country want us to be. We disregard the evidence of the world around us, even when that evidence is as close as a tattered wreck in front of one of our ghetto's bars. We dash into the coffeehouses and dish the boys over cappuccino. We wax rhapsodic over the Brazilian waiter's huge biceps; we notice how they burst out of his crisp white T-shirt sleeves like watermelons. We shake our heads when we read about the latest fagbashing. We are strangely confident that it will never happen to us. We hang out of the front windows of the bars on Sunday mornings like Persian cats in a solarium, waiting for something enticing to cross our paths.

*   *   *

We pretend that nobody is out to get us. *No amount of make-believe can help this heart of mine.* We will be safe, we reason, as long as we stay in our ghetto and do not push ourselves in the world's face. We win liberty. We lose love. We wander, looking for something we cannot quite place our fingers on. Jeremiads are so uncool. But *Kristallnacht* is sooner than we dream.

NOTES

1. Holleran, Andrew. "Preston." *Christopher Street,* 215, July 1994, p. 4.

2. Montaigne, Michel. *The Essays: A Selection.* Translated and edited by M.A. Screech. New York: Penguin Books, 1987, p. 233.

Learning the F Words

John Stoltenberg

THE FIRST F WORD I LEARNED WAS "FATSO"

I grew up a fat kid. I was tall for my age and way overweight. I was teased and picked on by older boys in the suburban neighborhood where my family lived. "Fatty, fatty, two-by-four, can't get through the bathroom door." The sing-song taunt stings like yesterday.

"Husky" was the euphemism for clothes my size in the Sears and Roebuck catalog. My corduroy pants always eroded to shreds where my thighs rubbed together, and by the time I got to junior high school I could not run a quarter-mile in gym class without throwing up.

My mother taught me to suck in my stomach—I can't recall exactly how, but I must have been very young, five or six. My mother also grew up fat, so in a way for her it was like passing on a grooming tip, a subtle way to conceal a few pounds. The lesson stuck; and almost involuntarily now, I keep my abdominal muscles held in.

My well-meaning mother also realized that I needed some vigorous physical activity to offset my otherwise vegetative interests. Sports were not to my taste; I much preferred imaginative play with puppets, my toy circus, magic tricks, and the like. So when I was five my mother sent me to dancing school, where I was not only the fattest kid in class but also the only male one. I took ballet and acrobatics at first, and rather enjoyed it. I especially got a kick out of the annual dancing school recitals. Within a few years my dancing teacher—the elegant and gray-coiffed Miss Phillips—intelligently advanced me to tap, a choreographic form in which my heavy footfalls could be put to some purpose. I had fun. I liked dressing up and performing.

I have a set of recital pictures showing me in various costumes—jester, snowman, cowboy, tuxedo—and at various proportions of body fat from the age of five to the age of fourteen. Flipping through that pile of photos, it's like watching me go through puberty on stage—now plump, now plumper, always smiling like a trouper and surrounded by dancing girls.

I LEARNED THE WORD "FUCK"
WITHOUT A CLUE WHAT IT MEANT

Throughout my early years in primary school, I always played with girls at recess. I remember one game in particular because we played it endlessly. A bunch of us would line up perpendicular to the school building with the last kid's back against the brick wall and the rest of us in a tightly packed row, each kid's front against another's backside. The kid at the head of the line had no one in front, until rhythmically we would chant, "Squish! squash! apple! sauce!" On each accented syllable, the whole row of us would bounce our collective weight backward against the kid nearest the wall. "Squish! squash! apple! sauce! Squish! squash! apple! sauce!" On each shout of "sauce!," the bouncing backward would become more intense. Then and only then did the kid against the wall have the option to duck out and take the place at the head of the line.

I have no idea why I was welcomed into this playful piling on, which was almost exclusively a girls' game. Roughhousing boys weren't interested anyway, I suppose; they tended to tear around, play ball, or climb on the jungle gym. And I don't recall any feelings during it other than fun, laughter, and physical acceptance. No one ever got hurt—that wasn't what we were trying to do.

Looking back (now that my sexuality has ostensibly "matured"), I can't imagine that a child's sex play could be more subliminally vanilla—at least with clothes on and in a public place. But I was as naive as they come. Front-to-butt, "Squish! squash! apple! sauce!"—the game went on and on, and I can't remember experiencing any specifically sexual sensations. Actually I can't recall any sexual feelings at all at that age.

What I do remember vividly is one day when we were playing as usual and we found a rude graffito on the school brick wall. Scrawled there in chalk where we always played "Squish Squash" were the words EAT ME FUCK YOU.

I'd never heard the word "fuck" in my life, and I had no idea what it meant. Some of the girls laughed knowingly, and so did other boys. The joke was somehow anatomical, I supposed, but beyond that I was in the dark.

I knew what "eat" meant—*to eat food,* of course. So what's the opposite of eating?—well, I deduced, that must be *to go to the bathroom number two.* So, in my mind, the vulgar scrawl translated: "Eat me, shit you." I'm sure I never said that out loud (I didn't even know the word "shit" yet). I just remember gaily laughing along, all the while thinking the naughty joke was about bodily elimination of solid waste.

One day at recess in late spring, in my second grade, my whole class was supposed to play an organized game of baseball. For some reason the teacher made us, all the boys and girls together. I had never played any kind of ball before in my life. Never played catch. Never practiced batting. Didn't even know the rules. So when I was up to bat and accidentally connected with a ball that was pitched in my direction, *I didn't know you were supposed to run anywhere.* I didn't know what first base *was,* much less that I should *get* to it. So there I stood, momentarily stunned and humiliated by other kids' jeers, until, frantically coaxed, I lumbered along in the direction of first base. Before I got there I was "out," owing to other boys' athletic prowess.

One day in fifth grade, my dreaded phy ed teacher—a balding, thick-necked, pot-bellied sadist named Mr. Sohaki—gave all the boys a health lecture while the girls were ushered off someplace else. It was a completely new experience to me and mostly inscrutable. Mouths agape, we boys sat quietly on the gymnasium floor as gruff Mr. Sohaki drew words and diagrams on a blackboard.

Afterward, at recess, another boy came up to me and we sat and talked on a grassy bank by the playground. He was much shorter than me, lithe and lean, dark-haired, a runt compared to our age mates, but to me he seemed good at sports and a real athletic boy. Billy, his name was. He sat behind me in class, and though he and I rarely spoke, I remember liking him. It turned out that on this particular afternoon, Billy was also perplexed by Mr. Sohaki's chalk talk. Mr. Sohaki had told us the word "scrotum," for instance, and wrote it on the board so we wouldn't forget.

"What do you think a scrotum is for?" Billy asked me, sitting there close and cross-legged on the grass. I didn't really know either, but I happened to guess right.

"I think it has something to do with having babies," I told Billy sagely.

"Oh," said Billy. And that was that.

FOR ME, "PHYSIQUE" COUNTED AS AN F WORD

My father, a warm-hearted and soft-spoken man, was a tool and die maker by trade. Though never athletic, he was always of normal weight for his height, and strong from working with his hands. He had a metal- and woodworking shop in the basement of our house, and he used to subscribe to magazines such as *Mechanics Illustrated* and *Popular Mechanics.* I often picked them up out of curiosity, and at a very young age I became an avid reader. By the time I was in fifth or sixth grade, I had my own subscriptions, given to me by my dad, which I kept receiving for years. I liked reading about all the do-it-yourself projects—the diagrams, the instructions—but soon I became more fascinated by the advertisements for mail-order, bodybuilding courses. I discovered in every issue, for instance, there were ads targeted to "90-pound weaklings," like Charles Atlas said he once was. Sometimes the ads were headlined, "Hey, skinny!"—never, "Hey, fat boy!" But these ads appealed to me viscerally because I was so unhappy with my body. I had soft rolls where I knew other boys' bodies had none. I was too heavy to do push-ups or chin myself in phy ed. When I looked at my belly and thighs in photographs, I didn't see a boy there; the fat I saw reminded me of my mother. "Fatty, fatty, two-by-four, can't get through the bathroom door." And in my enormous unhappiness I began keeping a collection of *Mechanics Illustrated* and *Popular Mechanics* in the bottom drawer of my dresser so that whenever I was alone in my room and the door was closed, I could take them out and look with lonely yearning at the tiny photographs of muscled torsos.

I discovered masturbation all on my own. I was in fifth grade, maybe younger. Most likely I was in my bed, rolling around with my pillows or the bedclothes, maybe happening to touch my penis maybe not, when suddenly I was overcome by whole-body paroxysms. I became delirious—and I promptly passed out. When I came to, I saw that something had squirted out of me. I had no idea what just happened. Not only had I never heard of masturbation (I was to discover the word in a dictionary years later); I didn't know relevant slang. Yet so overwhelming was this newfound pleasure that I was to continue doing it over and over, always alone in my bedroom with the door shut. Oddly, I cannot recall having been given a single "message" about masturbation pro or con. During my entire childhood, no adult or age mate communicated anything about it to me at all. Somehow—perhaps from this shroud of silence—I inferred on my own that this was something to be ashamed of, a pleasure I should keep strictly to myself, and I never exchanged a word about it with anyone till I was nearly an adult.

But perhaps I learned to be ashamed because I had begun masturbating while looking at those Charles Atlas ads. And then there were the men's underwear pages of the Sears and Roebuck catalog. And then there was that boy with the astonishing thick arms modeling a mail-order barbell set. And then there came those bodybuilding ads in the back of comic books, where the young men were teenage, and they stuck their wide chests out, and their biceps bulged, and they wore tiny, tight, swim briefs, and they tucked their clenched fists into sinewy, taut abdomens where their navel was an actual *button,* not a tummy tunnel like mine. At the drugstore in town . . . and then on the newsstand where I transferred buses coming home from church choir practice, and at the seedy used-magazine shop near the public library where I went downtown to research school papers, there were so-called physique magazines: *Demi Gods, Tomorrow's Man, Young Physique.* Page after page (once I stealthily got one home and cut open the plastic wrap), they showed muscular young men flexing incredibly developed bodies with their genitals pouched discreetly in a posing strap. I quaked and trembled inside when I saw them. Perhaps by the time I realized that these had become the photographs that I was compulsively masturbating to sometimes several times a day—filled with disgust for my body and bursting with longing for theirs—perhaps that was when I became so ashamed I often wished I was dead.

Well, no. It's not quite true that my postmasturbation wish was suicidal *per se.* My actual recurring fantasy of self-mutilation—just after carefully disposing of the Kleenex I'd used, just before concealing the magazines and comic books in a drawer until next time, and just before permitting myself to pass out and fall sleep—was that my left forearm would be chopped off, somehow accidentally severed, because that was the hand I always used.

I DON'T REMEMBER LEARNING THE F WORDS "FAG" AND "FAIRY" AND "FRUIT." BUT I DO REMEMBER LEARNING THE MEANING OF "FEAR."

By the time I got to seventh grade, I was trying not to look too long and longingly at the bodies of other boys in the locker room. I knew that if I did, I would have an unseemly erection. Shy in the shower and ashamed of my heft, I put my clothes back on as fast as I could. But sitting at my desk in class, I could admire those same male classmates and remember them naked, and my erection could be concealed in the corduroy that billowed up amply in my lap. My crushes were secret. Bob, Ron, all the rest of the athletes in their mesomorphic grace and breathtaking beauty—they never knew. I was terrified of being found out; but so far as I know, I was never suspected.

I cultivated a disguise as a normal, outgoing teenager. In eighth grade, our homeroom won a schoolwide contest for selling magazine subscriptions door to door. The grand prize was an after-school party, with soda pop and potato chips and a phonograph. Some of the kids brought their own records, and when they began to dance with each other, I looked on. I'd never danced socially, never been invited to a party where there was dancing, but to my amazement—from having taken dancing lessons since

I was five—I found I could pick up the dance steps easily. I'd watch for a few minutes, and it was as if I'd always known how.

The more "popular" kids—impressed with what appeared to be a dancing ability cultivated, like theirs, at private parties—invited me to join them. Within days Mom had bought me the saddleshoes, pink cords, and charcoal shirts then in vogue, and I was literally dancing my way to a social life.

Every other weekend, some kid would throw a party in his or her parents' basement. We always danced boy-girl, of course. I was not oblivious to the fact that the real stars of this social circuit were the very athletes on whom I had crushes, but nor do I recall being especially obsessed with them. I was simply caught up in an enormously gratifying social whirl, and I loved it. I liked going to the parties, I liked dancing with all my popular new friends, and I liked being accepted. I gained a lot of friends that year, and lost a lot of weight.

After school a bunch of us would periodically take a public bus ride way across town to a TV station that broadcast a local knockoff of *American Bandstand*. While the DJ spun a platter, we would dance for the cameras, and all over town teens watched us from home. Now and then some famous singer would come on the show. I especially remember watching Jimmy Rogers—as cute in person as in his pictures, with his curly black forelock—as he lip-synched his latest hit, "She had *(uh-oh!)* kisses sweeter than wine . . . " Who knew what a girl's kiss was? Who even knew what wine was (my Lutheran family only imbibed during Holy Communion)? Not me. I was only along for the dance.

Most of my new friends came from well-off families. The basements of all their suburban ranch houses were finished like living rooms or rec rooms, ideal for a party. In the basement of my family's home was a real basement; Mom and Dad couldn't afford to fix it up. I tried to assure them that I was really happy going to other kids' parties and it was just fine with me that I was never able to reciprocate all the invitations I got. And it really *was* fine, too. But I think Mom sometimes felt bad that I could never give a party for the crowd at our house. She especially recognized, I think, that something wonderful had begun to happen in my life, and she didn't want anything to stand in the way of my happiness.

When summer came, I went off for two weeks to Bible camp. It was a woodsy mix of swimming and softball, arts and crafts, sing-alongs by the campfire, and religious instruction. My folks had sent me there each summer for many years, and I had come to enjoy it. But that year, without my parents' foreknowledge, the college-age counseling staff had been recruited from an extremely fundamentalist Lutheran Bible institute. They were all attractive, athletic, eager, energetic—and determined to save our souls from hell.

My counselors were a young man and woman who seemed to be dating. In Bible class and small-group discussions under spreading oaks and tall pines, they kept harping on the urgency of committing your life to Christ. In particular, they reiterated dire warnings about the dangerous evil of dancing: "Who knows what it will lead to?"

Well I, for one, had absolutely no *idea* what dancing would lead to. I was a few years younger than most of the other campers that summer, and I was a sexual naïf to begin with (I'd only recently been given a book and a quiet talk by Mom about the facts of life). Perhaps more to the point, all that boy-girl dancing I was doing—my entrée to a whirlwind social life— was for me just a fun way to be with friends. I never associated it with anything remotely sexual. But that summer at Bible camp, zealous counselors put the fear of damnation in me. One night near the end, they held a big revivalist bonfire. Somberly the counselors exhorted us campers sitting around it to accept Jesus as our personal Savior. "Say yes to Jesus," they intoned, "say yes to Jesus." We sang songs, we prayed; it went on for hours, our brains on spin cycle. "Say yes to Jesus."

I was dying inside, choked up with fear and fervor because I so wanted to be saved, I so wanted the love of Jesus as my personal Savior just like my counselors said—but I knew that I could not honestly say yes to Jesus without also promising to give up dancing. In my heart of hearts, I knew that would be a lie, and Jesus would know. Sitting on a log and watching sparks fly up into the night sky, I wrestled with my fourteen-year-old conscience. When I finally whispered "yes," with a flood of private tears, it was with the inner conviction that when school started in the fall, I would no longer dance. I would swear it off for Jesus.

Truth to tell, I'd been making promises to Jesus for quite some time. In church services, especially during the confession part of the liturgy, I regularly promised to stop masturbating. Needless to say, I had not kept my word. But this decision about dancing was going to be different, I vowed. Soon after school started in the fall, I was invited to a party at the home of one of my popular friends as usual—but I didn't dance. I spent the night amiably sitting on the sofa and going back and forth to the chips and dip. When someone asked me, I declined politely, "No thanks, I'm not dancing." I was invited to just one other party that fall. Evidently a party-pooper, I was dropped from the social scene like a hot potato.

All that school year, my body bulged. Bankrupt of physical self-esteem, I turned with new desperation to those physique pictures in my bedroom, and they became my private image bank—arousing me, rebuking me. I could not resist them. And each time I masturbated to them, I memorized again my loathing of my own soft fleshiness.

It was about this time that, masturbating to a physique magazine in my bedroom as was my habit, I happened to pass out and fall sound asleep, carelessly not remembering to put the magazine back into a drawer. Then my father happened to enter my room on some errand or other. I'm sure he must have knocked, and I'm sure I must have mumbled in my stupor it was OK to come in—but immediately after he left I realized in horror that the magazine showing photographs of muscular men's bodies was still lying wide open on the hardwood floor, right where I'd just used it. My heart stopped. To my enormous relief, Dad never mentioned the incident (or maybe he didn't notice), but my shame sunk in deeper and my terror of discovery grew.

Though my social life in ninth grade was zero, my academic and extracurricular life was off the charts. I was in band (I played trumpet), a school musical based on Mark Twain stories (I played Pudd'nhead Wilson, a girth-appropriate role), science club, plus so many church youth group activities I can't remember them all. Near the end of the school year, at a convocation in front of the whole class (which numbered over 500), my name was announced: the faculty had voted me Most Outstanding Ninth Grade Boy. I was a walking cliché—happy on the outside, miserable on the inside. But I had kept my promise to Jesus not to dance.

Tenth grade began with a fateful augury. That fall, there was to be a formal dance, girl-ask-boy, and I got asked. Sue was her name. The spring before, she had been voted by the faculty Most Outstanding Ninth Grade Girl. I didn't know her well, but I admired her, and I was amazed and flattered. She did not belong to the élite circle that had dropped me (or surely she would have known better than to ask). Like me she was very tall (I had already reached what was to be my permanent height of six feet, unexceptional now, yet towering at the time); but unlike me, Sue was reedthin. Her need to find a suitable height mate may have had something to do with her invitation, but I think she also probably admired me and liked me from afar.

When Sue invited me, I no longer felt averse to social dancing. Sick of the social isolation that those damn camp counselors had put me through, I had begun to doubt whether the church I was raised in was for me—not to mention whether I was for *it*. Try as I might, I could not picture myself as a happy, crew-cut husband with a pert wife and 2.5 adorable kids. I now wanted to *know* what dancing could lead to. I wanted to experience those feelings I'd been warned about, those sexual feelings that a boy supposedly has with a girl while dancing, those uncontrollable feelings that must be saved for when you are *married.* I wanted to feel those feelings desperately, to know I was going to grow up normal and OK.

So I readily accepted Sue's invitation. She was to be my opportunity to experience those feelings for myself, up close and personal. What good luck.

Then a panic set in—*because I was afraid I'd forgotten how to dance.* It had been over a year, after all; I was no longer partying, no longer watching and instantly picking up new steps. A whole year of new hits had gone by, new moves, and I didn't know them. Then I had an idea . . .

Lyle was his real name, but everyone called him Pepper. Preternaturally peppy, he was by far the cutest, most popular boy in the entire class. He had dimples for days. And he was a fabulous dancer. Even in my eighth-grade prime, I could never dance as well as Pepper. Not so much an athlete, he was a natural leader and heartthrob—many a girl swooned over him and he was friends with all the jocks. I'd been to a party at his house, so I knew he was such a sharp dresser because his folks could well afford it. He was also always nice to me, and continued to be friendly even after I was disgraced from the party circuit. So one day I nervously asked Pepper for a favor. I told him I'd been invited to the dance and I was afraid I'd forgotten how and would he please give me a private lesson so I could brush up? Sure, he said, ever cheerful. And so it was that one day after school, Pepper and I snuck into the deserted auditorium, and there backstage among the hanging curtains—in theater jargon they're called "teasers" and "tormenters"—the cutest boy in school and I danced the latest steps.

The night of the dance, I drove the family car over to pick up Sue in her fancy new dress. The school lunchroom was mood-lit, festooned in crepe paper. Sue and I danced (it all came back to me, no problem), we drank fruit punch, we made small talk with classmates. Two tall overachievers, we looked for all the world like we were made for each other. But it was during a slow dance near the end—I was holding Sue's tiny waist in my right hand and her hairdo was gently nestling against my left ear—when I realized something terrible: I was not having those feelings that I had been warned about. I was not having any sexual feelings of any kind. I was going through the motions, and the only thing I was feeling inside was devastation. This was my big opportunity, my make-or-break moment; I was on the verge of making out with a girl I liked and a girl who liked me—and my groin was numb.

That night I learned for certain that something was horribly wrong with me. Inside I was terrified. I drove Sue home, awkwardly said good-night, and never spoke to her again.

I began to have to wear special orthopedic shoes for fallen arches. Under my weight, their snug fit began to incubate an athlete's foot infection that became so severe—fluid-filled blisters covered the bottoms of my feet and burst like bubble wrap when I walked—that I had to be hospitalized. I was eventually cured of the infection, but for a few months, I was on crutches or in a wheelchair, and in my inactivity I continued to gain. That spring, still in a wheelchair, I exhibited the results of an original experiment at the state science fair and won some sort of prize.

During eleventh grade, I slipped into an undiagnosed depression. The guidance office became alarmed when not only my schoolwork fell off (from straight As in eighth grade, I began getting Cs and a D) but I was bailing out on the school newspaper, an extracurricular activity I used to enjoy. The school counselors made me take a Minnesota Multiphasic Personality Inventory and a Rorschach inkblot test and sent me to a weird psychologist to try to find out what was going wrong with me. Nobody guessed what my real problem was—the shame that had no name—and I was determined not to talk about it with anyone. About this time I began to mentally check out of the church and religion I was raised in, and mercifully my parents respected my wishes when I told them I did not want to go talk to our pastor about whatever was bothering me. They also readily agreed when I told them I didn't want to go back to that weird shrink.

I determined to bury my pain and get on with my disguise as an active, intellectual, creative teen. I succeeded. I kept my private masturbatory life with pictures of bodybuilders a secret, even almost from myself—I learned to forget about it when I wasn't doing it. And by the time I got to college, I weighed in fatter than I'd ever been.

I LEARNED ABOUT FUCKING, AND THIS TIME I LEARNED WHAT IT MEANT

In my freshman year, for the first time in my life, I fell in love. He was a beautiful, sensitive loner, an acoustic guitar player named Ted. He knew I loved him, including sexually, because I told him so when we decided to room together off campus; but Ted did not feel comfortable reciprocating, so our friendship was chaste. Some of our most intimate talks were the ones we had in the morning in the bathroom, while I shaved and he lolled in the tub, his blond body a more languid and younger brother to Michelangelo's *David*. I was his Jonathan. I would sometimes masturbate under my covers at night, thinking about how close he was. For more than a year we were inseparable.

During those early years in college my mother gave me pills—some sort of weight-loss drugs prescribed her by her doctor, perhaps amphetamines (I never knew for sure). She always got extra and passed a supply on to me, and I popped one every day. By my sophomore year the buzzy drug allowed me to eat comfortably just one meal a day, breakfast, and my body got leaner than any time before or since.

I threw myself into theater—writing, performing, directing. My early stuff was satire, and it became a campus hit. I then formed a group called Playmakers that gathered on Saturday nights to do theater improv, and from this bohemian bunch I cast the full-length plays I wrote and produced. One was about a boy in a mental institution who—at least in my subtext—was in love with two fellow inmates, another boy and a beautiful girl. In real life, I fell in love with the woman who played the girl, and during our senior year, we got married. She was beautiful and very talented, and I was successfully sexual with her. Months before our wedding, both virgins, she and I first made love in my bedroom at my parents' home, site of countless other prior ejaculations. I thought marriage would straighten me out. It didn't. Two years into our marriage I confessed to her that I was homosexual. Understandably, she got hysterical.

We divorced amicably after five years of marriage (no fault, no children), and I moved out to a lonely one-room apartment. I'd got fat again while married, a new all-time high, so I joined a Y and began a workout regimen, and I lost weight drastically by permitting myself a dollar's worth of food daily. Slowly but surely, I began to come out.

By now, I was twenty-six years old. I didn't know the first thing about how to be gay, so I got myself a book, *Homosexual Handbook.* There was an astonishing section in it about anal intercourse, a completely foreign notion to me. Up to that point, my fantasy life with other men's bodies only involved being physically close to their physiques in some nonspecific way—or, better yet, having their body as mine and *being* them. I never imagined any particular "sex acts." But reading that book, I realized that if I was going to be gay, I had better learn how to be fucked.

I seized the opportunity one day while cat-sitting for my ex-wife in the apartment we'd recently shared. I happened upon a dildo she now had—a hard pink plastic thing, a battery-operated hummer. In this same bedroom where I once sporadically functioned as husband, I took my pants and underwear off and lay down on the wood floor. By trial and error I figured out how to voluntarily relax my rectum (you bear down as if you're trying to shit) so I could push the dildo all the way in.

This was New York City, circa 1971. My graduate studies in dramatic arts were about to end, and I was offered a job with an avant-garde theater company as administrative director, writing grants and managing tours. The man who offered me the job was to become my first time. His name was Joe, about eight years older than I. It happened one night in a motel on the road in Canada. Joe was charismatic, extremely sweet, and gentle. I admired and trusted him enormously, so I was overjoyed when he invited me to his room. Eager to please, I fellated him briefly (and by the book), myself too nervous to be aroused. But mostly I just lay naked with him in his arms. We touched and we hugged and we held and we talked and I was in heaven. Oddly what now comes back to me—the only thing I remember him saying to me that night—is "Why do you want to lose weight?" By the following morning, I had fallen in love.

The extent and variety of my sex life increased. I began going to dances sponsored by the Gay Liberation Front at a converted firehouse downtown, and there I would meet men and go home with them. Once I took a trip to an island off Venezuela, picked up a young man from Bogota in a dance bar, and brought him back to the ramshackle hovel where I rented a cheap room. He was the first man to fuck me—and he fucked me raw. I was much relieved to get that over with, and flattered that he wanted to keep seeing me, so we got together again over the next few nights, but each time he would fuck me with more aggression than before, and I became alarmed. Finally I told him I didn't want to see him anymore, and he got angry. For the rest of my stay, I slept alone in fear that he would break down my door.

Back in New York, I had several sexual liaisons, lasting from a night to a few weeks, and I was amazed that now and then at a dance or a bar or in the theater scene, I attracted a sex partner who embodied my ideal "type"—someone whose face and/or body resembled a photograph in my magazines.

I wrote a long letter to my parents. It started, "Dear Mom and Dad, I'm homosexual . . . " They took it as well as could be expected: Mom said she'd pray all the harder for me. I sent them a book, *Society and the Healthy Homosexual.*

During these promiscuous years, I remember that when my weight was down, I'd start to panic about being more available to the very sexual affection I desperately wanted with men. I'd get hit on and couldn't handle it, feeling ashamed of being queer. Out of homosexual shame, I'd then pack the fat back on for protection, so no one would want me. I'd then become ashamed of being fat again, sexually lonely, and crash diet. I yo-yoed a lot.

My collection of masturbation magazines was still with me, of course. (Even when I was married, I turned to it regularly, and I mentally called up images from it in order to function sexually with my wife.) By now they were no longer published under the euphemism of "physical culture"; increasingly targeted to a growing market of homosexual men, the magazines now displayed naked genitals, sometimes erect. The genitals held not so much appeal for me as did the abs, pecs, delts, biceps, and other body details that for me betokened mesomorphic masculinity. When I was leaner, I could sometimes masturbate by looking at my own musculature in a mirror. But when I was fat, I could not masturbate without looking at those posing bodies in gay male magazines.

One night during a lean period, a somewhat older man with an evident gym body, darkly mustached, followed me from bar to bar. When he finally caught up with me he offered to buy me a drink. Within the hour I was in his classy apartment on Washington Square and he was fucking me. Over breakfast he invited me to his weekend place on Fire Island in the posh Pines gay enclave. I went, flattered. My first night he took me to a house full of men who were premiering a new gay sex film—*Bijou,* by the maker of *Boys in the Sand*—and afterward he took me outdoors and fucked me on someone's waterbed. He was in the closet, and he fucked hard and fast. We didn't have much in common; he was an assistant Manhattan district attorney. He really just wanted to fuck, and when he was done he sent me home.

If anyone wanted to fuck me and I envied his body, I complied. I never got into being the fucker, though I did try occasionally, when that's what someone explicitly asked. If it would make someone happy, I gave it my best shot. But fucking someone, even to climax, never did a thing for me. All my previous anxious associations with marital coitus (will I get hard enough? will I get it in?) were still vivid. Perhaps as a result, I never felt closer to anyone fucking them—always farther apart.

I started going to the baths (this was long before AIDS pooped the party big-time) because, as I told myself, I was getting weary of all the inane small talk I'd been doing as a prelude to sex. Why not just go where no one talks at all, and cut to the chase? So there I was—a former fatty, with only a towel tied around my loins—nonverbally cruising and getting groped and probed in dark hallways, bed booths, and orgy rooms. Without our ever exchanging a word, a guy could have me on the floor, somewhere in the dark, doggedly trying to penetrate my butt. Even though I was nowhere near relaxed, I would put up with the pain and try to let him in. How else, after all, was I ever going to get to feel so close to such a built male body?

Being fucked the way I discovered I really liked it—which was much slower going, relaxed in a real bed, and with KY or other lubricant, not just his spit on his cock—I found I could not only relax my sphincter but also abandon restraint on my abdominal muscles. Letting go during sex meant letting my belly go, letting it stick out, unblocking my gut lock (that lesson I learned from Mom)—and this became for me a wonderful sensual pleasure. I also discovered the exquisite pleasure of having my prostate gland massaged within my rectum from intensifying thrusts of an erect penis. I sometimes climaxed just from that. Plus, being fucked felt like getting *stuffed,* filling up my innards the way overeating bloats the intestines. Was this some bizarre womb envy? some perverse female fantasy of being made pregnant? Quite the contrary. I grew up deathly ashamed of being fat, never feeling like a real enough boy, never feeling like a virile enough young man, never feeling like a potent enough husband—and now desperately trying to pass as a butch enough gay man. Apropos my particular manifestation of gender anxiety, when I was being fucked, I felt his masculinity *fill* me—literally pack me with every thrust, injecting me with the genderedness that I felt I lacked. Viscerally, going to the toilet afterward, defecating out globules of his pungent semen mixed with my own excrement, I recalled the excruciating pleasure of having just ingested and assimilated a load of genuine manhood.

Not long after, of course, I'd feel lacking again. Would I replenish my emptiness by stuffing myself with food, or would I starve myself to stay fuckable? I was always walking that line.

"Fatty, fatty, two-by-four, can't get through the bathroom door."

Food could fill me, numb my feelings, insulate my pain, shield me from my homosexual shame, blunt my homosexual desire—but it made me fat, which reminded me of my mother and filled me with self-loathing. When a man rear-ending me stuffed my insides, it was as if he filled me with masculinity, which for me was the opposite of fat.

If a man fucked me brusquely, or if a man fucked me painfully (such that there was blood in my next stool), or if a man climbed on top of me in my sleep and started fucking me (as once happened), no matter. I figured I'd better put up with it. I'd better withstand the pain. Because inside I was still a self-hating fatso—and I believed I should feel grateful that anyone hunky wanted to have sex with me at all.

FINALLY I LEARNED AN F WORD THAT SAVED MY LIFE

I had never been a political person. When SDS came to my college in the mid-1960s, I never knew for certain what the initials stood for (Students for a Democratic Society, I later learned). I was vaguely aware that some fellow students traveled southward to participate in the civil rights movement, but that was not for me; I was an esthete, into theater. By virtue of my Midwest pietist background, I grew up a political naïf as well as a sexual one. After college, when I began graduate studies at Union Theological Seminary in New York City, it was not out of any sense of mission or social activism or spiritual calling; it was to stay out of Vietnam, it was because both my wife and I wanted to live in New York, it was because Union had a drama department, and it was because I won a scholarship that paid my way. (I had long since abandoned any pretense of having a faith, because the Bible and the church were so blatantly antagonistic to a nonheterosexual like me.)

A lot changed for me my last year at seminary, the spring of 1969. That was when the black student caucus, demanding reparations from the white church, occupied the administration building. I was asked by the black student caucus to be their press spokesman (the word *spokesperson* hadn't been coined yet), and I was swept up and embroiled in their protest. I'd been recommended to them by a co-worker at the Interchurch Center, where I had a part-time job doing religious radio and TV production. So there I was, white-bread me, standing out on the street explaining to a CBS News crew the righteous demands of the students inside. When the students invited me into their closed strategy meetings, behind barricades built of church pews, I was deeply moved. I found myself on their side, completely identifying with their cause, in an explicit commitment to social fairness and a profound new embrace of principled friendship. That experience was my emotional/political "baptism."

Later that summer, outraged street transvestites rebelled during a routine police raid of a gay bar in the Village. I was not cognizant of that event at the time (the black student takeover at Union was to remain my personal landmark, my own rite of passage to political revolt), but indirectly I was its beneficiary. A few years later, seeking out some sort of politicized context in which to affirm my new identity as an out gay man, I found a group spawned in Stonewall's wake. One of my closest friends was Joe Chaikin, artistic director of the experimental Open Theatre, and he invited me to early meetings of what became the Gay Academic Union—a lively mix of young lesbian and gay students and older professors who gathered in members' homes. It was at one of these meetings, in Marty Duberman's brownstone on Charles Street, that Joe introduced me to a good friend whom he knew from anti-Vietnam War circles. Her name was Andrea Dworkin.

At first I thought that Gay Academic Union was exactly the forum I was seeking—not only a place to plumb fundamental questions of sexuality and politics but also a form for my coming out a whole person: someone with both meaningful values and a happy sex life. Within GAU, a men's caucus began, and I attended eagerly. I remember John D'Emelio was there, Jonathan Katz, Marty, a bunch of other early movement leaders and soon-to-be notables, plus several men with whom I had had or would have (or would like to have had) sex. Heady and spirited huddles, the meetings settled into a pattern: someone would present a topic for ten or fifteen minutes, then we'd spend the rest of the evening talking it through, thrashing it out.

At one point, I proposed that we talk about our attitudes toward women. It seemed to me, I said, that maybe that's something we should take a close look at—you know, our attitudes toward our women friends, our feelings about our mothers and women in general, how that might affect our feelings about ourselves . . . Enthusiasm for the topic was tepid, but since I had volunteered it, I was delegated to make a presentation.

I then wrote up a short paper, and besides the men at the next meeting who heard it, only two other people have ever seen the manuscript. It is my first nonfiction work on sexual politics, and it is so full of agonized disclosure that I have never wanted it published. Rereading it now, and looking back at my notes and drafts, I believe I have been correct to keep it in a file drawer for twenty-one years. Some things in it could hurt people—I wrote about the meaning to me of my mother's body, and the meaning to me of sex with the woman I was married to, for instance. So it is best left tucked away.

But there is a passionate passage near the end of it that still astounds me. It is so brutally honest, I still can't believe I shared it with anyone. It touches graphically on my feelings of femiphobia and my feelings about being fucked when I did not really want—all sensations I had no name for at the time. In my first draft, the passage read this way:

> My fear of women has taken many forms. I have been repulsed by their bodies, horrified of their cunts, chilled by their touch, smothered by their breasts, disgusted by the potential woman in myself, ashamed because they didn't turn me on, paralyzed and inept in bed. I have wished for some kind of exorcism. When I feel my fear, something inside collapses.
>
> There's a woman in me that I fear to become. But there's a woman in me that I honor. The woman I honor can't stand domination. The woman I honor can't stand it when a man puts the make on me. The woman I honor can't stand it when a man insists. The woman I honor can't stand the man who doesn't respect my right to say "no." Or "wait," meaning: "I'm not ready just yet." That woman is in me. And I am she.

Prior to the gay men's caucus meeting for which I was writing, I gave that draft to my new friend Andrea to read. We were just getting to know each other. She was about to have a book published, *Woman Hating.* We saw each other socially, at Gay Academic Union meetings, at War Resisters League events, and we were becoming close, fast friends. For a certain period, I recall, I was in love with Andrea and with Joe simultaneously.

I remember Andrea reading my draft, and I remember her coming to my apartment to talk about it. She spoke to me soberly, intently. "This sentence where you say, 'There's a woman in me . . . ,' " she began; "you can't really say *woman* there."

She paused and I nodded. Then she went on. "You have not lived the life of a woman. You don't know what that's like . . . "

I nodded, holding my breath, listening raptly.

"What you mean," Andrea said, "is the *feminist* in you—the *feminist* in you can't stand domination . . . "

The word was then brand-new to me. I was as oblivious to the early days of women's liberation as I had been to Stonewall. But the word made sense. I liked it. I revised the paragraph accordingly. I thanked her. And then on April 5, 1974, I read my statement to the group. It now concluded this way:

> I have wished for a kind of exorcism. When I feel my fear of becoming a woman something inside me bloats. When I feel my fear of going in to a woman, I tense, and my genitals get numb and retreat.
>
> I have chosen my gayness. I do not choose my fear of women.
>
> Gently, and slowly, I feel I'm becoming a feminist.
>
> There has always been in me a woman I honored, who for very practical reasons is a feminist. That woman I honor can't stand domination. Can't stand it when a man puts the make on me. Can't stand it when a man insists. Can't stand the man who doesn't respect my right to say "no," or "wait," meaning: "I'm not ready just yet." That woman is in me. And I am she.
>
> But I'm also trying to find out what it means to be a feminist man. How does he act? What does he do? What does he say? What does he pay attention to?
>
> How does he live through his profound fear of women?
>
> Because in a sense, the only appropriate attitude toward women I know of is feminism.

The question for me is can men learn how to be feminists among men, and it seems pretty clear men have to learn among women. To a large extent, *from* women.

I believe there need to be many forms of coalition among feminist men and feminist women. I once thought Gay Academic Union might be moving in that direction, but I'm no longer sure. There are structures for equal decision making and the men and women hardly know what to say to one another.

I wonder if we can talk about our fears of women. I wonder if we can talk about becoming feminists. I have absolutely no idea. I feel there's something here, in GAU, and in the Gay movement in general—something that's very stuck.

Trying to live as a feminist keeps me a little bit from despair.

Everyone pretty much hated hearing this. They squirmed throughout, and could not wait to get on to topics they much prefered—their attitudes toward *other men,* how to improve relations with men, *anything else.* After a short while, the group explicitly stopped discussing the topic I'd presented.

I felt dismayed by their determined refusal to look at what I had begun to perceive as a throbbing contradiction in "gay male liberation"—the underbelly of woman hating in much of our so-called love for men. Why were they being so defensive? I wondered. Why were they so annoyed at me for bringing up the obvious? I felt hurt and betrayed by men I thought were friends, enlightened allies I thought would understand. So I left that caucus meeting disenchanted, and I never returned.

That November I gave a notorious speech at a Gay Academic Union conference, analyzing and condemning the sexism that I saw pervading the gay-male-dominated movement. It was to be my public swan song. Duberman, D'Emelio, et al. were in the audience; they subsequently stopped speaking to me, and I became a pariah to the fledgling New York gay politico scene.

But it was Andrea who gave me the F word "feminist." And she first showed me how to use it meaningfully in a sentence of my own, about being fucked against my will.

FURTHERMORE . . .

This essay is an excerpt from a memoir in progress, in which I plan to tell the continuation of this story. On August 1, 1974, when I had just turned thirty and Andrea was twenty-seven, she and I began living together.

In the intervening years, my deepening understanding of the word "feminist"—and all that I have learned from women engaged in sexual and political struggle against male supremacy—allowed me to find real answers to my own sexual and political struggle. My profeminist activism and my published critiques of male-supremacist convictions, including many gay men's, became more widely known. Because I publicly allied myself with radical feminists on issues of pornography, prostitution, and sadomasochism, I was more reviled by antifeminist lesbians and gay men than I ever was by anyone for being queer and fat. And this time I was proud to be an outsider.

PART 13:
REENVISIONING MEN

Why I Hate The Beatles
and The Supremes

Ozzie Diaz-Duque

I look upon the steamy mirror,
and in circling motions with my hand
I seek the face of a twenty-year-old lad.
 . . . but there's a shock: another face is staring back!
"My God! Who are you?"—I ask.
And the man in the mirror shouts back:
"Honey, get a hold of yourself,
and just face the facts.
I don't mean to shock you,
I don't mean to laugh, but . . .
have you forgotten just how old you are?"

Now I understand why the young ones are aghast
when I tell them that I,
yes, me, really, in the flesh,
all grown up and already in college
saw The Beatles back in sixty-nine at Flushing Meadow Park.

"You saw The Beatles?",
says with incredulity a young man.

Yes, and The Supremes
at Forest Hills the year before that.
"You saw The Supremes," he adds,
as if I had just said I had gone to a concert aboard Noah's ark!

But, you know,
when I bring Lady Clairol home to cover my gray locks,
—really, my scalp, as there is not hair now to speak of—
I say to myself: why are you doing this?
Why do you fall in this trap? You don't look so bad!
God, how I hate The Beatles and The Supremes,
and those shocked young ones who still don't believe
that time does pass.
But, you know what? I don't look so bad.
Not for a forty-year-old queen, anyway,
and, besides,
Diana Ross is still seven years older than I!

If Only I Were Cute:
Looksism and Internalized Homophobia in the Gay Male Community

Andrew J. Feraios

LIFE AS A FAT GAY MAN

I am a thirty-two-year-old, gay, white man who has struggled all of his life with weight gains and losses and the subsequent social rewards and punishments thereof. For as long as I can remember, I internalized the fact that I was fat: as a young boy that meant that I had failed being a "normal" boy who ran, jumped, and played sports; but as a teenager and young adult, it meant that I was "just not good-looking enough"—especially to the gay male world. During my twenty-seventh year, I committed myself to an exercise plan that changed my body and my life but not in the ways I had intended or hoped when I began my quest. I lost over sixty pounds and worked myself into a physical shape that was clearly athletic. At first, the world opened up to me anew as I became aware that I was indeed attractive. However, in the midst of my transformation, I discovered the intractable role of looks in the gay male community, and I was never to see myself or the gay male community in the same light again.

Long before I developed a gay identity, I suffered the effects of growing up as a fat male child. My earliest memories are rife with adults' conversations about my weight, what I ate, how much I ate, and how great it would be if I would only turn away second helpings, stay away from sweets, get some exercise, or just lose a little weight. Since kids do not expect fat kids to be good at sports, I escaped being labeled a faggot, queer, or sissy. When my incipient sexual feelings drove me to look up the word "homosexual" in the dictionary, I knew it had dangerous implications for *who* I was and *what* I was going to be; and I was already gaining and losing weight.

Although I was a good swimmer, sports were difficult for me because I was not comfortable around groups of boys my age and I had been fat throughout my childhood. Exercise, food, sex, and my body image fueled the psychological struggle between my sexual attraction to men and my fear of being gay. Food was a way for me to push down feelings that I did not want to have and a way to insulate myself with layers of fat that would keep people at sexual distance from me. And when I gained weight, I could obsess over dieting, exercise, and losing weight in lieu of my constant fear of anything queer.

As a young adult, my weight fluctuated from fifteen to thirty pounds overweight while I lived in the center of the gay male community on Chicago's north side. The first few times that I ventured into the bar scene, I encountered a standard of bodies and looks that I felt was beyond my reach. One spring when I had lost some weight and sported a fresh tan from a vacation in California, I went out into the scene and noticed that I was more popular than I could ever remember. Nevertheless, I found solace in progressive politics, AIDS services, and the gay and lesbian community center. Concurrently, I went to graduate school where my studies and research included both the nature of coming out among young lesbians and gay men and adolescent males' knowledge and experience with HIV/AIDS.

I emigrated from the Midwest in search of an out-of-the-closet, politically active, intellectually stimulating community of lesbians and gay men. I entered a graduate program at the University of California at Berkeley in Psychology and went to the first meeting of the Gay/Lesbian/Bisexual Alliance (GLBA). Within the first several meetings, I was elected GLBA co-President and together with Stacye Raye, the lesbian also elected co-President, we built the largest single organization on campus. By the end of the year, we could boast that over 500 people were on our mailing list and that we could draw hundreds of people to rallies and dances. Pride in what we accomplished did not make up for the extra flesh on my thighs, butt, and gut: even as I developed a healthy gay identity, I secretly harbored a poor and festering body image.

Although I had a lover, I always felt that what made me popular was that I provided the social and organizational context for others to carry on a sexual and romantic life. During the academic year, I had been unhappy in my academic program and I had begun to gain weight. My pants grew tighter and I had to buy jeans with a larger and larger waist. At some point, the human body changes in shape when one becomes overweight, and jeans no longer fit the contours of one's body no matter what size one buys. By December of 1987, I stopped being able to wear jeans, the gay male uniform. My role as a campus leader afforded me protection from feeling that I was not attractive enough, but I was painfully aware that my status in the community was changing. When I went places with my lover, I saw that people treated us differently, as I was fat and he was not.

At the same time that we were building a campus organization, others in the community established a private party network for "cute" gay men called "Boy Parties." These parties were strictly by invitation only, and only those who were considered "cute" enough were invited. When "Boy Parties" came up, men would discreetly come to GLBA dances and coffee hours and selectively invite those they considered "cute." Those of us in the student movement took a hard line against the elitist and looksist nature of these parties, but they remained highly popular. Needless to say, I was never invited, and although many in the student movement eschewed the parties, they were nevertheless unhappy that they were not given an opportunity to turn down an invitation. The men who did attend these parties were often in the closet, in fraternities, considered "straight-acting" or "very cute." Personal ads often ask that anyone who answers be both "straight-acting" and "very cute," revealing the double oppression of internalized homophobia and the cult of gay male beauty. When I tried to discuss the link between looksism and homophobia, I felt that other men, particularly attractive men, did not take me seriously and had even been told, "You wouldn't feel that way if you got laid more often."

Shortly after the end of my graduate education, the AIDS Project of the East Bay in Oakland, California, hired me to do HIV health education. My weekend evenings as a health educator were spent in the East Bay gay bars, organizations, and bathhouses passing out condoms and safer sex literature, facilitating safer sex workshops, and conducting outreach. Occasionally, I would stay after my shift and note that I was "too fat" to interact with my age peers even in a casually friendly way. They let me know that I "wasn't cute enough" by looking through me as if I were invisible, avoiding eye contact, and enforcing physical distance. When my lover of many years and I went our separate ways, I was well aware of my status in the community, and I hated the image that stared back at me each day in the mirror.

By spring 1990, I was single and weighed 212 pounds. No matter what successes I achieved in my career, in relationships, or in my intellect, I was still fat. I would walk down Castro Street and would marvel at how unfriendly the community was; *no one ever smiled back at me.* At times, when I smiled at someone or asked someone a simple question, they would look down their noses at me, roll their eyes, and quickly let me know that I was not in their league. At one point or another, every age peer that I met would feel compelled to tell me that we were only going to be friends, whether or not I expressed a romantic interest in them. Occasionally, when I was in a gay environment as a patron rather than a health educator, I would see men laughing and looking my way. I looked the other way and feared what they might be saying about me.

IF ONLY I WERE CUTE

Over the course of my year as a health educator, I developed a very close friendship with my primary co-worker, an African-American gay man named Jay who was living with HIV. One very memorable evening he blurted out to me, "Look, either stop worrying about your weight or do something about it; you've complained about your weight for as long as I've known you, and you've yet to do something about it!" Angry but knowing he was right, over the next several weeks, I cut out all meat and as much fat as I could from my diet but was careful to balance my diet with complex carbohydrates and protein. I swam over a mile each day, and as my self-confidence grew, Jay dragged me out dancing three or four nights a week to increase my level of aerobic exercise.

As I went out, and as I began dropping weight, I noticed a subtle change in the way I was treated. Jay spent considerable amounts of time helping perfect the way I moved, the way I walked, my posture, and my attitude. He was my Pygmalion, and I was grateful for any advice he could give me, but I had internalized the idea that I was not attractive so I did not expect to be considered "cute" even if I lost weight. Nevertheless, I began to lose weight and watched my body change. The pool where I swam was outside, thus I soon sported a deep shade of brown. By the time I started seriously investigating the gay scene, I still experienced much rejection; I was tan, thinner, and I could dance, but I still was not able to meet men in a bar. By September 1990, when I had reached 180 pounds, I began to notice a distinct change in attitude toward me among the men in the scene and soon became obsessive about getting into shape. On my twenty-eighth birthday Jay gave me an ominous warning: "If you follow through on what you've started, your life will never be the same." He proceeded to choose a haircut for me, buy contact lenses for my birthday, and pick out clothes to wear. When I finally reached 150 pounds, I learned that I could be considered "hot."

Jay helped me adopt a style of dance that attracted attention and the "cutest" guys went for me. Suddenly, everywhere I went, men smiled at me, said hello to me, came over and asked my name, and winked at me. As my body grew more muscular, men's attentions became ever more focused on my body so that as a man introduced himself, he would grab my upper arm, touch my chest or butt, and try to determine just how good my body was. At my new weight, I had an opportunity to work as a health educator.

This time, young men, attractive men, the most attractive men in the bars now sat down next to me speaking of safer sex, and then ultimately asking what I was doing after I stopped working. Never again would I hear the words, "But, I am not attracted to you." Men I met professionally routinely asked me out, or if they were in a relationship, made less than discreet invitations for three-ways or tête-à-têtes.

Behind every corner of the bar I imagined that maybe there was a hotter and more interesting guy than the last. I stopped spending time with people I was close to so that I could go out more. I stopped having to walk up to people; all I had to do was smile and they walked up to me. Going out became a drug, where I felt continual validation. Suddenly, all of the men that I would never have dared approach were walking up to me and buying me drinks. Men that I had spoken to as a health educator and who had ignored me as a fat person hit upon me. When I tried to explain who I was and how I knew them, they couldn't remember me. One guy did remember me; when his moment of recognition came, he said, "You can't be the same person. . . . you're too cute!"

As I saw acquaintances out, few recognized who I was. Very few of them told me that I looked "good"; the usual refrain was "You look so different." Often the shock was translated not as a compliment, but rather as disbelief. Jay, who was my constant companion in the scene, explained, "Don't you see? They're threatened. They had decided that they were cuter than you and now they have to deal with you looking better than they do!" I felt like a spectacle. On several occasions while I was with dates, acquaintances approached me and said, "My god, I can't believe how much weight you have lost; how did you do it?" One Sunday afternoon at a tea dance, I ran into a gay male therapist whom I knew as a health educator. When he realized it was me, he asked if I had been ill—the gay male euphemism for AIDS. Another man who I had known while I was a health educator ran into me in line to enter a dance club. He did not recognize me, and I had to tell him my name. His mouth dropped open and he insisted that I must have had plastic surgery. He would not accept that I had not had surgery, raised his voice, and said, "No way . . . no one could change that much by just losing weight!" People in line took notice and I fled in embarrassment. In the same way that I felt people saw only my obesity, now it was its absence that dominated their perceptions.

I quickly found that being "hot/cute" did not garner me any more sustainable relationships, friendships, or otherwise than when I was fat. In fact, it became more difficult because when I was overweight, those who did become interested in me were doing so primarily because of who I was and not what I looked like. Suddenly, I found men keying into me because of my physical type or my image on the dance floor. Men who approached me thought I was in my early twenties, and my physical form and dance style projected a boyish image. Intimacy became even more elusive where physical attraction took up so much energy.

As the summer of 1991 approached, my drive toward physical perfection was monomaniacal. I spent forty-five minutes a day working on my abdominal muscles, swam six days a week for over an hour each day, purged all fat from my diet, and began working out on weights three times a week. My social life revolved around my bars and dance clubs of choice; daytimes were spent in the sun at the many places gay men lie out for tanning; when the sun began to go down, I hung out at the cafés in the Castro. Freed from my negative body image, nothing could have prepared me for my impending disillusionment.

DISILLUSIONMENT AND IDENTITY CRISIS

My identity crisis began quite unexpectedly during and after a series of experiences in June of that year. On Lesbian and Gay Freedom Night '91, I put on my tight, blue T-shirt and jeans, and I went to the Castro. Castro Street was blocked off between 17th and 18th, and there were thousands of men in the streets. I walked up Castro and I watched as eyes looked me up and down. I literally heard people say, "Cute!," "Blue T-shirt!," "Hey, baby," "You're too cute not to smile," all so that I could hear them. Some smiled at me in a genuine way, but most gawked. A carload of guys pulled up alongside me and invited me in for a blow job. Another man came up to me and invited me to come along to a party with him. I told him I was with a friend, which I was, and he said, "Blow him off, and come with us; we're all cute."

I ran into a friend and we had dinner. When he went to the bathroom, every man in the place checked me out. My space felt invaded; I felt empty and alone. When I was fat, I never doubted that people liked *ME*. We spoke about the gay community, about men, about the clubs, and about looksism. He was bitter toward me because he believed that I had gotten caught up into it all. I walked back down Castro alone and once again was cruised. I imagined myself fifty-five; I imagined myself with AIDS and Kaposi's Sarcoma; I imagined myself with scars on my face; I imagined myself 4'8". They would not be interested then. But I know that it is not ME they are interested in, I am an object, a thing to be had—to be done. I began to fear that I had spent a year making myself a sexual object only to find myself suspicious of why men want to get close to me.

I then went to the Stud for a total of ten minutes, felt alienated, and left. A young, attractive man ran up to me and handed me a free pass to ORGASM, the after-parade sex club; being cute affords men with innumerable social opportunities. Out of some morbid curiosity I decided to check it out. I ran into an HIV-positive friend of mine who has since died, and watched guys have sex. Jacking off and oral sex were the rule of the day, though I did see someone getting fucked. I wandered aimlessly, attracted to no one and mired in disillusionment. I chanced upon the two "hottest" guys in the place—young, buff, tanned, and "cute." They looked at me and invited me to join in by yanking off my shirt. They afforded me with "equal" status by smiling, kissing, and caressing me.

The three of us stood facing each other while blocking others who might try to join in. Men that were "less cute" hovered around us, watching and waiting for an opportunity to be included. Upon rejection from "equals" status, several dropped to their knees in the hope that they could perform oral sex upon one of us. One of the "less cute" guys tried to suck my dick; I lunged backward and tucked my shirt back into my pants. Another "cute" guy came up to me and cornered me. He wanted to kiss me; I hugged him and told him that I had to go and left. The hierarchy in a sex club is that the "cutest" guys assume dominance and are granted deference by others in the scene. Those who are rejected may choose to move on or may choose to prostrate themselves before those they consider "hot."

In the month following my Freedom Day '91 experience, I dated a man about whom I felt optimistic. He was a stunningly beautiful, highly educated, and sincere man who had been, in his own words, a "ninety-pound weakling." Gradually, I learned that he worked out for three hours each day, six days a week, ate two dinners each night to provide energy for his workouts, and ate a low fat diet so that he could eliminate all body fat. He complained that his relationships had not been going anywhere, as he kept finding himself dating bodybuilders with whom he had little in common. To each his own? I became aware that he hated his diet and exercise regimen; he increasingly complained about them with each new conversation. I finally asked him why he does it if he hates it so much. He retorted, "I like the way people treat me the way I am and I guess it's worth the trouble." Here was a man about whom everyone I knew remarked, expressed curiosity, and even jealousy. He had become an ideal sexual type, was miserable and unhappy, but was determined not only to continue but also to reach ever higher levels of physical perfection. Another man I became close to who spent untold hours in the gym reported in a vulnerable moment, "I have to work out if I want to be loved."

I continued going out to the bars despite how I felt, so ingrained they had become in my social life. My place in the looksist hierarchy ensured a drug of continual validation, where I could walk into a bar and collect phone numbers, be treated with deference, or have access to sexually attractive men. At the center of social life in the gay male community is the club or the bar; to reject the bar meant giving up the power I had so recently won. One evening in a very crowded bar, a hand grabbed my crotch so hard and with such force that I doubled over in pain. I grabbed the man's arm with both of my hands and thrust him off of me, turned to him, and angrily told him that he had hurt me. I quickly moved away from him, but before I had a chance, he grabbed my butt with even greater force. I clenched my fists and thrust my elbow into his gut with every ounce of strength that I had and told him to fuck off.

In the months that followed, I began to withdraw from the gay scene and to search out alternatives such as gay cultural events and gay rap groups. When I shared my story of sexual harassment with other gay men in a rap group at a gay support and social services center, a man in the group asked, "How were you dressed?" Another said, "Well, you know . . . you're very cute; you should be flattered that men are attracted to you!" With my anger barely contained, I blurted, "So . . . if I were a woman in a leather miniskirt, then I would deserve to get raped . . . right?!" It was here in a gay support and social services center, not in a sex club, bar, or bathhouse, where my final crisis of identity began.

During the social period before a rap group, I ran into a man with whom I had become friendly. One of the group facilitators, "Joe," began eyeing me from the other side of the lobby, walked over to me and said, "Isn't your name Drew?" I answered that it was and returned to my conversation. He remained close by and said, "Didn't you used to do safer sex workshops here?" I became anxious because I knew the direction of his questions and sure enough he inquired, "Haven't you lost a lot of weight?" I looked at him squarely in his face and said, "That is really rude." He countered with, "But you look so different; I didn't recognize you . . . you look really good." I responded, "Look, I really don't want to talk about it." He pleaded, "No, really, I meant it as a compliment!" I said, "I know that's what you thought you were doing, but that doesn't mean that it's OK to interrupt my conversation." He apologized and walked away.

I approached him a few minutes later, accepted his apology and explained that I was tired of people making my appearance and my weight a public issue. He said, "Well you're just going to have to get used to it because you really do look different." In a gesture of goodwill, my friend and I decided to attend Joe's support group, which he had entitled *Intimacy and*

Honesty. The group was participatory, and we were each to introduce ourselves with three pieces of information about ourselves to everyone in the room. Each participant was supposed to stand up and the others in the room would recount what they had learned about the person. When the first person stood up, someone in the group said, "Well I didn't get a chance to talk to him, but I think he is really cute!" Joe the facilitator said, "The point of this exercise is to share what we learned about the person who is standing; we should not comment on superficial issues or make observations about the person." When my turn finally came, I heard Joe say, "Well the first thing I have to say about Drew is that I didn't recognize him because he has lost so much weight." I slumped into my chair, composed myself, and said, "You really don't know how that feels do you?" He countered with, "But you look so good . . ." I became enraged and lost control and parted with the words: "How dare you comment about my weight and after I told you in the lobby not to, and after you said that we weren't going to be talking about appearances in this group!" I stormed out of the room feeling violated and enraged and wrote a letter in protest: it was too late; my gay identity was shattered and wounded.

THE PERSONAL IS POLITICAL

For the next several years, I withdrew from the gay male community, healed from my experience, and forged a new way for myself to live as a gay man. On Sunday, June 18, 1995, I went to the San Francisco Lesbian, Gay, Bisexual, Transgendered Freedom Day Parade for the first time since 1991, a time when I was running around in what I now call *Cute-Mode.* Not all individuals, who are more often than not regarded as highly attractive, are in *Cute-Mode. Cute-Mode* refers to an individual whose self-esteem, identity, behavior, stature, clothing, exercise, and eating habits are designed to project an image of sexual attractiveness to the world. *Cute-Mode* is an attitude; it is often what gay men refer to as "giving attitude." It is a statement to the world that I am better than other people because I am "hot." I lived in *Cute-Mode* for two years after having grown up and come out thinking that I was intrinsically unattractive.

For a long time after that Freedom Day in 1991 that left me so disillusioned, every time I began to exercise or eat more healthfully, I would notice changes in the way that I was treated by men in the gay male community. And as men started treating me with interest and deference based upon my looks, I found myself slipping back into *Cute-Mode.* Each time I felt that change I stopped taking care of myself and gained enough weight to keep sexual energy away from me. I learned to value men who were attracted to me and to my extra flesh, though I have remained single for the last three years and have dated only a few times.

A year ago, I decided to live my life for me and not for the possibility that I too would find a lover, a soul mate, someone to make me happy, which was at the root of my need to be "cute." Instead, I stopped doing all of the things that we gay men do in our never-ending search for Mr. Right. I had believed that if I were "cute" enough and if I went out into the bars and cafés enough, then surely I would be able to find my mate. Probably my greatest revelation of all was that I liked the people I met when I was heavier better than those I met when I was in *Cute-Mode*. I really believed that when I was fat there was something lacking in me, some sort of natural beauty that I just simply did not have. As I look back from where I am now, I see how easily I had traded in the feeling that I was unworthy because I was gay for the feeling that I was unworthy because I was fat. No matter how poorly gay men may treat each other in the game of sex, I did not like myself.

And then suddenly it dawned on me. All of those bodies that you see in the Saturday night dance clubs, the tans you see at the gay beaches, the bulked up arms and defined abs that you see wherever the "cute" guys go out looking for tricks, dates, and lovers—Could it be that poor self-esteem drives it all? "Maybe," I mused, "There is an inverse relationship between the size of one's biceps and one's self-esteem!" Now, when I see bulked up guys wearing shirts so tight that you can see nipples, muscle definition, and navels from across the room, I see not a desirable human; I see a human in *Cute-Mode*. When I gained enough weight that I couldn't choose to be in *Cute-Mode* any longer, I decided that I had to go out dancing to find out what that would be like with my extra weight.

I couldn't wear jeans because I couldn't fit into a pair that was comfortable enough to be able to dance, so I wore a large, black T-shirt and a pair of black sweatpants. I got out into the middle of the dance floor and started to dance. I could feel my chest, gut, and butt shake and jiggle, and I couldn't quite move the way I had in *Cute-Mode,* but I did enjoy myself. I ignored the scene, refused to make sexually charged eye contact, refused to give deference to anyone I thought was attractive, and I kept a genuine smile on my face, as I truly love to dance. Unlike when I danced in *Cute-Mode,* no one tried to dance with me, and no one stopped me on the floor to get my phone number. But I was there to be in my community, I was there to prove to myself that I would be willing to jiggle to the beat no matter what I looked like and no matter how anyone treated me. I refused to give deference to anyone and therefore did not feel oppressed! When I got crowded out of the dance floor, I ran up to the stage and danced before a room of hundreds of gay men, a full forty-five pounds more than when I was in *Cute-Mode*. I had triumphed over a lifetime living with a negative body image; I took back my power from those whom I had given it to, and I was free.

When I went to Freedom Day in 1995, I went with my closest gay male friend and three of my closest lesbian friends. I didn't go with the expectation that I would meet Mr. Right, and I didn't obsess about every "hot" guy that walked by. What I found, though, was a parade with a profoundly empowering theme: "A World Without Borders." And what I saw was a beautiful mix of people charged up by the resurgence of the Christian Right. The parade started at 11:00 a.m., and I remarked to my friend Frank, "What's wrong with this picture—something's missing." At first he looked confused but quickly responded, "No white T-shirts—the *Cute-Mode* guys aren't here! Where are they?" I answered, "If you were in high *Cute-Mode*, you would've gone to the Saturday night clubs last night, maybe one of the sex parties or underwear parties. It's a little early for them to be out. They'll show up in an hour or two." Sure enough, a few hours later walking up the street were guys with their shirts off displaying chest, tans, and definition, and drinking beer in paper cups. I knew because it is what I had done while I was in *Cute-Mode;* and when I was in *Cute-Mode,* the parade took on less significance: it was the parties that attracted me and the other guys living in *Cute-Mode.* The parade that year reflected the full range of bodies and ages of the community and stood in contrast to the crowds one finds at the gay bars and clubs. I felt like a regular person, not like a "cute" guy, not like a fat guy, and not like a sexual object. The looksist hierarchy does not work when we don't play the game.

Six months ago, I went to the gym for the first time in a year to swim. When I walked into the sauna to stretch, three guys with pumped up chests abruptly left, and one of them looked right at me and rolled his eyes; I was an unwelcome intruder in their cruise scene. I knew that it wasn't a reflection of my worth so I laughed out loud and got a place to sit! Six months later I went into the same sauna (it isn't a gay gym) fourteen pounds lighter and feeling healthy after several months of swimming. I stretched for a few minutes and looked up to find a muscular man groping his penis and checking me out. I motioned to him that there was another person present and he stopped. But when the other person left, he started to masturbate and he said, "Turn around . . . let me see that hot butt. Let me see the crack of your ass." I left and took a shower, knowing that the looksist hierarchy was the same as it was when I was fat, and when I was in *Cute-Mode*, but that I had disengaged from it as much as is possible for me at this time in my life.

As time passes and I become more removed from my own experience with *Cute-Mode* and from the looksist hierarchy, I sometimes forget the full impact of looksism upon the social conventions that bind gay men. On the fiftieth anniversary of the founding of the United Nations in San Francisco, the temperature hit a very unusual 99° Fahrenheit. I brought my journal to the very top of Buena Vista Park and waited for the ocean breeze to reach me. Buena Vista Park is a huge park in the center of San Francisco featuring a complex system of paths that lead up to a summit 500 feet or so above the rest of the city, and it is a notorious gay male cruise scene. All around me were men in *Cute-Mode*—tight, white muscle shirts, tans, muscles, baseball caps, and furtive eye contact. Straight couples were walking their dogs, and there were small groups of tourists. Two young men climbed up the stairs to the grassy center of the summit of the hill, took off their shirts, and exposed beautiful but not quite perfect male physiques. One was blonde and very thin and the other was shorter, chubby, and brunette. They began to do a complex form of partnered yoga and massage that *was the single most intimate and beautiful physical interaction I have ever seen between two men in public.*

The *Cute-Mode* guys tentatively observed them, cruised them, and returned to their pursuit of each other. I was so fascinated that I walked over to them and asked what they were doing. They explained that they were checking out the West Coast and that they were massage and yoga instructors from the Boston area. As our conversation progressed, they began asking me questions about San Francisco and where they might find like-minded people. At that point I asked if they were gay or straight. They answered that they were straight. The intimate physical contact that I saw them engage in stood in dramatic contrast to the cruise scene all around me. They were a handsome pair, but their bodies were not stylized; their body hair was not shaved and trimmed; their clothes were utilitarian and not fashionable; their touching and stretching had all the qualities of dance or of a complex Eastern art. Their physical closeness was matched by what was clearly a warm and intimate friendship. The *Cute-Mode* guys, circling, pacing, checking each other out, had perfectly stylized bodies, clothes, and hair but were all single. I tried to imagine them all in pairs on the grassy center laughing, holding each other, massaging each other, and I could not. When I walked down the hill, I passed by the crannies in the bushes where men have sex and saw at least half of the men I had seen passing above paired up in a bush discreetly trying to have sex.

CONCLUSION

As a man who has lived both as a "not cute" gay man, who felt he was not attractive enough for the standards of his community, and a gay man living in *Cute-Mode,* who tried very hard to live up to that ideal, I experienced what I consider to be the fundamental relationship between looksism and internalized homophobia. As a fat person, I had always suspected that the "cute" guys stood around making fun of me and people like me: as a "cute" guy, the other "cute" guys never ceased to amaze me in the amount of time and energy they spent putting others down on the basis of looks. When I listened to what they feared and what they loathed, I knew that their judgments were rooted in basic homophobia.

Young gay men have little support to unlearn all of the vile things they were raised to believe about gay men. When they come out, they carry with them the majority culture stereotype of the effete, old, and lonely gay man: even as young gay men are the strictest enforcers of fashion and attractiveness, they fear that one day they will grow old and be alone. Graffiti in public restrooms, bars, and bathhouses, and language in personal ads often use the phrase, *"No Fats, No Femmes, No Old Trolls,"* as they provide information for sexual encounters. Men who perceive themselves as not living up to the standards of the community internalize these judgments and often suffer from poor self-esteem.

Once I lost weight, I never lost sight of the fact that I was the same person that I had always been; it was the change in my image that had altered *other* men's perceptions. As I became a "sought after" gay man, I heightened my consciousness about what it was that manipulated the perceptions of others and tried very hard to live up to the gay male ideal. The ideal of the tanned, well-muscled, eternally youthful, masculine stud with a big dick (and a fast car) prevails in advertisements, in pornography, and in the collective mind of the gay community. At the same time, the gay male ideal stands in contrast to the societal stereotypes of wispy, wimpy, limp-wristed, lonely, and frivolous gay men by creating visual images of athletic, gay supermen.

Many of the young gay men I met expressed anxiety about turning twenty-five, told me they feared becoming an "old troll," and were already using products to prevent hair loss and lines in their faces. Concurrently, young gays often use disparaging remarks against those whom they do not consider "cute." My contrasting experiences allowed me to see how the image of the gay male ideal drives both the need to conform and the desire to judge others who fail to live up to unrealistic standards of physical perfection.

Repeated rejections on the basis of physical appearance compound the self-esteem problems that remain in the psyches of gay men after they come out. Men who are raised to believe that there is something sick or sinful about their nature easily trade in a fear of being homosexual for a fear of not fitting into their new community of acceptance. Since a large part of that community of acceptance is contingent upon physical appearance, men are left feeling that they will never fit into the community or that they must reinvent themselves through diet and exercise. Self-esteem issues originating in homophobia and looksism impact the gay community by encouraging substance abuse, compulsive sexuality, and HIV transmission: health educators and researchers report that the number one reason that gay men cite for having unsafe sex is that "he was really hot."

Societal homophobia and stereotypes about gay men drive feelings of hopeless unattractiveness, obsessive preening, compulsive exercise, and the need to put others down. Just as young men grow up feeling "less than" their heterosexual male counterparts, they also carry the division of "us" and "them" as they come out of the closet. The "cute" guys get to be "us," and older, overweight, and "unattractive" men become "them." The division between "us" and "them" represents a means for young men to reject being different or other but serves to create the looksist hierarchy within the gay male community. Pointing the finger at others who are different or who do not live up to the gay male ideal, creates the means for the young gay person to claim his place among the elect. And those who are not among the "cute" are humiliated by their peers and easily internalize the notion that they are of less value than their "cute" counterparts. When a young gay person accepts himself as gay only to find out that his peers reject him on the basis of looks, his internalized homophobia finds new expression in a poor body image and in accepting a subordinate status, or he can work out, lose weight, and do all of the things that he can do to conform, except of course drink from the fountain of youth. And it is equally true that men who perceive themselves as less attractive routinely subordinate themselves to men they view as further up the looksist hierarchy than themselves, thereby reinforcing the cult of gay male beauty.

When the lie of the gay male ideal was exposed in my mind, I began to see looksism in political rather than in personal terms and committed myself to writing about looksism and sharing my contrasting experiences with others, to name the problem that gay men face and to confront our own looksism. Now when I go swimming at the YMCA, when I go out dancing with friends, when I go to events in the gay male community, I refuse to maneuver myself to meet all of the "cute" guys, and I refuse to ignore those who do not seem attractive at first glance.

While it is clear to me that the "cutest" guys are not interested in me any longer, I am no longer intimidated by them, and I have enhanced my self-respect: a healthy dose of self-confidence actually makes up for the sin of love handles, undefined "abs," and a refusal to conform. In addition, I learned that if I treat other gay men as human beings, *only,* not as "cute" people or "not cute" people, they respond to me differently as well. Treating people equally forced me to stop making sexually charged eye contact with men whom I met. My struggle to treat everyone equally is an ongoing, everyday commitment, and all it takes is a moment to slip into old patterns.

If each of us in the gay male community were to treat every other person in our community as a fully equal partner in our struggle against homophobia, we could not treat those who are "cute" as sexual objects and those who are "not cute" as trolls. Now, as I go out with my friends, I do not care who looks my way and who gives me attitude. I have found that there is a very real difference between cruising and friendliness. Friendliness instead of cruising has no doubt cut down on sexual opportunity, but it has made me many new friends. I have learned to enjoy my interactions with other gay men out in public, even in dance clubs and at the gym. It is a choice that must be made each day and with each new interaction with another gay man, but it is a choice that is possible even without a profound change in the gay male ethos. As much as I believe that the looksist hierarchy exists and plays itself out, I also believe that individuals have the power to break free from the judgments that we feel when we look in the mirror or when we glance at another man on the street or in the gym.

My experience with looksism is not only a personal story, it is as political as any manifestation of homophobia. Where looksism and poor body image encourage unsafe sex, drug and alcohol use, and sap energy and strength, the gay male community is weakened and individuals are destroyed. A truly supportive gay male community would enforce the notion that to be cruel, dismissive, or judgmental of each other plays into the hands of those who actively promote an antigay agenda. A supportive gay male community would nurture each of us and would allow each of us to be in the bodies that we have without sanction. It would create new sanctions against abusive and judgmental behavior toward those who have committed the sin of losing their hair, gaining weight, possessing physical disabilities, or maturing with age. Each of us has the power to disengage from the looksist hierarchy, treat each other as equal partners in the struggle against homophobia, and accept the full range of bodies belonging to members of our community. We owe it to ourselves to fight homophobia in all of its forms, including the cult of gay male beauty, and to build a culture of resistance to gay male looksism if we are to fight for freedom from homophobia and stop HIV/AIDS from its relentless march.

More Than a Sum of Parts:
Rescuing the Male Body
from Fundamentalism

Darrell g.h. Schramm

Years ago when I was in college, one of my closest friends was deter-mined to make me "one of the guys." He and I had agreed to meet so that he could teach me how to throw and catch a hardball, something I had no interest in, but I valued his company and tried, therefore, to keep an open mind. It was a hot, summer day in the East Bay. When I arrived, he asked almost at once, "Why do you have to wear such skimpy shorts?"

"Because I like my body," I said, feeling the sting of his ball through my glove.

He was, it turned out, as disturbed by our exchange as I was—he by my answer and I by his question. His thinking was something like, "What good does it do to throw a ball like a man if you're going to dress like a queer?" And my thought was "If you're such a good friend, why can't you accept me as I am?"

This wasn't an isolated incident. He had once objected to the way I wore my shirts—unbuttoned, nearly to the navel. And he changed the subject whenever I began to speak about the male body. "Guys don't talk about other guys' bodies," he once gulped impatiently. I wondered if his Lutheran background was a cause for his distaste. Certainly homophobia was, though that word hadn't yet been coined. Homophobia, shame, or queasiness—the issue was the body. He was afraid of it (or, at the very least, uncomfortable with it), and I reveled in it.

Years later, I roomed with an architect who had been asked to help design and build a house on Orcus Island, where he spent part of the summer. I had planned to visit him until I received his postcard that stated, "When you come up, wear your loosest clothes, if you have any. Don't wear your tight jeans."

Tight pants were all I ever wore. I was not, and am not, afraid of my body, my sexuality, not afraid of who I am. I won't hide myself to play someone else's game, and I'll take the consequences. This is not to boast; after all, I do not have the body of a Greek god or hero nor the unnaturally pumped-up version of it extolled today. But I do like this skin, this flesh, this sensual being that is me.

We used to say in the 1970s, "If you've got it, flaunt it!" Nothing wrong in that, provided the flaunting isn't all there is. Life is not only physical, not only the obvious. Our very dissatisfactions, disappointments, depressions, and despairs, our elations, excitements, serenities, and yearnings are witness to more. We *feel* more than the physical. We *are* more than the physical body. We are body and more than body—eros and agape and logos. Those who believe they were created in God's image may be aware that their bodies represent something more than flesh and blood. Those who do not believe in Genesis—or God at all—are aware, given the crisis of AIDS, that the body is not enough to get us through our losses and longing and grief. "Is that all there is?" sang Peggy Lee. No, we gay men can say calmly, confidently. No. Metaphysical answers do not reside in the material body.

Love, acceptance, devotion, truth, peace, etc., are not found in the body per se. And yet, for years we tried—and some of us still try—to use the body to give us what it can't possibly give—immortality. We work at the gym to become Body Beautiful; that is, we attempt to show the world "This is who I am: these pecs, these biceps, these lats and abdominals—these are *me*." We sport a basket in tight Levi's (I'll be the first to admit it) to say, "This hot and eager cock is me." We bronze and groom and cream our bodies, saying, "This, what you see, is me." (Some women do the same with short skirts, slit skirts, décolletage, etc.) The photos on calendars and greeting cards that focus on only a part of the body, the pictured personal ads in gay newspapers and magazines—shots of the crotch, the ass, the torso, all usually without faces, without heads—speak to our fetishistic views of life. And so many of us have been or are disappointed that we did not find the satisfaction, the devotion, the love we crave. The metaphysical answer is not found within the body. It is not found in the body *alone*.

Paradoxically—and the human body is a paradox—there are those people who are so detached from the body that they hide it or hurt it out of shame, conditioned by experience or religion to think of it as a humiliation, an inadequacy, even a source of evil; or when engaging in any sex act, they justify themselves by saying, "This [body] isn't me. It isn't me, so I can do it—I can masturbate or fuck or suck, do anything I want." This is much like the traditional revelers at Carnival who behave without inhibition as long as they are in costume and mask. But this behavior is, again, the result of viewing a person as only a material thing.

How did we get to this point, this place where we try to force all meaning from the human body as a fetish? I suspect that to pursue all we are as gay men is terrifying for many homosexuals. I think it's a problem of courage. Near the end of his life, the psychologist Abraham Maslow said that out of fear people often evade their own destiny. They evade growth. How? By not thinking. By not going beyond the obvious, the material. Advertising and the accumulation of goods help to keep the obvious and the material before us, help to distract and evade.

Lost or hiding behind this "glut" of goods as poet James Scully (1988, p. 50) calls it, behind a swank apartment or house, a closet crammed with the latest fashions and a skeleton or two, a hutch of fine china and Baccarat crystal, a choice of gold chains and diamond rings, the perfect tan on the perfect body, etc., lost or hiding behind these is often an evasion of the depths of what a gay man—or any person—is. Or can be. To be fair, some of us do not so much hide behind the accoutrements of a lifestyle promoted by Madison Avenue as explore them as a way of being, but too often, we seem to stop within the limits of this exploration. We don't venture deeper into the cavern. This evasion becomes an avoidance of life's fullest intensity, an avoidance shared by most of the straight world. Our cup runneth over with things but lacks something still. And so where can we find some sense of satisfaction if not also joy, love, peace? Perhaps, in an expanded view of sex?

"That's what it's all about? Sex? Just sex?" asks one of Peter Weltner's characters in *Identity and Difference*. To which a second character replies, "Why not? I think so. Don't you?" Then the second character reveals he hasn't thought much at all about sex, its ramifications or its meanings. For sex in the human body has the potential to be more than just a conditioned or biological reflex (Weltner, 1990, p. 9).

Sex is fate. It is the body—the limited, finite body—that will die. It is this understanding (whether or not we have ever articulated it) that terrifies us. It is this understanding of *sex as mortal body* from which so many of us have tried to hide and to distract our daily lives. It is this distraction, this denial of death (as the cultural anthropologist Ernest Becker [1973] put it), that causes some of us to become enslaved by the sex act, obsessed by the body. Because of our capacity for physical pleasure, unthinking and uninhibited pleasure, some of us submit to the slavery of sex to avoid considering the fate of the body.

However, as I mentioned earlier, the body is a paradox. Sex is a paradox. Sex is a limitation defined by the body, a limitation of pleasure and a

limitation of life itself. But sex is also freedom. As gay men, many of us
have learned that sex offers a way to liberation from the social strictures
and mores that would prescribe and legislate the order of our lives, liberation from the censure mainstream society would have us adhere to, liberation from a narrow view of sex and the sex act. Whether exploring and
enjoying solitary, mutual, or communal sex—masturbation, fellatio, S &
M and all the variants of leathersex, handballing, etc.—we have done so in
an effort to transcend our limits. Our willingness to delve into the eroticism of the body is a way to acknowledge our love of the body. Knowing
this flesh and bones and blood will not last, it is yet a way to transcend that
very fate. How? By giving, by sharing, by desiring ecstasy in the other as
well as in oneself. (Ecstasy = out of stasis, out of stagnation or standstill,
i.e., into life.) We know the body is a playground of pleasure but not for
ourselves alone. True eros is communion. Unafraid of our animal nature,
we can enjoy the erotic side of ourselves and each other without inhibition.
By giving we are given; by freely giving we move beyond ourselves into
each other. We are alive!

Our sexual play can go beyond the animal release of "a fuck is a fuck,"
beyond physical pleasure; it can become a way to move beyond a mere
body that will die. Foucault (1980) tells us that the history of sexuality is
the rise of the body over the mind and spirit, which is to say that we have
limited our lives, our selves, each other. I maintain that we can embrace all
that we are—mind, spirit, *and* body. But that requires courage—courage to
move beyond the predictable worlds we have fashioned for ourselves and
each other. Dare we take the chance to do more than locate our meaning in
our physicality? To give up control, to risk, is, as I said, a cause for fear
and trepidation. But to give up control, to risk, is also to become more.

I can't help but consider the myth of Orpheus: Orpheus was a master
poet of Thrace. Personal disaster followed immediately upon his marriage
to Eurydice. Fatally stung by a serpent, Eurydice died on their wedding
day. Unwilling to accept death, Orpheus made his way to the underworld
where he charmed the God of Death who promised to return the bride to
him provided Orpheus trusted the god and would not look behind him to
ascertain whether or not Eurydice was following. Of course, he looked
back, and he returned to the mortal world without her. He is said to have
wept for seven months, all the while playing such beautiful music on his
lyre that he moved trees and rocks and soothed wild beasts. Avoiding
women after his loss, he became the first mortal to advocate homosexual
love.

But the story does not end there. Despised by a group of Thracian
women (the Maenads, followers of Dionysus) because he had not only

spurned them but also condemned their orgiastic promiscuity and Diony-sus' human sacrifices, he was stoned in an oak grove by these women and torn apart—dismembered. They flung his head and his lyre into the sea where both drifted to the isle of Lesbos (Graves, 1957, pp. 110-111).

This is the story of a man who loves, loses, confronts death, wins—momentarily—loses again, but becomes something more than he was. Orpheus does not remain in stasis or in the same place. He does not evade growth. If anything, he becomes even more alive. With his music, he touches stones, trees, wildlife, people. He grows attentive, grows beyond the person he was to notice the world around him, to notice he alone is not the world. He begins to see the world in another way. Life is more than self-indulgence; it becomes communal. He dares to have convictions. Among other things, he advocates men loving men. This, however, is anathema to much of the straight world, and so the heterosexual Maenads kill and dismember him. The head floats to Lesbos where it becomes oracular, and Dionysus, god of wine and orgies, honors it. (The felicity of a homosexual head on the lesbian island is not lost on me—but that's another topic.)

Notice that it is the head, the intellect, that is salvaged. Orpheus in the end resides with Dionysus, he of passionate sexuality. The two are together. In fact, several ancient records attest that Orpheus and Dionysus were actually the same being (Graves, 1957, p. 114). (The Orphic Mysteries are said to be homosexual.)

In addition, Orpheus is a poet, a singer, one who creates. The wonder of creation is of the spiritual realm. Thus, in the end, body, mind, and spirit are joined. It is a long, complex, multivalenced myth that speaks to sexual-ity, reason, emotion, and wonder.

Wonder—the body is also a source of wonder. "I am fearfully and wonderfully made," sings the ancient Psalmist (Psalm 139:14). We can be struck with wonder—the awe we feel at a thundering waterfall, a desert sunset, a towering redwood, a crocus, a newborn child. It is this sense of mystery that binds us even to strangers.

The other day, I sat with Mark on the very pinnacle of Buena Vista Park—the whites of houses cobbling the landscape below us, the deep blue of the bay beyond dappled with white sails, and the green of Angel Island risen from the water like a humpback whale, everything vivid and scintillating under a brilliant, Van Gogh sky. At first we shared the vista with only three others, but as the afternoon drifted on, more and more people made their way to the top, staring out in silence or speaking in undertones. What brings so many people together but this wonder? It is a magnet, something that pulls together, a bond. It is eros. It is a part of what I call spirituality.

Spirituality—a sense of mystery, a sense of connection, a sense of wholeness. This sense is a feeling, an outgoing emotion, that brings together and binds. It is something within and yet beyond ourselves. It begins with the body, but it doesn't end there. It reaches out. It connects. It embraces.

In *Where the Spirit Dwells* (1988), Tobias Schneebaum relates his spiritual journey among the Asmat tribes of New Guinea. Among the men of these tribes, it is the custom for a man to choose one other man as his special mate, often in addition to a wife. Sometimes that choice occurs in boyhood when two young men feel a mutual bond. It is not a matter of promiscuity but one of loyalty, of a union between two men devoted to each other. Schneebaum learns that balance is essential among these people, indeed, is essential to being human, and essential, I might add, to that dimension within us that is often called spiritual. "There must always be balance," Schneebaum writes, " between *mbai* [two men in this ritual relationship of friendship and adoption]. When one *mbai* sucks the penis of his friend, the two may not part until the friend turns around and sucks *his* penis. If one enters the ass of another, the other must turn around and enter *his* ass. *Mbai* must always give back what they take. When I bring fish to the house of Kayet, my *mbai*, he will bring me sago the next time he goes into the jungle" (1988, pp. 195-196). The spirit dwells in a place beyond the cul-de-sac of the takers and the self-involved.

A spiritual dimension, that is, one which consists of compassion, generosity, integrity, and balance, one that supplements reason with wonder, imagination, love, and justice, is essential to wholeness. (Of course this doesn't apply only to men.) Elsewhere in the book, Schneebaum describes a ritual in which a man is chosen by the other men of the tribe as a source or field of energy and power. The chosen man is a body that houses more than fluids and solids; his skin, toes, penis, nose, and other orifices are sucked by others in the belief that it will give them some of his life and spirit. Schneebaum states of the Asmat men that "in the process of their wanting part of me inside them and part of them inside me, we were all being made into a single being, . . . all our individual characteristics were being combined into a universal concept of life itself" (p. 190). In other words, we are more than the sum of our parts, not only as individuals but also as a human community. It's an ecstasy of communion, a cosmic union, a wholeness that I believe few attain.

To shortcut our lives because of fear of death or because of the fate of the body, to experience the body only as a territory to explore free of the strictures of our society—liberating and exhilarating as that is—is never to realize our potential. Beyond the exterior potential, an interior one awaits our realization.

To fit in, to conform, is to be safe, to keep control; it is to be closed off from the interior of ourselves. The physical life houses an interior no scientist can discern; its rooms are a labyrinth connected to the labyrinth of other lives, other worlds. To stop short of exploring it beyond getting one's toes wet is understandable. It's scary. What assurance do we have that we won't lose ourselves, won't be torn apart, and never be on familiar ground again? Yet, to explore and become all we can be as human beings and, more specifically, as gay men with a spiritual consciousness, means we must risk losing control. For to confront the miracle of who we are utterly is to confront more than our finite bodies; it is to confront the miracle of the world itself.

REFERENCES

Becker, Ernest. *The Denial of Death*. New York: Free Press, 1973.

Foucault, Michael. *The History of Sexuality: An Introduction*. Translated by Robert Hurley. New York: Vintage, 1980.

Graves, Robert. *The Greek Myths, Volume 1*. New York: George Braziller, 1957.

Schneebaum, Tobias. *Where the Spirit Dwells*. New York: Grove Press, 1988.

Scully, James. *Line Break: Poetry as Social Practice*. Seattle, WA: Bay Press, 1988.

Weltner, Peter. *Identity and Difference*. Freedom, CA: Crossing Press, 1990.

Skinny, "White" Chicks and Hung, Buff Boys: Queer Sex Spaces and Their Discontents

Jill Nagle

I was twenty-five, sitting in a café with Mandy, forty, my date, who looked something like what I might look like at her age. By chance, we had run into Patty and Liz, two ample, sensual queer women, one white and one black, considered attractive by many in the social circles we shared. The four of us discussed sex, orientation, settings for sex play, and an upcoming safer sex party[1] at which Liz said she hoped to encounter women other than "skinny, white chicks with short hair."

"Not that there's anything wrong with skinny, 'white' chicks with short hair," she added quickly. Mandy and I, who could both fit that description, looked at one another and grinned a little sheepishly. Liz explained that her criticism was not of "skinny, 'white' chicks," per se, but rather of their overwhelming, disproportionate presence and visibility in queer sex spaces.[2]

This made sense to me. Clearly, queers discriminate against one another on the basis of looks. We can be, well, looksist. But "skinny, white chicks?" The phrase caught me off guard. It reminded me of the phrase "straight, white men," and the reactions it sometimes evokes among heterosexual males of European descent who don't like having attention called to those attributes. I winced at the idea that I, too, might be eschewing membership in a socially valued group, with similar effects of hampering progress for the excluded. I wondered how, as a skinny, white chick, I might be a more conscious ally to the women of color and the women of size[3] I knew, loved and/or lusted for.

I began by acknowledging that, yes, at least some of the sexual attention that comes my way is based not in any innate magnetic essence oozing from my pores, but rather in how well I match certain sexual templates currently in fashion. My activist side wants me to wear buttons saying, "Imagine me with another fifty pounds/years," "I could be disabled," or "Don't assume I'm 'white,'" to call attention to the ephemerality and cultural embeddedness of our physical appearance and abilities and to get people to think about whether they'd still be interested in talking to me if I looked quite a bit different. Buttons such as those could be a way to challenge or deconstruct "skinny, white chick privilege." Young, hung, buff boys[4] could wear similar buttons.

Conversely (perversely?), my exhibitionist side wants to revel in most kinds of sexual attention I get in queer sex space. I love taking off my clothes, doing erotic readings, and putting on shows for predominantly queer, sex-positive crowds. I have time and again decided against public exhibitionism in straight spaces because I don't think I would particularly enjoy sexual attention from crowds of predominantly straight, white men. But I rarely refuse an opportunity to strip or do sexual perfomance art at a queer event.

As the reader might have gathered by now, the rest of this piece grapples with integrating the desire to be desired and the desire to honor my own desires, on the one hand, and the desire to create my ideal, sex-radical queer community, on the other. I have felt these desires as a tension between honoring myself as an actor, an agent in the world, and choosing to become more aware of myself as the product of a number of competing ideologies—some more oppressive than others.[5] Though rather rarefied environments, I believe queer, public, sex spaces (such as safer sex parties, sex clubs, and sexually oriented publications) provide a uniquely powerful, largely untapped source for examining queer notions of attraction, desire, appearance, and the like. By creating and participating in such environments, I have begun to work in interesting ways with that tension between honoring myself as a sexual agent and analyzing myself as a sexual product. Conversations such as the one with Mandy, Liz, and Patty in the café help raise the issues I want to be examining. I intend to continue having such conversations across, as well as within, queer, public, sex spaces.[6]

Partially as a result of the Mandy-Liz-Patty conversation, I conceded to myself that, yes, women of European descent with below average height-weight ratio, do, perhaps, compose a particular demographic cohort, privileged in some ways and oppressed in others. Whether or not I *feel* like or *want to be thought of* as a skinny, white chick is only part of the issue. Certainly there is a story to be told about my reaction to the term—the history and range of emotion it evokes. There is also a story to be told about the social conditions that make it possible for me to be perceived as a skinny, white chick and the power relations revealed in how the label is deployed. That story involves white supremacy, racism, ethnocentrism, male supremacy, sexism, fat oppression, thin privilege, ableism, ageism, economic oppression, and more.

In terms of my own story, throughout my healthy adult life, I have rarely thought of myself as skinny and don't believe I am perceived that way, generally. However, last I heard, the average woman in the United States was five feet, four inches tall and weighed 146 pounds. At five-six and 130-variable pounds, I am statistically on the thin side, regardless of how I view myself. Perhaps if age were held constant, I would be closer to the mean. I generally feel average to on the slim side. Yet, I definitely felt *thin* next to Patty and Liz, in contrast to whose full, rounded bodies I looked positively angular. I imagined how easy it was for them to see me as skinny.

Part of the irony for me in being implicated as a skinny, white chick is that as a child, I actually *was* skinny and gawky—terribly so, or at least it seemed. A late bloomer, I was teased for being flat-chested and for having no curves. "Snake hips," my stepmother called me, affectionately. Levi's corduroy jeans were the "in" thing to wear in my junior high. The twenty-five inch waist, the smallest they carried, was too big for my little girl's body. I wilted in the shadow of my best friend, whose firm and rounded body inspired my then-unnamed lust and admiration, as well as that of most of the boys we knew. So, skinny was a curse, a taint, a scarlet letter "S." Skinny meant invisible, undeveloped, unsexy, left out, and incomplete.

Theoretically, there must have been a time when my body was some-where between feeling too skinny and occasionally feeling too fat. Even now, there are times when, *during the same day*, I can glance in the mirror at the gym and see that gawky kid and feel too skinny all over again, when only that morning, I felt too fat wriggling into my freshly washed jeans.

The shift I recall as a teenager happened sometime around my tenth-grade year, when I could finally wear junior-sized clothes. I remember trying on a pair of expensive, second-hand, wool gabardine, pleated pants, nicer than any I had ever owned, and staring in shock at the figure in the mirror I scarcely recognized as my own. The pants defined and accentu-ated a slender torso and pelvis that resembled those I had admired on other *women*. Yet, I still thought of myself as a skinny *girl*. I slid a silver serpentine belt through the loops and fastened it in front, turning right and left in front of the mirror. My body had a female shape! I couldn't stop looking at my newly defined body. I bought more clothes—buttoned, hooked, and zipped them around my newly discovered waistline and bud-ding hips. I finally grew into my fiber-fill, A-cup brassiere.

According to Carol Gilligan's now famous Dodge Study,[7] this is about the time that (at least white middle-class) teenage girls lose the confidence so characteristic of their youth. That confidence gets replaced with extreme self doubt, which often correlates with unhappiness about weight and body image. With 150,000 women allegedly dying each year of anorexia,[8] and thousands more spending countless hours bingeing, purging, dieting, obsessing, and blaming themselves, the tyranny of thinness in women's lives weighs in heavily as a silent monster, omnipresent and severely underdiscussed. While once affecting primarily upper-middle-class women of European descent, eating disorders have begun branching out to afflict a wider range of women, and also men.

In *The Beauty Myth*, Naomi Wolf painstakingly details the way a very narrowly defined notion of beauty has replaced all other categories of achievement as the one thing women cannot live happy, fulfilled, sexually rewarding lives without. To the extent that women believe our worth to be equated with our rating on an artificially constructed beauty scale, the myth succeeds in robbing us of our humanity, our right to enjoy our inherent beauty, and our appreciation of ourselves as vital, sexual beings rather than as ranked commodities.[9]

I am heartened to know that not all cultures instill the doubt about appearance into their female members that Western, particularly U.S., cultures do. The following passage, written by an anthropologist, describes a young woman of the !Kung tribe,[10] a hunter-gatherer culture living in the Kalahari desert in southern Africa:

> One day, I noticed a twelve-year-old girl, whose breasts had just started to develop, looking into the small mirror beside the driver's window of our Land Rover. She looked intently at her face, then, on tiptoe, examined her breasts and as much of her body as she could see, then went to her face again. She stepped back to see more, moved in again for a closer look. She was a lovely girl, although not outstanding in any way except by being in the full health and beauty of youth. She saw me watching. I teased in the !Kung manner I had by then so thoroughly learned, "So ugly! How is such a young girl already so ugly?" She laughed. I asked, "You don't agree?" She beamed, "No, not at all. I'm beautiful!" She continued to look at herself. I said, "Beautiful? Perhaps my eyes have become broken with age that I can't see where it is?" She said, "Everywhere—my face, my body. There's no ugliness at all." Those remarks were said easily, with a broad smile, but without arrogance. The pleasure she felt in her changing body was as evident as the absence of conflict about it.[11]

Contrast the experience of the young !Kung woman with bell hooks' description of women of African descent in U.S. culture:

> Obviously, the dearth of affirming images of black femaleness in art, magazines, movies, and television reflects not only the racist white

world's way of seeing us, but the way we see ourselves. It is no mystery to most black women that we have internalized racist/sexist notions of beauty that lead many of us to think we are ugly. In support groups like Sisters of the Yam, all over the United States, I have seen black females of awe-inspiring beauty talk about how ugly they are. And the media has bombarded us with stories telling the public that little black children (and we are talking here primarily about girl children) prefer white dolls to black dolls, and think that white children are cleaner and nicer. The white-dominated media presents this knowledge to us as if it is solely some defect of black life that creates such aberrant and self-negating behavior, not white supremacy.[12]

White supremacy is the collection of ideas, customs, and systems that support setting people of European descent (and their image) as the standard of humanity, power, and civilization.[13] At the time of the late anthropologist Marjorie Shostak's writing above, presumably the !Kung tribe was sufficiently insulated from European culture to escape some of its more pernicious effects, although the !Kung were clearly aware of Europeans and on occasion expressed admiration of fair skin.

In U.S. culture, standards of female attractiveness reflect white supremacist as well as sexist backlash[14] notions of desirability. Both inter- and intraracial attractions are overdetermined by this context. Yet, along with both dubious and real privileges (heterosexual male attention, favoritism in job hiring, opportunities to earn money in the sex industry or as a model) accorded to socially defined attractive women of European descent and their look-alikes, also comes related oppression. Examples include unwanted sexual attention and detraction from or denial of "desirable" women's intellectual strengths in favor of an overemphasis on physical attributes.

Modeling and the sex industry (stripping, prostitution, adult films, etc.) are the only two arenas of labor in which women earn more money than men. This says that the contributions of women most valued relative to men are our "beauty" and our sexual services. That modeling and sex work are occupations currently unavailable to most women[15] further removes these erstwhile rewards from the reach of most women. Current work to reform laws, attitudes, and practices governing the sex industry are helping to bring about change in those fields.[16]

If beauty oppression feeds the backlash against women, it feeds another kind of backlash against men's health and the specter of AIDS. Since the onset of AIDS in the early 1980s, the "gym body" has become so much of an earmark as to be a cliche, an overwrought symbol of gay male attractiveness and health. AIDS affects men of color (and people of color, in general) far disproportionately to white people, yet most articles about people living with AIDS in mainstream queer publications do not mention this fact and disproportionately feature white men as spokespeople.

In contrast to most queer women's publications, cosmetic surgery—i.e., pectoral implant, liposuction, and penile enlargement—ads now jump out of queer men's publications. I have yet to see analogous female-targeted ads appear in a publication geared toward same-sex-oriented women. In yet another contrast to their female counterparts, image after image of young, hung, buff boys grace the pages and pages of phone sex advertisements at the back of men's magazines.[17] Any representations of men of color most often appear as fetishes for "white" men's interest.

Those queer women's publications that do feature photographs tend to at least try to present variations on traditional notions of beauty. This is likely by virtue of lesbianism's often organic entwinement with feminism. The now defunct *On Our Backs* magazine, whose subtitle read "Entertainment for the Adventurous Lesbian," has featured women of size and women of Asian, Latino, and African descent, as well as "skinny, 'white' chicks." However, I would love to see queer publications feature people of color (for want of a more accurate term) as clearly more than just sexy side dishes for their white readers. An article on interracial relationships, for example, written by a white woman, still ends up recreating a mostly white-centered perspective. The author acknowledges this context in her opening paragraph:

> When Jackie Goldsby wrote in *Outlook* magazine in 1990 that "dykes politicize race, gay men eroticize it," it rang true. Gay men have developed a verbal code for cross-race desire, with terms like "dinge queen," "snow queen" and "rice queen," evolving from slang that was considered offensive by the race conscious, to an ironic celebration of what society still finds troubling. It seems that lesbians glorify diversity to such an extent that it objectifies race in as problematic a way as gay men do when they sexualize it.[18]

Although many white queers feel that sexual desire for partners of another ethnic or "racial" background is evidence of having moved beyond the white supremacist context in which such desires take place, I have seen plenty of interracial relationships replete with racism, racial fetishism, and internalized racism. Just as loving a woman doesn't make a man a nonsexist, neither does loving a person of another racial or ethnic background make one nonracist.

Consensual sexual relationships and sexual spaces of many varieties can, however, be entryways to dialogue about their contexts. I know a man of African descent who has done some of his best one-on-one counseling and education combating white supremacy with men of European descent he meets through personal ads. Considered extremely attractive and captivating by people of many genders and races, Daniel uses the attention he gets for his attractiveness as a conduit to generating dialogue about issues he feels are important, such as white supremacy, self-love, safer sex practices, and AIDS.

Despite the queer community's outpouring of activism and compassion for people living with AIDS and its demands for better government and citizen response to the epidemic, queer sex spaces still practice looksist policies that adversely affect those living with visible symptoms of AIDS, as well as others who do not fit narrow definitions of attractiveness.

The first issue of *Steam: A Quarterly Journal For Men*, which covers popular and sex-related issues in the physical layout of an academic journal, bravely took on this topic in their first issue. In a point-counterpoint format, owner Allan Gassman defended his Los Angeles men's sex club: "The OBoys! door policy is 'looksist' and 'attitude-ist,' and somewhat 'ageist.' It is not racist." Because an individual's level of "beauty" shifts both with cultural attitudes and over time as the individual ages, "ugly" people, unlike "black" people or women, do not constitute what in legal terminology would be called a "suspect class." Neither does the culture at large have a very easy time discussing discrimination on the basis of looks. Part of this reason is that what we call "looks" is not just physical appearance but actually comprises a number of things. Quoting Body Electric's Jim Curtin, Gassman notes, "One of the great problems in our community is not just about looksism, it's about vampirism. There are people—and I understand why young, attractive men feel assaulted—who want to feed off that energy without contributing anything."[19]

I sympathize with this. At my first sex party in 1990, I was touched without consent by two strange men and felt relatively powerless to prevent it. Carol Queen, who hosts private pagan sex events with a mailing list of about four hundred, told me "Queen of Heaven parties started because the mixed-gender queer sex space that I had access to (the same one I attended in 1990) wasn't meeting my needs, for a variety of reasons."

I believe in, as Carol suggests, the "let 1,000 flowers bloom" approach. I started my own erotic performance/play parties, called "Sluts on Stage," because I wanted to have performance with high erotic energy followed by free sex play. I am heartened by the plethora of queer sex spaces available here in the San Francisco Bay Area, and I hope the series of experiments continues. I also feel that mailing lists in the hundreds create a de facto community, or constituency, and with the power of such a substantial following comes the responsibility to examine critically what kinds of "isms" our events (re)produce. In freeing ourselves from vampirism and feeling invaded, we may have also unwittingly created other hierarchies of oppression, even within a space intended to be liberatory for all.

Apart from vampirism, looksism also overlaps with ableism, racism, sexism, and other forms of discrimination. As I said, I believe it's true that some of what appears to be looksism masks self-protective attempts to circumvent vampirism, sexual harassment, and other ills. But these are behavioral, not visual problems. Carol Queen is correct in saying that we have an insufficiently developed vocabulary to discuss things such as "energy" and "sexual skill."

Gassman, however, attempts to conflate behavior with looks. The "troll" slur is primarily a visual, not a behavioral epithet; otherwise, it wouldn't work as a door policy. Too bad. First, I know at least one or two "young, attractive" men who *prefer* older men. Second, there is a catch-22 relationship between a group's pariah status and its lack of self-love. Witness the disproportionate levels of suicide and alcoholism among queer and same-gender-loving youth and adults. No one would feel comfortable in an environment in which they are rejected or the only one of their group. Policies have effects, and exclusion hurts, especially within an already outcast group one looks to for acceptance, community, and support.

Also, race is a social, not a biological fact. It sounds as though the OBoys! believe that admitting "men of color" that they want to fuck makes it okay to discriminate against those they don't want to fuck simply because it isn't on the basis of "race." Since "race" is a fiction anyway, what makes discrimination on the basis of one kind of fictional category ("race") reprehensible but the other ("troll-hood") okay? Again, "trolls" are not a culturally consolidated identity the way "race" is, but both are social realities correlated with painful discrimination.

Gassman defends OBoys! policy on the grounds that it is a private club. Hello!? In this country, private institutions hold most of the power. Fortune 500 companies, network television, and Condè Naste are institutions privately owned by heterosexual, white Christian men. Based on Gassman's reasoning, corporations and the media could justify excluding queers from whatever realms they chose. Appeals to privatized power risk being turned around at a moment's notice. For better or for worse, most queer activism appeals to notions of justice and to people's sense of empathy. We tell stories, we talk about our lives because we believe that if we remember our own, as well as our listener's humanity, hearts open and prejudices can transform. Studies show that people are less likely to be homophobic after encountering a queer person, even if the encounter was negative. The same must apply to outcasts within the queer community. The maintenance of a "troll" class may be a self-perpetuating phenomenon—exclude folks and they get hurt, resentful, and pissy, and you find it easier to maintain your illusions about them because you have no contact, let alone sex, with them.

At what point does a private institution become accountable to the community that it serves? One friend of mine, Rick, said that if *every* sex club adopted looksist door policies, then he would stop going or at least protest. As it is, he wishes that parties here in the Bay Area, such as mine and Carol's, for example, were *more* looksist. Carol acknowledged that the gay men's public sexual community is large enough to be pretty widely diversified. After all, she pointed out, there are no correlates for their degree of specialization among heterosexuals, or queer women for that matter. For example, "I have yet to see a *heterosexual* swingers piss-play club," she noted. But queer sex spaces are still few and far between enough that one controversy has large ripple effects. We need to be able to extend the very limited legal discourse of "rights" and "privacy" to discuss power, policy impact, and ethics within queer communities.

Since I started this discussion, I might as well confess. I, too, like young, pretty boys. I would like to be admitted to the OBoys! club. Although I respect men's *right* to male-only sexual space, and I think I understand the *social* reasons for such space, I have heard no corollary political argument made about men-only space analogous to why women need women-only sexual space. If anything, male-only sexual space helps reinforce some gay men's fear and horror of female sexuality. And with access to more money, the best play spaces generally end up being taken up by queer men who keep them men-only. How about a new ethic of queer sibling-hood, guys?

This extended diatribe is not a dispute about OBoys!' "right" to discriminate on the basis of looks or gender, nor is it an attempt to single out OBoys! as the only, or even the most extreme, example of looksist practices. As I said, I'd like to move beyond talk about only rights and privacy to creating dialogue and comparing visions of queer community. I use OBoys!' policies as a way to raise questions such as: Do you want to be a member of a club that will exclude you in x number of years? Is the focus on young, hung, buff boys a lunge toward immortality in the face of death? How many more years will the idea of two and only two sexes[20] be so real as to support excluding the "other" from sex space?

I know these are not easy questions. As a community built on nothing less than commonality of unacceptable desires, there is a tremendous resistance to examining our desires yet again. Quite understandably, many want to keep sexual desire as the last safe haven from political scrutiny. Gassman quotes AIDS activist and author Michael Callen from an NGLTF "Creating Change" conference:

> I would like to declare our sexuality to be the last natural preserve, where we are not required to justify why we are sexually attracted to somebody . . . I am not prepared to formulate an amorphous "everybody should be capable of having hot sex with everyone else" policy.[21]

Natural preserve? Does anyone really believe that the particulars of sexual desire are *natural*? And, having someone in the same space with you does not mean you are forced to have sex with them. It *could* mean, however, that you would be forced to expand your notion of what or who is considered sexy or allowed to be a sexual being. Gassman warns,

> The overweight, the unkempt, and the geriatric will not feel comfortable at our events and they would distract from the energy of the party . . . We only admit people who will contribute to the erotic experience we're trying to create.[21]

This comes from a population regarded by large chunks of mainstream North America as aesthetically repulsive. It could be rationalized that queers would "not feel comfortable" at straight events, as a way to keep queers marginalized as well. Heterosexism and looksism, not our own queerness or our own looks, make us uncomfortable. Perhaps it is easier to get one's rocks off by reproducing an oppressed class within, for the thrill of a false sense of security, specialness and belonging. Ideologically, we might as well build a sex club on a precipice. For those who wish us eliminated care not how tight our butts, toned our pecs or chiseled our features (however, those attributes make quite lovely advertising images for those in pursuit of the queer dollar bill). To the homo-haters, we are all disposable goods. It is in the context of being increasingly targeted by the very well-organized, well-funded Right that I so urgently want to envision the most humane ways possible of forging links across differences.

In his response article to Allan Gassman, Dave Johnson calls for the creation of inclusive community. He recalls his very inclusionary experience with "Healing the Body Erotic," a workshop offered throughout the country, based in Joseph Kramer's Body Electric School in Oakland.

> I remember my first time . . . I was not attracted to most of the men in the room, and I was terrified. But by the end of the weekend I felt comfortable in the arms of each and all of them, and would happily have not only hugged but made love to them all.[22]

I talked with Keith Hennessey, a San Francisco performance artist, community activist, and self-described "sacred intimate," through repeated Body Electric workshops, Keith has had "to relearn the same lesson over and over. You never know where the good touch is going to come from. Sometimes it comes from the older fat guy." Keith himself is another person considered by many, this author included, to be extremely sexually attractive. Yet, he declares, "I've never had a 'buff' boyfriend, and I've got a big attitude against exercise that people do in order to look better. I object to hegemony on all levels."

Keith sees the dominant aesthetic in this country as pornography, which has a very specific, limited view of sexual attractiveness. It extolls youth worship, hairless bodies, and muscles that are not a product of bodies used in the service of art or labor, but simply in pursuit of a cliched, "ideal, body type." Keith moans, "The monotype makes me sad. I want substance; I want history"—the kind that comes from engaging in contact improvisation (an interactive dance form), for example. Not surprisingly, Keith is pretty ho-hum about the OBoys! and encouraged me not to focus on them too much. Said a mutual friend of Keith's and mine, "I've met the OBoys! themselves. They were distinctly non-hot." Oh, say it isn't so! "They were, well, like *young trolls.*" I guess there's no accounting for taste, after all.

"Trolls" or not, I can safely say that neither Keith Hennessey, Carol Queen, Bayla Travis, former editor of *On Our Backs,* nor I would exclude them or anyone else from our queer sexual space based on appearance alone. I'll be the first to admit—I love being surrounded by people I'm attracted to, and those attractions often correspond to convention. Too, I definitely don't want to be harassed. But check this out. Of the many times I've been sexually harassed, most have happened on the street in broad daylight. And sometimes, when I have the energy and inclination, I have used the incident as an opportunity to engage, to transform the interaction into something more human and respectful. I believe that, on more than one occasion, I have influenced someone who harassed me such that he was less likely to then harass someone else—and I did it by remembering my humanity and the humanity of my harasser. I have also done on-the-spot education about attitude and scenario creation at my own sex parties and allowed people to remain and play if they seemed receptive to education, rather than kicking them out because they didn't get it right the first time. Finally, of the several truly awful sexual experiences I've had with men, most of the perpetrators lived in bodies considered more conventionally attractive than average.

First and foremost, I prefer to share sex space with folks who already know how to behave without making others feel uncomfortable. Yet, if, as a community of queer sex radicals, we are to bone up on such notions as "energy" and "skill" and bring higher levels of sophistication into our sexual vocabularies, those experts among us might do well to start sharing some of their insights with the less enlightened. Then, perhaps everyone is likely to feel more comfortable all around. I, for one, feel like a novice in a largely undefined field. I have seen a few workshops on sex party etiquette, and I'd like to see a whole lot more.

Some people do get what they want in their radical sex circles. Nicola Ginzler, a San Francisco performance artist and leather player finds the values of her S/M[23] culture a welcome respite from the world outside. "In the leather community," says Ginzler, "you're judged (as a sexual or play partner) not so much by what you've got, but by what you *do* with what you've got." Other players in similar communities confirm that experience, skill, confidence, and energy, not conventional attractiveness, determine a player's popularity. Perhaps, as it introduces notions of consensuality and negotiation into more mainstream discussions, S/M culture will lead the way to increased consciousness around the role of conventional attractiveness in pursuing a variety of sexual practices.

Good sex, says modern day sex guru Annie Sprinkle, is not about a particular look or even about body parts interlocking in particular ways. It is about "the energy between people."[24] There's that "e" word again. It would appear that this concept bears further investigation. How might we create spaces that seek to *transform "vampire" energy* rather than contributing to maintaining a class of "vampires?" What kind of radical potential exists in that, dare I say, *spiritual* choice?

My ideal queer community would both celebrate desire and also continually engage in dialogue about how we, as an oppressed group ourselves, reproduce oppression within our own ranks. It is not now and never was good enough to simply tell our stories and make our demands to those in relation to whom we are disenfranchised and oppressed; we must also listen to the stories and demands of those in relation to whom *we* are disenfranchisers and oppressors. We must see how we, too, can hurt others through our ignorance. This, of course, is not always as much fun as honoring our desires in the moment. After all, if we open our hearts to others' pain, we risk breaking them. But perhaps this is necessary. According to Cherie Brown, founder and director of the National Coalition Building Institute, "Each of us needs to be willing to let our hearts break at *all* of the injustices that have happened" (italics added).[25] Indeed, a "liberated," queer, sex-radical community that liberates only hung, buff boys, skinny, white chicks and those they fetishize is far from my ideal world.

With new conversations, stories shared, and the production of consciously created, countercultural, queer sex spaces, such as Body Electric workshops, radical faerie gatherings, and mixed gender parties, we are creating new contexts for our queer desire. I know that my own preferences have gradually shifted over the years in response to the cultures in whose values and images I have immersed myself. For example, I have come to appreciate the touch, presence, and energy of older people, in contrast to the often anxious, tense, preoccupied touch, presence, and energy of younger people. While I have always found older women attractive, I have only recently come to appreciate some of the special qualities of some older men. I learned a tremendous amount recently by playing with a fifty-plus-year-old man who was the most orgasmic person, male or female, I have ever had the pleasure of touching. I was mesmerized. My strap-on and I could have entertained him for hours without blinking. However, I was not impressed with his physical appearance on our first meeting. Round, balding, and with average, if sweet-looking features, I would easily have passed him by. As Keith Hennessey said above, this is a lesson I may have to relearn repeatedly. Yet it was a huge step for me.

I credit the counterculture I am helping to create. In negotiating the tension between honoring myself as an agent of desire and deconstructing myself as a product of culture, I can help create new contexts closer to my own ideals of queer, radical, sexual communities. In the process of generating counterculture, I reacculturate myself.

NOTES

1. Safer sex parties come in many varieties. The kinds with which I am most familiar are either private or not widely advertised, welcome queer and queer-friendly people of all genders, and have involved anywhere from twenty to two hundred or more people. The primary purpose of these gatherings is sexual pleasure in a safe environment. To that end, hosts enforce strict rules about behavior and the necessity of getting consent from prospective partners. They also supply and enforce the use of latex and other barriers for prevention of pregnancy and disease transmission.

2. I place the term "white" in quotes to indicate the fictionality of race constructs, which have no scientific basis; most people who get labeled "white" are actually people of European descent. The "queer sex space" encompasses sex parties, as well as any gathering of lesbian, bisexual, transgender gay people and those who favor marginalized sexual activities that encourage, require, or permit sexual activities, for example, a men's bathhouse.

3. For fat-positive politics, commentary, pictures, essays, and more on sexy fat women, see *FaT GiRL: A Zine for Fat Dykes and the Women Who Want Them,* Fat Girl, 2215-R Market Street #193, San Francisco, CA, 94114, (415) 567-6757, airborne@sirius.com.

4. I use the term boy as it is used among queer men whom I know—as an affectionate term for eighteen-plus-year-old men in their community.

5. Some may hear in this tension echoes of the essentialism versus constructionism debate. I reject this dichotomy and choose to work with the idea of a "virtual self," a work-in-progress, a process of negotiating what we *experience* as *our* desires, inclinations, and propensities against the backdrop of what we perceive to be authority sources—parental, institutional, religious, etc. This echoes Freud's tripartite model of the ego negotiating the superego (society) with the id ("base" desires).

6. I use the plural here to reflect the differences among women-only, men-only, and multigendered, queer, public sex spaces.

7. Gilligan, Carol. *Making Connections: The Relational Worlds of Adolescent Girls at Emma Willard School.* A report funded by the Geraldine Dodge Foundation, as summarized in *The New York Times Magazine,* January 7, 1990, by Francine Prose.

8. Brumberg, Joan Jacobs. *Fasting Girls: The Emergence of Anorexia as a Modern Disease.* Cambridge: Harvard University Press, 1988, as quoted in *WAC (Women's Action Coalition) Stats: The Facts About Women.* New York: The New Press, 1993. Though this figure has been widely cited, I have never seen the supporting documentation to verify it. Even if greatly exaggerated, however, it still staggers the mind—for example, if overestimated fully ten times, 15,000 young women perish each year from eating disorders alone.

9. Wolf, Naomi. *The Beauty Myth.* New York: Anchor Books, 1991.

10. The exclamation point at the beginning of "!Kung" represents a "click" sound made with the tongue that is part of !Kung speech.

11. Shostak, Marjorie. *Nisa—The Life and Words of a !Kung Woman.* New York: First Vintage Books Edition, 1983, p. 270.

12. hooks, bell. *Sisters of the Yam—Black Women and Self-Recovery.* Boston: South End Press, 1993, p. 84.

13. Manago, Cleo, personal conversations. This definition of white supremacy contrasts many people's images of white supremacy as confied to the Ku Klux Klan and similar overtly hateful groups. However, I use the term consciously to refer to the broader phenomenon that I believe affects, and thus implicates, all of us. This brings white supremacy home to roost, as it were, so that liberals and other well-intentioned folks cannot simply dismiss white supremacy as an isolated problem perpetuated by others more ignorant than them(our)selves.

14. My understanding of the backlash against women's recent social, political, and economic advances was profoundly influenced by Susan Faludi's acclaimed *Backlash.* Though narrow in scope of analysis (white, middle-class, heterosexual females), her journalistic exposé of the sexism of mainstream institutions and leaders supports her case very strongly.

15. Only one woman in 40,000 meets the physical criteria for modeling (*WAC Stats,* The New York Press, 1993, p. 20), while most forms of sex work are severely stigmatized, illegal, and/or have similarly stringent physical requirements.

16. For more information, contact U.S. Prostitutes Collective, P.O. Box 14512, San Francisco, CA, 94114, (415) 626-4114 or COYOTE (Call Off Your Old Tired Ethics), a sex worker's support, advocacy, and political organization, 2269 Chestnut Street Ste. 452, San Francisco, CA 94123, (415) 435-7950; send SASE for information. See also *Whores and Other Feminists* for writings by feminists in the sex industry (Jill Nagle, ed., Routledge, 1997).

17. See, for example, the *Advocate, Frontiers,* or the *Bay Area Reporter.*

18. Smyth, Cherry. "Crossing The Tracks—Interracial Sex Love is Not (Color) Blind," *On Our Backs,* Volume X, Issue 2.

19. The Body Electric School, based in Oakland, CA, offers a variety of pioneering workshops for men, women, and mixed groups on sexuality and massage.

20. For an expanded critique of the notion of two and only two sexes, see Nagle, Jill. "Framing Radical Bisexuality: Toward a Gender Agenda." In *Bisexual Politics: Theories, Queries, and Visions,* Naomi Tucker, ed. Binghamton, NY: The Haworth Press, Inc., 1995.

21. Gassman, Allan, Guest Editorial—The Wrestling Ring, "No Creeps or Trolls Allowed!" *Steam, A Quarterly Journal For Men,* Volume 1, Issue I, Spring 1993, p. 6.

22. Johnson, Dave, Guest Editorial—The Wrestling Ring, "A Call for Real Community," *Steam, A Quarterly Journal For Men,* Volume I, Issue I, Spring 1993, p. 7.

23. S/M is an abbreviation for sadomasochism, which generally refers more broadly to a wide range of practices involving consensual power exchange. For more information, see Pat Califia's *Sensuous Magic: A Guide for Adventurous Couples* (Richard Kasak Books, 1993).

24. Sprinkle, Annie. "Beyond Bisexual." In *Bi Any Other Name,* Loraine Hutchins and Lani Ka'ahumanu, eds. Boston: Alyson Publications, 1991, pp. 103-107.

25. Brown, Cherie, quoted in *Making A Difference: Newsletter of the National Coalition Building Institute,* Winter/Spring, 1994, p. 2. The National Coalition Building Institute, based in Washington, DC, trains trainers in their communities to conduct prejudice reduction, conflict resolution, and leadership workshops. I began work in 1994 to establish the San Francisco Bay Area Chapter of NCBI. For more information, call (202) 785-9400.

Index

*Body Talk = Survival: Intersections
    of Disability, Sex, and Race,*
    312
Body use, typology of, 6
Bonus, Nancy, 174
Boogeywoman, 177
*Boots of Leather, Slippers of Gold;
    The History of the Lesbian
    Community,* 236
Bornstein, Kate, 191
Boston/New York Aids Ride, 124
"Boy Parties," 417
Boye, 245-248
Boyish preppie, gay man, 369
Boys of Pattaya, porn video, 285-286
Boys in the Sand, 405
Breast-feeding, transsexual
    experience of, 196
Breasts, as female characteristic,
    190,192
Bright, Susie, 127
British Medical Journal,
    intersexuals, 215
Bronski, Michael, 347-349,350
Brown, Christy, 315
Brown, Laura S., *xxxv,*28,34
Brownmiller, Susan, 13
Bulimarexic, 389
Bulimia
    gay men, *xxxiii-xxxiv,*363
    lesbians with, 84,85,163-164,
        166,363
"Bull dyke," 55
Burnett, Carol, 182
But Some of Us Are Brave, 257
Butch
    appearance standard, 23-24,56,
        234,235-236
    class and race, 56
    gay man, 369
    hostility toward, 234
    lesbians
        feelings of exclusion, 23-24
        visibility of, 55,234-235
    as male-identified, 56

Butch *(continued)*
    role in lesbian community, 235
    sexuality of the, 160,234
Butch-femme
    concepts of, 9,64n.9
    dynamics, 229
    role-playing, 54-55,61,88
    as style, 20,21,233-234
    subculture, appearance norms
        in, 23,24,234,235-236

Callen, Michael, on sexual desire,
    347,448
Camp, lesbian, 54,57
Campaign, 328-329,330
Canada, intersexuals in, 215
Career
    gay male identity and, 83
    lesbian identity and, 81
Chaikin, Joe, 407
Chapkis, Wendy, *xxxi*
Chi-chi, 295,298
Christian, Meg, 58
Christian church, on the penis, 262
Christian fellowship, body image
    and, 148-149
"Chubby-chasers," 364,371
Cigarettes, abuse of, 120,133
Classism, deadly ism, *xxxix*
Clitoral orgasm, 49
Clitorectomy, 205,206,207,209,230
Clitoris, lesbian sexuality, 62
Clitoroplasty, 209
Clitpapers, 155
Clones, 380
Clothing, lesbian issue of, 9
"Codependency," 320
Coker, Syl Cheney, 267
Colette, 51,52,54-55
Coming out
    as bisexual, 183-184,223-224
    body image and, *xxxix,xli,*132
    as intersexual, 206,212
    lesbian, 255

Heterosexual women *(continued)*
  view of weight and, *xxxvii-xxxviii,*
  18-19,28
Heterosexuality, imposed, 47,49,51
"High yellow," as pejorative, 252
Hijra Nippon, 216
Holmes, Morgan, 215
HomeGirls, 257
"Hommo-sexuality," 57
Homophobia
  anorexia and, *xxxiv,*363
  body as issue, 431
  bulimia and, *xxxiv,*363
  and fat oppression, *xxxv-xxxvi,*
  369,417
  internalized, impact of, *xxx*
  lesbian experience of, 7,8,12
Homosexual Handbook, 403
Homosexuality, theories of, 328
hooks, bell, 442-443
Hotlanta, gay party circuit, 349
Hubbard, Ruth, 214
Hunger So Wide and So Deep, A, xl
Husky clothes, 393
Hwang, David Henry, 279

"Icon of despair," 310
Ideal female body, rejection
  of, 37-38
Ideal weight, *xxxvii*
Identity and Difference, 433
Identity House, 123
Image police, 380
In Living Color, 367
Incest, tattooing ritual, 127-128
Incongruity, queer body theory, 334
India
  movie depictions in, 271
  racial complexion, 271-272
Indigo girls, 114
Infibulation, 50
Inner Circle, porn video, 289

Intercourse, definition
  of heterosexual adequacy,
  210-211
International Olympic Committee,
  intersexuals and, 216
Intersex Society of North America,
  *xlvi,*208,215,217n.2
Intersex specialists, role of, 210,213
Intersexual, experience of, 221-226
Intersexual assignment, 208-209
Intersexuals, 205,206
  myths about, 232
Intimacy and Honesty, support
  group, 422-423
"Invisibly disabled," *xxxix*
"Isms," six deadly, *xxxix,*446

Jahn, Janheinz, 265
Japan, intersexuals in, 216
Jaws, wiring of, 60
Jeopardy, 117
Joan of Arc, 54
John Birch Society, 182
Johnson, Dave, 448
"Jungle fever," as pejorative, 252

Karhas, 275
Karyotypes, chromosomal, 216
Katz, Jonathan, 408
Kessler, Suzanne, 214
Kinsey Scale, 40,41,45n.4,77,228
Kristallnacht, 392
!Kung tribe, 442,443

Ladder, The, depiction of butches, 56
Ladies of Llangollen, 50-51,52
Lambda Legal Defense
  and Educational Fund, 279
Lambda Literary Awards,
  accessibility at, 317
lang, kd, 88,90,157
"Last Chance Syndrome," 340
*Last Harmattan of Alusine Dunbar,
  The,* 267-268